THALES TO SEXTUS

AN INTRODUCTION TO ANCIENT PHILOSOPHY

GARRETT THOMSON
COLLEGE OF WOOSTER

Long Grove, Illinois

For information about this book, contact:
Waveland Press, Inc.
4180 IL Route 83, Suite 101
Long Grove, IL 60047-9580
(847) 634-0081
info@waveland.com
www.waveland.com

Cover image: Vladimir Wrangel/Shutterstock

Copyright © 2016 by Waveland Press, Inc.

10-digit ISBN 1-4786-2776-X
13-digit ISBN 978-1-4786-2776-0

All rights reserved. No part of this book may be reproduced, stored in a retrieval system, or transmitted in any form or by any means without permission in writing from the publisher.

Printed in the United States of America

7 6 5 4 3 2 1

Contents

Preface xi

Historical and Cultural Introduction   1
The Archaic Period   3
The Classical Period   6
The Macedonian Empire   9
The Hellenistic Period   11
Philosophy   13
    Part I: The Early Ancient Greek Philosophers   14
    Part II: Socrates and Plato   14
    Part III: Aristotle   15
    Part IV: Hellenistic Philosophy   15

PART I
Early Ancient Greek Philosophy   17

1   The Milesians and Ionians   23
The First Phase: The Milesians   24
    Thales (ca. 624–545 BC)   24
    Anaximander (610–540 BC)   26
    Anaximenes (585–528 BC)   28
The Second Phase: The Ionians   30
    Pythagoras (570–497 BC)   30
    Heraclitus (540–480 BC)   34
Conclusion   41
Study Questions 41   *Discussion Questions* 42

2   Parmenides and Zeno   43
Parmenides (515–445 BC)   43
    The Journey   44
    The Way of Truth   44
    The Way of Seeming   47
    Discussion   49

Zeno (490–430 BC)   50
   The Midway Problem   50
   Achilles   51
   The Arrow   52
   The Moving Rows   52
   The Other Arguments   52
   Discussion   55
Melissus of Samos   58
Conclusion   59
Study Questions 59   Discussion Questions 60

3 The Pluralists, Atomists, and Sophists   61

The Fourth Phase: The Pluralists and Atomists   61
   Empedocles (492–432 BC)   61
   Anaxagoras (500–428 BC)   67
   Democritus (460–360 BC)   72
The Fifth Phase: The Sophists   77
   Protagoras (490–420 BC)   79
   Gorgias (485–395 BC)   84
   Discussion   86
Conclusion   87
Study Questions 87   Discussion Questions 88

PART II
Introduction to Socrates and Plato   89

4 Socrates in the Early Dialogues of Plato   95

The Socratic Dialogues   96
   The Socratic Knowledge Paradox   97
   Discussion   99
Philosophical Method   100
Philosophical Theses   102
   1. Happiness as the Greatest Good   102
   2. Functions of the Soul   103
   3. Virtue and Happiness   103
   4. Intellectualist Theory of Virtue   105
   5. Unity of the Virtues   105
   6. Harming Others Harms Oneself   106
   Conclusion   107
Sophism, Pre-Socratic Thought, and Religion   107
   Sophism   107
   Pre-Socratic Thought   108
   Religion   109

Socrates's Trial and Death   110
   Euthyphro   111
   The *Apology*   112
   The *Crito*   113
Conclusion   113
Study Questions 113   ∾   Discussion Questions 114

5 Plato's Views in Development   115

Introduction to Plato   116
Some Differences between Socrates and Plato   117
Plato's Arguments against Sophism   118
   The Need for Definitions   118
   The Analogy of the Arts and the Sciences   118
   Reductio ad Absurdum Arguments   119
   The Self-Defeating Nature of Sophism   120
   The Arguments for the Forms   120
The *Protagoras*   120
The *Gorgias*   122
The *Meno*   123
   Overview   123
   The Paradox of Inquiry   124
   Learning as Recollection   124
   Knowledge and True Beliefs   125
   Is Virtue Teachable?   126
The *Phaedo*   126
   The Argument for the Forms   126
   Arguments for the Immortal Soul   127
Conclusion   128
Study Questions 129   ∾   Discussion Questions 129

6 Plato: Metaphysics and Epistemology   131

The Theory of Forms   132
   Ontological Claim   132
   The Unity Thesis   133
   Exemplary Self-Predication   134
   The Reality of the Forms   134
Arguments for the Forms   136
   Arguments from Relativity   136
   Arguments from Predication   138
   Epistemological Arguments   139
   Semantic Arguments   139
   Sophism Is False   140

The *Republic* 140
   Overview 141
   The Analogy of the Sun 143
   The Divided Line 143
   The Analogy of the Cave 145
Conclusion 146
Study Questions 149 ◆ *Discussion Questions* 149

7 Plato: Justice and Love   151

The Challenges 151
   Element 1: The State 155
   Element 2: The Soul 156
   Element 3: The Form of Goodness 158
   Element 4: Characters 158
The Overall Argument 158
   The First Strand 159
   The Second Strand: Types of Character and States 162
   The Third Strand: Justice and Pleasure 163
Education 165
The Ideal State 166
The *Symposium* 168
   Interpretations 170
The *Phaedrus* 171
Conclusion 174
Study Questions 174 ◆ *Discussion Questions* 175

8 Plato: Later Period   177

The *Parmenides* 178
   The Critique 178
   The Deductions 181
The *Theaetetus* 182
   Knowledge as Perception 183
   Knowledge as True Belief 185
   Knowledge as True Belief with an Account 186
   Discussion 187
The *Timaeus* 187
   Creation 188
   The Receptacle 189
   Necessity 190
   Discussion 191
The *Sophist* and the *Statesman* 192
   Falsity and Non-Being 193
   The Problem of Non-Being Dissolved 194
   The Problem of False Statements Solved 194
   Discussion 195

The *Laws* 195
Conclusion 197
Study Questions 198 ~ Discussion Questions 199

PART III
Introduction to Aristotle 201

9   Aristotle: Logic and Science   **205**
Some Contrasts with Plato   207
The *Organon*: Scientific Method   210
The *Categories*   210
On Interpretation   212
  The Sea Battle   213
Logic: The *Prior Analytics*   215
  The First Step   215
  The Second Step   216
  The Third Step   217
  The Fourth Step   217
  The Fifth Step   218
  Meta-Conclusions   219
  Modal Deductions   220
  Overview of the *Prior Analytics*   220
  Summary   221
The *Posterior Analytics*   221
  The Need for Fundamental Principles   222
  The Necessary   223
  Deductive Explanation   226
  Definitions   227
  Empirical Knowledge   227
The *Topics*: Dialectic   229
Conclusion   230
Study Questions 231 ~ Discussion Questions 232

10   Aristotle: Physics and Biology   **233**
A Brief Overview of the *Physics*   233
The Possibility of Change   234
  Two Kinds of Change   234
  The Analysis of Parmenides   235
Natural Change and the Four Causes   236
  The Four Causes   238
  The Teleological, Chance, and Necessity   239
  The Defense of Teleology   240

Motion 241
The Infinite 242
Place 243
Time 244
Continuity of Motion 246
   Zeno's Paradoxes 247
   A Brief Summary 248
Causes of Motion 249
   First Cause, but No First Event 249
On the Universe 250
   On The Heavens: The Superlunary World 251
   The Sublunary World 253
Animals 257
   Classification 257
   Anatomical Descriptions and Physiological Processes 259
   Reproduction, Inheritance, and Growth 260
   The Movement and Perception of Animals 261
Conclusion 261
Study Questions 262 ⁓ Discussion Questions 263

11 Aristotle: Metaphysics   265

A Brief Overview 265
Wisdom and the Knowledge of First Principles 266
Being *Qua* Being 267
What Is Substance? 271
   In Search of Substance (Book VII) 272
   Actuality and Potentiality 275
   Discussion 277
Plato and the Pre-Socratics 278
Theology 279
   General Conclusions about the *Metaphysics* 281
De Anima 281
   Brief Overview 281
   Soul as the Form of the Body 282
   Discussion 284
Levels of Being Animate 285
   Plants 286
   Animals 286
Perception 287
Reason 289
   Interpretation 289
Conclusion 290
Study Questions 291 ⁓ Discussion Questions 292

12 Aristotle: Ethics, Politics, and Poetics — 293

An Outline of the *Nicomachean Ethics*   293

Happiness as the Ultimate End   294
- Ends and Good   294
- Ends Are Structured   295
- The Value of Ends   295
- Chains of Means Must Come to an End   295
- Happiness   296

Happiness and Virtue   297
- Is Happiness Inclusive or Exclusive?   298

Virtues and the Mean   299
- Specific Ethical Virtues   300

Responsibility   301

Practical Wisdom   302
- Unity of the Virtues   303
- Ethical Realism   304
- The Practical Syllogism   304

The Intellectual Virtues   305

Incontinence or *Akrasia*   305

Friendship   307

Pleasure and Contemplation   308
- The Problem   309
- The Overall Argument   310

Politics   311

Overview   311

The Household and the *Polis*   312
- Slaves   314
- Male–Female   314

Kinds of City-States   315

The Ideal City-State   316
- Commentary   318

The *Poetics*   318
- Art as Imitation   318
- Tragedy and Catharsis   319

Conclusion   319

Study Questions 320 ∾ Discussion Questions 321

PART IV
Introduction to Hellenistic and Roman Philosophy 323

13 Epicureanism: Epicurus and Lucretius 329
Epicurus (341–270 BC) 329
- Physics 330
- Theory of Knowledge 336
- Ethical Theory 337

Summary of Key Texts 340
Lucretius (99–55 BC) 341
Conclusion 342
Study Questions 343 ~ Discussion Questions 343

14 Stoicism: Zeno of Citium, Seneca, Epictetus, and Marcus Aurelius 345
Zeno of Citium (334–262 BC) 346
- Philosophy of Nature 346
- Ethics 352
- Cosmopolitanism 355
- Logic 357

Seneca (1 BC–65 AD) 362
Epictetus (55–135 AD) 364
Marcus Aurelius (121–180 AD) 367
Conclusion 368
Study Questions 369 ~ Discussion Questions 370

15 Skepticism: Pyrrho and Sextus 371
Pyrrho of Elis (367–275 BC) 371
Academic Skepticism 374
Sextus Empiricus (175–225 AD) 375
- Influences 378

Conclusion 378
Study Questions 379 ~ Discussion Questions 379

Timeline 381
Endnotes 385
Glossary of Some Key Greek Terms 397
Bibliography 399
Index 407

Preface

This book spans the period from Thales (approximately 624–545 BC) to Sextus Empiricus (175–225 AD). This is arguably the most exciting phase in Western philosophy because it comprises the birth and flowering of the subject. Many of today's philosophical problems have their roots in the philosophy conceived during this time. The twentieth-century thinker Bernard Williams claims: "the legacy of Greece to Western Philosophy is Western Philosophy."[1] While this doesn't imply that all contemporary thinking is simply a reworking of ancient thought, it does mean that most of the philosophical problems of today have their origin in ancient philosophy. It also means that many of the answers and the methods of contemporary philosophy have their source in the thinking of ancient Greece.

This testifies to the richness, breadth, and depth of much ancient thinking. It also means that the study of ancient philosophy is relevant to contemporary thought. By studying ancient philosophy, we can see many of the issues relevant to contemporary thinking in an especially direct and simple form, and in a different cultural context.

The Greeks pioneered the questions about ethics and politics that still plague us today. They also invented the basic concepts that we need to understand the natural world. It is difficult to remember that ideas as fundamental as, for instance, substance, cause, biological function and species, needed to be created. Today we have a vast and complex background of accumulated knowledge, ideas and concepts that we take for granted, which the ancient thinkers did not have and which they had to create. For them, there was a whole world to understand and explore, and it was all uncharted intellectual territory.

The very early Greeks in particular had a firm confidence that they could understand the world through their own intellectual capacities. They discovered that, through empirical observation and reasoning clearly and systematically, one can understand fundamental natural processes and their underlying laws, or how the world works. This might be humanity's greatest discovery because it is the prelude to science. It was a very powerful and liberating breakthrough for the ancient Greeks. It became more so when they applied it to human life itself, thereby inventing the rudiments of psychology and social science. This became the basis of the ethical theories of Plato, Aristotle and the Stoics that are still part of contemporary thought. It is probably for these reasons that ancient Greece gave rise to three of the greatest philosophical minds of all time: Socrates, Plato, and Aristotle.

One of the main purposes of most courses in ancient philosophy is to stimulate students to think about the basic philosophical issues that were real to the ancient Greeks. With this purpose in mind, this book is meant to accompany and guide the student through his or her reading of the primary texts. It is a companion text to the original works of the philosophers. Such secondary texts are an important guide in our reading of original works, because they provide a set of contexts and recount some of the major ways in which the texts have been interpreted and understood by scholars. Pedagogically, a comprehensive secondary work like this one frees up class time for philosophical discussion of these issues, time which might otherwise be taken up with explaining interpretations of the primary texts.

This book is a general introduction to the claims and arguments of the ancient philosophers, and it is designed to be accessible without being philosophically naive. It contains explanations of their central arguments in metaphysics, epistemology, ethics, and politics. Where appropriate, I have attempted to inform students of different, contrasting interpretations of the original texts, but without entering the quagmire of detailed exegesis.

At some key points the book also presents some standard critical assessments of the views and arguments of the philosophers. Offering a companion to the great philosophers without presenting some critical assessment of their ideas would mislead students as to the critical nature of philosophy itself.

The book is organized into four parts:

Part I: The early ancient thinkers, including the Sophists
Part II: Socrates and Plato
Part III: Aristotle
Part IV: Hellenistic Philosophy

Of course, ancient philosophy is not really divided into four neat, self-contained groups. However, this classification is useful and needs to be understood, even if it is ultimately rejected. This book recounts a standard narrative about Ancient Philosophy and, at the same time, it points out the shortcomings of such a portrayal.

In addition to the book's general introduction, each part has its own introduction. There is a brief biography of each of the philosophers. At the end of each chapter, two sets of questions appear: self-test questions to help readers assess their comprehension of the chapter; and discussion questions to help connect the material in the chapter to wider philosophical issues.

I am very grateful to many other writers whose texts have helped me in the writing of this one. These authors are listed in the bibliography and in the endnotes. I would like to thank the following people for their comments: Professor Richard Kraut on chapters 6 and 7 and Diana Hoyos on chapter 12. Professor Elizabeth Schiltz read through the whole manuscript and made many helpful and insightful suggestions and comments that have improved the work. Thank you! I am also very grateful to Gayle Zawilla and the team at Waveland, who have accompanied me on this writing journey. Gayle did a marvelous job of editing the whole manuscript.

Historical and Cultural Introduction

People from all over the Aegean came to the first recorded Olympic games held in 776 BC. This event marks a symbolic watershed in the history of Greece; it represents the growing of a shared awareness of Hellenic identity. The people in the area of the Aegean began to recognize themselves as Greek, sharing a common language, culture, mythology, and religion. To better understand the historical significance of this event, we need to step back to the earlier history of the region: to the so-called "Dark Ages" (spanning roughly 1100 to 800 BC), and to the period even before that, namely, the late Bronze Age, from roughly 1600 to 1100 BC.

During the late Bronze Age, the mainland cities of Greece, such as Mycenae, Athens, and Thebes, flourished alongside the yet older Minoan culture of Crete. There was widespread trade between these mainland Mycenaean cities and Crete, Cyprus, Egypt, Mesopotamia, and Western Europe. Around 1500 BC, the Mycenaeans built their famous beehive tombs to bury their noble families; these, and the gold and jewelry found nearby, attest to the wealth and culture of the period. Around this time, the Mycenaeans invaded Minoan Crete and took control of the palace of Knossos. They began to build similar palaces around mainland Greece, with frescoes and indoor plumbing. Mycenaean civilization consisted of a loose gathering of different regional centers, each of which consisted of a city and a hinterland containing villages and settlements. Each of these regional centers was controlled by a king and was organized centrally for rural agricultural production, as well as urban craft making and textile, leather, and metallic manufacture. The palace was the hub controlling these economic activities and was the center of religious and cultural activities. Many of the gods of later classical Ancient Greece date from the Mycenaean later Bronze Age period: Zeus, Poseidon, Hermes, Athena, Artemis, and possibly others.

By 1200 BC, this period of prosperity and culture was on the wane. A hundred years later, many of Mycenaean kingdoms no longer existed as the Dark Ages began. The palaces were destroyed, and with them the organization that ran the local economies. It was during this period that the city of Troy was sacked. Similar decline was experienced throughout the eastern Mediterranean, from Egypt to the Hittite Empire that straddled modern-day Syria and Turkey. This general decline in Greece, and the resultant Dark Ages, are sometimes attributed to the invasions of the Dorians from the north. However, it is likely that the causes were many. There may have been other contributing factors, such as natural disasters, reduction in trade, drought, and soil exhaustion. The result was that the Mycenaean later Bronze-Age civilization collapsed.

By around 800 BC, however, there were signs of a regional revival, such as the first Olympic games. As their sense of common identity grew, the Greeks developed a heightened awareness of a shared history and heritage. An important part of this heritage was the mythology that Homer articulated in the *Iliad* and *Odyssey* in roughly 700 BC. These epic poems express nostalgia for a mythologized earlier heroic age, before the Dark Ages, during the late Bronze Age. In fact, the battle for Troy may have actually occurred around 1200 BC, by which time Mycenaean civilization was already past its zenith. However, the Greeks remembered and romanticized their past. It was key to their growing sense of identity.

The renaissance of Greek society was due to many interrelated factors. The eighth century BC was a period of population growth. At the same time, the more fertile land, which had previously been communal, was appropriated and used by wealthier families for growing grain. As propertied aristocracies increased during a time of population growth, there was mounting pressure to find more land. So the Greeks started to settle in other parts of the Mediterranean. At the same time, there was an expansion in overseas trade, and Greeks founded trading outposts both west and east. Both of these factors led to an increase in economic activity. The whole area became wealthier.

The trading contacts led to important cultural developments. Possibly around 800 BC the Greeks invented their own alphabet based on that of the Phoenicians. This was used for recording property ownership, but also for writing poems. There are fragments of poetry scratched on pots in early forms of Greek from around 750 BC. Around this time the decoration on pottery became more varied, ornamental, and pictorial: we see paintings of battle scenes framed in oriental motifs as well as a greater variety of bronze statues. All of this indicates a culture that is beginning to bloom.

As trade with foreigners picked up, the contrasting sense of Greek identity deepened. During the eighth century, more religious festivals occurred in which Greek people from all over the region participated. There were famous shrines for Zeus and Hydra at Olympia, for Apollo and Artemis at Delos, and the oracles at Delphi. These festivals fostered the sense of common identity. Perhaps for this reason, by 750 BC an increased interest was evident in the tombs, heroes, and legends of the ancient Mycenaean period, including special shrines for Agamemnon at Mycenae and Helen of Troy at Sparta.

The Archaic Period

Contemporary historians have marked 700 BC as an approximate start for the so-called "Archaic period" of Greek history, which ends around 500 BC with the beginning of the Classical period. The Archaic period is characterized by the formation of the city-states, an increase in the colonization of the Mediterranean and the Black seas, and by the politics of cooperation and rivalry between the city-states.

Ancient Archaic Greece was not a single country but rather a collection of several hundred city-states, which gradually spread throughout the Aegean. This had many implications. It meant that each *polis* or city-state could be organized in a politically more inclusive way than a large country or empire. Land-owning aristocracies often governed the city-states. In any case, the city-state consisted an important departure from the centralized kingships of the Mycenaean period. The city-state conceived itself as a community of citizens with common interests, loyalties, and traditions. Even when the local aristocracies retained most of the power, the city-state was a political unity.

A glimpse into the spirit of this period is provided by the contrast between the heroic epics of Homer and the more pedestrian works of Hesiod. Although they were written down at roughly the same time, Homer's *Iliad* and *Odyssey* capture a romantic feeling for an earlier heroic period prior to the Dark Ages. The *Iliad* was probably written down about 760 BC and the *Odyssey* a little later; both are written records of older oral poems.

In contrast to the adventurous spirit of Homer's works, the writings of Hesiod are more matter-of-fact, especially the *Works and Days*. This is a poem about 800 lines long, in which Hesiod provides advice (to his brother Perses) about how to live, extolling the virtues and rewards of hard work. Hesiod was a farmer in Boeotia, a region in central Greece near the city Thespiae. Hesiod also praises the benefits of marriage to a local girl and cites the myth of Pandora, the first woman, who was created to punish the crime of Prometheus who stole fire from the gods. The myth says that Pandora opened the jar that contained the diseases and plagues of the world.

Hesiod probably wrote his other work, the *Theogony*, around 700 BC. The poem describes the origin and mythology surrounding the Greek gods. Its main theme is the ascent of Zeus to lasting dominance among the gods, including the battle that the twelve younger Olympian gods won against the traditional Titans. The original Titans were the children of Uranus and Gaea. Uranus was jealous of his children, and he tried to destroy or hide them. However, his son Cronus was able to defeat his father with the help of his mother Gaea, and he became ruler of the gods. Cronus in turn was jealous of the children that he fathered with Rhea and he swallowed them. However, the youngest son Zeus was able to escape with the help of Gaea. He freed his siblings and waged war against his father. After the 10-year Battle of the Titans, Zeus and the Olympians were able to defeat Cronus and the Titans. The twelve Olympian gods included: Zeus, Hera, Hestia, Poseidon and Demeter (5 of the 6 children of Cronus and Rhea), and various children of Zeus: Apollo, Artemis, Ares, Aphrodite, Hermes, and Dionysus. Although these are very grand themes, Hesiod's aim is pedestrian; he wants to compile, sort out, and recount a set of oral traditions. The main purpose of the *Theogony* is to bring the stories of the gods into the everyday lives of Greeks.

As the population in the Aegean increased, the city-states began to threaten each other, and this spurred tighter governance, more central organization of each *polis*, and the inclusion of the farms and villages of the surrounding region. Each state needed an army. This required a government, and the local aristocrats shared the administration of the city among themselves, each post with a limited term of office. The rulers were assemblies or councils of elders, who replaced the old chiefs and kings from the earlier period. Public office was restricted to male citizens. In practice, only the wealthy aristocrats held office.

By around 650 BC, the armies of the city-states consisted of foot soldiers, called "hoplites," drawn from the farmer class. They were organized in tightly packed formations—the phalanx. In battle, the two opposing phalanxes collided with each other like two walls of shields and helmets, with protruding spears. The soldiers had to stand firm against the enemy line so that their large shields could protect their companions by their side.

The most famous war involving city-states was between Chalcis and Eretria on the island of Euboea around 710 BC. The two cities fought for the fertile Lelantine Plain. Because of alliances, many of the Greek cities were drawn into this conflict. On the side of Chalcis were Samos, Corinth, and Thessaly, and on the other, Miletus, Megara and possibly Chios. As a result the fighting spread around Greece. There were also armed squabbles about land between Sparta, Argos and Corinth on the Peloponnese peninsula in southern Greece. Nevertheless, as the Archaic period advanced, the major Greek cities tended to sign treaties and to form alliances and federations to preserve peace in the region. For example, the Thessalian confederacy was the main power in northern Greece during the sixth century BC.

The major threat to oligarchic rule in Archaic Greece was the emergence of tyrants in several of the cities around 650 to 500 BC. This period is sometimes known as "the age of the tyrants." Most of these tyrants came from the aristocratic class, for example, Cypselus of Corinth and Orthagoras of Sicyon. They grabbed power when the city underwent some crisis, such as fighting amongst the aristocrats. Several tyrants may have had the support of the people for a while, presenting themselves as saviors of the population from the oligarchs. Some initiated land reforms, trade, and building projects that favored the general population. However, only a few of the tyrants managed to hand down power to their descendents. Tyranny is unstable in the medium term.

As the city-states grew more prosperous and populous, migration and trade increased. Many of the city-states were located on the sites of more ancient settlements in narrow valleys. As they grew, many needed to trade. For example, Athens is located in an area of poor soil and had to import grain. For these reasons, many of the Greek cities founded settlements or colonies. For instance, the Corinthians founded Syracuse in Sicily in 734 BC. By the end of the Archaic period, Greek settlements extended westward into Italy, southern France, Corsica, and even to Spain. Eastward, they extended to the Mediterranean coast of Turkey and around the Baltic Sea. Southward, they reached to Cyrene in contemporary Libya. The process of colonization was especially successful around the Black Sea, where there were few competitors and the land was fertile. Most of the colonies preserved some kingship, cultural, and religious links to the mother *polis*. All of the colonies retained their Greek character.

This expansion led to conflicts, especially with the Phoenicians, the Lydians in modern-day Turkey, and eventually with the Persians from modern-day Iran. Around 540 BC, the Persians invaded Lydia, where there were many Greek settlements. In 525 BC, the Persians conquered Egypt, and around 492 BC, the Persians moved into Macedonia and Thrace. In 499 BC, the Ionian Greeks, under the influence of the tyrant Aristagoras, rebelled against their Persian rulers. Having failed to convince the Spartans to join his cause, Aristagoras persuaded the Athenians and the Eretrians to assist the Ionians in their revolt, but they eventually lost in 494 BC. However, the Persian King Darius promised revenge on the Athenians and the Eretrians for burning his Ionian capital, Sardis. Thus begun the Persian Wars, which mark another turning point in Greek history.

In 490 BC, Darius sent a military expedition to invade mainland Greece. They defeated the coastal city of Eretria, and moved on to Marathon. Athens decided to fight. Allegedly, they sent the courier Philippides to seek support from the Spartans; he ran the 150 miles from Athens in a day and a half. The Spartans could not send reinforcements until after the festival of Apollo. But Miltiades, the leader of the Athenian force of about 11,000 soldiers, decided on a swift and strategic attack when he learned that the Persian cavalry were indisposed. Thus, the Athenians won the historic battle of Marathon against a Persian army outnumbering the Athenians by more than two to one.

After many years of preparation, the Persian King Xerxes, the son of Darius, sent a huge army and navy for a second attempted invasion of Greece in 480 BC. When the Greeks learned that the Persians were building ships and preparing for war, they held a congress in Corinth in 481 BC and formed the Hellenic League, comprised of 31 states, with Sparta in command. They decided to make a stand on land at Thermopylae and to place their ships at Artemisium in the north. Themistocles, the leader of democratic Athens, advocated the evacuation of the city; many people went to Troezen and the island of Salamis.

Remarkably, because Athens and Sparta worked together, and because of their superior organization the Greeks were able to resist a far larger Persian onslaught. In the battle of Thermopylae, a force of about 7,000 Greeks led by King Leonidas of Sparta resisted a Persian force reputedly numbering about 100,000 for several days. The most famous part of the battle occurred when the Greeks were outflanked, and roughly 1,300 remained with the suicidal mission of holding off the Persians for as long as possible. The Persians eventually won and conquered the evacuated city of Athens.

However, Themistocles coaxed the Persian fleet into the narrow straits of Salamis, where the Athenian navy won the decisive sea battle of Salamis in 480 BC. Xerxes retreated to Asia in order to regroup for a final onslaught the following year, 479 BC. The Greeks hurriedly prepared for this land battle, gathering an army of perhaps 100,000 men. It is possible that the Persians had a force of 250,000. In any case, the Greeks won this final encounter, the famous battle of Plateae, partly because many Persians became trapped when they pursued the Greeks whom they mistakenly thought were retreating.

Around the same time, the Greeks had sent a fleet to the island of Samos, where the Persians had their camp and naval fleet. At the battle of Mycale, the Greeks defeated the Persian forces and destroyed their ships. According to the ancient historian Herodotus, this victory occurred on the same day as the battle of Plateae.

THE CLASSICAL PERIOD

These events in 479 BC mark an important turning point in European history, after which victorious Athens enjoyed a golden age of greatness. Because of its newfound wealth, stability, and self-confidence, Athens attained new intellectual and cultural heights. Pericles, who held political office from 467–428 BC, led this process: he instituted more reforms to make Athens an economic and cultural center, as well as more democratic.

In 477 BC, about 150 Greek city-states formed the Delian League, a military alliance under the leadership and control of Athens, whose fleet had spearheaded the defeat of the Persians. While the aim of the league was to keep the Persians at bay, it gradually became more akin to an Athenian empire. Various islands and cities, such as Carystus and Naxos, were compelled to become part of the league and to pay a heavy tribute to its coffers. By 456 BC, Athens had control over a large part of the region.

At the same time, after the war, Athens was becoming more democratic, partly under the guidance of Themistocles until 471. Power could no longer reside only in the hands of the aristocratic few, in part because the lower classes made such an important contribution to the fleet. Traditionally, the Council of the Areopagus had been filled with aristocrats. However, back in 508 BC, Cleisthenes had started the reforms needed to make Athens more democratic. After the war of 479, the assembly passed more power from the Council of the Areopagus to other bodies, such as the Council of Five Hundred. Pericles continued this process of democratization. Under his influence, the general assembly met more frequently, sometimes with an attendance of around 6,000 people, which was about 12 percent of the population of the city and surrounding countryside. Various bodies or boards, consisting of men elected by lot for one-year terms, carried out the administration of the state. There were no permanent officials. Even service on a jury was spread among many people, perhaps several hundred. Pericles instigated the idea that people should be paid something for their public service in order to help widen the spread of public participation in the running of the state. Despite this, we need to remember that in Athens there were many slaves, and women had no explicit political participation. Additionally, successful generals and the rich had greater political influence.

During this golden period, the arts flourished. In 447, Pericles initiated the construction of the Parthenon. This was the period of the great tragic plays of Aeschylus (c. 525–456 BC), Sophocles (ca. 497–405 BC) and Euripides (ca. 480–406 BC), and later the comedies of Aristophanes (ca. 446–386 BC). This was also the time of the great philosophers, such as Empedocles, Anaxagoras, Democritus, the Sophists, and Socrates. In Periclean Greece, Herodotus and Thucydides produced their major historical works, the former on the Persian wars and the latter on the Peloponnesian Wars. Hippocrates wrote his systematic medical texts on the island of Cos.

However, under the leadership of Sparta, other Greek city-states, such as Corinth, challenged Athens' military and economic supremacy. One of the catalysts of these uneasy relations was the wealthy state of Megara, which was situated between Corinth and Athens. To protect itself from Corinth, Megara left the Peloponnesian League and allied itself with Athens; this gave the Athenians control of the port of Pegae on the Corinthian Gulf. The so-called "first Peloponnesian War," from 460 to 445 BC, consisted in various battles that punctuated the uneasy peace between the Athenian and Spartan (or Peloponnesian) leagues. In 451 BC, a five-year truce between Athens and Sparta was negotiated. In 445, Athens lost some of its empire because of a revolt in Euboea, and because Megara switched its allegiance. In these circumstances, King Pleistoanax of Sparta was on the verge of invading Athens. Pericles prevented him through diplomacy, possibly through bribes. Later that year, in 445 BC, Athens and Sparta signed a peace agreement, and the first Peloponnesian War ended. Despite many battles and much loss of life since the start of the war, Athens had not increased its territorial empire.

The peace was short-lived because it was fragile. When Corcyra approached Athens for help in a dispute with Corinth, and when in 433 BC the Corcyraeans defeated Corinth with Athenian help, the peace accord was on the verge of breaking. Similar disputes broke out concerning Potidaea and Megara. These events initiated the second Peloponnesian War (431–404 BC), which Sparta eventually won, after 27 years of fighting. At the start of the war, Pericles convinced the farmers and people of the state of Attica to abandon their farms and houses and move into the city walls of Athens. During the first Peloponnesian war, Pericles had ordered the building of a wall around Athens and the land connecting it to the nearby port city of Piraeus. This effectively made Athens invulnerable to invasion and sieges, so long as it could import provisions by sea through Piraeus, especially grain from its territories in the Black Sea. Now, in the second war, Pericles convinced the rural Athenians to crowd into the city walls and sit out the siege from the Spartans rather than engaging with them militarily. Unfortunately, during the second year of the siege, a devastating plague broke out within the city walls that may have killed as much as a third of the population. Pericles was blamed and removed from office. However, within a year, he was reappointed as the commander of the Athenian army. The same year, in 429 BC, he himself died from the plague. Athens was greatly weakened after so much loss of life.

The war continued wearily. By 421, there was the possibility of another peace accord between Athens and Sparta. However, the proposed Peace of Nicias fell apart mainly because it left the Athenian empire intact, and some of the other partners in the Peloponnesian League, such as Corinth, Megara, and Boeotia, could not agree to such terms. Hostilities resumed. Alcibiades, pupil of Socrates and great aristocrat, led Athens towards further disasters.

The turning point in the war was the Sicilian Expedition of 415–413. Under the leadership of Alcibiades, Athens hoped to capture the rich city of Syracuse on Sicily, which was a colony of Corinth, Athens' great commercial rival. Although Athens sent a huge fleet to Sicily, the expedition was a catastrophe; needed support from disaffected groups in Sicily never materialized, and Alcibiades defected to Sparta, after being accused of impiety towards traditional Athenian rituals. In the ensuing debacle, Athens lost half of her military and naval power.

However, this terrible defeat didn't spell the end of the war, which lasted another nine years. The defeat wasn't the end of Athens' misfortunes either; the loss in Sicily ignited a conflict between aristocracy and democracy in Athens itself, and in 411 BC various oligarchic councils replaced the democratic assembly: first, the Council of the Four Hundred and later a council of five thousand. Alcibiades had a hand in these events. After acting as a commander for Spartans, he became an advisor to the Persians, and then he tried to persuade the Athenians that the Persians would enter the war on their side if Athens became an oligarchy. When the council of five thousand was installed, it recalled various Athenian exiles including Alcibiades himself, who went on to lead the Athenians in a famous naval victory at Cyzicus in 410 BC. Later that year, democracy was restored in Athens.

The war took another turning for the worse for Athens when, in 407 BC, the Spartans formed a partnership with the Persians. Despite this, in 406, Athens won an important sea battle near the Arginusae Islands, close to Lesbos. This success was marred by a disaster in which a storm prevented the rescue of the survivors of 25 sunken ships and several thousand Athenians. Eight generals were tried unconstitutionally, and despite the protestations of the philosopher Socrates, who was chairing the assembly, they were sentenced and executed. The next year, in 405 BC, Athens lost her fleet during the naval battle of Aegospotami. The victorious Spartan commander, Lysander, sailed to Athens and held the city in siege. Without means of importing provisions, the Athenians suffered starvation during the blockade and were forced to surrender in March 404.

After the war, the Spartans established the oligarchy of the Thirty Tyrants to govern Athens. This included Critias, who was a pupil of Socrates and a relative of Plato. The Thirty were violent, and many Athenians with different political persuasions and allegiances fled Athens to Thebes and Megara, where they planned the restoration of democracy that occurred in late 403 BC. It was around this time (399 BC) that Socrates was executed for impiety.

The defeat of Athens in 404 marks the beginning of the end of the golden age of classical Greece. There was no stable peace under Spartan control. In 387 BC, Sparta signed a pact with the Persians that gave Sparta the protection of the Persians but ceded all the Greek cities in Asia to Persian control. This led to discontent among the Greek city-states, and Thebes won a famous victory against Sparta in 362, which allowed Athens to regain some temporary supremacy of the region around 360 BC. However, even though it was home to Plato and Aristotle, and despite its economic prosperity, Athens did not repeat the artistic and cultural achievements of its Periclean past, around 80 years earlier.

THE MACEDONIAN EMPIRE

In 360 BC, Philip II became king of Macedon. Macedon or Macedonia was a kingdom north of Thessaly and to the south and west of Thrace. The Greeks did not consider the Macedonians to be Greek, despite their linguistic similarities. There were several cultural differences between the two societies. For instance, whereas Greek society was a loose association of city-states, Macedonian society consisted of farmers who owed allegiance to local aristocrats who paid homage to an autocratic king. Although Macedonia had grown in wealth since the Persian wars, when Philip II took power in 360, it was politically unstable. Over the next decade, he consolidated his power through strategic allegiances with Thrace and Athens, which enabled him to defeat nearby Illyria to the west, and Paeonia to the north. He captured the Greek cities on the Macedonian coast, and the gold mines of Mount Pangaeus. He introduced sweeping military reforms, including to the organization and equipment of the army. In 352 BC, Philip won a decisive battle against Phocis and Pherae to the south, enabling him to be appointed as commander of the Thessalian League. Finally, he occupied Pherae and Phocis in 346. Through these victories, Philip II became a powerful force in northern Greece. Feeling the threat of his growing power, Athens negotiated a peace treaty with Philip in 346. By 340, Philip had won control of the Black Sea coast (in today's Romania) and was able to capture the entire shipment of grain destined for Athens. Finally, in 338, Philip won a decisive battle against Athens and Thebes at Chaeronea in Boeotia. One of the heroes of the day was the eighteen-year-old son of Philip, Alexander. Macedonia was now supreme in Greece.

Despite his victory, Philip was lenient with Athens, and he tried to establish friendly relations with the city. This enabled him to form the Corinthian League in 337, which included all Greek cities except Sparta. The aim of the League was to ensure peace between the Greeks and to fight Persia. Soon afterwards Philip started planning his invasion of Persia. However, in the summer of 336 BC, he was assassinated because of a family squabble pertaining to his seventh wife.

At this time, Alexander was 20 years old (356–323 BC). After quickly securing his succession to his father and consolidating his power within the Corinthian League, Alexander attacked the Illyrians to the west and Thracians to the east in 335 BC. The young king showed his ruthlessness when he quelled a rebellion in the city of Thebes in Boeotia, central Greece. He asked the neighboring cities in Boeotia to decide the city's fate, and when they requested that Thebes be destroyed and that the Thebans be sold as slaves, he complied. Only a few people were spared, including the famous poet, Pindar.

In 334 BC, Alexander began his conquest of Asia, with an army of around 37,000 soldiers. By the time he died in 323, he had conquered Egypt, the whole of the Persian Empire, and land eastward as far as the Indus River. The campaign began in earnest with the Battle of Issus in 333 (on the coast of today's Turkey), in which Alexander defeated the Persian King Darius III, who was forced to flee. From there he passed through the Phoenician cities of Tyre and Gaza. Tyre refused to surrender, and Alexander laid siege to the city for eight months. When he captured the city, he punished its inhabitants, slaying the men and selling the women and children into slavery. In 331 Alexander invaded Egypt without a fight and founded the city of Alexandria.

Alexander pushed on into Persia and conquered the cities of Babylon in late 331 BC and Persepolis in 330. Persepolis (near Shiraz in Iran) was the spiritual center of Persia and of the Achaemenid Empire. Alexander ordered that the city be torched. The Macedonian emperor continued east in pursuit of Darius III. In fact, Bessus of Bactria assassinated Darius later that year and had himself crowned king of Persia. After quelling resistance that lasted almost three years in Sogdiana (near the modern city of Samarkand) and Bactria (in today's northern Afghanistan) in 327, Alexander entered the valley of the Indus River in today's Pakistan. He won the Battle of the Hydraspes in 326 BC (in today's Punjab) against the army of King Porus, which included 200 elephants. Alexander continued his march eastward, but his army mutinied. In the face of this revolt, he agreed to return to the Indus, and he set off to conquer the area southward, to the mouth of the Indus, which he reached in July 325. From there, he returned to Persia along the coast via the desert area of Gedrosia (in today's Balochistan, West Pakistan). In the spring of 323, he arrived back in Babylon. In June that year, he suffered from a fever and died at the age of 33.

All these grand events are marked by an enormous wealth of detailed occurrences that need not concern us here. Nevertheless, there are some general themes that we can pick up on. First, Alexander became increasingly convinced of his own divine genealogy and exacted the appropriate obedience from the conquered peoples. Second, as his army trekked eastward, he made new allegiances and increasingly relied on soldiers that were neither Greek nor Macedonian to fill the ranks of his army. He also used conquered wealth to employ mercenaries. Third, although Alexander did have some plans for the management and continuation of his empire, they were insufficient. Throughout the lands he conquered, he appointed loyal friends as satraps or governors with military support to govern the surrounding area, or he used the allegiance of local dignitaries, such as King Porus, to maintain control in the region.

These extraordinary and relentless events changed the world of ancient Greece. It was no longer a collection of city-states but part of a vast, eastward-stretching empire that was in some ways Greek. Greek-speaking Macedonian leaders controlled the empire, and Greek cities, towns, and settlements were scattered throughout the vast territory.

The Hellenistic Period

The Hellenistic period starts from the death of Alexander the Great and ends with the domination of the region by Rome. Alexander's sudden death in 323 BC initiated a struggle for the succession of his empire. Alexander had a half-brother, Arrhidaeus, who was mentally deficient, and one of Alexander's wives was pregnant. A compromise was reached: Alexander's chief minister Perdiccas took charge as regent until, hopefully, the birth of the baby boy, at which time the baby and Arrhidaeus would be appointed as joint kings, Philip III and Alexander IV. Perdiccas had to quickly appoint satraps throughout the empire and quell rebellions in Asia and in Greece. To stabilize his position, he also appointed two other men to govern the empire in the name of the kings. When Ptolemy redirected Alexander's funeral cortege to Egypt, Perdiccas responded to this challenge by trying to retake Egypt in 321. He failed and was assassinated by his own officers. Antipater took control of the regency. Further struggles for control of the empire ensued after the death of Antipater: Antigonus fought the new regent Polyperchon and ruled until 301. By 280 BC, the empire had settled into three Macedonian kingdoms: the Ptolemies in Egypt, the Seleucids in western Asia, and the Antigonids in northern Greece and Macedonia.

The cities of mainland Greece were no longer self-ruled. They were part of a much larger empire, subject to political struggles beyond their control. This had several effects on the life, art, and philosophy of the Hellenistic period. Athens was no longer the cultural center of a self-contained Greek world. For example, Alexandria in Egypt became the home of the greatest library in the world, where funded scholars could study. Universities were established by Stoics in Rhodes and Tarsus. Artists and sculptors found patrons throughout the empire. At the same time, local culture influenced the Greek speakers living in the empire. For example, in Egypt the Greek pantheon of ancient gods was redefined to incorporate Egyptian elements, and Egyptian gods were altered to include Greek ingredients. As we can imagine, during the 300 years of the Hellenistic period, considerable symbiosis existed between the local populations and the Macedonian urban elites.

In 196 BC, Rome defeated the king of Macedonia and began to intervene more aggressively in the eastern Mediterranean. The last bastion of the Hellenistic empire was Ptolemic Egypt, which fell with the defeat of Cleopatra in 31 BC. Although Greece had a tremendous influence on Roman culture, by this time mainland Greece was a small part of the Roman Empire. By 188 BC, Rome was the power of the Mediterranean, and in 146 BC Greece became a protectorate of Rome.

In conclusion, we have examined very briefly the periods and some of the main events of the history of ancient Greece in order to have some context and background for our study of the philosophy of the time. As we have seen, we can divide the history conveniently but artificially into six stages. First is the late Bronze Age, from roughly 1600 to 1100 BC, which is marked by the Mycenaean civilization. Second is the Dark Ages, which span roughly from 1100 to 800 BC. Third, the Archaic period, from

700 to 500 BC, is marked by the expansion of Greek city-states around the Mediterranean and Black Seas, and by the Athenian and Spartan victory in the wars with the Persians. Fourth, the Classical period from 479 to roughly 338 BC is defined by a so-called *golden age* of greatness in Athens under the direction of Pericles. This period of greatness was halted by the Peloponnesian Wars, which Athens lost. Fifth, when Philip of Macedonia defeated Athens and Thebes in 338, a brief period began during which Alexander the Great conquered much of the known world. Finally is the Hellenistic period from 323 to 196 BC.

PHILOSOPHY

The intellectual culture of ancient Greece was optimistic and bold. In general, it lacked the cynicism and self-doubt that sometimes plagues our age. The early Greeks in particular had an extraordinary confidence that they could understand the world in all of its aspects through the application of their own intellectual capacities. They discovered that we learn some of nature's secrets just by reasoning clearly and systematically, based on empirical observation. This is probably humanity's greatest discovery. It was an extremely powerful, invigorating, and liberating breakthrough for the ancient Greeks. It was probably for these reasons that ancient Greece gave birth to three of the greatest minds of all time: Socrates, Plato, and Aristotle.

Thales, Anaximander, Pythagoras, and Parmenides all flourished within one century. Only about one hundred and fifty years separate the lives of Thales (624–545 BC) and Socrates (470–399 BC). Yet, during this short span, we can see many of the great ideas of Western philosophy in embryonic form. Indeed, ancient philosophy contains nearly all the major elements of Western thought.[1] Because of its simplicity, it is often more beautiful and edifying than later philosophical work, which tends to be cluttered with qualifications and sometimes contains ideological debates, such as those surrounding Christian doctrine. The ancient Greek philosophers pioneered many of the great ideas of humanity, and by studying these thinkers we may hope to regain the original force, freshness, and clarity of their insights.

This book is organized around a narrative that describes the development of ancient philosophy, which can be divided into four parts corresponding to the sections of this book. Any story is, by necessity, a selective simplification of what occurs. The story of ancient philosophy outlined in this book is quite standard, but we shall see later how it is partial, highlighting some aspects of ancient philosophy and ignoring others. Furthermore, scholars dispute how the views of the thinkers we shall study should be understood. At key points, the standard story of ancient thinking requires interpretations that are contested.

Part I: The Early Ancient Greek Philosophers

The first Western philosophers, Thales, Anaximander, and Anaximenes, came from the eastern provinces of the Greek empire. They tried to explain the universe by identifying the basic stuff out of which all things are made, and by specifying the fundamental organizing principles of nature. Around 500 BC, with the work of Heraclitus and Pythagoras, this philosophy became more metaphysically oriented.

Around 450 BC, Parmenides threatened this whole enterprise. He denied that natural philosophy describes the nature of reality. He and Zeno argued for the claim that the universe is an undivided whole in which change and plurality are impossible. As a consequence, natural philosophy is a description of illusion and not reality. Parmenides and Zeno provided powerful arguments for their counterintuitive conclusions. Later philosophers, such as Empedocles, Anaxagoras, and Democritus, had to try to answer these challenges in order to continue with the natural philosophy.

In about 420 BC, a new skeptical approach emerged: Sophism. Partly in reaction to the diversity of earlier metaphysical theories, the Sophists taught a form of relativism that spurned metaphysics and challenged the religious and moral views of the time. In simple terms, the Sophists argued that there were no metaphysical and ethical truths to be learned. Instead, they taught their pupils to debate persuasively.

Part II: Socrates and Plato

In about 420 BC, Socrates began to argue against Sophism. He took issue with its skeptical and relativist view of ethics, and he developed the idea that the life of virtue is the happiest. However, Socrates is most well known for creating and embodying a questioning and dialectical approach to philosophical inquiry based on the need for definitions.

In order to refute Sophism decisively, Plato argued for the existence of universal Forms. These Forms or Ideas are abstract objects that define the essence of terms, such as *justice* and *goodness,* and Plato believed their existence is required to explain knowledge and language. In many of his dialogues, Plato expounds the implications of the Theory of Forms for areas of knowledge, such as epistemology, education, theology, ethics, art, and politics.

Plato also rejected the Pre-Socratic tradition of natural philosophy, arguing that purely mechanical explanations never provide the reasons why things happen. In conclusion, Plato rejected the two main options of earlier thought, i.e., the physical mechanism of the natural philosophers and the relativism of the Sophists. In at least some his dialogues, Plato thought that this rejection requires the existence of universal Forms.

Part III: Aristotle

However, does the refutation of Sophism and mechanism really require the existence of universal Forms? Aristotle argued that it does not. He claimed that the denial of relativism does not require Platonic absolutism. Aristotle had a great interest in the natural world and the classification of species. He also classified uses of misleading philosophical terms, such as *to be* and *cause*, and this led him to conclude that things can be said to exist in different ways, which he explains through the concept of *categories*. In particular, the category of *substance* indicates what exists primarily, and other kinds of existence such as that of qualities or the forms are derivative. In other words, Aristotle believed that Plato was mistaken to treat the Forms as if they were substances. Furthermore, Aristotle explained form and matter as two inseparable aspects of substance: the form is its essence, and the matter, what it is composed of. This allowed Aristotle to transcend both Plato and the natural philosophy of the Pre-Socratics, who respectively and mistakenly treated form and matter as if they were independent substances. Aristotle thought that universals exist, but that their existence is derivative or parasitic on natural substances. The forms are immanent in the natural world.

Part IV: Hellenistic Philosophy

The period of brilliance in Greek philosophy did not end with Aristotle, even though the golden age of the city-states faded away. About twenty years after the death of Aristotle, three important new schools of philosophy emerged: Epicureanism, Stoicism, and Pyrrhonean skepticism. These philosophies grew in the Hellenistic period, during which Greece was a small part of the Macedonian Empire. When Rome became the central European power, these new systems—especially Stoicism—gained strength. Around 170 AD, the Stoic Roman emperor, Marcus Aurelius, gave grants to the four philosophical schools of Athens: Plato's Academy, Aristotle's Lyceum, Epicurus's Garden, and the Stoa of the Stoics. By this time, however, the philosophical originality of ancient Greece had been lost. Rome was already under the threat of invasion, and philosophy was about to decline.

PART 1

Early Ancient Greek Philosophy

Many of the first Western philosophers were naturalists who tried to understand the natural world in a systematic manner. It is common to contrast their work with the poetic and mythological writings of Hesiod. Given this contrast, the emergence of natural philosophy in the sixth century BC constituted a new enterprise of human understanding. But, from this beginning, philosophy soon grew in many new directions, and so early ancient Greek philosophy unfolds as a story about different visions of the basic principles of understanding. We can divide this narrative into five phases.[1]

In the first phase are the earliest Western philosophers: Thales (ca. 624–545 BC), Anaximander (610–540 BC), and Anaximenes (585–528 BC). They all lived in the coastal town of Miletus, which was in the Greek province of Ionia on the Mediterranean coast of today's Turkey. These philosophers identified the basic principles around which nature is organized, and they studied many varied natural phenomena, from planets to plants.

In the second phase of early ancient Greek thought, Ionian philosophy became more metaphysical. Pythagoras (570–497 BC) taught that the universe is mathematical and that the soul is immortal, transmigrating after the death of the body. He formed a school to teach people how to live in accordance with his semi-mystical views. Around 500 BC, Heraclitus (540–480 BC) wrote a series of caustic and mystical aphorisms that express an intriguing metaphysics based on change and the duality of opposites.

In the third phase, Parmenides (515–445 BC) and his followers argued that the very idea of a science of nature was based on an error. These thinkers from Elea, the Eleatics, argued that there could not be a plurality of things. Parmenides wrote a poem arguing for the existence of a single, indivisible, changeless thing. Zeno (490–430 BC) supported this position with many arguments, including the famous paradoxes of motion. The works of Parmenides and Zeno constitute a fundamental objection and challenge to early ancient Greek naturalistic thought.

The fourth phase consists of various responses to Parmenides, and in attempts to continue the tradition of natural philosophy in a similar manner to that of the Milesians. The main authors of this period are Empedocles (492–432 BC), Anaxagoras (500–428 BC), and Democritus (460–360 BC). Empedocles, for example, agreed with Parmenides that nothing can come into or go out of existence, but he argued that the eternal stuff of the universe, the four elements (earth, air, fire and water), could change and intermingle. Democritus argued for the existence of indivisible atoms.

In the fifth phase, the Sophists reject the idea of discovering truths about nature, substituting for it the aim of teaching the art of persuasion. Many Sophists embraced relativism and skepticism, and in so doing they set philosophy another fundamental challenge: Are there truths that can be discovered by reasoning? The replies of Socrates and Plato to this question constitute Part II of this book.

This five-phase story is a simplification that is almost a caricature. There are many prominent philosophers left out of this picture, such as Xenophanes of Colophon (ca. 570–475 BC), Melissus of Samos (born ca. 470 BC), Philolaus (470–385 BC), Isocrates (436–338), Diogenes of Sinope (ca. 412–323 BC), and several Sophists such as Hippias and Antiphon. Even in its later periods after Plato and Aristotle (examined later in the last part of this book), the story omits many Stoic and Cynic thinkers, as well as the work in the schools of Plato (the Academy) and Aristotle (the Lyceum) after the death of their founders. Also omitted in the story are all the thinkers one might consider as intellectuals who contributed to the culture of the time, including philosophers who are less well known.[2] In short, the story is very selective. More than anything else, however, in its five phases the story is told from the perspective of Socrates, Plato, and Aristotle.[3] It imposes a teleological end or a story line on the history. It is as if all Pre-Socratic thinking is a prelude to Socrates and his intellectual descendents, Plato and Aristotle.

Additionally, much of our knowledge of the early philosophers comes from Plato and Aristotle and their followers, and there are reasons to doubt the accuracy of some of the views they attribute to earlier philosophers. This is because Plato and Aristotle were primarily interested in how the work of earlier thinkers related to their own thought; they weren't trying to describe the history of philosophy.[4] For example, Plato paints the Sophists as moral relativists in ways that focus on some aspects of their views and ignores others. Plato does so in part to distance Socrates, his mentor and friend, from the Sophists, but also to show how Sophism is mistaken. Aristotle looks to the early ancient philosophers for precursors to his own views about causes and substance.

The early ancient Greek philosophers are often called the *Pre-Socratics*. This term is a modern invention that is misleading. First, some of the Pre-Socratics were contemporaries of Socrates; for instance, Democritus may have even outlived him. Second, it encourages the idea that all roads lead to Socrates and, through him, to Plato and Aristotle. This unfortunate misconception reinforces our tendency to see earlier philosophy merely as a prelude to later philosophy, which we assume to be better. Such a view might lead us to disregard earlier philosophers as thinkers on their own terms. It also blinds us to alternative ways of reading the history of philosophy.

However, despite these serious misgivings, this book will concentrate on the traditional picture of early ancient Greek philosophy. In part this is because to challenge the traditional portrait, one needs to know and understand it well. The standard portrayal of ancient Greek philosophy captures important developments. Therefore, to help overcome its limitations, we can note some of the relevant exegetical shortcomings and issues on the way.

The thought of the early ancient philosophers was extraordinarily diverse and rich, both in style and content. The fragments that remain from this period reveal many different styles of philosophical thinking and writing: scientific poems, paradoxical aphorisms, and wise sayings, as well as prose. They contain bright flashes of insight, detailed observations of nature, and speculations, as well as sustained argument. In early ancient thought, we can find many of the perennial debates of philosophy: the senses versus reason; the timelessness of reality versus its ever-changing nature; mathematics versus poetry; science versus religion; matter versus form; argument versus rhetoric, and the Absolute versus the relative. The early ancient philosophers were the first to formulate concepts that are now key to philosophy and other disciplines. In general terms, the works of these early philosophers contain the seeds of much later thinking. In part, this is simply because they were the first philosophers. It is also a reflection of the cultural wealth of Greece.

THE TEXTS

The original works of the Pre-Socratic philosophers have been lost. Our knowledge of their thought is based entirely on later reports, quotations, and commentaries. This means that the reliability of these sources is questionable and often disputed.

Luckily, we have 26 Platonic dialogues, many of which contain references to earlier thinkers, especially the Sophists. Unfortunately, however, Plato (427–347 BC) does not try to record their views with historical accuracy. His main aim is to dramatize philosophical discussions, in which the main character, who is usually Socrates, his teacher and mentor, shows the failings of other views. Plato is a major source of information regarding the Sophists, but one of his objectives is to show how Sophism is mistaken.

The writings of Aristotle (384–322 BC) are a vital source of information about many of the Pre-Socratic thinkers. He systematically reviewed the thinking of earlier philosophies in order to learn from them. So, for example, in his *Physics*, Aristotle examines the theses and arguments of Parmenides and Zeno in order to develop his own theory of change.[5] As this indicates, Aristotle's interpretations reflect his own reading of the development of thought because he studied the opinions of earlier thinkers in order to argue for and develop his own ideas. Nevertheless, Aristotle may be considered the first doxographer. Some of his pupils followed his interest in the history of knowledge; for instance, Meno and Eudemus wrote histories of medicine and mathematics.

Most significantly, Aristotle's pupil, Theophrastus (371–287 BC), wrote a great deal on the Pre-Socratic philosophers. Among his extant works is *On the Senses*, which discusses the views of several Pre-Socratic thinkers. Unfortunately, this is his only surviving work with a strong historical content. Theophrastus had a direct interest in the history of philosophy as such, and later commentators summarized and used as a reference his original works, which are now lost. In this way, some of his work was preserved, and indeed, much of the knowledge we have of the early ancient philosophers comes indirectly from Theophrastus.

Around 100 AD, Aetius wrote a work summarizing the views of the early philosophers. Such collections of ancient doxography are called *Placita*. Aetius's *Placita* was lost. However, it formed the basis of two later doxographies: that of pseudo-Plutarch and Stobaeus. Plutarch (45–120 AD) wrote papers and treatises about history, biography, literature, and philosophy, which contain quotations from the Pre-Socratics. Of special importance is the work *The Opinions of the Philosophers*, probably written in the second century AD after Plutarch's death, but which was falsely attributed to him and is now referred to as "pseudo-Plutarch." This work was based on Aetius's *Placita*. Likewise, in fifth century AD, Stobaeus (or John of Stobi) collected summaries and quotations from over five hundred ancient writers, based on the now lost work of Aetius.

Hippolytus of Rome (170–235 AD) was a Christian theologian who wrote *The Refutation of all Heresies*, in which he summarizes and quotes some ancient thinkers in order to show that they were heretical.

In the third century AD, Diogenes Laërtius wrote a work called the *Lives of the Philosophers*, which has survived and which is a valuable source of information about the early Greek philosophers, even though some of its stories are probably false. Another very important source of many of the original texts is Simplicius's commentary on Aristotle's *Physics*, written around 530 AD.

Towards the end of the nineteenth century, Alexander Diels and Walther Kranz collected the fragments of the Pre-Socratic philosophers, which were scattered in later writings such as those mentioned above. Their work, *Fragmente der Vorsokratiker*, was translated into English by Kathleen Freeman and published as *Ancilla to the Presocratic Philosophers*. The so-called "B-numbers" cited after each fragment in Freeman's work refer to the Diels-Kranz text. The *Ancilla* does not contain the commentaries of some of later ancient thinkers, which are sometimes also insightful and useful. Furthermore, most of the more contemporary commentators prefer more recent translations of the original Greek. Nevertheless, even when one does not rely on the *Ancilla*'s translation, the Diels-Kranz reference (cited in this text as DK) is a common way to pinpoint a text.

There are considerable and unavoidable problems in translating these ancient texts. First, abstract terms such as *logos* have significantly different senses in different contexts. *Logos* can mean *reason*, or *rational principle*, or *causal law*, or *organizing idea* in different texts. Second, none of our English equivalent terms may capture the nuances and ambiguities that the original Greek word may have had for an ancient reader. For example, *logos* has a connotation of the divine or godly that none of the earlier-mentioned English words have. Third, all words come with a history of usage, and many of our English philosophical terms have a Christian ancestry. For this reason, it is not exactly correct to translate the Greek term *psuchê* by using the English *soul*, or translating *areté* with the word *virtue*. For these reasons, readers should be careful in attributing contemporary meanings to the texts.

When reading the ancient Greeks, it is important to remember that we take for granted a vast and complex background of accumulated knowledge and concepts that the ancient philosophers did not have. For example, we know that the moon is smaller than the sun; we assume that all animals and plants are classified into species; we know how to explain the existence of clouds. In the ancient world, this complex web of background knowledge and concepts had yet to be discovered and formulated. For the Greeks, this presented itself as a challenge; there was a whole world to understand and explore.

1 The Milesians and Ionians

The first ancient Greek philosophers were interested primarily in the study of the natural world. They attempted to systematically describe and explain natural phenomena. This makes them in some sense both the first philosophers and the first scientists, even though such a claim is anachronistic.[1] They assumed that nature can be explained and understood because it is organized according to certain principles. Their main aim was to discover those principles.

This aim required them to invent or form concepts that we now usually take for granted. For example, they used the term *cosmos* to stand for the universe as an orderly whole. They employ the word *nature* (or *phusis*, from which we have derived the word *physics*) to stand for things that grow or are formed naturally, as opposed to artifacts, which are made. The aim of explaining natural phenomena may also involve the concept of natural essences. Natural things have certain fundamental properties, or an *essence*, in terms of which their other properties can be explained. The early philosophic enterprise also employs the notion of systematic explanation: the idea of explaining as much as possible assuming as little as possible.

These first thinkers advanced arguments in favor of their positions, and for this reason, they deserve to be called philosophers. They assumed that careful reasoning can yield knowledge of nature, and they implicitly distinguished reasoning from speculation. At the time, the idea of giving arguments for one's claims was novel. To highlight the dramatic nature of this innovation, contemporary writers about ancient Greece often contrast *muthus* (myth) with *logos* (reason). In this regard, we might compare the early philosophers with the mythical stories of Hesiod's *Theogony*. Hesiod's poem, which was probably written in the eighth century BC, charts the genealogy of the gods, starting with Chaos, Gaea (Earth), and Eros (Love). The mythology of this poem was a generally accepted part of Greek culture. It personifies natural forces and objects, and it tries to explain the origin of some natural phenomena such as day and night, the mountains, the sea, and people. For example, it describes how the mating of Earth and her son, Uranus (the Heavens), produced the first race, the Titans (see Historical and Cultural Introduction).

In contrast to this mythology, the early philosophers tried to make sense of nature without *ad hoc* appeal to the whims of the gods. They attempted to provide a single explanation of all natural phenomena, and to substantiate their claims with some reasoning or evidence. The idea that claims should be supported in such a way destroys the assumption that they should be accepted solely because an authority advances them. Arguments are revolutionary. In part this is because they allow for more freedom of thought than acceptance based solely on authority. As we shall see later, Heraclitus was one of the first philosophers to express such a rebellious attitude explicitly.

THE FIRST PHASE: THE MILESIANS

As we saw in the introduction, early ancient Greek philosophy can be conveniently, but slightly artificially, divided into five phases. The first phase was concentrated around Miletus, which is a city in the Greek province of Ionia, located on what is now the western coast of Turkey. Miletus was a wealthy seaport, a focal point for commercial activity, and partly because of this, there was increased leisure that permitted thought, discussion and art. Miletus became a cultural center, and the first western philosophers were from there.

Thales (ca. 624–545 BC)

We do not know much about the life of Thales, and nothing of his work remains except fragments reported by later writers such as Aristotle, and Herodotus, the fifth century AD historian. However, Thales was named as one of the seven sages of the early ancient Greeks, and he was known not only as a philosopher and scientist but also as a political advisor.[2] He urged the Ionians to establish a single council located at the center of the province.[3] During the Persian war, when the army of Croesus could not cross the river Halys, Thales ordered the digging of a channel and dam that diverted the river so that it was fordable.[4] He was also an astronomer who allegedly predicted the eclipse of 585 BC, as well as discovering some of the first theorems of geometry (such as that in every isosceles triangle the angles at the base are equal). Reportedly, he once fell in a ditch when looking at the stars. The woman he was with exclaimed: "Do you think, Thales, that you will learn what is in the heavens, when you cannot see what is front of your feet?" In contrast, it is claimed that he wanted to show that it is easy for a philosopher to become rich: he foresaw a good early olive crop and hired all the olive presses, which he rented out at great profit.[5]

According to Aristotle, Thales claims that all things are made of water. In this standard view of his ideas, Thales introduces the claim that the universe is composed of a fundamental material, and he conjectures that this was water. Thales proposes the idea of one fundamental substance-kind as a simple and unified way to explain all natural phenomena. In the *Metaphysics*, Aristotle writes:

> Most of the first philosophers thought that principles in the form of matter were the only principles of things. For they say that the element and the first principle of things that exist is that from which they all are and from which they first come into being. . . . Thales, the founder of this kind of philosophy, says that this is water. (983b6–9) (DK11A12)[6]

Moreover, just after the quoted passage, Aristotle suggests that Thales may advance an argument for his position, namely, that all things have their nourishment and seeds in something moist, and that the origin of things is the principle of all things. Aristotle also notes that Thales thinks that the earth rests on water. This brief mention is a reference to the problem of the stability of the earth that we will revisit when we discuss Anaximander.

This standard interpretation of Thales is challenged by some of today's scholars primarily on the grounds that Aristotle interpreted the earlier philosophers in light of later ones, such as Anaximenes, who were more clearly concerned with the basic stuff out of which the universe is composed.[7] Furthermore, Aristotle himself makes it clear that he is reviewing the work of the early philosophers to see to what extent they anticipate his own insights about the different kinds of cause. Some contemporary scholars argue that we cannot conclude that Thales thinks that water is the basic stuff of the universe from the assertion that it is the origin of all things.[8] "All things are made of water" doesn't follow from "all things come from water."

In *On the Soul* (*De Anima*), Aristotle also claims that Thales asserts that all things have a soul:

> Some say that it [i.e., soul] is intermingled in the universe. That, perhaps, was why Thales thought that all things are full of gods." (*De Anima* I 411a7) (DK11A22)

According to Aristotle, Thales's argument for this claim is that magnets can move iron, and that anything that is capable of initiating movement is thereby animate.[9] By definition, anything that is animate has a soul. The Greek word *psuchê* (soul) comes from the word *empsuchos*, which means animate. When reflecting on this thesis, we must avoid imposing on Thales the Christian conception of the soul as a conscious spiritual substance. Thales's idea is that all things are to some degree animate, and that, therefore, there is no strict dividing line between what is alive and what is not.[10] If this is his view, then he may have held that the cosmos is in some sense alive, a form of what was later called *hylozoism*. If this is a correct interpretation, it isn't right to portray Thales straightforwardly as a materialist philosopher.

Anaximander (610–540 BC)

Anaximander was reportedly a student of Thales. He wrote an ambitious, wide ranging work called *Concerning Nature*, which included a cosmology; a natural history of the Earth; a description of many kinds of natural phenomena, such as rain and wind; an account of the development of animals, and a work on geography, including a famous map of the world.[11] Unfortunately, only a few sentences of this work have survived.

We can summarize the basics of Anaximander's natural philosophy with four points. First, he claims that the fundamental constituent of the universe is something infinite or without limits. This is usually taken to mean that it is something spatially infinite, and eternal or infinitely old. In the *Physics*, Aristotle says:

> It is with reason that they all make (the infinite) a principle . . . for everything is either a principle or derived from a principle. But the infinite has no principle—for then it would have a limit. Again, it is ungenerated and indestructible and so is a principle. . . . And it is also divine; for it is deathless and unperishing, as Anaximander and most of the natural scientists say. (203b6–11) (DK12A15)

In this passage, we find an argument, which is probably Anaximander's, for the need of an infinite first principle:

1. Everything must either come from a first principle, or itself be such a principle.
2. The unlimited cannot be derived from a principle, for then it would be limited by that principle.
3. Therefore, the unlimited itself must be a principle from which other things are derived.

As another passage from Aristotle indicates, Anaximander probably also argues that the primordial substance-stuff of the universe is infinite in age because change is perpetual, and all change is the alteration of some pre-existing substance (Physics, 203b13–30) (DK12A15).

Second, a selection from Simplicius sheds light on another aspect of Anaximander's thought. Simplicius contrasts the views of Anaximander with those of Thales, reporting of Anaximander:

> He was the first to introduce this word "principle." He says that it is neither water nor any other of the so-called elements but some different infinite nature from which all the heavens and the worlds in them come into being . . . It is clear that he observed the change of the four elements into one another and was unwilling to make any one of them the underlying stuff . . . . (*Commentary on the Physics*, 24.13–23) (DK12A9)

This passage provides an argument based on the premise that the basic stuff the universe must underlie all changes. Since all of the so-called elements (earth, water, air, and fire) can change one into the other, none of them can be the basic substance of the universe.

1. The basic substance-stuff underlies all change and, therefore, it cannot change into something else.
2. Each of the elements does change into the others.
3. Therefore, the basic substance-stuff of the universe is not one of the elements.

Since the basic substance of the universe is not one of the four elements, and given that these elements are defined by their properties, it follows that Anaximander probably views the basic substance-stuff of the universe as indeterminate.[12]

Third, Simplicius also says that Anaximander "accounts for coming into being not by the alteration of the element, but by the separation off of the opposites by eternal motion" (*Commentary on the Physics*, 24.23–25). Probably the point is that the four elements have opposing qualities; for example, air is cold and fire is hot; water is moist and earth is dry. It is these opposing qualities that explain change.

In this context, Simplicius apparently quotes a passage from Anaximander's original work; speaking of these opposites, he says: "they give justice and reparation to one another for their injustice in accordance with the arrangement of time." If this citation is indeed directly from Anaximander's original text then it is the earliest surviving written piece of Western philosophy. The idea is probably that any imbalance between the four elements is eventually restored to equilibrium. A predomination of one element will be compensated by a period of predomination of its opposite.

Fourth, we find in Aristotle's *Physics* an argument that if the universe is unlimited, it cannot be composed of any one of the four elements (204b22–9). The argument is that if any one of these elements were unlimited, then it would have destroyed the others, since the four elements are opposed to each other in their qualities. So, for example, if water were fundamental then its moisture would eradicate the dryness of earth and fire, and its coldness would eliminate the heat of air and fire. Given enough time, everything would turn into water. Since none of the elements have been destroyed, we may conclude that the basic constituent of the universe is not one of these elements.

1. The basic substance-stuff must be infinitely old.
2. If the basic substance-stuff were one of the elements, then it would have destroyed the other elements in an infinite amount of time.
3. All four elements can be observed to exist.
4. Therefore, the basic substance-stuff is not one of the elements.

This argument neatly brings together the first three strands of Anaximander's thought outlined above, namely: (a) the unlimited must be a principle, (b) the principle can't be one of the elements, and (c) the opposing elements must be in balance. Even though this argument looks like one that Anaximander would give, we cannot be sure that it is from Anaximander.

Anaximander is also famous for his ingenious explanation of the fact that the Earth hangs in empty space, apparently without physical support and apparently without moving. This is sometimes called "the problem of the stability of the earth": how can the Earth be stationary in space? As we saw, Thales tries to solve this problem by suggesting that it floats in water. Anaximander argues that if the Earth is mid-way between all other things, then there could not be a reason for it to move one way rather than another. Consequently, if the Earth is the center of the universe, then it must stay where it is.[13] This argument appeals to what was later called the *Principle of Sufficient Reason*, the claim that there must be a reason why things are so and not otherwise.

Anaximander claims that the Sun, Moon and the stars came into being when the part of the universe that produces heat split off so as to cause spheres of flame to surround the Earth (DK12A10). He says that the circle of the Sun is 27 times the size of the Earth, while that of the Moon is 18 times. We don't know how he arrives at these figures. He claims that the rings of the stars are closest to the Earth and the ring of the Sun is furthest, with the Moon in between (DK12A11). Again, we don't know why he thinks this. It might be because the Sun contains the greatest amount of fire and, as fire is opposite to earth, the Sun needs to be far away from our planet in order to maintain equilibrium between the two.

The few surviving fragments that mention Anaximander suggest that he had a very wide range of interests in the natural world. For example, he discusses winds, rain, clouds, and lightning. Thunderstorms arise when the wind has been compressed within a dense cloud and breaks out (DK12A23). He also tries to account for the origin of life and species, suggesting that the first creatures were fish-like animals that arose from heated water and earth and which became more fitted for a drier environment as the earth dried up (DK12A30).

Anaximenes (585–528 BC)

Anaximenes may have been a student of Anaximander. Apart from the fact that he was Milesian, very little else is known about his life. Like his predecessors from Miletus, Anaximenes proposes that there is a single substance-stuff out of which everything is made. In his commentary on Aristotle's *Physics*, Simplicius presents Anaximenes as saying that:

> The underlying nature is one and infinite, but not undefined as Anaximander said, but definite, for he identifies it as air—and it differs in its substantial nature by rarity and density. Being made finer it

becomes fire, being made thicker it becomes wind, then cloud, then (when thickened still more) water, then earth, then stones,—and the rest come into being from these. He, too, makes motion eternal, and says that change, also, comes about through it. (DK13A5)[14]

According to Anaximenes, apparently Anaximander's views are not explicit enough in two crucial ways. First, Anaximenes claims that the elemental substance-stuff is unlimited air. In other words, he substitutes Anaximander's indeterminate substance for something determinate and gaseous. Second, Anaximenes is more explicit than his predecessors concerning the processes through which ordinary things are generated from the one substance. These processes are condensation and rarefaction. Through compression, air thickens and progressively becomes clouds, water and earth. Through expansion, air becomes thinner and turns into fire. This view implies that the different properties of the things we observe (such as liquids and solids) are due to differences in their relative density. In this way, Anaximenes tries to explain meteorological phenomena such as wind, clouds, hail, lightning, and rainbows, as well as earthquakes.

Anaximenes says that air is infinite in extent and surrounds the cosmos. In *On the Heavens*, Aristotle claims that Anaximenes says that the existence of air explains how the flat Earth is stable: it is supported by air from below (DK13A20; DK13A7). Hippolytus also reports Anaximenes as claiming that the Earth and other heavenly bodies ride on air because they are flat.[15]

Plutarch reports that Anaximenes claims that our souls are made of air. He cites what *may* be a quote directly from Anaximenes:

> For example, our soul, being air, controls us and breath and air contain the whole cosmos. (DK13B2)[16]

It is worth noting that the Greek word *aēr* does not adequately translate into the English term *air*. Clearly, Anaximenes is referring to a rarified gas that we breathe. Nevertheless, it also has a primordial role in his conception of the universe and is responsible for the animation of living things. Similar points apply to the translation of the relevant Greek words as *water, fire,* and *earth*.

We may conclude that the Milesians are the precursors of scientific enquiry because of the broad scope of their interest in nature. They initiate a long tradition of examining and explaining a wide range of natural phenomena, from stars to mountains and from plants to animals in a unified and systematic manner. As we shall see, this tradition continues in the ancient period until *On the Nature of Things* by the great Roman poet Lucretius (99–55 BC). However, we can also see Descartes' book, *The World* (1633), as a continuation of the same tradition because it seeks a unified account of all natural material phenomena, such as fire, light, the movements of the planets, the tides, and human physiology.

The Second Phase: The Ionians

Ionia was the region of ancient Greece on the coast of central modern Turkey; Miletus was one of the Ionian Greek settlements. Despite their geographical proximity, the Ionians had ideas that are significantly different from the earlier Milesians, such as Thales and Anaximenes. The philosophies of the Ionians such as Pythagoras and Heraclitus reach beyond the scientific philosophy of the earlier Milesians because the Ionians are concerned with metaphysics and, to some extent, with ethics. As we shall see, this modulates their approach to the natural world. For example, in the case of Heraclitus, his aim is not only to describe and explain changes in the natural world, but also to show how human life, ethics, and politics fit into this natural world order, and thereby to describe wisdom.

Pythagoras (570–497 BC)

Pythagoras was born on the Ionian island of Samos in the eastern Aegean, located between Miletus and Athens. Some sources claim that, as a young man, Pythagoras traveled in the Middle East and Egypt.[17] Around 530 BC, he moved to Croton in southern Italy, where he established a community of followers. The community grew and acquired political importance and power in the region. As a consequence, after about twenty years a revolt occurred against the Pythagoreans.

Pythagoras wrote nothing, but his later followers wrote much, attributing to him diverse views. Pythagoreanism became a popular philosophy and, in part because of this, it is impossible to define exactly what Pythagoras himself thought because the later Pythagorean schools tend to attribute their own teachings to the master. According to later accounts, after his death, Pythagoras's disciples split into two groups: the *akousmatikoi* and the *mathematikoi* (DK18, 2).[18] By the fourth century AD, Pythagoras was considered as a philosopher at least equally important as Plato and Aristotle.[19]

The Akousmatikoi

The first Pythagorean School, called the *akousmatikoi*, followed Pythagoras's religious teaching concerning the soul and the right way to live. This school regarded Pythagoras as a sage or spiritual master. Central to Pythagoras's teachings is the claim that the soul is immortal, and that it transmigrates on the death of the body, a claim called *metempsychosis*. The soul may even be reborn in animal form. Indeed, Xenophanes, a contemporary, teases Pythagoras for this aspect of his teaching: he reports that when Pythagoras saw a puppy being beaten, he took pity on it and claimed that the puppy was the soul of a friend of his, recognizable by its shouting (DK21B7). Unfortunately, we know little of Pythagoras's view of the soul. For instance, we don't know whether, in his view, the soul is personal, what its relation to consciousness might be, and whether all or only some souls are transmigrated. Presumably his view implies that personal identity is constituted by the soul. According to such a claim, a person literally *is* his or her soul rather than it being something that a person *has*. This difference is important, as we shall soon see.

The little we know of Pythagoras himself comes largely from lost works by Aristotle on the history of the Pythagoreans, which are quoted by later writers. The early sources indicate that Pythagoras preached a way of life that involved a moral code and sets of rituals. For instance, Isocrates, a contemporary of Plato, reports that Pythagoras studied with the Egyptians, and that "He was concerned, more conspicuously than anyone else, with matters to do with sacrifice and temple purifications."[20]

In his *Histories*, from around 440 BC, Herodotus says that Pythagoras, like the Egyptians, forbad the wearing of woolen garments for burial and in temples (DK14, 1). Another example of a possible Pythagorean ritual is the prohibition of eating beans. Diogenes Laërtius quotes a fragment from Aristotle claiming that the Pythagoreans prohibited touching a white rooster and breaking bread (DK58C3). Beyond such details, we know little about the morals and rituals of the Pythagorean sect; they were sworn to secrecy.

Pythagoras's doctrine of the soul apparently means that we are not mortal beings but rather immortal souls, and that we are not really at home in our bodies. Philolaus, a later Pythagorean, claims that "the soul is yoked to the body and buried in it as in a tomb" for the sake of punishment (DK44B14).

Pythagoras's view of transmigration implies that the animals are our kin. According to Porphyry, Pythagoras thinks that "all living things should be considered as belonging to the same kind" (DK148A).[21] For this reason, the later Pythagoreans consider the eating of flesh as a form of cannibalism; it is possible that the early Pythagoreans did not follow strict vegetarianism.[22]

Some aspects of Pythagoras's teaching regarding the transmigration of the soul are similar to the views of the Orphic religious tradition. Orphism was a religious cult based on the mythical poet and musician Orpheus. Sometimes Orpheus is represented as a god whose music could charm wild animals and who visited the underworld. Sometimes he is represented as a real person who established a religious movement, the secrets of which were revealed only to the initiated. Part of the Orphic tradition was that the soul is imprisoned in the body, and that rituals and purifications are needed to clean the soul from the bodily influences. Although the Orphic tradition has its roots earlier than the Pythagorean, there seems to be no decisive evidence to settle the question of whether or not Pythagoras was influenced by Orphism.[23]

In any case, Pythagoras was the first Western philosopher to articulate clearly the idea of a soul distinct from the body, which found full expression in the works of Plato. Furthermore, like Plato after him,

Pythagoras stressed the moral importance of the soul. These Pythagorean ideas became part of Western culture because of the later marriage of Neo-Platonism and Christianity through the works of St. Augustine.

In the *Phaedo*, Plato discusses the Pythagorean view that the soul is a harmony or attunement of opposites. In this discussion, Plato rejects the claim that the soul is the harmony of the elements of the body, a claim that implies that the soul is not immortal. The view that Plato rejects perhaps might be Pythagorean, but Pythagoras himself almost certainly thinks that the soul is immortal and may also think that it is composed of air. Pythagoras conceives of the soul as distinct from the body and, nevertheless, perhaps tainted by being associated with it. If this is the case, then it is probable that he thinks that, by following the right way of life, one may struggle to be a good moral agent freer from such bodily impurities.

In this tradition, as a spiritual teacher, Pythagoras is credited with some extraordinary powers. For example, Diogenes Laërtius, writing in roughly 300 AD, reports that Pythagoras could remember and recount his previous lives (DK14, 8).[24] Diodorus's *Universal History*, which was written about 60 BC, claims that when Pythagoras was at Argos, he wept when he saw a shield from Troy, because he had himself carried it in a previous life when he was Euphorbus.[25] According to one account, Pythagoras even appeared in two places at the same time (DK14A7). Such are the incredible powers attributed by later writers to Pythagoras.

The Mathematikoi

The second group of Pythagoreans was interested in the study of mathematics, music, and astronomy. The key to their ideas is that the universe consists of a harmony that should be studied mathematically. In this, they reject the Ionian idea of trying to discover the basic stuff of the universe, replacing it with the study of form. In this study, the numerical ratios between sounds in the musical scales provided an analogy for the harmonious development of the whole universe. In other words, according to this second group of Pythagoreans, we can understand the universe, including the soul, by knowing the numerical relations that express the harmonic ratios according to which everything changes.

This vision of a mathematical cosmology influenced Plato, especially in his later work, the *Timaeus*. However, contemporary German scholar Walter Burkert argues that there is no evidence to support the claim that Pythagoras himself was a mathematician or an advocate of a rational cosmology.[26] For instance, we can find no such support in the works of Plato or Aristotle. Plato mentions the *Pythagoreans* as claiming that mathematics, astronomy, and harmonics are "sister sciences."[27] His only mention of the individual person Pythagoras himself is to assert that he was beloved for his instruction and that he taught a way of life.[28] Burkert argues that there is no evidence to support the claim that Pythagoras had a mathematical philosophy, even though later Pythagoreans did.

Philolaus, who was born in Croton around 470 BC, a century after Pythagoras, did set down in writing the idea that the universe has numerical structure and harmony. His book was supposed to have started as follows:

> Nature in the universe was harmonized out of both things which are unlimited and things which limit; this applies to the universe as a whole and to all its components. (DK44B1)

The even numbers represent the unlimited, and the odd numbers the limiting (DK58B4 and B5). According to Philolaus, the harmony of the cosmos is numerical because "nothing can be known or understood without number" (DK44B4). These harmonies consist in the ratios that correspond to the three basic musical ratios: the octave 2:1; the fifth 3:2, and the fourth 4:3. The numbers when added together constitute the perfect number $1+2+3+4=10$, which is called the *tetractus*. The tetractus can be represented as an equilateral triangle with four units at the base, ascending followed by three units, two units, and at the apex, one.[29] This triangle is a symbol for the musical ratios that provide the order of the universe.[30]

This number constitutes the basis of the Pythagorean cosmology of Philolaus (DK58B4). The centre of the universe consists in fire, around which orbit 10 spheres: the fixed stars; the five planets; the Moon, Sun and the Earth (DK44B7 and B17). According to Aristotle, the Pythagoreans added an invisible counter-Earth, bringing the number to 10 (DK44A16).[31] Notice that in this system, the Earth orbits around the fire, and its position relative to the Sun produces day and night (DK58B37). The movement of the bodies around the central fire instantiates the three basic ratios, thereby producing what was later called "the music of the spheres" (DK58B35). In this way, according to Philolaus, the cosmos has a mathematical order.

About fifty years later, Archytas was renowned as a Pythagorean mathematician and scientist. Aristotle wrote three books on the philosophy of Archytas, which are lost except for some fragments; and Aristotle's pupils, Eudemus and Aristoxenus, wrote works on Archytas's geometry, his physics, and his life. Archytas was a companion of Plato, and he is credited with having saved the life of Plato by arranging for him to escape from Dionysius of Syracuse in 361 BC.[32] Even though only a few fragments and reports of his writing remain, Archytas is known for his work on three-dimensional geometry and ratios, as well as on acoustics and mechanics. Clearly, he had an important influence on Plato.

So far we have represented the Pythagoreans as being concerned with harmonies or patterns of the universe, rather than the substances out which things are composed. However, there may be another aspect to Pythagorean thought. According to Aristotle, the Pythagoreans assert the existence of numbers as abstract entities. Furthermore, they claim that everything consists of numbers or that the whole universe is constructed out of numbers.[33] Aristotle even says that they claim that number is the substance of everything.[34]

We cannot be sure that Aristotle is accurately reporting a Pythagorean view on this precise point, namely, that all things are made up of numbers. In this part of the *Metaphysics*, Aristotle reviews earlier philosophers, mainly to show how they failed to properly distinguish between form and matter, in order to present his own views. He is not primarily concerned with portraying their views sympathetically. Nevertheless, it is more reasonable to attribute to the Pythagoreans the milder claim that numbers exist as nonphysical entities. In other words, the Pythagoreans affirm the existence of nonmaterial abstract objects. This claim was an important influence on Plato, who argues for the existence of abstract universals or Forms.

From later Pythagoreans, such as Philolaus and Archytas, we have the picture of Pythagoras as a brilliant mathematician who invented the theorem that, in any right-angled triangle, the square of the hypotenuse is equal to the sum of the square of the other two sides. Pythagoras was portrayed as applying his mathematics to music and astronomy and, thereby, developing a metaphysical system based on number.

It is contentious to what extent this rational cosmology based on number is attributable to the historical person Pythagoras himself. According to one view, championed by Burkert, advocated earlier by Zeller, and more recently by Huffman, Pythagoras was a semi-religious leader with quasi-religious teachings based mainly on tradition and myth. According to this view, the mathematical cosmology is a later rationalization. Another interpretation is that the *akousmatikoi* and the *mathematikoi* both represent strands of Pythagoras's original teachings.[35]

Heraclitus (540–480 BC)

Heraclitus was born in Epheseus, a town on the western coast of Ionia, between Miletus and Colophon. Colophon is where the traveling poet/philosopher Xenophanes was born (ca. 570 BC). It is worth digressing to briefly examine Xenophanes, whose philosophical poems probably influenced Heraclitus. Like Heraclitus, Xenophanes has views that directly challenge those of the Greek religion of the time and would have shocked many of his contemporaries. He lampooned traditional beliefs that anthropomorphized the gods by claiming that if cows and horses could draw, then they would sketch the gods as cows and horses (21 B15). According to Theophrastus, Xenophanes argued that god is the universe and that it is one and neither finite nor infinite nor changing nor changeless.[36] This is a view in some ways similar to that of Parmenides, as we shall see in the next chapter.

Returning to the discussion on Heraclitus, we are told that he was of noble birth and that he gave up opportunities to pursue politics in order to practice philosophy. He wrote his main philosophical work in about 500 BC. Of this, about 125 fragments remain.[37] These sayings are culled from later writers, such as Sextus Empiricus, who quote from Heraclitus. This means that we do not know the order of the short sayings of Heraclitus, except for the first two at the very beginning of the book. Of course, the order of the fragments affects their interpretation; consequently, this is a contentious issue among scholars.

Heraclitus was a polemical and enigmatic thinker who was scornful of the popular beliefs of the many, and who rejected the authorities of the time. He wrote in a playful, poetic style, sometimes using apparently paradoxical sentences and at other times employing memorable aphorisms. This, coupled with his rebellious attitude, makes Heraclitus a source of inspiration for many diverse later writers. His philosophy ranges over many topics, including the place of human life in the universe, the nature of knowledge, and ethics. In part because of the difficulties of interpretation, it is simplest to begin with his philosophy of nature, which can be summarized with five general propositions.

1. Everything happens in accordance with *logos,* a general principle of nature.
2. Everything is in constant flux.
3. The underlying nature of the universe is fire.
4. There is a divine intelligence governing the universe, and a spark of this intelligence exists in human reason.
5. Opposites exist as a unity.

The fifth of these propositions, sometimes called *the unity of opposites,* requires a more lengthy explanation because Heraclitus's main point is more obscure.

First, everything happens in accordance with a general principle of nature (the Greek word is *logos*). The first fragment begins with the following claim:

> Of this principle, which holds forever, people prove ignorant, not only before they hear it, but also once they have heard it. For although everything happens in accordance with this principle, they resemble those with no familiarity with it, even after they have become familiar with the kinds of accounts and events I discuss. (DK22B1)

The Greek word *logos* has many meanings, and Heraclitus exploits the richness of the term. It can refer to a piece of language, ranging from a single word to a narrative. It can also mean a proportion, a reckoning, a piece of reasoning, and an evaluation. It can also signify an account and, in this sense, it can mean something close to law.[38] For this reason, it is often translated as *principle.* Several fragments reveal Heraclitus's general understanding of this cosmic principle: it is clearly objective and governs all events.[39]

Heraclitus also claims that "all things are one" (B50). This suggests that he thinks there is a single rational order to the universe, governed by the principle. At B64, he says that "thunderbolt steers all things," suggesting that the rational ordering is intelligent. Furthermore, B32 suggests that this order has divine aspects: it is "both unwilling and willing to be called by the name of Zeus." By this, Heraclitus may mean that the intelligent principle that governs the universe is divine because it is eternal, but that it shouldn't be identified with the traditional gods of mythology. The principle is divine but immanent.

Heraclitus also speaks of the *logos* of the cosmos as a language that we can listen to and understand. Those who understand it are wise, and are able to behave in accordance with the principle.

So far we have looked at Heraclitus's general descriptions of the principle or law that governs nature. But what does the general law actually mean? What is its content? Heraclitus provides with us some clues and tantalizing glimpses. To piece these together, we need to continue our review of his natural philosophy.

The second general proposition of Heraclitus's natural philosophy is his thesis that everything is in flux, even when the change is imperceptible. Famously, he affirms that it is impossible to step into the same river twice (B91). Heraclitus's thesis may be that all things are constantly changing. This is the view that Plato attributes to Heraclitus in his dialogue, *Cratylus*, when he says that "everything moves and nothing rests."[40]

According to Aristotle, Cratylus, a pupil of Heraclitus, claims that all perceptible things are *constantly* in flux.[41] Thinking that this claim implies that nothing is stable and that it is impossible to refer to anything, Cratylus allegedly refused to speak and merely raised his finger. Cratylus criticizes Heraclitus on the grounds that it is not possible to step into the river once.[42] Cratylus's reasoning for this claim seems to be that (a) everything is changing at all times *in all respects,* and (b) that to refer to X, there must be some property of X that isn't changing at the time of the reference.[43] Given this premise, the conditions for referring to something aren't satisfied.

In contrast, Heraclitus's more modest view is perhaps that we can grasp and refer to objects, even as they change. This is suggested by the testimony given in B91:

> According to Heraclitus one cannot step twice into the same river, nor can one grasp any mortal substance in a stable condition, but by the intensity and the rapidity of change it scatters and again gathers.

This indicates that, although substances are never in a stable condition, one can grasp them by differences in the intensity and rapidity of their change. If this is the case, then Heraclitus's view may be that we should conceive of the universe as a set of processes rather than as consisting of things or entities. Again, this is a contentious point.

Third, Heraclitus asserts a monism, according to which the underlying nature of the universe is fire. However, if Heraclitus means to assert that there are no permanent entities because everything is in flux, then it may be incorrect to think of fire as a permanent underlying substance out of which everything is composed. If this is the case then Heraclitus's view is probably that the cosmos is a process rather than a static substance. The process would be one of burning and quenching, which perhaps can be divided into processes of heating up and cooling, and of drying and becoming moist (B126). If this is his view, then everything is fire in the sense that the cosmos consists of processes of burning and quenching (and *not* in the sense that fire is an underlying permanent substance). He says:

> No god and no human being made this cosmos, but it was always and is and will be an ever-living fire, getting kindled in measures and getting quenched in measures. (B30)

In short, it seems that the underlying process of the cosmos is one in which fire cools and becomes liquid and solid, and heats up again to eventually become lightning. As the quoted passage B30 indicates, these processes of heating and cooling are in measures, and the following quote suggests a balance in these interchanges, reminiscent of Anaximander:

> All things are repayment for fire and fire for all things, just as goods are for gold and gold for goods. (B90)

The fourth general proposition of Heraclitus's natural philosophy is that there is a divine intelligence governing the universe. To this, he adds the important idea that a spark of this intelligence exists in human reason. Let us take these two points in turn. First, as we saw earlier, Heraclitus thinks that the principle or rational ordering of the cosmos is intelligent. He uses intentional verbs such as *steers* and *grasps* to describe this ordering or regulatory action. Apparently, he also identifies this intelligent and divine principle with lightning or fire. As we saw earlier, he proclaims: "Thunderbolt steers all things" (B64), and he also claims: "Fire as it progresses will discriminate and grasp all things" (B66).

Second, Heraclitus also believes that this divine fire is at work in the soul.[44] He says that it is death for the soul to become moist (B77) and that the soul functions best when it is dry:

> Dry light-beam is soul at its wisest and best. (B118)

This implies that, for Heraclitus, knowledge of the soul and knowledge of the order of the cosmos are united, for the fundamental nature of each is the same.[45] This has fundamental implications for his ethics and epistemology. Heraclitus's idea of fire as the divine guiding aspect of the cosmos and of humans, and his claim that eternal laws govern the universe, had an important influence on Zeno of Citium, the founder of Stoicism. Stoic philosophy became very popular in ancient Rome, and the Roman

Empire was receptive to Christianity in large part because of these Heraclitean aspects of Stoicism, as we shall see in chapter 14.

To understand the fifth general proposition of Heraclitus's natural philosophy, we need to step back and take a broader view. It is possible to read Heraclitus's work as a search for wisdom. At B101, he affirms, "I went to search out myself." In the very first passage of the work he disdains the ignorance of the multitude, but this may be primarily to draw our attention to the need for wisdom. As he says, "Everyone has potential for self-knowledge and sound reasoning" (B116), but few attain it. He claims that wisdom is speaking the truth and acting with knowledge that accords with nature (B112). He also describes wisdom as knowing "the intelligence by which all things are steered through all things" (B41). Wisdom is possible because humans are part of the natural order, which has an immanent divine guidance. In a similar fashion, the human soul receives such guidance.

These points shed a very different light on the natural philosophy of Heraclitus. He is not merely working in the tradition of the Milesians, but rather trying also to show the meaning of the natural order for human life and for wisdom. As we shall see now, this line of interpretation, which is due to Charles Kahn, helps us to better understand the fifth point, namely, his idea of the *unity of opposites*.

In several passages Heraclitus affirms the presence of apparent opposite qualities in the same thing. In some of these passages, he draws our attention to the co-presence of opposites by comparing the needs, tastes, and desires of humans with other species, such as fish, donkeys, and pigs. For example:

> Sea water most pure and most tainted, drinkable and wholesome for fish, but undrinkable and poisonous for people. (B61)
>
> Donkeys would prefer refuse to gold. (B9)

These passages indicate that some of our judgments are true only relative to our perspective and invite us to see things from another perspective. In other passages, Heraclitus makes similar comparisons from within human experience:

> It is not better for men to get everything they want. Disease makes health pleasant and good, as hunger does being full, and weariness rest. (B110 and 111)

The positive term (e.g., health) has value only in relation to its contrary, the negative term (i.e., disease). These and other quotes are not appeals to relativism but rather indications that all desires and pleasures essentially involve opposites.[46] This point suggests that the path to wisdom does not lie in pursuing one's desires: pleasure will always require suffering. Indeed, Heraclitus says that to be temperate is the greatest excellence (B112).

The above quotes also reveal the partial or limited nature of the human perspective—for instance, things that are poisonous to us may be food to other animals. In other places, Heraclitus also points out the perspectival nature of human perception (B3). Duality is not only part and parcel of human desire; it is integral to the very experience of living. This is probably implied when Heraclitus says:

> A road: uphill, downhill, one and the same. (B60)

This quote indicates that up and down are perspective-relative terms and that underlying these opposites there is a unity, namely, the road. We can generalize the point: how things appear from one point of view may be the opposite from another point of view, but there is an underlying unity beyond these opposites.

This point suggests that wisdom involves both transcending the limited perspectives of the opposites and seeking the unity beyond them. This is the purpose for which Heraclitus affirms that there is a unity behind these oppositions: to highlight its importance for wisdom. As evidence for this interpretation, consider, for example, his complaint against Hesiod, who regards some days good and others bad, "not understanding that the nature of every day is one and the same" (B106). In conclusion, wisdom requires transcending the limited perspective-relative view of things and grasping the unity behind them.

Let us examine the nature of this unity in more depth. The quote about the road may also allude to the cosmic processes of fire quenching and kindling. In other words, if this allusion is intended, then Heraclitus's point is that opposites are a reflection of the pattern of the cosmos, which consists in kindling and quenching of cosmic fire.[47] In other words, Heraclitus's idea seems to be that the process of fire quenching and burning manifests itself in human experience as a set of inescapable dualisms pertaining to our desires, pleasures, and perceptions.

The same quote (i.e., B60) also indicates that from the divine perspective of the cosmos, these oppositions are a unity: the road is the same. The divine nature of the unity is suggested in other passages:

> The god: day night, winter summer, war peace, hunger satiety. It changes as when mingled with perfumes it is named by the pleasure of each. (B67)

This passage indicates that God is the unity beyond the dualities of day-night, and so on . . . and that this underlying unity changes into sets of dualities when it is named according to the pleasures of beings. Although these dualisms are essentially part of human experience, from the cosmic perspective all is one. To gain wisdom, it is necessary to understand this cosmic perspective and to grasp the unified *logos* of the cosmos, which is beyond the dualisms, as the complaint against Hesiod mentioned earlier indicates. In support of this reading, we can note that Heraclitus also claims:

> To God all things are beautiful and good and just; but humans have supposed some unjust and others just. (B102)

This reiterates the earlier point: from the divine perspective of the cosmos, all things are one, and the dualities of human experience are transcended. This doesn't mean that Heraclitus is denying the oppositions that constitute human experience. He isn't saying, for instance, that justice is an illusion.[48] He is simply affirming that such dualities depend on a perspective, and that from the divine point of view of the cosmos there is unity.

According to Heraclitus, the divine law of the cosmos has value implications for individual behavior. He says at B2 that we must try to follow what is common (i.e., the divine principle that gives order to the cosmos). He also affirms that the divine principle has implications for politics because social laws should be in keeping with the divine law. He says:

> Those who speak with intelligence must stand firm by that which is common to all, as a state stands by the law, and even more firmly. For all human laws are in the keeping of the one divine law; for the one divine law has as much power as it wishes, is an unfailing defense for all laws, and prevails over all laws. (B114)

Let us now turn briefly to Heraclitus's epistemology. As we have seen, he thinks that it is possible for humans to know the intelligible order. In several places, he compares the divine order to a language that speaks to us and which we can hear, or not. He implies that any person has the capacity to hear and follow the principle of the cosmos. Nevertheless, he thinks that most people live as if they were in a private dream-world, as if they were asleep (B89); they do not listen to the principle that is common to all, and they lack sound judgment. As we saw, in several fragments he scorns the ignorance of the multitude. Additionally, he rejects many of the traditional authorities, including Homer. Of Pythagoras and Hesiod, he says that much learning does not teach the mind (B40). At B50, he says, "When one listens, not to me but to the *logos*, it is wise to agree that all things are one." In so doing, he disclaims authority for himself.

Heraclitus thinks that learning comes from firsthand experience, from hearing and seeing (B55). However, such learning does not suffice for wisdom; the mind must know how to interpret what the senses see and hear. He says:

> Bad witnesses are eyes and ears to people, when they have souls that do not speak the right language. (B107)

This is how it is possible for people to ignorant of the principle of nature. He says that fools hear as if they were deaf (B34); they do not know how to listen (B19).

CONCLUSION

The earliest Greek philosophers, the Milesians, had the revolutionary idea that all changes in the natural world could be explained in terms of alterations in a basic substance. Thales identifies this substance as water; Anaximander argues that it was something indeterminate and Anaximenes contends that it is air. These thinkers initiate a long tradition of natural philosophy that attempts to explain a broad variety of natural phenomena in a unified and systematic manner. This tradition stretches through ancient thinkers such as Aristotle and Lucretius to the modern precursors of natural science, such as Galileo (1564–1642) and Descartes (1596–1650).

The Ionian philosophers Pythagoras and Heraclitus constitute the second phase of early ancient Greek philosophy. They approach philosophy with a more metaphysical and ethical orientation. Pythagoras taught that the soul is immortal and that when the body dies, the soul transmigrates to another body including those of animals. Pythagoras devised a spiritual way of life based on this set of beliefs. Later Pythagoreans claim that the universe is a harmony based on mathematical patterns, which can be found in astronomy and music. We cannot be sure to what extent this tradition of the *Mathematikoi* is based on the teaching of Pythagoras himself.

Heraclitus claims that wisdom is to be found in the unity of opposites. The conflict between opposites defines human experience. Wisdom consists in transcending the limitations or partiality of such dualities. It consists of attaining the cosmic perspective from which these opposites are unified and from which one can grasp the divine *logos* of the cosmos as a whole.

Study Questions

1. Why is it important that Thales may have claimed that everything is composed of water?
2. What argument did Thales provide for the claim that soul is intermingled in the universe?
3. How did Anaximander argue that the unlimited must be a first principle?
4. What was Anaximander's main argument for the claim that the basic substance of the universe cannot be one of the four elements?
5. Given that the four elements are in balance and given that the universe is infinitely old, what may we conclude?
6. Why does Anaximenes claim that the basic substance is air?
7. What were the two groups of Pythagoreans?

8. According to the Pythagoreans, what are the main ethical implications of the transmigration of the soul?
9. Why does Philolaus claim that the universe is numerical?
10. When Heraclitus claims that everything happens in accordance with *logos*, what does he mean?
11. How does Cratylus criticize Heraclitus's claim that one cannot step into the same river twice? How might Heraclitus respond?
12. What is Heraclitus's theory of the unity of opposites?
13. How does this theory relate to the divine perspective and the search for wisdom?

Discussion Questions

1. Do we need the notion of a basic substance that underlies all change?
2. How does such a notion relate to the principle of the conservation of energy?
3. Does the notion of the transmigration of the soul make sense?
4. Must our understanding of human life depend on a metaphysical view in the ways that Heraclitus's does?

2 Parmenides and Zeno

The Eleatics gave ancient Greek philosophy a tremendous shock. They argued that the universe cannot be as it is described by the Milesians. For the Eleatics, reality could not consist in a plurality of things that change. It must consist in only one unchanging thing. For this startling conclusion, they gave the best and most challenging arguments that we have seen so far.

The main Eleatics were Parmenides and his pupil, Zeno, who were both from Elea. In this chapter, we also briefly discuss the views of Melissus of Samos, who followed their views.

PARMENIDES (515–445 BC)

Parmenides was born in Elea, a Greek city in southern Italy. He was reportedly a student of Xenophanes and may have studied with the Pythagoreans, but he followed neither. He wrote a long poem in Homeric hexameters, of which about 150 lines have been recovered. In addition to the recovered lines of the poem, we also have some testimonial reports of Parmenides's views.[1] Among others, these include Plato's dialogue *Parmenides*, and some mentions of Parmenides in other Platonic dialogues such as the *Theaetetus* and *Sophist*. There are also references to Parmenides in some of Aristotle's works such as the *Physics* and *Metaphysics*. Of course, all the fragments of Parmenides's poem are extracted from quotations in later texts.

Parmenides's poem is a watershed in the history of early Western philosophy. It radically changed philosophy. It challenges the Milesian tradition by offering strong arguments for the view that the scientific investigation of nature is at best only a study of appearances and not of reality. Reality itself is something quite different: it is indivisible and changeless. Future thinkers face the fundamental challenge of how to overcome Parmenides's arguments in favor of his strange position.

The poem is divided into three parts: the first part is the prelude that describes the journey of an unnamed young man to meet the goddess of wisdom. The rest of the poem consists largely in the message of the goddess. The second part of the poem describes the Way of Truth, and the third, the Way of Opinion, which characterizes a false and deceitful manner of thinking.

The Journey

The young man journeys towards the light, on a chariot pulled by "wise mares" and accompanied by maidens from the house of the Night. They arrive at the great gates of Night and Day, where the maidens persuade the gatekeeper, Justice, to let them in. The young man then meets the goddess of Wisdom, who declares:

> Come and I will tell you (and listen and pass on my words): there are only two routes of inquiry for thinking. One: that it is and that it cannot not be; this is the path of Persuasion (for it attends on truth). The other: it is not and it is necessary that it not be. This latter I say to you is a completely un-learnable way, for you could not know what is not (for that cannot be done) nor could you say it. (DK28B2)

In other words, the goddess promises to show him both the Truth and the unreliable opinions of mortals. She indicates that mortals confuse appearances with reality, as we shall see.

The quoted passage is immediately followed by the important claim: "For thinking and being are the same" (DK28B3). By this, the goddess means that if something is not thinkable then it does not exist, and if something is thinkable then it may exist. For example, a round square is not thinkable and does not exist. What exists can only include what can be spoken and thought of. So, if something cannot be spoken or thought of then it does not exist.

Notice that the quoted passage above sharply makes the contrast between the two ways: the goddess implies that the Way of Truth shows us what exists and *must* exist, and the Way of Opinion shows us what doesn't exist and *cannot* exist. The goddess implies that what exists must exist, and what doesn't exist cannot exist. To see why, we need to examine the arguments from the Way of Truth.

It is important to note that, although Parmenides employs the poem to portray his understanding as if it were a divine revelation, the goddess provides comprehensive arguments for her conclusions. Indeed, she entreats the young man not to rely on habit born of experience but rather to "judge by reason" her "heavily contested refutation" (DK28B7). Parmenides is the first philosopher we know of to employ an extended argument to support his conclusions. For this reason, it is perhaps surprising that he presents his ideas through the mouthpiece of a divine authority.

The Way of Truth

In the Way of Truth, the goddess argues for a seamless, changeless, finite universe. In effect, she argues that there can only be one thing or, in other words, that all plurality is an illusion. The argument for this conclusion is based on the premise that we cannot speak of or think about that which does not exist.

> That which is there to be spoken and thought of must be,
>
> For it is possible for it to be,
>
> But not possible for nothing to be (DK28B6).

The implication of this sentence is that it is not possible to think of nothing, which implies that whatever we think about must be something, or an existent. Every subject of inquiry and thought must exist. In contemporary terms, one cannot think about what does not exist because if one can refer to something, then it exists. Parmenides's argument at the beginning of the Way of Truth, couched in today's idiom, would look like this:

1. To think about something, one must be able to refer to it.
2. One cannot refer to what does not exist.
3. Therefore, one cannot think about what does not exist.

From this conclusion, at the beginning of fragment 8, the goddess argues for several signs for or features of what exists.

First, she argues that what exists must be ungenerated and imperishable. It cannot be generated for two reasons. First, if it were generated then at the time before it came into being, there must have been what does not exist. But this is impossible because what does not exist cannot even be thought of: the concept of the nonexistent is impossible. Consequently, the idea of the existent coming into being from nothing relies on an impossible idea. This first argument can be laid out as follows:

1. The claim that what exists came into being requires the concept of the nonexistent.
2. The concept of the nonexistent is impossible.
3. Therefore, the claim that what exists came into being cannot be true.

Later in fragment 8, the goddess reiterates this conclusion by claiming that what is not can only give rise to what is not (B8, lines 12–14).

As for the second argument, the goddess asks the rhetorical question: "What necessity would have stirred it up to grow later rather than earlier, beginning from nothing?" (B8, lines 10–11) This is implicitly an argument of the form:

1. There can be no reason for what exists to have come into being at any one time as opposed to any other.
2. There must be a reason for what is.
3. Therefore, what exists did not come into being at any time.

In this second argument, Parmenides is appealing to the principle that everything must have a reason why it is so and not otherwise. As we saw in the previous chapter, Anaximander employs the same principle to explain why the Earth hangs midway in space without support.

These two arguments conclude that what exists cannot come into being. Parmenides implies that similar reasoning can show that what exists cannot perish. For instance, what exists cannot perish because then there would be a time in which nothing exists, which is impossible.

Second, given that what exists hasn't come into being and cannot go out of being, it follows that the existent must be eternal at least in the sense that it is everlasting. This means that there is no time at which it doesn't exist. However, Parmenides adds the phrase, "it never was nor will it be" which suggests that what exists is eternal not in the sense of being everlasting, but rather in the sense of being timeless (B8, line 5). In other words, this part of the text suggests that what exists does so timelessly rather than existing at all times. This conclusion seems to be supported in lines 17–21 of fragment 8, where the goddess asks rhetorically, how could what is be in the future and come to be?

In this part of fragment 8, Parmenides argues that all change or coming to be is impossible. Change is impossible because any change requires either that something comes from nothing, or that something comes to not exist. Both of these requirements are impossible because the nonexistent is inconceivable.

1. The claim that what exists can change requires the concept of the nonexistent.
2. The concept of the nonexistent is impossible.
3. Therefore, the claim that what exists can change cannot be true.

In short, the goddess argues that what exists is unchanging. This conclusion may be thought to support the idea that Parmenides thinks that what exists is timeless.

Third, since it is impossible to think about what does not exist, the existent must be seamless or without gaps because the idea of gaps presupposes the nonexistent, which is impossible. The whole is "all full of what it is," meaning that there is no more or less regarding any parts of it (B8, lines 23–24). Indeed, Parmenides's goddess argues that the whole is not divisible into parts at all, "since it is all alike" (B8, line 21).

Lines 29–30 imply that motion is impossible. This conclusion is already entailed by the claim that what exists cannot change. But the goddess adds:

> Remaining the same in the same and by itself it lies and so stays there fixed; for mighty Necessity holds it in the bonds of a limit which pens it in all around. (B8, lines 26–31)

Finally, Parmenides apparently claims that the existent whole is unique. He says that it remains the same "by itself." Furthermore, he adds that it cannot be incomplete: "it is not lacking" for if it were, "it would lack everything" (B8, lines 30-33).

Notice that Parmenides's poem does not contain an argument against the existence of empty space, from which he might also have argued that motion is impossible. Such an argument was given in fact by his follower Melissus, as we shall see below. In summary, Parmenides concludes that the universe is a seamless, indivisible, unchanging whole.

Given the above, we can see why Parmenides's assertion that one cannot refer to that which does not exist continued to haunt philosophy for many centuries. How can we refer to Santa Claus when he does not exist? How can we refer to the nonexistent? As an answer to this question, in the nineteenth century, Meinong (1853-1920) argued for an ontology that included nonexistent objects; he said that such objects absist. In 1919, the English philosopher Bertrand Russell (1872-1970) formulated his famous Theory of Descriptions as an ontologically less extravagant answer to the question. In brief, Russell's idea was that sentences such as "the present King of France is bald" are in fact a conjunction of three distinct sentences: (1) There is a thing which is the present king of France, (2) There is only one of them, and (3) That thing is bald.

The Way of Seeming

In the third part of Parmenides's poem, the goddess outlines the Way of Seeming, which describes the erroneous views of mortals, who mistake appearances for reality. The account begins towards the end of B8 at line 50:

> At this point I stop for you my reliable account and thought concerning Truth; from here on, learn mortal opinions, listening to the deceitful ordering of my words. (B8, lines 50-52)

Fewer fragments of this part of the poem survive, and for this reason it is more difficult to interpret. This section of the poem apparently offers a scientific account of the cosmos similar in tone and aim to those provided by the Milesians. The goddess intends to describe the world as it appears so that "no mortal opinion may ever overtake" the young voyager (B8, Line 61). In other words, the goddess describes the cosmos, which is the way the one reality appears, but by giving a description that is better than those of previous natural philosophers.

The mistake of mortal opinion is to have posited a duality: "two forms of which it is not right to name one" (B8, line 54). This duality consists in the contrast between, on the one hand, fire—which is ethereal, bright, and light—and on the other hand, heavy and dark matter (B8, lines 56-59). The goddess indicates that this distinction creates separate identities—each of the two elements is distinct from the other, and it is identical with itself. In other words, the false duality creates distinct identities. This distinction also provides order to the world of appearances, for everything in that world is composed of mixtures of these two elements, which Parmenides names *light* and *night*.

Fragments 10, 11, and 12 indicate that Parmenides has an intricate cosmology explaining how the Earth, Sun, Moon, planets, and stars came into being, including the aether that contains them. Fragment 12 mentions the goddess who governs all things, who is perhaps the same as Necessity.[2] She is situated in "the middle of all things" and is responsible for the creation of all things in the world of appearance. Around this middle are narrow rings of fire, which themselves are surrounded by wider rings of the darker element, night, intermingled with some fire or light. The goddess at the middle rules over the union of all things including "hateful birth" and "the sending of female to unite with male and in opposite fashion, male to female" (B12). Parmenides thinks that the light of the moon is a reflection from the sun. The goddess who governs all things, Necessity, creates the other gods including the goddess Love.

It is a contended point how one should understand the relation between the second and third parts of Parmenides's poem. Although few lines remain from the third part of the poem (44 lines), there are enough to deduce that the original contains an account of the cosmos, the origin of the celestial bodies, and an account of the biology of animals and humans. There is an extended report from Theophrastus, the pupil of Aristotle, regarding Parmenides's account of sensation, which is based on the physical balance of the body: knowledge that comes from the warmer parts of the body is better than that coming from the colder parts.[3] In short, the third part of Parmenides's poem comprises all the elements that one would expect from a Milesian work, *On Nature*. Obviously, Parmenides thinks that his account of the cosmos is superior to those of his predecessors. Yet it does *not* describe reality.

One interpretation is to claim that Parmenides's views require a sharp distinction between reality and the realm of appearances. Parmenides's assertion that reality is an unchanging unity must be contrasted with the idea that the world of plurality and change is merely an appearance. We find echoes of this kind of distinction in later philosophy. In some ways, Plato's Theory of Forms adopts some Parmenidean-like claims. As we shall see in later chapters, Plato contrasts the realm of the unchanging and timeless universal Forms, known through reason, with the ever-changing realm of the particulars of sense-experience. The former is reality; the latter are appearances. We find a view that is similar in some ways in the philosophy of Kant (1724–1804). He makes a radical distinction between noumena and phenomena. The world as is it in itself consists of non-spatial and non-temporal noumena, transcending the categories or the conceptual framework that makes experience possible. The spatiotemporal world of everyday objects or phenomena is in some sense an appearance because it is relative to the categories, which make experience possible.

Another interpretation of the relation between the Way of Truth and the Way of Opinion tries to eschew ascribing pseudo-reality to the Way of Opinion. The idea isn't that Parmenides is describing two realms; appearances aren't a separate realm. Rather, Parmenides's intention with the Way of Opinion is to offer his reader the best understanding of the natural world, but only to dismiss it as erroneous. According to this view, the function of the third part of the poem isn't to accurately describe the realm of appearances but rather to prevent the reader from falling back into the errors of the mortals.

Discussion

It is worth pointing out a few of the philosophically important implications of Parmenides's poem. First, in order to argue for his startling thesis, Parmenides introduces a new and more rigorous approach to philosophy, namely, that of providing deductive arguments based on an understanding of key terms, such as *is* and *exists*. Given this approach, it is not surprising that Parmenides causes a revolution in ancient philosophy. To reply to his arguments, Aristotle has to employ a similar kind of approach. In arguing against Parmenides, Aristotle is careful to distinguish between uses of the same term, and to base his own argumentation on such analysis in the *Physics* and *Metaphysics*, as we shall see in chapters 10 and 11.

Second, Parmenides's sharp distinction between reality and how the world appears implies that sense perception is systematically misleading or deceptive. It leads us to believe that there exists a plurality of things that change, when reality is a single changeless whole without parts. Sense perception cannot provide us with knowledge of reality. At best, it can tell us about the nature of appearances only. As we shall see in chapter 6, Plato continues with this Parmenidean idea by arguing that because sense perception depends on contextual and relative factors, it can never provide knowledge of reality.

Third, Parmenides's position in the second part of the poem implies that the true nature of reality is revealed only by reason. Knowledge of reality must be acquired by reasoning carefully, even when that reasoning runs against common sense. Parmenides's argument in the second part of the poem is a priori: it is based on logical deduction from necessary truths. It describes how things *must* be.

Perhaps surprisingly, Parmenides's thesis that everything is an indivisible whole has had an enormous influence on philosophy. It introduced many fundamental new concepts to Western thought that have had a lasting effect, and it is an early precursor of pantheism and deism. For instance, Plotinus conceived of God as the Parmenidean One and launched a pantheistic understanding of God as an alternative to mainstream Christian orthodoxy. Parmenides's claim that everything is a seamless whole is also echoed in the Stoic claim that the universe is one.

This Stoic assertion influenced the seventeenth-century metaphysician Spinoza, who argued for the existence of only one indivisible substance—namely, nature as a whole—which he called "God."

Zeno (490–430 bc)

Zeno also came from Elea. He was about 25 years younger than Parmenides, and the two may have been lovers. In 450 BC they visited Athens together and probably met with Socrates, who was about 20 years old. Plato's dialogue *Parmenides* reconstructs these fascinating discussions (if they took place).[4] In this dialogue, Plato portrays the character Parmenides criticizing the Theory of Forms, which is Plato's own theory. We know little else about Zeno's life except that, after participating in a rebellion to overthrow a tyrant, he was captured and, despite being tortured, he refused to betray his companions.

We are told that Zeno had forty arguments in his work *Attacks*, but of these only 8 or 9 survive (DK29A15). Some of these surviving arguments are often called *paradoxes*, although they are not really paradoxes at all. A paradox is an apparently inescapable contradiction. Typically in a paradox one has a seemingly valid argument from apparently undeniably true premises for a conclusion that is a contradiction. As such, a paradox invites a solution or resolution. Instead, as far as we can tell, Zeno's treatise advances arguments designed to prove the startling and counterintuitive conclusion that everything is one. Zeno aims to support Parmenides's conclusion that there is only one thing by showing that the existence of a plurality leads to contradictions or absurdities. In this way, Zeno makes Parmenides's challenge to philosophy even greater.

Of Zeno's eight famous arguments against motion, four are stated by Aristotle in his *Physics*.[5] The four arguments are: the Midway Problem, Achilles, the Arrow, and the Stadium. Zeno's basic strategy is to show that the commonsense view that more than one thing exists leads to absurdities or contradictions, thereby supporting Parmenides's claim that there can only be one thing.

The Midway Problem

This argument is sometimes called the *dichotomy*. Aristotle reports the argument as follows:

> First is the argument that says that there is no motion because that which is moving must reach the midpoint before the end. (Aristotle *Physics*, VI, 9, 239b11–13)

Imagine that you have to cross a room by traveling half of the distance across it, then half of the remaining distance and half of the remaining distance, and so on *ad infinitum*. As Aristotle remarks later in the *Physics*:

> It is always necessary to traverse half the distance but these are infinite, and it is impossible to get through things that are infinite. (Aristotle *Physics* VIII, 8, 263a5–6)

You will never actually cross the room because it requires completing an infinite set of tasks. The journey cannot be completed. However, the argument applies to *any* journey and, therefore, no journey or movement can even begin, not even the first step. In effect, Zeno argues as follows:

1. For anything to move requires its completing an infinite number of tasks.
2. It is impossible to complete an infinite number of tasks.
3. Therefore, movement is impossible.

According to the first premise, moving requires an infinite number of tasks because space is continuous, and hence infinitely divisible. This means that between any two points there are an infinite number of points. This in turn implies that to move between any two points requires completing an infinite number of steps or tasks. Concerning the second premise, it might seem that Zeno's point is that it is impossible to complete an *infinite* number of tasks in a *finite* amount of time. However, his real point is that it is impossible to complete an infinite series because, by definition, an infinite series has no last member.

Achilles

This argument is sometimes known as "Achilles and the Tortoise." The Achilles paradox is essentially similar in form to the midway problem. The tortoise has a head start in a race with Achilles, the faster runner. The argument claims, however, that Achilles can never catch the tortoise. In order to catch up to the tortoise, Achilles must first reach the point from which the tortoise started. However, during the time that he does that, the tortoise has advanced another shorter distance. So, in order to catch up the tortoise, Achilles must first reach this second point. But during the time he does that, the tortoise has advanced yet again, albeit another still shorter distance, and Achilles has to reach this third point, and so on *ad infinitum*. This argument can be represented as follows:

1. To catch the tortoise, Achilles needs to perform an infinite number of tasks or steps.
2. It is impossible to complete a task consisting of an infinite number of steps.
3. Therefore, Achilles cannot catch the tortoise.

We can generalize this particular conclusion to support the claim that motion is impossible. The concept of motion implies that if any body is traveling faster and in the same direction as another, then it will overtake it in a finite amount of time. But the Achilles problem has apparently shown that this condition is impossible to meet.

The Arrow

Imagine an arrow flying through space. Zeno argues:

1. At any moment, the arrow occupies a space that is equal to its own size.
2. Something that occupies a space equal to its own size is at rest.
3. Therefore, at any moment, the arrow is at rest.

This conclusion can be generalized to show that no motion is possible.

The Moving Rows

This argument is sometimes called "the Stadium." There are different interpretations of the details of the argument, but they agree on its basic form. There are three groups of blocks, all of equal size. Group A is stationary. The two remaining groups move with equal speed in opposite directions. Let us suppose that each group has two blocks. After a period of time T, one of the B blocks has moved past all two Cs and only one of the As. Hence, the following argument applies.

> Block B1 moves past a single A in time T.
> Block B1 moves past two Cs in time T.
> Blocks A, B and C are equal in size.
> Blocks C and B move with equal speed.
> Time = distance divided by velocity.
> Therefore, T = 1/2 T.

From this absurd consequence, Zeno concludes that motion is impossible.

It is worth noting that the underlying strategy of the first two arguments, or paradoxes, is different from the second two. The first two, the paradox of the Midway Problem and that of Achilles, are concerned with the infinite divisibility of a determinate quantity. Zeno is trying to show us that we cannot move from the many to one. In contrast, in the paradoxes of the Arrow and Moving Rows, he tries to show that one cannot go from the one to the many.

The Other Arguments

Zeno has four or five other arguments to show that a plurality is impossible, but these additional arguments do not pertain to motion.

The first argument is reported by Simplicius in his *Commentary on Aristotle's Physics*, and it tries to show that if there is a plurality then each member or unit of this plurality has the contradictory properties of being both infinitely large and infinitely small in size.[6] Zeno starts with the premise that any thing X is the same as itself, and if something were to be added to it, then it would not be X but rather X + Y. He also argues that everything must have magnitude or size. From these two assumptions, the argument is supposed to branch in two opposite directions. In the first branch, he tries to argue that everything with a size must be infinite or unlimited in size. The idea is that any part Z of that X must also have a size. Likewise any part of Z must itself have a size. Similarly, any part of the part Z must have a size, and so on *ad infinitum*. He says that "no part of it will be the last" (DK29B1). In other words, any thing that has a size must have infinite parts, each of which will have a size. The sum of an infinite number of magnitudes must be infinite. Therefore, any single thing must have an unlimited large size.

Unfortunately, we don't have a clear record of Zeno's argument for the second branch, for the opposite conclusion that any single thing must have an infinitely small size. However, if both branches of the argument are sound then any one member of a plurality must have contradictory properties: it would be both infinitely large and infinitely small. This allegedly shows that whatever exists cannot be a member of a plurality.

The second argument, which is also reported by Simplicius, tries to show that if there are many things then they must have the contradictory properties of being both limited and unlimited in number.[7] Despite their similarities, we can treat this second argument as distinct from the first because it is about number and the first concerns their magnitude or size. The first limb of the second argument states that if there are many things, then they must be limited in number because there must be just as many as there are, not more or less. There is a definite number of them and therefore, they are limited.[8] According to the second limb, however, this set will also be unlimited because:

> There are always others between the things that are, and then again others between those, and so the things that are are unlimited. (DK29B3)

The idea seems to be that between any two things, there is always a third; between these three, there is always another two, and between these five, another four, and so on *ad infinitum*.[9] In conclusion, this limited set has an unlimited number of members.

A third argument concerns place. The idea that many things exist requires the idea that there are places in which these things can exist. However, Zeno argues that this last requirement is impossible to meet. In other words, there cannot be places. The following reasoning is supposed to show that this is so. Everything that exists must have a place. Therefore, if place exists then it is in a place. However, this regress continues to infinity and therefore, place does not exist. This argument is reported in Aristotle's *Physics*, as well as in Simplicius's commentary.[10] The argument can be represented as follows:

1. If there is a plurality of things then there must exist places (for them to exist in).
2. Everything that exists must have a place.
3. If place (N) exists, then N also must exist in a place, N+1.
4. If the existence of any place N depends on an infinite regress of places, then place N does not exist.

5. Therefore, there is no plurality of things.

Premises 3 and 4 need some explanation. Premise 3 is a generalization that follows from premise 2. The idea is that because everything that exists must have a place then even a place must exist in a place. We can express this idea by claiming that if place 1 exists then it must also exist in a place, which can name "place 2." However, if place 2 exists then it too must also exist in a place, which we can call "place 3," and so on *ad infinitum*. In other words, the requirement expressed by premise 2 inevitably sets up an infinite regress. This infinite regress idea is expressed by premise 3. Premise 4 asserts that if there is such an infinite regress then no place can exist. This premise is plausible because the regress is one of dependency: in other words, in order to exist, place N depends on the existence of place N+1. Zeno may be assuming such dependencies cannot consist in an infinite regress.

A fourth argument appears in Aristotle's *On Generation and Corruption*. Aristotle doesn't attribute it to Zeno, but Simplicius does.[11] Aristotle employs this argument to show why some later Pre-Socratic thinkers were convinced that indivisible atoms must exist. As such, we shall discuss it in greater length in chapters 11 and 14 of this book.

For Zeno, this argument shows that what exists must be a unity and without parts. It cannot be a plurality. The argument asks us to imagine that we have divided a body completely or "through and through." If a body is divided completely, then what remains? We cannot claim something with a magnitude remains, because the original assumption was that the body was *completely* divided; if something with magnitude remains, then that contradicts the original assumption. So what remains? It looks as if we only have two possible answers. The first is that nothing remains, but then we would be forced to the absurd conclusion that a body is composed of nothing. The second answer is that what remains are dimensionless points, but, in this case, we would be forced to the absurd conclusion that a body is composed of points that do not have magnitude. Either way, we are forced to an absurd conclusion, so we had better give up the original assumption that what exists is a plurality. In summary:

1. If what exists has parts then it must be infinitely divisible.
2. The claim that X is infinitely divisible logically entails absurd conclusions.

3. Therefore, what exists cannot have parts.

Chapter Two—Parmenides and Zeno   55

The fifth argument takes us back to Plato's dialogue, the *Parmenides*. Towards the beginning of the dialogue, Plato mentions, and attributes to Zeno, an argument to the effect that if things are many then they must have the contradictory properties of being both like and unlike. The idea seems to be that if there are two objects A and B, then A is like A and B is like B but also A is unlike B and B is unlike A. Therefore, each object is both like and unlike, which is impossible.[12] A bit later in the dialogue, the character Socrates replies to Zeno's argument by presenting his own Theory of Forms.[13] According to this theory, which we will examine in detail later in this book, in addition to particular objects there also exist universal Forms, such as whiteness, largeness, and circularity. Plato argues that particular objects partake in these Forms; for instance, circles partake in the Form of circularity. Plato applies this idea to Zeno's argument by claiming that there exists a Form of likeness and one of unlikeness. Particular things, says Socrates, can participate in both of these Forms; he asks rhetorically, "what's astonishing about that?" (129d). Plato argues that in a similar fashion, a particular can participate in both the Form of Oneness and the Form of Many, without contradiction.

It is important to point out that we have adopted a standard reading of Zeno, which follows the claim at the beginning of Plato's *Parmenides*: the character Socrates asserts that the thesis of Parmenides (that there can be only one thing) and Zeno's arguments (that there cannot be a plurality) amount to the same claim. In the dialogue, the character Zeno replies that his treatise is indeed a defense of Parmenides's argument. In contrast to this, some authors (e.g., Jonathan Barnes) have disputed the claim that Zeno presented all his arguments systematically in favor of the claim that there is only one thing.[14] We have presented Zeno's arguments as showing the absurd consequences of the claim that there is a plurality of things and therefore as a defense of the Parmenidean claim that there is only one thing.

Discussion

Zeno's paradoxes indicate deep puzzles about the nature of infinitesimals, such as points in space and time. Does a line or a distance consist in an infinite number of dimensionless points? Does a period of time consist in an infinite number of moments? As we shall see in a moment, these questions still persist today, though in a different way.

Like his teacher Parmenides, Zeno set a new standard of rigor in philosophical argument. To attempt to answer Zeno, Aristotle had to attain at least the same level of precision. As we shall see in chapter 10, Aristotle contends that Zeno's arguments are fallacious because they rely on the false view that time is composed of indivisible instants. It is still a debated point whether this is a correct or fair way to understand Zeno's arguments.[15]

In any case, Zeno and Aristotle did not have the concept of a convergent series, and Cantor's notion of infinite sets, which are required to attempt a mathematically precise reply to Zeno's arguments. Briefly, the central point is that we can calculate the sum of an infinitely long series of numbers if the series converges on some limit. The sum of an infinite convergent series of numbers will be finite. For example, the infinitely long series $1/2+1/4+1/8+1/2n\ldots$ has a sum, which is 1. In other words, concerning Zeno's midway problem, the sum of the half, plus the half of the half, and so on is 1, and so one is able to cross the room. The main point is that, to begin to answer at least some of Zeno's paradoxes, one requires mathematical concepts that were not developed until the seventeenth and nineteenth centuries, and perhaps even beyond.

The contemporary standard solution to Zeno's paradoxes assumes that motion is a continuum, as described in calculus and standard analysis. Motion is a function that has a continuous input of real numbers that represent time, and which has an output of real numbers that represent position in space. A continuum is represented in a mathematical line, which is represented by the real numbers. The real numbers are: all the rational numbers (such as 1, 2, 3, etc., and the fractions, such as 4/3), all the irrational numbers (such as the square root of 2) and the transcendental numbers, such as *pi* and *e*. The infinite points on a continuous line have a one-to-one correspondence with the real numbers. Due to the work of several mathematicians, including Cantor and Dedekind, the notion of a real number and of a continuum has been given a rigorous definition in terms of set theory.[16]

Effectively, the standard solution to the paradox of Achilles and the Midway problem is to affirm that a person can complete an infinite number of tasks in a finite time. In short, in an infinite number of instants Achilles goes to an infinite number of places or spatial points, but the sum of the relevant infinite series is finite.[17]

The standard solution to the Arrow is to assert that there can be motion at an instant in the sense that a body can be in motion at an instant in time. However, motion is not intrinsic property of a body; it is relational. Therefore, to describe the motion of a body as such requires describing the spatial position of the body at different times. According to the standard solution, these spatial positions and times are described as points on a continuum.

While the majority of mathematicians and philosophers would accept some version of the standard solution to Zeno's paradox, the fundamental philosophical issues do not necessarily die here. Some thinkers believe that the conceptual questions at the heart of Zeno's paradoxes are not solved by standard analysis.[18]

First, consider the question, "Do mathematical objects really exist independently of us?" The idea that there exists a transfinite set of real numbers requires a positive answer to this question. It assumes what one might call "a Platonic theory of mathematics," a term that we shall encounter later in chapter 6. The standard solution assumes that, in some sense, infinitesimals and infinities exist.

Do actual infinities really exist? As we shall see in chapter 10, Aristotle argues that the answer to this question must be negative, and he uses this answer to try to solve Zeno's paradoxes. Most contemporary mathematicians will argue that the answer to this question must be positive. The mathematician Georg Cantor (1845–1916) showed the existence of different infinite sets and transfinite numbers, the mathematics of which has been developed considerably since then.

This kind of view assumes a Platonic theory in the philosophy of mathematics, namely, that mathematical objects such as numbers or sets really exist. In contrast, there is a constructivist tradition in the philosophy of mathematics that would give a negative answer to the question, "Do mathematical objects really exist independently of us?" According to this tradition, mathematical objects do not exist independently of us; they are constructed. Constructivists typically reject the idea that infinitesimals exist, claiming that instants and points are not real. In which case, they will deny that the standard theory really solves Zeno's paradoxes.

Second, does the physical world really contain continuums? Quantum mechanics seems to imply that it doesn't. According to some realist interpretations of quantum mechanics, there exist physically minimal units of space and time, which are usually defined in terms of Planck's constant. In other words, according to these interpretations, space and time are essentially granular, an idea proposed and rejected by Aristotle (see chapter 10) but accepted by Epicurus (see chapter 13). So, does the physical world really contain continuums? Part of the issue here is that two apparently contradictory mathematical languages exist. One is the mathematics of continuums, which consists of calculus and also tensor theory. This is the mathematical language of Einstein's theories of relativity. The other is the mathematics of discrete units, which is the mathematical language for quantum mechanics. In short, we seem to have two fundamentally different mathematical languages: those that postulate infinite continuities and those that are committed to discrete entities.[19] What is the relationship between these two languages and physical reality?

Concerning Zeno's paradoxes, many writers assume that Zeno's arguments have a flaw and that the problem is to identify that flaw. Other commentators say that Zeno's paradoxes identify deep conceptual problems that resist a purely mathematical solution.[20] Arguably, the mathematics for the sum of an infinite convergent series does not solve all the conceptual problems raised by Zeno's paradoxes. This is because the mathematics itself has metaphysical assumptions built into it, such as the existence of infinitesimals. "Can those assumptions be defended?" is a different question.

MELISSUS OF SAMOS

It is important to note that Melissus of Samos also made an important contribution to Eleatic thought. Samos is an island in the Aegean Sea, where Pythagoras was born. So Melissus was not an Eleatic by birth. Nevertheless, he followed the views of Parmenides and argued for the thesis that what exists is a single, seamless and indivisible whole. Melissus was born around 470 BC, and in 441 BC, he was commander of the Samian naval fleet that won two battles against the Athenians, led by Pericles. Apart from this, we know little about his life.

There are a few notable differences between the views of Parmenides and Melissus. Parmenides thinks that the One is timeless, or at least there is only one eternal moment in which the One exists. In contrast, Melissus claims that the One is eternal in the sense of existing always (DK30B2). So, although they agree that the One cannot be created or destroyed, the two thinkers differ in several ways:

First, Melissus seems to be committed to the existence of infinity of moments, which Parmenides denies. Second, Melissus argues that the One is spatially infinite or at least infinite in magnitude (DK30B3). The One is infinitely large and hence lacks a beginning and an end in space. Third, Melissus argues that what-is must be full, and what-is-not must be empty. He argues that what-is-not does not exist, and therefore he denies the existence of the void. If there is no empty void for things to move into, motion is impossible (DK30B7, sections 7 and 10).

Finally, it is important to note that Melissus lived a generation after Zeno and that he is a contemporary of the pluralists, Anaxagoras and Empedocles. Because of this, he is able to provide an Eleatic reply to some of the points that the pluralists raise as objections to Parmenides. For instance, Melissus claims that the One cannot be rearranged, as the pluralists suppose. This pluralist idea presupposes that the One can be altered, which contradicts Parmenides's original argument negating the possibility of change.

In a similar vein, Melissus argues that the One must be seamless and "all alike" or qualitatively uniform. If it were unalike, then it would have different parts, and it would be a plurality rather than a unitary one (DK30A5). The One must be indivisible because if it had parts then it would be a plurality, which is impossible.

This same point rules out the claim that what-is can be more or less dense or rarefied (contrary to the Milesian Anaximenes). The concept of being more or less dense or rarefied contradicts the claim that the One must be "all alike" and thus also contradicts the claim that it is a single unity without parts. However, the concept of different densities is also ruled out by Melissus's negation of the empty void. He says that something could only have less density if more parts of it were empty rather than full

(DK30B7, line 8). It would be erroneous to attribute different densities to the One because that would require the existence of the empty void.

Conclusion

The Eleatic tradition comprises the third phase in the story of early ancient Greek philosophy.

The poem of Parmenides is a watershed in Western philosophy. Parmenides challenges the natural philosophy of the earlier Milesians by arguing that reality must consist of a single unchangeable and indivisible whole. Change is impossible because one cannot refer to what does not exist and change requires the idea of something not existing. Given that reality is an unchanging single whole, natural philosophy must be the study of mere appearances.

Zeno adds depth and strength to Parmenides's challenge to natural philosophy. He does so through his famous paradoxes of motion, which are usually understood as powerful arguments that support Parmenides's claims that reality is a single undivided whole and that plurality is impossible. Zeno provides other arguments to show that a plurality of things is impossible. One of these contends that if reality has parts then it must be infinitely divisible, which is impossible.

Study Questions

1. What does Parmenides mean by the claim that thinking and being are the same?
2. How would Parmenides support the claim that we cannot think about what does not exist?
3. How does Parmenides support the view that change is impossible?
4. Why does Parmenides think that reality cannot be divided?
5. What are Parmenides's conclusions about the nature of reality?
6. What is the purpose of Parmenides's Way of Seeming?
7. What is Zeno's argument in the Mid-way Problem? What is he trying to show us?
8. What is Zeno's argument concerning the Arrow?
9. How does Zeno argue that if there is a plurality then each member must be infinitely large?
10. What is Zeno's argument concerning place?
11. How does Zeno argue that what exists cannot have parts?
12. How does Melissus employ the claim that reality is seamless to argue against the pluralists?

Discussion Questions

1. How might one best respond to Parmenides's argument that change is impossible?
2. Which of Zeno's arguments against the possibility of motion is the strongest? How might one best respond to it?
3. Which of Zeno's arguments against the existence of a plurality is the strongest? How might one best respond to it?
4. Why does it matter whether reality is one or a plurality?

3 The Pluralists, Atomists, and Sophists

As mentioned in the Introduction, early ancient philosophy can be divided conveniently into five phases. After the first phase, the natural philosophy of the Milesians, comes the more metaphysical thinking of Heraclitus and Pythagoras, the Ionians. The third phase comprises the challenge provided by the work of Parmenides and Zeno. In the fourth phase, Empedocles, Anaxagoras, and Democritus continued to think philosophically about nature, following the earlier Milesian tradition. However, to do this, it was necessary that they respond to the challenge of Parmenides and Zeno. To do so, they argued that the basic being or substances of the cosmos are immutable, and they introduced a principle of change external to that being.

THE FOURTH PHASE: THE PLURALISTS AND ATOMISTS

Anaxagoras and Empedocles argue for a pluralistic view of substance. Although they are philosophers of nature who continue the Milesian tradition, they argue that there are several different kinds of substance-stuffs that constitute the world, rather than only one single basic kind, as the Milesians claimed.

In contrast to the pluralists, Democritus, following his teacher Leucippus, advances an atomistic theory of nature. The world consists of indivisible physical atoms. Leucippus is said to have written two books, *On the Mind* and *The Great World System*, but no fragments of his work remain and almost nothing is known about his life. Nevertheless, his atomism is expounded by Democritus and explained by Aristotle as well as by later ancient writers, such as Simplicius.

Empedocles (492–432 BC)

Empedocles came from a wealthy family in Acragas, Sicily. He himself had some political influence, supporting democracy against the aristocratic interests of his own family. However, he is famed for this extravagant personality, his flamboyant dress, and his remarkable deeds. He is reported to have kept a woman alive for a month when she was without a pulse and to have diverted two streams to rid the city of Selinus of plague. He himself claims to be an immortal god (DK31B112). Diogenes Laërtius reports that Empedocles died when he threw himself into the volcanic crater of Mount Aetna while trying to prove his god-like nature.

Empedocles wrote several works, of which only two poems survive in part: *On Nature* and *Purifications*. In the poem *On Nature*, Empedocles describes many natural phenomena, including the working of the eye, the action of breathing, and the development of the universe. He tries to explain biological and psychological phenomena in terms of different effluences or liquids fitting, or failing to fit, different pores or inlets in parts of the body. In short, Empedocles continues the tradition of natural philosophy started by the Milesians. In the poem, *Purifications,* Empedocles advances a Pythagorean-inspired view of human spirituality. For instance, he describes the fall of humankind. Originally, we were spirits who enjoyed a life of bliss. As a consequence of some error, we are destined to live as incarnate beings, reborn in animal and sometimes even plant form.

In around 320 AD, in the *Lives and Opinions of the Philosophers*, the biographer Diogenes Laërtius mentions that Empedocles wrote these two poems. In the early twentieth century, Diels and Kranz follow Diogenes's lead: they assign the fragments numbered as B1–111 to Empedocles' poem *On Nature*, and B112–153, to the *Purifications*. However, as we shall see, it is quite possible that the two poems comprise a single larger work and we can treat them as such.[1]

One reason that might motivate our regarding them as two works is that their subject matter is so different. However, as we have seen with both Heraclitus and Parmenides, the early ancient thinkers do not make the distinction between scientific and spiritual or religious works about the soul. Another reason why they perhaps might be considered as two distinct works is that they appear to reach contradictory conclusions. In particular, Empedocles's natural philosophy affirms that only the four elements are indestructible, while his spiritual work affirms the immortality of the soul. Either way the argument is spurious. If there isn't a contradiction in Empedocles's thought, we don't need to postulate two separate poems. If there is a contradiction, it does not vanish by placing it in two separate poems. Another piece of evidence in favor of there being two poems is that, apparently, they are directed to different audiences: *On Nature* addresses Pausanias (B1) and *Purifications* the citizens of Acragas (B112). The controversy about the poem was fuelled in the 1990s by the discovery of new lines of Empedocles on a papyrus in Strasbourg.[2]

Either way, many fragments of Empedocles's poem or poems exist; in fact, we have more of his work than that of any other Pre-Socratic philosopher.[3] Nevertheless, the existing fragments are quotes from various later secondary sources, and these generally do not indicate the order of the selections.

Chapter Three—The Pluralists, Atomists, and Sophists   63

Empedocles claims that the universe consists of four basic elements: fire, air, water, and earth, which are operated on by two forces, Love and Strife, or attraction and repulsion. Empedocles calls the elements the *roots*, and he also refers to them by the names of gods, Zeus (fire), Nestis (water), Hera (air), and Aidoneus (earth) (B6). He employs other names of the gods: Helios, Hephaestus, and Elektor for fire; Pontos and Thalassa for water; Ouranos for air; and Chthon, Aia, and Gaia for earth.[4] He considers them the basic indestructible stuff of the cosmos, and in this sense, the term *element* (used by Aristotle) is not too misleading, despite its modern allusions to contemporary chemistry. It is possible that Empedocles uses the term *earth* to refer to certain kinds of solids, *water* to pick out basic liquids, and *air* for gases. In any case, we shouldn't think of these terms (earth, water, air, and fire) as having modern meanings and references. The primary important points are that these roots are everlasting, all compounds are composed of them, and only and all the compounds are destructible.

Love is the force that forms the compounds by mixing the roots, and Strife the force that separates them. Whereas Love brings together things that are dissimilar, Strife separates them and brings together things that are similar. For Empedocles, these opposite forces are equal in the cosmos. If they were not, then one of the two would ultimately prevail and the cosmos would consist either only in entirely separate elements (or roots) if Strife were more powerful, or only in a huge intermingled mixture if Love were dominant.

It seems that the cosmos undergoes alternating periods in which one of the forces is dominant (DK31B17). In a famous passage, Empedocles says:

> I will tell a double story. For at one time they grew to be only one out of many, but at another they grew apart to be many out of one. Double is the generation of mortal things, and double their decline. For the coming together of all things gives birth to one and destroys it and the other is nurtured and flies away when they grow apart again. And these never cease continually interchanging, at one time all coming together into one by Love and at another each being borne apart by the hatred of Strife. (DK31B17)

Empedocles believes that the development of the universe is cyclical and eternal. Under the influence of the attractive force, the universe forms itself into a unified seamless sphere (B27). Under the influence of the repulsive force, Strife, the universe splits into the different elements, separated from each other (B35). In between these two extreme states, both forces influence the cosmos. This process of union and division is repeated an infinite number of times for eternity.

How does Empedocles conceive of the two forces? Apparently, they are physical insofar as they have a spatial location, and he thinks that their presence is necessary for the processes of mixing and separation. Some passages suggest that the physical presence of the force of Love is necessary to fuse together a compound from its elements or roots (B96 and B98). Referring to the formation of bones, he says that the elements are "fitted together divinely by the glues of Harmonia" (B96). However, at the same time, Empedocles apparently considers these two forces as immaterial and more than physical. He describes these forces and their effects in anthropomorphic terms; for instance, things affected by Strife are "enemies". Furthermore, the two forces have moral properties that have good and bad effects on human relations, including psychological love.

It is possible that, like Aristotle after him, Empedocles thinks the elements have natural tendencies to move: air and fire upwards, and water and earth downwards. If so, then the forces of Love and Strife are not agents for all change, but rather only for the mixing and separation of compounds.[5] In fact, Empedocles seems to think that the relevant quantities of each element in a compound can be specified; for instance, he claims that bone is made of four parts fire, two parts earth, and two parts water (DK31B96), and that flesh and blood consist of fire, air, and water in equal ratios (B98). He seems to think that the compounds formed by mixing have new properties, and he compares these compounds to the colors formed by mixing the primaries (B23). He compares the cosmic forces to two painters who

> take in their hands many-colored substances, mixing in harmony some more, others less, they produce from them images which resemble all things. They fashion trees and men and women and beasts and birds and water-bred fish and long-lived gods, best in honor. Just so, let no deception seize your mind that there is any other source of all the countless mortal things you see. (DK31B23)

This quote suggests that, like two painters, the two forces are intelligent and experience desire as a motive for their actions. However, it is important for Empedocles that, in this process, the elements cannot be destroyed, and this implies that the making of new compounds cannot constitute the creation of something that annihilates the original elements.

This point is important because it is part of Empedocles's implicit response to Parmenides. As we have seen, Parmenides argues that change is impossible given that we cannot refer to what does not exist. Empedocles answers Parmenides, first by agreeing that absolute creation and destruction are impossible and, consequently, that the basic elements have always existed and always will (B8). His second response is that changes in the world are simply the reorganization of what already exists, namely, the four basic elements.

> There is coming-to-be of not a single one of all mortal things, nor is there any end of destructive death, but only mixture, and separation of what is mixed, and nature is the name given to them by humans. (DK31B8)

In other words, Empedocles would claim that such changes do not violate the Parmenidean principle that we cannot refer to what does not exist: "For it is impossible to come to be from what in no way is" (B12). Third, like the Eleatics, Empedocles claims that it is impossible for there to be empty time and space (B14 and 16).

As mentioned earlier, Empedocles provides a cosmogony and a zoogony. In other words, he provides an account of the origin of the cosmos and of the generation of animals. The cycles of the cosmos can be divided into four phases: the two extreme static stages in which either Love or Strife predominates (described earlier), and two transitional phases in which both forces are active—one in which the elements are unifying and Love is increasing, and the other in which the elements are separating and Strife is on the ascendency.

Many interpreters think that Empedocles's position implies that the cosmos has a different cosmogony and zoogony according to whether it is in the process of unification or differentiation. When the cosmos is in the process of increasing separation, the formation of compounds and animals is the reverse of what it is when the universe is in a process of increased unification. This is the standard view.[6] Other interpreters claim that Empedocles implies there is only one cosmogony and zoogony, irrespective of the overall direction of the process.

Aristotle reports Empedocles as saying that the cosmos is currently in a period of increasing Strife (DK31A42). Aristotle also claims that Empedocles doesn't provide the details of what would be a backward cosmogony, although there is a brief and general description at B35. Aristotle says: "For he would not be able to put together the heaven by constructing it out of separate things and making the compound through Love" (DK31A42).[7] Other early ancient Greek cosmogonies are based only on the process of separation; they assume that the universe was originally a unity, and they describe the process of differentiation from that initial state.

Empedocles describes the process of cosmic differentiation: "the air was separated off and it flowed round in a circle" (DK31A30). Afterwards came the separation of the fire, earth, and finally water, so that, in the center there is earth, with seas on its surface, air above that, and a region of fire still further above. Empedocles claims that the Moon was formed from solidified air rather "like hail," and that its light is reflected from the Sun (A30).

He claims that animals are generated in four phases or steps (A72). In the first, the parts of animals are formed separately through the combining of the elements in definite ratios under the influence of Love. In this first stage, there are arms without shoulders, eyes without foreheads, and faces without necks (B57). In the second stage these organs and limbs combine in random ways through the influence of Love, producing, for example, the head of a human with the body of an ox, beings with two faces or with chests on both sides (B61), or cattle with many hands (B60). However, this random process resulted in combinations that were apt for survival, as well as those that were not. In other words, there were combinations that "fulfilled each other's needs," such as teeth for softening food, stomachs for digesting it, and livers for turning it into blood (B61). Apparently Empedocles describes the third phase as a process in which "whole-natured forms" rose out of the earth combined with some water and heat, thrown up by the separation of fire. Initially these beings did not have distinct limbs or sexual organs (B62). In the fourth stage, after sexual differentiation emerged with "much wailing," animals were generated by sexual reproduction.

Empedocles's descriptions of the four stages raise several questions. It is difficult to understand the relation between the first two stages and the third: why is the third stage necessary, given that the second can produce functioning whole organisms? Furthermore, the processes of stages 1, 2, and 4 require the attractive force of Love, while the third occurs during a period of Strife. Empedocles seems to think that the cosmos is currently undergoing a period of increasing Strife, but his account of the generation of animals seems to require an increase in the influence of Love. In this way his cosmogony and his zoogony apparently require different views about which of the two forces predominate. Perhaps, his idea is that both forces work at the same time at different levels, so that while Strife leads a process of separation at a cosmic level, Love can work a process of integration at the level of individual organisms.

The passage at B112 appears to be the opening of the *Purifications*, in which Empedocles addresses the citizens of Acragas (currently, Agrigento in Sicily). If the *Purifications* and *On Nature* are really one piece, then this may be the start of the poem as a whole. In the subsequent passages, Empedocles claims divine status for himself and direct access to truths inaccessible to ordinary mortals. He claims himself to be a *daimōn*, a divine spirit exiled from the gods for a fixed period of 30,000 seasons for some offense, such as shedding blood or swearing a false oath. He describes himself as a fugitive from the gods, "the blessed ones," and as a wanderer who placed "his reliance on raving Strife" (B115). This claim reinforces the idea that Empedocles attributes moral properties to the two forces, Love and Strife. Elsewhere, Empedocles suggests that human history contains more bloodshed and violence as the force of Strife increases in the universe and that there was a golden age of peace when Love reigned (B128) and "friendliness burned brightly" (B130). In several passages, Empedocles describes the fall of the *daimōnes* in terms of the suffering of an outcaste (B121–126). He says: "while wandering in harsh evils, you will never relieve your spirit from wretched distress" (B145).

It is possible that Empedocles views the transmigration into different living beings as integral to the process of banishment from the gods. In this, his view is similar to that of the Pythagoreans of his native Sicily.

Empedocles himself claims to have born previously as a girl, a fish, a bird, and a bush (B117). He argues against animal sacrifice on the grounds that a person might be killing a close relative who has transformed into an animal form (B137). He apparently argues that all meat eating is potentially a form of cannibalism (B136). Empedocles offers all sorts of advice to help exiled *daimōnes* return to their blessed state and find freedom from banishment. These include Pythagorean injunctions such as to stay away from beans (B141) and laurel leaves (B140) and, more generally, to fast from evil (B144).

Anaxagoras (500–428 BC)

Anaxagoras came from Clazomenea in Ionia (today, Uria in Turkey). Like the earlier philosophers from Ionia, Anaxagoras's main interest was in the philosophy of nature and the cosmos. At the age of twenty he moved to Athens, where he remained for thirty years. His book *On Nature* was proclaimed the greatest scientific work of the period. Only about a thousand words of this work survive, mostly preserved by Simplicius. Anaxagoras wrote it in prose instead of poetry. It is said that he predicted the fall of a meteorite, and he claimed that the sun was a red-hot ball of stone rather than a god. He had a passion for astronomy. He was a friend of the famous statesman, Pericles, who was the founder of democracy in Athens. He also taught the playwright Euripides. Anaxagoras's apparently materialist and anti-religious views were unpopular, and he was charged with impiety by Pericles's opponents and subsequently exiled from Athens.

The natural philosophy of Anaxagoras can be divided into two parts. First is his philosophy of substance and second, his view of *Nous* or mind. Regarding substance, Anaxagoras accepts the Parmenidean claim, "what-is cannot not be" (B3), and consequently that creation and destruction are impossible. Consequently, nothing can come from nothing, and everything has always existed. Anaxagoras argues that all change is simply the reorganization of what already exists. Aristotle says:

> Anaxagoras . . . accepted as true the common opinion of the physicists that nothing comes to be from what is not. That is why they say: "all things were together," and why Anaxagoras makes the generation of a thing of a certain sort into alteration. (DK59A52)[8]

Anaxagoras takes the principle of Parmenides, that nothing can be created, more to heart than Empedocles does. As we saw earlier, Empedocles claims that new substances, such as bone and flesh, are formed when the four elements combine in definite proportions. In contrast, Anaxagoras denies that new substances can be created in this way. He asks rhetorically:

> For how . . . can hair come from what is not hair, and flesh from what is not flesh? (DK59B10)

In other words, hair cannot come from something that doesn't contain hair. Indeed, for this reason Anaxagoras claims that all substances are always intermingled. For example, a small piece of gold contains all of the other kinds of substances, and those tinier pieces of the other substances contain all of the others.

> Since these things are so, it is right to think that there are many different things present in everything that is being combined, and seeds of all things, having all sorts of forms, colors, and flavors. (B4)

In a similar vein, at B11 Anaxagoras says, "In everything there is a portion of everything." He argues for this conclusion about intermingling on the basis of the observation that anything, or rather any kind of substance, can come from any other. For example, water can come from clouds; air can arise from fire; and wood can originate from water. In short, from any single substance-kind, any other stuff can be extracted. To this empirical observation, we must add the principle that if one can extract a substance from some object then that object must contain some of that stuff. In short, Anaxagoras argues:

1. From any substance-stuff, one can extract any other substance-kind.
2. If one can extract a substance-kind from some object, then that object must contain some of that kind of substance.
3. Therefore, any piece of a substance contains all other stuffs.

In other words, the world is a thoroughgoing and infinitely divisible mixture. This implies that there is no smallest portion of any substance-stuff. According to Simplicius, Anaxagoras gives this argument, defending premise 1 on the grounds that anything can come from anything, even if the change is not immediate or it has to happen in a definite sequence (DK59A45). The second premise might be defended on the grounds that if it weren't true, it would be like magic, a change without sufficient reason.

It seems clear that, for Anaxagoras, there are basic things out of which everything else is composed, and which are infinitely intermingled. Nevertheless, within these general parameters, interpretations of Anaxagoras vary. For instance, what are these basic elements? One interpretation of Anaxagoras claims that these basics are confined to the opposites, some of which he mentions later in B4: the wet and the dry, the hot and the cold, and the bright and the dark. He says:

> Before there was separation off, because all things were together, there was not even any color evident; for the mixture of all things prevented it, of the wet and the dry and of the hot and the cold and of the bright and the dark, and there was much earth present and seeds unlimited in number, in no way similar to one another. For no one of the others is similar to another. Since these things are so, it is right to think that all things were present in the whole. (B4)

Chapter Three—The Pluralists, Atomists, and Sophists   69

Given this passage, it is probable that Anaxagoras thinks of the opposites as substances or as kinds of stuff, like the Milesians. In which case, the wet would be a substance-kind that moistens other things.[9] According to this interpretation, all of the other things mentioned by Anaxagoras are composites of these basic opposites.

A second interpretation doesn't restrict the basics things only to these opposites. In particular, the basics may include what Anaxagoras calls the *seeds*, referred to in the first quote from B4 cited earlier. With the term "seeds," Anaxagoras probably refers to various substance-kinds, such as hair and flesh, and indicates that their presence in minute quantities allows for the kind of changes described earlier. In other words, if my hair grows because of the food I ingest then this indicates that the food must contain seeds of hair. Likewise, if my bones grow because of the food I eat, then the food must contain tiny pieces of bone that function like seeds. The term "seeds" isn't necessarily restricted to the biological; it might also refer to non-biological substances such as gold. According to the second interpretation, Anaximander's basic ontology includes both the opposites and other things, such as the seeds.

One of the differences between these two interpretations is that the second posits bits of the substances that are in principle countable, whereas the first doesn't. The first conceives mixtures only in terms of proportions, rather like mixed liquids, and does not include countable parts. The second interpretation seems to posit countable bits, such as fragments of gold or bone or hair. Which of these two interpretations one might best accept depends on some unanswered questions. For instance, when Anaximander suggests that there are seeds of hair in food, how literally does he mean that? Are there literally such seeds present, as the second interpretation would indicate? Or rather does he mean simply that the opposites present in hair are also present in the food I eat, as the first interpretation would suggest? We will return to these questions later after we have looked at Anaxagoras's thought in more depth.

Even though all things are intermingled, Anaxagoras thinks that they are mixed in different proportions in different things. So, for example, blood must have a specific proportion of hot and cold, and so on. In this way, even though every other substance is present in a piece of blood, only certain elements predominate in blood; the others are merely latent. Likewise, in a piece of gold, some basic elements predominate and others are latent, despite the fact that every basic thing contains all basic substances. There is no smallest portion, but each thing is manifestly what it contains in the largest proportion. In short, differences between various objects are due to differences of proportion (B12).[10]

We don't know how many basic things there are, according to Anaxagoras. In addition to the opposites, there could be the seeds, such as hair and flesh, as we have discussed. However, he also mentions air and aether in B1, and also earth, water, cloud, and stone Possibly, Anaxagoras thinks that there is an indefinite number of basic things.

He does distinguish these basics from compounds, such as the Sun, the Moon, and the stars, which are fiery stones (DK59A42), and dwellings and cities, which are also compounds. However, because he claims that there is a portion of everything in everything, we should not conceive of Anaxagoras's basic things as irreducible elements or indivisible atoms. For Anaxagoras, there is no smallest portion. In this sense, it is misleading to call his basic things "elements." Thus, in Anaxagoras's theory, change cannot be conceived as a rearrangement of basic elements, as it can in Empedocles's system. For Anaxagoras, change must be alterations in proportions, so that smaller portions become larger, and vice versa.

Anaxagoras's claim that there are no smallest portions may constitute a partial agreement with and reply to the arguments of Zeno. As we saw in the previous chapter, Zeno claims that every thing is infinitely divisible, and as a result, when such a division is carried out completely (albeit hypothetically), the resultant parts would have no size, which is absurd. Zeno apparently uses this argument to conclude that there cannot be a plurality. Zeno argues that if there were a plurality then, because of infinite divisibility, absurd consequences would follow.[11]

Anaxagoras agrees with Parmenides's claim, "what is cannot not be"—i.e., what is must be. He cites this as the reason why there can be no smallest part (B3). Therefore Anaxagoras apparently agrees with Zeno that if what exists has parts then everything is infinitely divisible. However, Anaxagoras disagrees with Zeno, affirming that there cannot be an infinite number of resultant parts from such an infinite division, because he claims that an infinite division cannot be carried out completely.[12] Thus, Anaxagoras says that things cannot be "split apart with an axe" (B8). In short, he tries to defuse Zeno's argument that there cannot be a plurality by arguing that infinite divisibility is impossible and therefore, it doesn't entail absurd consequences.

At B3, Anaxagoras has the strange saying:

> And the large is equal to the small in extent, but in relation to itself each thing is both large and small.

One might read this as claiming that, although there is a *larger proportion* of gold in a nugget than there is a proportion of water, nevertheless, one cannot say that there are *more bits* of gold in a nugget than there are bits of water. There are infinite amounts of both bits of gold and water in a nugget of gold. Likewise, there are an infinite number of bits of gold in a drop of water. This conclusion means that we cannot refer to finite countable bits in the basic things in the cosmos (because they are always infinite); we can only refer to greater or smaller proportions. This conclusion follows from Anaxagoras's claim that everything is infinitely intermingled, which is part of his reply to Zeno.

Chapter Three—The Pluralists, Atomists, and Sophists   71

The second part of Anaxagoras's philosophy is his view on the nature of the Mind, or *Nous*. According to Anaxagoras, the Mind or *Nous* is separate from all material things. It is not intermingled with anything material: it "has been mixed with no thing, but is alone itself by itself" (B12). *Nous* is infinite and self-controlling (B12, line 2).

The main function of *Nous* in Anaxagoras's philosophy is that it is responsible for all changes. The claim that it is so responsible may be regarded as a partial reply to Parmenides's view that change is impossible. In reply to Parmenides, Anaxagoras claims that any alteration in material substances requires the external agency of mind; in short, Parmenides is right insofar as material things cannot change on their own, but he is mistaken insofar as change is possible through the external agency of *Nous*. In this respect, Anaxagoras's conception of *Nous* is similar to Empedocles's notion of the two forces, Love and Strife: they are required for change to be possible at all. However, there are important differences between the thought of Anaxagoras and Empedocles. First, *Nous* is infinite and apparently all-powerful and all-knowing. Here is how Anaxagoras describes it:

> It is the finest of all things and the purest, and indeed it maintains all discernment about everything and has the greatest strength. (B12)

Anaxagoras argues for this claim on the grounds that *Nous* initiates change by controlling things, but it would not be able to do so if it were mixed with anything else, because then it would be thwarted. It would be thwarted because if it were mixed with anything, then it would have to be mixed in with everything physical, since all the basic physical things are intermingled. Thus, *Nous* must be separate from all the physical things of the cosmos (to be able to control them). We can represent Anaxagoras's argument as follows:

1. *Nous* initiates all changes by controlling the basic physical things.
2. If *Nous* were mixed with anything physical, then it would have to be mixed with everything physical (because all basic physical things are intermingled).
3. If *Nous* were mixed with everything physical, then it could not control physical things.

---

4. Therefore, *Nous* is not mixed with anything physical.

In contrast, Empedocles seems to attribute both physical and psychological characteristics to the two motivating forces of Love and Strife. In brief, the distinction between matter and mind seems sharper for Anaxagoras than it does for Empedocles. Nevertheless, it would be incorrect, as well as anachronistic, to claim that Anaxagoras conceives of *Nous* as an immaterial substance. Like Empedocles's forces, *Nous* is present in space. At B11, he says: "there are some things in which *Nous*, too, is present." Anaxagoras's description of *Nous* as "the finest of all things" imputes to it physical attributes.

Second, Empedocles ascribes moral characteristics to the forces of Love and Strife. Anaxagoras doesn't characterize *Nous* in moral terms. Nevertheless, he does describe *Nous* as imposing order on the cosmos, which might suggest purpose, and even purpose directed towards the good. Furthermore, Anaxagoras attributes the power of judgment, knowledge of the future, and even omniscience to *Nous*. Again this suggests that *Nous* has intentions and purposes, but Anaxagoras never affirms this explicitly, as far we know. As we shall see in later chapters, in Plato's *Phaedo*, Socrates complains that Anaxagoras treats the cosmic Mind mechanically rather than teleologically. Aristotle makes a similar complaint in his *Metaphysics*.[13] In brief, the role of Anaxagoras's *Nous* seems to be restricted to setting up a mechanical process.

Anaxagoras characterizes the working of *Nous* primarily by describing his cosmogony. He begins his work by declaring, "In the beginning, all things were together unlimited both in amount and in smallness" (B1). He proclaims that "nothing was evident" (B1) because "the mixture of all things prevented it" (B4). By this he means that because things were completely intermingled, nothing stood out as distinct from anything else. Everything was a homogeneous whole. In the passage B12, Anaxagoras states that *Nous* caused this whole to rotate, which began a process of separation or differentiation that permitted identifiable things to emerge. The rotation of this vortex caused the forces that brought the basic things of the same kind together in greater concentrations or proportions. According to Anaxagoras, this rotational movement and the subsequent forces increased over time, as did the area rotating (B9).

In the first passage of his work, Anaxagoras says that early in the history of the cosmos "air and aether dominated all things" (B1). This claim may seem anomalous given that everything is intermingled. One possible explanation, suggested by B2, is that air and aether were the first to be separated by the forces of the rotating vortex. Anaxagoras apparently thinks that lighter things tend to move towards the periphery of the cosmos because of the vortex (B15, B16). However, Anaxagoras also thinks that the stars, planets, and Moon are fiery stones, and this presents another apparent incongruity in Anaxagoras's cosmogony. Anaxagoras had evidence for his claim about the planets and the stars: in 467 BC, a large meteorite fell to Earth near Aegospotami, in modern Turkey, which Anaxagoras explained in terms of his theory. He explains the motion of the planets and the heavenly bodies in terms of the force of the swirling vortex.

Democritus (460–360 BC)

Democritus was born in Abdera, in Thrace (in Northern Greece). We don't know when he was born, but Diogenes Laërtius claims that Democritus was 40 years younger than Anaxagoras. Allegedly, Democritus

Chapter Three—The Pluralists, Atomists, and Sophists 73

lived to over the age of 100, and if he was born in 460 BC, he was 9 years younger than Socrates. During his long life, he traveled widely in the ancient world, although the reports that he visited India are probably false. He was a prolific writer. Diogenes Laërtius lists over sixty works written by Democritus, including his famous *Maxims*. His interests extended far beyond natural philosophy and atomism. He discussed the nature of humans as cultural and social beings, what today we would call "anthropological studies." He wrote treatises on poetry, mathematics, and various technical matters, such as farming, diets, medical judgment, and military tactics. He also wrote nine works on moral and political philosophy. Although we have many fragments and sayings from Democritus, these are primarily regarding his ethics and political ideas.[14] Concerning his atomism we must rely largely on the testimony of later writers. In particular, Aristotle makes frequent comments about the atomism of Democritus throughout his own works. Indeed, he wrote a work on the physics of Democritus, which is lost but is quoted by later commentators such as Simplicius. However, Aristotle argues against the atomism of Democritus and needs to be regarded with caution as a source.

Democritus was a pupil of Leucippus, who was the first atomist and who wrote the works *The Great World System* and *On Mind* somewhere around 440–430 BC, which makes him roughly a contemporary of Empedocles and Anaxagoras. Like them, Leucippus tried to reframe natural philosophy in a way that answers the arguments and challenge of Parmenides. It is difficult to distinguish the views of Leucippus from those of his pupil Democritus. However, it is probable that, while Leucippus developed the basic theory of atomism, Democritus applied it systematically to natural phenomena, including human perception and knowledge.

According to Leucippus and Democritus, the cosmos consists only of two basic things: the void and atoms. The Greek word *atomos* means something that cannot be cut or divided. Leucippus and Democritus claim that there are an infinite number of indivisible atoms. They are solid, and they have a size and a shape. They cannot be destroyed or created.

In claiming that atoms cannot be destroyed or created, Leucippus and Democritus agree with Parmenides. Each atom is like an unchanging Parmenidean world, which cannot be destroyed or created. They also agree with Parmenides insofar as they claim that each atom is homogeneous, changeless, and indivisible, like the Parmenidean universe. However, Leucippus and Democritus disagree with Parmenides in that they argue that there are many atoms and that they move. Leucippus and Democritus try to substantiate this view. They accept the Eleatic premise that motion requires that we can refer to what is not. Whereas Parmenides argues that this means that motion is impossible because we cannot refer to what is not, Leucippus and Democritus argue that we can refer to what is not. The what-is-not is simply empty space or the void, about which we can speak and think (DK67A7).

Aristotle presents this argument as an attempt to explain or save the phenomena. In other words, the atomists assume that the appearance of motion is not an illusion, but to maintain this claim, they must explain how motion is possible given the challenge of Parmenides. They do this by claiming that the void is what is not. About Leucippus, Aristotle says:

> Agreeing on these matters with the phenomena and agreeing with those who support the One that there could be no motion without void, he asserts that void is what-is-not and that nothing of what-is is not. (DK67A7)

In other words, the void and only the void is what-is-not. In short, the argument of Leucippus and Democritus can be represented as follows:

1. Motion requires the existence of what-is-not.
2. What-is-not could only be the void.
3. There is motion in the universe.
4. Therefore, the void exists.

In this argument, Parmenides would agree with premise 1. Premise 3 assumes the reality of the phenomena of motion and is anti-Parmenidean.

Concerning the conclusion 4, Simplicius reports that Leucippus posits "what-is is no more than what-is-not, and both are equally causes of what comes to be" (DK68A38). In this sense, atoms and the void are equally existent. What is the void? Democritus calls the void "nothing" (DK68A37). Although Aristotle identifies the void with empty space, this identification is open to question because Democritus apparently locates the void in empty space.[15] According to the atomists, despite being nothing, the void or what-is-not exists. This is perhaps the most fundamental point of contention between the atomists and Parmenides.

Having argued for the existence of the void, Leucippus and Democritus can now also contend that the cosmos consists in a plurality of things rather than a single undifferentiated whole as Parmenides claims. There can be many things because the void allows them to be apart (DK, 67 A7). Without void, all matter would be one single mass. In conclusion, the existence of the void allows for motion and plurality but at the same time respects the sharp Parmenidean separation of what-is from what-is-not. Where there are atoms there is no void, and where there is void there are no atoms. The individual atom contains no void.

We can also see the postulation of atoms as a partial answer to Zeno. The atomists accept Zeno's contention that apparently absurd consequences follow from the claim that finite objects are infinitely divisible. They reply by positing the existence of indivisible atoms that have no parts. In so doing, they avoid the argument given by Zeno to show that any single finite thing must have an unlimited large size. As we saw in chapter 2, Zeno's argument depends on the claim that finite things are infinitely divisible and that any part must have a size.[16] Democritus rejects that assumption. As we mentioned in chapter 2, in *On Generation and Corruption*, Aristotle claims that Democritus appears to have been persuaded by Zeno's argument that the idea of a complete division of a body leads to apparently absurd consequences and thus postulates the existence of indivisible atoms (DK68A48).[17]

According to Aristotle, Democritus claims that atoms differ only in their shape, arrangement and position: the letter A differs from N in shape, "'AN' from 'NA' in arrangement, and 'N' from 'Z' in position" (DK67A67). To this list we can add size as another fundamental property of atoms (DK68A47). Although in principle a single atom could be any size, in fact they are all minute and unobservable.

To this list we might also include two non-fundamental properties, although these are contested: weight and solidity. Since atoms are made of the same stuff, it stands to reason that bigger atoms will weigh more than smaller ones (DK68A60). This property of atoms shouldn't be confused with the heaviness and lightness of compound bodies. Likewise, the infinite solidity that atoms have because of their indivisibility shouldn't be confused with the hardness and softness of compound bodies, as we shall see.

In short, the atoms can only differ primarily from each other in their size and shape, and they can vary only in their arrangement, position, and motion. They are indivisible and have no parts. Furthermore, each individual atom is changeless. They have no intrinsic qualities to change except their size and shape—these cannot be altered, and each atom is indestructible.

This limited nature of atoms means that they do not have perceptible qualities such as hardness or softness, color, and taste. More importantly for the context of early ancient Greek thought, they do not have the perceptible properties of hot and cold or wet and dry, which define the traditional four elements earth, water, air, and fire. This makes atomism radically different from the thought of Empedocles and Anaxagoras and the earlier Milesians. It also means that the atomists need to explain how compounds of atoms can give rise to such perceptible qualities.

Democritus begins this task by claiming that the motion of the atoms in the void constitutes our familiar world. Sometimes, when they collide, the atoms cohere together to form more complex compound bodies. The atoms can hold together because of their shapes because "some are hooked, others concave, and others convex" (DK68A37). According to Democritus, "each of the shapes produces a different composition when arranged in a different compound" (DK68A38). In this way, they form the building blocks of everything we perceive. Compounds, unlike the atoms that compose them, will also contain void. Democritus explains the hardness and softness of objects in terms of the gaps of void between the atoms, and he explains the weight of materials in a similar fashion: he claims that iron must have more void per unit of volume than lead (DK68A135).

Why do atoms move in the void? Although Aristotle complains that the atomists don't answer this question satisfactorily (DK, 67 A6), Democritus does claim that the universe is infinitely old, and that atoms have always been in motion (DK67A16). In other words, there is no first cause. The atoms cause each other to move simply by colliding with or knocking against each other (DK68A47). This means that in the cosmology of the atomists, there are no forces such as Empedocles's Love and Strife and no place for Anaxagoras's *Nous*. Accordingly, all things happen "as a result of a reason and by necessity" (DK67B2).

Democritus distinguishes the universe as a whole—which is unlimited—from a cosmos. A cosmos is a world system, which is limited in space and time. So, for instance, the Earth, the Moon, the planets, and stars constitute our cosmos. The infinite universe contains an unlimited number of cosmoses (DK67A1). These cosmoses may be quite different from each other: some without a sun, others without a moon, and others without animals (DK68A40). They are scattered randomly throughout the universe. Democritus describes the typical generation of a cosmos like ours as follows: the atoms

> . . . collect together and form a single vortex. In it they knock against one another and move around in all different ways and they separate apart, like moving towards like. (DK67A1)

The swirling vortex throws out the smaller atoms to the periphery while the remaining larger ones gather in the center. In this way, the Earth is formed at the center of the cosmos, and the smaller atoms towards the outside of the whirl form the fixed stars. The process by which cosmoses form is purely mechanical, and clearly, in an infinitely large and infinitely old universe, there is nothing special about our cosmos.

One of the most remarkable features of Democritus's philosophy is his theory of perception. Diogenes Laërtius cites works by Democritus on flavors, colors, and shapes, as well as a general treatise on the senses. Democritus realized that his atomism had dramatic implications for perception. The only real things are atoms. Since these are colorless, color and other similar perceptual properties must be illusions. Consequently, our senses continually deceive us; the world itself is very different from how we perceive it to be.

It is important to note that the term *atom* is used differently throughout the history of physical theory. The contemporary conception of atoms is *very* different from that of Democritus. In contemporary physics, atoms are not indivisible particles. Contemporary physical theories involve a multitude of subatomic particles, such as neutrons, protons and electrons, and the protons and neutrons are further composed of quarks. Atoms have a complex internal structure and are not homogeneous. They have quantum mechanical properties. Furthermore, even the corpuscles as conceived by the early modern philosophical scientists are not the same as Democritus's atoms. For instance, Galileo (1564–1642) and Descartes (1596–1650) argued that corpuscles are divisible because they are located in space, which is conceived of as continuous and infinitely divisible. Perhaps Newton's (1643–1727) conception of atoms comes closest to Democritus's. According to Newton, the world must consist of indivisible atoms because the assertion that matter is infinitely divisible is physically problematic. Anything made of bits or parts cannot transmit forces instantaneously and will not be perfectly rigid, and, thus, cannot satisfy the requirements of Newton's theory, which involves forces acting at a point. In short, Newton's theory of motion requires the existence of atoms that do not have parts.

It is also worth noting that the impact of Democritus's atomism on the history of thought has been largely indirect through Epicurus (341–270 BC) and the influential writings of the Epicurean poet philosopher Lucretius (99–55 BC), whose views we will examine in chapter 13.

THE FIFTH PHASE: THE SOPHISTS

As we said in the introduction to the first part of this work, early ancient philosophy can be divided into five phases. The first two consist in the natural philosophy of the Milesians and the metaphysics of the Ionians, Heraclitus and Pythagoras. The third consists in the challenge of Parmenides and Zeno. The fourth is the reply of the pluralists (Empedocles and Anaxagoras) and of the atomists (Leucippus and Democritus). The fifth and final phase constitutes a change of direction.

Sophism is more directly concerned with ethics and politics than most of the earlier ancient Greek philosophy. The Sophists include Protagoras, Gorgias, Hippias and Antiphon, among many others. The Sophists don't constitute a school of thought even in the loose way that the Milesians do. They are individual thinkers who share a common general outlook. More precisely, they are traveling teachers who taught, among other things, the arts of persuasion and rhetoric, and who made their living this way.

The Persian Wars ended in 478 BC. After this time, Athens enjoyed supremacy among Greek states and throughout the Aegean. The city became wealthy and powerful. In 458 BC it also became democratic. Political power shifted away from officials towards the assembly of citizens and to the jurors of the law courts. Sophism resulted in part because of this increasing prosperity and political sophistication of Athens in the late fifth century BC. These developments led to a demand for forms of education that went beyond the elementary training in literature, music, arithmetic, and gymnastics offered in the schools of the time. Young people wanted to be trained in the arts of rhetoric and argumentation in order to gain influence in the city. In response to these demands, the

Sophists worked as travelling teachers, offering instruction in persuasion, and transmitting their analyses of morality and politics.

The Sophists tend to have a critical attitude to prevailing moral and religious beliefs. They often articulate some form of individual or cultural relativism, denying objective moral claims, and claiming that moral beliefs arise solely through social conventions. They tend to contrast social convention (*nomos*) with the objectivity of nature (*phusis*).

The view that moral claims are based on nature or on the reality of things (*phusis*) provides those claims with objectivity, a necessity and an authority that may seem to make them beyond challenge. In contrast, the view that such claims are purely conventional suggests that they have no such authority. The historian Herodotus cites the case of the Persian king Darius, who asks the Greeks if they would eat the corpses of their dead fathers. He also asks the Kallatiai Indians, who do eat their dead parents, if they would be willing to cremate the corpses of their parents, as do the Persians. Both answer with a resounding and horrified *no*. Herodotus concludes that such moral views are merely based on *nomos* or custom.[18] In part such a claim denies that there is any necessity to such conventions.

Sophists tend to employ the distinction between *phusis* and *nomos* in two different ways. On the one hand, those who support nature or *phusis* tend to argue that by nature, each person pursues his or her self-interest, and the strong naturally will succeed against the weak if allowed to do so. According to this kind of view, *nomos* consists of a bogus set of social laws that protect the weak and deny the authority of the natural law that prescribes the pursuit of one's own advantage. Callicles in Plato's *Gorgias* and Thrasymachus in the *Republic* embrace different versions of this kind of rational egoist view.[19]

On the other hand, Sophists who support *nomos* tend to advocate either some form of cultural relativism or the idea that morality is a social contract for the sake of mutual benefit. In each of these different scenarios, the Sophist view of morality challenges the claim that morality is a fixed law of nature.

In these two different challenges to morality, we can also see the seeds of a radically new type of confrontation with traditional religion. The rationalism and materialism of early scientific Greek philosophy challenges the traditional mythological religious beliefs in a particular way. Rationalism defies the authority of traditional belief because it requires that claims about the cosmos be supported by evidence or argumentation. Any view that is not so supported is merely superstition. It is in this vein that Heraclitus spurns traditional religious views of the gods and that Xenophanes ridicules their anthropomorphism, claiming that horses would portray the gods as horses. The materialism of early philosophy also challenges traditional religious beliefs by providing natural explanations for phenomena that don't require divine intervention. When Anaxagoras claims that the Sun is hot rock, he is denying that it is a divinity. Democritus's atomism requires no god. Although naturalistic philosophy already rebels against traditional religious views, Sophism adds new dimensions to this confrontation. It adds the idea that religious views and rituals are socially relative.

Our sources for the Sophists are sparse. There are very few surviving fragments from their writings, and Aristotle mentions them infrequently. We are forced to rely on the dialogues of Plato. Plato wrote several dialogues that are explicitly named after Sophists: the *Enthydemus*, the *Hippias*, the *Gorgias* and the *Protagoras*. Other dialogues are at least in part about Sophism including the *Theaetetus*, the *Sophist*, and not least the *Republic*. As we shall see in chapter 5, Plato wrote much to refute Sophism, having a tendency to weaken the views of the Sophists in order to make them easier to defeat. Plato tends to portray the Sophists as superficial thinkers who taught solely for financial gain. Thus, we need to treat his portrayals with caution.

Originally, the term *sophist* came from the word *sophia*, meaning wisdom. The Sophists were regarded as people of wisdom. However, later the term *sophist* became associated with the word *sophon*, which means cleverness.[20] In this way, the Sophists came to be portrayed as purveyors of cleverness rather than as philosophers, lovers of wisdom.

Protagoras (490–420 BC)

Protagoras proclaimed himself as the first Sophist. He came from Abdera, an Ionian colony on the coast of Thrace. In his *Life of the Sophists*, Philostratus (ca. 172–250 AD) reports that Protagoras's father was an associate of the Persian king, Xerxes, and that Protagoras was educated by Zoroastrians from Persia. It is possible that Protagoras knew Democritus, who was born in the same town. In any case, Democritus was about 30 years older than him and argued against Protagoras's subjectivism. As a young man Protagoras went to live in Athens, and in 443 BC, he was asked by Pericles (495–429 BC) to form a constitution for the Greek colony Thurii in Southern Italy. Pericles was the foremost Athenian statesman during the golden age of Athens. Philostratus also reports that Protagoras was banished from Athens for professing agnosticism or impiety and that he drowned when he was chased at sea. This account of a heroic death does not square with Plato's *Meno*, which says that Protagoras died with a good reputation (91d).

Although he probably wrote 18 works (12 of which are listed by Diogenes Laërtius), there remain only a few sentences and phrases of these works. The works of Protagoras include the volumes *On the Virtues* and *On the Political Constitution*, as well as a work on truth, one on argumentation, and one on wrestling. Diogenes Laërtius reports that Protagoras made a classification of speech acts into assertions, questions, commands, and so forth.[21] Plato reports that he wrote on the correctness of language, and Aristotle reports that he classified grammatical genders.[22]

Plato discusses Protagoras's thoughts at length, especially in the dialogues *Protagoras* and *Theaetetus*, although he is not present as a character in the latter.[23] From these and other sources it is possible to tentatively reconstruct some aspects of his philosophy.

Protagoras is well known for his claim that:

> A human being is the measure of all things—of things that are that they are and of things that are not, that they are not (DK80B1).

This brief saying raises many questions of interpretation. Does it refer to humans as a species or to individual people? The Greek word *anthrôpos* could be used for either. Does it mean *that* things are or *how* they are? To answer these questions, we must turn to Plato's discussion in the *Theaetetus*. In this dialogue Plato argues against Protagoras's view, as we shall see in chapter 8. Therefore, we need to be careful not to assume that his characterizations of Protagoras's views are always accurate.

From Plato's discussion of the saying in the *Theaetetus*, Protagoras probably means that the phenomenal qualities of a thing are relative to the individual perceiver.[24] Plato interprets Protagoras's view to be: "As each thing appears to me, so it is for me, and as it appears to you, so it is to you" (152a). For instance, the same wind might feel cold to one person and warm to another. On Protagoras's behalf, Plato says that rather than asserting that the wind is cold (or not) by itself, it is better to affirm that it is cold for the one who feels cold (152b). In short, "things are for the individual such as he perceives them." Later, Plato seems to be willing to generalize this view beyond perceptual judgments on Protagoras's behalf. He suggests that Protagoras's view is that whatever a person judges is true *for him* (158e).

Probably, Protagoras argues for this subjectivism as follows: if the wind feels cold to one person and warm to another, what are the options with regard to the qualities of the wind?

1. We could argue that one person is right and the other is mistaken; but this would be arbitrary because we have no more grounds for the claim that the wind is warm than we do for the contradictory claim that it is cold, and vice versa.

2. We could argue that we cannot know whether or not the wind is cold. But this is an unsatisfactory option because we do have evidence that it is warm in that it feels so to one person, and likewise, we do have evidence that it is cold.

3. We might claim that neither is right (i.e., that the wind is neither warm nor cold). Again, this alternative seems unsatisfactory, because, as we just said, we do have evidence that it is warm in that it feels so to one person, and likewise for cold.

4. We could argue that the wind is both warm and cold. But this view would attribute to the wind itself contradictory properties,

and there is good evidence that Protagoras accepts the principle of non-contradiction.[25] Thus, this view is unacceptable.

5. Finally, there is the option that each judgment is true for the person who makes it. In other words, we cannot make absolute affirmations such as "the wind is cold"; we can only make relative ones such as "the wind is cold for person P".

Protagoras would argue for the fifth option on the grounds that all the other alternatives are unsatisfactory. Unlike the fourth, the fifth option doesn't involve a contradiction because the two relativized claims—"the wind is cold for P" and "the wind isn't cold for Q"—don't contradict each other.[26] Generalizing this conclusion, all truths must be taken as relative to the experience or judgment of the person making the judgment.

If this characterization of his view is correct, then Protagoras is not arguing that the very existence of an object depends on the mind of the observer—for example, that the tree you see only exists in your mind as a set of private perceptions. Instead, he is claiming that any judgment about how an object is must be relative to the person who is making the judgment.

Later in the *Theaetetus,* Plato apparently imputes to Protagoras the claim that:

> Whatever in any city is regarded as just and admirable *is* just and admirable in that city so long as that convention maintains itself. (*Theaetetus,* 167c)

This is similar to the earlier view that truths must be taken as relative. However, in this case, they are relative to a society or a city rather than to an individual. This kind of cultural relativism may be similar to individual subjectivism, but it is important to note that the two views are incompatible (because an individual might reject the accepted view of a city).

There is other evidence that Protagoras affirmed individual subjectivism. As already mentioned, Sextus Empiricus reports that Democritus argues against Protagoras's subjectivism.[27] In his *Metaphysics,* Aristotle also apparently imputes such a view to Protagoras, claiming that he says: "it is equally possible to affirm and to deny anything of anything."[28]

In an apparently similar vein, Protagoras thinks that for every argument in favor of a proposition, there is another argument for the opposite statement (DK80A1). This claim underlies one of the teaching methods of Protagoras.

> Protagoras made the weaker and stronger argument, and taught his students to blame and praise the same person. (DK80A21)

Plato objects to this on the grounds that such a procedure teaches people to win a victory in a debate, but without trying to discover the truth. Aristotle also complains that Protagoras teaches his students to make the weaker arguments stronger.[29] Given these criticisms, it seems that Protagoras's view is that there are no independent objective criteria to which one can appeal to determine which is the right answer, and therefore, all views are equally contestable.[30]

Nevertheless, other aspects of what we know about Protagoras suggest that his view is more sophisticated than simple individual subjectivism. For instance, Protagoras also was a teacher of *areté* or virtue. He trained his students to exercise good judgment in the management of their own lives and of the city, claiming:

> Education is not implanted in the soul unless one reaches a greater depth (DK80B11).

He emphasized the importance of habit in training. He taught them to act in a way that would have beneficial effects. In the dialogue *Protagoras*, Plato has Protagoras claim to the young Socrates:

> If you associate with me, the result will be that the very day you begin you will return home a better person, and the same will happen the next day too. Each day you will make constant progress toward being better. (DK80A5, 318a)

Protagoras specifies the relevant progress as the management of the household and of the city's affairs, so that the person may be powerful in action and speaking. The passage from Plato doesn't seem to suggest that Protagoras is an ethical subjectivist who thinks that all value claims are merely a matter of opinion or that they are relative to a culture. It hints at some objective notion of "better," at least when applied to self-improvement and self-interest. This point is reinforced by Protagoras's so called "great speech" later in the Platonic dialogue named after him. In this speech, Protagoras argues that society requires that we must exercise the virtues of political wisdom, justice, and self-restraint. This would seem to imply, therefore, that Protagoras's view is that, in debate, a wise person would use his or her oratory skills to promote the view that will have the most beneficial effects. While we must be careful about imputing a view to the historical figure Protagoras based on the character portrayed in Plato's dialogue, Plato's text suggests that Protagoras wasn't a subjectivist about at least some value claims.

As we have seen, Plato more readily imputes subjectivism to Protagoras in the *Theaetetus* than he does in the *Protagoras*. Nevertheless, even in the *Theaetetus* there are passages that suggest that Protagoras holds some limited form of objectivism. In particular, in reply to the objection that usually experts know better than ordinary people on relevant matters, Socrates tries to answer on behalf of Protagoras that some views are better than others even if they are not truer (167a–b). For instance, an educator will help his or her students make judgments that are better for them. This suggests that Protagoras's view presupposes some form of objectivism about "better." In sum, the passages from the dialogue *Protagoras* seem to indicate that Protagoras has a pragmatic view that allows for some objectivity with regard to what is useful or better. According to this pragmatism, Sophist teaching enables us to hold views that are better, or most beneficial for us.

These tentative characterizations of Protagoras's views are further complicated by his agnosticism regarding the gods. He says:

> Concerning the gods, I am unable to know either that they are or that they are not or what their appearance is like. For many are the things that hinder human knowledge: the obscurity of the matter and the shortness of human life. (DK80B4)

This passage is interesting for its implications. It doesn't advocate a subjectivist stand about the existence or nature of the gods. It doesn't imply radical or thoroughgoing skepticism. It simply suggests that, in this kind of case, we cannot have knowledge because of our limitations. The implicit suggestion of this passage might be that we should turn our attention away from mythology and theology towards the study of the human.

In this section, we have discussed in what ways it is accurate, and not to attribute to Protagoras some form of individual subjectivism. It is important to note that Protagoras's method of making the weaker argument stronger doesn't imply subjectivism. In fact, it contradicts it. First, if one argument really is stronger or weaker than another, this seems to indicate that it is objectively so. Second, if one person argues for the conclusion that X is F for him, and another person argues that X is not F for her, then their arguments are directed to different conclusions and they don't contradict each other.[31]

Protagoras's famous assertion that the human is the measure of all things marks an important watershed in the history of thought. It not only constitutes a rejection of objectivism, but it also indicates a humanism and pragmatism. Protagoras moves philosophy towards more human concerns and away from the naturalism of earlier thinkers. This shift away from the more narrowly scientific expands the scope of ancient philosophy and permits the more integrated approaches of Plato and Aristotle.

Protagoras's approach has a similar effect in the philosophy of later periods. For example, his famous saying was taken to articulate an idea central to the development of humanism during the Renaissance of the fifteenth century. The saying captures a shift of emphasis away from the standards of the divine and of otherworldly realm of Platonic Forms towards the human. This was one of the great insights of the Renaissance: we must understand things in human terms, and humanity should be devoted to the study of itself. Likewise, Protagoras's approach and saying has been seen as a precursor of the nineteenth-century pragmatist claim that truth must be regarded in terms of usefulness for human purposes, and that it cannot consist in a metaphysical correspondence between our beliefs and reality.

Gorgias (485–395 BC)

Gorgias was born in Leontinoi, an Ionian colony in Sicily. Around 427 BC, Leontinoi was at war with the city of Syracuse. Gorgias was sent to Athens as part of an envoy from his native town to seek the support of Athens. Apparently, he astonished the Athenian assembly with his rhetorical skills, and he succeeded in winning the help of Athens for the war. He traveled throughout the Greek world, lecturing and teaching. In Athens his teaching brought him great financial success. Of the eleven works he wrote, we have two summaries of his book *On the Non-Existent*, one attributed perhaps incorrectly to Aristotle and the other to Sextus Empiricus.[32] Although they are similar, we can stick to the passage from Sextus Empiricus, which is generally held to be more reliable.[33]

In this work Gorgias argues for three extraordinary claims, corresponding to the three parts of his treatise:

- Nothing exists (nothing is).
- Even if something does exist, we humans could not know it.
- Even if something does exist and could be known, it cannot be communicated.

Gorgias's ingenious argument for the first thesis can be outlined as follows (DK82B3):

1. What exists must be either what-is or what-is-not or some combination of these.
2. What exists cannot be any of these three alternatives.
3. Therefore, nothing exists.

Concerning the second premise, the claim that what exists cannot be what-is-not is at least intuitively plausible. The difficult task for Gorgias is to show that what exists cannot be what-is. He tries to accomplish this as follows: what-is must be either eternal or generated, and what exists cannot be either of these.

Why can't what exists be eternal? Because something eternal must be ungenerated, and something ungenerated must be unlimited. However, something unlimited must be nowhere and, of course, something that is nowhere does not exist. Why must something unlimited be nowhere? This is because if it were somewhere, then it would have to be contained or enclosed in something bigger than itself, which is impossible.[34] Consequently, the eternal must be nowhere, and thus it does not exist.

We can now turn to the second alternative, namely, that what exists is generated. Gorgias presents us with two options: it is generated either from what-is, or from what-is-not. It cannot be generated from what-is because what-is already is. In other words, if what-is is generated then it must come to be, which implies that it wasn't before; therefore, what-is cannot be generated from what-is. However, additionally, it cannot be generated from what-is-not because what-is-not cannot generate anything.

In conclusion: first, what exists cannot be what-is because what-is cannot be either eternal or generated; second, what exists cannot be what-is-not; and third, neither can it be a combination of these two. Therefore, nothing exists.

Gorgias's second thesis is that, even if something existed, we could not know it or understand it. His argument is based on the idea that we cannot affirm that what we think about exists. If we could do so, then we would be committed to the claim that all the things we think about exist, including flying men and chariots racing in the sea. Thus, we must conclude that it is impossible that what a person thinks about exists. From this conclusion, Gorgias infers that what exists cannot be thought about.

> For if things that are thought of, says Gorgias, are not things-that-are, what-is is not thought of. (DK82B3, line 77)

He argues for this on analogy. If things we think of were white, for example, then that would imply that white things have the property of being thought of. In a similar way, if things that we think of have not-being, then things that have being will have the property of not being thought of.

The third thesis is that even if something could be comprehended, that comprehension could not be communicated. Gorgias argues that we communicate through *logos*, but *logos* itself is not the things that are. *Logos* and external objects are quite different in kind. To suppose that we could communicate directly the things that are is like supposing that we could hear the visible. Here, in this comparison, Gorgias is presupposing that each sense has its own objects: in other words, what one sees, one cannot hear, and what one tastes, one cannot touch.

What are we to make of these strange arguments? Let us start with the first. Does Gorgias really think that nothing exists? Some commentators, such as McKirahan, think that Gorgias's argumentation is a parody of the Eleatics. He is making fun of them. According to this view, at best, Gorgias is illustrating how Eleatic-type arguments can be employed to reach absurd conclusions. There is some circumstantial evidence for this interpretation, namely, that Gorgias composed his arguments around the same time that Melissus wrote in support of Parmenides in the late 440s.[35]

Other commentators, such as Paul Woodruth, take Gorgias's first thesis more seriously. Often it is regarded as a criticism of Parmenides, who claims that only being can exist and that non-being or what-is-not cannot exist. In critical reply, Gorgias is arguing that neither being nor non-being can exist.[36] At the same Gorgias's argument is also directed towards the pluralists who claim that what exists is composed of infinite elements. Instead, it is composed of nothing.

Philosophically, Gorgias's second argument is supposed to indicate a systematic, logical gap between our cognitive states and reality. The contemporary commentator Kerferd interprets Gorgias as denying that thoughts can refer to objects.[37] He says that, according to Gorgias, we cannot know things directly. Knowledge is always mediated by perception and language and, therefore, we have no direct contact with reality. Likewise, Gorgias's third argument is probably based on the idea that words do not convey the things that they refer to (if they could refer). The word *table* can never give one a table.

Discussion

What is Sophism? Are there some philosophical claims that are sophist? Of course, it is very hard to draw any firm conclusions. To begin with, we have only briefly examined two sophist thinkers; there are many others we haven't looked at. Additionally, we have seen that these two are very difficult to interpret. However, concerning moral claims, we have mentioned four kinds of Sophist view.

First, there is individual subjectivism, which claims that each person is right for him or herself in whatever judgment he or she makes. In other words, the truth of a judgment is relative to the person who makes the judgment. Protagoras may have held this view.

Second, there is cultural relativism, which claims that each culture is right in the moral conventions that it accepts. In other words, the truth of a moral claim is relative to the culture or city that makes the claim. It is less likely that Protagoras held this view.

Third, there is a pragmatic view that affirms that moral claims cannot be true or false, but rather should be judged according to whether they are beneficial to the person making them. When we are trained in the virtues, we learn to make judgments that benefit us. This seems to be Protagoras's view according to Plato's dialogue, the *Protagoras*.

Finally, there is the rational egoism of Callicles in Plato's *Gorgias* and of Thrasymachus in the *Republic* that prescribes the pursuit of one's own advantage. As we saw earlier when we discussed *nomos* and *phusis*, according to this kind of view morality is a bogus set of conventional social laws that seek to protect the weak and to deny the natural law of egoism.

Although these four views are different from each other, they do have in common the denial that moral claims can be true or false *simpliciter* (in or by themselves). However, the third and fourth views seem to imply some form of objectivism about what is advantageous for a person. In this context, *objectivism* means that there are true claims about what is good for a person, and that it is not merely a matter of opinion.

In stark contrast, Gorgias argues that seemingly commonsense claims are just false. In other words, his conclusions seem to rely on some notion of true or false *simpliciter*. Nevertheless, his second and third theses reject the idea that we can represent and communicate objective truths about the world. They deny that we can refer to things or have communicable meanings about things, and in this way they indicate a radical rejection of realistic conceptions of truth and representational epistemologies.

CONCLUSION

The fourth phase in early ancient Greek thought consists largely of the attempt to continue the earlier tradition of natural philosophy, but in ways that answer the objections of Parmenides and the Eleatics. In this vein, Empedocles and Anaxagoras argue that the universe consists in a plurality of substances. They are called "the pluralists." Empedocles argues that the universe consists of the organization of the four basic elements through the operation of the two forces, Strife and Love. Anaxagoras claims that the universe consists of an infinite intermingling of different substances directed by a nonmaterial cosmic mind, or *Nous*. The Pluralists try to answer Parmenides by contending that everything that exists is composed of something indestructible.

In this regard the atomists are similar. For instance, Democritus argues that everything must consist of different arrangements of indestructible atoms and void. The arrangement of these atoms will explain the observable features of the world, such as hardness and softness, color and taste. In this way Democritus establishes a tradition that came to fruition in the science of the modern period, especially the work of Isaac Newton (1643–1727).

The fifth and final phase of early ancient Greek thought consists in the teachings of the Sophists. Sophism takes philosophy in a new direction by arguing that moral claims are culturally relative or are based on individual self-interest. Protagoras seems to take this relativism further by arguing that all judgments must be relative to the person making the judgment; a human being is the measure of all things, he says. Gorgias extends the skepticism of Sophism even further by arguing that nothing exists, and even if something does exist, it could not be known or communicated. Sophism presents philosophical thought with a new set of radical challenges, which Socrates tries to answer.

Study Questions

1. Why does Empedocles postulate two forces as well as the four elements?
2. How does Empedocles try to answer the challenge of Parmenides?
3. Describe in what ways Empedocles might be called a "Pythagorean?"
4. What does Anaxagoras mean when he asserts that all things are intermingled?

88   Part I: Early Ancient Greek Philosophy

5. How does Anaxagoras argue for the claim that all things are intermingled?
6. What does Anaxagoras mean by *seeds*? How does this relate to the claim that all mixtures are only proportions rather than being countable?
7. How does Anaxagoras argue for the existence of *Nous*?
8. How does Anaxagoras argue that *Nous* is not mixed with anything physical?
9. How does Democritus argue that the void must exist? How does this argument relate to his reply to Parmenides?
10. How does Democritus argue that indivisible atoms must exist?
11. What properties do atoms have, according to Democritus?
12. How does Democritus distinguish between the universe and a cosmos?
13. What is the Sophist distinction between convention and nature?
14. Explain the two ways in which Sophists use this distinction.
15. Explain the meaning of Protagoras's claim that man is the measure of all things.
16. How does Protagoras argue for subjectivism?
17. What evidence is there that Protagoras wasn't an individual subjectivist?
18. What are Gorgias's three claims?
19. How does Gorgias argue that nothing exists?
20. Distinguish four kinds of Sophist views.

Discussion Questions

1. Do Empedocles, Anaxagoras, and Democritus adequately answer the challenges to natural philosophy posed by the arguments of Parmenides and Zeno?
2. Does natural philosophy require a notion like Anaxagoras's *Nous*?
3. Can all of the features of the observable world be explained in terms of the basic properties of atoms and void?
4. Does it make sense to affirm that claims about what is valuable are merely a matter of opinion?

PART II

Introduction to Socrates and Plato

Socrates and Plato take philosophy to an entirely new level. Up to this point, early Greek thought consisted largely of natural philosophy, the attempt to identify the principles and concepts needed to explain natural phenomena in a systematic fashion. This was the project of the early Milesians, of the pluralists Anaxagoras and Empedocles, and of the atomists, Leucippus and Democritus. Arguably, it was a partial aim of Heraclitus, and perhaps even of Pythagoras.

Despite the fact that one can see definite advances in this project from Thales to Democritus, there were three major failings or shortcomings. First, there are still unresolved problems within this naturalistic enterprise. For instance, how can we explain conscious phenomena such as awareness and reason? There also are lurking metaphysical questions regarding, for instance, the nature of space and time: these aren't things made of the elements, so what are they? There are also implicit epistemological questions that need to be asked and answered, such as "How can we even know what the universe consists of?"

Second, there is the challenge of Parmenides and Zeno. Empedocles, Anaxagoras, and the atomists try to reply to this challenge in part by accepting Parmenidean principles, and by modeling a naturalistic philosophy within those new parameters. Despite this, however, it is fair to affirm that up to this point there has not been a definitive reply to the extraordinarily powerful arguments of the two Eleatics. Often in philosophy we find that the reply to such profound challenges requires a radically new point of departure and approach.

Third, early ancient philosophy is narrow in its scope. Up to this point, there has been very little systematic philosophical thinking about ethics, politics, society, art, and culture, and the meanings of human life in general. Of course, we must acknowledge that Heraclitus does present a vision of human wisdom that includes such themes. We must also recognize that Pythagoras was also concerned with these topics, as was Democritus. Nevertheless, the point still stands: prior to the Sophists, such human issues were not central to most philosophy. Even religious issues were periphery. The Sophists changed this. They placed human concerns at the core of their thinking, but arguably, they did so in a fundamentally unsatisfactory way. Their approach might seem deeply unsatisfactory insofar as it eschews or avoids questions of truth. Thinking people want answers to philosophical questions about what we should value, about what is valuable in life and why. This implies that one wants answers that are truer and less false, and that are supported by some reasoning and evidence. At least as portrayed by later writers, the Sophists didn't address these concerns in this way.

With regard to this third shortcoming, Socrates takes the art of philosophy to a new level. As characterized by Plato in many of his dialogues, Socrates systematically investigates value questions central to human life, such as: "What is friendship?" "What is virtue?" "What is justice?" "Is pleasure the ultimate good in life?" "Should we always obey the state?" and "Does the soul survive death?"

Moreover, Socrates does this in a way that presumes there are answers to be found, and that it really matters that we find them. His deep concern for truth drives a relentless questioning that is systematic and honest. Socrates is always willing to admit that he doesn't have an answer to his own questions. Some of his explorations end in an impasse. Through his conversations and interrogations, Socrates develops a new and powerful philosophical methodology, which we describe in the next chapter. Suffice to say that it permits for arguments of even greater penetration and precision than those of Parmenides and Zeno. The intense conversations of Socrates show that he lived for philosophy. He died for it too, for he was perhaps the first secular martyr.

Socrates revolutionized and renewed philosophy. Plato organized and extended it. He took the energy, lessons, and ideas of his teacher and fashioned from these a whole worldview that embraces all aspects of human knowledge from politics to art, from science to literature, from psychology to education. This worldview is still with us today. Plato argues systematically for a metaphysics that transcends the naturalism of the Pre-Socratics, tries to answer the Eleatics, and presents a rich and positive vision of nearly all aspects of human life, from friendship to love, from morality to politics. Nevertheless, Plato retains the intellectual energy of his teacher and frequently challenges and probes his own ideas.

In this part of the book, we will examine the philosophies of Socrates and Plato. Most of what we know about Socrates comes from Plato's dialogues. So chapter 4 is devoted to the philosophy of Socrates as revealed in some of the early dialogues of Plato. After the death of Socrates, Plato started to develop his own views, and some of his dialogues are considered as transitions to his own mature philosophy. We examine these transitional dialogues in chapter 5. Plato's mature thought, as revealed in his famous dialogues (e.g., the *Republic*), requires two-part coverage: first, the metaphysics and epistemology (chapter 6) and second, his views on love, ethics, and politics (chapter 7). Towards the end of his life, Plato's philosophy shifted at least in emphasis, and possibly in content. For this reason, we need to treat these later dialogues separately from the others, and this is the theme of chapter 8.

THE LIFE OF SOCRATES (469–399 BC)

Socrates was born about 469 BC in Athens, the son of a stonemason (Sophroniscus) and a midwife (Phaenarete). His family background was humble, and he learned his father's craft as a young person and worked as a stonemason early in life. He married Xanthippe and they had three sons. During the Peloponnesian Wars, he served as an infantryman or hoplite on three campaigns: Potideae (432 BC), Delium (424 BC), and Amphipolis (422 BC). He is reported to have been a brave soldier who saved the life of Alcibiades, the famous general and statesman, in the battle of Potideae.[1]

In 406 BC, Socrates served as a member of the Athenian council of citizens, and as an official he resisted the attempt to hold an unconstitutional trial against the eight generals who abandoned their ships during the battle of Arginusae earlier that year. In 404 BC, Athens was defeated by Sparta in the Peloponnesian War, and the Thirty Tyrants were elected as the government. During their short-lived reign of terror, Socrates refused to cooperate in the arrest of Leon of Salamis.

We cannot tell when Socrates took up philosophy. Plato reports that Socrates described himself as a gadfly who attaches himself to the city to challenge and arouse it through philosophical questioning. Furthermore, he reports that Socrates regarded this as his divine mission: to interrogate citizens deeply regarding how they should live. Socrates practiced his art in public places, such as the agora; by the time he reached his forties, he was already notorious in the city for this role. As we shall see, some of Plato's dialogues portray Socrates in this function. Plato also reports that, occasionally, Socrates heard a "divine" voice or sign that guided his actions or prevented him from harmful behavior, and that Socrates had heard this voice since childhood.

Socrates attracted a following of young people eager to learn from him. This following included, of course, Plato. It also included members of Plato's aristocratic family, Critias and Charmides, who were members of the government during the time of the Thirty. Among Socrates's entourage was also the famous statesman and military commander, Alcibiades (mentioned earlier), who betrayed Athens in 415 BC during the Peloponnesian Wars. Alcibiades later re-defected, became an Athenian general in 411 BC, and returned home to the city in 407 BC. Alcibiades was a close friend of Socrates, and his love for Socrates is described in Plato's dialogue the *Symposium* (see chapter 7).

In 399 BC, Socrates was indicted on a charge of impiety and corrupting the young. Possibly this charge was politically motivated, perhaps because of his association with members of the government of the Thirty or because of his friendship with Alcibiades. In any case, Socrates was indicted and sentenced to death. After refusing several opportunities to escape into exile, Socrates drank the poison hemlock and died. In a series of dialogues Plato describes these dramatic events, including the events leading up to the trial, Socrates's speech at his trial, and his philosophical conversations on his deathbed.

THE LIFE OF PLATO (427–347)

Plato came from a prominent aristocratic Athenian family. His mother was a descendent of Solon, the great seventh-century BC poet and statesman who initiated constitutional reforms, wrote many of Athens's laws, and celebrated Athenian democracy in popular poems. Plato's name was "Aristocles"; "Platon" was his nickname (based on his broad physique).

Plato received the best education available to prepare him for a great political career. He excelled in poetry, music, and wrestling. However, his path towards politics was disturbed by the 27-year long Peloponnesian Wars between Athens and Sparta which began in 431 BC. One of the crucial turning points occurred in 413 BC, when Athens disastrously lost its forces in the Sicilian expedition aimed to capture the city-state of Syracuse. This loss caused panic in Athens, which now seemed to be at the mercy of the Spartans. In 411 BC democracy fell, to be replaced by an oligarchy. These events happened during Plato's adolescence. He himself served in the military from 409 to 405 BC.

When Athens surrendered in 404 BC, a new post-democratic government was set up, later called the "Thirty Tyrants" (or "The Thirty"). Two of Plato's relatives were involved in this government: Critias, his mother's uncle, was part of the group; and Charmides, his own uncle, was a leader in nearby Pireaus. The Thirty only remained in power for perhaps less than a year, but their rule was oppressive and cruel. The restoration of democracy in 403 BC involved more upheavals and reprisals, despite an amnesty.

During this turbulence and violence the young Plato grew disillusioned, and he spurned the idea of a life dedicated to politics. Instead, he turned to philosophy, having been influenced by the sophist Cratylus, and having studied Protagoras, Heraclitus, and the Eleatics. He became a pupil of Socrates in around 407 BC, when Socrates was 60 years old. However, it is probable that Plato had known Socrates since his own childhood. Around 402 BC, life in Athens returned more or less to normal, and many of the conversations of the Socratic dialogues are set after this date. However, in 399 BC, his beloved teacher Socrates was condemned to death, when Plato was around 28 years old.

These events profoundly affected the young philosopher, who left Athens about three years afterwards for nearby Megara, 34 km to the west. There he began writing his famous dialogues. He met with mathematicians and thinkers, and sometime before 390 BC they formed an informal study group, which was the precursor to Plato's Academy and which met on land that Plato had inherited.

In 385 BC Plato was invited to and visited the court of Dionysius I in Syracuse, Sicily.[2] The king enjoyed having intellectuals around him. Apparently, Plato was not impressed by the tyranny of the king and the decadence of the court. However, he struck up a friendship with the king's young brother-in-law, Dion, who was very willing to learn from the philosopher.[3] There is a story (probably unreliable) from later sources that Plato left Syracuse because he angered Dionysius I, and that he was sold into slavery and was purchased and released by Anniceris of Cyrene.[4]

After his stay in Sicily, Plato returned to Athens in 383 BC and established his famous school, the Academy, a center for the advancement of wisdom and learning. The Academy was set outside the city walls of Athens and included a grove of olive trees, said to be sacred. We believe that the Academy included strong mathematical and scientific components in its curriculum, and that it charged no fees. It was probably more like a community of intellectuals, who worked together, rather than a modern teaching university. One of the most famous scholars or students was the mathematician Eudoxus of Cnidus. Aristotle became a student in 367 BC. The period from 383 BC until roughly 361 BC is sometimes called Plato's middle period, when he may have written his most famous dialogues such as the *Republic*.

At around the age of sixty, in 367 BC, Plato received an invitation to train the newly appointed king of Syracuse, Dionysius II, to become a philosopher-king, following the model of Plato's work the *Republic*. Plato's friend Dion, who had since married the daughter of Dionysius I, was now an advisor to the newly crowned king. At first Plato was reluctant to travel, but Dion persuaded him, and in 366 BC Plato sailed for Sicily for the second time. In 365 BC, the political climate of Syracuse became full of intrigue. Dion was exiled, his family was imprisoned, and eventually Plato returned to Athens.

Four years later, in 361 BC, Plato was summoned to return to Syracuse by Dionysius II. He was very reluctant to go but eventually was persuaded to do so, against his better judgment, with promises of support from the King. In reality, these promises were false and Plato had to flee Syracuse almost immediately after his arrival, fearing that his life was in danger. In fact, these events were a part of a prelude to the overthrowing of Dionysius II by Dion and a general (Heracleides).

After this fiasco Plato settled down to the final phase of his life, during which he worked with colleagues in the Academy, wrote several dialogues, and looked after his family. Plato never married, but his brothers and sisters did, and when two of his nieces died Plato became partly responsible for four grandnieces.

Socrates in the Early Dialogues of Plato

Socrates (469–399 BC) is possibly the most famous of all philosophers, a sage who is sometimes even compared with great religious figures such as Buddha and Christ. Initially, this is a bit puzzling. Socrates wasn't the first philosopher, and he didn't write a philosophical treatise. He wasn't the founder of a philosophical school, let alone a religion. Who was this person, Socrates, who has inspired generations of thinkers? This question is sometimes known as the Socratic problem.[1] If we could know Socrates the historical person, we might be able to explain his enduring appeal.

Our knowledge of Socrates comes from four principle sources: Plato's dialogues, in twenty of which Socrates is the main character; Xenophon, who wrote the *Memorabilia*, which claims to record several Socratic conversations; Aristophanes, who wrote a comedy, the *Clouds*, featuring Socrates; and finally, Socrates is mentioned several times by Aristotle, who was born 15 years after the great man's death. There are also passing references to Socrates in other sources, such as in some remaining fragments from Aeschines, one of his followers who wrote several dialogues.

Aristophanes was a Greek comedy playwright, and the *Clouds*, produced in 423 BC, features Socrates as the protagonist. Aristophanes mocks the intellectuals of his day. He paints Socrates as a disbeliever in the gods of the traditional Greek religion, and as a sophist who teaches "unjust arguments" to his pupils. He also portrays Socrates as a researcher in scientific questions about nature, such as in astronomy and natural history. This conflicts with the accounts of Xenophon and Plato, who show Socrates to be interested almost exclusively in the nature of happiness and the good human life. In short, although he may not be reliable about the historical Socrates, Aristophanes reveals a strand of popular opinion about Socrates during his lifetime.

Xenophon was a pupil of Socrates during the last decade of the latter's life. He wrote four Socratic works to defend Socrates against popular prejudice. He portrays Socrates above all as a purveyor of moral advice. He also paints him as a pious believer. Apparently, Xenophon was not very interested the philosophical life of Socrates; he was more concerned with receiving practical advice from the teacher. This has led some recent scholars to question his closeness to Socrates.[2]

Despite the fact that he never met him, Aristotle is a very important source of information about Socrates because he explicitly contrasts Socrates with Plato. He tells us that Socrates claimed to know nothing and asked questions without answering them (*Sophistical Refutations* 183b6–7). He says that Socrates was concerned only with ethical matters and not with nature. He also claims that Socrates was the first to seek universal definitions by asking questions such as "What is virtue?" Unlike Plato, he did not separate these universals (i.e., Plato thought of universals as independently existing abstract objects [*Metaphysics* XIII, 4,1078b29–30]). Aristotle also informs us that philosophers other than Socrates influenced Plato.[3] Plato studied with Cratylus, thus becoming familiar with the views of Heraclitus, especially with the claim that the world of perceptible objects is always in flux. Pythagoras inspired Plato too in that Plato adopted the older thinker's belief in the existence of abstract objects, which explain the ordinary objects of perception, as we shall see in the next chapter.[4]

Plato is by far the most important source of information about Socrates. Indeed, some twentieth-century writers, such as Gregory Vlastos, argue that Socrates the historical person resembles, and can be identified with, the character that appears in the early dialogues of Plato.[5] This is a substantial and contentious claim, since the representations of Socrates in Xenophon and Aristophanes conflict in many ways with Plato's portrayal. Moreover, one could counter-argue that Plato's Socrates in the early dialogues is mostly a literary invention of the author. Plato wasn't merely recording Socrates's conversations in these early dialogues. He was also defending and exploring his teacher's views. Even with these early dialogues, we can't be sure to what extent they are a reliable source of information about the historical Socrates.[6]

THE SOCRATIC DIALOGUES

The claim that the historical person Socrates is portrayed by the character in the early dialogues of Plato raises two important issues. First, it assumes the idea that Plato's dialogues should be divided into early and later periods. In fact, many commentators today agree that the dialogues should be split into three periods: early, middle, and late. In the middle and some of later dialogues, Plato has Socrates express many rich philosophical views that are Plato's own theories rather than his teacher's. Only in the early, so-called "Socratic dialogues," does Plato try to understand and explore the views of historical Socrates.

Out of the 26 existing Platonic dialogues, the early Socratic ones are usually listed as follows:

Chapter Four—Socrates in the Early Dialogues of Plato 97

Apology	*Protagoras*
Charmides	*Ion*
Crito	*Hippias Major*
Euthyphro	*Hippias Minor*
Euthydemus	*Menexenus*
Laches	*Republic, Book I*
Lysis	*Gorgias*

The *Meno*, which we will examine separately, is usually considered as a transitional dialogue, taking us from the early to middle period. The *Gorgias* was probably the last work of the early period, and some writers classify it as a transitional work too. Both dialogues show a Pythagorean influence, possibly due to Plato's visit to Sicily in 387 BC.

As portrayed in the early dialogues, Socrates was almost exclusively concerned with the question of how a person should live his or her life. For example, in the *Laches, Charmides, Hippias Major*, and *Euthyphro*, he searches for an answer to this question, even though the dialogues end inconclusively in an impasse. The ancient Greek term for this kind of ending is *aporia*.

The Socratic Knowledge Paradox

A second issue is raised by the thesis that the early dialogues portray the historical Socrates. The thesis requires an answer to a problem. Did Socrates have philosophical knowledge? To see the importance of the question, let us contrast two points.

First, on the one hand, in the early dialogues, Socrates is represented as someone who proclaims ignorance and professes not to have special knowledge. He is fascinated by philosophical questions and goads those around him into thinking. However, rather than forming his own theories, he provokes his interlocutors into offering a definition of a key idea, such as justice or virtue, and then asks brilliantly penetrating questions of them. He persists with his cross-examination until either he arrives at a satisfactory answer or he has revealed a hidden contradiction.

This representation of Socrates exemplified in the early dialogues has given rise to the philosophical method, often called *elenchus*, or "argumentation and refutation." This portrayal of Socrates fits with the fact that he had many pupils with differing views; some were hedonists (Aristippus) and others were Pythagoreans (Simmias and Cebes).[7] It also accords with Plato's later description of Socrates in the *Theaetetus* as a midwife of philosophical ideas. His aim wasn't to have babies of his own, but to help others in this process of giving birth to theories.

Second, on the other hand, the early dialogues also represent Socrates as having important and substantial philosophical views of his own. These views mostly concern the way people should live, and they might be summed up with the saying, "the unexamined life is not worth living for a human being" (*Apology*, 38a). So, we are left with a problem: can we square Plato's picture of Socrates as a person without wisdom with the portrait of Socrates as having positive philosophical views?

There are four general types of answer to this question:

The first argues that Socrates's claims to ignorance are *not* inconsistent with his holding the philosophical views he does. Socrates can be ignorant and still have some philosophical knowledge. The two are compatible. We will examine this first response in more detail below. It is exegetically the most generous type of answer.

The second response to the problem is to claim that Socrates is being ironical when he claims that he knows nothing. Certainly, Socrates uses irony in many of Plato's dialogues. For example, in the *Republic*, Thrasymachus accuses him of it, referring to Socrates's "well-known irony" (336e–337a). In the *Symposium*, Alcibiades says that Socrates's life is one big "game of irony" (216d–e). The issue is: do these and other quotes provide us with a good reason for thinking that Socrates is being ironical when he says that he is ignorant to the extent that he does not really mean it? Or put another way: is he disingenuously exaggerating his own ignorance?

Another possibility, of course, is that Socrates's claims to ignorance really are incompatible with his holding the philosophical theories that he does. This view would maintain that Socrates is just wrong to claim that he is ignorant.

The final possibility is that we just do not know. In other words, there is not enough evidence to know what Socrates thought and whether or not his views were contradictory.[8]

Let us return to the first of these general possibilities, namely, that Socrates's claims to ignorance are compatible with his philosophical views. There are three kinds of replies along these lines. To introduce the first, let us consider the following story. In the *Apology*, Socrates reports that the oracle in the temple of Apollo at Delphi had affirmed that he is the wisest person. This greatly surprised Socrates, and so he decided to cross-examine the leaders of Athenian society. He found that such people are ignorant of things that are worthwhile to know, just as he is himself. The only difference is that he *realizes* that he is ignorant. Finally, he felt that he understood the strange pronouncement of the oracle that he (Socrates) was the wisest Athenian: he was wise because he realized that he was ignorant (*Apology*, 21b–22e). These passages in the *Apology* suggest that:

1. Socrates knows that he is ignorant about significant things.[9]

From this statement, two *apparently* contradictory conclusions follow:

2. In virtue of statement 1, Socrates is ignorant about significant things; and

3. In virtue of statement 1, Socrates has meta-knowledge because he has knowledge of his lack of knowledge.

Statements 2 and 3 might appear contradictory, but they are not really so. "Person A doesn't know that p" doesn't contradict the proposition "Person A knows that he doesn't know that p." In fact, the second claim entails the first.

How could Socrates have this second-order knowledge and still remain ignorant about the important things in life? One suggestion is that Socrates is ignorant because he doesn't know the definitions of the relevant key terms. To have knowledge of X, one must be able to give a reasonable answer to the question "What is X?" One must be able to provide a definition of X. For instance, one cannot have significant knowledge of justice and of what things are just unless one knows what justice is. The point is that, unlike his fellow Athenians, Socrates actually knows that this is a requirement of knowledge. Furthermore, unlike his fellow Athenians, he knows that he lacks the relevant definitions. This knowledge allows Socrates to know that he is ignorant.

We see this idea at work in *Laches* at 190b–c. Socrates claims that knowledge about the best way to acquire virtue requires that one first know "what virtue is." Likewise, at *Republic* I, 354b–c, Socrates says that he had been mistaken to try to discover facts about justice before defining "what justice is."

There is a second way to reconcile Socratic ignorance with Socratic philosophy. It is possible that there are two kinds of knowledge involved. Vlastos argues for this solution (in "Socrates's Disavowal of Knowledge"). Accordingly, Socrates implicitly distinguishes between knowledge as certainty and *elenctic* knowledge. One has *elenctic* knowledge when one has a true belief that has survived a cross-examination or a process of *elenchus*. One's true belief has not been defeated, but this doesn't amount to knowing with certainty. In short, when Socrates professes ignorance, he uses the term *knowledge* in the first way: he doesn't know with certainty. When he advances positive philosophical views, he is implicitly claiming knowledge of the second kind: his views have survived the *elenchus*.

A third solution along these lines is to distinguish between knowledge and true belief. Although Socrates disclaims moral knowledge, it is compatible with this idea that he has beliefs which are true and for which he has some justification, so long as these do not amount to knowing (Fine, 2000).

Discussion

In summary, let us return to the very first points: why is Socrates the most famous of all philosophers, and who was he? The claim that Plato's early dialogues accurately portray the historical Socrates explains Socrates's preeminent position as a philosophical figurehead in three ways. First, there is the extraordinary and intriguing force of Socrates's personality as revealed by Plato, which embodies a philosophical approach or method. Second, Socrates's standing is partly due to the nature of his philosophical conclusions about human life. Third, there are the remarkable events that surrounded Socrates's trial and death. The legendary nature of his death exemplifies the philosophical values that he lived and argued for. Let us now examine each of these points in more detail.

PHILOSOPHICAL METHOD

Socrates's method, or the *elenchus*, has two aspects. The first is that he often asks his interlocutor for a definition of the key moral term. When the young man Euthyphro confesses that he is prosecuting his own father in the law courts because piety requires it, Socrates asks, "What is piety?" Likewise, in the *Lysis* he asks, "What is friendship?"; in the *Gorgias*, "What is rhetoric?"; in the *Charmides*, "What is temperance?"'; and in the *Meno*, "What is virtue?" The dialogues testify that such questions are not easy to answer.

We can take these "What is . . . ?" questions as requests for definitions or for a set of necessary and sufficient conditions. Using the example of piety, a necessary condition is what all examples of piety must have. In other words, a necessary condition of piety (N) will satisfy the following schema: if X is pious then X will be N. A sufficient condition of piety is that which: if something has it (S) then that thing will be pious. In other words, it will satisfy the following schema: if X is S then X will be pious. So, while being a sibling is necessary for being a brother, being both a male and a sibling is sufficient.

In the early dialogues of Plato, Socrates seems to be committed to what contemporary commentators call the *Priority of Definitional Knowledge*, which says that if a person doesn't know what F-ness is, then she cannot *know* of any particular thing that it is F.[10] Note that a person might have true beliefs about what things are F without having knowledge because the latter requires that one has a kind of justification. This is a point that we will return to in the discussion of the *Meno*.

The second part of Socrates's philosophical method consists of challenging the views of his partner in conversation (or his victim!) through three steps. First, he gets his interlocutor to express what he claims to know (call this P). Second, Socrates asks questions which elicit other beliefs from the interlocutor (call these Q). Third, Socrates argues that these other beliefs are inconsistent with the first claim to knowledge. P and Q are incompatible.

Here is a simple example: Euthyphro defines piety as what pleases the gods. Socrates elicits from the young man the assertion that one thing cannot be both pious and impious, and also the claim that the gods disagree in what they like. The three claims are inconsistent. In other words, the following propositions cannot all be true:

a. Piety is what pleases the gods.

b. Something cannot be both pious and impious.

c. The gods disagree in what pleases them.

At least one of these must be false. Confronted with this point, Euthyphro provides another definition of the term *piety*. He revises proposition a.

Notice that we did *not* assert that Socrates tries to argue that the original belief (P) (or in this case proposition a. above) is false. If Socrates were to argue for this strong claim, then he would have to show that the other relevant beliefs (Q) are true (in this case propositions b. and c. above).[11] In other words, the strong view would require that Socrates's arguments have the following shape:

Schema A:

1. Not (P and Q)[12]

2. Q

3. Therefore, not P

This argument-form would require asserting and defending the truth of both premises 1 and 2 in order to conclude statement 3. In contrast, we have characterized the Socratic method, more mildly, as undermining the interlocutor's claim to know P. This milder, less onerous, view does not require Socrates to show that the other beliefs (Q) are true. As such, this milder interpretation fits well with Socrates's claims to ignorance. According to this milder view, Socrates's job is simply to elicit the beliefs P and Q from his interlocutor, and to show that they are inconsistent. He tries to show that premise 1 above is true, but not premise 2.

Let us apply this idea to the example of *Euthyphro*. The three original propositions were:

a. Piety is what pleases the gods.

b. Something cannot be both pious and impious.

c. The gods disagree in what pleases them.

Socrates claims that propositions a., b., and c. are inconsistent. According to the strong view of the *elenchus*, Socrates also wants to conclude that Euthyphro's definition (claim a.) is actually false. Consequently, following Schema A above, Socrates would need to argue as follows:

1. The first claim is inconsistent with the second and third propositions—i.e., Not (P and Q).

2. Propositions b. and c. are true.

3. Therefore, proposition a. is false (i.e., *piety* can't be defined as what pleases the gods).

In sharp contrast, according to the milder view of the elenchus, Socrates doesn't want to prove that the definition of piety (i.e., claim a.) is false. Consequently, it is *not* part of his method that he should try to show that propositions b. and c. above are true. Socrates's method is more modest and dialectical in its aims: to challenge the definition (claim a.) by showing that it is inconsistent with other beliefs that the interlocutor holds.

In summary, we have seen that Socrates's method has two sides. There is the need to first, define key terms, and second, show that the interlocutor has beliefs that contradict a central claim. To bring the two aspects of the Socratic method together, we might say: Socrates applies question-and-answer interrogation to the definitions of key moral terms. In other words, the key claim that is questioned is usually a definition. Although this pattern fits most of the early dialogues, it is not always a definition that is tested or rejected. In the *Crito*, the view that is scrutinized is that Socrates should escape from prison. Likewise it is not always a definition that is rejected. In the *Laches* (197ac), Socrates examines the definition of courage as wisdom. Through the interrogation, this definition is kept, and the claim that lions are courageous is dropped.

Philosophical Theses

According to the portrayal of Socrates in the early Platonic dialogues, Socrates affirms various substantial philosophical theses. Socrates was concerned primarily with the nature of the good life and its relation to virtue or excellence (*areté*), regarding which he advances at least six main claims.

In reflecting on these claims, it is important to remember that the evidence we have for what Socrates thought is controversial. We have to rely mainly on the early dialogues of Plato, but we shouldn't think that Plato was merely reporting his teacher's views in those dialogues. Plato was exploring philosophical positions for himself, and the dialogues are literary forms in which Socrates is a literary character.

1. Happiness as the Greatest Good

Socrates claims that the greatest good for humans is *eudaimonia*, or happiness (*Crito*, 48b–d; *Lysis*, 220a–b). Anything that is good is good only insofar as it contributes to this goal. The ultimate goal for each person is his or her own happiness.[13]

At *Lysis* 219c–d, there is an argument for this last claim. Socrates argues that when we desire something for the sake of something else, there must be something that we desire for itself (or not for the sake of something else). Otherwise, there would be an infinite regress of wanting for the sake of something else. This, he says, implies that there must be an ultimate end, which is one's own happiness.

It is important to note that Socrates's claim is not equivalent to contemporary hedonism. Hedonism is the view that pleasure and the absence of pain is the only non-instrumental good. Socrates does not identify happiness with pleasure.[14] There is more to *eudaimonia* than feeling pleasure. This is suggested by Socrates's view is that happiness is excellence or virtue (which we will examine in a moment). Socrates's view of *eudaimonia* contains the idea of practicing the art of living well, which is an idea that would not be reducible to living a life of pleasure. Other values seem to be involved, such as friendship and being noble. Furthermore, Plato uses Socrates as a mouthpiece to argue against hedonism in the *Gorgias*, *Phaedo*, *Republic* and *Philebus*, and this also suggests that Socrates was not a hedonist. However, the evidence about Socrates's views is both scant and controversial. The point is contentious in part because there is a well-known passage in the *Protagoras* in which Plato seems to identify happiness with pleasure (351b–e). We will examine Plato's own views about hedonism in a later chapter.

Socrates's view about happiness is not equivalent to contemporary psychological egoism. Psychological egoism affirms that each person acts only out of self-interest—defined in terms of one's own pleasure or desires. Socrates's view appears to be quite similar. He seems to affirm that each person acts for his or her own *eudaimonia*. However, as we just saw, *eudaimonia* is not to be identified with feelings of happiness, nor with getting what one wants. It is equivalent to living well, and as such it can include non-instrumental concern for others. Indeed, as we shall now see, Socrates's conception of living well contains a strong ethical component, which makes it different from psychological egoism.

2. Functions of the Soul

In the early dialogues, Socrates often compares the art of living well with various crafts or practical sciences such as horse training and medicine. Each of these sciences has a good that is its goal. Socrates thinks that this is an analogy for the soul. The soul is the person's instrument for living, comparable to the way that a knife is the instrument for cutting and the bow for archery.

This helps us to understand his view of virtue. What makes a knife good or virtuous is that it cuts well. It performs its function (or *ergon*) well. Likewise, what constitutes or makes a soul good or virtuous is that it lives well, in accordance with the functions of the soul. This is the second Socratic claim: virtue or excellence consists of living in accordance with the functions of the soul. But what are the functions of the soul? Frustratingly, the early dialogues don't contain an explicit reply to this question. Perhaps the most direct answer comes in Book I of the *Republic*: "taking care of things, ruling, deliberating . . ." (353e).

3. Virtue and Happiness

Socrates's thesis is that *eudaimonia* partly consists of, or is attained through, the exercise of the virtues (*Apology*, 28b and 30a–b). To live happily, we must live virtuously.

To understand this claim, we need to consider that the translation from the Ancient Greek is tentative and delicate at this point. The term *eudaimonia* is sometimes translated as "flourishing" rather than "happiness," because the latter seems to refer to how we feel, whereas the former contains the idea of living well. Likewise, although the Greek term *areté* is usually translated as "virtue," it might also be interpreted as "excellence." The difference is that the former is overlaid by a strong suggestion of Christian morality that is not present in the Greek.

Furthermore, contemporary commentators understand Socrates's view of the relationship between virtue and happiness differently. We can single out three such interpretations.

First, Terence Irwin advocates the view that, for Socrates, virtue is purely a means to *eudaimonia* or happiness. This means that the value of virtue is purely instrumental (Irwin, 1977, 1995). This seems to fit well with the craft analogy we examined earlier: the virtues produce happiness.

Second, Gregory Vlastos argues that, for Socrates, virtue is part of one's happiness; this opposes the instrumentalist reading of Irwin (see, e.g., Vlastos, 1991, ch. 8). Vlastos's idea is that the virtues are not external *means to* living well; their relation is more intimate: exercising the virtues *constitutes* living well (at least in part).

To explain the idea that virtue is a component of happiness, Vlastos argues that, according to Socrates, virtue is central in several ways. It is worth looking at these.

Being virtuous is a necessary condition of happiness. No one can be happy without virtue. At *Gorgias* 4.13, Socrates claims: "I say that the admirable and good person, man or woman, is happy, but that one who's unjust and wicked is miserable. If 'all happiness depends on justice,' then no one is happy who lacks justice." For a later echo of this view, we can turn to *Republic* 353d–354a, where Socrates says, "Therefore, a just person is happy, and an unjust one wretched."

According to Vlastos, Socrates thinks that virtue is a sufficient condition for happiness. Nothing else is needed. This view seems to imply that a virtuous person cannot be harmed. Obviously, this is not a very plausible claim, and there are passages in the *Apology* that appear to contradict it. Probably, Socrates means that a just person cannot suffer harm to the soul. In other words, the soul that is good can never be harmed when a person is virtuous.

According to Vlastos's reading, other goods such as wealth, honor, and health can become bad when they are in the service of bad ends (*Meno*, 78c–d). This is not true of the virtues of the soul, such as wisdom and justice. Virtue is a power that transforms something that wouldn't otherwise be good into something good (such as intelligence). Socrates advances this view in *Apology* 30a–b: "Wealth does not bring about excellence, but excellence brings about wealth and all other public and private blessings for men, both individually and collectively." Power, wealth, and honor can be either beneficial or damaging to our well-being; it depends on whether one is wise or ignorant (*Euthydemus*, 281a–e).

The third interpretation of the relation between happiness and virtue is the idea that for Socrates, happiness consists in the performance of right actions, and virtue produces those actions. The value of virtue is its power to produce right action (Brickhouse, 1994, p. 143). Gail Fine advances this kind of interpretation.

4. Intellectualist Theory of Virtue

Socrates argues for the thesis that knowledge of goodness is necessary and sufficient for virtue. Socrates argues for this fourth claim based on a theory of motivation: people always desire what they think is best for them in the circumstances (*Protagoras*, 352a–c).[15] The thesis implies that a person will never do wrong intentionally: we always will do what we perceive as good (*Gorgias*, 467d–468b; *Meno*, 78b). As a consequence, there is no such thing as incontinence, or doing what goes against one's best judgment (*akrasia*).

It is common for the Greek term *akrasia* to be translated as "weakness of the will": when a person knows what he or she ought to do but doesn't do it, then this is a sign of weakness of the will. The problem with this translation is that it is anachronistic.[16] The concept of the will as a distinct function of the human soul or psyche is a later concept introduced explicitly into philosophy by St. Augustine (AD 354–430), and possibly by earlier Roman writers such as Lucretius and Seneca. As we shall see in chapter 9, Aristotle recognizes the concept of choice and voluntary action, but even in his case, it would be misleading to translate *akrasia* as weakness of the will.[17]

According to Socrates, *akrasia* is impossible. Harmful actions that go against our self-interest arise only because the person has false beliefs about what is good for him or her under the circumstances. This is so because if a person always desires what is good for him or her in the circumstances, and given that those beliefs are true, then it follows that the person would want what is best for him or her.

Likewise, morally wrong actions necessarily arise only from ignorance or lack of intellectual understanding. Socrates thinks that people act immorally because they mistakenly believe that what they are doing is actually good for them. Wrongdoing is the result of ignorance of the harm that morally wrong actions cause the agent.

This is sometimes called an *intellectualist view of virtue*. It contrasts with the views of Plato in the later dialogues. For example, in the *Republic*, Plato thinks that training of the emotions and the non-rational parts of the soul are necessary for virtue.

5. Unity of the Virtues

Socrates's fifth thesis concerns the unity of the virtues. Most fifth-century BC Greeks believed that there are five cardinal moral virtues—

piety, courage, temperance, justice, and wisdom. Socrates follows this tradition; what is new is that he affirms their unity. As a minimum this means that a person who is virtuous cannot lack any of the virtues; for example, a just person must be also courageous and temperate; likewise, to be courageous one must also be just.

It is usual to distinguish two claims here:

First, there is the identity claim, which is supported in the *Protagoras* (349a–d) (Penner, 1973). According to this claim, all the virtues are literally identical (Devereux, 1992).[18] Therefore, there is only one virtue: knowledge of the good. This theory of the unity of the virtues follows from the intellectualist theory of virtue outlined above: since knowledge of the good is necessary and sufficient for any of the virtues, there is only that one virtue, and what appear to be other virtues are just different aspects of the one virtue.

Second, more modestly, there is the claim of the reciprocity of the virtues.[19] According to this claim, each virtue is constituted by a different set of behavioral dispositions, and therefore, the names of the virtues do not refer to the same thing. Even if they are all forms of knowledge, they are not the same. For instance, the moral knowledge that makes a person just is not the same as that which constitutes piety. Nevertheless, wisdom makes the unity of the virtues possible. It is like a central hub because it is a necessary condition for the possession of any of the other virtues, and second, because it is sufficient for the possession of each of the others as well.

We might ask which of these two theses is best supported by the texts of the Socratic dialogues. One might also ask which of the two is a more plausible thesis. Either way, the theory might be contrasted with Plato's *Republic*, in which it is possible for the military class to have courage, and the merchant classes temperance, without wisdom. The latter is a virtue apparently reserved for the ruling class.

6. Harming Others Harms Oneself

Perhaps the most important thesis that Socrates advances in the early dialogues is that, by harming others, one harms oneself. Furthermore, he claims that the harm is so great that it is never in one's interest to harm others. For example, in the *Apology* Socrates asks his accuser, Meletus, if he believes that he (Socrates) corrupts the youth willingly. Socrates says that if he does, then "I do know that by willingly corrupting the youth, I am doing myself harm."[20] In the *Gorgias*, Socrates argues that acting unjustly towards others is always worse that having others act unjustly to oneself. He says to Callicles that injustice is worst for the person who commits it (509b).

Why does Socrates think this? Following Brickhouse and Smith, we can tentatively piece together an answer from scattered elements in the early dialogues. Socrates says that unjust action destroys the soul (*Crito*,

47d3–5).[21] For Socrates, there is nothing more important than the condition of one's soul. As we saw earlier, the soul's function is to live well. According to Socrates, this requires that the soul rule over our appetites rather than being ruled by them. Unjust actions harm us because they strengthen our appetites and make it impossible for the soul to function well.[22] Perhaps the most explicit argument to this effect is in Book I of the *Republic*.

The claim that it is never in one's interest to harm others appears to be false, and Socrates doesn't give definitive systematic support for his claim. These points set a challenge that dominates much of Plato's own thinking. How can we justify justice? How can we show that wrongdoing harms the agent? As we shall see, especially in the *Republic*, Plato tries to answer these Socratic questions with ideas that go beyond those of Socrates.

Conclusion

Given these six claims, we can see why Socrates thought that study of the good was supremely important for our lives. We can also see that Socrates did indeed hold substantial philosophical views, even though his claim to wisdom was based on his own ignorance.

Sophism, Pre-Socratic Thought, and Religion

One way to think about these Socratic philosophical claims in the early dialogues is to consider their denial, or what Socrates was rejecting. It is important to see how Socrates disagrees fundamentally with both Sophism and the Pre-Socratic naturalistic philosophers, and how his rejection of each has a common core.

Sophism

First, Socrates rejects Sophism. As we saw in an earlier chapter, Sophism may be characterized as the view that all claims to truth are subjective in the sense that all opinions are equal in value. As a result, Sophists claim that the aim of argumentation is simply rhetorical: to convince. In other words, rhetoric should aim at persuasion and not at truth.

Part of Plato's aims in the early dialogues was to defend his teacher against the indictments and popular opinions that led to his prosecution. As described in the *Apology*, Socrates was accused of corrupting the youth, and many people viewed him as a Sophist teacher who taught unjust argumentation. Plato wants to show that this is the reverse of truth: in fact, Socrates was opposed to Sophism. Socrates claimed that certain things have supreme value, and that this is not merely a matter of opinion. Therefore, Socrates did not corrupt the youth.

Not only does Plato want to show that Socrates wasn't a Sophist: he also aims to show that Socrates has powerful arguments against Sophism. The two earliest dialogues most directly concerned with the rejection of Sophism are the *Protagoras* and the *Gorgias*. Plato argues that Sophism implies the false claim that all value questions related to the human good concern only means. Ends are only a question of what the individual chooses as good. According to Sophism, there can be no argumentation about ends. As a result, Socrates argues that Sophism cannot teach us what is really desirable and therefore cannot provide guidance about the good life and virtue.

Socrates supports this view by arguing that the science of virtue or of taking care of one's soul is not neutral about ends. This claim is inherent in his comparing it to various other sciences such as medicine, which have definite ends. First, medicine is not neutral about health; it seeks to improve a person's health as a good. Second, it is not merely a matter of opinion what is good for a patient's health. In other words, there is a body of knowledge that allows us to distinguish between those who know medicine and those who do not. Against Sophism, Socrates is making similar claims about virtue and the care for the soul.

We return to Plato's own arguments against Sophism in more detail in the next chapter. Some of his arguments against Sophism go beyond the teachings of Socrates. This applies even to the *Protagoras* and the *Gorgias*, which are considered as Socratic dialogues, as well as to the later dialogues.

Pre-Socratic Thought

Second, Socrates fundamentally disagrees with the naturalism of the Pre-Socratic philosophers. In the *Phaedo*, Socrates recounts how as a young man he was initially attracted to study these early philosophers to better understand the causes of natural things (96a). He narrates how, later, he came to realize that he had been made quite blind to things that he and others thought they knew (96c). The context makes clear here that Socrates is referring to the life of the soul and the good life. Many of the naturalistic Pre-Socratic philosophers held the view that the world consists only of matter in motion. This seems to imply that human psychology must be understood in terms of the movement of material particles. Socrates claims that he was not suited to the study of earlier naturalistic philosophy because it left out what is most important: the study of the good. Socrates tells us how he was delighted to hear of a book by Anaxagoras in which the mind organizes and is the cause of everything (97b). He assumed that such a view would give primacy to the study of what is excellent and best (97d). Of course, Socrates was disappointed because Anaxagoras's philosophy was concerned primarily with natural causes.

Socrates's approach to Sophism and to the Pre-Socratics has a common core. Both fail to address questions about the soul and how we should live. The first rejects the idea that there can be objective claims about what is good. The second fails to understand the existence and functions of the soul, and hence cannot address the important issues in life concerning how we should live.

Religion

Third, we need to examine Socrates's supposed rejection of religion. As we saw in earlier chapters, it is interesting, but not always revealing, to contrast philosophy with religion, or *logos* with *muthos* (reason with myth). In the particular case of Socrates, we have conflicting evidence. For example, in his trial, Socrates was indicted with impiety and atheism or "of not believing in the gods that city believes in."[23] At the same time, in the *Apology* Socrates describes his own mission in life as god given. Additionally, he describes the wisdom that he lacks as god-like. Was he religious or not? Let us examine these conflicts to see if we can make sense of them.

On the one hand, there are many signs of Socrates's deeply religious nature. He consults the oracle—a purified woman, filled with the spirit of Apollo, who delivered divine prophecies. These prophecies might consist of enigmatic sayings and riddles, which were usually interpreted by male priests. Although Socrates tries to falsify the oracle's claim by looking for someone wiser than himself, he also states that disobeying the oracle would be tantamount to atheism (*Apology*, 29a3–5). Moreover, Socrates professes true beliefs about, and even intimacy with, the divine. For instance, in the *Apology* he says that the god has placed him in the city to perform some function: to be a gadfly (30e2). Socrates testifies to hearing a divine voice that guides him throughout his life. Later in the *Apology* he claims that his divine voice has prevented him from doing wrong (40a2). It prevented him from entering public office and from other acts harmful to himself and others. Socrates says that he received no sign that he should try to avoid his trial and consequently, "it is better for me to die.... That is why my divine sign did not oppose me at any point" (41d 3–6).

Additionally, in some of the later dialogues Plato stresses the spiritual character of Socrates. For example, in the *Phaedrus* Plato has Socrates affirm that he is a seer (242b8). When Socrates offends the gods by giving a speech against love, his divine sign or voice tells him to make atonement for an act that was "close to being impious." In the *Symposium*, Socrates is described as having supernatural powers and experiences. Agathon wants to touch him to gain some of his wisdom. Plato's texts suggest that Socrates might be viewed as an intermediary between the gods and normal people. Socrates himself rebuffs this kind of suggestion. Nevertheless, in the *Symposium* the priestess Diotima characterizes love as a *daimonion*, as an intermediary between the divine and the human.

On the other hand, Socrates is portrayed as anti-religious in many respects. He is scornful of the popular conception of the gods. He thinks that the gods are completely wise, and that this excludes their being jealous and vengeful. He rejects the popular idea of the gods as immortal beings with both a body and a soul (*Phaedrus* 246c–d). Furthermore, he is clearly a free thinker who is willing to challenge religious authority. To Crito, Socrates says, "Not now for the first time, but always, I am the sort of man who is persuaded by nothing in me except the argument which appears to be the best when I reason about it" (46b).

One of the problems is that Socrates claims to follow reasoning as best he can, and yet he has a divine voice sometimes guiding him. Can these two claims be reconciled, and if so, how? Socrates's views would make sense if he saw reason as something divine. Indeed, in the *Memorabilia*, Xenophon portrays Socrates as claiming that "the human soul partakes of divinity" (4.3.14). In short, Socrates may have regarded the divine as rational, and the human capacity to reason or reflect as divine too. In which case, Socrates might think of his divine signs as compatible with the demands of reason.[24]

Socrates's Trial and Death

Earlier we said that Socrates is the father of philosophy because of three factors: his personality and method, his philosophical views, and the story of his death. Many regard Socrates as the paradigm philosopher partly because of the extraordinary events surrounding his death, which exemplify his philosophical method and views. He is a great philosopher because his fundamental convictions are reflected equally in both his life and his death.

Socrates's questioning was perceived as impious, threatening, and rebellious. In 399 BC, Meletus, Anytus, and Lycon accused him of impiety. The charge had three parts: corrupting the youth of Athens, not recognizing the gods of the city, and introducing new divine things.[25] At the time, Socrates was 70; he was married and had three sons. Socrates repeats the charges against him, insults his audience, and ridicules his accusers. He is found guilty by a vote of 281 to 220. Meletus proposes the death penalty. Socrates, who has the right to propose an alternative punishment, suggests a lifelong pension! Of course, the jury is almost forced to decide the death penalty, and does so with 80 more votes. Despite the fact that he could have easily escaped, Socrates drank the poison and died.

These events occurred five years after the defeat of Athens in the Peloponnesian Wars. Athens was still in a period of political turbulence. In 404, the Council of Thirty assassinated many democratic Athenians and suppressed freedom of speech. However, in 403, democracy was restored to the city. The indictment against Socrates may have had political motivations: one of his pupils, Critias, was the notorious leader of the Council of Thirty. Furthermore, Alcibiades was Socrates's lover, and Alcibiades was the leader of the disastrous Sicilian military expedition, who became a traitor by defecting to the Spartans and later to the Persians.

The dramatic scenes surrounding Socrates's death are immortalized in four of Plato's dialogues. The *Euthyphro* portrays Socrates on his way to court; the *Apology*, the trial itself; the *Crito* shows Socrates's refusal to escape from prison; and the later *Phaedo*, the last conversation and the death of the old master. We will briefly examine the first three of these in this chapter. (The *Phaedo* is probably a different kettle of fish because it contains some arguments and views that belong more to Plato than to Socrates. We will examine it in the next chapter.)

In addition to these four traditionally cited dialogues, we might also add parts of the *Theaetetus*, one of the dialogues of the middle period, which also has several allusions to the impeding trial of Socrates that help set the scene for the death sentence.[26] Towards the beginning of the dialogue, when Socrates is coaxing Theaetetus to explain his view of knowledge, Socrates compares himself to his mother, who was a midwife. Socrates describes himself as one who helps others give birth to ideas. He expounds upon the features of his profession that explain why he is sometimes blamed and hated. First, those who leave his guidance too early lose their ideas (or metaphorically their unborn babies), and reproach him. Second, he is often blamed for the birth pains that accompany false pregnancies, when someone does not really have an idea to give birth to. Third, midwives aren't themselves pregnant, and likewise, Socrates himself is barren of ideas. For this reason, he himself is not wise.

Euthyphro

This dialogue takes place shortly before Socrates's trial and subsequent execution in 399 BC. Euthyphro is a young religious man who believes that piety requires him to prosecute his own father. The father, a rich landowner, accidentally caused the death of a slave who had murdered another slave. Euthyphro's father left the murderer tied up in a ditch while he went to call the authorities, and the slave died. Euthyphro thinks that he is required to accuse his father of manslaughter. This is how the dialogue begins.

If we take his words at face value, Socrates is impressed by Euthyphro's commitment to moral justice and piety. Socrates asks Euthyphro to teach him the true meaning of piety, so that he can better defend himself against his own impending charge of impiety. However, none of Euthyphro's answers satisfy the persistent and skeptical Socrates.

First, Euthyphro gives an example of piety—that is, his own actions: prosecuting someone for some wrongdoing. Socrates points out that an example is not a definition. A definition is a general statement that can then be used to determine whether or not some particular action is pious. To understand a general concept such as piety requires more than citing examples, because knowing the meaning of the concept is necessary for classifying the examples.

Euthyphro then tries to rectify his mistake by giving a definition. Pious actions, he says, are those that please the gods, whereas impious actions are those that displease the gods. Instead of challenging this definition, Socrates asks another question: do the gods sometimes disagree? Euthyphro says that they do. Socrates points out that an action that pleases some gods will anger others so that, based on Euthyphro's definition, a particular action can be both pious and impious, which is contradictory.

1. An action cannot be both pious and impious at the same time.
2. The gods disagree in what pleases them.
---
3. Therefore piety cannot be defined as what pleases the gods.

Euthyphro replies that on some things all the gods agree. Instead of raising objections about how we might know this, Socrates asks one of the most famous and penetrating questions of philosophy: Is an action pious because it pleases the gods, or does it please the gods because it is holy? In other words: is some action, X, right because God says so or does God say so because X is right?

This question forces Euthyphro into a dilemma: on the one hand, if being pious is right only because it pleases the gods, then it is not the merits of piety itself that makes it right or wrong. This makes the difference between right and wrong arbitrary. On the other hand, if the nature of pious acts makes the gods love such acts, then this means that the approval of the gods is irrelevant to what piety itself is. Some acts are pious independently of what pleases the gods. Socrates's persistent questioning has brought the hidden problems of Euthyphro's view to the surface.

The *Apology*

The *Apology* portrays the defense of Socrates at his trial, against the charge of corrupting the youth of Athens. The prosecution speaks first, outlining the charges. After the prosecution has spoken, the accused speaks in his defense. The jury consists of 501 representative citizens, who must decide his guilt. If the accused is found guilty, the prosecution must propose a punishment and the defendant may propose an alternative penalty, after which the jury must decide which punishment to apply.

The *Apology* contains a rendering of the extraordinary speech Socrates gave in his defense at his trial (the Greek word for apology means "defense" rather than "request for forgiveness"). The charges against Socrates were corrupting the minds of the young, and impiety.

In the dialogue, Socrates claims that he has spent his life trying to understand virtue, but that he has not been able to come to a wise conclusion. The only wisdom he can profess is that of knowing that he does not know. Knowledge of the virtues is probably only possessed by the gods. We humans must recognize the limits of our moral understanding.

Although he is able to reject false claims, Socrates is not able to reach a positive conclusion. He is wise because he realizes this.

The *Crito*

In Athens, a death sentence would usually be carried out immediately after the sentencing. But Socrates's trial took place during an important religious festival, and for this reason he was detained in prison for a month. It was probably expected that, during this time, Socrates would flee from prison and live the remainder of his life in exile. In the *Crito*, his friends come to plead with him to escape. Socrates refuses, arguing that he is morally obliged to stay. Crito appeals to Socrates's own self-interest. Socrates replies on behalf of moral obligation, until Crito can no longer contest the logic of his argument.

CONCLUSION

Socrates is the patron figure of much Western philosophy. This is in part because of the extraordinary nature of his character, life, and death, which embody a critical attitude and a dialectical method that has been central to much Western philosophy since.

As far as we can tell, despite his claims to know nothing, Socrates advances some philosophical beliefs. In particular, he holds that virtue is supremely important. To live happily, one must live virtuously, and virtue consists in living in accordance with the functions of the soul. To be virtuous, it is necessary and sufficient to have knowledge of goodness. For this reason, the virtues are a unity.

Socrates transcends the main dichotomy of the Pre-Socratic thinkers. On the one hand, he rejects Sophism. He denies that all opinions are equal in value. In medicine, health is a good and expert doctors know what is conducive to good health. Likewise, with regard to the soul, happiness is the good end, and virtue is conducive to that end. Contrary to Sophism, there are important truths to know or to be mistaken about. On the other hand, Socrates rejects the naturalism of the earlier Pre-Socratics because a purely mechanical account of nature cannot help us to understand the functions of the soul. For this reason, it is deficient in understanding virtue.

Study Questions

1. How can we reconcile Socrates's claim that he knows nothing with his philosophical claims about virtue?
2. What is the *elenchus*?
3. What are the three steps by which Socrates typically challenges the views of his interlocutor?

4. Apply these three steps to the dialogue the *Euthyphro*.
5. What is the *Priority of Definitional Knowledge*? Why is it important, according to Socrates?
6. According to Socrates, what is the relation between *eudaimonia* and virtue?
7. How does Socrates defend the claim that knowledge of the good is sufficient for virtue?
8. What does the unity of the virtues mean?
9. According to Socrates, what are the functions of the soul?
10. How would Socrates defend the claim that by harming others one harms oneself?
11. In what ways does Socrates reject Sophism?
12. How does Socrates argue against Pre-Socratic naturalism?
13. In what ways is Socrates anti-religious? In what ways is Socrates religious?
14. In what ways is the death of Socrates philosophically important?

Discussion Questions

1. Is Socrates right to claim that there is nothing more important than the condition of one's soul?
2. Is Socrates right to claim that it is never in one's interests to harm others?
3. Was Socrates right to have drunk the hemlock?

Plato's Views in Development

*P*lato is the first philosopher to have an integrated view of philosophy as a separate discipline. He combines all of the elements of philosophy discussed by the Pre-Socratics and Socrates, and more besides, into a single unified vision that encompasses the theory of knowledge, metaphysics, language, mind, mathematics, science, art, education, morality, and politics. Philosophy reveals the existence of and the need for objects that are inaccessible to the senses, and these Forms show us how we should transform our own individual lives and the politics of the state. From this vision, philosophy emerges as the most important of all studies.

This grand vision is based foremost on the existence of the Forms. These are abstract, eternal, and changeless entities that exist independently of us, that can be known through thought, and which define the essence of things in the world. A question such as "What is Justice?" seeks to understand the Form of Justice. The basis of morality and wisdom is to know the Form of the Good.

Before we examine the theories of the mature Plato in the following chapters, it is important to sketch the intellectual journey that brought him there. The main evidence that we have of this voyage consists in the dialogues sometimes classified as transitional. In these transitional dialogues, Plato's own thought begins to emerge but does not yet attain the full maturity of the middle period. Among this transitional group, the most prominent are the *Meno* and the *Phaedo*, both of which we discuss in this chapter. In the *Meno*, Plato argues that learning is really the recollection of knowledge that the soul acquired prior to birth. In the *Phaedo*, Plato argues for the immortality of the soul, thinking that the true benefits of living virtuously can only be received after the death of the body.

In this chapter we also discuss Plato's own rejection of Sophism. As we saw in the previous chapter, Socrates argued against Sophist doctrines. However, as Aristophanes's play and Socrates's trial suggest, Socrates himself was branded as a Sophist by Athenian society. Plato regards this as unfair, and he takes up the challenge of this gauntlet in several of the early dialogues by showing how Socrates argued against Sophism. In addition to this, Plato also wants to show for himself or for his own sake that Sophism is a mistaken philosophical view, and this is a reoccurring theme in several dialogues throughout his life. Among the most important of these are the *Protagoras* and the *Gorgias*, which are often considered to be from the early period.

Introduction to Plato

Many scholars of Plato argue for a developmentalist approach to Plato's dialogues that divides them into three periods: early, middle, and late. The main gist of this classification is as follows. First, in the early dialogues Plato dramatizes the kinds of philosophical conversations that Socrates held. These Socratic dialogues are the most reliable source for our knowledge of Socrates. In the case of the dialogues of this early period, Plato had views close to those of Socrates, even though Plato actively and dramatically explores those views rather than just passively representing them. We examined some of these early dialogues in the previous chapter. Second, in the middle period dialogues Plato develops his own views, which are significantly different from the views advanced by Socrates, even though the main protagonist of the dialogues is still the character Socrates. It is worth noting that Plato himself never appears as a character in any of his dialogues. Third, in the late period Plato distances himself from his own theory of Forms. He either revises parts of it or has a more skeptical attitude towards it. During this period, Socrates is often not the main protagonist of the dialogues.

The developmentalist approach emerged as standard in the Anglophile world in the 1960s. This classification is based on stylometric evidence as well as analysis of the content of the texts. Stylometry investigates various features of writing style, such as vocabulary and prose rhythm.[1] The results of this approach accords well with what Aristotle says about the differences between Plato and Socrates. For example, according to Aristotle, Socrates inquired exclusively into ethics. In contrast, Plato was interested in other philosophical themes, such as metaphysics. Socrates advanced no philosophical theories of his own. In contrast, Plato did. Furthermore, Plato drew inspiration from Pythagoras and Heraclitus (through Cratylus), and not only Socrates.[2]

Nevertheless, it should be noted that the developmentalist strategy for reading Plato's works as a whole has problems as well as strengths. First, alternative approaches that reject the attempt to place Plato's works into periods stress the unity of his work. Placing the dialogues into a fixed historical order encourages the idea that there are fundamental breaks in Plato's works, and it forces us to focus more on the differences than the similarities. Second, although the classification of the dialogues into the three categories is a relatively standard approach, there are controversies about the placing of individual dialogues. There isn't a standard agreed-upon list based on clear evidence.[3] Nevertheless, some agreement does exist. We listed what are often regarded as the early dialogues in the previous chapter. One grouping of the middle and late dialogues might be as follows:

The middle dialogues:	The late dialogues:
Cratylus	*Parmenides*
Phaedo	*Critias*
Phaedrus	*Laws*
Republic	*Philebus*
Symposium	*Politicus*
Theaetetus	*Sophist*
Timaeus	

Even if we renounce the attempt to assign more specific chronologies within each of the three broad groupings, nevertheless, there are controversies. For example, G. E. Owen places the *Timaeus* as a middle-period dialogue. Despite the dangers, difficulties, and uncertainties of the standard developmentalist view of Plato's dialogues, nevertheless it has become the standard view among many Plato scholars.

SOME DIFFERENCES BETWEEN SOCRATES AND PLATO

The developmentalist view enables the idea that Socrates and Plato were quite different as philosophers in their methods, views, and style. Given this, let us contrast the two. Some of the important differences[4] between the early Socratic dialogues and the other dialogues of Plato that emerge are:

1. The earlier dialogues do not come to a positive philosophical conclusion. They are *aporetic*. The middle and later dialogues argue for definite, and often ambitious, philosophical conclusions.

2. The early Socratic dialogues are concerned almost exclusively with ethics, virtue, and care of the soul. The later dialogues cover many other philosophical areas such as metaphysics, mathematics, epistemology, art and literature, and politics, as well as ethics.

3. In the early dialogues, Socrates is represented as having an intellectualist theory of motivation and virtue, as we discussed in the previous chapter. In contrast, Plato later regarded the human psyche as a combination of rational and irrational elements. Only the rational elements necessarily desire the good. Appetitive desires can be blindly irrational and resistant to changes in belief. As a result, Plato is not committed to the Socratic views that all desire is for the good and that so-called "weakness of the will" is solely a question of ignorance. In short, Socrates rejects and Plato accepts the possibility of incontinence, or *akrasia*.

4. Accordingly, Plato rejects Socrates's idea that an intellectual perception of the good is sufficient for virtue. In keeping with this rejection, whereas the Socratic dialogues argue for some strong version of the unity of the virtues, this view is not present in Plato's middle and later dialogues. For instance, in the *Republic*, the lower class has temperance and the military class has courage, but neither has wisdom. They can have the one without the other.
5. Socrates's *elenchus* is usually directed specifically to the beliefs of a particular interlocutor. Plato's method is still dialectic, but it is more impersonal.
6. There are substantial differences in tone and feeling between the earlier and later dialogues. The earlier ones are more mischievous and energetic, while the later ones are more scientific and ponderous.[5]

PLATO'S ARGUMENTS AGAINST SOPHISM

The rejection of Sophism was a major preoccupation of Plato throughout his life. Many of Plato's early dialogues are explicitly named after Sophists: the *Enthydemus*, *Hippias*, the *Gorgias*, and the *Protagoras*, which we briefly examine below. Furthermore, in many later dialogues, especially the *Theaetetus* and the *Sophist*, Plato is still arguing against Sophist positions. Plato keeps returning to Sophism throughout his thinking life because he regards the position as worth refuting. Indeed, as we shall see, it is arguable that Plato felt that he had to depart from Socratic minimalism in order to defend basic Socratic principles against Sophism.

The Need for Definitions

A challenge against Sophism that arises directly from Socrates is based on the *elenchus*. As we saw in the previous chapter, Socrates's method often deploys the idea that one cannot have knowledge of X unless one knows how X should be defined. For instance, one cannot know what piety is like and what actions are pious, unless one knows what piety is. This method directly challenges Sophism because it presupposes that piety (for example) has an essential nature, captured with a definition, about which one could be mistaken.

This point in itself does not constitute an argument against Sophism. It merely shows that the Socratic Method presupposes that Sophism is false.

The Analogy of the Arts and the Sciences

In the Socratic dialogues there is an argument against Sophism, which is sometimes called *the analogy from the arts*. The idea is that there are certain arts or crafts that deserve the name "science." A minimal requirement for this is that they should be directed to some good. So the art of being a doctor is a science in part because there is a good pursued by such activities, namely, health.

This aim implies that health is a good that is objective in the sense of its being independent of people's opinion about it. Because of this objectivity, a person can make mistakes about what is healthy, and because of this, we seek experts when we are ill. In other words, not all opinions on these matters are equal.

Plato seeks to apply this kind of argumentation to refute Sophism with regard to the good. Here Sophism can be taken as the view that rhetoric aims at the good, which is persuasion (rather than truth), and that the power to persuade is a good because it helps a person to obtain what he or she wants. In other words, according to a Sophist, rhetoric aims at the good, namely, getting what one wants. The good consists in getting what one wants.

In reply, Plato argues that this view is based on an erroneous view of desire. There is a difference between what a person declares that he or she wants and what he or she really wants, which is the good. In other words, we must distinguish between what a person thinks the good is and what the good really is. We shouldn't assume that what a person claims to want and thinks is good really is good. He or she might be mistaken.

Reductio ad Absurdum Arguments

In Book I of the *Republic*, the sophist teacher Thrasymachus advances a relativist definition of justice according to which justice is only the advantage of the stronger (331c). Plato employs a *reductio ad absurdum* argument to refute this definition (339b–e). A *reductio* argument proposes that a position is mistaken by trying to show that it implies an absurdity, such as a contradiction. The argument in the *Republic* proceeds as follows:

1. Justice is only the advantage of the strongest.
2. If premise 1 were true, then it would be just to obey all laws.
3. Lawmakers can mistakenly pass laws that are not to their own advantage.
4. If it is just to obey all laws and if premise 3 is true, then it would be just to obey laws that disadvantage the strong.

---

5. Therefore, premise 1 is false.

Premise 1 states Thrasymachus's definition of justice. Premise 2 states an implication of that definition given the assumption that the strongest people in a society are those who make its laws.

According to the *reductio* argument, the original definition in premise 1 leads to a contradiction when combined with the turning key of the argument, namely, the third premise. This premise relies on the idea that anyone, including even powerful rulers, can make mistakes. The argument reveals how Sophism is incompatible with this commonsense claim. This third premise picks up a reoccurring Platonic theme: the idea that Sophism is incompatible with error. Sophism implies that mistakes are impossible. Because errors are always possible, Sophism is a false theory.

Plato advances this form of argumentation quite explicitly in the *Theaetetus*, arguing that Protagoras's dictum, "Man is the measure of all things," ignores the fact that some people are wiser than others. Furthermore, he argues that the claim that all beliefs are true cannot be right because someone could believe that "Not all beliefs are true." If someone had this belief, then according to the Sophists it would have to be true, in which case not all beliefs would be true (171a–b).

The Self-Defeating Nature of Sophism

In the *Theaetetus*, Plato tries to apply the sophist thesis to itself in order to show its absurdity. Plato takes Protagoras's thesis that man is the measure of all things and then applies it self-referentially to itself. Is the thesis itself true? Well, if the thesis is true, then man is the measure of all things and man is the measure of the thesis itself. This implies that whether the thesis is true depends on what people believe about it.

The Arguments for the Forms

Fundamentally, Plato argues against Sophism by trying to show that—and why—the Forms must exist. If there are nonmaterial Forms that define, for instance, what justice and goodness are, then Sophism is mistaken.

THE *PROTAGORAS*

When Hippocrates enthusiastically suggests that he and Socrates should go to see Protagoras, one of the great Sophist teachers, Socrates suggests that Protagoras is a "merchant who sells provisions to nourish the soul." The implication is that a merchant is a salesman who isn't concerned for the truth of his claims.

When they meet Protagoras, the great Sophist explains that he teaches his pupils how to have good judgment in both private and public life. Socrates interprets this to mean that Protagoras thinks he teaches the virtues of good citizenship. Socrates then expresses doubt concerning the claim that virtue can be taught, claiming that if it could, then Pericles and other statesmen would have imparted it to their sons.

Protagoras replies to this with a long discourse, known as "the great speech" (320c–328d), which contains a myth and a philosophical account. In the myth, the god Epimetheus hands out all the powers and talents to the creatures, but he has none left over when he comes to the humans. Seeing this, Prometheus stole fire and practical wisdom from the gods to give to the humans. However, he could not provide them with political wisdom, the art of living together, which was guarded by Zeus. Consequently, although humans developed materially, they lacked this virtue. To remedy this, Zeus sent Hermes to distribute a sense of justice and shame to *all* people. Consequently, Protagoras claims, there are no special experts in the field of justice, contrary to what Socrates suggests.

Protagoras aims to show that this sense of justice needs to be developed through teaching (323c). He argues that people are punished for wrongdoing because punishment is a deterrent, and this presupposes that virtue can be taught. Likewise, the educational system assumes that virtue can be taught.

Nevertheless, Socrates seems unwilling to accept the conclusion that virtue can be taught, and he steers the discussion in an apparently quite different direction, towards the question of whether the virtues are one (329b). He argues that a person who has any one of the five virtues (temperance, courage, wisdom, piety, and justice) must have the others (328d–334c).

In the course of trying to show that all the virtues are knowledge, Socrates attempts to debunk the popular idea that people are overcome by pleasure when they act weakly or out of weakness of the will. Socrates tries to show how the popular view of weakness of the will is inconsistent with the other popular and hedonist view that pleasure and pain are the only things of intrinsic value and disvalue. According to the hedonist view, when people think that they are being overcome by pleasure, in fact what is going on is miscalculation. People think that pleasures in the near future are greater than they really are when compared to pleasures of equal strength in the distant future. Current pleasure appears greater than an equal pleasure next year. These perspectival differences make the distant pleasures appear lesser and the near ones appear larger. Consequently, we are apt to miscalculate what actions are most conducive to pleasure in a way that favors immediate pleasures. In short, what appears to be an incontinent action is in fact a lack of knowledge.

Arguing against Socrates's thesis of the unity of the virtues, Protagoras claims that a person can have courage without possessing the other virtues. Socrates replies with a long argument spanning from 358D to 360D, concluding that courage is knowledge of fearful and non-fearful things. In other words, courage is a form of wisdom.

The dialogue concludes with an observation that turns it upside-down. In the first part, Socrates doubted that virtue could be taught. However, he now notes that because he has argued that all the virtues are one because all are knowledge, therefore, he should conclude that the virtues are teachable. Likewise, Protagoras originally argued that virtue could be taught. However, in the second part, he has argued that the virtues are not knowledge, and thus, should conclude that virtue cannot be taught (361b). In this way, the discussion has been "topsy-turvy."

THE *GORGIAS*

This dialogue contains Plato's main arguments against Sophism. It was probably written after the Protagoras, which itself is probably one of the later dialogues from the early period.[6] It is remarkable as an early dialogue because Socrates gets quizzed and questioned. Socrates disputes with three interlocutors, Gorgias, Polus and Callicles, in that order.

When Socrates asks the elder Gorgias about his craft, Gorgias defines oratory or rhetoric as the producer of persuasion concerning justice (453a). To challenge Gorgias, Socrates argues that there are two kinds of persuasion: one that results in belief and the other in knowledge. Rhetoric is the former and not the latter. In other words, rhetoric doesn't result in knowledge of what is just. Thus, the Sophist is not an expert on justice (454d–455a).

To this, Gorgias responds by highlighting the power of being able to persuade, citing the example of how he was able to convince a previously unwilling patient to have the surgery the doctor recommended (456b). To defend rhetoric further, Gorgias compares rhetoric to the art of boxing. Neither the teacher nor the art itself are responsible for how the student uses his acquired skills (456d–457c). However, Socrates challenges this analogy by arguing that rhetoric about justice requires knowledge of justice, and that a person who has such knowledge would be just. Therefore, rhetoric wouldn't be like boxing.

Polus jumps to the defense of his teacher and turns the table on Socrates by questioning him. He asks Socrates what kind of craft *he* thinks rhetoric is. Socrates replies that rhetoric is not really a craft at all. It is a knack that aims at flattery and pleasing others without considering what is best (465a). He says that rhetoric is to the health of the soul as pastry-baking is to medicine.

Furthermore, Socrates claims that rhetoric doesn't confer power to its practitioners. This is because power must be good, but rhetoric is not directed towards the good. Likewise, people only want things insofar as they are good but rhetoric doesn't aim at that; so it doesn't help people achieve what they really want (468b–e).

Socrates enounces the famous claim that "doing what is unjust is the worst thing that there is" (469b) and that consequently it is worse to commit injustice than to suffer it. Polus is incredulous and cites the example of Archelaus, ruler of Macedonia, who committed heinous crimes but lived happily afterwards. Socrates replies that doing what is unjust is more shameful than suffering it, and this isn't because the first is more painful, but rather because of its badness (475c). Socrates adds the idea that having a corrupt soul is the most shameful thing, but again this is not because it is the most painful (477b–e). Finally, Socrates claims that the happiest person is "the one who does not have any badness in the soul" (478d). Given these three claims. Socrates is able to dispel the claim that the unjust Archelaus is happy (479e).

The brash and frank Callicles now enters the discussion, accusing Socrates of a systematic sleight of hand—confusing what is just by law and by nature. Because of this, Polus shouldn't have agreed that acting unjustly is more shameful than suffering injustice. Polus meant that it is true according to the law, but not by nature (natural morality). Callicles proceeds to outline why it is naturally worse to suffer injustice than to commit it. Nature shows that it is just for the stronger to rule and have a greater share than the weaker (482d–484e).

Socrates challenges Callicles's defense by questioning him regarding the word *stronger*, showing how people can be stronger than others in some respects but not in other respects (490a–491d). Socrates introduces the idea of self-rule. But Callicles embraces the idea that each person's ultimate good is to purse his own pleasure (494a–495b). Socrates tries to refute this hedonistic position by arguing that some pleasures are better than others (499b). Those that are better are beneficial in that they lead to the good. This establishes a distinction between the good and the pleasant (500d). Socrates argues that all actions are performed for the sake of the good (499e) and consequently, even pleasant actions are done for the sake of the good (500a). From this conclusion, Socrates repeats his own criticisms of rhetoric and, in particular, the claim that rhetoric is a knack rather than a craft because it aims to please rather than the good *per se*.

The *Gorgias* is probably one of the last of the early dialogues. Its style is slightly different from the other early dialogues because Socrates is more willing to set out his own views in a more systematic way than before.

THE *MENO*

The *Meno* is probably one of the first dialogues in which Plato expresses more of his own views rather than those of Socrates. It is a transitional dialogue, a bridge from Plato's early Socratic works to his own mature reflections. It was written probably around 386 BC, when Plato was in his early forties. It shows Plato's deep interest in mathematics, something not present in the earlier Socratic dialogues and which reveals a Pythagorean influence.

Overview

In the first part of the dialogue (up to 81a), Meno asks Socrates whether virtue is teachable. Socrates insists that we need a definition of virtue first. Meno tries to challenge this insistence (and the priority of definition, discussed in the previous chapter). He claims that Socratic argument actually numbs perplexity rather than stimulating it (79e). He also raises the famous paradox of inquiry, namely, that a person cannot discover what he knows or what he does not know. If one does not know what an F is, then one cannot know anything about Fs, and thus, one cannot know what one seeks to discover or recognize an F even if one finds one (80d–e). We will return to this point in a moment.

The main concern of the second half of the *Meno* is whether knowledge is innate or acquired. Plato wants to prove that the knowledge of certain basic principles is innate, and that what we call learning is really a recollection of what the soul knew before birth. To demonstrate this, he shows how an ignorant slave boy can display significant knowledge of geometry by answering suitable questions. Plato claims that this result is evidence that the slave is recollecting propositions he already knew, rather than learning them for the first time.

The dialogue introduces the important distinction between knowledge and true belief. True belief becomes knowledge by being "tied down," a process of "working out the reason," which requires recollection (98a). In other words, knowledge requires knowing why a true belief is true, and this involves knowing the basic principles that lie innate in the soul and which can be recollected.

The Paradox of Inquiry

The *paradox of inquiry* can be viewed as a challenge to the Socratic method that Plato himself tries to overcome. A paradox is an apparent contradiction. In this case, the contradiction is that there is an apparently sound argument for the conclusion that inquiry is impossible, which contradicts the seemingly obvious claim that we can inquire or learn. The argument occurs at (80a–d) and can be stated as follows:

1. For all p, either one does, or one does not know that p.
2. If one already knows that p, one can't inquire into p.
3. If one doesn't know that p, one can't inquire into p.
4. Therefore, for any p, inquiry is impossible.[7]

The first premise states the law of excluded middle concerning knowledge. The second premise states that one cannot learn what one already knows. The least obvious premise is the third. It is based on Socrates's view of the priority of definition, which we examined in the previous chapter. Accordingly, for instance, if one does not know what virtue is then one cannot examine it or ask questions about it. Plato resolves the paradox in the second half of the dialogue, and in so doing, he defends the Socratic idea of the priority of definition, but with a theory that goes beyond Socrates's own views.

Learning as Recollection

Plato answers the paradox by trying to show how all learning is really recollection. He tries to support the idea through Socrates's discussion with a slave boy about geometry. Socrates assists the boy to think through a geometrical proof simply by questioning him. The fact that the uneducated boy can complete a proof without any previous learning of geometry is meant to show Meno how the slave boy had prior knowledge of geometry, which he recollects in the course of the proof. In this way, Socrates tries to support the theory that learning is merely a recollection of knowledge already acquired by the soul. In order for the example to work, Socrates mustn't teach the slave boy, but merely facilitate his recollection of something he knew before but had since forgotten.

Given that what we call *learning* is (at least sometimes) a recollection, Plato has a reason for rejecting premise 3 in the above argument. One's inquiry can be guided by recollection. In this way, he defends the assumption of the early Socratic dialogues that one can inquire even if one lacks knowledge. Plato defends the Socratic method, but to do so he needs recourse to a metaphysics (i.e., the theory of recollection) that goes beyond the Socratic dialogues.

Knowledge and True Beliefs

Later in the dialogue, Plato distinguishes true beliefs from knowledge (97a–98c). The difference is that, to know that p, one must have an explanatory account of why p is true. In the dialogue, Plato says that knowledge is "fastened by the tie of cause," and this fastening is recollection.[8] In other words, a person who knows can explain why what he or she knows is true; this requires knowing the relevant definitions. Mere true beliefs that don't amount to knowledge lack this element.

However, Plato insists that true opinion or belief can be equally useful in guiding action as knowledge. A person who does not know the way to Larisa might have true beliefs about the right road to take and would still be a good guide, even though he or she lacked knowledge.

The distinction between knowledge and true belief helps to show why Plato thinks that premise 3 of the argument for the paradox is inadequate. Knowledge isn't necessary for inquiry; true beliefs will suffice. This also shows how Plato defends the elenchus in the *Meno*. Even if definitions are needed for knowledge, one can inquire into something (such as the nature of virtue) even if one lacks those definitions because one's inquiry can be guided by true beliefs. As we noted in the previous chapter, this distinction may help in resolving the paradox about Socrates's ignorance.

The *Meno* provides what is probably the first distinction between knowledge and true belief in the history of Western philosophy. It is a distinction that Plato returns to in other dialogues such as the *Republic* and the *Theaetetus*. Implicit in the *Meno* is the idea that knowledge is a special kind of true belief: one that is backed up with an explanatory account. This is roughly equivalent to the contemporary claim that knowledge is justified true belief: to know that p, it is necessary and sufficient to believe that p is true, when "p" is true and to have adequate justification for this belief.⁹ This point will emerge as important later on in our discussion.

Is Virtue Teachable?

The theory of recollection can help us answer the fundamental question of the dialogue: Is virtue teachable? The importance of this question is as follows. On the one hand, a sophist position will automatically imply that virtue cannot be taught: all opinions about virtue are equal. On the other hand, if virtue can be taught then this means that, in principle, there are some people more versed in virtue, and who ought to be its teachers. In other words, not all opinions about virtue are equal; some are better than others. Clearly, of the two, Plato favors the second view. In this regard, he compares virtue to medicine and other crafts. In medicine there are better and worse opinions, and for this reason there are experts, called "doctors."

THE *PHAEDO*

If the *Meno* introduces the theory of recollection then the *Phaedo* makes its metaphysical basis more apparent. The latter argues for the immortality of the soul. Dramatically, the dialogue takes place on the deathbed of the poisoned Socrates. It portrays his last conversation and the death. In this way, the *Phaedo* forms the last of a series of dialogues consisting in the earlier *Euthyphro* (which portrays Socrates on his way to the court), *Apology* (the trial), and *Crito* (Socrates refusing to escape from prison).

Nevertheless, most commentators regard the *Phaedo* as a transitional dialogue in which Plato is flexing his own philosophical muscles. For the first time, Plato explicitly argues for the existence of changeless and eternal forms, known only through thought. This dialogue was probably written after the *Meno* but before the *Republic*.

Contemplating his own death, Socrates calmly argues for the separation of the soul and the body, and for the immortality of the soul. After death, the philosopher will be able to attain the wisdom he or she sought in this life, which he or she was not able to gain before because of the confusion created by the body and its desires.

The Argument for the Forms

Plato presents his first argument for the Forms in the *Phaedo*. The Form of Equality itself cannot be identical to equally sized sticks, or any such observable object. We could be mistaken about the equality of two sticks, but we could not think that Equality itself was unequal. In other words, there must exist a Form of Equality that is distinct from all equal particular things. Furthermore, Plato argues that the Form of Equality is superior to all particular equal things. The latter are equal because they participate in the former. It is the universal form of Equality that makes equal things equal. Therefore, the Form of Equality is a paradigm of equality. In similar vein, Plato affirms the existence of the Forms of Justice, Beauty, Goodness, Health, and Strength (65d). We will examine these arguments in the next chapter.

Arguments for the Immortal Soul

Plato provides three main arguments for the existence of an immortal soul that can survive bodily death.

First, he combines his new theory of Forms with his theory of recollection to demonstrate the existence of the soul (74b–d). The Forms can only be understood through thought, although we are reminded of them in sensory perception. For example, seeing two equal sticks reminds us of the Form of Equality. Without that prior knowledge, we could not see the sticks as equal. That knowledge cannot be acquired through any sense perception and is a recollection. Consequently, we must have known the Forms prior to birth. Thus, we have evidence that a non-material soul exists. There is an implied supposition that such a soul is immortal (premise 4 below). With this supposition, we have an argument in favor of the existence of a soul that is distinct from the body.

1. Knowledge requires recollection.
2. Recollection requires the apprehension and existence of non-material Forms.
3. The only thing that could apprehend non-material Forms is a non-material soul.
4. If the soul is non-material then it is immortal.
5. Thus, an immortal soul exists.

Of course, the idea that the soul must have existed before birth to apprehend the Forms (and thereby explain how we can know anything) does not automatically imply that this soul is immortal and will survive the death of the body.

Second, perhaps to allay this criticism, Plato argues that there is a certain affinity between the soul and the Forms (78c–80c). The Forms are eternal, indivisible, and unchanging, distinct from the destructible things of the perceptible world. Plato suggests that, because these Forms are perceived only by the soul, the two must be similar. Therefore, the soul too must be eternal and distinct from the transitory world presented to the senses. If this is so, then the soul is immortal.

1. The Forms are non-material, indivisible, and eternal.
2. The soul can perceive the Forms.
3. For this perception to be possible, the soul must be similar to the Forms.
4. Therefore, the soul is non-material, indivisible and eternal.

Plato's third and final argument for the immortality of the soul is based on the claim that the soul (*psuchê*) is the principle of life (104c–107b). The soul necessarily always brings life; it animates. Since life is the opposite of death, the soul cannot die.

1. The soul is the animating principle of life.
2. A principle cannot give rise to its opposite.
3. The opposite of life is death.
4. Therefore the soul cannot give rise to death, and thus, it is immortal.

In reply, Simmias argues against the immortality of the soul. He agrees that the soul is non-material. However, because it is like the harmony produced by a lyre, dependent on the body as much as the tune is on the instrument, it is not immortal (85e–86b). Socrates replies to this challenge by arguing that the soul is not like a harmony (92e–93b):

1. The soul moves and directs the physical body.
2. A harmony cannot move or direct the physical thing it depends on.
3. Therefore, the soul is not a harmony.

In other words, our thoughts and decisions can affect changes in our bodies. If the soul were an epiphenomenal harmony then it would not be able to have this kind of effect on the body. A tune cannot change the lyre that it is played on.

Socrates provides a second and third reply to Simmias (93b–94b). The second argument is that harmonies are different in kind from souls because harmonies can come in degrees but souls cannot. In other words, an instrument can be more or less harmonious, but a soul cannot be more or less a soul. Therefore, the two are not analogous (93b). The third argument is that the soul can be evaluated qualitatively in ways that harmonies cannot. For instance, the soul can be evaluated as intelligent and virtuous (94a–b). The argument can be represented as follows:

1. All harmonies are purely quantitative relations.
2. Quantitative relations are not subject to qualitative evaluations.
3. The soul is subject to qualitative evaluations.
4. Therefore, the soul is not a harmony.

Conclusion

In this chapter, we have examined some the dialogues and argumentation that constitute the transition from the views of Socrates in the early Platonic dialogues to the views of Plato during his middle period. The early Socratic dialogues already contain the seeds of arguments against Sophism, but in a set of dialogues that are usually considered transitional, Plato shapes those criticisms for himself. In this way, he develops positive ideas that go beyond the teachings of Socrates.

For instance, in the *Meno*, Plato argues that learning is a recollection of knowledge acquired by the soul prior to birth. He contends that the idea of recollection can solve the paradox of inquiry. To develop this idea further, he distinguishes knowledge and true opinion or belief, arguing that the former requires some kind of account. The metaphysical basis of the theory of recollection is made explicit in the *Phaedo*, where Plato argues for existence of the Forms and for the existence of a nonmaterial and immortal soul.

Study Questions

1. What are the main differences between the middle and early dialogues of Plato?
2. How does Plato argue against Sophism?
3. What is Protagoras's great speech?
4. In the *Protagoras*, how does Plato defend the claim that there is no weakness of will?
5. When Gorgias compares rhetoric to boxing, how does Socrates reply?
6. How does Plato argue against hedonism in the *Gorgias*?
7. What is the paradox of inquiry in the *Meno*? How does Plato dissolve or answer the paradox?
8. In the *Meno*, how does Plato answer the question "Can virtue be taught?"
9. In the *Meno*, how does Plato distinguish knowledge and true belief?
10. What is Plato's argument for the existence of the Forms in the *Phaedo*?
11. What are the three arguments for the existence of the soul that Plato provides in the *Phaedo*?
12. How does Plato reply to the claim that the soul is a harmony?

Discussion Questions

1. Does Plato's analysis reveal the problems with Sophism? Do his arguments show us that Sophism is mistaken?
2. Are Plato's points against hedonism convincing?
3. Is Plato right to argue that the soul is immaterial? How should we assess his arguments in the light of contemporary neuroscience?

Plato
Metaphysics and Epistemology

*P*lato argues that there exist abstract, non-material entities, called *Ideas* or *Forms*. These Forms make worldly objects what they are. When a predicate term that classifies reality into different types is applied to many things, there is a Form corresponding to that term. For example, all square things are squared because they participate in the Form of squareness.

According to Plato, the existence of this realm of Forms has great ethical significance. Wisdom consists in understanding this realm, especially the Form of the Good. Knowledge of this Form will make a person virtuous and happy and, thereby, such knowledge is valuable for the political life of the community. In the *Republic*, Plato employs this point to try to show that leading a virtuous life is beneficial, quite independently of its implications for the afterlife appealed to in the *Phaedo*.

Plato's middle-period philosophy is above all about the Forms. It tries to support the idea that there are Forms, and it tries to show how their existence transforms our understanding of value, virtue, education, politics, and art. According to Plato, a proper understanding of mathematics, language, science and knowledge requires the existence of the Forms. Following most commentators, we can call this body of writing *Plato's Theory of Forms*, so long as it is understood that Plato never developed a fully-fledged theory.

We can see Plato's theory as showing what is wrong with both the naturalism of the Pre-Socratics and with Sophism. Both kinds of theory are inadequate because they lack the Forms. Pre-Socratic naturalism cannot explain why X is F by citing the ways that matter moves. In this sense, explanations couched in terms of material causes are insufficient. To explain properly why X is F requires citing what F-ness is. In other words, naturalistic philosophy lacks the necessary appeal to abstract universals—specifically, the Forms. As an integral part of this lack, naturalistic philosophy cannot account for the role of the mind or the soul in understanding: there must be a soul to grasp these Forms.

In a parallel manner, Sophism is mistaken because it denies that there are objective value claims about what is good. At most, it can only inform us how to get what we want. It cannot tell us what is desirable and why. Thus, it cannot help us to understand what the good life is, and how this relates to justice and the state. Such understandings require comprehension of the Form of the Good, and to show how humans can come to know Goodness. In more general terms, Sophism is also inadequate because it cannot account for how false claims are possible because it lacks the Forms; it makes all claims relative to opinion, at least in some versions of Sophism.[1]

In a similar fashion, we can see how Plato thinks that the Theory of Forms allows him to go beyond the limitations of the Socratic method and Socrates's views. Plato retains a fundamentally Socratic interest in showing why Sophism is mistaken, and in showing why it is never good for the soul of a person to commit wrong acts. However, as our study of the *Republic* will show us, Plato thinks that the Theory of Forms provides a powerful way to argue these points that was not available to Socrates.

The middle period dialogues include the *Republic*, *Phaedrus*, and *Symposium*. The *Parmenides* and *Theaetetus* are usually also classified as middle period dialogues, but they also mark Plato's transition to the later period. For this reason, we will examine them in the last chapter on Plato. The *Republic* is Plato's most famous and complete work. In it, Plato tries to show how justice is its own reward, and in so doing he develops a theory about the ideal state and the principles that should govern it. He also develops a theory of the soul and its relation to the Form of Goodness. The *Phaedrus* contains two contrasting speeches of Socrates about the nature of love and its relation to the beautiful. These themes also form the backbone of the *Symposium*, in which at a party Socrates reports on his discussion with the poetess Diotima. In this chapter, we will restrict ourselves to the metaphysics and epistemology of the middle period dialogues. We will save ethics, politics, beauty, and love for the next chapter.

The Theory of Forms

It is not so easy to determine what exactly Plato's Theory of Forms is. Plato doesn't formulate it as an explicit theory until the *Parmenides*, by which time he is ready to criticize it. Nevertheless, despite the lack of clarity, it is possible to discern four or five theses that constitute the theory.

Ontological Claim

The first we can call the *ontological thesis*, according to which, for some property F, there exists an abstract universal F-ness, which we can call the *Form of F-ness*. In other words, there is a realm of unchanging abstract universal objects, which exist distinctly from the realm of changing material perceptible objects and independently of us.

There are at least three important contrasts in this claim. First, universal versus particular: the Form is a universal in the sense that it can be shared by many particular things but is not identical to any of them. For example, the Form of Circularity is universal because all particular circles participate in that Form. Plato argues that the universal Form is not identical with any particular instance that instantiates it. The Form would exist even if no particular instances of it did. According to this view, there is a Form of a chiliagon (a two-dimensional figure with 1,000 sides) even if no such figure exists in physical reality.[2]

A second contrast is between the changing and the unchanging. The world of particulars is in flux. In contrast, the Forms are changeless. The Forms constitute an eternal realm distinct from the ever-changing physical world. This attempts to reconcile the conflict between the views of Heraclitus and Parmenides: the former was right to claim that the world of perceptible objects is ever-changing; the latter was right to claim that reality is changeless. Both were right and mistaken, each in their own way, about distinct domains.

The claim that Plato reconciles the conflict between Heraclitus's and Parmenides's views needs an important qualification. Plato does not give the two equal weight. In a sense that we are about to explore, Plato gives priority to the unchanging world of the Forms. The perceptual world of changing particulars is in some sense less real than the eternal Forms. This is why, according to Plato, human development consists in ascending from becoming to being, as we shall see in the next chapter.

Third, the ontological thesis about Forms carries with it an epistemological contrast. In brief, there is a contrast between the sensible objects known by perception and the abstract objects known by thought. This epistemological contrast between perception and thought is contentious, and we shall return to it later.

The Unity Thesis

The Form of F-ness is what makes F-things F. It is what all the particular things that are F have in common, and what makes them Fs. For instance, the universal Form of Justice is what makes just actions just. This is sometimes called the *Unity Thesis* because the Form F brings unity to all the disparate instances of F.

Because of the Unity Thesis, the Forms have definitional significance. To know the definition of the term *F* it is necessary to know the Form of F-ness. As we saw, F-ness is what all Fs have in common. Thus, knowing the Form will constitute knowing the definition of the relevant property word, which requires us to know the essence of the thing or kind in question. To know the definition of *justice*, one needs to know the Form of Justice, which provides us with the essence of Justice. This essence is what all and only just actions must have in common. Thus, the definition of justice consists in a set of necessary and sufficient conditions. From this we can conclude that the Form is what makes just actions just. It explains what makes just acts just. F-ness is what makes F-things F.

Exemplary Self-Predication

According to Plato, each Form F itself has the property of being F. For example, the Form of the Beautiful is itself beautiful; the Form of the Good is itself good. Plato's reasoning for this thesis is probably that what makes all F-things F must itself be F. Furthermore, in addition to being self-predicative, the Forms are paradigms or standards of the quality in question. The Form of Goodness is the perfect or paradigm good; the Form of the Just is the perfect exemplary of justice; the Form of Beauty is beautiful par excellence. In short, the third thesis is that the Form of F-ness is F-ness in its perfection. For the sake of clarity, we might divide this third thesis into two parts: self-predication as such (i.e., the Form F-ness is itself F) and the exemplary thesis (i.e., the Form F-ness is the perfect paradigm of being F). We shall explore what the latter means in a moment.

The Reality of the Forms

The Unity Thesis and the Exemplary Self-Predication Thesis together suggest the idea that the Forms are more real than the world of particulars. If the Form of F-ness is a perfect paradigm of being F and given that all F things are F because of that Form, we can begin to see why Plato would think that the realm of Forms is more real than the transitory world of things that we perceive.

As we shall see, according to Plato, the world of particular just actions has a relationship to Justice that is similar to the relationship between the shadow of a rose and the real rose. Particular things are like passing shadows. The world we normally live in is imperfect. For example, perfect beauty belongs only to the Form, the beautiful itself. One way to interpret this is to claim is that sensible Fs are only approximately F; they are not really F. What we regard as beautiful particulars are only approximately or ambiguously beautiful.[3]

Because of the above discussion, the existence of the Forms has an enormous epistemological, ethical, and political significance. Their existence establishes a contrast between perceptual opinion on the one hand, and real knowledge on the other. Mere perception of circles cannot provide knowledge of what it is to be a circle. Such knowledge must come from an intellectual apprehension of the Forms. Indeed, such apprehension must be prior to birth. Because of this, we can be sure that the soul is distinct from the body and is immortal. Furthermore, the existence of the Forms has a huge ethical and political importance, which we will examine in the next chapter. In short, to be good, it is necessary to know the Form of the Good. A just society should be organized around this simple point. Indeed, Plato depicts life as a journey out of a metaphorical cave towards the Forms, from darkness to light.

Some Problems of Interpretation

We have taken Plato's metaphysical theory of the Forms to consist in four main theses. However, it is debatable what they mean, and to what extent these views really are Plato's. In this section, we will look at three such questions.

Which Properties? Are there Forms for all properties or only some? Certainly, in the middle dialogues, Plato typically argues for Forms in the cases of abstract moral properties such as Justice, Beauty and Good. However, in the *Republic*, apparently, he affirms that: "whenever a name is applied to many different things, there is a Form corresponding to the name" (596a). In that dialogue, he postulates forms for artifacts such as beds.

In sharp contrast to the *Republic*, there is the suggestion in the *Cratylus* that Plato restricts the word *name* so that something is a name only if it picks out a real property or kind. This passage suggests that Plato's idea might be that forms are properties that "carve at the natural joints" (265e12)—in which case, there are forms only for natural properties.

Furthermore, many commentators think that Plato tries to clarify explicitly these aspects of his Theory of Forms only in the later dialogues, such as the *Parmenides, Statesman,* and *Sophist*. In the *Statesman*, Plato says that if a name indicates a non-arbitrary classification of reality then there is no Form corresponding to it. For example, there is no Form *barbarian* because the group non-Greek is not a genuine whole, and the Greek vs. non-Greek division is arbitrary (262c–e). Therefore, it is possible that Plato changed his mind to become more ontologically conservative in his later period.

Properties or Meanings? Are the Forms properties or meanings, or, perhaps, both? The idea that they are meanings might be explained as follows. A general word must have a non-particular meaning, and it does so by referring to or naming a universal Form. For instance, the term *circularity* doesn't refer to particular circles. Its meaning is the universal Form that it refers to. According to this view, there is a Form for every meaningful general term.[4]

We can see how Plato might have arrived at this idea through an analogy based on the contemplation of mathematical objects as follows. Nothing in this world is a perfect circle. Yet there must exist such an object in order for the word *circularity* to have meaning and in order for us to be able to explain what ordinary circles have in common. However, as we shall see later, it is debatable whether Plato regards the Forms, or even some of them, as semantic meanings. The point is that if Plato thinks that the Forms are only natural properties then they are not meanings. In other words, if the former view is true, then Plato thinks that there are Forms corresponding only to properties such as "being water" and perhaps mathematical properties such as "being a triangle." On the other hand, if the latter view is true, then Plato thinks that there are Forms corresponding to every meaningful predicate-term such as "is a unicorn."[5]

Self-Predication. What does Plato mean by saying that the Form F is itself F (i.e., by self-predication)? Taken at its simplest, the idea might be that Form F is F in much the same way that a particular is F, except perfectly. For example, the Form of Goodness is good in much the same way that a wise person is good, except only perfectly. *Perfectly* in this context probably means unambiguously. Even the wise person would be unwise in some respects and therefore will not be unambiguously wise or good. In contrast, the Form of Goodness itself would be perfectly good.

This simple way of interpreting Plato's idea of the self-predication of the Forms is open to some serious objections. For instance, it seems to make the Forms both universals and particulars at the same time. It would make the Form a particular insofar as it is the subject of the predicate.

There is, however, another more sophisticated way to understand Plato's conception of self-predication. The idea is that when Plato asserts that the Form F is itself F, this should not be understood as asserting that the Form is F in a manner similar to the way that particular things are F. In other words, for example, the Form of Largeness isn't itself really big in size.[6] The idea is that the Form of F is itself F only in the sense that it explains why all F things are F. In other words, the Form of F is intrinsically F. So, for instance, the Form of Largeness isn't itself something huge, but rather it is intrinsic to the concept of largeness that anything that is large is big in size because of its relation to the Form of Largeness.

Arguments for the Forms

Plato provides us with various arguments for the ontological claim that the Forms exist separately from the sensible world of particulars.

Arguments from Relativity

Plato's most explicit argument for the existence of Forms as distinct from perceivables occurs in the *Phaedo* at 74b–c.3. We can summarize the argument as follows:

Argument A:

1. Any two equal sticks can appear equal to one person and not to another.
2. Equality itself cannot appear unequal.
3. Therefore, equality itself is distinct from any perceptible equal things.

Any perceptible equal things can appear unequal. For example, two equal sticks that appear equal at a distance will look unequal under a microscope. However, equality itself cannot appear unequal, even sometimes. If it did, then it would not be equality anymore but rather inequality, which is absurd. Plato concludes that the Form of Equality must be distinct from particular objects and that perceptibles are only "deficiently" equal. This argument can be extended to other perceivable properties.

Another similar argument for the claim that the Forms are distinct from perceptibles occurs at *Republic* 475c–480a. Plato refers to large and small, heavy and light, and hard and soft as "contraries," and he claims that perceptibles can present contrary appearances simultaneously (523b–c, 524d–525a). For instance, he maintains that every perceptible thing that appears beautiful can also appear ugly (479a–c). The same applies for "just," "double," "large," and "heavy." He concludes that sensible objects are "no more are than they are not what one calls them" (b9–10). That is, says Plato, a perceptible thing no more is F than it is not F.

This suggests the following interpretation. Plato is trying to point out, first, that when we say that something X is F, the implication is that X is F is independent of both the viewpoint of the judger and the circumstances of the object. In other words, the idea that X really is F implies that it is so, irrespective of both context and point of view. Second, however, judgments about perceptible objects fail to meet these criteria. Judged in one way, something is beautiful; judged in another way, it is not. Thus, we cannot claim that a perceptual object X really is F.[7] Perceptual objects are always ambivalently F, that is, "it is impossible to think of [them] . . . as being or as not being or as both or as neither" (479C3–5).

If this way of reading Plato captures an aspect of his thought, then we can represent his argumentation in the *Phaedo* and *Republic* as follows:

Argument B:

1. The claim "X really is F" implies that X is so, irrespective of context and point of view.

2. All judgments about any perceptible object being F fail to meet these criteria.

---

3. Therefore, all perceptual objects are ambivalently F.

This argument helps us to understand how Plato disagrees with the Sophist. According to the Sophist, the fact that water appears or feels cold to one person and not to another implies that the water is cold to the first person and not to the second. This means that Sophism denies the first premise of Plato's argument. In so doing, it implies that no one can be mistaken, as Plato points out in the *Protagoras* (sometimes this is called *infallibilism*). At the same time, the above argument allows us to see that Plato and the Sophists actually agree on a fundamental point. Sophism draws our attention to the fact that our judgments about the object of perception are ineluctably relative to context and point of view (i.e., to premise 2.). In this regard, Plato and the Sophists agree.

The above way of reading Plato's argumentation may avoid the objection (originally from Owen) that Plato fails to recognize that judgments like "X is cold" and "X is small" are implicitly relational.[8] According to this criticism of Plato, a judgment such as "X is cold" really means something like "X is colder than Y," even though the comparison with Y is left implicit. According to the criticism, Plato fails to recognize this point in the relevant passages in the *Phaedo* and *Republic* mentioned above. In other words, he treats these implicitly relational properties as if they were monadic (or non-relational). Plato's argument is flawed because of this mistake.

However, this way of reading the key passages in the *Republic* seems to be too unsympathetic. Plato does recognize the difference between relational and non-relational properties in other contexts.[9] Thus, if there is a more charitable way of interpreting these passages, then we should adopt it. Argument B above does exactly this.

Arguments from Predication

Plato often says that perceptible objects "partake" or "participate" in Forms. This seems to imply that F-ness is not identical to the many F-things. This is because those F-things must have something in common, and this one something must be distinct from any of those particulars.

There is another argument for the existence of the Forms based on explanation. In the discussion with Cebes in the *Phaedo*, Socrates says:

> It seems to me that if anything is beautiful besides the Beautiful-itself, [that other thing] is beautiful for no other reason than because it participates in the Beautiful-itself, and that this applies to all [these other] things. (100c3–8)

This passage suggests that Plato's idea is that we should explain why X is beautiful as follows. Consider the following reasoning:

Argument C:

1. Anything that participates in the Form of Beauty is beautiful.
2. X participates in the Form of the Beautiful.

---

3. Thus, X is beautiful.

The idea is that we must explain the conclusion 3 by citing the two premises (1 and 2) that entail it. In other words, conclusion 3 is explained by premises 1 and 2.

This idea can be used to argue for the Forms because the explanation of why X is beautiful requires the claim that there exists a Form of Beauty independent from any beautiful thing. You can see that premises 1 and 2 assume that the Form of the Beautiful exists. Consequently, if things are beautiful, then there must exist a Form of Beauty. More slowly: if things are beautiful, then there must be an explanation of why this is so, and as Plato says, this explanation must involve the Forms, and so they exist. This argument in favor of the existence of the Forms can be generalized for other Forms apart from Beauty as follows:

Argument D:

4. If the explanation of some claim B requires the existence of F, then if B is true F really exists.
5. B is true.

6. Thus, F really exists.

Premise 4 restates what we said about Beauty in more general terms. As we saw, Plato claims that an explanation why X is beautiful requires the existence of the Forms (i.e., to explain 3 above, one must invoke 1 and 2, which assume the existence of the relevant Form). Premise 4 simply says that if the explanation of some fact (*B*) would involve the existence of a Form (*F*), then given that fact (*B*), then F exists. Premise 5 affirms that the fact (*B*) is indeed given (such as the one referred to in premise 3, namely, that X is beautiful).

Epistemological Arguments

As we have seen, the *Phaedo* contains an argument to the effect that knowledge requires the existence of Forms. This claim is also elaborated in the *Republic*. To have knowledge of F-things as such, one must know the essential nature of F-things, and this requires knowing the Form of F-ness. For instance, to have knowledge of good things (as such or with respect to their goodness) requires that we know what goodness is, and this requires existences of the relevant Form.

Plato may have another argument for the Forms based on knowledge. It appeals to the impossibility of knowledge in an ever-changing Heraclitean world. According to this argument, since sensible or perceivable objects are always changing, there cannot be knowledge of them. Nevertheless, we do have knowledge and, consequently, there must be unchanging Forms that constitute the objects of such knowledge.

Aristotle attributes this argument to Plato.[10] However, there are some reasons for thinking that Plato would not argue in this manner. In particular, as we saw in chapter 1, there is an extreme view that claims that all things are constantly in flux *in all respects*; although Cratylus may have held this view, it is probable that Heraclitus didn't. To argue that we cannot have knowledge of sensible things because they are ever-changing requires the extreme view that they are always changing *in all respects*, and there is no direct textual evidence that Plato held such a view.

Semantic Arguments

If Plato thinks that Forms were meanings, then he might argue for the existence of the Forms from the meaning of general terms. To see the idea, take the sentence, "Homer is blind." According to what we might call today a *referential theory of meaning*, in order to be meaningful the relevant parts of the sentence must refer to or name something. The name

"Homer" refers to a particular individual (i.e., Homer) and derives its meaning through this reference. According to a referential theory of meaning, in order to be meaningful the word "blind" must also refer to something. Clearly, it does not refer to an individual or particular. Thus, it must obtain its meaning by referring to a non-particular or to a universal that can be shared between individuals.

Does Plato actually employ this kind of argument? The textual evidence is meager. *Republic* (X, 596a67) suggests this semantic form of argumentation; Socrates says:

> We are, I suppose, in the habit of positing some one form for each group of many things to which we apply the same name.[11]

This suggests there is a Form for very general term, but it doesn't claim that the Form is the meaning of the term or that the existence of the Forms is necessary for general terms to have meaning. In contrast, if Plato restricts the Forms to only natural properties (i.e., he doesn't include meanings), then the semantic argument for the Forms would not be available to him.

Sophism Is False

If Plato thinks that the only alternative to his theory of Forms is the subjectivism inherent in Sophism, then his arguments against Sophism would count as arguments for the Theory of Forms. In other words, Plato might think that, in absence of Forms, Sophism would be true or all claims would be merely a matter of individual judgment, as Protagoras seems to claim. If he makes this assumption, then all his arguments against Sophism would *ipso facto* be arguments in favor of the Theory of Forms.

THE *REPUBLIC*

This is the most important dialogue of the middle period and is arguably Plato's greatest work. The dialogue gives us an overview of Plato's grand theory from epistemology to metaphysics, and from ethics to politics and art. Plato's thought reaches its maturity in the *Republic*. He tries to resolve the fundamental ethical problems raised by Socrates without appealing to the afterlife as he had done in the earlier *Phaedo*. (However, this isn't exactly right because Plato includes an appeal to the afterlife in Book X—but by this time, the main arguments for the Socratic claim that it is better to be just are already completed).

We will examine Plato's theory of justice and of the state in the next chapter. Before we look at the issues pertaining to metaphysics and epistemology in this chapter, let us briskly review the layout of the *Republic*. To present the overall structure of the book, here is a brief synopsis of the work. It consists of ten books. The main unifying theme is that it is better, or more advantageous, to be just than unjust, but many other illuminating ideas revolve around this central theme.

Overview

In Book I, Socrates tries to define justice and apparently fails on the first round. In contrast to Socrates, Thrasymachus (a Sophist) affirms that justice is not necessarily beneficial to the person who performs just actions. He defines justice as "the advantage of the stronger" and "the good of another" (338c and 343c). Although Socrates argues against Thrasymachus's view of justice, Book I seems to end inconclusively. Plato now has a challenge to meet: to argue that justice is beneficial to the person who acts justly. Many commentators claim that the fact that Book I fails to reach a definitive conclusion is important. It indicates Plato's changing relationship to Socrates. It signals that, in order to answer the challenge of Sophism, Plato needs to use a method of argumentation and to employ concepts (such as the Forms) that were not part of Socrates's philosophy. In other words, Plato is drawing attention to the shortcomings of Socrates's method.

Book II defines the challenge of Sophism more definitively. The two brothers, Glaucon and Adeimantus, add to Socrates's task by arguing that one should act unjustly if one can get away with it by using the imaginary example of the ring of Gyges, which makes a person invisible. In reply, Socrates affirms that to understand justice, we must examine it first in the case of the state (386c–369a). In other words, Plato proposes to answer the challenges concerning the just individual by examining justice and the state. He describes a model of the perfectly just city-state.

In the remainder of Book II and in Book III and IV, Plato portrays a society consisting of three groups: artisans and merchants; soldiers; and rulers. Plato's main thesis in this part of the book is that the society he describes would be just because the three social elements would be working harmoniously, each fulfilling its proper role according its nature. The reader should beware because, at first, Plato calls the military class "the guardians," but later he reserves the term for the ruling class only, and he calls the military class "auxiliaries." Part of Plato's discussion (from 376c–403c) concerns the role of poetry and myths in the education of the guardians.

In Book IV, Plato introduces the idea of a tripartite division of the soul. He argues for the principle that the same thing will not be able to undergo opposites in the same part of itself at the same time (436b). He employs this principle to conclude that the soul must have three parts: desire, the spirited, and reason. He then compares the divisions of the soul with the three parts of the state, and he argues that justice for the individual also consists in the three elements of the soul working harmoniously, each fulfilling its role according to its nature (423b-436b and 441c–445e).

In Plato's political philosophy, a good political community is one that promotes the well-being of all its citizens. The basis of political power is not the consent of the governed because people may not understand well what is in their best interests, and may accept a system that is not beneficial to them. In contrast, the leaders must have such understanding, and it is their duty to educate the people. In Plato's republic, the leaders have great power, but this does not mean that they should abuse it. For this reason, Plato recommends abolishing private property and the family for the ruling class. The city-state should be designed for the happiness of all the citizens, and not for just one group.

Book V begins with a controversial discussion of the status of women within the society. Around section 472, Plato begins to argue that the rulers of the society should be philosophers, or lovers of wisdom.

In Book VI, in order to show what a true philosopher is, Plato distinguishes between opinion and knowledge, arguing that the latter requires acquaintance with the Forms. Around section 507, he introduces his famous simile that compares the Form of the Good to the Sun. The Form of the Good makes the Forms knowable, just as the Sun makes physical things visible. Around 510, he uses the Divided Line analogy to describe four types of access to reality in order to clarify his distinction between knowledge and opinion.

In Book VII, Plato draws the famous Analogy of the Cave. He compares the situation of most people to that of prisoners in a cave who can only see things as shadows cast by torchlight. Like these prisoners, we are subject to a systematic illusion, believing that transitory ordinary objects are real, while in fact these are only the shadows of the Forms. Plato's analogy implies that the world of ordinary everyday objects is less real than that of the Forms. This shows the real importance of virtue. By coming to know the Forms, we can acquire virtue and thereby escape from the cave or from illusions.

Book VIII considers different imperfect societies and compares them to the imperfections of an individual person. Plato describes four political systems, in addition to the ideal one already discussed. These four are timocracy, oligarchy, democracy and dictatorship. In each case, Plato compares the problems of one of these societies to the nature of the corresponding personality or character type.

Book IX contains the final argument for the main conclusion that the just person would be happier than an unjust person.

In Book X, Plato discusses art. He distinguishes three uses of the word *bed*. It can apply to the painting or image of a bed; to a physical bed; and to the Form. Plato suggests that the relation between the image and the physical bed is similar to the relation of the physical bed to the Form: in both cases the former is less real than the latter. Only the Form is completely real. The physical bed is less real than the Form because it depends on the latter in a manner similar to the dependency of the image on the bed. Plato uses this comparison to argue that poetry and art do not give us real knowledge and can corrupt the soul. Finally, he gives an argument for the immortality of the soul and tells the myth of Er, which describes the rewards in the life after death for the just person.

The Analogy of the Sun

In Book VI, Plato tries to characterize a wise person. In order to do this, towards the end of *Republic* V, he distinguishes between belief and knowledge. He also argues that knowledge requires the existence of the Forms. These passages in the *Republic* are followed by the famous analogies of the Sun, the Line, and the Cave.

In the Analogy of the Sun, Plato compares the Form of Goodness to the Sun (507c–509b). Just as the Sun illuminates and makes possible vision of all other objects, the Form of Goodness makes it possible for us to apprehend or know the other Forms. In this analogy, just as the Sun makes sight possible, the Form of the Good makes knowledge possible. Likewise, just as the eye makes seeing possible, so do reason or intelligence make knowing possible. Because of its role as preeminent among Forms, the Good is the pinnacle of existence. Socrates says that it is "beyond being" (509b).

Why does Plato think that the Form of the Good makes knowledge of the other Forms possible? In part answer, remember that each of the Forms defines a perfect ideal. The Form of F is F perfectly. For instance, the Form of the Circle is circularity at its perfection. Consequently, to grasp each Form requires knowing the Form of Goodness. If each Form is perfectly F, then goodness or perfection is involved in each of the Forms. A more complete reply requires reference to one of Plato's later dialogues, the *Timaeus*, which we examine in chapter 8.

The Divided Line

The idea of the priority of the Forms is made clearer in the subsequent section on the Divided Line (509d–511e). Socrates draws a line in the sand, which he divides into four unequal parts. On the left-hand side of the line, he writes four types of objects: the Forms, mathematical objects, sensible objects, and images. The main point of this aspect of the analogy is to show that the lower level of objects depends asymmetrically on the next higher level. Images depend for their existence on objects, but not vice versa, much in the way that a shadow depends on an object. Likewise, sensible objects depend on mathematical objects in an asymmetric manner, which in turn depend on the Forms.

Why does Plato have four kinds of objects? Why are mathematical objects different from the Forms? In his *Metaphysics*, Aristotle provides an answer. He says that, according to Plato, mathematical objects lie between sensible objects and Forms. Both differ from sensible objects in that they are eternal and unchangeable. However, mathematical objects differ from Forms in that "they are many and alike" (1.6 987 4–18).

On the right-hand side of the line, Plato names four types of cognition, which correspond to the four objects. These consist of two kinds of knowledge (*episteme*): thought and intelligence, and two kinds of belief (*doxa*): imagination and trust. Imagination might be characterized as the cognitive state in which one accepts conventional views without critical review. Trust is when one has some reason for thinking that one's beliefs are true, but this justification is not yet sufficient for knowledge.

The Analogy of the Divided Line also postulates two kinds of knowledge: thought and intelligence. Thought is a lower kind of knowledge in the sense that one has to rely on certain assumptions or hypotheses to justify one's beliefs. In other words, the justification for one's beliefs is limited because it requires assumptions. Plato thinks that this kind of knowledge constitutes the sciences and mathematics. In contrast, intelligence is the highest kind of knowledge, where one grasps the Forms directly and understands how they relate to the Form of the Good.

In summary, in the Divided Line, Plato characterizes four kinds of objects and four kinds of cognitive state as follows:

Kinds of Existence:
Form   Mathematical Objects   Objects   Images

Kinds of Cognition:
Intelligence   Scientific Knowledge   Trust   Imagination

Socrates divides the line unequally. This point has significance. The first act of dividing cuts the whole line (K–N) into two parts: knowledge and opinion. The first part, knowledge (K–O), is a larger segment than the latter one, opinion (O–N). This inequality represents the great clarity of knowledge over opinion. In the second act of dividing, each of the two parts (knowledge and opinion) are themselves subdivided in the same proportions as the first cut. In the illustration below, Knowledge is cut into K–T (intelligence) and T–O (thought) and Opinion into O–I (trust) and I–N (imagination). This indicates, for instance, that with regard to knowledge, intelligence is clearer than thought in the same proportion than knowledge is clearer than opinion.

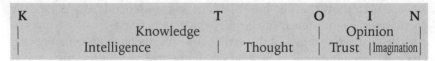

Returning to Socrates's original line, the ratios between the left-hand side (ontological) and right-hand side (cognitive) of the lines will be the same. In other words, the intelligible and visible realm of objects will be similar in proportion to the difference between what is known and what is believed.

In these passages, Plato appears to make knowledge correspond with the Forms, and mere belief with sensible objects. It seems then that, in these passages, Plato expounds a Two-Worlds Theory according to which knowledge is restricted to the Forms, and belief to sensible objects. This renders knowledge and belief mutually exclusive.[12] In other words, we cannot have knowledge of sensibles, or mere beliefs about Forms.

If this is Plato's view in the *Republic*, then it conflicts with the more moderate claims of the earlier dialogue the *Meno*, according to which knowledge is a special kind of true belief. In the *Meno*, Plato doesn't restrict knowledge to the Forms. They aren't the only objects of knowledge even if, to know anything, one must know the relevant Forms. Remember that in the earlier dialogue, Plato implies that one can have knowledge of the road to Larissa. In other words, we can have knowledge of particulars in the *Meno*.

The same epistemological issue arises in the *Timaeus*. In this dialogue, Plato seems to embrace a Two-Worlds epistemology, in which he distinguishes between true opinion and understanding as part of an argument for the existence of the Forms (51b–d). Understanding involves a true account and is unmoved by persuasion, unlike true opinion. In other words, to understand something, it is not sufficient to have true belief, but one must also have a true account, which specifies why the claim in question is true and which requires appeal to the existence of the relevant Forms. In the course of this exposition, he says that the Forms cannot be perceived but are only the objects of understanding.

The Analogy of the Cave

We now come to Plato's famous allegory of the Cave, rich with many layers of meanings. In the allegory, Plato postulates four levels or conditions of human existence.

First, in the Cave, the prisoners are only acquainted with the shadows or images of real things, which are of puppets cast by the artificial light of a fire. In this sense, the prisoners live a dream-like existence: they systematically confuse the shadows or images thrown on the wall for real things. They cannot turn around to see the objects or puppets whose shadows are reflected on the wall.

Through education, some people are at least able to turn their heads, and they realize that the shadows or images are reflections of objects. Unfortunately, these objects are only puppets: artifacts or reproductions of animals and persons. Furthermore, what they see is by courtesy of the artificial light of the fire, and not the natural illumination of the Sun. Although these people are not chained, they still remain in the Cave, unable to make the steep path out of the Cave into the sunlight and the real world.

Those who are able to escape the Cave are at first dazzled, but finally they are able to adjust their eyes to the sunlight and eventually, they can see the originals of which they had previously seen only reproductions (and worse, shadows of reproductions). Nevertheless, they are not able to fully understand their situation because they are still fettered by their desires.

Fourth, those who are most free are able to see and contemplate how the Sun is the cause of all sight. These people are lovers of wisdom.

We will return to an important aspect of the allegory in the next chapter: Plato's description of the moral ascension from the Cave to the Sun. This ascent has its metaphysical and epistemological aspects, but it is also a journey of liberation from desire. These lovers of wisdom are the guardians of the city.

Plato's allegory of the Cave has several political aspects. First, the prisoners in the Cave are prisoners of others, who manipulate the images. Second, Plato portrays those who find enlightenment as under an obligation to return to the cave in order to help free the prisoners and administer the state (519d–521b and 540a).

There are some similarities between the four kinds of human existence described in the Analogy of the Cave and the four sections of the Divided Line. For example, the Cave represents the visible world. However, there are differences; the analogies do not match up and Plato probably did not intend that they do so. For instance, the Line distinguishes between Forms and mathematical objects; the Cave does not. In the Cave, there is a distinction between, for instance, an animal and a puppet or model of that animal. This distinction does not occur in the Line.

Conclusion

Much contemporary analytic philosophy would tend to reject the dualism inherent in Plato's Theory of the Forms. Plato's theory is dualistic in that it postulates the existence of two realms, one nonmaterial and the other material. Many contemporary thinkers argue against dualism on the grounds that nonphysical entities could not have any causal effect on the physical. How can the nonmaterial Forms have causal influence on our bodily existence? As we have seen, Plato would answer this by claiming that there is a nonmaterial soul that grasps the Forms. However, this raises the similar question of how a nonmaterial soul can influence the body. Finding no satisfactory answer to this kind of questioning, many contemporary philosophers argue that the appeal to nonmaterial abstract objects and nonmaterial souls are explanatorily redundant. Such appeals cannot help explain observable physical phenomena.

Despite this, versions of Plato's Theory of Forms are popular in several areas of contemporary philosophy. Any view that postulates the existence of abstract objects distinct from material objects and distinct from states of consciousness may be called *platonic*. For instance, mathematical Platonism is the claim that there exist abstract entities such as numbers and sets. It is an important view in recent philosophy of mathematics, advanced by the great logician Gödel and contemporary mathematician Roger Penrose, among many others. Penrose's book, *The Emperor's New Clothes*, contains a popular exposition of his philosophy of mathematics.

Another contemporary platonic view claims that propositions exist as abstract entities. When two or more assertions have the same meaning, for instance, "Il neige," "Esta nevando," and "It's snowing," we say that they express the same proposition. A proposition is the meaning of an assertion or a declarative sentence. Gottlob Frege (1848–1925) argued for the existence of propositions or senses as abstract objects distinct from material objects and states of consciousness. Several contemporary philosophers of language hold a similar view. This is a platonic claim. Furthermore, the claim that there exist possible worlds as abstract entities would also count as a platonic view. In this manner, the recent theory called *possible world semantics*, which tries to explain semantic meaning in terms of possible worlds, has a tendency towards being platonic.

Philosophers today still question the nature of properties and universals. In what sense are properties real? The idea that they can exist apart from particulars (for example, that there exists the property of being a dodo, even though no such birds exist because they are extinct) seems to provide support for a quasi-Platonist position regarding properties or universals. Some contemporary thinkers, such as David Armstrong and Michael Tooley, argue that a realist position regarding universals is required for understanding causal laws. Such laws express a relationship of necessity between universals that exist independently of physical objects.

Plato's direct influence is felt in many other areas of contemporary philosophy. For example, he defined knowledge as justified true belief, and this definition was accepted widely until the 1970s, when causal and other theories of knowledge also became popular. His claim that sense perception cannot yield understanding of the reasons why things are as they are expresses a dissatisfaction with empiricist accounts of perception and knowledge that has been expressed by many thinkers over the generations. This dissatisfaction is voiced at times in terms of the need for innate concepts or abilities, and sometimes as the need for universal principles.

Stepping back to the broader picture of the history of philosophy, it is difficult to underestimate the overall influence of Plato on the history of thought, especially his views concerning the reality of the Forms, and the nature of the soul and knowledge. Additionally, we have mentioned already how the ideas of Pythagoras and Parmenides entered Western thought largely through Plato. At the same time, as we shall see, Plato had a huge influence on the thought of Aristotle, despite the major differences between them, and Aristotle has an extraordinarily wide impact on Western thinking.

Plato's direct influence on the history of philosophy came in three major waves: the first, around 380, in wedlock with Christianity; the second, around 1450, in opposition to the doctrine of the Church; and the third in the form of seventeenth-century rationalism.

The first wave began with Plotinus (205–270 AD), who argued in favor of Platonism and against Stoicism and Epicureanism. Broadly speaking, Plotinus identified Plato's form of the Good with God, with which the inner part of the soul has direct contact. In brief, Plotinus's influential Neo-Platonism highlighted certain affinities between Plato's thought and the emerging Christianity. Augustine (354–430), who studied Plotinus and Plato before converting to Christianity, made those affinities more explicit by trying to reconcile Platonism and Christianity. In the process he produced a theology that dominated Christian and, hence, Western thought until Aquinas, around 1260. Because of Aquinas, Plato's influence was eclipsed by that of Aristotle, whose works (which had been largely unknown in Europe) were reintroduced into the continent by Arab thinkers through the Moors in Spain.

However, two hundred years later, a second wave of Platonism broke upon Western thought. During the Renaissance, Europeans scholars rediscovered their forgotten ancient pagan heritage—including much of Plato's philosophy, which, as a consequence, for the second time had a major impact on the history of thought. In 1441, Cosimo Medici established a platonic academy in Florence, which was attended by the artist Michelangelo and the thinker Pico della Mirandola, who wrote *On the Dignity of Man*. Cosimo also funded Marsilio Ficino to devote himself to the translation of Plato's works. This revival of Plato helped to establish the humanism of the fifteenth century and end the supremacy of Scholastic philosophy based on Aquinas's interpretation of Aristotle. The humanism of the Renaissance focused attention away from God and towards the individual. Consequently, it drew inspiration less from Plato's otherworldly theory of forms but more from his theory of the soul, which emphasizes the noble nature of a person, as well as from the breadth and literary quality of Plato's dialogues.

In turn, humanism enabled the scientific revolution that marked the transition from medieval to modern philosophy in the later half of the sixteenth century. At this stage in the development of thought, Plato's writings became influential for another reason: like the thought of Pythagoras, they stress the mathematical order of the universe, which inspired scientists such as Galileo and Kepler to formulate their scientific theories in precise mathematical terms.

The third surge of Platonic thinking occurred in the seventeenth and eighteenth centuries. Rationalists such as Spinoza and Leibniz opposed empiricist thinkers, such as Locke, who argued that all knowledge and concepts must be derived from sense-experience. In opposition to this, the rationalists were impressed by the platonic arguments for the conclusion that sense-experience is illusory. Moreover, according to these rationalists, sense-experience never provides knowledge of real causes, which requires appeal to general principles (such as the Principle of Sufficient Reason, which can be known through reason alone).

Study Questions

1. According to Plato, in what ways do Pre-Socratic naturalism and Sophism suffer from a similar defect?
2. What is Plato's Theory of the Forms?
3. Explain the self-predication thesis about the Forms.
4. How does Plato argue for the existence of the Forms based on the relativity of perception?
5. How is the existence of the Forms supposed to explain why things have the properties they do?
6. According to Plato, is there a Form for every property?
7. How does the existence of the Forms make knowledge possible?
8. What is Plato's Analogy of the Sun in the *Republic*?
9. What is Plato's Analogy of the Divided Line in the *Republic*?
10. Explain the purposes of the Analogy of the Cave in the *Republic*.

Discussion Questions

1. Is Plato right when he claims that we need to postulate the existence of Forms?
2. What are the main problems with Plato's Theory of Forms?
3. Does the Analogy of the Cave tell us something significant about human existence?

7

Plato
Justice and Love

The central unifying theme of the *Republic* is the nature and value of justice. Plato argues for the claim that it is better to be a just person who suffers misfortune than an unjust person who enjoys benefits such as a good reputation and fortune. Plato's argument for this claim is based on his explanation of the nature of justice in the state: it is the harmony amongst the parts. Plato argues that justice in the individual likewise consists of the harmonious functioning of the parts of the soul. On this basis, he then argues that being a just person is preferable to being an unjust person. Central to this argument is the just person's relationship to the Form of Goodness. Plato's overall argument raises many interesting issues concerning, for instance, the nature of education, the value of art, different kinds of government, and family life.

THE CHALLENGES

In Book I and at the start of Book II of the *Republic*, Plato sets out the challenges that he will try to answer later in the work. Book I looks like an early Socratic dialogue that ends inconclusively in *aporia*. It appears to be a puzzling false start. Socrates discusses the nature of justice with Cephalus and Polemarchus but to no conclusion. Finally, Thrasymachus argues against the view that justice is a virtue that it is advantageous to have. Socrates tries to reply to his skeptical arguments, but the replies are not presented as successful.

His replies are Socratic in that they conform to the method and views of Socrates as portrayed in the early dialogues, as we outlined in an earlier chapter. Consequently, one way to read Book I of the *Republic* is that Plato is setting up the rest of the dialogue by showing the limitations of the Socratic method and views. By implication, Plato thinks that these Socratic replies are inadequate or, at least, need supplementing; the rest of the work presents Plato's own theory that provides a better answer to the challenges. Understood this way, Book I is more than just a Socratic *elenchus* that ends inconclusively, because it reveals Plato showing how the Socratic method and views are incomplete.[1] In other words, Plato is indicating the need to go beyond Socrates.

This way of reading Book I has some support. Plato has Socrates participate in a discussion with the elder person Cephalus and his son, Polemarchus. The discussion is inconclusive in part because Socrates's method is dialogical: it works by convincing people; it doesn't aim at truths acceptable to *anyone*. It only works when people are disposed to be convinced. Cephalus is too settled in his ways, and Polemarchus is too young and inexperienced to be persuaded. If this is the right idea, then Plato is drawing our attention to the limitations of the Socratic method.

Socrates's discussion with Thrasymachus in Book I is more poignant. He taunts Socrates by accusing him of talking drivel and pretending to be ignorant. Thrasymachus doesn't try to define "justice" but rather claims that the main characteristic of the idea of justice is that it is used by the strong to further their own advantage.[2] His main support for this claim is as follows (338d–339a):

Argument T:

1. In all countries, the strongest is the ruler or government who makes the laws.
2. Those laws always advantage the rulers or government themselves.
3. In all countries, justice is taken to be obeying those laws.

4. Therefore, in all countries, justice provides advantage to the stronger party.

The theory Thrasymachus advances is similar to what today is called *positivism* and to what in political theory is called *realism*. Positivism in the social sciences avoids any value judgments about how society ought to be, and merely tries to describe how it is. Positivism sticks to the facts, usually quantitative ones. Political realism adds the idea that nation states or political actors always try to act in their self-interest. In a similar vein, Thrasymachus states his view: "A person of great power outdoes everyone else" (344a).

Socrates challenges both this reasoning and the resultant conclusion with an argument that we presented and discussed in chapter 5 in the section on *reductio ad absurdum* arguments against Sophism. Plato's argument against Thrasymachus is as follows:

Argument RT:

1. Justice is only the advantage of the stronger.
2. If premise 1 were true, then it would be just to obey all laws.
3. Lawmakers can mistakenly pass laws that are not to their own advantage.

4. If it is just to obey all laws and if premise 3 is true, then it would be just to obey laws that disadvantage the strong.

5. Therefore, premise 1 is false.

Plato argues against the definition of justice given in premise 1 in RT on the grounds that it leads to an absurdity if one also admits that governments can make mistakes in identifying laws that serve their own interests (339c–e). In other words, Thrasymachus's definition of justice looks viable only given the Sophist assumption that governments cannot make such mistakes. In short, in RT Plato attacks the general Sophist assumption that the relevant authority cannot make mistakes in its/his/her judgments.

Plato also rejects the specifics of Thrasymachus's own argument T by denying premise 2 in argument T above. Of course, ultimately, Plato will reject premise 3 in argument T because he is seeking an alternative conception of justice.

Plato also argues that each craft is designed for the benefit of something other than itself. For instance, medicine doesn't seek to benefit itself but rather to benefit the body (342c). A doctor is a practitioner of the craft of medicine. So, each doctor, *insofar as he or she is acting as a doctor*, seeks to benefit his patients rather than himself (342d). In general, the practitioner of a craft *as such* aims to benefit his or her subject. Additionally, the subject of the craft (i.e., the patient) is weaker than the practitioner (i.e., the doctor) *with respect to that craft*. So we can conclude that the practitioner of a craft seeks to benefit the one who is weaker rather than the stronger one (himself). We might layout this argument as follows:

1. The practitioner of any craft *as such* aims to benefit his or her subject (i.e., the patient) rather than himself.

2. The subject of the craft is weaker than the practitioner *with respect to that craft*.

3. Thus, the practitioner of a craft seeks to benefit the one who is weaker rather than the stronger one.

This argument applied to rulers or governments supports the contradictory position to that of Thrasymachus's premise that rulers seek to benefit themselves.

Towards the end of Book I the discussion takes a significant turn in direction, focusing on the question of whether the just life is better or more beneficial than the unjust one, or vice versa, as Thrasymachus holds (347e). In defending his views, Socrates anticipates some later themes of the *Republic* in four steps. First, he argues that justice in a city will make it strong and united, and that injustice will render it divided and "incapable of achieving anything as a unit" (351e–352a). Second, he then applies the same idea to the individual: injustice will make him incapable of acting as a unit "because he is in a state of civil war and not of one mind" (352a). Justice is the virtue of the soul. Third, Socrates tries to support this position by arguing that the virtue of anything consists in its performing its function well. For instance, the virtue of the eye is to perform its function of seeing well (353b). Likewise, the virtue of the soul is to take care of things, to deliberate, and to live well (353d). If the virtue of the soul is to live and if the virtue of the soul is justice, then the just person will live well. Furthermore, and fourthly, such a person would be happy. Consequently, the just person will be happy (353e–354a). In brief the argument can be represented as follows:

Argument S:

1. Justice is the virtue of the soul.
2. The virtue of anything consists in its performing its function well.
3. The function of the soul is to live as a person.
4. Therefore, the just person lives well.
5. To live well is to be happy.
6. Therefore, the just person is happy.

These Socratic ideas should be familiar as such from chapter 5. Then, right at the end of Book I, there is another remarkable and abrupt twist: Socrates disavows his own argument, claiming that the result of the argument is that he knows nothing because the notion of justice was not defined from the outset. For this reason, commentators claim that Book I ends inconclusively with *aporia*. As we said earlier, one way of reading this puzzling ending is that Plato is representing Socrates's own position and arguments as incomplete. He signals that we need a fresh start.

Book II redefines the challenge of Thrasymachus. First, Glaucon asks Socrates to show that the just person is happier than anyone else. Second, Glaucon and Adeimantus add to Socrates's task by arguing that one should act unjustly if one can get away with it. Recall their example of the mythical ring of Gyges. When invisible, one can get away with the consequences of acting unjustly, without fear of being discovered. Most people would claim that, under such conditions, there would be no reason to refrain from acting unjustly. People should act justly only to avoid being treated unjustly by others, and the ring of Gyges removes this motivation. In summary, this second challenge is to show that acting justly is better for the person than acting unjustly, even under the hypothetical conditions of the ring of Gyges. Third, part of the point of Glaucon's example of the ring is to show that justice is only an instrumental good—good for what it brings to the individual—rather than an intrinsic good.

Plato's main project in the *Republic* is to respond to these three challenges. First, Plato will show that the just person is happier than anyone else. Second, he will explain why unjust acts harm the soul of the person who commits them, even when those acts are unseen. Third, he will show why justice is an intrinsic good (apart from its consequences).

Plato's extended reply to these challenges consists of several steps. The first is to define justice; he does so first by examining the example of a perfectly just state. Justice is harmony among the parts of the society. Second, Plato argues that a justice in the individual is analogous. It consists of harmony among the parts of the soul similar to the harmony of a just society. Third, Plato argues that justice in the individual requires knowledge of, and dedication to, the Form of Goodness. Plato argues that the Form of Goodness is necessarily incomparably good. Fourth, Plato tries to show how a life dedicated to the Form would be a happier life.

This whole argument is embedded in a very rich text with many other issues at play. Furthermore, the overall structure of Plato's main argument is a matter of contention. Before we look at that overall shape, let us examine the different elements of the argument. To be more explicit, we will now introduce four elements that Plato needs in order to construct his main argument. After that, we will look at the arguments themselves.

In Book X, Plato argues for the immortality of the soul and for the claim that the just person will receive reward for his or her moral behavior in the afterlife. This argument does not count as a reply to the challenges of Book I because it is based on rewards.

Element 1: The State

To answer Glaucon's challenges, Socrates argues that we need to understand justice. His strategy is to examine justice as exemplified in the state and then extend that analysis to the soul (386c–369a). To characterize the just state, he sketches how a perfectly just *polis* (Kallipolis) might function and why it is just.

In the last part of Book II and in Books III and IV, Plato describes Kallipolis, which consists of three social groups: the artisans and merchants, the soldiers, and the rulers. He argues that a *polis* must have these three classes. A society must have artisans and merchants to produce and trade all the material goods necessary for the persons living in that society. This class includes farmers. A society must have a military class because it needs to protect the good and wealth produced by the artisans from other city states that are potential invaders. The ruling class is necessary to ensure the functioning and harmony of the other two classes. For example, the ruling class must be responsible for the legal and educational systems that make such a society possible.

Plato's main thesis in this part of the book is that the utopian society he describes would be just because the three elements would be working harmoniously, each fulfilling its proper role according to its nature. As noted earlier, in reading the text please be careful. At first, Plato calls the military class "the guardians." Later he employs the term *guardian* exclusively for the rulers and he calls the military class "auxiliaries."

Plato says that the main aim of a state is to promote the well-being of all its citizens. This is the basis of political power. It is not the consent of the governed. Individuals may not understand what their best interests are and may accept a system of governance that isn't good for them. To know what is good for people, one needs wisdom, which requires special education. The rulers need this understanding to govern the city wisely and to educate the people. To appreciate the power of the guardians in Plato's ideal *polis*, consider what he says about the use of myths and poetry in education (376c–403c). The guardians must select what stories children and young people are told so that such stories contribute to the general good. Because the guardians have this kind of power they need to be wise. This requires that they not have private property and family. The ruling class shouldn't have such special interests. At 472, Plato begins to argue that the rulers should be philosophers or lovers of wisdom.

Based on the division between the three social groups, Plato identifies the virtues of the city that enable it to flourish. These are moderation, courage, wisdom, and justice. Wisdom is constituted by the guardians' knowledge of what is best for the whole (428c–429a). Courage consists in the ability of the auxiliaries or military class to know what should and should not be feared (429b–430c). Moderation consists in everyone knowing who is wise and so who should rule (432a). Finally, justice consists of each group carrying out its proper function (433a).

Element 2: The Soul

In Book IV, Plato introduces the idea that the soul is divided into three parts: the rational, the spirited, and the appetitive. He argues for the principle that the same thing will not be able to undergo opposites in the same part of itself at the same time (436b). Plato asserts that it is possible for someone to be thirsty without being willing to drink. Effectively, the person both wants and does not want a drink at the same time. Therefore, these must be different parts of the soul. The argument is:

1. It is possible for a person to want to drink and not want to drink at the same time.
2. Wanting to drink and not wanting to drink at the same time are opposites.
3. The same thing will not be able to undergo opposites in the same part of itself at the same time.
4. Desires take place in the psyche.
5. Therefore, the desire to drink and the desire to not drink must be in different parts of the psyche.

In such a case, there must be something in the psyche that bids a person to drink and something that forbids him or her from drinking. The former is an appetite and the latter is a calculation. Therefore, from the principle, the soul must have at least two parts: the appetitive and the rational.

Plato employs this principle and similar reasoning to conclude that the soul has three parts: the rational, the spirited, and the appetitive. To distinguish the appetitive and the spirited, Plato cites the story of Leontius, who noticed some corpses (439d). He wanted to look at the bodies but he was also disgusted. Finally, when he was overpowered by the desire, he was angry. Plato concludes that anger "sometimes makes war against the desires." Plato also cites examples in which a person's sense of honor allows him to overcome his appetitive wants.

Plato's separation between the three parts of the soul shouldn't be assimilated to the modern distinction between reason, emotion, and desire. According to Plato, each part of the soul has its own characteristic desires, feelings, thoughts, and pleasures. Reason is defined by its desire for wisdom and for the good of the soul as a whole. The spirited part of the soul is characterized by aspiration and the desire for honor and reputation; and the appetitive by the satisfaction of the appetites for food, drink, sex, and other physical pleasures. In other words, each part of the soul (the rational, the spirited, and the appetitive) has its own characteristic type of desire.

In fact, later in the dialogue, Plato distinguishes appetitive desires into three groupings: necessary, unnecessary, and lawless. Necessary desires are those we are unable to deny, but we could avoid unnecessary desires if we trained ourselves from youth (559a). Lawless desires are those that are free of all control by shame and reason (571b).

We can now see how Plato rejects the Socratic ideas that all desires are rational and consequently that weakness of the will is impossible. According to Plato, not all desires are directed towards the overall good, and it is possible for a person to act on an irrational desire and knowing that it is irrational. This is why the guardians need extensive training or education that includes the non-rational parts of the soul.

Plato gives a temporary account of the four cardinal virtues: temperance, courage, wisdom, and justice. He then compares the divisions of the soul with the three parts of the state, and he argues that justice for the individual also consists of the three elements of the soul working harmoniously, each fulfilling its role according to its nature (423b–436b and 441c–445e).

The Analogy

Plato clearly thinks that there is some kind of similarity between justice in the state and in the individual. But what does this similarity consist of? The idea is structural, namely, that the kind of relations between the three parts of the just state is similar to the kind of relations between the three parts of the just soul.

In this regard, we might understand Plato as implicitly advancing an overall theory of the Good: goodness consists in a harmonious functioning of the parts. This would be what justice in the state and the individual have in common. This interpretation would fit Plato's conception of health (as harmonious order of the body). More contentiously, one might think that Plato is advancing a view of the Forms, according to which the Form of Goodness harmoniously orders the other Forms.[3]

Element 3: The Form of Goodness

In Book VI, to show what a true philosopher is, Plato distinguishes between opinion and knowledge, arguing that the latter requires acquaintance with the Forms. As we have seen, he employs the Analogy of the Divided Line to describe four types of reality and to argue that the Forms are the most real. Furthermore, he introduces his famous simile that compares the Form of the Good to the Sun. The Form of the Good makes the Forms knowable, just as the Sun makes physical things visible. In this sense, the Form of Goodness is the pinnacle of existence.

To emphasize the importance of this point for human life, Plato draws the famous Analogy of the Cave in Book VII. He compares the situation of most people to that of prisoners in a cave who can only see things as shadows cast by torchlight. Like these prisoners, we are subject to a systematic illusion, believing that transitory ordinary objects are real, while in fact these are only the shadows of the Forms. Plato's analogy implies that the world of ordinary everyday objects is less real than that of the Forms. This shows the real importance of virtue. By coming to know the Forms we can acquire virtue and thereby escape from the cave, or from illusions.

Element 4: Characters

Books VIII and IX consider different imperfect societies and compare them to the imperfections of an individual person. Plato describes four political systems, in addition to the ideal one already discussed. These are timocracy, oligarchy, democracy and dictatorship. In each case, Plato compares the problems of one of these societies to the nature of the corresponding personality or character type, as defined by the tripartite division of the soul and his distinction between different kinds of desires, mentioned earlier.

The Overall Argument

We have outlined four elements that make up the background to Plato's replies to Glaucon. The text of the *Republic* presents at least three separate lines or strands of argumentation to support the conclusion that justice is good apart from its rewards. In very brief summary:

First, at the end of Book IV, Plato argues that justice is the harmonious working of the parts of the soul. As such, it pertains to the soul in the way that health pertains to the body (444c–445c). Justice is the health of the soul.

Second, in Books VIII and IX, Plato compares five types of people: the timocrat, the oligarch, the democrat, the tyrant, and the wise philosopher. He argues that the philosopher is the happiest of them because he can rule himself (580a–c).

Third, in Book IX Plato argues that the philosophical life is more pleasurable than any other. He does so on two grounds. First, the philosopher prefers the pleasures of the philosophical life to all the other types of life, and his or her preference is informed because he or she can compare the pleasures of these different types of life (580c–583a). Finally, the pleasures of the philosophical life are greater than the others because they are more real (583b–588a).

There is considerable debate about how these three strands relate to each other, and how they relate to the four elements that we introduced above, including Plato's discussion of the Form of Goodness. So, we need to examine each of the three strands of argumentation in turn.

The First Strand

It is tempting to think that Plato has almost completed his reply to Glaucon by the end of Book IV when he concludes that justice in the individual consists of a psychological harmony or health. It seems like a short step from there to the conclusion that it is better to be just than unjust. However, this interpretation has a couple of problems.

The first is that, so portrayed, Plato's argument may have a flaw, sometimes called the *Fallacy of Irrelevance*.[4] The essential idea is that if this were Plato's argument then it would be irrelevant to Glaucon's original challenge. In short, Plato would have redefined the term *justice* to suit his own thesis. Glaucon was asking about the value of justice in the ordinary sense of the term, and Plato has replied by redefining it as a kind of psychological health.

One might reply to this objection that Plato's definition of justice is a revisionary one: he is arguing that we should revise our understanding of justice.[5] As evidence for this interpretation: when Socrates argues that justice in the *polis* consists in the harmonious working of the parts, he contends that this conception of justice has similarities to the ordinary conception. For example, he notes that no individual should be deprived of what is his own and should have what belongs to another (433e).[6] In other words, Plato is aware that his conception of justice is different from the normal one, but he is trying to show how it should be redefined. Of course, this doesn't mean that Plato's revisionary definition is successful as such.

There is a second reason for thinking that Plato's argument at this stage (the end of Book IV) is incomplete: he has yet to introduce the core of his philosophy, namely, the preeminent position of the Form of

Goodness. Plato says that the account of justice he provides at the end of Book IV is only partial, and that there is "a longer way" to a more complete account (504b). Indeed, as we shall see, this longer route is necessary to reply properly to the objection that Plato has committed the Fallacy of Irrelevance.

Given that the argument is incomplete at the end of Book IV, how do the different elements fit together into one argument? The overall reasoning might be represented as follows, as two linked arguments:[7]

Argument A:

1. The just person has the parts of the soul functioning together harmoniously.
2. This requires that reason rules over the other parts of the soul.
3. This requires that reason has knowledge of the Form of Goodness.

4. Thus, the just person must have knowledge of the Form of Goodness.

- In Argument A, Plato would support premise 1 through the analogy with the state. In other words, the first element about justice in the city-state serves mainly to support the second one, namely, the claim that, in the individual, justice is the harmonious functioning of the parts of the soul.
- In premise 2, Plato supports the idea that in the ideal person, reason rules over the other parts of the soul by comparing his ideal character type with those associated with other political systems in Book VIII.
- In premise 3, in order to rule wisely over the other parts of the soul, reason needs to have knowledge of what is good for the soul as a whole. Such knowledge requires knowledge of the nature of goodness, and hence the Form of the Good.

Argument B:

4. The just person must have knowledge of the Form of Goodness.
5. Knowledge of the Form of Goodness requires a life devoted to it.
6. The Form of Goodness is indefeasibly the greatest good that there is.
7. A life more devoted to the indefeasibly greatest good will always be (*ipso facto*) happier than a life that less so.

8. Therefore, the just person will always lead a happier life.

- In Argument B, premise 4 is the conclusion of argument A.
- Premise 5 is supported by Plato's philosophy of education. The idea is that knowledge of the Form of the Good requires lifelong training, which includes liberation from non-rational, unnecessary, and lawless desires.

- Premise 6 is supported by the conception of the Forms as paradigms that we discussed in the previous chapter. The Form of the Good is the supreme good in the sense that all other things are (imperfectly) good by virtue of it.
- Premise 7 is a key premise. The idea is that what kind of life we should lead is determined by which "goods" we should pursue.[8] The greatest happiness, or *eudaimonia*, consists in pursuing the greatest good.

Some Objections to the First Strand

One objection to Plato's strategy in the first strand is that justice pertains to one's relations with others, but Plato makes it self-directed, about one's relationship with oneself. We might say that justice is normally regarded as an other-regarding feature of actions and not as a self-regarding feature of the soul. This is an amplification of the Fallacy of Irrelevance objection presented earlier.

In reply, Plato's idea is that a healthy soul requires good and fair relations to others. This is because, to be healthy, the soul needs to be close to the Form of Goodness. Once the soul is so close, it will want to promote all kinds of goodness including, of course, benefiting others and having just social institutions.[9] In short, the distinction between self-regarding and other regarding is not mutually exclusive; and indeed, having a healthy or harmonious soul requires being just. This is the reason why we might claim that, although Plato's ethics is *eudaimonistic*, nevertheless it is not egoistic. In other words, Plato's ethics concerns the *eudaimonia* of the person, but his conception of *eudaimonia* isn't self-centered because it includes virtues such as love of Justice and Goodness.

The reply given above, on Plato's behalf, is sometimes called the *impartial justice approach*: the individual with a just or harmonious soul directly wants to bring about the impartial good, and so would not act unjustly.[10] This reply has a problem. The objection is that this account means that the person would have to sacrifice his or her self-interest in order to bring about the impartial good. If this were the case, then Plato would have failed to show why it is in our self-interest to be just. In other words, the pendulum has swung too far to the other side: first, Plato was not able to deal with the other-regarding nature of justice, and now, in appealing to the Form of Goodness, his reply does not allow him to explain well how it is in our self-interest to be just.

One reply to this new objection is that Plato is trying to redefine self-interest. Normally, we would think of self-interest in terms of getting what one wants most. But Plato explicitly argues that this is a mistaken view of self-interest. One has to inquire into the nature of the desires in question and, specifically, how they relate to the harmony of the soul. Plato's alternative conception of self-interest claims that it is in our self-interest to have *eudaimonia*, and this requires coming to know the Form of Goodness, despite the tremendous effort that this involves.

An allied objection is that there is a gap between the virtue of justice and just actions. In other words, the just person need not always perform just actions. However, in reply to this objection, Plato doesn't need to show that the just individual will *always* perform just actions. Rather, he needs to show that the person with a harmonious soul will be thereby motivated to perform just actions, and this is a point that we have already covered. Additionally, Plato is not claiming that, to perform just actions, one must have a just soul.

Another objection to Plato is that his abstract and otherworldly conception of the Good is too distant from everyday human affairs to be recognized as something important or worthy of our concern. If something is to count as good then it must be something that we have reason to choose in our everyday lives, such as pleasure and health.

Plato's reply to this objection would be to reiterate the claim that the Form of Goodness is the supreme good. It is supremely good in the sense that it explains why anything else that is good is good. Plato's idea is that a person who has spent his or her life dedicated to knowing or apprehending this Form will thereby (*ipso facto* tend to) want to facilitate all the common-garden things of goodness, such as pleasure, health, love, and justice.

One might wonder whether Plato's understanding of *eudaimonia* is too elitist. According to Plato, to be happy requires that reason govern the other parts of the soul, and this requires that one know the Form of Goodness. In this sense, Plato seems to imply that only the wise person can be happy. This indicates that ordinary people such as the merchants, artisans, and soldiers cannot have a happy life. In some sense, happiness requires that one lives one's life dedicated to knowing the Form of Goodness.

In reply, Plato would accept this as a consequence of his theory but reject the idea that it constitutes an objection. He might insist that happiness or *eudaimonia* really does require the development of reason and knowledge of the Good, and although it is unfortunate that most people do not attain this state, this is not a fault of his theory.

Plato would also remind us that the ideal state would be established for the benefit of everyone, and not just for one class. He would emphasize that anyone who has the capacity to be wise would receive the training to become a guardian.

The Second Strand: Types of Character and States

Plato has characterized the just city and the just soul. There are relational correspondences between the two. In Books VIII and IX, he describes four types of unjust cities and unjust souls: timocracy, oligarchy, democracy and dictatorship. Plato presents these as a hierarchy with dictatorship or tyranny as the most degenerate kind of political regime and soul.

In a timocracy, the rational part is unable to rule over the other two. So, as a compromise solution, the military class governs. In such a society the wise are unable to rule, and society becomes over-concerned with honor and victory. Likewise, in the timocratic individual, the spirited part of the soul rules over the others, thereby allowing considerations of honor to displace the good.

In an oligarchy, the productive part rules over the other two, and this means that the society is dominated by the desire for money. Because of this, only the richest members of the society have power in an oligarchy. In a parallel fashion, in the individual, an oligarchical soul is ruled by the appetitive desires, even if these are necessary ones; such desires are those connected to one's health and well-being.

Democracy is the rule of freedom, understood as the ability to do what one wants. This means that there is no governing class. In the name of liberty, all members of society have equal voice. As a result, there are no shared values or public virtues, except toleration. In a corresponding way, the democratic soul cannot choose between different desires; it treats them all as equal, in the name of liberty. Thereby, the democratic soul cannot distinguish between necessary and unnecessary desires, and so it is dominated by the latter.

Dictatorship is defined by absence and disregard of law. It has no ruling value at all. Likewise, the corresponding individual soul has no dominant end, and it is characterized by lawless desires. This means that the tyrant allows his or her desires to grow unconstrained, and this results in frustration, fear, and anguish (579a–d). In short, to supplement the argument of strand 1, Plato shows that a life of injustice, characterized as that of a tyrant, is unpalatable. This provides a psychological argument against Glaucon that is independent of the metaphysics of the Forms.

As an aside to our main point, Plato also describes the processes by which the higher forms of government degenerate into the lower ones. Without entering into the details, the descent from an ideal republic through successive stages and finally into dictatorship is marked by the rule of increasingly lower forms of desire. At the pinnacle, the ideal republic is ruled by the rational desire for the Good, both in society and in the individual, and at the bottom, lawless desire rules both the regime and the person.

The Third Strand: Justice and Pleasure

In Book IX Plato argues that the life of the just person will be more pleasurable (in some sense) than that of the unjust person. However, before we look at Plato's arguments about justice and pleasure in the *Republic*, we need to briefly examine his attitudes towards hedonism in some of the earlier dialogues.

Hedonism might be defined as the view that the only things of intrinsic value are pleasure and the absence of pain, and that better pleasure is identical with more pleasure (all other things being equal), and worse pain is identical with greater pain. In other words, the notions of better and worse can be identified with quantities of pleasure and pain.

Plato was aware of the strengths of this theory. In the *Protagoras*, Socrates claims that such a theory allows us to resolve disputes about the good and the bad because pleasures and pains can be measured and weighed (356b–357a). The theory implies that ethics is a science with determinate goods. Such a view would also support the Socratic claim that the virtues are constituted by knowledge of the good. In the *Protagoras*, Plato has Socrates advance these and other points apparently in favor of hedonism. Protagoras tries to resist these and to advance objections to hedonism but, in this work, the objections to hedonism seem to fail.

This is surprising because in other dialogues, such as *Gorgias*, *Phaedo*, the *Republic*, and the later *Philebus*, Plato's rejection of hedonism seems unequivocal. These dialogues are later than the *Protagoras*, and so some commentators think that Plato changed his mind. Others claim that Plato only appears to endorse hedonism in the *Protagoras*, because in the relevant passages of that dialogue, Socrates is assessing popular opinion, which includes the claim that most people think that hedonism is true (351c).[11] Plato is not portraying Socrates as accepting this opinion.

In the *Gorgias*, as we saw in chapter 5, Socrates tries to refute the hedonistic position of the Sophist Callicles through examples, such as the pleasure of a coward who flees a battle. These examples convince Callicles that some pleasures are better than others (501a), and this premise forms the basis of Socrates's argument that hedonism is mistaken. If some pleasures are better than others, aside from their being greater, then there must be some other value or positive good apart from pleasure. In the *Phaedo*, Plato identifies pleasure with bodily enjoyments, which he views as part of what imprisons the soul in the body. To attain wisdom, one must be free of such mundane pleasures.

The *Republic* advances a more nuanced view. Plato retains the key anti-hedonist idea of the *Gorgias* that some pleasures are better than others. He distinguishes different kinds of pleasure for each of the three parts of the soul, and he argues that the pleasures of the rational part of the soul are better and greater than those of the other two. In contrast to the *Phaedo*, in the *Republic* Plato claims that the pleasures of the non-rational parts of the soul may be good, so long as they are ruled by reason.

Plato offers two arguments for the claim that the pleasures of the rational part of the soul are better than those of the lower parts. The first is an appeal to the authority of the philosopher. The pleasures of the rational part of the soul concern learning; those of the spirited part of the soul concern honor, and those of the appetitive part focus on money. To discover which of these three kinds of pleasures is best, we must ask a competent judge who knows all three and who can make a reasoned judgment. Only the philosopher satisfies these criteria of judgment, and he or she prefers the rational pleasures of learning. Consequently, we can conclude that the pleasures of the rational part of the soul are better than the others.

One of the weaknesses of this first argument is that it is simply an appeal to authority. It doesn't inform us *why* the philosopher prefers the pleasures of the rational part of the soul. What is it about those pleasures that makes them better? Plato's second argument for the claim that the pleasures of the rational part of the soul are better fills this gap. It starts with a distinction between pleasure and relief from pain. Liberations from pain are upward motions towards a calm midpoint from below. In contrast, true pleasures are an upward motion of the soul starting from the middle state (584d). Plato argues that most bodily pleasures are really liberations from pain and not true pleasures. In contrast, those of the philosopher are true pleasures that start from the calm middle state.

Does Plato need these two arguments concerning pleasure? Isn't the first strand of argumentation presented earlier sufficient to show that Glaucon is mistaken? One answer is as follows. Remember that Plato's first line of argumentation appeals to the notion of happiness as *eudaimonia* (in premise 7). Plato realizes that a skeptic such as Glaucon might reject the idea that the best life for a person is the happiest in this *eudaimonistic* sense of "happy." Therefore, it is incumbent on Plato to appeal to a thinner conception of happiness that the skeptic can agree to, namely, happiness as pleasure. Otherwise, without the thinner conception the skeptic would not be convinced by the argument. This doesn't mean that Plato is adopting a hedonist position in Book IX. It just means that Plato would assert to the statement that the just life is more pleasurable than the unjust one.

It is worth noting a possible third argument lurking in the background of these passages. Plato switches metaphor at 585b–e. He speaks of pleasures as a filling up, and claims that truer pleasures consist in being filled with objects that are more real. In other words, the more real the object of one's pleasure is, the truer is the pleasure. Therefore, the virtues provide the truest pleasures. In this brief passage, Plato links true pleasure to the degrees of reality as outlined in the analogies of the Line and the Cave. Plato seems to be affirming that pleasures that arise from the higher levels of reality are better than those from the lower ones. Obviously, this line of argumentation is not independent of his metaphysics.

Education

Plato's theory of the government of the ideal state is also a theory of education. In the ideal state, the guardians will be wise people, who know and love the Form of Goodness. (Plato calls them *philosophers*, but here the term has its original meaning: lovers of wisdom; he doesn't mean contemporary academics.) The guardians need wisdom in order to know what is best for the city as a whole. This requires extensive training or education. It will take fifteen years of study to come to know the Form of the Good. This study would include mathematics, astronomy, harmonics, and dialectic (522d–535a).

However, Plato's educative process is not only intellectual. Because it is a question of bringing the soul into harmony, it also is a process that involves a transformation of all three parts of the soul. Plato's idea is that, through this education, the non-rational parts of the soul must serve the philosophical life, or the love of wisdom. The training enables the person to become liberated from the domination of the appetitive and spirited parts of the soul.

Such processes are necessary to attain an orderly soul. The other side of the same coin is that the preparation also involves being able to appreciate the order among the Forms and to love the Form of Goodness. This is why Plato characterizes education as the art of turning around, as a turning away from the world of becoming towards the world of being. He describes it not as an art of producing intelligence but rather one of turning it around (518d). In Book VII, Plato characterizes the kinds of study that would turn the soul away from the realm of becoming towards the realm of being. For example, if it taught properly, arithmetic could enable the soul to think about numbers themselves rather than simply the number of visible things. In so doing, it "leads the soul forcibly upward" (525d). Plato also mentions geometry as a subject that can compel the soul to study being (526e).

Plato insists that no one should be forced to learn. He says: "nothing taught by force stays in the soul" (536e). We should use play rather than force also because in this way the teachers will be able to see what each child is naturally suited for.

In characterizing education in this manner, Plato describes the moral life-journey of the individual. It is an ascent from illusion to reality, from fragmentation to unity and from pleasures to happiness. This process is also a political prerequisite: for the ideal state, it is necessary that the guardians have been through it. In the ideal state, the rulers must be wise and such a person would be free from material and competitive self-interest.

THE IDEAL STATE

Plato's sketch of the ideal city-state has been both criticized and praised from many angles. Sometimes it is accused of a misplaced communism. Plato's idea is that the ruling guardian class should not have private property or families so that they can better serve the interests of the whole of the city without having distracting personal interests. The guardians will have property and family in common (423e–424a). This view of how the ruling class should live might be justified both politically and in terms of the good life. Politically, for the sake of the harmony and unity of the state, the rulers should be without any personal interests beyond those of the common good. This requires abandoning private property and individual family. In terms of their own lives, the rulers have dedicated themselves to knowing the Form of Goodness, and this requires transcending the desires of self-interest, such as family and property.

However, these replies meet a deeper challenge. The arrangements for the soldier class also mean that these parents and children will not know each other, and that the rulers choose which couples shall mate as a type of selective breeding. The ruler class uses a false lottery to disguise this fact (460a). Indeed, Plato says that the "rulers have to make considerable use of falsehood and deception for the benefit of those they rule" (459c).

For reasons such as these, Plato's state is indicted for being totalitarian, for instance, most famously by Karl Popper in the *Open Society and Its Enemies*. Roughly, the idea of totalitarianism is that the state wields total authority over the lives of individuals. A problem with this charge against Plato is that totalitarianism is not such a clear doctrine, and thus the criticism isn't either.

First, totalitarianism can mean that the rulers aim to promote the interests of the state without regard to the well-being of the individual citizens. So, for example, if the rulers promote the prestige and power of the state at the expense of the well-being of its citizens then this would be totalitarian. However, in this sense of the term, it would be unfair to claim that Plato's view is totalitarian. Plato envisages the guardians as ruling the city in a way that cares for the happiness of all the citizens. Plato says that the aim of the ideal city isn't the happiness of any one class, but of all (420b–421c).

Second, totalitarianism can mean that the main function of the state is to look after the welfare of its citizens. This second kind of totalitarianism is paternalistic, but unlike the first, it does *not* treat the state as a super-entity that has interests of its own, separate from those of its citizens. It is paternalistic because, in this regard, it deprives the individual of autonomy. It is fair to say that Plato's theory is totalitarian in this second sense.[12] According to Plato, the happiness of the citizens is best served by the governance of the guardians who know best what is in the interests of each group.

For this reason, it is clear that Plato's utopia is opposed to a liberal theory of the state. According to this liberal idea, the state should remain neutral between competing visions or conceptions of the human good. Its role is to provide a just but neutral social framework that enables people to freely pursue their own conceptions of happiness or the good life. In sharp contrast, Plato has a definitive vision of the human good, perhaps best encapsulated in the Allegory of the Cave. This vision shapes the structure of the ideal society.

Likewise, Plato's city-state is not democratic. Nevertheless, it might be misleading to call it *totalitarian* for that reason alone without some qualifications. For one thing, all citizens, regardless of their sex and background, have equal opportunity to become guardians. They are educated in the same way, and anyone who shows the relevant abilities for ruling during this long training can become a guardian. So, although the guardians chose the guardians, they do so on the basis of their wisdom and ability.

There is a general problem with using terms such as *communist, totalitarian, liberal,* and *democratic* when thinking about Plato's utopia. These concepts have developed in the context of the large nation-state and industrial societies, or in the context of a set of conditions that are very different from those of Plato's city-state. Therefore, we always need to qualify these terms very carefully to avoid being misleading, or avoid using them altogether.

Plato has been seen as a champion of feminism because he thinks that women should have equal opportunity to become guardians. The gender of a person is irrelevant to whether he or she should become a ruler (456a–e). However, we need to be wary of calling Plato a feminist.[13] First, insofar as some forms of feminism require the upholding of equal rights for women, Plato's Kallipolis is not a society that respects the notion of individual rights. Plato's concern is primarily whether women would serve the state well. Second, Plato dissolves the family, at least for certain classes, and with it the traditional caring of motherhood. Some radical feminists might claim that the institution of the nuclear family is oppressive to women and is best eradicated. Others might argue that Plato's dismissal of the family reflects a profound misunderstanding and lack of appreciation of the love that children need and that mothers give. Thirdly, although Plato does think that people should have the social roles that most befit them irrespective of their gender, nevertheless, he also claims that on average women have inferior abilities. Finally, when Plato says that the guardians will have women in common, he talks as if women were the property of men (457c10–d1).

THE *SYMPOSIUM*

The *Symposium* consists of an account of a dinner and drinking party, held in 416 BC, at which the distinguished guests discussed the nature of love. The dialogue consists in the secondhand report given by Apollodorus based on the account of Aristodemus, who was present at the party. The dialogue was probably written around 385 BC.

At the party, Phaedrus and Eryximachus propose that each of the guests should give a speech in praise of love and Eros, the personification of love. The speeches were delivered by Phaedrus, Pausanias, Eryximachus, Aristophanes, Agathon, and, finally, Socrates. At the end of Socrates's speech, Alcibiades enters with some drunken friends. He gives a speech praising Socrates. Finally, more drunken people arrive at the party and, after a while, Aristodemus falls asleep. When he awakes in the morning, he finds Agathon, Aristophanes, and Socrates still drinking and talking.

Phaedrus begins by claiming that Eros is the oldest god, one of the first to be born after chaos (178b). For this reason, love bestows great benefits including courage and honor. The next speaker, Pausanias, distinguishes between two versions of the goddesses Aphrodite: the heavenly and the common. Correspondingly, there are two kinds of love (181b–c). The latter is purely physical and is generally bad. In contrast, the love of the heavenly Aphrodite is concerned to make the loved one better and wiser. Such love, which seeks virtue, is usually between men.

At this point, there is a break in the original planned sequence, as Aristophanes has a bad attack of the hiccups, and the doctor, Eryximachus, speaks in his turn (185c). Eryximachus agrees with and wants to extend the distinction between common and heavenly love (186a). He makes it akin to a cosmic principle. He analyses medicine in terms of the two kinds of love within the body: one producing illness, and the other, health (186d). Heavenly love is harmony between the antagonistic parts of the body. He applies a similar analysis to music, the seasons, and astronomy (188a).

Afterwards, Aristophanes, the famous comic playwright, delivers a speech, having recovered from his hiccups (189d). He describes a myth according to which our ancestors were created as double what we humans are today. For instance, they had four arms, four legs, and two heads. Because these beings threatened the gods, Zeus decided to cut them in half to reduce this menace (190d–e). As result, humans search for their other half, in an attempt to regain their original nature. "Love . . . tries to make one out of two and heal the wound of human nature" (191d). This explains why we care so much for our partners: we have a deep need for our other half, which transcends our sexual appetite (192c). Furthermore, according to the myth, the original beings had three genders: male, female, and androgynous (190b). So people seeking members of the opposite sex were originally androgynous; men who are interested in other men were originally male, and similarly for women.

The poet Agathon announces his intention to describe the nature of Love itself rather than its beneficial effects (194e–195a). He gives an eloquent speech that praises the different virtues of Love. Love is the happiest, most beautiful, and youngest of the gods, he says (195a–c). Love is just and moderate.

Socrates declares that he will not engage in a contest of rhetorical skill with Agathon. Nor will he praise Love if this means describing it with the grandest qualities "whether it actually has them or not" (198e). He declares that, instead, he will make a plain statement about love (198c–199b). In quizzing Agathon, he notes that love is always *of* something: it has an object. Furthermore, this object is desired and lacked. Socrates notes that the love of beauty indicates the lack of beauty, and therefore it cannot be beautiful, contrary to what Agathon supposed (201b–c).

After questioning Agathon, Socrates delivers his speech, which consists in a report of a dialogue between him and a wise woman called Diotima (201e). When Diotima declares that love is neither beautiful nor good, Socrates is at first horrified to think that it must ugly and bad. But Diotima corrects him, pointing out that there are intermediaries between good and bad, and between beautiful and ugly. In a similar vein, correct judgment is neither understanding nor ignorance, but lies in between the two (202a). Likewise, love is not a god or a mortal either; it is an intermediary between the two. Diotima describes love as an intermediary or bridge between the world of the Forms and that of sensible objects.

She claims that love is the desire to possess the good forever (206a). This implies that love contains a desire for immortality, which we see manifest in our desire for reproduction and offspring (206b). The goodness that love is directed to is the beautiful. Diotima describes how love can pass from the desire for particular beautiful bodies to the love of beautiful bodies in general, to the love of beautiful souls, to the love of the beauty of knowledge, and finally, to the love of Beauty itself, or the Form of the Beautiful (210a–211d). The object of love is always beauty, and beautiful things in the sensible world lead the lover to seek the Form of Beauty itself, which is identical to the Form of the Good. This ascension Plato calls "the art of loving." The contemplation of the Beautiful is a mystical experience, which Plato describes towards the end of the speech.

At this point, there is another break in the proceedings. The politician Alcibiades stumbles into the party drunk, and after some kerfuffle or commotion he agrees to speak; but rather than praising love, he praises Socrates. Alcibiades describes the extraordinary emotional effect that Socrates has on him to make him cry, to feel shame, and how he cannot live with him or without him. He describes the inner beauty of Socrates and how Socrates was immune to his attempts to seduce him (217e–218e). He describes Socrates's indifference to the bitter cold and his bravery as a foot soldier.

Interpretations

First, Plato seems to separate the first three speeches from the second three through the device of Aristophanes's fit of hiccups. Why does he do this? What is this separation? One plausible suggestion is that the first three speeches rely on some distinction between good and bad love. In contrast, the second three do not.

Second, we can also see a progression in the second set of three speeches. Socrates's speech combines elements from those of Aristophanes and Agathon. Aristophanes characterizes love as a yearning for wholeness, and Agathon praises it for its intrinsic qualities or virtues. In effect, Socrates unites these two ideas: for Socrates, the nature and qualities of love are explained by what it is a desire for. Socrates says that love has the virtues that it does because it is a yearning for the Beautiful.[14]

Third, the entrance of Alcibiades clearly constitutes another break or shift. The significance of Alcibiades's speech is contentious. Is the main point that the speech reveals Socrates's indifference to interpersonal love, a detachment that is necessary to attain higher love of the Form of Beauty? Or, perhaps, is Plato showing us, through Alcibiades, that real love must be first of an individual person rather than primarily of a Form? In other words, is Plato suggesting a criticism of his own view of Platonic love?[15]

THE *PHAEDRUS*

The *Phaedrus* is one of Plato's most beautiful works, the central part of which returns to the nature of love and beauty. The *Phaedrus* can be divided into two parts. The first consists of three speeches about love, two of them from Socrates. The second part is about good speech making, rhetoric, and the relative virtues of the spoken and written word.

Socrates is alone with Phaedrus in an attractive spot by a stream and some trees outside the city. Phaedrus reads out a speech about homosexual love originally given by Lysias, which he has written down. This point is important in view of the conclusions about writing in the second part of the dialogue. In brief, Lysias's speech lists some arguments for the view that it is better "to give your favor" to a non-lover than to a lover. That is, Lysias argues that it is better to give one's sexual favors to a person who is not overcome with love and who is not in need of one's love, but who is simply willing to return a favor. Socrates sarcastically praises the speech and flatters Phaedrus. A discussion follows about the merits of the speech, in which Socrates criticizes the content of Lysias's work; and flirting with Phaedrus, he agrees to make his own speech on the same theme as Lysias's (234e–236b).

In this first speech, Socrates aims to show how someone might persuade a boy to give his favors to a man who does not love him rather than to the one who does (237b–241d). He says that each person is ruled by two principles: the innate desire for pleasure and the judgment about what is best. Sometimes these two principles agree; but when the desire takes control, the result is outrageousness, of which there are many kinds, such as gluttony (327d–328c). When the desire is directed to the beauty of the human body, it is called *eros*. From this analysis, Socrates argues that it is better for the boy to give his favors to someone who does *not* love him. This is because the person who loves him would be overcome with the desire of *eros*. Such desire would drive out any good will towards the boy. The purpose of a lover driven by *eros* is simply to sate his hunger like a wolf with a lamb. Socrates concludes that this is how lovers befriend a boy (241d).

However, after completing his speech, Socrates has a radical change of heart. He hears a voice, "a familiar divine sign," telling him to make amends for the offense given to the gods by the two speeches, Lysias's and his own (242c–e). Socrates explains to Phaedrus that he (Socrates) is a seer, albeit not a very good one, who is prevented from performing wrong actions by a voice. He says that the two speeches were terrible because they were offensive to the divine nature of love; they were "close to being impious." He intends to give a new speech to rectify his mistake, and he urges Phaedrus to listen, for "otherwise he may be too quick to give his favors to the non-lover" (243e).

In his second speech, Socrates praises love (244a–257b). He claims that madness is often divinely inspired and declares that he will show that love is one of the (four) kinds of madness given to us by the gods (245b). He begins by trying to prove that the soul is immortal. He argues that the soul is essentially a self-mover. Something that is a self-mover will always continue in motion. This is because it cannot have a beginning, and because of this, it cannot be destroyed. Hence, it is immortal (245b–e).

In order to show how love is a divine madness, Socrates describes the structure of the soul through his Analogy of the Soul as the union of a charioteer with two winged horses (246a–b). In the case of humans, one of the horses is good and beautiful, while the other is the opposite; this makes driving precarious for humans. Socrates compares the life of the gods, who know the reality of the Forms, with that of the other souls who have to struggle to rise up and to fully know the Forms. The feathers are nourished by the truth, so that a soul with wings in good condition can fly and maintain itself high up in the heavens. However, if the charioteer is unable to control the bad horse, its heaviness will drag the soul down. If the soul falls, then it will no longer be able to know the reality of Forms, and its wings will lose their nourishment. As a result, the soul inevitably will fall even further until it becomes embodied. Embodied souls are reincarnated. However, if a soul is able to practice the love of wisdom for three cycles of one thousand years each, it will re-grow its wings. The process of loving wisdom by coming closer to the divine makes a person "stand outside human concerns" (249d). Such a person is no longer concerned with the mundane features of life and is often judged as disturbed.

From within this metaphorical framework, Socrates characterizes love as a divine madness. When a person sees the physical beauty of another person as a reminder of the Form of Beauty, his soul wants to fly up towards that Form, but it cannot. Some souls are more easily reminded of real Beauty, but they may become "besides themselves" because their experience is beyond their comprehension (250a). Among the Forms, Beauty is most visible, and it may inspire our love. When it does, this love will stimulate the place in the soul where the wings once grew, which Plato calls "a stump." This causes aching, which is only relieved by the sight of the loved one, producing joy. This mixture of pain and joy causes the kind of anguish which we know emotionally as the madness of love (251a–252b).

Phaedrus lavishly praises the speech of Socrates, and this provokes them to discuss the art of speechwriting (259e). Socrates warns against the power of rhetoric, which is inferior to the true method of inquiry, dialectic. He compares rhetoric to praising a donkey by calling it a horse when the audience does not know what a horse is (260b–d). The genuine art of speaking requires a grasp of truth, even when the speaker's aim is to deceive his audience (262c). Otherwise, it is artless.

Socrates applies these points to his own speeches and to that of Lysias. Socrates criticizes the speech of Lysias for omitting a definition of "love," the key term, and for lacking an organic order. He notes how his own speeches were based on relevant distinctions such as the difference between ordinary and divinely inspired madness (265a–c). Phaedrus and Socrates also analyze the writings of orators of the past. Socrates reiterates that the art of rhetoric requires a grasp of the nature of the soul (270b–c). This is because the person who knows the truth knows best how to make the appropriate definitions and determine relevant similarities (273d).

Socrates shifts the discussion to writing (274b). He notes that the written word, like a painting, cannot engage in conversation. It cannot explain or defend itself when "it needs its father's (i.e., its author's) support" (275e). The written word is only an image of "the living breathing discourse of the man." In other words, Plato points to the inherent limitations of written philosophical works compared to dialectic or philosophical conversations. Such written works can only serve as reminders for those who already know. A true lover of wisdom must be able to defend his writing in person, and must understand that writing has little worth.

Let us briefly compare the tripartite division of the soul as given in the *Phaedrus* with that of the *Republic*. In what is presumably the earlier dialogue, the *Republic*, Plato presents a three-way distinction between the rational, the spirited, and the appetitive parts of the soul. The later dialogue, the *Phaedrus*, seems to present a different classification with his Analogy of the Chariot. However, the two might overlap. They would do so if we can identify the appetitive part of the soul with the bad horse, the spirited part of the soul with the good horse, and reason with the charioteer. Plato may be suggesting this identification when he writes that the good horse is "a lover of honor with modesty and self-control," and that the bad horse is "a companion to wild boasts and indecency" (253d–e). Furthermore, he portrays the bad horse as driven by sexual appetite. If this is a good reading of Plato's text, we can take the discussion of the soul in the *Phaedrus* as an extension of that in the *Republic*. Indeed, it might even be an improvement because in the *Republic*, Plato characterizes each part of the soul as if it were independent. In contrast, in the *Phaedrus* he seems to acknowledge that the soul must be a unity. He speaks of the three parts as a "natural union" (246a).

Conclusion

A central thesis of Plato's philosophy is that a proper understanding of morality requires knowledge of the supreme Form of Goodness. According to Plato, this thesis is required to refute the ethical subjectivism inherent in some kinds of Sophism. While many contemporary philosophers agree with Plato in rejecting ethical subjectivism, fewer have followed Plato's thesis regarding the Form of Goodness. One of the notable exceptions is the British/Irish philosopher and novelist Iris Murdoch (1919–1999), whose famous works *The Sovereignty of the Good* and *Metaphysics as a Guide for Morals* are explicitly platonic in parts.

However, any philosopher who is willing to affirm that some things are better than others in an absolute or non-relative sense has a platonic strand to his or her thinking. In this manner, many contemporary ethical theorists have platonic threads running through their work. For example, a non-Platonist might claim that one thing can be better than another only when relative to a type of organism. For example, a social life is better for humans but not for more solitary animals such as tigers. For such a non-Platonist, the judgment that it is better to be a human than a tiger wouldn't make sense because such a claim wouldn't be relative to a type of organism. In contrast, a Platonist would be willing to affirm that some value judgments are unqualified.

For Plato, the defining feature of politics is that the city-state should be just in the sense that all the parts function harmoniously for the good of the whole. This implies that only the wisest persons should govern. These are the people who are able to put aside self-interest and know the Form of Goodness. In many ways this is an antidemocratic political vision. Political thinkers of both the left and right have drawn inspiration both from Plato's positive political vision and from his negative criticism of democracy.

Study Questions

1. Towards the end of Book I of the *Republic*, Plato provides a Socratic argument for the claim that the just person will be happy. What is this argument?

2. What are the challenges that Plato faces from Glaucon in Book II of the *Republic*?
3. What are the three social groups of the just city-state, and what virtues do they embody?
4. How does Plato argue for his tripartite division of the soul?
5. What are the three strands of argument in the *Republic* for the claim that the just person will always be happy?
6. What is Plato's main argument for the claim that the just person will always be happy?
7. How does the existence of the Form of Goodness comprise part of this argument?
8. What are the differences between the four imperfect societies (timocracy, oligarchy, democracy, and dictatorship) and their associated character traits?
9. What is Plato's view about hedonism in the *Republic*, and how does it differ from his view in the *Phaedo*?
10. What is the educational process whereby the guardians learn to become wise?
11. How do the guardians live in the ideal city-state?
12. Is Plato's view of the state totalitarian?
13. How does Socrates portray love in the *Symposium*?
14. What does Alcibiades's speech tell us about love in the *Symposium*?
15. In the *Phaedrus*, how does Plato describe the soul?
16. In the *Phaedrus*, how does Plato characterize love as divine madness?
17. According to Plato in the *Phaedrus*, what are the limitations of philosophical writing?

Discussion Questions

1. Does Plato answer the challenges of Glaucon in a satisfactory way?
2. Are Plato's criticisms of democracy well founded, and can we criticize Plato's ideal city-state for being undemocratic?
3. Is there a divine aspect to love?

8 Plato
Later Period

Plato's later dialogues are usually held to be the *Timaeus, Critias, Sophist, Statesman, Philebus,* and *Laws*. The *Statesman* is later than the *Sophist*; it is its sequel. Likewise, the *Critias* is a sequel to the *Timaeus*, and it is unfinished. Diogenes Laërtius, from the third century AD, depicts the *Laws* as Plato's last dialogue. Recent stylometric evidence suggests that this is so, and it too seems to be unfinished, like the *Critias*.

Socrates plays a minor role in the *Timaeus, Critias, Sophist,* and *Statesman*, and has no role at all in the *Laws*. This is sometimes thought to indicate that Plato is trying to distance himself from of his own views in the middle period. Many contemporary writers think that Plato modifies his Theory of Forms towards the end of his life, though there is considerable debate concerning what that modification consists of. In the *Philebus*, Plato exams the role of pleasure in the good life (a Socratic theme), and Socrates has a major role in that dialogue.

In this chapter we also examine two middle-period dialogues, the *Parmenides* and *Theaetetus*. Plato wrote these after the *Republic*, and both take a critical stance towards topics central to the *Republic*. In the *Parmenides* Plato criticizes aspects of his Theory of Forms, and the *Theaetetus* seems to adopt a different understanding of knowledge from the *Republic* and *Phaedo*. For these reasons, some commentators take the *Parmenides* and *Theaetetus* as two transitional dialogues in which Plato examines critically his own assumptions about the Forms and knowledge and, as a result of which, he modifies some aspects of his Theory of Forms.

However, these claims are highly contentious and need examination. There is also a related scholarly debate over the dating of the *Timaeus*. There is stylometric evidence to suggest that it is a later dialogue. However, in the dialogue, Plato seems to revert to the full Theory of Forms that he himself criticized earlier in the Parmenides. For instance, in the *Timaeus*, Plato refers to the Forms as paradigms. For this reason, G.E.L. Owen, a well-known Plato scholar, argued that the *Timaeus* must be a middle-period dialogue, written after the *Republic* but before the *Parmenides*.[1] The alternative seems to be to claim that Plato did not think that the criticisms of the theory of Forms given in the *Parmenides* were fatal to his theory.² If this is so, then there is greater continuity between the so-called middle and later periods of Plato's thought.

THE *PARMENIDES*

The *Parmenides* is possibly Plato's most intriguing dialogue. The dialogue is often understood as a criticism by Plato of his own Theory of Forms, which he later amends in light of this self-criticism. However, the interpretations of this dialogue are contentious. In part this is because it is not obvious how the earlier and later stages of the dialogue are related to each other, as we shall soon see.

The dialogue consists of a report at third hand of a conversation between Parmenides, Zeno, and Socrates as a youth, in which the older Parmenides grills Socrates. Cephalus has heard that someone can remember this conversation in detail and, together with Plato's half brothers Adeimantus and Glaucon, he visits Antiphon, who recounts the conversation that he himself had heard from Pythodorus, at whose house the (fictional) conversation took place. For the sake of simplicity, we can divide the dialogue into two parts: Parmenides's critique of the Theory of Forms, and the long and complex section that follows.

The Critique

The conversation starts with Zeno defending Parmenides's monism. Zeno claims that if there are many things, then they are both alike and unlike. Since nothing can be both, then there cannot be many things. Socrates objects to Zeno's reasoning arguing that things can indeed be both like and unlike because these qualities are contraries and are not contradictory. Socrates argues that perceivable objects can participate in both of the Forms, likeness and unlikeness. As we saw in earlier dialogues, Plato thinks that sensible things can have contrary properties, although the Forms themselves cannot. In short, Socrates states the Theory of Forms (128e–130a). Parmenides now launches into six criticisms of the theory.

How Many Forms Are There?

Parmenides starts to question this theory by asking what kinds of things have Forms. Socrates claims that there is a Form for every predicate. Parmenides questions this. The young Socrates admits there are Forms for moral qualities such as Beauty, Justice and Goodness.

Part/Whole

Later, Parmenides asks another difficult question: when individual things participate in the Forms, does each individual thing participate in the whole of the Form or only part of it? Can we even think of the Forms being divided or shared? Once again, it seems that Plato is noting a lack of clarity in his own theory. Neither of these two lines of questioning, however, amounts to a refutation.

Third Man Argument

However, following these passages, Plato seems to give an argument against an aspect of his own Theory of Forms (131e–132b). Although Plato's argument concerns largeness, it is known as the *Third Man Argument*, following a similar argument advanced by Aristotle (*Metaphysics* 1079a). The argument requires the self-predication assumption, namely, that any Form of F-ness itself has the property F. For example, in earlier dialogues, Plato claims that the Form of the Good is itself good or that the Form of Beauty is itself beautiful. These forms serve as paradigms or models. Such claims imply self-predication regarding the Forms.

One interpretation of the Third Man Argument is as follows.

Step 1:

1. If several objects have the property of being F, then there is a Form of F-ness (in virtue of participating in which, they are all F).
2. Several objects (i.e., a, b, and c) are large.
3. Therefore, there is a Form of Largeness (call it L1).

Step 2:

4. The Form of Largeness is itself large (this is called the assumption of self-predication).
5. There exists a set of things, a, b, c, and L1 itself, that are all large.
6. Therefore, by premise 1 above, there exists a second form of Largeness (i.e., L2).

Step 3:

7. The same steps (1–6) can be repeated infinitely for L2 and for any Form Ln, thus generating an infinity of Forms.

The above interpretation probably reflects the text quite well. In brief, it shows that three claims central to Plato's theory generate an infinite series. The first of the three claims is the Unity thesis; when several objects are all F; this is because they participate in the Form of F-ness. Second, there is the claim that the Form F is not identical to the particulars that are F. Third, there is self-predication. Together these three claims generate an infinite regress of Forms.

The interpretative problem is twofold: first, why is an infinite series of Forms a problem for the theory? And second, how does Plato use this overall argument? Regarding the first question, the infinite regress might be damaging because it contradicts the claim that there is only one Form for every property.

In answer to the second question, there are three general kinds of interpretation concerning how Plato's understanding of the Forms changed:

1. Plato's aim with the Third Man Argument is to criticize his own Theory of Forms insofar as it involves self-predication. Given this view, having made this criticism, Plato abandons this aspect of his theory. In the later period, Plato still believed in the existence of the Forms but altered his view about their nature with regard to self-predication. However, this interpretation is made problematic by the apparent fact that Plato seems to accept a self-predicated view of the Forms in the later dialogue, the *Timaeus*. At least, he says that sensible objects resemble the relevant Forms.
2. Plato saw some of the problems with his Theory of Forms, but he did not explicitly or significantly alter his theory. This is because he thought that there were good replies to the objections. After all, in the dialogue, Parmenides himself says that these objections can be answered by anyone with sufficient philosophical training (135a–d).
3. Plato abandoned his Theory of Forms in the later period because he recognized problems with the theory.

Forms as Thoughts

Socrates suggests an escape route, which is that the Forms are thoughts that occur in minds (132b). He suggests that this might halt the regress by restricting each Form to one thought. The regress would stop when the person has no more of the relevant thoughts. Parmenides quickly closes this escape route, however. Thoughts must be of something and be about some single character that "is over all the instances." Parmenides concludes that Socrates's suggestion would lead to absurd conclusions given the claim that all things, including the unthinking, partake of the Forms. It would imply that all things think or are composed of thoughts.

The Likeness Regress

Socrates now switches direction and suggests that Forms are patterns set in nature. Things partake of the Form by being like the pattern (132d). Forms are immanent paradigms. Parmenides points out that this also leads to an infinite regress as follows:

1. Things partake in the Forms by being like them.
2. Thus, the Form and the thing are like each other.
3. Thus, both partake in the Form of Likeness.
4. This partaking itself would be constituted by another likeness (because of premise 1).
5. This would require another Form: Likeness2.

6. Likeness2 and Likeness must be like each other, and
7. A repetition of premises 3 and 5 would generate Likeness3.

The "Greatest Difficulty"

Parmenides outlines what he calls "the main difficulty" with the idea that one posits a Form every time one makes a distinction between things (133b), namely, that the Forms become unknowable.

1. Forms are what they are, in themselves (each Form is itself by itself).
2. None of those Forms are in us, and none are what they are in relation to things that belong to us.
3. Therefore, neither do we have the Forms, nor do they belong to us.
4. To have knowledge of the Forms, one must have Knowledge itself (134a).
5. Knowledge itself is a Form (134b).
6. Therefore, we don't have knowledge of the Forms.

Whereas premises 1 and 2 entail 3, premises 3, 4, and 5 are supposed to entail the conclusion 6. The core nub of this argument is a combination of two points: first, that the Forms have an absolute kind of existence that precludes us having them, and second, that any knowledge of the Forms would have to be knowledge itself (i.e., the Form of Knowledge). From this conclusion, Parmenides tries to show that the divine gods would not have knowledge of human affairs. Being divine, their knowledge would be restricted to the Forms.

The Deductions

At 134c the dialogue takes a surprising turn. We might expect Parmenides to conclude that there are no Forms. However, he apparently argues for the opposite, claiming that there must "a character that is always the same" in order for dialectic to be possible. Presumably this means that language itself requires the existence of properties that remain the same.

Parmenides then proposes a methodology for thinking about the Forms, which consists of examining the consequences of postulating the existence of a Form, both for the putative Form considered in itself and for its relations to other things. From this methodology, Parmenides presents eight arguments or so-called *Deductions* that constitute a rubric or schema for examining the consequences of the existence of a Form. This part of the dialogue is very intricate, quite puzzling, and contested. However, the underlying general idea is that the older and wiser Parmenides provides the younger Socrates with an antidote to the tendency to postulate the Forms too quickly, namely, a set of exercises for thinking through the consequence of postulating them. Understood this way, the second part of the dialogue provides a method for answering the objections of the first part, but without directly replying to them. For instance, Plato doesn't directly answer the question, "What Forms are there?" but does so indirectly by providing a method for determining this. The Theory of Forms is not saved, but it is not condemned either.[3]

Another possibility is that Plato intends to distinguish between two kinds of predication, and to apply this distinction to self-prediction in order to dissolve the problems that result from it.[4] The two kinds of predication arise from the two ways of thinking about the consequences of the postulation of a Form: "in relation to itself" and "in relation to the others." The former is an intrinsic predication, and the latter, an extrinsic one. One might say, for instance, that being large in size is intrinsic to the concept of being large or that being good is intrinsic to the concept of being just. One might express this idea by claiming that Justice is good. However, this type of predication should be distinguished from applying the same predicate extrinsically (or "in relation to others") such as in the judgment, "Sophocles was a good man."

Let us stand back to see the bigger picture. If the second part of the *Parmenides* is at least an undefeated attempt to reply to the objections presented in the first part of the dialogue, then the distinction between the middle period and later dialogues becomes less drastic. Plato maintained or refined his theory rather than abandoning or modifying it substantially. If this is so, then, as a consequence, the timing of the *Timaeus* is no longer such a problem. The *Timaeus* presents the Forms as changeless objects known by reason, which are the paradigms from which the divine craftsman creates the sensible world. In short, in the *Timaeus* Plato seems to affirm his Theory of Forms much in the same shape that he did in the middle dialogues. Thus, there are three propositions that form an inconsistent triad, assuming that Plato didn't contradict himself:

1. The *Parmenides* presents an undefeated argument against the existence of self-predicated Forms.
2. The *Timaeus* assumes the existence of self-predicated Forms.
3. The *Timaeus* is a later dialogue than the Parmenides.

In other words, a consistent interpretation of Plato would require us to give up one of these three propositions. If we deny (1) by claiming that, in the second half of the *Parmenides*, Plato answers his own objections, then we can maintain (2) and (3) without problem.

THE *THEAETETUS*

The *Theaetetus* was probably written after the *Parmenides* and, like it, may be considered as a transition to the later period. It contains Plato's analysis of knowledge. It is often considered to be his most intricate and sophisticated dialogue. Plato offers us three definitions of knowledge, and in the end he rejects all three. Towards the beginning of the dialogue, Plato has Socrates compare himself to a midwife (this analogy was discussed in chapter 4). This suggests that Plato is preparing his audience for an inconclusive or *aporetic* ending. The dialogue consists of a long conversation between Socrates and Theaetetus, with some interventions from Theodorus. This conversation is supposed to have taken place in 399 BC but is read out by a slave from the memoirs of Eucleides thirty years later, in 369 BC.

Knowledge as Perception

First, Socrates rejects Theaetetus's definition of knowledge as perception (151d–186e). The most direct argument for this rejection is that to know something requires the judgment that something is so and so. Judging is different from perceiving because it involves thought and concepts such as sameness, difference, and existence, which are not acquired through the senses (183e–187a).

Prior to this argument, Plato provides a more indirect and complex argument: the view that knowledge is perception implies Protagoras's Sophist thesis that man is the measure of all things, which in turn implies Heraclitus's assertion that everything is always changing (160d–e). As both of these theses are false, so is the claim that knowledge is perception (160e–186e).

We can start with the Sophist view of perception. The wind blows; one person feels it as cold, another as warm. Both have equally good credentials for their respective judgments. But we wouldn't want to conclude that the wind itself was both cold and warm, because that is a contradiction. So Protagoras concludes that we cannot make absolute affirmations such as "the wind is cold"; we can only make relative ones such as "the wind is cold for person P." In other words, all judgments are true for the person who makes the judgment, or "man is the measure of all things."

Applying this argument to all perceptions, we can conclude that, according to the Sophist theory, there are no stable objects with enduring properties. First, we cannot make non-relative judgments about objects in themselves; we can only make relativized claims about how things appear to different people. In effect, this means that we can only make claims about appearances or perceptions. In other words, we must give up the ontology of objects in themselves beyond appearances. Second, given this, what we typically consider as changes in the properties of enduring objects in fact becomes only changes in perceptions. Since perceptions are always altering, and there are no stable objects behind those appearances, the Sophist view of perception implies an ontology of constant flux, similar to that of Heraclitus. Therefore, the Sophist view of perception implies that there exists only a constant flux of subjective perceptions and that there are no stable objects with enduring properties.

As we indicated in chapter 6, one might be tempted to think that the issue at stake is that both Sophism and Heraclitus provide partial or incomplete truths. According to this idea, Heraclitus was right to stress the ever-changing nature of the world of sensible things but wrong to conclude that the world as a whole was in constant flux, because this ignores the realm of the Forms. Heraclitus was partially right. Likewise, the relativism of Sophism is also a partial truth, true of the sensible world but not of the Forms. According to this idea, Plato can claim that both Heraclitus and the Sophists are right about the world's sensible particulars but mistaken about the Forms.

However, this tempting idea doesn't fit well with the text of the *Theaetetus*. In this dialogue, Plato doesn't mention the Forms. His basic argumentation goes beyond this point about the incompleteness of both Sophism and Heraclitus's view. The idea is that these twin views are radically mistaken, even about the sensible world. In large part this is because they cannot account for error (see 160b–d). They imply that perception is infallible.

From these observations, we can see that when Plato argues against the claim that knowledge is perception, he is attacking a view that is similar to the much later view called the *Empiricist Theory of Perception*. According to this view, perception consists in the passive reception of sense-data. These sense-data or perceptions are infallible in the sense that one cannot be mistaken about having one. Empiricists also claim that all knowledge is derived from these sense-data. In other words, the thesis under consideration, that knowledge is perception, is a proto-Empiricist view of perception. It is this view that implies Sophism and a Heraclitean ontology of flux.

Plato provides several arguments against both of these views (i.e., Sophism and Heracliteanism). We have already examined the main ones against Sophism in chapter 5. The main critique of Heraclitean ontology of flux is very interesting. Plato argues that if there were only a continuous flux of perceptions or appearances, then no meaningful statement could be made. As we just saw, the Sophist view of perception rejects the ontology of objects. Given this, the thesis that everything is in continuous flux concerns perceptions rather than objects. In other words, there exist only subjective perceptions, and these are in constant flux. Plato seems to be affirming that, given that such a view were true, no statement would be possible.

There are at least two ways to reconstruct Plato's idea in this argument. The first and more modest one aims to show that, under such a view, reference is impossible.[5] One cannot refer to something unless re-identification of the same thing is in principle possible, but re-identification is not possible in this constant Heraclitean flux of perceptions. A richer reconstruction is aimed at the level of meanings. The idea is that

Heraclitean flux excludes the existence of stable meanings and because of this, meaningful statements would be impossible.⁶ Notice how someone who thought that Plato's Forms include meanings as abstract objects and who also thought that Plato doesn't abandon the Theory of Forms in the later works would find this second reconstruction appealing.

Knowledge as True Belief

Having rejected Theaetetus's definition of knowledge as perception, Plato next argues against the definition of knowledge as true belief or judgment. Towards the end of the section (at 200d–201c), Plato argues directly against the claim on the grounds that a judgment can be true by sheer luck; in which case it does not count as knowledge. Plato uses the example of a jury that makes a true judgment, but without knowing its truth. He says that a skillful lawyer can persuade the jury into true belief "about things that only someone who sees them can know" (201b).

As an aside, this latter claim contradicts Plato's view, apparently outlined in the *Republic*, that the only things we can know are the Forms. However, as we saw in the discussion of the *Republic*, Plato may have thought that knowledge was not confined to the Forms.

In the first part of this section of the *Theaetetus*, Plato continues to argue against perception-based or empiricist accounts of knowledge. He argues that such theories cannot provide an adequate account of false belief. Of course, if they cannot do so, then they cannot explain how believing is possible at all.

Plato's first argument for the claim that theories cannot account for false beliefs or judgments is based on the hypothesis that such errors might arise from misidentification. Plato argues that, on perceptual theories of knowledge, misidentifications are impossible (187e–188c). He argues for this as follows. On the one hand, if the person does not know the objects (that are supposedly misidentified) then there is a problem: according to such proto-empiricist theories, one can only make judgments about things one knows. On the other hand, suppose the person knows the objects (that are supposedly misidentified). If the person knows them, then he or she can't misidentify them.

Plato's second argument is based on the idea that false belief consists in judging that which is not. But that which is not is nothing. Consequently, according to this view, false beliefs are beliefs about nothing. But there can be no beliefs about nothing because to be a belief at all, it must be about something. In contemporary language, a belief must have content. In short, the proto-empiricist claim that knowledge is perception leads to an absurdity. This is because, on such a view, knowledge is a form of perception. However, one cannot see what is not present to be seen. In this sense, one cannot see nothing. The same applies to other kinds of perception: there is no perception of nothing. Consequently, for the thesis that knowledge is perception, there can be no false beliefs. As Plato says,

"Knowledge lies not in the effects [of the senses] upon us, but in our reasoning about them. For it is, it seems, possible in the case of the latter to lay hold on reality and truth, but not in the case of the former" (186d).

Knowledge as True Belief with an Account

Finally, Plato discusses the claim that knowledge is true belief with an account, or *logos* (from 201c–210a). This broadly means that knowledge requires knowing why the relevant belief is true. This section of the dialogue has two main parts.

In the first part, Socrates recounts a dream that he had, which contains an explanation of knowledge. He dreamt that all things are either primary elements or complexes (compounds), and that accounts can be given only for the complexes but for not the simples. This means that there is knowledge only of complexes and not of simples. Simples can be perceived but not known (202b).

Plato provides two objections to the theory given in Socrates's dream. The first objection goes as follows (202d–205e). A complex whole either is or isn't identical to its parts. Given that it is identical, it does not make sense to assert that one can know the complex whole but not the simples out of which it is entirely composed. Suppose that we say the whole isn't identical to the parts. This would imply that the whole is a single thing or unit. If this were so, it would have no parts, and it would itself be a simple—in which case, it would be unknowable too. The second objection is the claim that we learn about complex wholes by knowing their parts, i.e., knowing parts is more basic than knowing complex wholes (206a–c). If so, then we may have knowledge of simples too, contrary to Socrates's suggestion.

In the second section of this part of the dialogue, Plato tries to understand what "giving an account" (or *logos*) means (from 206c). He considers three alternatives, of which the third is the most favorable. The first says that giving an account is making one's thoughts vocal. The second alternative, which probably refers back to the theory given in Socrates's dream, is that providing an account consists of enumerating the elements out of which a complex is composed (207a). The third analysis claims that providing an account of X consists of being able to distinguish X from everything else (208c–e). According to this third explanation, to know P is to believe P when P is true and to be able to explain how P is different from anything else.

Socrates criticizes this third analysis. On the one hand, he says that if we mean that the person must make an additional correct judgment about how the thing in question differs from everything else, then this is an absurd requirement (209d–e). It is absurd because it adds nothing. On the other hand, we could require that the person has to *know* how the thing in question differs from everything else (209e). However, this would make the definition of "knowledge" circular.

The dialogue seems to have a puzzling, inconclusive ending. Socrates concludes that knowledge is neither perception, nor true judgment, nor true judgment with an account (210b). The apparent *aporetic* (or inconclusive ending) to the dialogue is perplexing. The claim that knowledge is true belief plus an account is similar to Plato's own views as argued for in the *Meno*, *Phaedo*, *Republic*, and *Symposium*. Why then does the *Theaetetus* reject this claim? There is an important difference between the later dialogue and its predecessors: in these early dialogues, the account is one that provides reasons why the belief in question is true. This specific claim is not mentioned in the *Theaetetus*.

Discussion

One of the notable features of the *Theaetetus* is that it does not explicitly mention the Forms. The significance of this fact is disputed. On the one hand, it seems that Plato is trying to provide an understanding of knowledge that does not require the existence of the Forms, unlike the theories of knowledge given in the *Phaedo* and *Republic*. This might be because he is distancing himself from that theory, after the unanswered objections directed towards it in the *Parmenides*. Such a reading, of course, supports the idea that there is a sharp break between the middle and later dialogues.

On the other hand, if there isn't such a sharp break and if Plato thinks that the objections to the Theory of Forms in the *Parmenides* can be answered, then we might read the *Theaetetus* in a very different way. The dialogue fails to come to a definition of knowledge because such a definition requires the Forms. In other words, the *aporetic* conclusion is an indirect argument for the claim that a definition of knowledge requires mention of the Forms, and hence for the Forms themselves.

The *Timaeus*

At the beginning of the *Timaeus*, Socrates, Timaeus, Critias, and Hermocrates agree to exchange speeches. The *Timaeus* consists in Socrates's summary of his own speech given the day before, and a long speech by Timaeus. The *Critias* is presented as the sequel to the *Timaeus*, and in it Socrates suggests that Hermocrates would speak after Critias (108a). Thus, it is possible that Plato conceived a project consisting of three dialogues: the *Timaeus*, *Critias*, and *Hermocrates*. However, Plato never wrote the last of these three dialogues. The second one breaks off in the middle of a sentence. Only the *Timaeus* is complete.

The *Timaeus* presents a myth of creation based on Plato's metaphysics and epistemology. The conversation between Socrates and Timaeus is set the day after Socrates's speech covering the themes of the *Republic* (19a). After Socrates reviews the conclusions of the previous day, Critias recounts a story, as reported by Solon, of a city on the lost island of Atlantis, which bore many resemblances to Plato's utopia as described in the *Republic*. However, the majority of the dialogue is actually a long speech delivered by Timaeus, an astronomer who "has made it his business to know the nature of the universe" (27a). We can divide the account into three parts: Creation, the Receptacle, and Necessity.

Creation

Timaeus begins by distinguishing between the eternal (which is grasped by reason alone), and the changing, or that which comes to be and never is (which is sensible or perceived by the senses) (28b–c). Anything that changes must have a cause. Thus, the world must have a cause, or a maker (28c). However, a maker needs a model, and the only good model of this world is something changeless. Consequently, this world of becoming is a changing image or likeness of an eternal world of being upon which it is modeled (29b).

Timaeus recounts how the god or the Craftsman is supremely good and therefore wanted the best for the world, insofar as its nature would allow (30a). So he "took over" all that was visible and in discordant motion and brought it to order (30b). He reasoned that the world would be better if it were intelligent, and that to be intelligent, it had to be endowed with a soul.

Accordingly, the god brought into being a world as a living thing, endowed with soul and intelligence, which contains all living things (30c–d). There couldn't have been two or more of them because then there would have had to be another living whole to contain these others, and we would be back to there being only one (31a–b).

This living being needed a solid, tangible and visible body. Thus, it needed to be created from earth (tangible) and fire (visible). To be a three dimensional (solid) unity, it had to be mediated by water and air. The living whole has a spherical, smooth, self-sufficient and self-contained body (33a–34c).

The god made the soul of the living world as follows. This world soul is composed of being that is the intermediary between the indivisible, eternal Being and the divisible, ephemeral realm of Becoming (35a). The demiurge created the world soul from this intermediary being mixed together with a mixture of the Same and the Different.

Next, the demiurge distributed the world soul throughout the universe according to various harmonious and disharmonious relations, thereby setting the entire cosmos into motion (35b–36d). This motion consists in the world soul permeating the whole cosmos and then returning to itself and, through this circular motion, it creates within itself individual consciousness, perception, and thought (37b–d).

The god wanted the living world to be more like its eternal model. But a created thing cannot be eternal. So the god made time, as a model of eternity moving according to number (37d). In this way, time and the universe were begotten together. The universe was made sempiternal or everlasting so that it would be most like the non-temporal or eternal model (38b–c). The temporal nature of the universe allows Timaeus to explain the creation and nature of the Sun, Moon, and planets, which serve as markers of time (38c). He postulates the fixed but revolving stars as gods, and it is these gods who create other living beings (41c–d). Timaeus describes these processes, including the creation of souls and their capacity to perceive.

The Receptacle

Timaeus's account needs a third basic component: a receptacle of all becoming, which serves as the underlying substance or stuff, and also as a spatial field for the body of the living universe (49a–51c and 52b–53b). This receptacle underlies the processes whereby the elements change into one another; for instance, water condenses into earth, or air ignites into fire. He calls this receptacle "what is such" (49e). Furthermore, this substratum receives the imprints of the eternal Forms so as to form the temporal copies or perceptible things. Therefore, the nature of the receptacle is to be available to be shaped and reshaped by the Forms, and it must be devoid of any characteristics in itself (50b–51b). For this reason, commentators on Plato normally would not call this substance *material*. It is interesting to note that Timaeus says it is perplexing and mysterious how the receptacle receives the imprinting from the eternal Forms. In any case, in conclusion, there are three components to the creation of the universe: (1) the eternal Forms or Being, (2) the receptacle or Space, a fixed state for all things that come to be, and (3) the things that become (52a). The first two are like the Father and Mother and the third, their offspring.

During this part of his speech, Timaeus presents the outline of an argument for the Forms as follows (51d–52a):

1. If there is a distinction between understanding and true opinion, then the Forms exist.
2. There is a distinction between understanding and true opinion.
3. Thus, the Forms exist.

Timaeus argues for the second premise, claiming that there is a clear distinction between understanding and true opinion: unlike the latter, the former requires a true account and is not moved by persuasion. We can have the first without the second (51d–e).

This argument needs to be set in the context of the earlier parts of the *Timaeus*. In those earlier passages, Timaeus distinguishes between, on the one hand, the eternal—that which always is and never becomes, and on the other, the changing—that which becomes and never is (28a). The former is grasped by reason and constitutes knowledge, and the latter is sensible, or perceived by the senses, and constitutes at best true opinion (28b–c). In light of these earlier passages, the argument at 51d acquires a new significance: seemingly, it attempts to establish that the objects of knowledge and true belief are different. Knowledge requires a true account (51e), which requires reference to, and hence the existence of, the Forms. True belief does not require such an account. It doesn't require reference to the Forms, and it is made and can be undone by persuasion.

Necessity

Having presented space or filled space as an elementary component of the universe, Timaeus sets out how various geometrical shapes define the four elements and also their different varieties (53b–61c). He also explains how the various sensible properties, such as the various tastes and colors, arise from the characteristics of the different elements and their combinations (61c–68d). Part of the point of these descriptions is to emphasize the necessity of things (69a).

The passages that set out how the four elements are defined by geometrical shapes are remarkable. Timaeus argues that the qualities associated with the four elements depend on the shape of the corpuscles that constitute that element as follows.

- *Earth*: The heaviest element is comprised of corpuscles shaped as a cube.
- *Water*: It is constituted by icosahedrons; this is a 20-sided figure of 20 equilateral triangles.
- *Air*: It is composed of corpuscles shaped as octahedrons, consisting of eight triangular faces.
- *Fire*: It is consists of tetrahedrons (pyramids of four triangular faces).

Timaeus explains how the elements may transform into each other according to their shapes. For instance, two fire corpuscles may be changed into one air, and vice versa. The only element that cannot be so transformed is earth, and this impossibility can also be explained in terms of its shape: one cannot make triangles out of cubes. He also applies these ideas to explain the formation and nature of compounds solely on the basis of their shape and size, and their combinations. He also explains the perceptible qualities of each element in terms of its shape. For example, fire must be hot, bright, and light because of what the Form of fire is, and the most appropriate shape that embodies these qualities of the Form is the tetrahedron.

These passages are notable for a couple of reasons. First, while it is clear that Plato is not an atomist, nevertheless he is showing how features of atomism can be incorporated into the more traditional metaphysics of the four elements, without losing the explanatory necessity of the Forms. Let us unpack this complex point. It is important to remember that Democritus's atomism is a fundamental departure from and challenge to the traditional metaphysics of the Pre-Socratics, which postulated four elements each with different basic qualities: hot versus cold and wet versus dry. In sharp contrast, Democritus claims that we can explain all perceptible qualities solely in terms of the arrangement and motion of differently shaped and sized atoms. Democritus's atoms have no intrinsic properties except their shape and size. In the *Timaeus*, Plato forges a middle position between the traditional four elements and atomism. He attempts to explain the qualities of the four elements in terms of the shape and size of corpuscles. To this extent, he is embracing Democritus's project.

At the same time, it is clear that Plato doesn't accept the basic features of Democritus's theory. Plato continues to argue that any explanation of why things are as they are must involve reference to the changeless Forms. As we saw earlier, the eternal Form of fire has an essence that needs to be embodied in matter of a certain shape. The Platonic point that the physical world is an imperfect and ever-changing embodiment of the perfect and eternal Forms remains unscathed. Any purely mechanical explanation of observable phenomena would be essentially incomplete, according to Plato. Indeed, as we shall see, perhaps the main message of Plato's *Timaeus* is that explanation must involve the Form of Goodness and therefore must be teleological or involve purpose.

There is a second reason why the passages concerning the shape and size of corpuscles are important. Plato's physical explanations are precursors to modern chemistry. Take, for example, Robert Boyle (1627–1691), who might be considered the grandfather of chemistry.[7] Boyle thinks that all physical states of matter can be explained in terms of the combinations and the motions of particles whose intrinsic properties are only shape and size. Boyle uses this point to distinguish between mere mixtures such as oil and water, and compounds, such as chalk, silica and, of course, water, as Lavoisier (1743–1794) realized.

Discussion

In terms of Plato, the importance of the *Timaeus* is that it brings to fruition an idea present but undeveloped in the *Republic*, namely, that the Form of the Good is necessary for all knowledge. The fundamental principle of the creation myth in the *Timaeus* is that everything is made for the best. The Craftsman created the living world because he wanted everything to be good and nothing to be bad insofar as this is possible (30a). From this principle, the nature of the soul and the physical universe are deduced in quite some detail. In other words, the *Timaeus* provides a teleological explanation of the nature of the world. This shows why the Form of the Good is necessary for all knowledge.

In providing a teleological explanation of the nature of the world, Plato also brings to fruition a seed planted in the *Phaedo*. In that dialogue,

Socrates recounts how he was dissatisfied with the mechanistic approach to explanation advanced by the earlier naturalistic thinkers (the Pre-Socratics). He was especially disappointed by the work of Anaxagoras, who had said that the mind is the cause of everything; Socrates had wrongly assumed that this meant that Anaxagoras would provide teleological explanations of nature instead of mechanistic ones.

Plato's plan with the *Timaeus* and *Critias* was to supplement the *Republic* in various ways. First, Plato's idea in the *Timaeus* was to give a metaphysical grounding for his theories of ethics and politics. The order in the universe is reflected in the harmony of the soul, and so human morality must accord with the cosmic order. He gave the account of creation in the form of a myth in order to describe the rational order in the universe without imputing literal truth for his claims. Second, in the sequel, Critias offers to supplement the theoretical characterization of the ideal city-state given by Socrates with a description of the functioning of that state during a time of war. He proposes to do this by recounting how Athens worked when it fought with Atlantis 9,000 years earlier. According to the story, Atlantis was an island in the Atlantic, near the entrance to the Mediterranean Sea, and it had already conquered and was dominating much of the region (108e). However, the dialogue only contains Critias's introductory remarks, and it ends abruptly before the main description starts.

The *Sophist* and the *Statesman*

The dialogue the *Sophist* is set on the day after the discussions of the *Theaetetus*. In this dialogue, Socrates asks an unnamed visitor from Elea and others whether the philosopher, the statesman, and the sophist are three different kinds of intellectual person or a single one. The visitor answers the question in two dialogues: the *Sophist* and the *Statesman*. Plato never wrote a third dialogue, the *Philosopher*, and we cannot be sure whether or not he intended to. The two dialogues take place sequentially on the same day between the visitor from Elea (who is a follower of Parmenides), Theaetetus, and a young person called "Socrates." (Socrates, the teacher of Plato, has almost no role in these two dialogues.)

The aim is to define *sophist*. After some discussion, as an interim conclusion, the visitor notes that they have arrived at six different common characterizations of the sophist (231d–e). He is described as a hired hunter of rich young men; as a wholesaler of learning about the soul; as a retailer of learning about the soul; as a seller of his own learning; as an athlete in verbal combat, distinguished by his expertise in debating; and as someone who cleanses the soul of beliefs that interfere with learning. These are the appearances of sophistry. The visitor challenges the adequacy of these six appearances by arguing that the sophist claims to know or to be an expert in everything by imitating knowledge. Towards the very end of the dialogue, the sophist is defined as the person who produces copies of the truth that are false, and yet he makes them appear to others to be the truth. In other words, the art of the sophist is one of deception.

Falsity and Non-Being

To arrive at this conclusion, the visitor recognizes that he must show how false statements are possible, given that they are about what is not. Remember that he is from Elea, the town of Parmenides (who famously argued that it was impossible to think and speak about what is not). Furthermore, we need to remember that Plato's main critiques of Sophism are based on the idea that Sophism does not permit false statements. To defend those critiques, Plato needs to show how falsity is possible. In other words, to show how Sophism is mistaken, it is necessary to show how Parmenides was wrong. In other words, through the analysis of the visitor, Plato argues as follows:

1. Sophism implies that false beliefs are impossible.
2. False beliefs are possible.
3. Therefore Sophism is mistaken.

To argue for the conclusion, Plato needs to defend the second premise. This point provides the inroad to the discussion on false statements and non-being for which the dialogue is well known.

Plato sketches some puzzles about non-being. He claims that these puzzles also infect our thinking about being too (243c, 250e). The commentator G. E. L. Owen coined the phrase the *Parity Assumption,* according to which any understanding of or confusion about non-being will be equally an understanding of being, and vice versa.[8] Likewise, an account of how statements can be false also will be one of how they can be true.

The first puzzle about non-being is: To what does the phrase *that which is not* refer? The puzzle is that one apparently cannot answer this question without absurdity. On the one hand, the phrase cannot refer to something that is, and thus it appears that it can't refer to something. On the other hand, a person cannot be talking about nothing; a person who says nothing does not even speak (237b–237e). We seem to be trapped in a contradiction.

The second puzzle concerns number. On the one hand, numerical terms such as *the one* and *the many* only apply to what is (i.e., to being and beings).[9] On the other hand, the very terms *those which are not* and *that which is not* are themselves numerical and thus apparently apply only to what is (238a–c). Once again, we are ensnared in a contradiction.

Third, we cannot even conclude that it is impossible to speak and think about that which is not. Even to assert that proposition implies that the phrase refers to some thing that is not or to a set of things that are not. Apparently, we cannot even frame the propositions that affirm that non-being has us locked into contradictions.

In line with the Parity Assumption, Plato also notes some paradoxes about being. One of these concerns change. He notes that the philosopher ought not accept that everything is changeless (Parmenides) but also should reject that everything changes in all ways (Heraclitus). Thus, the philosopher should accept that *that which is* includes both the unchanging and the changing (249d). This sounds very reasonable, but Plato notes a puzzle with this line of thought. We might conclude that *that which is* is a third thing, distinct from both rest and change themselves (250c). However, this implies an apparently absurd result: if *that which is* is not changing, then it needn't be at rest. Likewise, it implies that if *that which is* isn't at rest, then it needn't be changing (250d).

Plato's reply to these puzzles has two parts. In the first, he tries to solve the problem of being by providing a preliminary account of non-being (258e), and in the second, he gives us an account of how false statements are possible (260d).

The Problem of Non-Being Dissolved

Regarding the first part of the reply, Plato argues that the various puzzles arise from a couple of erroneous assumptions. First, there is the assumption that only one name can correspond to one thing (251a–d). This leads, for instance, to the idea that it is impossible for the one to be many, and the many, one. Second, there is the assumption that negation signifies the contrary (257b–d). For instance, we shouldn't assume that *not* attached to *large* indicates small; it only indicates something other than large. This point applies to "that which is." The negation of the phrase does not indicate its contrary, but rather something other than "that which is" (258b).[10] Plato expresses this point with a paradoxical twist by saying that "that which is not" is.

Now we can see how the rejection of the first assumption about names also kicks in. *The different* doesn't name one thing. There are myriad ways to be different. So, there are many ways to be different from that which is. Thus, there are many ways to be "that which is not."

We might conclude that *those which are not* are. Furthermore, "that which is not" is really "each part of the nature of the different that is set over that which is" (258e). In other words, the phrase "those which are not" indicates ways of being that are different from "that *which is*."

The Problem of False Statements Solved

Regarding the second part of his reply to the various puzzles, to explain how false beliefs and statements are possible, we need the idea that statements are complex and have a structure. In it simplest form, a statement must have a name and a verb (262a). Consequently, a mere list of names (e.g., lion, stag, horse) or of verbs (walks, runs, sleeps) does not constitute a statement. Furthermore, a statement is an affirmation of how things are. With a statement, the speaker doesn't just name, but he or she asserts something by "weaving verbs with names" (262d). How do these two points explain falsehood? First, falsity is possible even though the statement refers to something, because the combination is mistaken. *Theaetetus flies* is false, even though the statement refers to Theaetetus. Second, the assertion is false because it asserts how things are, but differently from how they actually are (263b).

Having shown that false statements are possible, the visitor from Elea can now complete his characterization of the sophist as merely an imitation of the wise person (268c): he is an insincere producer of speeches that copy appearances without knowledge (268d).

Discussion

In order to show that the sophist, statesman, and philosopher are indeed distinct, the sequel dialogue characterizes the statesman as the person who has specialized, expert knowledge of how to run a city-state.

One of the very important threads running through both dialogues is Plato's elaboration of the method of division, or collection and division. The method aims to characterize the verbal definition of a kind by looking for relevant dichotomizing divisions. The visitor proposes to illustrate the method by taking an easier example or model case before attempting to define the more elusive kind, *sophist* (218d). He employs the example *angler*. The method proceeds by dividing activities into expert and non-expert, expert actions into acquisition or production, acquisition into exchange and taking possession, the latter into combat and hunting, and so on. Each division into two types helps specify more accurately what the activity of the angler is (218e–221c). In the *Statesman*, the visitor presents refinements to the method, such as how to divide a class into real as opposed to merely conventional subclasses: the division between Greek and barbarian is conventional.

THE *LAWS*

Towards the end of his life, Plato wrote his longest dialogue, the *Laws*, dedicated again to the theme of an ideal political system and legal code. There are some sharp contrasts between this later work and the *Republic*, which we shall briefly explore in this section.

The dialogue begins with three elderly characters, Clinius from Crete, Megillus from Sparta, and an Athenian who is walking from Knossus to Mount Ida in Crete. On the journey, the Athenian quizzes his colleagues about the purposes of their civic institutions. The state does not exist solely for the purpose of war, but more importantly, for the sake of education, training for the virtues of peacetime. At the end of Book III, Clinias says that he is one of the commissioners entrusted to make the laws of a new city on Crete. This announcement changes the direction of the conversation: the Athenian offers his advice on the legal code needed to achieve the purposes outlined earlier. Perhaps the most important aspect of the dialogue is the discussion of the preambles to each law. These prologues explain the purposes of each piece of legislation so that citizens will conform willingly to the law. The texts of the laws contain commands backed by the threat of punishment, and without a preamble such laws would not be appropriate for free persons (Book IV).

As we have seen throughout this chapter, a reoccurring theme concerning Plato's later dialogues is the Theory of Forms. Do the criticisms of the theory in the *Parmenides* lead Plato to substantially alter his theory? Or does he think that he has answered those criticisms in the later part of the *Parmenides*? If the answer to the first question were yes, then we would expect a radical break between the dialogues of the middle period and those of the late. Such a break would be confirmed by the lack of reference to the Forms in many of the later dialogues. In sharp contrast, if the answer to the second question were yes, then we should *not* expect a radical break, and the comparative lack of mention of the Forms in many of the later dialogues would be a question of emphasis: the theory of Forms is part of the assumed background.

Bearing these points in mind, one of the differences between the *Laws* and the *Republic* is that whereas the *Republic* is centered around the Forms, they are hardly mentioned at all in the *Laws*. In discussing the Nocturnal Council, Plato describes the higher studies expected of the council, such as mathematics, astronomy, theology, morals, and jurisprudence. He mentions that they must learn how to look for a common shape or form among dissimilar instances. Apart from that fleeting allusion, the Forms are not referred to at all in the dialogue. Nevertheless, it would be rash to simply assume that this means that Plato has abandoned his Theory of Forms or reevaluated their moral and political significance, as we shall soon see.

There is a second important difference. Plato's *Republic* characterizes an ideal city-state, a utopia, without reference to whether it could be put into practice. For example, we might question whether the level of self-interest expected of the guardians is a practical possibility. In contrast, the *Laws* seeks a practical utopia, which is called *Magnesia*.

This second difference underlies a third. In the *Republic*, the guardians can rule without laws and without the consent of the citizens because of their wisdom. In a similar vein, in the *Statesman*, Plato refers to rule through a code of laws as a second-best system of governance. In contrast, Magnesia is a "law state" and much of the dialogue is devoted to describing the details of its legal code. Although it requires political wisdom to frame laws, following them does not.

Fourth, in the *Republic*, power is concentrated entirely in the guardians. In sharp contrast, in the *Laws*, every citizen has some legislative role. Even though power is unequally divided in the society, there is some concession to the need for democracy, and some recognition of the need to distribute power more widely in society. It is less elitist. It is described as halfway between monarchy and democracy. For example, the Nocturnal Council constitutes the intellectual aristocracy of the city. However, the Guardians of the Laws are elected through a vote in presence of the citizens. All citizens are members of the Assembly and they all vote for the members of the executive council of the Assembly. However, the Council has four classes of members based on wealth and, unlike the voting of the richer classes, those of the poorer classes is not compulsory. The general effect is to favor the political participation of the wealthier.

This doesn't necessarily mean that Plato has changed his political views. It might rather indicate that his project is less idealistic. His aim might be to describe a second-best, but more achievable, city-state.

Despite these four very important differences, there are also similarities between the politics of the two dialogues. In both cases, moral education is an important function of the state. Book VII of the *Laws* is devoted entirely to this theme. The prescribed education is different, with less emphasis on mathematics in the later dialogue. Second, in both dialogues, there is little toleration for views and practices that would undermine the virtue of the citizens. Both societies have a single ideology or political doctrine, which, apart from the differences already mentioned, is fundamentally similar: the health of both societies depends on the virtue and the *eudaimonia* of its participants. In Book X, Plato describes a set of religious beliefs that all Magnesians should accept on pain of legal penalties. The idea is that these beliefs are necessary for the stability of the state. Third, Plato's *Republic* is famous for making the guardian class open to women. The *Laws* follows the same principle: women are voting citizens and all public offices are open to them.

Conclusion

What conclusions should we reach about later dialogues? There are some striking differences compared to the middle-period classics.

1. The absence of Socrates as the main protagonist is a notable change.

2. There are also noteworthy differences in style. The *Timaeus* and the *Critias* contain long speeches, and in the Sophist and the *Statesman*, the interlocutors are relatively passive and quiet.

3. The previous point might indicate a more general and profound trend. In the early dialogues, Socrates's method was inherently dialogic. As we saw in chapter 6, the middle-period works try to

overcome the limitations of the Socratic dialogical method to support more universal conclusions, many of which are Socratic in spirit. The later dialogues introduce even more systematic and quasi-scientific approaches.

4. The later dialogues are less metaphysical in content. For example, the definitions and essences pursued in the *Sophist* and the *Statesman* are not linked explicitly to the transcendent Forms. We should not automatically conclude from this that Plato abandoned, or even significantly modified, his Theory of Forms. If the second half of the *Parmenides* contains the framework of a defense of the theory from the criticisms given in the first, and given that the myth of Timaeus relies on the Forms as paradigms, then the later dialogues exhibit a shift of emphasis rather than a change of direction. Plato is no longer elaborating and defending a grand metaphysical scheme but is more concerned with its worldly applications. Even the discussion of being and non-being in the *Sophist* is more concerned with clarifying language use than theory construction. Its metaphysics is immanent rather than transcendent.

5. This general point is also echoed in the political content of the later period. As we just saw, the aim of the *Laws* seems to be more pragmatic and less idealistic than that of the *Republic*.

Despite these differences between the middle and late dialogues, the continuities may seem more important. For instance, the *Timaeus* and the *Critias* are a continuation of the project of the *Republic*. Even the *Laws* might be best understood in this light—as a compromise: a description of a city-state that best serves the *eudaimonia* of its participants given the practical reality that concentrating so much power in the hands of a guardian class.

Study Questions

1. What is Plato's Third Man Argument?
2. What is the greatest difficulty with Plato's Theory of Forms according to Parmenides?
3. In the *Parmenides*, how does Plato reply to the challenges to his Theory of Forms given by Parmenides?
4. In the *Theaetetus*, how does Plato argue against the claim that knowledge is perception?
5. How does he argue that the thesis that all knowledge is perception entails a Sophist view of perception, which in turn implies a Heraclitean view of flux?
6. How does Plato argue that the thesis that all knowledge is perception entails that false beliefs are impossible?

7. In the *Theaetetus,* how does Plato criticize the thesis that knowledge is a true belief and an account?
8. Describe Plato's creation myth in the *Timaeus.*
9. In what ways is Plato's description of the natural world teleological in the *Timaeus,* and why is this important philosophically?
10. In the *Sophist,* Plato defends the claim that false beliefs are possible. How and why does he do this?
11. In the *Sophist,* how does Plato dissolve the problem of non-being? Why does he need to do this?
12. What is Plato's method of division?
13. Describe some of the main differences between the ideal city-state of the *Republic* and that of the *Laws.*

Discussion Questions

1. In what ways is it contrary to contemporary science to describe the world in teleological terms as Plato does in the *Timaeus*? Can Plato salvage his claim that all knowledge depends on the Form of Goodness from such criticisms?
2. Does Plato really answer Parmenides and dissolve the problem of non-being? Are there nonexistent things?
3. Does the *Laws* present a better political theory than the *Republic*?

PART III

Introduction to Aristotle

Plato's philosophy seems to provide the necessary antidote to the subjectivism inherent in some Sophist thought. It allows us to think that there are true answers to important questions concerning the meaning of human life, the nature of justice, and the best way to organize a society. Even if we don't know what they are, in principle there are answers to discover. At the same time, Plato's theory also allows us to transcend the narrow naturalism of some of the Pre-Socratics. It apparently shows us why naturalism cannot explain the form of things, and how the organization of the natural world requires appeal to non-natural eternal principles. It also permits us to resolve some of the problems of Pre-Socratic philosophy, such as the conflict between the changing, temporal world of Heraclitus and the eternal, timeless world described by Parmenides. Given these points, the thought of Plato may seem close to the summit of philosophy. Plato provides good solutions to old problems, combining the strengths of Pre-Socratic and Sophist thinking while avoiding their limitations.

However, Aristotle brings a perspective that ascends to an even higher plane. Central to this new vista is the following question: in order to avoid the subjectivism of the Sophists and the naturalism of the Pre-Socratics, do we *need* to postulate the existence of Platonic Forms? Plato contends that we do. He assumes that we can only avoid the different kinds of Sophism, such as egoism, pragmatism, and subjectivism, by showing how there must exist a nonmaterial, eternal Form of Goodness, separate from the world of particular objects.

There are two kinds of challenges to Plato's assumption. First, doubts start to creep in when we consider some of the problems associated with Plato's Theory of the Forms. For instance, can we affirm that there must be one Form of Goodness when different things are good in different ways? Must goodness be univocal in order to be objective? Could there be objective goodness without one Form? There are several other problems associated with the Theory of Forms. For instance, Plato postulates the existence of the Forms to explain knowledge. But how do human beings grasp the Forms, given that the latter are immaterial and eternal and that we are temporal beings? How can knowledge of the eternal explain beliefs about changing particulars?

Second, Aristotle provides a whole new set of considerations, a fresh approach that rejects the subjectivism of the Sophists without accepting the absolute nature of Plato's Theory of Forms. As we shall see, Aristotle had the insight to make classifications based on fundamental principles in many areas of human knowledge, including our use of language. In each of these areas, Aristotle emphasized the role of systematic empirical observation but without rejecting the need for organizing principles.

The review of this vast panorama of Aristotle's thought will engage us for the next four chapters as follows. In chapter 9, we examine Aristotle's methodology, his logic, and his philosophy of science. In chapter 10 we look at his physics and biology. His physics includes his work on the four causes, the infinite, and space and time. It also covers his work on astronomy, and what we today call chemistry. Aristotle's biology is mostly concerned with animals. In chapter 11, we investigate his metaphysics, including theology, and his arguments against the Pre-Socratics and Plato. This chapter will also cover his philosophical work in psychology, including perception and reason. Finally, chapter 12 will examine Aristotle's ethics, his politics, and (briefly) his aesthetics. One of the alluring characteristics of Aristotle's work is that his key concepts bring together all these themes under one unified approach.

THE LIFE OF ARISTOTLE (384–322 BC)

Aristotle was born in Stagira, in Macedonia (today in northern Greece). His family was wealthy; Aristotle's father, Nicomachus, was personal physician to the king Amyntas III of Macedonia in Northern Greece. His father died when Aristotle was a boy, and his uncle became his guardian. In 367 BC, the seventeen-year-old Aristotle went to Athens to study at Plato's Academy. We know very little of Aristotle's time there, but he probably studied astronomy, mathematics, and political theory, as well as the traditional subject areas of philosophy such as metaphysics, epistemology, and ethics.

In 347 BC, Plato died. Plato's nephew, Speusippus, became head of the Academy, and Aristotle left Athens to embark on a new independent life of intellectual exploration, probably in part because, under the direction of Speusippus, the Academy would acquire an even greater mathematical orientation. Aristotle moved to Assos, on the western coast of modern Turkey, for three years. There he married Pythias, the niece of King Hermeias; they had a daughter also named Pythias. During those three years, Aristotle established an academy and probably studied the local marine life. When King Hermeias was deposed, Aristotle moved to the nearby island of Lesbos, in northwestern Turkey. On Lesbos, he established a collaboration and friendship with Theophrastus, who was from the local town of Mytilene. During this whole period, Aristotle made many biological observations. He collected information regarding approximately 500 animal species.

In 343 BC, he was summoned by Philip of Macedonia to return to his homeland to tutor his son, Alexander the Great, who was then aged 13. Aristotle's tutoring of Alexander was probably intensive for about two years because, when he was 15, Alexander was appointed Regent. Nevertheless, Aristotle remained in this post for another five years, until 336 BC, when Alexander himself became the king of Macedonia and began his conquest of the ancient world. It is probable that, while Aristotle remained at the court of Philip, he continued his biological explorations with the help of all the king's fishermen, hunters, and farmers.

In 334 BC, at the age of 50, Aristotle returned to Athens to establish his own school, the Lyceum, in a grove in the north of Athens. The return to Athens marks the mature period of Aristotle's intellectual life, during which he composed most of his famous works. Although he was a prolific writer, only fragments of his published writings remain. However, his unpublished writings have survived in the form of lecture notes used by his students. He produced groundbreaking texts on many subjects: metaphysics, logic, argumentation, physics, astronomy, meteorology, taxonomy, biology, perception, psychology, ethics, politics, and aesthetics.

The Lyceum was a center of teaching, learning, and investigation. Aristotle gathered around him fellow students of nature and lovers of understanding, and he coordinated a systematic investigation covering almost all areas of human knowledge, which continued after his death. Aristotle also collected hundreds of manuscripts, maps, and natural specimens, and the Lyceum became one of the first libraries and museums. We know, for example, that it contained the constitutions of 158 city-states.

During this period, Aristotle's first wife died, and he married Herpyllis, with whom he had a son called Nicomachus. Aristotle's *Nicomachean Ethics* are named after his son. When Alexander died in 323 BC, Athens became a center of anti-Macedonian feelings. Aristotle was accused of impiety, apparently for a hymn praising Hermeias, the king of Assos. He decided to leave Athens for Chalcis, on the island of Euboea in the north of Greece. The following year he died at the age of sixty-two.

9

Aristotle
Logic and Science

It is astounding that, within the space of about 100 years, ancient Greek philosophy produced three thinkers as profound, wide-ranging, and influential as Socrates, Plato, and Aristotle.[1] However, it might be reasonably claimed that Aristotle was the greatest philosopher of the trio on all three counts, despite his reliance on his predecessors. Certainly, the range of his work was extraordinarily wide. The collected writings of Aristotle consist of 32 works. Following is the list of Aristotle's mature writings as known to us today.

- Logic: *Categories, On Interpretation, Prior Analytics, Posterior Analytics, Topics, Sophistical Refutations*
- Metaphysics: *Metaphysics*
- Natural Philosophy: *Physics, Meteorology, On the Heavens, On Generation and Corruption*
- On Animals: *History of Animals, Parts of Animals, Movement of Animals, Progression of Animals, Generation of Animals*
- On Humans: *De Anima, Sense and Sensibilia, On Memory, On Sleep, On Dreams, On Divination in Sleep, On Length of Life, On Youth and Death, On Respiration, On Breath*
- Ethics and Politics: *The Nicomachean Ethics, Eudemian Ethics, The Politics, The Constitutions*
- Aesthetics: The *Rhetoric, Poetics*

Three other types of works are not included in this list:

1. *Aristotle's early works*: Diogenes Laërtius lists 19 dialogues, written during the first period of Aristotle's adult life in Plato's Academy, which probably reflect Plato's views.[2] For some of these dialogues we have only fragments.[3] For others we only have only the names.[4] Cicero praised Aristotle's dialogues for their style, and they were considered to be equally as good as Plato's own dialogues.[5] Aristotle was famous during antiquity for his dialogues.

2. *Possible missing works from the mature period*: Three lists of Aristotle's works from antiquity exist. The oldest is that of Diogenes Laërtius from the early third century AD[6] Earlier lists have not survived. Diogenes cites 143 titles, and the catalogue does not include some of Aristotle's important works that have actually survived.
3. *Works possibly not by Aristotle*: There are several writings that are probably not authored by Aristotle but are included in the general collection of his works.[7] With some, it is unclear whether Aristotle wrote them at all. For instance, while some scholars argue that Aristotle was the author of the *Magna Moralia*, others disagree.

None of these lists are definitive. One of the main reasons for these uncertainties is that, in about 60 BC, the last head of the Lyceum, Andronicus of Rhodes, edited the manuscripts, grouping them together according to their relevant subjects. Consequently, many of Aristotle's works as known today may be compilations gathered from several shorter pieces. This is true of, for example, the *Metaphysics*. This may be part of the reason why Diogenes's list of the works is so much longer than ours.

For this reason too, it is notoriously tricky to date Aristotle's writings. Some of them may consist of parts composed at different times. For instance, some parts of Aristotle's mature works were penned before he returned to Athens in 334 BC: this may be true of the *Eudemian Ethics*, the *Metaphysics*, and parts of his writings on logic. Despite the difficulties in dating, it is clear that some of the works, such as the *Categories*, come from the early period when Aristotle was at Plato's Academy (367–347). The biological works may date from a middle period, roughly 347–335, when Aristotle was away from Athens. Many of Aristotle's most famous works were composed during the last third of his life, after he established the Lyceum in 335.

In general, these later works were notes that were probably written for the students and scholars of the Lyceum, who had already attended the relevant lectures. They are not books intended for the general public. Because they are lecture notes, they are often cryptic and difficult to understand, and many controversies exist concerning their interpretation. Most of Aristotle's writings are divided in books, and each book is subdivided into chapters. Sometimes the chapters are only a paragraph or two in length.

To appreciate the breadth of Aristotle's work, we might also sketch the activities of the Lyceum, a center of teaching, learning, and investigation founded and run by Aristotle. Aristotelian philosophers are sometimes called the *Peripatetics* (from the word *peripatoi*, which means covered walk) because in the mornings Aristotle and his pupils would walk up and down the gardens discussing philosophy. In the afternoons and evenings, there would be lectures. The Lyceum was a research institution that covered most areas of knowledge. For example, Meno wrote the history of medicine. Theophrastus complemented Aristotle's research on animals with an equally extensive investigation of plants. Strato worked on dynamics and mechanics, studying the lever, the pulley, and the wedge. The constitutions of Greek cities were catalogued. The Lyceum contained hundreds of manuscripts, maps, natural objects, and specimens; it was in effect one of the first libraries and museums, as well as being a research institute.

Some Contrasts with Plato

Let us begin our study of Aristotle by noting six very general features of his philosophy that characterize his thinking in contrast to that of Plato.

First, Aristotle's general philosophical approach is very different from Plato's. Plato's work is often otherworldly, and his method of philosophical investigation is rational rather than empirical. This is basically because of his Theory of the Forms and its rationalist epistemology: reasoning is required beyond the realm of things known through the senses.[8] In contrast, Aristotle develops the idea of the systematic empirical investigation of nature. He displays detailed knowledge of animals, physics, and other natural phenomena. Aristotle often starts his philosophical reflection by describing the relevant phenomena as they appear to us. He is unwilling to disregard and discard those appearances. For example, in reaction to Parmenides's claim that all change is an illusion, Aristotle retorts that it is self-evident that natural things change (*Physics* II, 1, 193a3–6). His reply to Socrates's claim that weakness of the will is impossible is similar. In both cases, he attempts to explain how these observable phenomena are possible, despite the arguments of earlier philosophers.

Although Aristotle thinks that the scientific understanding of nature requires empirical observation, he is not a modern empiricist. Scientific knowledge also requires comprehending first principles and understanding what follows from them. Thus, reasoning from principles is an important part of science too. Aristotle's method involves both building up an understanding of principles from sense experience, and reasoning about observations from those principles.

A second characteristic of Aristotle's approach is that he finds and defines problems concerning an area of study. Consider his approach to time in the *Physics*. Before he outlines a view of time, he systematically outlines the different problems that make the nature of time difficult to understand. Again and again, Aristotle shapes his discussion of an area of philosophy around a set of problems.

A third feature of Aristotle's method is that when addressing a problem, he surveys the views and arguments of earlier philosophers on the same issue. This method of reviewing past opinions is called the *endoxa*, which means "credible beliefs" Aristotle says:

> *Endoxa* are those opinions accepted by everyone, or by the majority, or by the wise—and among the wise, by all or most of them, or by those who are the most notable and having the highest reputation. (*Topics* 100b21–23)

Aristotle carries out such reviews because he thinks that there is much to learn from the work of earlier thinkers. Even when he disagrees with them, he finds in their thought some truth or insight that helps him towards a new analysis and solution, and of course, he tries to learn from their mistakes as well. For this reason, in disputes between two sides, often Aristotle concludes that both sides are right in one way and wrong in another. This adds nuance to his thought and helps to provide strategic depth.

Often, this strategic feature of Aristotle's thinking allows him to construct a third position that avoids an apparent dichotomy. For example, Aristotle's form/matter distinction allows him to avoid the dichotomy between the naturalism of some of the Pre-Socratic philosophers and the formalism of Plato. Both have something right about them, but both are fundamentally mistaken. Likewise, we might look at Aristotle's ethics in part as carving out a third way, avoiding the dichotomy between the subjective approach of the Sophists and the absolutist approach of Plato, as we shall see in chapter 12.

A fourth characteristic of Aristotle's thinking is his use of classification, which extends from his work in biology to areas of philosophy such as metaphysics, language, ethics, and politics. For example, he classifies different categories, logical inferences, explanations, virtues, and political systems. One reason why Aristotle's thought is so penetrating is that he applies a classificatory approach, at a meta-level, to the concepts relevant to the phenomena under study. It is distinctive of his thinking, for instance, that he asserts that things can be said to exist in many ways. It is also typical when he says that he must begin the study of the infinite by distinguishing the ways in which the term *infinite* is used (*Physics* 204a3–204a6). This meta-classificatory feature adds nuance to his thought. For example, because things can exist in many ways, Aristotle can affirm that Plato's claim that the Forms exist is correct in some respects and wrong in others. It is characteristic of his approach that he should seek clarity concerning an issue by asking in what ways the relevant key words are used. For example, when investigating whether heavenly bodies are indestructible, he investigates in what sense we use the terms *heavenly* and *indestructible* in Book I of *On the Heavens*.

Fifth, Aristotle rejects the Platonic thesis that there is a separate nonmaterial realm of Forms or Ideas. He argues that the forms exist only as the essence of things in the natural world. In short, Aristotle replaces Plato's dichotomy between the Forms and appearances with his own form/matter distinction. This aspect of Aristotle's thought is sometimes called *hylomorphism*. Provisionally, it is the view that particular substances are complexes of form and matter.⁹ The form and matter of a natural object are simply two aspects of its existence, which are separable only in thought. They are not two independently existing things. Provisionally, we might conceive of Aristotelian form as the structure or organization of a natural thing. For example, the form of an animal is the way the matter of its body is organized, such that it has the power to grow, perceive, and move in the way it does. This constitutes the essence of the animal. The matter is the material out of which the substance or object in question is composed. Matter cannot exist without form, and form requires matter.¹⁰

Returning to an earlier point, Aristotle's hylomorphism allows him to build a third alternative to the metaphysics of the naturalists of the Pre-Socratic period and to that of Plato. Put simply, the early Pre-Socratics identify substances with the matter out of which they are composed, while Plato identifies substances with the Forms. In this they share a similar error: thinking of one aspect of substance as if it were substance. Let us look into this a little more deeply. On the one hand, according to Aristotle, the early naturalist Pre-Socratics identify substance with the matter, or the stuff of which everything is composed. They treat matter as the primary existent. Against these Pre-Socratics, Aristotle argues that individual substances, such as plants and animals, are not reducible to the matter of which they are composed. On the other hand, Plato claims that reality consists in eternal Forms and treats universals as if they were substances. Aristotle denies that universals are substances. Form is an aspect of a substance. In this manner, Aristotle is able to develop a position distinct from those of the Pre-Socratics and Plato. He is able to avoid the dichotomy according to which denying the naturalism of the Pre-Socratics requires embracing the formalism of Plato.

This brings us to an allied sixth aspect of Aristotle's thought. He is master of the concept of *qua*. (Qua means *with respect to*.) The word *qua* specifies under what aspect something is studied or thought about. For instance, physiology studies humans *qua* body; psychology studies the human *qua* mental states and behavior; and sociology studies human beings *qua* members of society.

Aristotle's use of *qua* allows him to answer questions in a nuanced way. For example, is a bed something artificial or natural? Aristotle answers that, *qua* its form, a bed is an artifact, but *qua* its matter (i.e., the wood out which it is made), it is something natural. This idea of *qua*, or of different respects, allows Aristotle to treat mathematics in a way quite different from Plato. According to Aristotle, mathematics concerns itself with the physical world abstracted from physical change. In other words, it deals with substances *qua* (or with respect to) number, line, and geometrical figure, but not *qua* their physical nature (see *Physics* II, 3). This avoids the need for distinct mathematical objects. Likewise, Aristotle can refer to a substance *qua* its form or *qua* its matter without supposing that these are distinct objects.

As a broad and simplistic generalization, Plato was more analytic, humanistic, and religious, with an eye cast towards mathematics. Aristotle was more synthetic, scientific, and secular in his epistemology, with an eye directed towards logic.

THE *ORGANON*: SCIENTIFIC METHOD

Aristotle's scientific methodology is presented in six works that were later compiled as the *Organon*, which served as a definitive text until the sixteenth century. The *Categories* concerns the basic types of words, which are the parts of complete statements. *On Interpretation* is about these whole statements, which form parts of syllogisms. The *Prior Analytics* is a work in the logic of syllogisms. The *Posterior Analytics* explains the use of these syllogisms in scientific investigation. Finally, the *Topics* and the *Sophistical Refutations* systematize the use of arguments in dialectics and identify some informal fallacies. Presented in this way, the compilation has an obvious order, though it is one imposed by later thinkers.

This cumulative work constitutes an achievement that is hard for us to appreciate. In the *Sophistical Refutations*, Aristotle himself writes about informal logical fallacies and the syllogism:

> Of our present subject, however, it would not be true to say that part had already been worked out and part had not; it did not exist at all. (183b34)

What he says here might be extended to the whole idea of the systematic scientific investigation of nature, which hardly existed before. As well as carrying out such research, Aristotle described the methodology of these investigations; he invented a philosophy of science.

THE *CATEGORIES*

The *Categories* is probably an early work. The first four chapters of the *Categories* explain the general concept of a category, and the remaining chapters (5–14) discuss each particular category. The fifth chapter concentrates on the primary category of substance.

To discuss the different ways in which things can be or exist, Aristotle first defines *synonymy*, *homonymy*, and *paronymy* in chapter 1 of the *Categories*. Two things are synonymous when the same word is used to name them in virtue of the same characteristics. For example, man and ox are synonymous with regard to being animals. Two things are homonymous when they have the same name in common, but in virtue of different characteristics. For instance, a human and a picture of a human are homonymous because both are said to be animals but in virtue of different features. In other words, homonymy occurs when the same term is used in absence of a single common defining feature.[11] Two things are paronymous when the two names do not pick out the same thing and do not have the same definition, but the one term is derived from the other. For example, the term *grammarian* is derived from *grammar*.

Although Aristotle first explains homonymy in the *Categories*, he makes little explicit use of it in that text. Nevertheless, it is a central concept of Aristotle's thought. For example, in *Metaphysics*, Book IV, chapter 2, Aristotle explains how different things may be said to be healthy (1003a33–1003b18). Sports, athletes, complexions, and diets are all healthy, but they are so in different but connected, ways. These are healthy in a secondary or a derivative way. The primary way of being healthy is to have a body in excellent functioning shape. The secondary ways of being healthy derive from this primary way. In such a case, the same name does not pick out the same quality and does not have the same definition, but the use in the one case is derived from the other. In the *Metaphysics*, Aristotle uses this analysis of health to better understand existence. He explains how existence and being are (core-dependent) homonymous. Things can exist in a primary and secondary ways. In other words, what is it is to exist as a substance is quite different from what it is to exist as a quality or as a relation.

Should this phenomenon be called homonymy? There are two difficulties. First, today, homonymy indicates that the same word can be used in two unrelated ways, such as *bat* and *bank*.[12] Clearly, Aristotle typically isn't using the term to refer to such outright ambiguities. He is trying to identify a middle ground between strict synonymy and strict non-univocity. Recently, Christopher Shields has advocated the term *core-dependent homonymy* for the phenomenon that Aristotle has identified.[13] Second, the contemporary terms *synonymy* and *homonymy* apply to words. In contrast, Aristotle intends his distinction to be applied primarily to things rather than to words.[14] Consequently, the categories indicate primarily different ways that things can be, rather than only different kinds of words.

In chapter 2 of the *Categories*, Aristotle distinguishes between what may be said without combination and with combination. Those said with combination are whole propositions, such as *man runs*, that can be true or false (2a5–2a12). Those things that are said without combination are, for example, man, ox, runs, and wins. Things can be so said in different ways, and these ways are the categories. Aristotle lists ten of them in chapter 4 (1b25–2a4). These are:

1. Substance, or what is it? (e.g., *horse*)
2. Quantity, or how much? (e.g., *is four feet tall*)
3. Quality, or what kind? (e.g., *is white*)
4. Relations, or in relation to what? (e.g., *is larger than*)
5. Where? (e.g., is in the marketplace)

6. When? (e.g., *yesterday*)
7. Position? (e.g., *is upright*)
8. Having? (e.g., *has shoes on*)
9. Doing? (e.g., *is running*)
10. Being affected by? (e.g., *is being ridden*)

This list is repeated in the *Topics* (I, 9, 103b23). In other places, Aristotle cites eight or six categories (dropping *having* and *position*).[15] In the *Topics*, Aristotle says that the list is of categories of predication. According to this idea, the categories define different ways in which predicates may say something about their subject. For example, they may say what the subject is, what it is like, where it is, and so on.

The most fundamental category is the first, substance (*ousia*) (chapter 5, 2a13–4b19). Aristotle argues that substances are the basic or primary constituents of reality, and this point is central to his metaphysics. This means that all the other categories indicate dependent existents. Aristotle says, "All the other things are either said of the primary substances as subjects or in them as subjects" (2a35–6).

This is why substance is always included in all lists of the categories, in addition to quality and quantity. In the *Categories*, Aristotle examines the categories in turn, dedicating chapter 5 to substance, chapter 6 to quantities, chapter 7 to relations, chapter 8 to qualities, and chapter 9 to doing and being affected.

Although there are many interpretations of what the categories are, the primary debate is whether they constitute different kinds of existence or different kinds of predications. Fundamentally, is the list ontological or semantic? If it is both, then Aristotle's list is of the different ways in which things can exist (ontological), as well as being a list of the basic types of predications (i.e., semantic). If it is both, then is one of these primary?

The reasoning that leads Aristotle to conclude that the list of the basic type of existents is the same as that of the basic predicates may be as follows. If we ask what blue is, the answer is "a color." If we ask what color is, the answer is "a quality." However, we cannot ask for a higher classification for quality itself. For this reason, it is a category, an ultimate classification. The basic predicates indicate the fundamental classes into which all things fall. Therefore, they indicate fundamental types of things.[16]

ON INTERPRETATION

On Interpretation is primarily about things said in combination, such as sentences, statements, affirmations and negations. In chapter 1 he points out that names and verbs on their own "without combination" are neither true nor false (16a10–16a18). In chapter 4 he distinguishes between sentences and statements. A sentence is a significant combination of words. A statement is a sentence that affirms or denies a predicate of a subject. For example, the statement "Socrates is bald" affirms the predicate *bald* of the subject *Socrates*. Clearly, not all sentences are statements. For example, prayers, commands, and questions are sentences that are not statements (17a1–17a7).

One might claim that all statements are by their nature true or false; not all sentences are. This, however, is not right, according to Aristotle, because there are some statements that aren't true or false (yet), namely, those concerning the future, as we shall now see.

The Sea Battle

In chapter 9 Aristotle notes that, apparently, for any statement, necessarily either it or its denial is true (18a28–18a33). This is called the *law of excluded middle*.[17] Logically, it is expressed as "Either P or not P." Does this principle apply to statements about particular future events? Aristotle thinks not. He says, "With particulars that are going to be it is different" (18a33).

His argument for this claim has two parts. In the first part, Aristotle presents a piece of reasoning that concludes: if the law of excluded middle were true concerning statements about the future, then the future would be fixed (18a34–18b16). In the second part, Aristotle rejects this reasoning and tries to show that, to avoid the idea of a fixed future, we must abandon the law of excluded middle with regard to statements about the future (19a23–19b4).

First Part

Suppose that I predict that there will be a sea battle tomorrow. Is my prediction now true, or is it false? Either way, there is a problem. On the one hand, necessarily, if the prediction were now true, then there will be a sea battle tomorrow. Given that the statement is true now, there is no alternative: necessarily, the sea battle will take place. On the other hand, suppose that the prediction is already false: assume that it is false now that there will be a sea battle tomorrow. Once again, necessarily, if my prediction is now false, then there will not be a sea battle tomorrow. Given that the prediction is now false, then there is no alternative outcome. Either way, it looks as if the future is fixed or predetermined, or that there is no possibility of chance or contingency, given that the law of excluded middle applies to particular predictions.

This conclusion does not depend on the fact that we do not know what the future will hold. We are ignorant about what will happen tomorrow. However, this ignorance is irrelevant to the argument. Even if we are ignorant about the future, given that the above piece of reasoning is sound, the future is fixed. To be clear, we can express the argument of the first step as follows:

Argument A:

1. Necessarily, it is now either true or false that there will be a sea battle tomorrow.
2. If premise 1 is true, then the future is fixed and there is no contingency.
3. Therefore, the future is fixed and there is no contingency.

Second Part

Aristotle argues that the first premise is false regarding future events. In other words, he claims that the law of excluded middle is false concerning statements about the future. His argument for this conclusion might be summarized as follows:

Argument B:

a. Because there is contingency and the future is not fixed, conclusion 3 is false.
b. Because Argument A is valid, at least one of the premises must be false.
c. Premise 2 is true.
d. Therefore premise 1 must be false.

In other words, because the future is not fixed, and given the truth of premise 2 (i.e., that the law of excluded middle entails that the future is fixed), it follows that premise 1 is false. In this way, Aristotle concludes that statements about particular future events are not true or false now. He says:

> Take a sea-battle: it would have neither to happen nor not to happen. These and others like them are the absurdities that follow if it is necessary for every affirmation and negation . . . that one of the opposites be true and the other false, and that nothing of what happens is as chance has it, but everything is and happens of necessity. (18b25–19a7)

Aristotle's argument has generated much debate, most of which is focused on the third premise (c) above or premise 2 in Argument A, which Aristotle thinks are true. Some commentators argue that Aristotle's reasoning for this premise is faulty because it relies on a modal fallacy.[18] Modal logic deals with inferences that employ the concepts of necessity, possibility, and impossibility. A modal fallacy is a piece of modal reasoning that is invalid. The alleged fallacy in Aristotle's argument is to go from:

1. Necessarily (either the sea battle will take place or it will not.)
2. Either necessarily the sea battle will take place or necessarily it will not.

In other words, it is fallacious to pass from:

1. N (Either P or not P) to
2. Either N (P) or N (not P), where N means necessarily.

The problem is that the law of excluded middle states (1), whereas the claim that the future is fixed requires (2). Therefore, if (1) does not imply (2), then fatalism does not follow from the law of excluded middle. In which case, Aristotle cannot argue for the third premise (c) in Argument B above, which means that he cannot argue that premise 2 in Argument A is true. In other words, he cannot argue for the claim that if the law of excluded middle were true of particular future events, then the future is fixed.

In conclusion, the law of excluded middle says that necessarily, for any statement, either it or its negation will be true. According to the law, there is no option apart from truth and falsity. Aristotle tries to argue that the law of excluded middle is false with regard to statements about particular future events. If his argument is as we represented it, then we have seen that the argument fails. Of course, this failure doesn't prove that the law of excluded middle is always true. It only shows that this attempt to show it to be false has been defeated.

Logic: The *Prior Analytics*

In the *Prior Analytics*, Aristotle develops his theory of the syllogism or of deduction, which he defines as:

> A deduction is a discourse in which, certain things being stated, something other than what is stated follows of necessity from their being so. (24b19–24b22)

In other words, the *Prior Analytics* concerns logically valid arguments, arguments in which the conclusion follows necessarily from the premises. In chapters 1 through 7 of Book I, Aristotle's aims are to determine which arguments are logically valid syllogisms, which are not, and to explain why. He achieves these aims by classifying the different types of syllogisms in order to explain what their validity consists of. In order to simplify the complex and difficult text, we can divide his presentation into five steps. Later, we provide a brief overview of the *Prior Analytics* as a whole.

The First Step

The first step is presented in *On Interpretation* chapter 7, and in the first three chapters of Book I of the *Prior Analytics*. Aristotle classifies all propositions, which can form the premises of any syllogism. He says: "A proposition, then, is a statement affirming or denying something of something" (24a16). He assumes that all statements are of the subject-predicate form and classifies them according to quantity and quality—in which case, any statement would either be universal or particular (their quantity) and either affirmative or negative (their quality). Consequently, there are four types of such propositions:

A	Universal affirmative	All humans are mortal.
E	Universal negative	No humans are mortal.
I	Particular affirmative	Some humans are mortal.
O	Particular negative	Some humans are not mortal.

AEIO are the letters used by later medieval philosophers to indicate each of these kinds of statements. In *On Interpretation*, Aristotle treats singular statements about individuals, such as "Socrates is mortal," as a third type of quantity. In the *Prior Analytics*, this type is absorbed by the second, the particular. Also in the *Prior Analytics*, he includes indefinite propositions, which we can ignore because they are indeterminate between universal and particular statements (I, 2, 25a1–4 and *Topics* III, 6, 120a6–20). In chapter 3 of Book I, he also discusses modal propositions, which assert that something is necessary or possible. We can leave aside modality for the moment and return to it later. One of the difficulties in reading Aristotle's text is that, instead of saying "All S is P" or even "P is predicted of every S," he says that P belongs to every S.

Aristotle notes the logical relations between the four statement-kinds (*On Int.* 717b16–26 and I, 2, 25a4–25a27). To help simplify, we can represent what he says using the later medieval letters and contemporary logical terminology as follows:

1. **A** and **O** are contradictories and **E** and **I** are contradictories.
   They cannot both be true and they cannot both be false.
2. **A** and **E** are not contradictory: they are contraries.
   They cannot both be true, but they could both be false.
3. **I** and **O** are sub-contraries;
   They can both be true but they cannot both be false.

The Second Step

The second step consists of the classification of different syllogistic forms or structures based on the position of the middle term, which is the word the two premises have in common (shown in bold below) (I, 4, 25b32–26a2). For example, in argument C, the middle term is *animal*.

> Argument C:
>
> Major premise: All *animals* are mortal.
>
> Minor premise: All humans are *animals*.
>
> Conclusion: All humans are mortal.

In any syllogism, the middle term appears in both premises. It does not appear in the conclusion. Aristotle calls the terms in the conclusion the *extremes*. The major term is the predicate in the conclusion (i.e., *mortal*) and the minor term is the subject in the conclusion (i.e., *human*). The premises are named major and minor accordingly (I, 4, 26a21–3).

Aristotle realizes that the validity of formal arguments depends entirely on their form or structure, and he uses the concept of the middle term to classify the general types of syllogisms based on the formal relations between their premises. There are three forms of combination, which Aristotle calls the *three figures*. The middle term must be either a subject or a predicate in each of the two premises of any syllogism, and so there are three possibilities. In the first figure, the middle term is the subject of one premise, and the predicate of the other (I, 4, 26b21–26b33).[19] In the second, it is the predicate of both premises (Book I, chapter 5); and in the third, it is subject of both premises (chapter 6 and I, 23, 41a13–16). The structure of the three figures can be depicted as follows.

	First Figure Subject-Predicate	Second Figure Subject-Predicate	Third Figure Subject-Predicate
Premise	Bs are A	Bs are A	Cs are A
Premise	Cs are B	Cs are A	Cs are B
Conclusion	Cs are A	Cs are B	Bs are A

In the first figure the middle term is B, and it is the subject in one premise and predicate in the other. In the second figure the middle term is A, and it is the predicate in both premises. In the third figure the middle term is C, and it is the subject in both premises. In each case, the space before the proposition would be occupied either by *all*, *some*, *not all*, and *none*, as we shall now see.

The Third Step

Aristotle's third step is to combine the two classifications (I, 4–6). In other words, the three figures described in the second step must be filled in with the different kinds of statements from step one. For each of the three figures, both of the premises could be a statement of one of the four forms: A or E or I or O. For example, the following example would be a syllogism for the first figure with two universal affirmative premises (statements of type A):

All Greeks are animals.

All Athenians are Greeks.

Therefore, all Athenians are animals.

There are three types of syllogistic figures; and for each of these, both of the premises could be a statement of one of the four forms, as mentioned above in the first step. Therefore, each of the three figures has 16 possible combinations. Thus, there are 48 possible combinations.

The Fourth Step

In the fourth step, in the *Prior Analytics* (I, 4–7) Aristotle shows which of the 48 syllogistic forms are valid and which are not. He works methodically through all 16 combinations for each one of the three figures. He claims that some deductions are obvious; these he calls complete or perfect syllogisms (I, 1, 24b22–6). He deduces which of the other syllogisms are valid from these perfect syllogisms. Medieval thinkers gave each of the four perfect syllogisms a name, as follows.[20]

Barbara	Celarent	Darii	Ferio
All Bs are A	No Bs are A	All Bs are A	No B is A
All Cs are B	All Cs are B	Some C is B	Some C is B
All Cs are A	No Cs are A	Some Cs are A	Some C is not A

Aristotle derives 10 other valid syllogistic forms from these four, giving a total of 14 types of valid syllogism. (These are listed together with their medieval names at the end of the chapter.) The conversion rules for deriving the 10 other valid forms from the four perfect syllogisms are:

If every S is P, then some S is P.

If some S is P, then some P is S.

If no S is P, then no P is S.

The imperfect syllogisms are deduced by making it obvious that they can be reduced to a syllogism that is perfect (i.e., one of the four forms above) through a series of clear steps.

The Fifth Step

In the fifth step, for the sake of completeness, Aristotle also needs to show that the 14 forms mentioned above are the only valid syllogisms. He does this by argument from counter-examples, showing that the other 34 syllogistic forms are not valid because they can have true premises and a false conclusion. He does this by showing how the relevant two premises cannot validly yield a conclusion of any of the four forms. For example, he says:

> But if the first term belongs to all the middle, but the middle to none of the last term, there will be no deduction in respect of the extremes; for nothing necessary follows from the terms being so related; for it is possible that the first should belong either to all or to none of the last, so that neither a particular nor a universal conclusion is necessary. But if there is no necessary consequence, there cannot be a deduction by means of these propositions. As an example of a universal affirmative relation between the extremes we may take the terms animal, man, horse; of a universal negative relation, the terms animal, man, stone. (I, 4, 26a3–8)

Let us unpack this very dense passage to illustrate his argument from counter-examples. In this quote, Aristotle considers arguments with the two premises; "A belongs to every B" and "B belongs to no C" (where B is the middle term). In other words, the premises under consideration are "All Bs are A" and "No Cs are B."[21]

Aristotle's contention is that, from such premises, no conclusion can be validly drawn with respect to the extreme terms C and A. This isn't possible because the "first should belong either to all or to none of the last, so that neither a particular nor a universal conclusion is necessary." In other words, this is not possible because the conclusion would have to be either of the form **A**, **E**, **I**, or **O**, and none of these is possible. To show that no conclusion of these four forms is possible, Aristotle asks us to consider two examples, each of three propositions.

The first set of three propositions is: All men are animals, no horse is a man, and every horse is an animal. The first two propositions have the required forms as the premises under consideration: All Bs are A and No Cs are B. The third is a proposition of the form **A** (i.e., All horses are animals, or All Cs are A).

Since, in this specific case, all three of these propositions are true, the two premise forms under consideration *can be* consistent with a conclusion of the form **A**. But this means that the two premises would have to be inconsistent with a conclusion of form **E** and **O**. (Remember that **A** and **O** are contradictories, and **A** and **E** are contraries).

E Universal negative   No horse is an animal.
O Particular negative Some horses are not animals.

In other words, conclusions of the form **E** and **O** cannot follow from the premises.

The second example is: All men are animals, no stone is a man, and no stone is an animal. Since in this case these three propositions are all true, the two premises under consideration *can be* consistent with a conclusion of the form **E** (which is the form of the third proposition, "No stone is an animal"). This means the two premises would have to be inconsistent with a conclusion of form **A** and **I**.

A Universal affirmative   All stones are animals.
I Particular affirmative Some stones are animals.

In other words, conclusions of the forms **A** and **I** cannot follow from the premises. With the first example, we saw that no conclusions of the forms **E** and **O** follow from the premises. In summary, from the premises All Bs are A and No Cs are B, no conclusion can be validly drawn with respect to the terms C and A.[22]

This is an example of Aristotle's method for showing that the 34 other forms are not valid syllogisms. In other words, using this counter-example method, he is able to show that the 14 valid forms are the only ones.

Meta-Conclusions

In his discussion of each figure, Aristotle arrives at some meta-conclusions about the valid form in each of the figures. For instance, only in the first figure can universal affirmative conclusions be reached. In the second figure, only negative conclusions can be established, and in the third, only particular. In chapters 7 and 23–24, he also offers some general meta-conclusions, such as:

> No deduction contains two negative premises.
>
> A deduction with a negative conclusion must have a negative premise.
>
> A deduction with an affirmative conclusion has two affirmative premises.
>
> A deduction with a universal conclusion needs to have two universal premises.
>
> No deduction has two particular premises.

He also concludes that all valid arguments in the second and third figure must be deduced from the two universal arguments of the first figure (i.e., Barbara and Celarent) (I, 7, 29a30–29b26).

Modal Deductions

Concerning modality, Aristotle distinguishes three kinds of statements:
1. A necessarily belongs to B (e.g., Necessarily all humans are mortal.)
2. A may belong to B (e.g., Possibly all humans are mortal.)
3. A belongs to B (e.g., All humans are mortal.)

The first is necessary, the second possible, and the third, assertoric. In Book I, chapters 8–22, Aristotle extends his theory of the syllogism to these modal statements. He does so by considering that each premise could have one of the three modalities. The relevant five possibilities are: two necessary premises; one necessary and one assertoric; one necessary and one possible; two possible premises; and one possible and one assertoric. Aristotle then determines whether these possibilities will yield valid deductions for the 14 valid figures considered in the simple assertoric modality.

A complication needs mention. In *On Interpretation*, Aristotle uses *possible* so that "P is possible" is equivalent to "not necessarily not P" and "P is necessary" would be equivalent to "not possible not P" (*On Int.* chapter 13, 22a14–22a32). However, in the *Prior Analytics*, he employs the term *possible* in a different way: "P is possible" is equivalent to "Not necessarily P and not necessarily not P."

Overview of the *Prior Analytics*

Since the text is complex, let us briefly review the overall structure of Book I of the *Prior Analytics*. The first part of Book I, chapters 1–26, Aristotle shows which deductions are valid and why. In chapter 1, he provides definitions of key terms. Chapter 2 gives the rules for conversion, and chapter 3 does the same for modal propositions. Chapter 4 shows which deductions can and cannot be validly made in the first figure.

Chapter 5 does the same for the second figure, and chapter 6 for the third. In chapter 7, Aristotle draws some meta-conclusions. In chapters 8–22, he repeats more or less the same process for the modal syllogisms. Chapters 23–26 draw some meta-conclusions regarding what kinds of deductions are valid and invalid. In chapter 26 Aristotle concludes that he has shown how all deductions are produced (43a16–43a19).

In chapter 27 Aristotle defines a new aim: explaining how to construct syllogisms that are useful in finding knowledge. These are called *demonstrations*. Chapter 30 outlines how to establish the fundamental principles that are needed in any subject area (e.g., astronomy). Chapter 31 criticizes Plato's method of division. These topics are also treated in the *Posterior Analytics*.

In chapters 32–46 Aristotle shows how to construct syllogisms so that all deductions can be reduced to the figures. He says that, once this is done, "our original project would be brought to a conclusion" (47a6). Much of the discussion in chapters 32–35 concerns how to articulate the relevant propositions and chose the relevant terms clearly. Chapter 45 carries out the reductions to the first figure. The structure and aims of Book II are much less clear.[23]

Summary

In the first chapter of Book I, Aristotle's aim is to determine which syllogisms are valid and which are not, and to explain why. To achieve this, he divides subject-predicate propositions into four kinds, and syllogistic forms into three figures, according to the position of the middle term in the two premises. To show which forms are valid, he isolates four perfect syllogisms and uses them to derive 10 other imperfect syllogisms.

Perhaps Aristotle's main achievement in logic was that he was the first person to use symbols to stand for words in an argument. This is a very simple but deep insight, because it amounts to seeing that the validity of an argument depends on its logical form and not on its content.

Despite being systematic, Aristotle's logical theory is not complete. In particular, it lacks a branch of logic that concerns the logical connections between whole propositions, which we now call *propositional logic*. Specifically, there are inference patterns governed by the connectives *or*, *and*, *if . . . then*, and *not*. For example, "if P then Q" entails "if not–Q then not–P." The Stoics studied such inferences, as we shall see in chapter 14.

The *Posterior Analytics*

In Book I of the *Posterior Analytics*, Aristotle develops his theory of demonstration (*apodeixis*), which is the use of deductions to gain knowledge (*epistêmê*). In this case, *epistêmê* is usually translated as scientific knowledge or as understanding. He says:

> By demonstration I mean a scientific deduction; and by scientific I mean one in virtue of which, by having it, we understand something. (I, 2, 70b18–9)

Aristotle thinks that such scientific demonstrations must meet three conditions. First, he says that we have scientific knowledge only

> When we believe we know the cause of the thing's being the case—know that it is the cause of it—and that it could not be otherwise. (I, 2,71b9)

In other words, understanding must take the form of an explanation by citing the cause of something, which will explain why it is so by showing why it must be so.

Second, to be a scientific demonstration, the premises of the deductive argument must involve fundamental principles. They must

> Depend on things that are true and primitive and immediate and more familiar than and prior to and explanatory of the conclusion. (I, 2,71b22)

According to Aristotle, if the premises of an argument do not satisfy these conditions, we should not call the deduction a *scientific demonstration*. Aristotle explains each of these conditions in turn (70b25–72a5). However, provisionally we can say the idea is that the premises of the demonstration must involve fundamental principles that explain the phenomenon in question by making it intelligible or familiar (71b33–72a5). A principle is fundamental or basic (or *immediate*) when it cannot be demonstrated.

Third, Aristotle claims that the premises of the demonstration must include necessary truths:

> Demonstrative knowledge comes from necessary starting points—for what is known cannot be otherwise. (I, 6,74b5)

As we shall see, this probably means that scientific explanations must involve the real essences of the phenomena in question. These principles will be concerned with universals rather than particulars.

The Need for Fundamental Principles

In Book I, chapter 3, Aristotle argues that scientific understanding requires that there are fundamental principles. These fundamental principles are primitive and prior in the sense that they cannot be demonstrated (70b34–72a9). This means that there are no higher-level principles that explain them. Furthermore, Aristotle also says that it is necessary for scientific demonstration that one is more convinced of the principles than of the conclusion that one is trying to explain through them (72a32–72a36).

Aristotle argues for the conclusion that there are fundamental principles by rejecting two alternative views. The first view claims that there cannot be any understanding, because it would require a grasp of primitive or primary principles, an impossibility. Such a grasp is needed because otherwise there would be an infinite regress of demonstrations. To halt this regress, we need first principles, but these are unknowable because they cannot be demonstrated. The second view is that all knowledge requires demonstration, and that therefore there are no first principles, but rather circular and reciprocal demonstrations (72b7–72b14).

With regard to the first view, Aristotle argues that it is correct to reject the possibility of an infinite regress of demonstration; demonstration must come to a stop at some point.[24] However, the view is incorrect to reject the idea of non-demonstrable principles which are prior or basic (72b19–72b24). In short, Aristotle argues as follows:

1. Understanding is possible.
2. Understanding requires that there are non-demonstrable basic principles (otherwise there would be an infinite regress).
3. Understanding requires that we know the principles on which demonstration depends (because we must grasp what is prior).
4. Therefore, there are non-demonstrable basic principles that can be known.

Against the second view, he argues that it would make the idea of prior and more intelligible principles impossible. Demonstration in circles renders the same propositions both prior and posterior at the same time. According to such a view, one can only assert that "this is the case if this is the case," which is a claim too easy to prove (72b25–35). To make this point, Aristotle considers a circular deduction with three terms: A, B, and C. If A requires B which requires C, and C is the same as A, then the deduction only shows that if A is the case then A is the case. In words, such reasoning is circular and doesn't show anything.

In contrast, Aristotle affirms that conclusions must be demonstrated from premises that themselves cannot be demonstrated, although they can be known. He divides the starting points or basic premises of any demonstration into three kinds: axioms, definitions, and hypotheses (72a15–72a24). Axioms are principles without which reasoning would be impossible. For example, the law of excluded middle says that any predicate must either be truly affirmed or truly denied of any subject. Definitions state the meaning of the terms, and a hypothesis is an assumption about what exists. For example, in geometry we assume that points and lines exist.

The Necessary

In chapter 4, Aristotle argues, "Demonstration, therefore, is deduction from what is necessary" (73a24). If a demonstration shows why something is necessary, then the relevant deduction must include at least one premise consisting in a necessary claim. To support the claim that demonstration requires a necessary premise, Aristotle distinguishes the essential and the accidental. The accidental is what belongs to something not because of what it is (73b10–73b15). In contrast, the essential belongs to something because of what it is.

> I call universal whatever belongs to something both of every case and in itself and as such. It is evident, therefore, that whatever is universal belongs from necessity to its objects. (73b25–28)

Aristotle claims that the understandable consists in properties that belong to things necessarily or because of what they are (73b16). In other words, to understand a phenomenon as such, for what it is, requires citing its non-accidental or essential properties.

In chapter 6, Aristotle argues that necessity is needed because the point of a demonstration is to explain. He insists that citing a chance factor or an accidental feature will not explain (75a18–75a28). To understand something, one must know its explanation. He says:

> Since, then, if a man understands demonstratively, it must belong from necessity, it is clear that he must have his demonstration through a middle term that is necessary too; or else he will not understand either why or that it is necessary for that to be the case. (75a12–75a17)

Aristotle's claim that the premises must be necessary *seems* to remove the empirical and contingent elements from scientific demonstration. Apparently, it restricts science to necessary truths, and from a contemporary viewpoint this *seems* to imply that science is non-empirical. Let us consider this problem with Aristotle's theory.

We can see why Aristotle's view of explanation has some appeal despite the fact that it is counterintuitive. To thoroughly explain something, we must show why it *has* to be like that given all the right conditions. If we didn't do so, then there would some aspect of the phenomenon that has not been explained. Given this, to explain something is to prove that it has to be the way it is. Hence, Aristotle assimilates explanation to a specific kind of deduction (i.e., demonstration).

From the point of view of interpreting Aristotle, this reply still doesn't answer the problem that even if an explanation has to show why an event must happen given all the causal factors, this does not mean that those causal factors are themselves necessary. In other words, we need a more complete explanation of why Aristotle assimilates explanation to demonstration.

A better approach is to give up the assumption that in this context the Greek word *epistêmê* corresponds to what we mean now by science and knowledge. Today we think of the natural sciences as the empirical investigation of nature. In contrast, Aristotle means something akin to the pursuit of systematic knowledge that is universal and essential. In other words, according to Aristotle, we have scientific understanding when we grasp the fundamental or basic principles of a field and see their explanatory implications or relevance for different kinds of phenomena. This is important in two ways.

First, such understanding is holistic, and thus might be contrasted with atomistic propositional knowledge. In other words, in contemporary terms, we tend to conceive of knowledge as knowing that P where "P" is a single proposition that we can know or not independently of other truths. In contrast, Aristotle's conception of *epistêmê* is holistic. One cannot have understanding of a field unless one grasps the basic underlying principles and their explanatory implications or relevance for a range of relevant phenomena. *Epistêmê* cannot pertain to a single proposition or even to a single demonstration.[25]

In chapter 7 of the *Posterior Analytics*, Aristotle claims that each science has its own genus and subject matter: astronomy deals with the stars, arithmetic with numbers, biology with living things. As a consequence, each science has its own principles appropriate to that subject matter. So, for instance, the fundamental principles of plant biology will be quite different from those of astronomy, optics, music, and arithmetic. This is because understanding will consist of grasping the fundamental principles that pertain to the relevant essences of the genus (75b3–75b21). Aristotle says that, in demonstrating, it is necessary for the extreme and middle terms to come from the same genus. Otherwise, the explanation would be of accidentals, which as we have already seen is impossible (75b12–3).

As Aristotle notes in chapter 10, the idea that each science has its own fundamental principles and assumptions, which are proper to the relevant genus, does not preclude the claim that there are some overarching common principles that can be employed by all the sciences. He mentions the principle, "When equals are subtracted from equals, the remainders are equal" (76a41) and the law of excluded middle (77a30).

Second, for Aristotle, as he argues in chapter 8, there is no scientific demonstration of particulars *as such*. Demonstration is about the relation between universals. It starts from basic and abstract principles, and from those it deduces the relations between more specific properties. In other words, scientific demonstration can show the implications for specific properties, but it does not consist in knowledge of particulars as such.[26] Aristotle acknowledges this when he says:

> It is obvious that if the propositions from which a syllogism is derived are universal, the conclusion of such a demonstration must itself be an eternal truth too. So there can be no demonstration of perishable things, nor scientific knowledge of them strictly speaking, since the attribute does not hold of the thing universally, but at some time and in some way. (I, 8, 75b22–25)

Of course, we can give demonstrations of natural events, such as eclipses, insofar as they constitute a universal kind that can reoccur but not *qua* a particular event (75b33–75b36).[27]

These two comments may help us understand how Aristotle's conception of scientific demonstration differs from contemporary conceptions of science. However, it does not answer two related questions. First, how does the empirical investigation of nature fit into Aristotle's conception of scientific demonstration? This question is important because, as we shall see in the next chapter, Aristotle conceived of science as empirical. Indeed this is one of the important contrasts between him and Plato. For example, Aristotle's biological works show that we need to *look* to understand how an organ functions. Science starts from observation. The second question is: how can we know basic principles when, by definition, these cannot be known by demonstration? Aristotle has argued that explanation needs basic principles, and scientific understanding requires that we know them. So, how do we know them? The answers to these questions emerge towards the end of Book II of the *Posterior Analytics*.

Deductive Explanation

Aristotle thinks that scientific demonstrations are deductions that explain. In chapter 13, he gives the example of the nearness of the planet. Suppose the planets do not twinkle because they are so close to the Earth. Given all this, the following would be a valid syllogism with true premises:

Argument D:
1. Planets do not twinkle.
2. All heavenly bodies that do not twinkle are near.
3. Therefore, the planets are near.

For Aristotle, despite the fact that this syllogism is sound, it does not constitute a scientific demonstration, because it does not explain. Premises 1 and 2 do not explain the conclusion 3. The fact that the planets do not twinkle does not explain why the planets are near; rather it is the other way around. Consequently, argument D is merely "a syllogism of the 'that'" and it is not "a syllogism of the because." In contrast, the planets fail to twinkle *because* they are so near. Thus, argument E is a syllogism in which the premises explain the conclusion. In this respect, it is a scientific demonstration (78a30–78b3).

Argument E:
1. The planets are near.
2. All heavenly bodies that are near do not twinkle.
3. Therefore, the planets do not twinkle.

Definitions

In much of Book II of the *Posterior Analytics*, Aristotle examines the role of definitions in science. As we have seen, because of the nature of the syllogism, explanations rely on the middle term (90a8). In chapters 3 and 7 of Book II, Aristotle distinguishes demonstrations and definitions: definitions state what a thing is, and demonstrations explain. However, in chapter 4, Aristotle argues that the middle term in a demonstration consists of or presupposes a definition. In chapter 8, Aristotle shows how providing a definition can itself constitute an explanatory demonstration:

> What is thunder? Extinction of fire in cloud. Why does it thunder? Because the fire in the cloud is extinguished. (93b8)

However, as he makes clear in chapter 9, some demonstrations involve citing something else as the explanatory middle term of the demonstration (93b26–8).

In *Prior Analytics* I, 31, Aristotle criticizes Plato's method of division. In some of his later works, such as the *Sophist* and the *Statesman*, Plato defines and employs a method for making definitions by looking for relevant dichotomizing divisions. In the *Prior Analytics*, Aristotle criticizes Plato's method for making unwarranted assumptions. For example, it assumes of all animals that they must be either footed or footless, and that if man is animal then he *must* be either footed or footless. But this is an unwarranted conclusion because it isn't *necessary* that man should be footed. This quality (or the lack of it) isn't part of his essence. Thus, Plato's method isn't a reliable way of classifying or making definitions. Furthermore, it doesn't provide deductions for, as Aristotle says, the method begs what ought to be deduced. (46a32–46b25). Aristotle repeats this critique in chapter 5, Book II of the *Posterior Analytics* (91b13–91b27).

In contrast, Aristotle thinks that reality consists primarily of natural kinds of objects, such as individual plants and animals of different species. These natural kinds have a real essence (without which they would not be what they are). For example, the real essence of a human being is to be rational. Based on these real essences, there are real definitions of each natural kind; for example, by definition, humans are rational animals. In this vein, Aristotle outlines the method for arriving at definitions in Book II, chapter 13 of the *Posterior Analytics*. First, we must look for essential features of a genus, such as bird. Then we must seek the essential differences that distinguish the species in question from other species in the same genus. In this way, the definition does not need to consider nonessential differences (96b25–96b27).

Empirical Knowledge

Most of the *Posterior Analytics* is dedicated to the nature of scientific demonstration based on fundamental principles, but towards the end of the book (Book II, chapter 19), Aristotle asks how we know these universal principles. He starts with a puzzle.

Understanding through demonstration requires knowledge of the primitive, immediate principles. But how can we know them? On the one hand, it would absurd to postulate such knowledge as innate because that would require our having knowledge without noticing it. On the other hand, it seems impossible that we should gain knowledge of them without learning them from pre-existing knowledge. But that pre-existing knowledge would seem to require them (99b20–99b34).

Aristotle says that the solution is that we have an innate capacity for perception. Some animals have the capacity to remember what they perceive, and to make discriminations or conceive differences based on the memory of perceptions. Through such cognitive processes, we can ascend from particular sense experiences to knowledge of universal statements by induction (*epagôgê*) (100a15–100b5). He says:

> Thus it is clear that it is necessary for us to become familiar with the primitives by induction; for perception too instills the universal in this way. (100b3–5)

He contrasts induction with deduction. Scientific demonstration can provide understanding of specifics, downwards from that of more general universals. Induction provides knowledge of universals upwards from the perception of particulars. It is by induction that we gain the knowledge for the axioms, definitions, and hypotheses on which deduction is based.

In this regard, we might compare the philosophy of Aristotle with that of Plato. For Plato, universals are separate from the world of particulars; for Aristotle, they are immanent. According to Plato, we have innate knowledge of universals through reason, a view that Aristotle rejects. Aristotle believes that scientific knowledge is derived from sense perception and induction, even if such knowledge consists in demonstrations. For example, in the *Generation of Animals*, Book III chapter 10, he writes about the life of bees:

> Such appears to be the truth about the generation of bees, judging from theory and from what are believed to be the facts about them; the facts, however, have not yet been sufficiently grasped; if ever they are, then credit must be given rather to observation than to theories, and to theories only if what they affirm agrees with the observed facts. (760b29–760b33)

However, despite his insistence on the need for and importance of perception for scientific knowledge, this does not mean that we can call Aristotle an empiricist.[28] This is because he does not have a modern empiricist view of perception, according to which perception merely consists in the passive reception of sensory impressions. In the *Metaphysics*, Book IV, chapter 5, Aristotle stresses that perception is more akin to making a judgment, which can be erroneous. In *De Anima*, Book III, chapters 1–3, he argues that there must be a central judging faculty that can combine and compare the perceptions of the different senses and which enables them to belong to a single self-reflective awareness. In these works, addressed in the next chapter, Aristotle stresses that perception is an active process of making judgments about objects, a view that is non-empiricist. Towards the end of the *Posterior Analytics* (Book II, chapter 19) he says, "Even though it is the particular that is perceived, the perception is of the universal" (100a18–b2). In short, part of perception is to recognize the universal qualities of what we perceive, so that we can make judgments about them. This view of perception is non-empiricist. So, although Aristotle argues for the need for empirical knowledge in science, this does not make him an empiricist.

Although the process of induction relies on perception, according to Aristotle it also involves cognitive capacities such as the abilities to remember, to discriminate, and to group together perceptions, which are allied to perception in humans (99b35–100a9). In the last paragraph of the *Posterior Analytics*, Aristotle describes the cognitive state of grasping the basic principles, which results from the inductive process. He distinguishes understanding (*epistêmê*) and comprehension (*nous*), arguing that the latter is more fundamental. As we have seen, understanding relies on demonstrations that depend on basic principles. In contrast, comprehension of those basic principles cannot rely on demonstration (otherwise they wouldn't be basic). Aristotle argues that, because demonstration itself is not a principle of demonstration, understanding itself cannot be a principle of understanding. He says: "comprehension will be the principle of understanding" (100b6–100a19). This marks one of the limits of scientific demonstrative understanding. It cannot understand itself.

THE *TOPICS*: DIALECTIC

Dialectic is the art of systematic discussion and of using deduction from reputable opinion. Aristotle's work on dialectic is contained in the *Topics* and the *Sophistical Refutations*. The aim of the *Topics* is to:

> Find a method by which we shall be able to argue about any proposed problem from probable premises and shall ourselves under examination avoid self-contradiction. (100a20)

The word *probable* signals a contrast with scientific syllogisms, which have immediate premises. The dialectical syllogism has premises that are reasonable in the sense that they commend themselves as probable to most people.

For Aristotle, dialectic is an important tool of enquiry. First, it deals with claims that we do not know for certain, but which are probable.

Because of this, it is useful. For example, when discussing the nature of reality, Aristotle uses the conclusions of earlier philosophers as a starting point for his own investigation. He looks to see what these views have in common and uses that as a base. Also, sometimes he appeals to what is commonly held. In addition, Aristotle sometimes tries to discover what is true in the philosophical views he opposes. These are all hallmarks of Aristotle's pragmatic or commonsense approach to knowledge.

Second, the dialectical method is necessary for finding first or fundamental principles. In this way, it is part of the philosophical method. These first principles have a very important role in knowledge for Aristotle. Real understanding requires appeal to causes and, ultimately, first principles.

The *Topics* is like a catalogue of advice concerning the art of arguing. It focuses on different kinds of conclusions, definitions, and commonplace rules for arguing in ethics, or regarding species, and for the arrangement of questions. For example:

> It is a good rule also, occasionally to bring an objection against oneself; for answerers are put off their guard against those who appear to be arguing impartially. It is useful too, to add that so and so is generally held; for people are shy of upsetting the received opinion. (VIII, 156b18)

In the *Sophistical Refutations* Aristotle classifies common fallacies in argument. There are two kinds; those based on language and those that are not. Among those based on language, there are:

Equivocation—when a single word is ambiguous
Amphiboly—when the structure of a sentence is ambiguous

Among the fallacies that are not linguistic, Aristotle identifies *begging the question*—illicitly assuming what you set out to prove, and the false dichotomy—offering your opponent only two alternatives when there are others, such as (as we have seen) "to be or not to be." This is a false dichotomy because there are many ways in which something can be and the dichotomy only offers two alternatives.

Conclusion

In this chapter we have examined the main works by Aristotle concerning language and logic and the application of logic to scientific methodology. *The Categories* concerns the basic types of words, or ways in which things may be said to be. In his work *On Interpretation*, Aristotle examines what may be "said in combination," and in particular, whole statements that can be true or false. The *Prior Analytics* develops the logic of syllogism or of deductions using such statements. In this work, Aristotle determines which deductions are valid and which aren't, and explains why. These determinations are based on a systematic and complete classification of the different kinds of syllogisms.

In the *Posterior Analytics*, Aristotle examines when deductions count as scientific demonstrations through which we can gain knowledge. Demonstrations must be explanatory or cite a cause and in so doing, they must involve fundamental principles and contain necessary truths. Scientific explanations are deductive.

In the *Topics* Aristotle examines the art of using of deductions from reputable opinion to draw conclusions about what is probable. He calls this art *dialectic*. Aristotle provides advice for good dialectical reasoning and in the *Sophistical Refutations*, he classifies common informal fallacies in dialectical reasoning.

Study Questions

1. Outline some of the main differences between the philosophies of Plato and Aristotle.
2. What is Aristotle's concept of *qua*?
3. What is Aristotle's hylomorphism?
4. What is homonymy, according to Aristotle?
5. What is a category? What role do categories play in Aristotle's philosophy?
6. What does the example of the sea battle supposedly tell us about the law of excluded middle?
7. In the *Prior Analytics*, what are the four types of assertions?
8. In a syllogism, what is the middle term? How does the middle term define the three figures?
9. What are the four perfect syllogisms?
10. How do the four perfect syllogisms relate to the 10 imperfect syllogisms?
11. What is a scientific demonstration? How is it different from a deduction?
12. How does Aristotle argue for the claim that there are basic principles?
13. How does Aristotle distinguish the accidental and the necessary? Why is this distinction needed?
14. What are Aristotle's criticisms of Plato's method of division?
15. According to Aristotle, why does each science have its own basic principles?
16. How does Aristotle distinguish induction from deduction?
17. What does Aristotle mean by *dialectic*? Why is it an important method of inquiry?

Discussion Questions

1. Is Aristotle right to argue that scientific knowledge requires premises that are necessary in order for it to be explanatory?
2. Aristotle claims that each science has its own basic principles. Is this a true claim? Does it depend on an essentialist view of reality?
3. Why is it a mistake to call Aristotle an *empiricist*? Why would it also be misleading to call him a *rationalist*?

Types of Syllogisms

Contemporary writers on Aristotle's logic often use a medieval notation to represent the syllogisms. "All Bs are A" is equivalent to "A is predicated of every B" and "A belongs to every B." For this reason, "all Bs are A" is written shorthand as AaB. Likewise, for the other types of propositions:

A	Universal affirmative	All Bs are A	A belongs to every B
E	Universal negative	No Bs are A	A belongs to no B
I	Particular affirmative	Some Bs are A	A belongs to some B
O	Particular negative	Some Bs are not A	A doesn't belong to some B

Using this notion we can represent the 14 syllogisms, each of which has a name. These medieval names are mnemonics for the form: **Barbara, Celarent**, and so on, according to the vowels. The 14 valid syllogisms are:

First Figure
Barbara   AaB, BaC, therefore AaC
Celarent AeB, BaC, therefore AeC
Darii   AaB, BiC, therefore AiC
Ferio   AeB, BiC, therefore AoC

Second Figure
Cesare   CeB, AaB, therefore AeC
Camestres CaB, AeB, therefore AeC
Festino   CeB, AiB, therefore AoC
Baroco   CaB, AoB, therefore AoC

Third Figure
Darapti   BaC, BaA, therefore AiC
Felapton BeC, BaA, therefore AoC
Disamis   BiC, BaA, therefore AiC
Datisi   BaC, BiA, therefore AiC
Bocardo   BoC, BaA, therefore AoC
Ferison   BeC, BiA, therefore AoC

10

Aristotle
Physics and Biology

Aristotle divides knowledge into the theoretical, the practical, and the productive; the first is concerned with understanding for its own sake; the second with the good, and the third with the beautiful. Theoretical knowledge is divided into physics, mathematics, and theology. Physics deals with things which have a separate existence and which change; mathematics with things that do not change and do not have a separate existence. Theology concerns that which has a separate existence and does not change (i.e., God) (*Metaphysics* VI, 1).

Aristotle's *Physics* deals with the fundamental general principles of nature, which consists in those things that change. As such, the work is also about the nature of change and the physics of motion. The *Physics* might be grouped with his other works about the physical universe: *On the Heavens* (or *De Caelo*) which deals primarily with the movement and nature of the stars; *On Generation and Corruption*, which concerns the coming to be and passing away of substances; and the *Meteorology*, which tries to explain sublunary physical phenomena, such as the weather and the sea.[1] The *Physics* can also be grouped together with Aristotle's biological works, which we will examine towards the end of this chapter.

A Brief Overview of the *Physics*

The *Physics* itself has eight books. Very broadly speaking, we can divide them into four themes. Book I concerns the nature and possibility of change. Chapter 1 claims that understanding nature requires us to grasp the principles of natural change. In chapters 2–4 Aristotle tries to refute Parmenides's view that change is impossible. Chapters 5–7 analyze the nature of change primarily to show the need for the form/matter distinction, and also to show the nature of Parmenides's error.

Book II examines how we should explain physical changes. In chapter 1 Aristotle contrasts the notion of a natural object with that of an artifact, and in chapter 3 he lists four types of cause or explanation: the material, formal, efficient, and final causes. In chapter 8 he argues against a purely mechanistic view of nature and in favor of a teleological or purposive view.

The third theme is the infinite, and the continuous or the infinitely divisible. This topic spans Books III–V. In Book III, chapter 1, Aristotle distinguishes the potential and the actual, and in chapter 4 he argues that there are no actual infinities, but only potential ones. Book IV examines the nature of space and time. Book V examines different kinds of change and motion, and Book VI discusses the continuous and discrete nature of motion, space, and time, culminating in a discussion of Zeno's paradoxes.

The fourth theme is the causes of motion, introduced in Book VII. Book VIII concerns the limits of the universe in time, and chapters 5 and 6 contain Aristotle's famous argument for an unmoved mover.

The Possibility of Change

Early Greek naturalistic philosophy was deeply threatened by the arguments of Parmenides and Zeno. Parmenides denied the existence of change and, as we saw in chapter 2, his basic main argument was simple:

1. The nonexistent is impossible.
2. Change requires the nonexistent.
3. Therefore, change is impossible.

Parmenides's argument challenges the basis of Aristotle's philosophy, even his classification of knowledge. According to Aristotle, nature is the totality of natural objects, which are things subject to change, and so to understand nature one must grasp the principles of natural change. In Book I of the *Physics*, Aristotle sets out to show how Parmenides's arguments and position are mistaken. In the process, Aristotle's analysis of change leads him to formulate the form/matter distinction, which is at the core of his metaphysics and philosophy of mind.

Two Kinds of Change

To arrive at the basic principles for understanding change, Aristotle reviews earlier Greek schools of thought. He notes that they all recognize contraries (such as solid and void, up and down) as among the first principles. Aristotle claims that this point makes perfect sense just because of what first principles are: like contraries, they cannot be generated from each other, for otherwise they would not be *first*. Furthermore, all other things must be generated from the first principles (Book I, 5).

Without discussing what the primary principles of nature actually are, Aristotle argues that there must be at least two because they must involve contraries. He then notes that things can be said to be or exist in many ways, and that contraries are adjectival. Thus, the adjectival contraries presuppose a substance in which they inhere. Consequently, there are three basic principles of natural change: substance and two contraries. Every change involves three elements: the thing that changes, how it was before, and how it is after the change. Aristotle concludes that change requires the idea of opposites, and something undergoing the alteration (Book I, 6).

In chapter 7 of Book I, Aristotle argues that there are two kinds of change. He distinguishes:

1. X comes to be Y.
2. Y comes to be from X.

The first change is alterations in a substance. A person learns music; she becomes musical. She changes from being unmusical to being musical. As argued a moment ago, such alterations involve three elements: the person, musical, and unmusical.

The second kind of change involves the coming into being of a new thing. These changes are called *substantial generation*. Unlike alterations, this second kind of change does not involve a new condition of a preexisting thing. It involves the generation of a new thing. Aristotle claims that only substances can go through this second kind of change. They come into being by having form imposed on matter. For example, a statue comes into being when bronze is given a form. This kind of change requires the form/matter distinction (191a3–12).

The Analysis of Parmenides

Aristotle employs his account of the two kinds of change to argue against Parmenides. The key idea is: Parmenides claimed that change requires that being could not come from non-being and that, because of this, change is impossible (I, 8–9). Aristotle examines in what ways change does, and does not, involve the idea that something comes from nothing.

Do alterations (the first kind of change) involve being coming from non-being, as Parmenides supposed? When it is described in terms of the quality alone, the answer is yes. In this respect, the change originates from what is not (i.e., the musical comes from what is not musical). However, Aristotle has argued that such alterations must be understood in terms of three principles. They must be described in terms of the two contrary properties *and* the substance that undergoes the alteration. And, when the alteration is described in terms of the substance, the answer to the question is no. Alteration does not require that something come from nothing. The starting point of change is something that already existed, namely, the person who becomes musical. So, in this case, Parmenides is mistaken: the change does not involve being coming from non-being.

Let us move on to the second type of change. Does substantial generation require being coming from non-being? Aristotle's reply is that it depends on how completely the change is described. In the second type of change, a new substance comes into being. For example, a new tree grows. Described in this way, it appears as if something is coming into being from nothing. However, when it is characterized more completely, the change does *not* involve something coming from nothing. This is because, through such changes, something permanent persists, namely, the relevant kind of matter. Think of the making and shaping of a bronze statue. Something that previously did not exist comes into existence, but this is because the matter acquires a new form. So when substantial generation is described in this latter way, Parmenides is once again mistaken.

Parmenides might object that, despite all this, both kinds of change do involve something coming from nothing, at least in one respect. The non-musical becomes musical, and a statue pops into existence. To reply to this objection, Aristotle introduces the distinction between actual and potential.[2] He claims that all change involves the turning of something potential into something actual. Concerning alterations, when a person becomes musical, he or she was potentially musical before the change. With the change, this potentiality becomes actualized. Concerning substantial generation, the situation is similar. A block of bronze is potentially a statue. When it is shaped into a statue, that potentiality becomes actualized. Similarly, the seed is potentially a tree. When it grows, that potentiality is made actual. Both kinds of substantial generation involve a potentiality becoming actualized. Parmenides fails to take into account this aspect of change. What Parmenides would call *non-being* is really *potentially being*.

Natural Change and the Four Causes

In Book II, chapter 1 of the *Physics*, Aristotle argues for a distinction between natural objects and artifacts. Things that exist by nature have a principle of change within them. The principal cause of change is internal: it is their nature. For example, trees grow according to their nature. Such things include living organisms, their parts, and the four elements. In contrast, the cause of change for artificial things *as such* is something external. For instance, a bed needs to be made by a craftsman. It is artificial, even though *qua* its matter (the wood), it is natural (193b10).

Form and matter are not two independently existing things. Provisionally, we can say that they are two aspects of any substance or particular thing, and these two aspects are separable only in thought. Matter cannot exist without form, and form requires matter, with the possible exception of the divine, as we shall see later. In the next chapter we examine the metaphysics of the form/matter distinction in more detail. However, initially we can conceive of form as the organization of a natural thing, and its matter as that out of which it is composed.

Aristotle argues that the nature and principle of change in natural objects is their form. He does so through an analogy between such natural objects and artifacts. He notes that the nature of an artifact is its form rather than its matter. The nature of a bed is not wood; a piece of wood is only potentially a bed. The craftsman makes it actually a bed by imposing a form onto the relevant matter, the wood (II, 1, 193a32–193b8). In an analogous way, a natural object acquires a form through a process of generation or growth through which the form is imposed on the matter (except without the need of a craftsman). The form constitutes the natural end of the process of growth or development. This form or nature exists as a potentiality in the growing organism, and it defines the direction or tendency of the developmental process (194a29–31).

It is important to note that, although we can *provisionally* characterize Aristotle's notion of form (as the principle according to which the matter is organized in a substance), this requires several important qualifications. First, the form cannot be reduced to the matter. This is because the form is a principle of organization that provides unity to an entity. Such a principle cannot be reduced to the matter in which it is embodied. Nevertheless, because form and matter are simply two aspects of individual entities, we cannot think of the form as separate entity. It is a non-reducible aspect of substances. In this way, Aristotle is neither a dualist nor a reductionist with regard to the form/matter distinction. We need to return to these points later.

Second, we need to remember that the form is the *relevant* way in which the matter is organized. It is the principle of organization that permits the entity or substance in question to be and to behave as that entity. It is the essence. So, for instance, if humans are rational animals, then part of our essence is to be rational and to do the kinds of things that rational beings do. That is the relevant principle of organization. Because we are rational beings, our bodies are organized in a certain way. The form determines what kind of matter an organism can be composed of.

Third, the provisional characterization needs to be amended to include the role of natural forms in processes of natural development and growth (193b12–19). This means that the structure of an egg cannot be its form: the form is the principle of organization for the mature chicken that the egg will become. The form is the inner principle of change that constitutes the nature of an organism.

Fourth, Aristotle says that the distinction between form and matter is relative (194b9). This means that the matter of an entity is already organized. For example, an animal's body is composed of organs. These constitute the matter out of which the animal is composed. However, the organs themselves have a form, and they are composed of flesh or tissue. Flesh itself has both form and matter. Even the simple elements, earth, water, air, and fire, have form and matter. In short, the distinction between form and matter must be drawn at different levels.

The above points mean that science should not study only matter, as some of the naturalist Pre-Socratics seemed to think (194a17–28). It is the investigation of nature; and as such, it should also research the nature of things, which means their form (193b7). Furthermore, it must investigate the principles of change, and this means understanding forms. Since the forms of natural things constitute the natural ends of their development, the forms define the direction in which they change (194a28–30). In conclusion, against the reductionist tendencies of the naturalist Pre-Socratic thinkers, Aristotle argues that physics must study natural forms. It must also investigate matter, at least insofar as this helps understand how the form is realized physically. For example, a doctor has to know how health is realized differently in various parts of the body (194a23). In sum, physics requires us to understand nature, and this requires us to be able to explain change, and not all explanations concern the material.

The Four Causes

In chapter 3 of Book II, Aristotle turns to the nature of explanation. To understand things in physics and the sciences generally, we must know how to explain them (194b17–20). To this end, Aristotle distinguishes four different kinds of causes—or rather, ways of explaining things.

1. The term *cause* can be applied to "that out of which a thing comes to be and which is present as a constituent in the product" (194b25). We can explain by citing what the thing is made of. For example, the fact that a sphere is made of bronze explains many of its other properties. Commentators often call this the *material cause*.

2. *Cause* is also applied to the form, or "the formula of what it is to be the thing in question" (194b27). We can explain by citing the essence of the thing. For example, we explain many things that people do by citing the fact that to be human is to be a certain kind of animal. By specifying what something is, we can explain why it does what it does. This is usually called the *formal cause*.

3. The word *cause* can also indicate "from which comes the immediate origin of the movement or rest." For example, a person constructing is the cause of a building, and the father is a cause of the child (194b32). This is sometimes called the *efficient cause*, though this misleadingly suggests that Aristotle's third kind of cause is similar to the modern notion of efficient cause. Following the Scottish philosopher Hume (1711–1776), some contemporary writers think of efficient causation as a relation between two events: an earlier event causes a later one. In contrast, Aristotle thinks of the efficient cause as a substance that causes a process concurrently. The activity of the builder is concurrent with the actual building process, even though the former causes the latter.[3] So if we call Aristotle's third type of cause *efficient*, we must be careful to distinguish it from contemporary efficient causation.

4. A cause can also be the end or aim of the thing in question (194b33–195a2). We can explain by specifying that for the sake of which something is done. For example, artifacts are made for a purpose; we can explain artifacts in terms of the purpose for which they were made. We can explain organs or the parts of plants in terms of their usefulness for the animal or plant itself. This is called the *final cause*.

It is best to think of these four causes as different types of explanation that are not necessarily mutually exclusive. Aristotle says that the art of statue making and the bronze can both be causes of the statue, though in different ways. For the most part, all things have all four types of cause or explanation.

> The student of nature should know about them all and it will be his method, when stating on account of what, to get back to them all: the matter, the form, the thing which effects the change, and what the thing is for. (198a22–24)

Furthermore, the same factor can count for more than one type of explanation. Referring to the four causes, Aristotle says that the last three often coincide (198a25). As we have already seen, the form serves as the final cause as well as the formal cause; this is because it defines the end of the development of a natural substance. Also, the form can be the efficient cause too. For instance, humans give birth to humans (198a26). In this case, the formal and efficient causes coincide. Furthermore, matter itself has a formal aspect: each of the four elements has a natural tendency or movement. Fire tends to move towards the outer circumference of the universe and earth towards the center.[4]

The Teleological, Chance, and Necessity

Aristotle thinks of nature in teleological terms. Natural things, such as organisms and the elements, have final causes or ends, which define their growth. However, this claim needs some qualifications.

First, there are exceptions. In fact, despite what he says in Book II, chapter 1, Aristotle does not think that all natural things can always be explained in terms of the teleology of the thing in question. For example, in *On the Heavens*, he explains some of the behavior of the heavenly bodies in terms of the desires of the divine. Additionally, in the *Meteorology*, he explains some sublunary physical phenomena, such as the weather, solely in terms of necessity, chance, and the nature of the relevant kinds of matter.[5]

Second, things do happen by chance. In Book II, chapter 4, Aristotle claims that there are some natural events that do not happen naturally or habitually (or "for the most part") but rather, they occur concurrently or accidently. For example, if A causes B, but B just happens also to be C, then A causes C accidently. This, however, does not mean that chance is an additional cause. It is an incidental connection between events.

Third, many things occur in the way they do because of simple necessity. They happen because of the nature of the matter concerned. Aristotle says that the rain falls from necessity (198b17–21). Furthermore, not all things serve a purpose. For example, although eyes serve a purpose, their color does not perform a function and cannot be explained by citing a final cause (*Generation of Animals* V, 1). So not all aspects of natural things are teleological. Some occur through necessity.

Mechanical necessity and teleology do not always oppose each other. To make this point, Aristotle contrasts simple with hypothetical necessity in chapter 9 of Book II. Something is hypothetically necessary when it must be how it is because of some end that it serves. So, for example, in order to cut, a saw must be made of a metal such as iron. The necessity is hypothetical or conditional on the ends. Such hypothetical necessity is important in biological functioning because it shows the primacy of teleological explanation over material necessity. Physiological processes are directed by the relevant ends.

Note that, despite his anthropomorphic language, Aristotle's view is not that inanimate objects have desires. It is rather that all natural things have a nature, which is their form, according to which they tend to develop. This natural development is an end. Therefore, we can explain the growth of a tree teleologically, in terms of the end of its nature, without affirming that it has desires. As we have seen, this teleological explanation is at the same time a formal explanation, because it requires the concept of the form of the tree.

The Defense of Teleology

In Book II, chapter 8 of the *Physics*, Aristotle tries to defend his claim that natural things have an end or purpose. He contrasts his view to that of Empedocles (495–435 BC), who thought that nature and its diverse forms were the result only of mechanical laws, without reference to ends (see chapter 3). Foreshadowing Darwin's theory of natural selection, Empedocles claims that natural phenomena came about "by coincidence" so that:

> When all turned out just as if they had come to be for something, then the things, suitably constituted as an automatic outcome, survived; when not, they died. (198b29–31)

Aristotle rebuffs this view, claiming that all natural things come to be as they are "always or for the most part" and nothing that is the outcome of luck does that (198b35–199a1). The phrase "always or for the most part" means, in general, that it happens regularly, though there may be exceptions. In short, Aristotle argues a teleological view of nature on the following grounds:

1. Natural changes occur in a regular way.
2. By definition, things that happen by chance involve a lack of regularity.

3. What does not happen by chance must happen for an end.

4. Therefore, natural changes happen for an end.

The weakness in this argument is the crucial third premise, because it does not consider the alternative that things can happen regularly because of mechanical causal laws.[6] However, Aristotle has a reply to this criticism, as we shall see in a moment.

Aristotle also argues for his teleological view of nature on the grounds that nature is analogous to human art (199a9–20). Just as works of art are made for a purpose, so are the works of nature. If a house were to grow naturally, we would still view it as serving an end.

> If, then, the swallow's act in making its nest is both due to nature and for something, and the spider's in making its web, and the plant's in producing leaves for its fruit, and roots not up but down for nourishment, plainly this sort of cause is present in things which are and come to be due to nature. (199a25–30)

The argument is that works of art and artifacts are made for a purpose and natural objects are analogous because if an artifact were natural, we would still regard it as serving a purpose. Therefore, natural objects can be regarded as teleological.

At the root of both of these two arguments is the idea that any purely mechanical or material explanation of things would be insufficient to explain their form.[7] This idea is suggested when Aristotle says:

> And since nature is twofold—nature as matter and nature as form— and the latter is an end, and everything else is for the end, the cause as that for which must be the latter, the form. (*Physics* II, 8, 199a31)

A purely mechanical view of nature wouldn't be able to explain the form of natural things. It would be confined to their matter. This is the limitation or shortcoming of the Pre-Socratic naturalistic philosophers. They treat substances as if they were aggregates of matter without a form. This point applies preeminently to organisms or living systems. We need to understand an organism, its parts, and its overall development primarily in terms of purposes. When we understand the purpose of an organ, we will be able to understand why it has the material composition that it does. The form and the final cause are primary (*Parts of Animals* I, 1, 642a1–642a24). We shall return to these points when we discuss parts of organisms (see page 260).

MOTION

In Book III of the *Physics*, Aristotle examines the nature of change or motion.[8] In chapter 1, he says that motion is continuous, and for this reason it is considered infinitely divisible. Furthermore, motion presupposes time and space, and according to some, the void (200b15–200b21). This preliminary analysis sets the agenda for the next books of the *Physics*: Aristotle will investigate the infinite, place, time, and the void, before returning to the topic of motion and its causes. We will follow suit in the following sections.

What is motion? Aristotle claims that it is not an entity over and above things that move or change:

> There is no such thing as motion over and above the things. It is always with respect to substance or to quantity or to quality or to place that what changes changes. (200b33–201a3)

Aristotle defines motion in general as the actualization of potential *qua* movable (201a28 and 201b4). In this sense, motion is *in* the movable. Furthermore, as the above quote indicates, all changes must be with respect to the relevant categories. Hence, there are as many types of motion or change as there are types of being (201a9). As we saw earlier, changes in substance are processes of generation and destruction rather than alterations. Aristotle reserves the term *locomotion* for change of place (208a32).

THE INFINITE

In Book III, chapter 4, Aristotle claims that apparent contradictions result, whether we suppose the infinite to exist or not to exist (203b31–203b35).

On the one hand, in chapter 5, he claims that an infinite body is impossible. Every body must be bounded by a surface, and no infinite body could be so bounded (204b5–204b9). He also argues that an actual infinite body could be neither a simple nor a composite (204b13–204b21). Therefore, there is no body that is actually infinite (206a7–206a8). It is impossible that there should be a thing that is in itself infinite, separable from sensible objects (204a8–204a16).

On the other hand, in chapter 6 Aristotle argues that the claim that the infinite doesn't exist in any way also leads to obviously absurd consequences. First, it would mean that there is a beginning and an end of time. Second, it would mean that a magnitude would not be infinitely divisible, and third, that number could not be infinite (206a9–206a13).

To resolve this antinomy, Aristotle concludes that the infinite *cannot* exist as an actuality, but that it *must* exist as a potentiality. This apparently satisfies both sides of the apparent dilemma and avoids a contradiction.

However, this solution requires explaining what *potential* means in this context. Clearly it doesn't mean what it usually means for Aristotle: a piece of bronze is potentially a statue in the sense that it could become a statue. In contrast, a potential infinity isn't potentially an actual infinity! (He argues that infinity cannot exist as an actuality).

To explain what he means by a potential infinity, Aristotle compares the infinite in the processes of addition and division (206a14–18). At first sight, the two appear to be quite different. In the case of addition, to any set of numbers we could always add an additional number. In the case of division, we have, let us say, a line of a given length, and we can divide it indefinitely. In the second case, there is a given totality and in the first there isn't. However, in both cases, we have a process that could be carried on indefinitely, and in this sense the two cases are not so different: both yield a potential rather than an actual infinity (206b4–206b12).

In his denial of the actual infinite, Aristotle says that he is reversing the traditional conception of infinity. Ancient thinkers tended to think of the infinite as that which contains everything and, in this way, as something complete. On the contrary, says Aristotle, the infinite is something that is never complete:

> The infinite turns out to be the contrary of what it is said to be. It is not that of which nothing is outside it is infinite, but what always has something outside it. (III, 6, 206b330)

Some thing complete has nothing outside of it, but the infinite by definition cannot be completed. Nothing is complete that has no limit or end.

Place

In Book IV, chapter 1, Aristotle notes how puzzling place is. It isn't a body and doesn't have a body, and yet it has three dimensions. It isn't an element and isn't composed of the elements, and it isn't one of the four causes (209a14–22). So, what is it? Furthermore, as Zeno noted, apparently, if it exists, then it must be somewhere; in which case, it has a place. If place has a place, then an infinite series is generated (209a23–209a25).

By *place*, Aristotle doesn't mean space as a container.[9] However, he does distinguish place that is common to all bodies and place that is particular to each, which is a boundary or limit (209a31–209b4). In fact, he takes the second of these conceptions of place as primary. He tries to avoid a view of place that renders space as a separate object from particular substances. Nevertheless, he also argues that place cannot be identified with the objects that occupy it. Otherwise, objects would not be able to move their position. So place isn't identical to bodies, but neither is it some entity entirely separate from them. This is the provisional result that Aristotle reaches by the end of chapter 2 of Book IV, and this attempt to avoid two extreme positions defines his approach to place: place isn't identical to the objects in it, but neither is it a separate object or entity in itself.

In chapter 4, Aristotle lists some of the main features of the concept of place in the second or the particular sense of the term. The place of an object contains the object and is exactly the same size as the object it contains. It is not part of the object; it is something distinct from the object (210b34–211a5). From these considerations, Aristotle proposes four candidates for the role of being place: the shape of an object, its constituting matter, the extension between the extreme parts of an object, or the outer boundary of the body (211b10–211b13). He discards the first three of these. The first two he declines partly on the grounds that shape and matter are aspects of the object, and therefore, they are not separate from a body in the way that place is (209b5–29). He rejects the third on the ground that this idea assumes that the extension is a thing over and above the body itself, and that this is false (211b14–29).

So, Aristotle concludes that place is the boundary of the containing body at which it is in contact with the contained body. The contained body can be moved, but the boundary that constitutes its place (at that time) cannot. Thus, place is a motionless limit. "Hence the place of a thing is the innermost motionless boundary of what contains it" (212a20). Interestingly, Aristotle realizes that this means that, although everything in the universe has a place, the universe as a whole does not. Thus, the only way to suppose that the universe moves is that it turns.

Place and time are both presuppositions of movement. The existence of place is shown by the fact that movement involves displacement. For example, water moves in and displaces the air. Such displacement presupposes place.

Aristotle also discusses the void (Book IV, chapters 6–9), which is thought by some to be a presupposition of motion. Aristotle argues that there is no absolute void or vacuum, even though each of the elements can exist in different degrees of density.

This conclusion about the void supports Aristotle's decision to define place in terms of the boundary or limit of particular bodies rather than in terms of the common place occupied by all. If there is no void, all places are occupied. Furthermore, if we can define place in terms of the places of particular bodies, then this helps to avoid the reification of space as an entity distinct from all bodies.

TIME

Chapters 10–14 of Book IV are devoted to the study of time. Like place, it is a very puzzling concept. For instance, Aristotle notes that the change of each thing is only in the thing that changes, but time is present equally everywhere (218b12–218b14). From such puzzles, he concludes that time is neither identical to movement nor independent of movement (Book III 11, 219a3). Time is something that belongs to movement in some yet unspecified way.

Next, Aristotle notes that we only apprehend time when we perceive a "before" and an "after" (219a22–219a29). Without the conception of

Chapter Ten—Aristotle: Physics and Biology 245

before and after, there could be no time. Second, likewise, there would be no time without "now," and vice versa (220a1–220a4). Nevertheless, the now is not a *part* of time, just as points are not parts of a line (only a line can be part of a line). To apprehend time requires that there is a perception of two "nows," or in other words, before and after. The perception of a single "now" wouldn't suffice to permit a perception of time. Because of this, the perception of time is a perception of motion.

For these reasons, Aristotle concludes that time is the number of motion with respect to "before" and "after." By the phrase *number of motion*, Aristotle doesn't mean that time is motion, but rather that it is possible motion insofar as it can be counted or enumerated (212a30–b9). Time is that aspect of possible movement that can be counted. This is why Aristotle says that time is a measure of motion and of being moved (220b33–221a8).

According to Aristotle, this conclusion explains why time is continuous. Since time is a measure of movement (with respect to the before and the after), and movement is continuous, like magnitude, time also must be continuous (219a10–219a14 and 220a25–220a26).

Also, this account of time explains the special nature of the "now" or present moment. The *now* limits, links, and unifies.

> So the "now" also is in one way a potential dividing of time, in another the termination of both parts, and their unity. (222a18–222a20)

In other words, the present moment *now* divides time into past and future; it also constitutes the end of the past and the beginning of the future, and it unifies the past and the future into one time (222a10–222a17).

This means that, in terms of division, time is infinite only potentially. If it is an instantaneous instant, the present moment isn't a part of time. Any finite time period isn't composed of an actual infinity of instantaneous present moments.

Likewise, time is only potentially infinite in terms of addition. It can be added to indefinitely. In this sense, there is no last event. Likewise, we can go back in time indefinitely: in this sense, there is no first event. However, these two features of time (no beginning and no end) do not make time an actual infinity, because successive moments do not co-exist. As we have seen, for Aristotle, the nature of time is defined by *now*, as being what exists. It is only in relation to the now that we can specify past and future. Different times do not co-exist at the same time. Therefore, time itself is not an actual infinity. Its infinite nature is merely potential: for any moment, it is possible to find an earlier and later moment.

One of the puzzles about Aristotle's treatment of time is that time is counted but it is also a continuum. Counting seems to require the idea of discrete units. However, he maintains that time is a continuum, which implies that it is not discrete. Aristotle circumvents this puzzle by distinguishing two ways in which something is countable. On one hand, there are the numbers with which we count, such as the natural numbers, which require a plurality of discrete entities. On the other hand, there is the kind of number that is merely countable, which applies to things that are continuous. In something continuous, we count potential divisions.[10] For Aristotle, time is countable in the second sense only.

Aristotle affirms that time is a requirement of motion. However, the two cannot be identified, because there are many movements, but only one time. Only things that could be in motion can be in time. Things that are eternal and immobile are not. Aristotle uses this point to argue that time itself is eternal—it never began and it will never end. This conclusion is important for Aristotle in establishing the nature of the unmoved mover (see below).

CONTINUITY OF MOTION

Having analyzed the concepts of place, void, and time, Aristotle returns to the theme of motion in Books V and VI. He revisits the classification of different kinds of change. There are three kinds of change: the creation of and the destruction of a substance, and changes in the substance (225a1–20). The first two kinds of change are best *not* called *motion* because they involve the coming to be or cessation of a substance (225a20–36). For the third kind of change, the term *motion* is appropriate, and there are three kinds of motion: qualitative, quantitative, and local (225b9).

In Book VI, chapter 1, Aristotle argues that nothing continuous can be composed of indivisibles. In Book V, chapter 3, and at the beginning of Book VI, he defines the terms *continuous*, *in contact*, and *in succession* as follows: things are continuous if their extremities are one; they are in contact if their extremities are together, and they are in succession if there is nothing of their own kind intermediate between them. Aristotle says that, given these definitions, nothing that is continuous can be composed of indivisibles. For example, a continuous line cannot be composed of indivisible points (231a18–231a28).

He reaches this conclusion because if that which is continuous were composed of points, these points would have to be either continuous or in contact with one another. Both of these conditions are impossible to satisfy. The first condition is impossible because indivisibles cannot be continuous. The second is impossible because if the points were in contact with each other, it would have to be as whole to whole (since points don't have parts). However, if points were in contact with each other as wholes, they couldn't constitute a continuous line because a continuous line has spatially distinct parts. They couldn't overlap. To conclude, a continuous line cannot be composed of indivisible points (231a29–231b17).

Aristotle says that similar reasoning applies to lengths, motion, and time (231b18). Each is continuous and cannot be composed of indivisible parts (232a23). These sections of the *Physics* make it clear that, for Aristotle, spatial magnitudes or lengths are continuous and, because of this, movements are also continuous: movement is across places. Likewise, because of the continuous nature of movement, time is also continuous. However, Aristotle also says that if time is continuous, then magnitude must be too (because length or distance travelled is motion multiplied by time) (233a13–233a21) (see also Book VI, chapter 4). He concludes that the nature of the continuous is that it is always divisible into parts that are themselves always divisible (232b22).

In chapter 3 of Book VI, Aristotle contends that the now is indivisible. He argues that the now is indivisible on the grounds that it is the extremity of the past and of the future. If the two extremities were different, the one could not be successor of the other. This means that if the now were divisible, part of it would be in the past, and part of it would be in the future. To avoid this absurd result, we must suppose that the now is indivisible. The conclusion that the now is indivisible might appear to contradict the claim that time is continuous. However, it does not, because Aristotle rejects the claim that time is composed of indivisible nows.

Aristotle claims that, because place, time, and motion are all continuous, Zeno's famous arguments against the possibility of motion are fallacious. This is the main theme of Book VI, chapter 9.

Zeno's Paradoxes

As we saw in chapter 2 of this volume, Zeno's so-called "paradoxes" are not really paradoxes at all. A paradox is an apparently inescapable contradiction, and Zeno does not uncover or reveal such contradictions. Instead, he constructs a set of arguments designed to prove the startling conclusion that motion is not possible. He does so in order to support Parmenides's claim that motion is impossible and that the universe is one whole, indivisible, and unchanging thing.

Zeno states four arguments for his conclusion: the Midway Problem; Achilles; the Arrow; and the Stadium. Despite their important differences, the four arguments have a similar form, and we shall concentrate on Aristotle's critique of the Midway Problem and the Arrow.

The Midway Problem

As we saw in chapter 2, the argument has the following structure. Imagine that you have to cross a room, by travelling half of the distance across it, then half of the remaining distance and half of the remaining distance, and so on. According to Zeno, you would never actually cross the room. The journey consisting of an infinite number of such steps cannot be completed. However, the same is true of *any* journey, and therefore no journey or movement can even begin.

The general form of this argument is:

1. For anything to move requires that it complete an infinite number of tasks.
2. It is impossible to complete an infinite number of tasks.
3. Therefore, movement is impossible.

According to the first premise, moving requires finishing an infinite number of tasks because space is infinitely divisible. This implies that between any two points there are an infinite number of points. This in turn implies that to move between any two points requires completing an infinite number of steps or tasks. With regard to the second premise, Zeno's point is that it is impossible to complete an infinite series because such a series has no last member.

In reply, Aristotle rejects the notion of an infinite number of tasks. As we have just seen, a line does not consist in an actual infinite number of points; a line is a continuum that can be divided indefinitely. Therefore, in relation to the first premise, for something to move does not require it completing an actual infinite number of real tasks. Rather, the distance moved can be divided indefinitely.

The Arrow
Imagine an arrow flying through space. Zeno argues:

1. At any moment, the arrow occupies a space that is equal to its own size.
2. Something that occupies a space equal to its own size is at rest.
3. Therefore, at any moment, the arrow is at rest.

This conclusion can be generalized to show that no motion is possible. Aristotle's reply is:

> Time is not composed of indivisible nows any more than any other magnitude is composed of indivisibles. (VI, 9, 239b8)

In other words, Aristotle rejects the very idea of something being either at rest or in motion at an instant. The first premise of the above argument is therefore based on a mistake, because of the phrase "at any moment." A period of time does not consist of an actual infinity of instants or nows, just as a line does not consist in an actual infinity of points. A period of time can be divided indefinitely, but this makes a potential infinity and not an actual one.

A Brief Summary

Book I of the *Physics* starts with the idea that physics is the study of things that change. Aristotle needs to show, against Parmenides, that change is possible; and he does so by distinguishing two kinds of change, which in turn requires him to distinguish form and matter. The distinction between form and matter shows the need for four types of explanation and the priority of the teleological, which are explained in Book II. To understand what change is, Aristotle proposes to analyze continuity, place, and time. In each case he does so in the context of his theory about infinity, namely, that infinity cannot exist as an actuality but it must do so as a potentiality. This enables him to try to resolve problems regarding space and time, including Zeno's paradoxes. This summary takes us to the end of Book VI.

Causes of Motion

In Book VII, Aristotle turns to the causes of motion. As we have seen, he thinks that all natural objects have an inner tendency to movement, without which they would not move. This applies to natural inanimate objects as well as living things. This is what it means for them to be natural—they have a natural tendency to move. Aristotle thinks that the four elements have a natural place: fire moves up and earth moves down; each will come to rest in their natural place. Air and water are intermediaries, and they rise or fall accordingly. Artifacts have a natural tendency to move because of their matter, the material out of which they are composed.

Nevertheless, Aristotle argues that all motion must be initiated by the action of an external body. All motion requires a mover. Despite their natural *tendencies* to move in certain ways, even the natural elements need a mover to actualize those tendencies. Accordingly, for Aristotle, force is necessary to maintain a body in motion. He claims that a body can only move when it is in contact with the mover (VII, 2). There is no action at a distance. He realizes that this presents a problem regarding projectiles: one throws a stone, and it continues to move after one has let it go (VIII, 10, 266b–267a). According to Aristotle, it continues because of the effect of the movement on the air particles. The power of movement is communicated through those particles. However, this power decreases as the distance from the mover increases, and the stone will come to rest, quite independently of any opposing forces or resistance.[11] In summary, both the inner (the form and the end) and outer (the impulse or external force) components are necessary for change. Aristotle says that inanimate things have in themselves "a beginning of being moved" but not "a beginning of causing movement."

First Cause, but No First Event

In *Physics* VIII, Aristotle argues that there must be a first cause of all change, which itself is eternal and changeless. Motion has no beginning in time, but nevertheless, there must be a source of movement in the universe as a whole. There is a first cause, but no first event.

Aristotle tries to establish that change has always been happening and always will. In effect, he argues that there is no first event. His initial argument against a first event is that every change must have an explanation.

This explanation must always refer to a previous event. To explain how temporal things come into being, we must assume some other earlier change; otherwise, there would be nothing to explain the change. In short, any change requires an explanation of why it happened, and this explanation must refer to a previous event. Consequently, there cannot be a first event. Aristotle presents another argument for the same conclusion. This is based on the nature of time. Time itself cannot start or end. It is eternal. However, time is just the possibility of change. Therefore, change itself cannot have begun and cannot end, just like time. Thus, there is no first event.

In Book VIII, he famously tries to establish the need for an unmoved mover or for a first cause with the following argument:

1. There is motion.
2. At each instant, all movement requires a mover.
3. Whatever is moved must be moved by something else.
4. The primary cause of movement in the universe could not be a moved mover, because this would lead to an infinite regress.
5. Therefore, there must be an unmoved mover.

In this argument, the fourth premise should not be read temporally. We have already seen that, according to Aristotle, there is no first event; change has no beginning. Thus, we should not understand premise 4 as requiring a first event. It is articulating the need for a completion of explanation. To see this, consider an infinite series of stationary things, each one of which has the following feature: it needs to be pushed in order to move. Such a series could not move of its own accord. Therefore, if an infinite series of such things is moving, it must be because it was or is moved by something else that doesn't itself need to be pushed to move.

In the *Metaphysics*, Aristotle tries to argue that the unmoved mover is divine. He claims that the unmoved mover must be pure actuality. All movement implies potentiality. However, the cause of the movement must be something else that is actual. For example, to heat something up, one must use something that is already hot. The thing that is heated has a potential (to become hot), but the thing that heats it is actually hot. We can generalize this point to the claim that the actualization of something potential must be caused by something else that is itself actual. In this way, Aristotle tries to establish that the unmoved mover must be something that is completely actual. As we shall see, this is the first step towards showing that the unmoved mover should be called *God*.

On the Universe

The *Physics* articulates the principles of change. Aristotle's other works about the physical universe, *On the Heavens* (or *De Caelo*), *On Gener-*

ation and Corruption, and the *Meteorology*, apply these principles to different aspects of the natural world. *On the Heavens* concerns the movement and nature of the stars as well as the elements. One of its main points is to divide the universe into two worlds: the superlunary and the sublunary. The superlunary world begins at the moon, going upwards, and it consists of the stars and planets. The sublunary world, below the moon, is one of change and decay; this is the main concern of Aristotle's other works, the *Meteorology* and *On Generation and Corruption*.

On The Heavens: The Superlunary World

In Book I, chapter 2 of *On the Heavens*, Aristotle argues for the distinction between the superlunary and the sublunary based on the observation that the stars are in an eternal, constant, circular motion and that they are otherwise unchanging, which is why they are called the *fixed stars*. He argues that there are only two kinds of simple or basic movements: in straight lines or circular. All other movements are a combination of these two (268b11–268b26). Aristotle also claims that simple bodies move according to their own nature (268b27–269b17). Each of the four elements (earth, water, fire, and air) moves naturally in straight line; the natural motion of fire and air is upward, water and earth downward. Therefore, to explain the primary circular motion of heavenly bodies, there must be a fifth element.

In the *Meteorology*, Aristotle presents a different argument for the existence of a fifth element. The distance between the earth and the stars is great, and if this space was filled with one of the four sublunary elements, say air, then there would be an imbalance between the qualities of hot and cold, and wet and dry, in the universe (*Met*, I, 3, 339b29–340a18). He concludes that this space could not be filled with one of the four sublunary elements. Since there is no void, there must be another or fifth element.

Aristotle claims that this fifth element has divine features. In chapter 3, Book I of *On the Heavens*, he tries to show that this new element would transcend the categories *heavy* and *light* because necessarily, everything that possesses lightness or heaviness in some relative degree moves either up or down. So, any body that naturally moves in a circle cannot be heavy or light.

He also argues that heavenly bodies are indestructible and exempt from alteration (270a13–270a34). He does so on the basis that creation and destruction of a substance requires the changing of contrary properties. But the heavenly bodies do not have a contrary movement "because there can be no contrary motion to the circular." Therefore, these heavenly bodies are not destructible. This indicates that they will not also be subject to changes in quality because, says Aristotle, all bodies that change their properties are subject to increase and diminution in quantity. Therefore, the heavenly bodies are unchanging except for their circular motion.

Towards the end of chapter 3, Book I of *On the Heavens*, Aristotle is ready to draw his conclusion that the heavens must be made of a fifth element that is some ways divine. He says that "our distant ancestors" gave this special element the name *aether* because it runs on for an eternity. In chapters 9 and 10, he argues explicitly for the eternal nature of the heavenly. First, everything ceases to move when it reaches its end or natural resting place. However, in contrast, circular motion does not have a starting and an end point; therefore, the motion of the heavenly bodies must be unceasing or without end. In chapters 10–12 Aristotle argues that it would be impossible for something that was generated to be eternal; generated things always get destroyed (279b17–279b32).

In short, according to Aristotle, to explain the simple, ever-constant, circular movement of the stars requires the postulation of a fifth element, which is so different from the other four that one is required to make the division between the two worlds. Nevertheless, Aristotle hastens to add that these heavenly bodies must be finite. In chapters 5, 6, and 7 of Book I, he argues that the heavenly bodies cannot be infinite. In chapters 8 and 9 he claims that there can be only one heaven, and that there is no time, place, void, or matter outside of the universe.

The universe consists in concentric spheres. The outer one of these is heaven, which rotates uniformly (II, 6). It contains the so-called "fixed stars" and, in its rotation, it carries the stars along with it (II, 7–8). This perfect circular motion of the heavenly outermost sphere is due to God. At the center of the universe is the still Earth, which is the natural position of the heavy element earth, which tends to fall towards the center of the universe (II, 13–14). The Earth is naturally spherical, but not as big as the stars (297b14).

The constant circular motion of the outermost sphere and the "fixed" stars is simple compared to the sometimes irregular and complex motion of the planets, the Sun, and the Moon. How should this irregular motion be explained? Fundamentally, the cause of these irregularities is the motion of the other concentric spheres, which rotate in directions that are different from the heavenly outer one (II, 12).

In this point, Aristotle draws on the work of earlier astronomers, as we can see from chapter 8, Book XII of the *Metaphysics*. In Plato's Academy, Eudoxus had tried to solve the problem of the complex and irregular motion of the planets by postulating a number of concentric spheres, inclined at slightly different angles, and rotating at different speeds in different directions. He postulated four spheres for each planet (at that time only Jupiter, Saturn, Mars, Venus, and Mercury were known), and three each for the Sun and Moon. In this way, he was able to explain a large amount of observational data, including the rotation of the Sun and the Moon, and the mentioned irregularities. Aristotle's astronomer friend Callippus refined this model.[12] The result is that Aristotle thinks that there are 55 rotating spheres, each of which is moved by an unmoved mover, which Aristotle conceives as a nonmaterial, intelligent being, inferior to the prime mover, God (*Metaphysics* XII, 8 1073b36–1074a30).

The Sublunary World

In Books III and IV of *On the Heavens*, Aristotle turns to motion in the sublunary world, which is the world of change and decay. He distinguishes the four elements by their heaviness and lightness, and their corresponding tendencies with regard to motion (III, 5). Without intervention, earth will fall downwards, in a straight line towards the center of the universe. Without intervention, fire will rise upwards, away from the center of the universe. In this way, each of the elements has its own proper or natural position, or place. The remaining two elements, air and water, are intermediary in terms of their natural positions (IV, 3–5). Consequently, it makes sense to think of the Earth as a body at rest at the center of the universe around which, below the moon, lie concentric layers of water, air, and fire.

These points also help us understand part of Aristotle's resistance to the idea of an infinite universe. All natural movements must come to an end. This requires the idea of a natural resting place for the elements. However, the idea of such a place does not make sense in an infinitely large universe that has no center and no extreme ends. For this reason, according to Aristotle, in an infinite universe there could be no distinction between heavy and light, because this depends on the idea of a natural resting place (*Physics* III, 5, 205a19–20).

The Four Elements

In *On Generation and Corruption*, Aristotle tries to establish that there are four sublunary elements and that they are sufficient for explaining the behavior of all compounds.

The theory of the four elements was derived from Empedocles. The main competing theory of the time was that of the Atomists, especially Democritus. He claimed that the physical universe consists of fundamental particles, whose differences in shape, position, and arrangement underlies all other physical differences. Aristotle opposes the Atomist theory on the grounds that matter is a continuum, like space. According to Aristotle, there are no ultimate, indivisible particles in continuous space.

Aristotle says that atomism is motivated by an unsound argument. According to this argument, the claim that matter is infinitely divisible generates a contradiction, and therefore, there must be atoms (*De Gen.* I, 2, 316a11). To see why some philosophers argue this, suppose that an infinite division of matter were completed. In which case, what would one be left with? There are only three options: either there would be parts with no magnitude, or there would be nothing at all, or there would be parts with an indivisible magnitude. The first two options are absurd. The first is absurd because something without a magnitude could not constitute something with a magnitude. The second is absurd because something cannot be constituted out of nothing. Therefore, the only remaining third option must be the correct one. However, it contradicts the claim that matter is infinitely divisible; it assumes that there are atoms, after all. Since the other two options do not make sense, there must be indivisible atoms.

Aristotle rejects this argument for atomism (*De Gen.* I, 2, 317a). He does so by making a point that is similar to the one he employs in refuting Zeno's Paradoxes. He claims that to reject the idea of indivisible atoms does not require one to accept the idea of actual infinity of parts. Matter is infinitely divisible only potentially; the division of matter can never be completed. Thus, the claim that matter is a potential infinity does not mean that it is an actual infinite collection of parts. An infinite division of matter cannot be completed.

Having rejected the competing theories in the field, Aristotle develops his own theory.[13] In *On Generation and Corruption* (II, 2), he tries to show that all perceptible qualities in objects are tangible ones (e.g., heavy–light, hard–soft, viscous–brittle, rough–smooth), and that these tangible qualities reduce to four basic ones: hot and cold, and dry and wet. These are the four basic powers that explain all other physical properties, such as weight, roughness, and malleability. For example, brittleness can be reduced to dryness, softness to the wet, and hardness to the dry.

In summary, Aristotle explains the four elements in terms of the combination of these four basic powers. Earth is cold and dry; water is cold and wet. Air is hot and wet, and fire is hot and dry (*De Gen.* II, 2–3). These four are the simplest bodies. Because of this, the form/matter distinction applies to them only in thought or abstractly.

It is important to note that the four elements shouldn't be identified with their English equivalents. For instance, Aristotle's element fire is a rarified and highly flammable gas that surrounds the Earth, and it isn't literally what we now call "fire," which is in fact an excess of heat according to Aristotle.

These four elements can transform one into another (*De Gen.* II, 4). For example, water becomes air (steam) by being heated up—for instance, by the rays of the sun. The process is reversed during condensation. Likewise, earth is transformed to water and fire to air, both by becoming wet (*De Gen.* II, 4, 331a).

In *On Generation and Corruption* (II, 7–8), Aristotle tries to explain the behavior of all compounds from the actions of these four elements. To do so, he distinguishes two kinds of compounds: those with similar parts and those with dissimilar parts. The first, homogeneous compounds, such as hair, have parts that are alike (*Met.* IV, 10, 388a14–388a21). The second kind of compound has parts that are dissimilar; they are heterogeneous.

The division between these two kinds of compounds reflects the two processes through which compounds are formed: mixing and combination.

The first is just a mixture of two or more components that can be separated. For instance, a pile of seeds contains a mixture of the different sorts of seeds. Mixtures aren't homogeneous; they are heterogeneous. Because they can be separated, mixtures don't constitute a chemical reaction.

In contrast, the second process, combination, brings about the existence of a new substance, which may have properties quite different from its constituents. One of Aristotle's examples of such combination is the formation of bronze from tin and copper (*On Gen.* I, 10). The results of such combinations are typically homogeneous or uniform: a bit of blood is still blood.

All compound bodies are composed of all of the four elements (*De Gen* II, 8, 334b). The combination of the four elements explains the composition of compounds such as blood, tissue, milk, bark, stone, and gold. In Book IV of the *Meteorology*, Aristotle investigates the nature of specific compounds and gives an elementary classification of all compounds. For example, substances that solidify in the cold and are dissoluble by fire are mostly water based. Those that are solidified by fire are mostly earth based (*Met.* IV, 10).[14] This classification constitutes a demonstration that all chemical reactions can be explained in terms of the four elements.

Natural Phenomena

In the *Meteorology*,[15] Aristotle extends the theory of the four elements to give a generalized explanation of various natural phenomena. The book begins with an ambitious vision of a unified program.

> It is concerned with events that are natural, though their order is less perfect than that of the first of the elements of bodies. They take place in the region nearest to the motion of the stars. Such are the Milky Way, and comets, and the movements of meteors. It studies also all the affections we may call common to air and water, and the kinds and parts of the earth and the affections of its parts.... When the inquiry into these matters is concluded, let us consider what account we can give, in accordance with the method we have followed, of animals and plants, both generally and in detail. (*Met.* I, 1 338a23–339a8)

This grand opening suggests that Aristotle seeks a unified explanation of all natural phenomena of the sublunary world in terms of the four elements. However, Aristotle's vision is fundamentally non-reductionist, as we shall see.

The theory of the four elements explains various physical changes. For example, when water boils, it changes from the wet and cold (water) to the wet and hot (air). In other words, the cold becomes hot (*Met.* I, 3–4). In the *Meteorology*, Aristotle applies such ideas to a variety of physical phenomena such as, among others, shooting stars (*Met.* I, 4), comets (I, 6–7), the Milky Way (I, 8), clouds (I, 9), snow and hail (I, 11–12), the winds (I, 13 and II, 4–6), rivers (I, 13–14), and the sea (II 1–3).

Book IV of the *Meteorology* is concerned with the physical chemistry of compound substances, such as gold and silver. As we have just seen, Aristotle classifies the compounds according to their composition, and describes their reaction to heat and cold, and dryness and wetness (*Met.* IV, 10–11). Towards the end of the book, he discusses organic compounds, such as flesh and blood (*Met.* IV, 12). These passages make it clear how Aristotle avoids reductionism in his theory of the formation of compounds. Things cannot be reduced to the matter out of which they are composed, even at the elemental level. Even physics, which is concerned *mainly* with the matter out of which things are composed, is not exclusively concerned with matter.

There are two reasons for this. First, as we saw when we discussed the four causes, Aristotle retains the distinction between form and matter at all levels, even in physics. Any substance has a form that defines its essence and its natural end, as well as being composed of its constituent matter. Form and matter are two aspects of a substance, separable only in thought. In Book IV of the *Meteorology*, Aristotle emphasizes again that the form/matter distinction should be applied at all levels: it applies to the person, to the flesh and bone out of which he or she is composed, and to the elements out of which that flesh and bone are composed. He adds the idea that

> For the end is least obvious there where matter predominates most. If you take the extremes, matter is pure matter and the essence is pure definition; but the bodies intermediate between the two are related to each in proportion as they are near to either. (*Met.* IV, 12)

The second reason why Aristotle's physics is not reductionist is that he separates the matter/substance distinction from the part/whole distinction. Chapter 12 of Book IV of the *Meteorology* makes it clear that the two questions "What is a body composed of?" and "What parts does it have?" are distinct. The first question concerns the matter out of which something is composed. It seeks the material cause. In the case of compounds, this matter is homogeneous or uniform: bones, skin, milk, and tissue are uniform. Additionally, the matter or stuff is not countable; we do not count milks or bloods. In contemporary terminology, matter is referred to with a mass noun rather than a count noun.

In contrast, the second question concerns the parts of a whole. Such parts (e.g., organs and hands) depend on the whole: we can only understand them by knowing their function within the whole. Furthermore, they are not uniform; they are heterogeneous: part of a hand is not a hand. Additionally, the parts of an animal or plant can be counted, unlike the matter.

In summary, Aristotle's theory is not reductionist partly because he recognizes the importance of the distinction between the parts of an organism and the matter of which the organism's body is composed. He recognizes that this distinction involves two different kinds of explanation. To explain the parts of an organism, one needs to refer to its formal and final causes. We explain the heart by showing what it does and how it works, and not by specifying what it is composed of. Aristotle says:

> Now heat and cold and the motions they set up as the bodies are solidified by the hot and the cold are sufficient to form . . . the homogeneous bodies, flesh, bone, hair, sinew, and the rest. . . . But no one would go as far as to consider them sufficient in the case of the non-homogeneous parts (like the head, the hand, or the foot), which these homogeneous parts go to make up. Cold and heat and their motion would be admitted to account for the formation of copper or silver, but not for that of a saw, a bowl, or a box. (*Met.* IV, 12, 390b3–390b14)

In other words, Aristotle argues that material causes cannot explain everything. This point supports an important assumption implicit in his argument for a teleological conception of nature, which we saw earlier in this chapter (see pages 239–241). This key point about the insufficiency of purely material explanations is very clearly evident in his studies of animals.

Animals

As the beginning of the *Meteorology* testifies, Aristotle regards the study of organisms an integral part of the scientific study of the natural world, proceeding with the same principles of investigation as physics. In his studies of animals, Aristotle employs his philosophical work on form and matter, the four causes, hypothetical necessity, potential and actual, and part and whole. Science is about understanding causes, not just gathering facts. It is about understanding natural phenomena, substances as a whole, not just the materials out which they are composed (*PA*. I, 5, 644b).

Much of Aristotle's scientific work is dedicated to biology. There are his works about animals: the *History of Animals, Parts of Animals, Generation of Animals, Movement of Animals,* and *Progression of Animals*. Additionally, there are the works about human biology and psychology: *De Anima, Sense and Sensibilia, On Memory, On Sleep, On Dreams, On Divination in Sleep, On Length of Life, On Youth and Death, On Respiration,* and *On Breath*. We will discuss Aristotle's psychological studies in the next chapter, after looking at his metaphysics.

Aristotle's work in animal biology is directed towards understanding four broad areas: classification; anatomy and physiological processes; reproduction, inheritance and growth; and the movement and perception of animals.

Classification

The *History of Animals* appears to be a loosely organized compilation of data concerning the similarities and differences between species, and as such it is often viewed as a prelude to Aristotle's more organized works, such as the *Parts of Animals* and the *Generation of Animals*. The *History* begins with a familiar point: animals have heterogeneous parts, such as their organs, and these are composed out of homogeneous matter, such as flesh and bone (*HA.* I, 1). Aristotle reviews some of the differences between animals: some differ with regard to their parts or organs; their parts may be composed of different kinds of matter; animals differ in modes of subsistence and habits; they differ in their behavior and modes of living, and in their character (*HA.* I, 1–6). In chapter 6 of Book I, Aristotle sets out a program: he will consider the differences and similarities between different species and discuss their causes, focusing on the parts of animals (*HA.* 491a6–491a18). This suggests that Aristotle is interested in the classification of animals primarily as a way to organize, in groupings, the functioning and purpose of the parts of animals.

In the first book and chapter of *Parts of Animals*, Aristotle affirms that the natural scientist should study primarily the final causes or purposes of biological phenomena "presented by each group of animals" (*HA.* 640a16). Once we know the essence of a species, we can understand what parts it must have in order to survive, and from that understanding we can work out what its process of development must be (640a33–640b4). This will enable us to study the material causes, the matter out of which the relevant parts are made (640b18–640b29).

In Book I and chapters 2–3 of *Parts of Animals*, Aristotle rejects Plato's attempt to classify by dichotomous division, through pairs of opposites, such as "winged" and "wingless," following the methodology outlined in the *Sophist*. According to Aristotle, such a classification has no structure, and there are natural groupings, such as birds, that should not be broken up, and which Plato's classification would violate (642b10–642b21). For instance, aquatic and terrestrial birds might appear as distinct kinds of animals rather than different species in the same genus. Additionally, privations or negations, such as footless or featherless, don't admit of classification. Aristotle concludes that "we cannot get at the indivisible species of the animal, or any other, kingdom by bifurcate division" (643a18).

In chapter 4, Aristotle defines his own method: first, to describe the functions common to all animals; second, those that belong to a general genus, such as birds, and—only then—third, those that are specific to a particular species, such as human (644a35–644b7). He makes it clear that he wants to follow "an order of exposition which conforms . . . to the order of nature" (646a4). Aristotle notes that the large generic groups, such as birds, fish, cephalopoda (squid), and testacea (with shells), are defined by the organs they share (644b8). Between different genera, the similarities between organs are often analogical; for instance, the arm, foreleg, the wing, and the fin are analogous. Different species of the same genus have the same bodily parts, and the differences between them are ones of degree. Differences between individuals within a species serve no biological purposes (644a13–27).

How should animals be classified? In Book II of *Generation of Animals*, he argues for placing animals on a natural scale according to their state of development when they are born (733a32–733b16). This, he thinks, depends on the animal's body heat, which depends on blood. He therefore divides all animals into two broad groups: those with, and those without blood. His classification looks roughly like this:

With Blood
1. Humans
2. Hairy quadrupeds (land mammals)
3. Sea mammals (cetacea)
4. Birds
5. Reptiles and amphibia
6. Fish

Without Blood
7. Cephalopods (octopus and squid)
8. Crustacea (crabs and lobster)
9. Insects
10. Mollusks
11. Zoophytes (e.g., sea anemones)

The first three types are capable having newborn babies that are similar to the adult (viviparous). In contrast, animals in the range from birds to crustacea have eggs (oviparous). Birds and reptiles have perfect eggs that do not grow after being laid. Fish, cephalopods, and crustacea have imperfect eggs, which need to develop even after being laid. Lower still come those animals that have grubs or larva, which Aristotle thinks of as a primitive pre-egg (Aristotle was not aware that grubs come from eggs) (733a32–733b16). Lower still come those animals that reproduce asexually. The lowest kinds of animals generate spontaneously from the mud and earth (*PA*. III, 11, 761a13–761a31).

Although Aristotle thinks of the differences between natural species as fixed, when he mentions sponges and sea anemones he claims that there is no strict boundary between animals and plants, and even between life and not life.

Thus, nature proceeds little by little from inanimate things to living creatures, in such a way that we are unable to determine the boundary line between them (*HA*. VIII, I, 588b4).

Anatomical Descriptions and Physiological Processes

Aristotle starts Book II of the *Parts of Animals* by discussing the method of biology. He argues that, in biology, the final cause is more important than the material cause: "The formal nature is of greater importance than the material nature" (640b29). The heterogeneous parts of animals, such as their organs, exist for the sake of the different purposes or functions they serve. These parts are composed out of homogeneous matter, such as tissue and bone, and this matter exists for the sake of the organs that serve the organism (*PA*. II, 1, 646a13–647a13). Aristotle insists on the importance of this point for understanding the formation and development of these parts: such growth processes are to be explained in relation to the functions that the organs serve. In a similar fashion, Aristotle looks for natural purposes to explain physiological processes. For example, the *History of Animals* (III, 3–4) contains a description of the heart and the blood vessels and their function.[16] Breathing cools the heart. Higher animals are naturally hotter, and so they need to breathe a lot, and for this reason they have lungs. Fish fulfill the same functions by taking in water. For this reason they have gills.

As we have seen, the purposes of the different parts of the organism all serve an end, which is the form of the organism itself. In other words, they serve the purpose of being that kind of organism (i.e., that of growing, reproducing, perceiving, moving and living as that type of organism does). The end is the form.

Even though purpose and form are primary and irreducible, Aristotle also seeks material explanations and efficient causes for such phenomena. For example, he compares the lungs to bellows powered by the heat of the heart. The natural scientist needs first to understand the purpose of such processes, and also how materially such processes occur. As we saw earlier, fish need gills because they live in water, and they need a breathing organ adapted to water in order to regulate temperature. In other words, the form directs the physical process. This was the point of Aristotle's notion of hypothetical necessity as explained earlier.

However, although these points apply to the characteristics that define and are common to a species, they do not apply to differences between individuals within a species. In the *Generation of Animals*, Book V, chapter 1, Aristotle says that to explain such individual variations, such as eye color, we must refer to mechanical or material causes. Likewise, deformities and imperfections are caused by the variations and limitations of the matter.

Reproduction, Inheritance, and Growth

In the *History of Animals* (VIII, 1) Aristotle says, "The life of animals, then, may be divided into two parts, procreation and feeding; for on these two acts, all their interests and life concentrate" (589a4). In the *Generation of Animals* he claims that there are three kinds of reproduction: sexual from two parents, asexual from a single parent, and spontaneous generation (*GA*. I, 1). Regarding the former, Aristotle argues that the male provides the form in the semen while the female provides the embryological matter. The semen provides the organization that molds the indeterminate raw material (*GA*. I, 2–4). He argues for this claim on the basis that it best explains several observable facts better than the competing theories, such as the view that the contribution of the parents is from the whole body (or pangenesis) (*GA*. I, 17, 721b6–721b12). This purely bodily view can't explain, for instance, why sometimes offspring resemble remote ancestors rather than their parents (*GA*. I, 18). In brief, Aristotle claims that no purely material transmission could explain how the organization and later development of material parts is inherited (*GA*. I, 19).

The Movement and Perception of Animals

In the *Movement of Animals* Aristotle claims that movement is the fundamental characteristic of animals that distinguishes them from plants. Animals are moved by thought and desire; he says:

> Now we see that the living creature is moved by intellect, imagination, purpose, wish, and appetite. And all these are reducible to thought and desire. (*MA*. 6, 700b15)

Animals are motivated to act by the objects of their desires. Their actions are initiated by being for the sake of something; they are essentially teleological. Furthermore, to be so motivated requires that the animal can perceive or sense the things that it wants (*MA*. 6, 701a43–6). In modern terminology, purposeful action requires both motivation and cognition. Animals are beings that can desire and perceive because they can initiate purposeful action.

In this regard, Aristotle compares animals to the unmoved movers in the heavenly sphere. This is because that which initiates action (rather than just transmitting it) must be a mover that itself is not moved (*MA*. 2–3). This is a primary movement that occurs in animals when they reach maturity. It is for the sake of this that their growth and development occur (*MA*. 5).

Conclusion

Physics is the study of things that change. Every substance can be thought of *qua* both its form and its matter, and this distinction even applies to the ultimate constituents of the sublunary world, the four elements. Each of these is defined primarily by the nature of each of the elements—its natural tendency to move within the universe; the heaviest, earth, is lower and the lightest, fire, moves upward. This point illustrates the primacy of formal and teleological explanations within Aristotle's physics. In this way, the nature of things explains the order in the universe. It also illustrates the importance of place within Aristotle's view of the universe. Each element has its natural place.[17]

A basic idea of Aristotle's theory is that all things in the sublunary world are either mixtures or compounds of the four elements. There is a fundamental difference between the two. When the elements are mixed, they can be separated. In contrast, the process of combination that forms compounds creates a new substance that cannot be reduced to the combinations that created it. This is important because all substances in the natural world are formed by iterative combinations of the four elements.

However, in each case, we can distinguish between form and matter. This means that the explanation we must seek of the order in the universe must have two levels. First, we should explain the behavior of each compound in terms of what its nature is (i.e., its formal and final causes). Second, to explain *how* such behavior occurs, we must seek the material and efficient cause in terms of the matter that the compound is composed of.

This central point shows how Aristotle's theory attempts to reconcile the differences between those of Plato and Pre-Socratic naturalism. Plato's theory is anti-materialist because the Forms are nonmaterial. The theories of the early Greek naturalists are materialist, but also reductive: all explanations must cite only the substance out of which all things are made. In contrast to both of these, Aristotle's account of the formation of the sublunary world is materialist without being reductionist because of the way that he distinguishes form and matter.

In this regard, Aristotle's notion of hypothetical necessity is important because it shows how form has physical implications. In other words, the physical features of something are hypothetically necessary when its physical characteristics must be as they are because of the nature or form of the thing in question. The physical necessity is hypothetical or conditional on the formal cause. For example, humans are rational animals, and this means that we must have a certain kind of body (e.g., with a heart). In other words, what it means to be human is what imposes the physical limitations. Such hypothetical necessity applies to all substances, not just to organisms. In short, according to Aristotle, physics is the study of any change, but all changes must involve a formal aspect that defines which material aspects are possible and necessary.

Study Questions

1. How and why does Aristotle distinguish alterations in substance from substantial generation?
2. How does Aristotle employ the actual/potential distinction to argue against Parmenides?
3. What is Aristotle's form/matter distinction? How does Aristotle's distinction undermine much Pre-Socratic natural philosophy?

4. What are the four causes?
5. How does Aristotle defend the claim that all natural phenomena have a teleological explanation?
6. What is the antinomy regarding the infinite and how does Aristotle solve it?
7. How does Aristotle define place?
8. How does Aristotle conceive of time? What problems is he trying to resolve?
9. For Aristotle, is time infinite?
10. How does Aristotle argue that that which is continuous cannot be composed of points?
11. How does Aristotle employ this conclusion to resolve Zeno's paradoxes?
12. How does Aristotle argue for the existence of an unmoved mover?
13. How does Aristotle support the claim that there is a fifth element (aether)?
14. How does Aristotle distinguish between heavenly and sublunary bodies?
15. Why does Aristotle reject atomism?
16. Why and how does he distinguish mixing and combining?
17. How does Aristotle distinguish the form/matter distinction from the part/whole distinction? Why is this important?
18. What are the principles that Aristotle employs to classify animals? Why does he want to make such a classification?
19. How do teleological functions enter into physiological descriptions?

Discussion Questions

1. To what extent does contemporary science need Aristotle's conception of form?
2. Is Aristotle right about the nature of infinity?
3. In what ways is Aristotle an anti-reductionist, and is that a plausible view?

11
Aristotle
Metaphysics

The title of the work *Metaphysics* does not come from Aristotle. In fact, it is not a term that he uses. The book that we have of this name is a compilation of different shorter pieces written at different points in Aristotle's later life.[1] Nevertheless, they are all concerned with the study of "first principles" or what we today call *metaphysics*. Aristotle's overarching aim of the work is to create, define and defend this systematic study. In reviewing the *Metaphysics*, we will cover the following four main areas:

1. Metaphysics as the investigation of first principles
2. Metaphysics as the study of being *qua* being
3. Metaphysics as the search for substance
4. Metaphysics as theology

The third area turns out to be complicated but interesting because Aristotle examines the notion of substance in the light of two distinctions: form/matter and actual/potential.

Additionally, in this chapter we evaluate Aristotle's metaphysics in terms of one of its aims: to overcome the dualism of Plato and the reductive naturalism of some of the Pre-Socratic thinkers. This last point will lead us naturally into Aristotle's work *De Anima*, or *On the Soul*. The last part of this chapter is devoted to Aristotle's discussion of the soul and psychology in *De Anima*.

A Brief Overview

The *Metaphysics* has 14 different Books with different aims. The overall work is more like a collection of essays than a single text. The books of the *Metaphysics* are sometimes known by their Roman number and sometimes by their Greek letter. These books are:

- Book I or A (Alpha), which introduces the idea of a science of first principles

- Book II or α (little alpha), which discusses the methodology of such a science
- Book III or β (Beta), which sets out 15 problems with arguments on both sides (for and against possible solutions)
- Book IV or Γ (Gamma), which concerns metaphysics as the study of being *qua* being and tries to show how the principle of non-contradiction is an assumption of meaning itself
- Book V or Δ (Delta), which is a lexicon explaining the different senses of about 40 philosophical terms
- Book VI or E (Epsilon), which includes some brief remarks on truth
- Book VII or Z (Zeta), which concerns substance and its relation to the form/matter distinction
- Book VIII or H (Eta), which also concerns the form/matter distinction
- Book IX or Θ (Theta), which concerns substance and its relation to actuality and potentiality
- Book X or I (Iota), which is about unity and plurality
- Book XI or K (Kappa), which consists of a summary of previous points and parts of the physics
- Book XII or Λ (Lambda), which concerns the notion of unchangeable substances and the unmoved mover
- Book XIII or M (Mu) and
- Book XIV or N (Nu), both of which concern the existence of numbers and a criticism of Plato's ontology

Despite the fact that the *Metaphysics* isn't a single work, there is some unity between the different books. First, they have common aims. Much of the *Metaphysics* is an attempt to create a new science of first principles and to define its subject area. The work shows how the study of the most fundamental principles is possible and what it consists of, and part of this aim is to avoid the errors of the metaphysical thinking of the Pre-Socratics and Plato. Second, in Book III Aristotle outlines a list of problems that the science of metaphysics should solve, and most of the books of the *Metaphysics* deal with these problems.[2]

WISDOM AND THE KNOWLEDGE OF FIRST PRINCIPLES

Aristotle starts chapter 1 of Book I of the *Metaphysics* with the famous claim that all humans by nature desire to know. For this reason, like animals, we take delight in our senses, but humans also have the capacity to learn through experience, and thus to connect different memories together. The higher animals have these capabilities too, and so what distinguishes human beings is the higher-level capacity for practicing arts, by which Aristotle means the ability to make universal judgments that guide practice (e.g., as in medicine). Also, human beings have the capacity to understand causes, which he calls *science*.

In chapter 2 Aristotle asks what kind of knowledge deserves to be called *wisdom*. Wisdom is clearly more than the sensory experience of particulars, because understanding requires that we must know how to group particular things according to systems of classification and that we know their causes. But beyond this, what is wisdom? To answer this, Aristotle characterizes the wise person. First, such a person knows everything, without knowing every particular fact. Second, the wise person knows what is the most difficult to know; to really understand as a wise person, one must be able to give the most comprehensive explanation of things and in every branch of knowledge. Third, wisdom consists in understanding for its own sake. In this way, wisdom is different from technical knowledge gained for the sake of some practical purpose. From these considerations, Aristotle concludes that wisdom is the highest degree of universal knowledge. It must involve knowing for its own sake the most fundamental principles and the most primary of all causes (982a4–982b28). Aristotle believes that a science investigating wisdom must be divine-like, because God is thought to be among the first causes and principles.

Aristotle reviews the relevant theories of the Pre-Socratics (in chapters 3–5) and of Plato (chapter 6), concluding that they all have some inkling of the four causes (discussed in the previous chapter), but that none has a good understanding of how form or essence is a principle of change. In his search for the fundamental principles, Aristotle criticizes his predecessors' views (in chapters 8 and 9); we will examine these arguments later. Towards the end of chapter 9, after the critique of Plato, he concludes:

> In general, if we search for the elements of existing things without distinguishing the many senses in which things are said to exist, we cannot succeed. (992b18)

Aristotle picks up on this vitally important point in *Metaphysics* IV.

BEING QUA BEING

In Book IV (Γ or Gamma) Aristotle defines a general science that studies being *qua* being, or being as being. This science is what we would now call *metaphysics*, and in this part of the work Aristotle is concerned primarily with describing the nature of this study and showing that it is possible.

Aristotle thinks that he needs to show that such a science is possible. Normally, sciences concentrate on what distinguishes their subject matter from other areas of investigation. For example, biology concerns the living rather than the dead. Usually, specific sciences investigate a specific type of thing.

What does the most general science study? One might doubt that metaphysics is possible because it has no specific subject matter. What does the phrase "being *qua* being" signify? It means that the things that exist but with respect to their being. The word *qua* delineates under what aspect the thing in question is studied. For example, physiology studies the human being *qua* body, psychology the human being *qua* his or her behavior and mental states; sociology *qua* member of a society. Therefore, "being *qua* being" does not denote a special or separate ontological realm that is studied in metaphysics. Metaphysics does not appear to be about anything precisely because it is about everything.

What could this most general of all studies consist of? Aristotle answers this question with two points. First, he links metaphysical investigation to the study of substance. In chapter 2 of Book IV, he reminds us that there are many senses that things are said to be, "but they are related to one central point" (1003a33). To explain this, he uses the analogy of "healthy," which we described when we discussed the categories.[3] Sports, athletes, and diets are all said to be healthy, but they are so in different but related ways. He writes:

> Everything healthy is so-called with reference to health—some things by preserving it, some by producing it, some by being signs of health, some because they are receptive of it. (IV, 2, 1003a34)

These different ways of being healthy are connected. Diets, sports, and complexions are healthy in a secondary or derivative way. The primary way of being healthy is to have a body in excellent functioning shape. The central point is the health of the body.

Likewise, in an analogous fashion, there are many senses in which a thing is said to be.

> So too there are many ways in which things are said to exist, but they all refer to a single starting point. (IV, 2, 1003b4)

The single starting point regarding existence is substance. So, some things are said to be because they are a substance, others because they are qualities of substances, and still others because they are processes towards substance. In short, there is a primary type of existence as well as secondary ones. He concludes that the philosopher must grasp the principles and causes of substances (1003b18).

Second, Aristotle argues that, because it concerns being *as such*, metaphysics must study unity. A person is not different from *one* person and so "unity is nothing apart from being." However, because of this, first philosophy must also investigate the opposite of unity, namely, plurality (1004a10)[4]. Because there are many ways in which a thing may be said to be one, and many ways it can be many, the new science must investigate concepts such as contrariety and difference, and finally negation in general. Aristotle says that these are essential modifications of unity *qua* unity and of being *qua* being.

With this second point in mind, Aristotle argues that the science of metaphysics must investigate general principles that apply to everything, such as "the most certain of all principles." This will include the highest principles of negation, namely, the law of non-contradiction and the principle of the excluded middle.

The Principle of Non-Contradiction

This principle states that it is impossible for the same attribute to belong and not belong to the same subject, in the same respect and at the same time (1005b9–1005b33). For instance, the snow cannot be both white and not white in the same way, and at the same time.

Aristotle says that this principle is the starting point for all deductions and all other axioms. Today we call it the *law of non-contradiction* because it is equivalent to saying that a contradiction cannot be true. In *On Interpretation* (chapter 6) Aristotle defines a contradiction as a pair of opposed statements, one of which is an affirmation and the other of which is a denial. Aristotle regards this as a metaphysical principle of being *qua* being.

Because it is presupposed in all deductions, it would be circular to try to deductively prove this principle (IV, 4, 1005b34–1006a11). This is not a problem because all deductions must assume something: "the starting point of demonstration is not demonstration" (1011a13). The principle of non-contradiction is assumed in all deductions, and so any attempt to prove it deductively would be circular. The principle is so basic that it cannot be proved.

Nevertheless, Aristotle claims that one can provide a negative proof of the principle by arguing that anyone who tries to deny the principle would presuppose it in making such a denial. If this is so, then the principle is literally undeniable.

To get this argument off the ground, Aristotle assumes that a skeptic wants to say something meaningful. If someone asserts something meaningful, then he or she is denying the opposite of what he or she asserts (IV, 4, 1006a29). Otherwise, he or she would not be saying anything. Therefore, to affirm something meaningful P, one must be denying not P, and therefore the principle of non-contradiction is a precondition of meaningfulness. For example, to assert that someone is human, one must be denying implicitly that this someone is not human (in the same sense of the word *human*). Otherwise the original assertion would not have any meaning. In short, the principle of non-contradiction is a necessary condition of the meaningfulness of any claim. Aristotle's argument may be represented like this:

1. It is a necessary condition of asserting something meaningful P that one deny not P.

2. To affirm that the meaningful assertion of P requires denying not P is to presuppose the principle of non-contradiction.

3. Therefore, to assert anything is to presuppose the principle of non-contradiction.
4. To deny the principle of non-contradiction is to assert something meaningful.
5. Therefore, to deny the principle of non-contradiction is to presuppose the principle of non-contradiction.

To repeat, Aristotle is well aware that such an argument assumes the principle of non-contradiction and therefore is circular. He also asserts that this negative argument for the principle of non-contradiction does not depend on the proposition that each word has only one meaning. If a word has many meanings, then the same argument would apply to each. But to say that a word has an infinite number of meanings would be to imply that it has no meaning. Aristotle also claims that this argument only applies to someone who is willing to assert something. The skeptic who is unwilling to do this will escape the argument. However, anyone who denies the principle of non-contradiction thereby asserts something meaningful (namely, its denial of the principle) and in so doing, presupposes what he is trying to deny.

The remainder of Book IV discusses the principle of non-contradiction in relation to the Pre-Socratic thinkers who attempted to deny it in various ways. In chapter 5 Aristotle applies his reasoning about the principle of non-contradiction to the view of Protagoras that all appearances are true. As we saw in earlier chapters, Protagoras claims that something can appear sweet to one person and bitter to another, or to the same person at different times. If a person cannot be mistaken about what she perceives while she is perceiving it, then it apparently follows that no one perception can be truer than any other (1009b1). In other words, all appearances are true.

The conclusion that all appearances are true seems to contradict the principle of non-contradiction. This is because if X appears to be F to person A, and if X appears to be not F to person B, and if all appearances are true, then it follows that X is both F and not F. So, if all appearances are true, this seems to threaten the principle of non-contradiction.

Aristotle's reply to this argument is to deny that all appearances are true on the grounds that we should distinguish sensation from knowledge:

> In general, it is because these thinkers suppose knowledge to be sensation, and this to be a physical alteration, that they say that what appears to our senses must be true. (1009b14–5)

Aristotle's analysis locates two possible sources of error. First, he distinguishes the sensation in a perception from the appearance and argues that even if the first cannot be false, this doesn't apply to the second (101b1–3). By this he means that the sensations we feel when we perceive something should be distinguished from the judgment about how the perceived object appears. The simple sensation we feel when we perceive is like a physical change in that, on its own, it doesn't amount to a judgment that can be true or false. Second, Aristotle argues that sensation is not of itself (i.e., one doesn't sense a sensation). Because of this, there must be a distinction between the sensation and the object perceived (101b34). This distinction (e.g., between the perception of a table and the table) is required by the claim that when we perceive, we are making a judgment about how things appear. This distinction introduces another source of possible error: how the table appears to one might not be how it really is.

In contemporary terms, at the risk of anachronism, we might say that Aristotle rejects the idea that perception is just sensation or physical alteration on the grounds that perceiving involves judging how objects appear. Perception must be *of* something other than itself. This implies that perceptions can be mistaken.

What Is Substance?

Book V (Δ or Delta) contains a lexicon of different concepts that are key to the science of first principles, which Aristotle is trying to define and invent. As we have seen, one of the key ideas is that of substance. Aristotle must show us what kinds of things are substances. To do that, he first tries to find general criteria that something must satisfy to count as a substance and then, second, to discover what things satisfy those criteria.

To find these criteria, Aristotle defines *substance* in Book V of the *Metaphysics*:

> Things are called substances in two ways: a substance is whatever is an ultimate subject, which is no longer said of anything else, and a substance is a this so-and-so, which is also separable. (V, 8, 1071b23)

What does he mean by the first way? As we saw in the previous chapter, Aristotle says that all statements have a subject-predicate form. They consist in the assertion that a certain predicate is true of a subject—for example, the predicate "is white" is true of the snow (the subject of the sentence). But now consider the statement, "White is a color." In it, "white" appears as the subject (the predicate is "is a color"). In other words, "white" can appear both as a predicate and as a subject. In this sense, is it is not an ultimate subject and therefore is not a substance.

The second way: a "this so-and-so" or a "this something" is a strange phrase invented by Aristotle (a *tode ti*). What he means is that a substance is a particular—it is a *this*. It is also a so-and-so, because the individual thing has general characteristics that define what it is. It has a form or essence. Finally, he adds that such substances must be separable. This means that their existence must be explainable without reference to the existence of other things. On this criterion, a smile is not a substance because it exists only because someone is smiling, and so a smile is not separable.

As we shall see, later in Book VII of the *Metaphysics*, Aristotle discards the first way as an inappropriate way to define substance. This leaves us with the second way: with the criterion that substance must be a primary and separate existent and that it must be a "this so-and-so."

After the lexicon, Aristotle returns to the theme of the science of being *qua* being. In chapter 1 of Book VI (E or Epsilon), he argues that this science of first philosophy may also concern itself with immovable substances. The science of first philosophy must be concerned with substances that are not formed by nature, if there are any (1026a30–3). This is an anticipation of the topic of Book XII. In the rest of Book VI, Aristotle dismisses the accidental as irrelevant to the study of metaphysics (chapters 2–4) and turns to the question of substances in Book VII (Z or Zeta).

In Search of Substance (Book VII)

Aristotle begins Book VII by noting that substance is primary. As we have seen, all other kinds of existing things depend on the existence of substance. Consequently, he thinks that metaphysics involves the study of substance. We have seen his definition of substance. Now we must discover what satisfies that definition. Accordingly, in chapter 3 he lists four general candidates for the title *substance*: subject or substratum, essence, universals, and genus (1028b33). We shall consider each of these in turn.

Substance as Subject or Substratum

In chapter 3 of Book VII, Aristotle considers the idea, advanced in the *Categories*, that substance is an ultimate subject of predicates. This idea needs to be revisited in terms of the form/matter distinction. Which is primary: matter, form, or the combination of the two? (1029a4–6)

Aristotle ultimately rejects the definition of substance as a pure or ultimate subject, an idea canvassed back in Book V and the *Categories*. In the statement, "The sphere is large," the subject is "the sphere" and the predicate is "is large." A pure or ultimate subject would be something that is not a predicate of anything else. For example, "the sphere" would not count as an ultimate subject because it can be a predicate of something else. For example in the statement "That thing is a sphere," "sphere" is no longer the subject but rather is a predicate. According to Aristotle, the only thing that could satisfy this definition of an ultimate subject is bare matter, something which in itself has no characteristics but which supports all properties. This would be an indeterminate substratum (1029a24).

Aristotle rejects this proposal. He argues that this substratum of bare matter is not substance because substratum does not have independent existence. Pure substratum cannot exist independently of the things that are putatively made out of it, and therefore, it is not a substance.[5] Furthermore, substratum is not a particular, whereas substance is. In conclusion:

> Both separability and individuality are thought to belong chiefly to substance. And so, form and the compound of form and matter would be thought to be substance, rather than matter. (1029a28–1029a30)

Aristotle then also rejects the idea that substance is the combination of form and matter, saying that it is "posterior" (1029a33). Consequently, the only remaining candidate (in this first option) is substance as form. This idea, he says, is "the most difficult," and he returns to it in chapters 7 and 17 of Book VII.

Substance as Essence

In *Metaphysics* VII, chapters 4–6, Aristotle turns to essence as a general candidate for the title "substance." Essence is what a thing is said to be in virtue of itself. It is its being *per se*. In the *Categories* and *On Interpretation*, in his study of predication Aristotle distinguishes between essential and accidental predication.[6] Suppose the essence of being human is to be a rational animal—in which case, when we affirm that humans are rational animals, we are not just predicating a property of a subject. Instead, we are identifying what the subject really is by specifying its essence. Aristotle calls this "true in virtue of itself." In an accidental predication, we attribute a nonessential property to a subject. For example, when we affirm that some human beings are musical, we are not specifying their essence; we are merely attributing a property to them. So, by specifying essence, we identify what the subject really is.

Aristotle argues that only substances really have essences; all other things have essence in a secondary way. Furthermore, to have an essence, a thing must be strictly definable. According to Aristotle, the only things that meet this criterion of being strictly definable are species. Therefore, he concludes that only species have essence, and the only substances are members of species.

Clearly, Aristotle is working with a notion of real essence, as opposed to a merely verbal essence. The species *human* has a real essence, which is to be a rational animal. Anything that is a human has to be a rational animal. In contrast to this, a tailor does not have to be a tailor. A tailor is only a person who happens to make clothes. He could change his occupation without ceasing to be. Being a tailor is not part of a person's essence. Aristotle concludes:

> In the primary and strict sense only substances have definition and essence, but other things have them also, only not in the primary sense. (VII, 4, 1029b13)

In other words, tailors, heroes, and philosophers are not substances. Human beings and other species are.

Second, what is the relation of essence to the individual? In chapter 6 of Book VII Aristotle claims that things are identical with their essence. This seems to indicate that individual things in the natural world can have essences. For example, "Socrates is human" makes an essential attribution to the individual, Socrates. This is part of his essence; it identifies what he is.

Here there is a radical difference between the philosophies of Plato and Aristotle. Plato denies that individual particulars have essences. According to Plato, essences belong to the separate world of Forms, and essential predications can only be made of the Forms. In contrast, according to Aristotle, essences are in the natural world; consequently, understanding must be directed towards this world and not to a separate realm of Forms.

Substance as Universals

In chapter 13 of Book VII Aristotle argues that universals should not be considered as substances. He says:

> But it seems impossible that any universal term should be a substance. For the substance of each thing is what is peculiar to it and does not belong to anything else; but a universal is common.... (VII, 13, 1038b6)

Aristotle extends this argument against the claim that universals are substances into chapters 14–16, where he also criticizes this aspect of Platonism. These arguments will be examined later. Having rejected universals as a candidate for substance, Aristotle can also reject genus, since the genus of a thing is a type of universal. (If *human* is the species, then the relevant genus is *animal*).

Substance as Form

In chapter 17 of Book VII Aristotle says that the investigation needs a new start. So he applies a new approach to the claim that substance is form. Briefly, it is to consider substance as principle and cause (1041a6–9). For instance, if we ask "why are these materials a house?" then the answer must cite the essence of being a house.

> Plainly we are seeking the cause. And this is the essence (to speak abstractly), which in some cases is that for the sake of which, e.g. perhaps in the case of a house or a bed, and in some cases is the first mover; for this also is a cause. (1041a28–32)

Likewise, when we ask "why do these parts form this whole?" we are seeking "the form by reason of which the matter is some definite thing" (1041b7–8). From this point, Aristotle argues that a substance is a unity; it is not like a heap or pile. A syllable "ba" isn't simply a collection of two letters "b" and "a." It is a unity. This unity cannot be thought of as an additional element or ingredient or as a collection of ingredients: to conceive it so would only repeat the problem. What makes the substance a unity is its nature, which is a principle (1041b11–1042a2). The principle that defines a substance provides its essence. The argument of Aristotle's fresh approach in chapter 17 can be constructed as follows:

1. A substance is a unity or whole.
2. A whole is defined by a principle that specifies its nature (and not by its elements).
3. A principle that specifies the nature of something constitutes its essence.
4. The essence of something is its form.
5. Therefore, a substance is defined by its form.
6. The essence of something is what it is.

---

7. Therefore, a substance is its form.

As laid out, the argument has two steps. Though Aristotle does not separate them, we need both to arrive at the conclusion that substance is form. The first step shows that a substance is defined by its form (proposition 5). Crucial to this first step is the premise that a whole is defined as such by a principle rather than by its components. This second premise is supported by the argument that a whole is not merely a collection of elements E1 to En, and therefore that the addition of an extra element would be adequate to define the unity of a substance. We will return to that argument later. The second step moves from the claim that substance is *defined* by its form (proposition 5) to the conclusion that it *is* that form (proposition 7).

Aristotle concludes that substance is identical with definable form. In summary, he argues this on the grounds that the form of a thing is what makes it what it is. This is what essence is, and primary substances are essences (chapter 4, Book VII).

Actuality and Potentiality

In chapter 6 of Book VIII Aristotle reiterates the central idea of Book VII, chapter 17 that unified substances are more than mere aggregates:

> In the case of all things which have several parts and in which the whole is not, as it were, a mere heap, but the totality is something besides the parts, there is a cause of unity. (VIII, 6, 1045a8–10)

As we have seen, the cause of the unity is the form. Aristotle concludes that for things made of matter, "the proximate matter and the form are one and the same thing, the one potentially, the other actually" (1045b21–2). In other words, matter is potential and form is actuality.

This means that matter is only potentially something. To exist, it must be something, which means that it must have an actuality or a form. For example, bronze is only potentially a statue or a cup, but to be, it has to be a "something" made out of bronze. Once it has the form of a statue then it is a statue, and this is its actuality. In short, substance is form, which is actuality. This conclusion is important because it will help us better understand Aristotle's idea of metaphysics as theology, the topic of Book XII.

Interpretations

There are divergent interpretations of Aristotle's claim that primary substances are forms. In part, the difficulty is that Aristotle has made two major demands of the concept of substance. First, we have seen that substances are primary, because they have independent existence. Second, substances must be definable and knowable; hence their link to essence. These appear to be conflicting demands. The first makes us think that substances are individuals or particulars. The second might lean us towards thinking that substances are universals. This difficulty has led to very different interpretations of Aristotle, which we may broadly divide into three types, centered on how we should understand the crucial notion of form.

Form as Universal. According to the first view, the matter/form distinction should be understood as follows: matter is identified by a "stuff" term, such as "bronze." Form is identified by a property or universal term, such as sphericality. The resulting composite thing is a bronze sphere.

According to this interpretation, Aristotle's claim that primary substance is definable as form should lead one to conclude that he thinks of substances as universals (e.g., sphericality). This idea makes good sense of the claim that substance must be definable. However, it makes less sense of Aristotle's claim that the existence of universals is dependent upon that of particulars, which is a fundamental difference between him and Plato. Consequently, the above interpretation of "primary substance is definable form" seems to contradict the claim that substance is an independent existent.

Form as Neither Particular nor Universal. Some readers think that in Book VII of the *Metaphysics*, Aristotle is trying to define a position that identifies form neither with universals nor with particulars. According to this view, with his notion of substantial form, Aristotle is trying to forge a midway path between Platonic Forms on the one hand, and on the other hand his own earlier view (in the *Categories*) of individuals as basic. According to this claim, the world does not fundamentally consist in individual people, animals, and plants, but rather in the species themselves—the natural kinds. The world is really divided into these kinds, and these are basic.

Form as the Particular. According to the third interpretation, the form is the individual thing itself.[7] For example, the form of a house is a dwelling. According to this interpretation, the matter/form distinction is the distinction between the constituent and the thing constituted. The matter is the constituent (i.e., the bronze); the form is the thing constituted (i.e., the sphere). The form is a particular thing, the sphere, and not the universal, sphericality. For a form to exist is for matter to be differentiated in a certain way.

This third interpretation would fit well with the idea that, according to Aristotle, essences also are particular things. It should be pointed out again that if Aristotle does think that individual things have essences, then it might be more accurate to claim that these things *are* their essence, rather than that they *have* an essence. This is because essence is what a thing is *per se*. In this case, when Aristotle speaks of essences he is referring to individual things. If this view is right, then Aristotle's dual characterization of substance as essence and of substance as form would imply that substances are particular things.

Very tentatively, one general view that makes good overall sense of much of the text is that primary substances are individuals or particulars, but only insofar as they are members of natural kinds. Returning to the original definition in Book V (or Delta), substances must be a "this so-and-so." The "this" indicates that they are individuals, and the "so-and-so" specifies that they are natural kinds or species. In other words, we identify a particular individual as a primary substance if and only if we refer to it as a natural kind or species.

Discussion

Aristotle restricts what may count as substance to what we might call natural objects as individuals belonging to natural kinds.

1. He excludes matter or stuff, such as gold and blood. These are not individual things. They are what some individual things are made of. Hence, they are dependent existents and are not substances.
2. On the same grounds, he also rules out substratum.
3. He rejects universals on the grounds that they are dependent existents (VII, 13).
4. He excludes things that by their nature are only parts and hence are dependent existents. For example, a hand is essentially a body part; what it is should be defined in relation to the whole body. Hence, it is not a substance.
5. He excludes collections of things; for example, a flock of geese is not a substance. Its existence depends on that of the individual geese.
6. He excludes artifacts from the list of primary substances on the grounds that they are not formed by nature (VIII, 3, 1043b15–1043b23).
7. He also excludes particular things described in nonessential ways. For example, a soldier is not a substance. The essence of the individual, who happens to be a soldier, is to be human. Therefore, it is humans who are substances and not soldiers (VII, 4).

At the beginning we said that we would cover the following four areas: (1) metaphysics as the investigation of first principles; (2) as the study of being *qua* being; (3) as the search for substance, and (4) as theology. It remains now to investigate metaphysics as theology, the topic of Book XII. However, before we do so, let us briefly compare Aristotle's metaphysics to those of the Pre-Socratics and Plato.

Plato and the Pre-Socratics

According to the naturalism of the early Pre-Socratics, reality consists of the stuff that underlies all change. Thales identified this as water, Anaximenes as air, and Anaximander as an indeterminate stuff, more primitive than any of the four elements. Aristotle rejects these answers wholesale. In effect, he argues that such theories do not tell us what reality consists of. They only describe what things are *composed of* and not what they *are*.

The argument of Book VII, chapter 17, helps explain why this distinction is so important. First, the form is a principle that defines the essence of the thing in question. As we saw earlier, it cannot be an extra element that the thing is composed of, and for this reason, form cannot be reduced to matter. Second, it is the form that makes a substance a whole or a unity. Without it, nothing could be an organized whole; everything would be like a heap or a pile.[8] Consequently, substances are not identical with, nor reducible to, the matter out of which they are composed. The modified argument can be laid out as follows:

1. A substance is a unity or whole.
2. A whole cannot consist only of a collection of elements $E1$ to En.
3. The matter that a substance is composed of is only a collection of elements.
4. Therefore, a substance is not identical to the matter out of which it is composed.

In sharp contrast to the Pre-Socratics, Plato thought of reality as ultimately consisting of eternal Ideas or Forms, such as beauty, justice, and goodness, transcending the realm of particulars in space and time. These Ideas are universals, and particular objects are merely imperfect embodiments of them.

Aristotle denies Plato's theory, but he does not deny the existence of forms or universals or even abstract objects, such as numbers. Aristotle's view is subtler. Universals exist, but not in the way that Plato says they do, as independent existence. Plato is mistaken because universals have only derivative existence.

In Books XIII and XIV of the *Metaphysics* Aristotle defends this approach with regard to mathematics. About mathematical objects, he says:

The subject of our discussion will not be whether they exist but how they exist. (XIII, 1, 1076a36)

Aristotle tries to refute the Platonic claim that numbers are things distinct from the everyday objects that we can count. Likewise, geometrical figures are not things distinct from the surfaces, lengths, and volumes of the physical bodies we see. In this way, Aristotle hopes to show how mathematics is compatible with his naturalistic ontology, and to undermine what might seem to be an important support for the Platonic notion of the Forms.

According to Aristotle, there are no ideal triangles and circles. The mathematician studies ordinary physical circles and triangles. He or she does not study them *qua* (or as) physical things but rather as idealized and abstracted from the conditions of physical change. An ideal circle is nothing distinct from a real circle idealized. Mathematics and physics deal with the same substances, but *qua* different aspects.

In this way, Aristotle avoids two problems inherent in Plato's theory. First, if mathematical objects exist as abstract objects in a separate realm, how can we use them to describe everyday things? More generally, one of Aristotle's main arguments against the Forms as separate substances is that they have no explanatory power. Second, if numbers are substances separate from the world of concrete objects, then how do we know them?

As we saw in previous chapters, Plato argues for his Theory of Forms in part to avoid two problematic trends in Pre-Socratic thinking: first, to avoid the subjectivism inherent in the Sophist view of classification; and second, to avoid the reductive materialism inherent in the naturalism of the Milesians and the Atomists. In this Aristotle agrees. He rejects both the subjectivism of the Sophists and the reductive materialism of the Pre-Socratics, but he also denies Plato's Theory of the Forms. Both the Pre-Socratics and Plato are mistaken. To avoid one, it is not necessary to accept the other. Aristotle can steer a middle path between the Pre-Socratics and Plato mainly because he recognizes that there are different ways in which things can be said to exist, and because of his form/matter distinction. Form and matter are different aspects of substance; and as such both are necessary, and neither can be reduced to the other. The mistake of the Pre-Socratics was to think of matter as substance. The error of Plato was to think of the universal Forms as substances. Both of these are dependent existences, and hence neither constitutes substance on their own.

THEOLOGY

Metaphysics Book XII takes a new direction: Aristotle defines a science of theology, a study of the eternal substance that does not change. As we saw in the *Physics*, all things that change must have matter; even the indestructible heavenly bodies that move in space are composed of a fifth element: aether (XII, 1, 1069b26–1069b28). However, substance that is eternal and unchanging will not be composed of any matter, as we shall see.

In chapter 6 of Book XII, Aristotle repeats the argument of the *Physics* that there must be an unmoved mover. He concludes that this must be an eternal and unchanging substance. Aristotle's argument for this conclusion has three premises. First, if all substances were destructible, everything would be destructible, because substances are primary existents. Second, time and movement cannot come into being nor cease to be. Consequently, there must be an indestructible unchanging substance. Third, this substance must be capable of producing eternal change, unlike Plato's Forms (1071b22–1072a1).

Aristotle argues that this unmoved mover must be "an eternal principle whose essence is actuality." To be completely actual, the eternal substance must be without any un-actualized potentialities. This must be so, says Aristotle, because "that which is potentially may possibly not be" (1071b4). In other words, to explain eternal motion, it is not enough to cite the existence of something that is potentially an unmoved mover, since that is compatible with there being no movement at all.

This eternal unmoved mover cannot be made of matter. There are three reasons for this. First, because it has no potentialities, the unmoved mover cannot be composed of matter. Remember from our discussion of change that matter is potentiality: for example, a piece of bronze is potentially a statue. Second, things formed of matter or the four elements belong to the realm of generation and destruction. Even things in the realm of the eternal circular movement of the heavens are made of an element, albeit not an earthly one. Something unchanging must be without matter. Third, the prime unmoved mover is pure activity. This cannot be physical because all physical movement implies a contact of mover and moved, and hence a movement of the mover. Thus, the unmoved mover cannot cause motion in a physical way. Therefore, its actuality must consist of a purely spiritual activity.

In chapter 7, Aristotle begins to call the eternal substance *God*. He argues that there must a source of unceasing motion, and the only unending motion is in a circle. This circular motion of the outermost stars must be caused by an unmoved mover. The only way something can move without being moved is by being the object of thought and desire. The unmoved mover must cause change by being loved (1072a19–36). This establishes the nature of the eternal substance: it must be something essentially good. Furthermore, being pure actuality, it cannot be otherwise than it is (1072b17). Consequently, Aristotle claims that the unmoved mover

> exists of necessity; *qua* necessary its being is good and it is in this way (as good i.e. as object of love and desire) that it is a principle. (XII, 7, 1072a26)

Aristotle argues that the only possible unchanging, spiritual activity of God is pure thought or contemplation (1072b31–1073a3). He tries to isolate the "divine element which thought seems to contain." Because He is essentially good, God's eternal thoughts must be directed towards what is best. But what is best is simply God's thought. So God must contemplate His own thought. If He were to think about something else, then this would imply either one of two impossibilities: either that He could think about something less than the best or that there is something better than God's thought. Neither of these two options is possible. So, with the divine, there is no difference between the object of thought and the thought itself: "the thinking will be one with the object of its thought" (1075a8–10). Therefore, God thinks about Himself thinking: "so throughout eternity is the thought which has itself for its object" (XII, 9, 1075a24).

In chapter 10 of Book XII, Aristotle seems to assert that the contemplative activity of the divine is reflected in the order of the universe. He says:

> And all things are ordered together somehow, but not all alike—both fishes and fowls and plants; and the world is not such that one thing has nothing to do with another, but they are connected. For all are ordered together to one end. (1075a24–1075b10)

As we shall see, the ideal of divine active thought is an important notion for Aristotle's view of human nature, and consequently for his ethics. Aristotle argues that humans are capable of attaining divine-like active thinking, and this capacity is important for the nature of human flourishing.

General Conclusions about the *Metaphysics*

Aristotle's main aim in the *Metaphysics* is to define and defend a new area of study. Unlike other sciences, metaphysics does not investigate a specific class of things such as animals or numbers, but rather it studies being *qua* being. Aristotle claims that it can do this in three ways: first, through the first or basic principles of any investigation, such the principle of non-contradiction; second, by studying the general nature of substance, the primary existents; and third, by investigating the nature of the unmoved mover, the eternal source of all change.

DE ANIMA

Brief Overview

De Anima contains three Books. In Book I, Aristotle sets out the problems concerning the soul and reviews the theories of previous thinkers. In Book II, chapter 1, he outlines his own general theory that the soul is the form of the body. In chapter 3, he describes different levels of *psuchê* (the soul): plants, animals, and humans. In chapter 4, he describes the soul of plants: the powers to eat, grow, decay, and reproduce.

In the remainder of Book II, Aristotle discusses the soul of animals, which have the power of sense perception as well as the capacity to desire and perform actions. Chapters 5 and 6 of Book II explain sense perception in general terms. The sense organs receive perceptible forms; they have the capacity to become similar to the thing affecting them. After the general explanation, Aristotle discusses each of the five senses one by one: sight in chapter 7, hearing in chapter 8, smell in chapter 9, taste in chapter 10, and touch in chapter 11. Chapter 12 returns to the general nature of sense perception.

In general, Book III discusses the soul of humans, but in chapters 1 and 2 Aristotle completes his treatment of perception by discussing the perception of perception and the unity of the senses. Chapter 3 deals directly with the human soul by comparing understanding and thought with perception. Chapter 4 discusses thinking or passive intellect, which works by acquiring the form. In chapter 5, Aristotle distinguishes passive from active intellect. Active reason works by making all things. Aristotle compares it to light, which makes potential colors actual. He suggests that, as such, active reason is necessary for passive reason. Aristotle also claims that active reason is immortal, divine, and does not depend on matter for its functioning. Chapters 6 and 7 discuss the faculty of thinking. In chapter 8, Aristotle summarizes some of his main conclusions. In chapters 9–11 of Book III, Aristotle discusses the movement of animals and desire, wish and appetite. Chapters 12 and 13 discuss the relation of the senses to the bodies of animals, especially the necessity for the senses of touch and taste.

Soul as the Form of the Body

After reviewing the views of previous thinkers in Book I, Aristotle presents his own theory in Book II of *De Anima*. He claims that every living person is both a form and matter. The psyche or soul is the form of the person, and the flesh and bone are the matter of which the person is composed. Thus, to understand the relation between the soul and the body, we must grasp the relation between form and matter, which was explored in the *Metaphysics*.

To remind ourselves of the previous discussion, let us again consider the example of a bronze sphere. The object itself is a substance, which *is* both form and matter. Form is the thing constituted, and the matter is the constituent. The form identifies what the object essentially is. Therefore, the form is the sphere itself. The matter is the stuff of which it is composed (i.e., the bronze). This view needs to be stated carefully. We did not claim that the bronze sphere is *composed* of two *elements*, form and matter. If we had, this would suggest wrongly that the form and matter were things that could exist independently of the sphere. Also, we did not affirm that the bronze sphere *has* a form. It is more accurate to say the sphere itself *is* the form, since the form is not a universal. Aristotle's view is that there is only the thing. Described *qua* matter, it is bronze; described *qua* form, is it a sphere. *Qua* both, it is a bronze sphere.

Aristotle denies that form and matter are things independent of the individual substance. Given this, there are two mistakes to avoid: first, thinking of the form as an additional nonmaterial thing, in the way that Plato does; and second, reducing the sphere to its matter (i.e., the bronze) as do some of the Pre-Socratics. The example illustrates the relation between substance, form, and matter and thus helps us to understand Aristotle's view that the psyche or soul is the form of the body.

In the case of the soul, the form is more complex, but basically the relations between substance, form, and matter remain the same. The important point is: there is only one thing, namely, the individual person. Described as form, this person is soul identified by its essential functions. Described as matter, this person is flesh and bone. Neither the form nor the matter should be thought of as distinct. We cannot think of the soul as an entity distinct from the embodied person, but we cannot reduce the person to his or her body. Aristotle explains the soul as form in four related ways:

The Soul in Terms of Essence

Any particular thing or individual substance can be characterized as a form, which is its essence. *Essence* means the characteristics that a thing must have to be what it is. Since things are always definable in terms of their essence, and only things with an essence can be defined, essence itself cannot be defined. The soul *is* an essence; it does not *have* one.

The Soul in Terms of Actuality

Aristotle defines the psyche also in terms of actuality. After characterizing the psyche as "the form of a natural body which potentially has life" (412a20), he also describes it as "the first actuality of a natural body which potentially has life" (412a27). Aristotle says that form is to matter as actual is to potential: an undifferentiated piece of bronze (i.e., matter) is only potentially a statue. When it has the form of a statue, then it actually is a statue. In other words, matter is merely potential; form is actuality.

There are two ways of drawing the potential/actual distinction relevant to the soul. First, a being can have the required capacities without exercising them. For example, consider a scientist who is asleep. Is she actually intelligent? Yes, because she has certain capacities, even though she is not using them now. Second, the person can be actually exercising the capacities in question. Of these two kinds of actuality, the first one corresponds to knowledge and the second to the act of reflecting (412a22–3). Aristotle asserts that the soul or psyche is actuality in the first of these two ways, rather than the second. It consists in having the relevant capacities (knowledge) rather than the exercise of those capacities (the act of reflecting). A person has a soul even when he or she is asleep. Likewise, the eye has the capacity of sight even when it is not actually seeing. Thus, he says:

> Waking is actuality which corresponds to cutting and seeing, the psyche is actuality corresponding to sight, that is the capacity of the organ. (412b27)

To achieve this actuality (of having the relevant capacities), a body must have the appropriate organs. According to Aristotle, every capacity requires an organ (except possibly the vexed case of *nous* or active reason which we will discuss later). Therefore, Aristotle's account of the soul requires a description of the functioning of the organs.

The Soul in Terms of Final Cause

To explain the idea of form, Aristotle says that the soul is the end that the body and its parts serve. He compares a natural body first to a tool, and then to the eye.

> Suppose that a tool, e.g. an axe, were a natural body, then being an axe would be its essence and so its psyche; if this disappeared from it, it would have ceased to be an axe.... Suppose that an eye were an animal—sight would have been its psyche.... (412b11–22)

This explanation in terms of final cause is closely linked to the reference to organs, because organs perform various functions to serve the final end of the organism as animate being. Aristotle says:

> All natural bodies are organs of the soul. This is true of those that enter into the constitution of plants as well as of those which enter into that of animals. This shows that that for the sake of which they are is soul. (II, 4, 415b15–415b21)

The Soul in Terms of Motion

The soul is the principle of animation of a living body. It is cause of the movement of an animals and humans, and of qualitative change in plants (as we shall see) (II, 4, 415b22–415b27).

Discussion

These Aristotelian insights are still illuminating today. They cut across simplistic versions of the debate between the dualist and reductive materialist. A dualist regards the soul as a nonmaterial thing. Aristotle would insist that this kind of dualism involves treating the form of a person as though it were a separate substance. Reductive materialism, on the other hand, treats the person as though they were nothing more than the matter out they are composed and ignores form.[9]

In more contemporary terms, we might express Aristotle's theory as follows. A person can be described in two radically different ways: physically and psychologically. The psychological descriptions are given in terms of what the person wants, believes, hopes, feels, and does. Such descriptions do not indicate the existence of a separate entity, the mind. They apply to the person. However, the psychological descriptions cannot be reduced to descriptions of the person's physical and neurological state.[10]

Although Aristotle's view of the soul is relevant to the contemporary mind-body problem, the two are quite different. First, Aristotle does not have a modern view of matter. Since the seventeenth century, matter has been conceived scientifically as an inert substance obeying mechanical causal laws in determinate patterns. Such a conception seems incompatible with the idea of oneself as a self-conscious being who freely chooses his or her actions. This disparity defines part of the contemporary mind-body problem: how can a conscious being consist of inert matter? In contrast, Aristotle thinks of the physical universe as teleological rather than inert and mechanical. Every natural thing has an end. Given this teleological conception of matter, everything natural must have (or be) a form; and so in a sense, there isn't such a radical difference in kind between humans and the rest of the natural world. In this manner, Aristotle does not have the contemporary mind-body problem to solve.

Second, given some important qualifications, Aristotle views humans as animals with distinctive biological functions, such as the capacity to speak and think. In other words, he doesn't think of persons as something distinct from the natural world in the way that later thinker such as Descartes and Kant do. As a consequence of this, Aristotle isn't concerned with the modern all-or-nothing distinction between the mental-physical, but more with the different grades of differences between the physical elements and the human being. As a result, according to Aristotle, any understanding of the human being must include the nutritive soul with functions such as nutrition, respiration, and digestion, as well the animal soul with functions such as perception, memory, and desire. These points are, however, subject to an important qualification regarding the active intellect, which, as we shall see, is a divine-like faculty.

Given these two points, the Greek word *psuchê* shouldn't be translated as *soul*, because the English word is permeated with the Christian idea of a nonmaterial substance fundamentally distinct from the body. The word *mind* has similar connotations. Consequently, this translation doesn't do justice to Aristotle's idea of the principles of different degrees of animation.

Levels of Being Animate

All living things are animated. The principle of animation is the soul, but what the soul consists of depends on what kind of living thing is in question. This is because the soul is the essence of the living being:

> The soul is the cause or source of the living body. The terms cause and source have many senses. But the soul is the cause of its body alike in all three senses which we explicitly recognize. It is the source of movement, it is the end, it is the essence of the whole living body. (II, 4, 415b9–415b11)

The essence of a plant is different from that of an animal, and that of a human is different again. In saying of plants that they are alive, we mean that they have the capacity for nutrition, growth, and decay (II, 1, 412a12–17). In addition to these minimal nutritive capabilities, animals also have the capacity to perceive. Additionally, humans have the capacity to reason, since the essence of a human is a rational animal.

These essential characteristics of the different kinds of living things define what each of them is. Aristotle thinks that this approach is more appropriate than a single general theory of the soul. He says:

> It is now evident that a single account can be given of *psuchê* only in the same way as it is for figure. For, as in that case, there is no figure apart from triangle and those that follow in order, so here there is no *psuchê* apart from those just mentioned. (II, 3, 414b20)

Plants

Plants are the simplest form of life. They have the powers of nutrition: to eat, grow, decay, and reproduce. These functions define the nutritive soul. Aristotle says:

> Since nothing except what is alive can be fed, what is fed is the animate body and just because it is animate. Hence food is essentially related to what has *psuchê*. (II, 4, 416b9)

Eating food is not just a passive taking in. Food must nourish, and so even in the case of plants, it is changed by the process of digestion so that it becomes part of the body and hence it is linked to growth. In other words, the body acts on the raw food so that it may be nourished (416a19–416b9).

Animals

Animals have the same nutritive capacities as plants. However, in addition, they have the power of sense perception, and because of this they have imagination, which is a decayed form of perception. In turn, they have desire, which is stimulated by perception and imagination. Finally, because of desire, they have the capacity to do things, to move or to perform actions. According to Aristotle, these animal functions (perception, desire, and action) are conceptually linked. The last could not exist without the second and the first. Perception provides desire with its objects, and desire could not exist without pursuit.

> It follows that no body that has a soul is able to move but unable to perceive. (III, 12, 434a37)

Furthermore, perception would have no point without desire, and desire would have no point without the power to pursue.

Perception

Aristotle discusses perception in Book II, chapters 5–12; and Book III, chapters 1–3. As one might expect, after a general discussion, Aristotle treats perception sense by sense: sight in chapter 7, hearing in chapter 8, smell in chapter 9, taste in chapter 10 and touch in chapter 11. In Book III, chapters 1–3, he turns to the unity of perception.

The basis of the animal psyche is perception. Aristotle clarifies that we can use words such as *perceive*, *sense*, and *sentient* in two ways. An animal is a perceiving being even while it is asleep, because it has the capacity to perceive even though it is not currently exercising those capabilities (417a10–417a21).

Having noted that the senses need to be stimulated by external objects to produce sensation, Aristotle claims that

> What has the power of sensation is potentially like what the perceived object is actually; that is, while at the beginning of the process of its being acted upon the two interacting factors are dissimilar, at the end the one acted upon is assimilated to the other and is identical in quality with it. (417b29–418a6)

The distinctive capacity of the sense organs is to receive "perceptible forms without matter, as wax receives the ring's seal engraving without its iron or gold" (II, 12, 424a18). Basically, this means that the organs have the capacity to become similar to the thing affecting them. We perceive an object when that object causes the sensible faculty of the person to receive a sensible form that is the same as the form of the object.

According to Aristotle, a proper explanation of any mental function will identify the object of the relevant condition. We can refer to the object of perception in three ways. First, there are the objects specific to a particular sense: for example, color is the object of sight, and sound of hearing. Second, there are the objects that are common to several senses, such as movement and magnitude of objects. Finally, we can describe the object of sense incidentally: when we see the son of Diares, his being such is incidental to our perceiving him.

The object of sight is the visible. When we describe the object of sight as such, we identify it as a color. However, this does not mean that we can see only colors, because the object of sight can be described incidentally, as a person or as some object. In this way, it can be said that we see ordinary objects. By definition, the eyes must be capable of seeing, and to see, they must have a transparent element. Consequently, the material make-up of the eye is an essential part of a theory of vision.

In general, a proper account of a mental function will be also an embodied account. For example, a philosopher might define anger as the desire to return pain caused. The physician might define it as the boiling of blood around the heart. An embodied account of anger would involve both the formal and the material descriptions of the state (I, 1, 403b1). Likewise, in the case of each of the senses, Aristotle describes a psychical and physiological process. Referring to Plato, Aristotle says that to describe the functions of the psyche without giving any specification of the bodily conditions is an absurdity (I, 3, 407b12). This is because what a thing is composed of places physical constraints on what it can do. To do its job, an axe must be hard. In a similar way, mental functions require the physically appropriate organs.

Having described each of the five senses, Aristotle turns to the unity of perception in Book III, chapter 1. In the case of the common sensibles, there couldn't be a separate sense to perceive them (for if there were then they would be sensibles specific to that sense and no longer common). Thus, there is a common sensibility that allows us to perceive them non-incidentally. This common sensibility is necessary because all of our senses form a unity. By this, Aristotle means that we can judge an object to have disparate qualities; for instance, we judge bile to be both yellow and bitter. This judgment is not the act of either of the two senses, vision and taste (III, 1, 425a27–425b4). The common sense allows us to unite these disparate qualities as belonging to one object.[11] This shows that the whole sensory system of an animal is really one, because it is the animal itself who touches, sees, hears, and so on.

In chapter 2, Aristotle discusses the self-reflexive nature of perception—the fact that we perceive our own perceiving. Aristotle takes the case of seeing and argues that the seeing of seeing cannot be because of some other new sense. If this were the case then the sense that sees seeing would also see color, and we would have a regress. Aristotle concludes that "the sense must be percipient of itself" (425b14). He claims that the perception of a perception is not some thing distinct from the perception itself.

Later in the chapter, Aristotle argues that this self-reflective perceptual capacity is due to the unification of the senses: the common or central sense is aware of our sensing. He argues this on the grounds that we can discriminate between, for instance, white and sweet. Both qualities must be present to a single self-identical something that is capable of perceiving and judging both qualities simultaneously, at any one time. In short, there must be a common sense that is able to discriminate and integrate the perceptions of the five senses. This unity of sense would explain how awareness of perception is possible.

Reason

After discussing imagination in chapter 3, Book III of *De Anima*, Aristotle characterizes the nature of thinking in chapter 4 in order to define reason, the distinctive function of human beings. He compares thought to perception: thought is related to the thinkable as perception to the perceivable. Both are the capacity to receive the form of something (429a13–429a17).

Because everything is thinkable, it follows that this aspect of the soul must be free of qualities itself. The presence of such qualities would limit what could be thought; since everything is thinkable, the thinking part of the soul must be free of qualities when it is not thinking anything. The mind or the thinking aspect of the soul is not in actuality anything until it thinks something. It is only possibility.[12]

For this reason, Aristotle says of thought that "it cannot reasonably be regarded as blended with the body" and calls it "the place of the forms," but only potentially and not actually (429a24–28). In this sense, thought is *not* like perception: it doesn't depend on the bodily organs. This is why thought does not become dulled by overstimulation unlike the senses (e.g., after loud noises, one cannot hear well).

In chapter 5 of Book III, Aristotle distinguishes passive from active intellect. Passive intellect works by becoming all things. It acquires the form. In this sense, reasoning is like perception, in which we receive a perceptual form or likeness of the object perceived except that, for reason, the form is intelligible. It is the essence or definition of the thing. Passive reason is like a perceiver of definitions. It contemplates essences.

In sharp contrast, active reason works by making all things. Aristotle compares it to light, which makes potential colors actual (III, 5, 430a14–430a16). The essence of active reason (*nous poietikos*) is activity. For this reason, it "is separable, impassible, unmixed." By this Aristotle means that active reason does not depend on matter for its functioning. Later he claims that when it is separated from the body, it is immortal and eternal.

What Aristotle claims about active intellect in *De Anima* is reminiscent of his assertions about the divine unmoved mover in *Metaphysics*, Book XII. Both are pure form without matter. Both are pure actuality and activity. In *De Anima*, Aristotle seems to be saying that with active intellect, to think that P is *ipso facto* to make it true that P. He says that actual knowledge is identical with its object (430a20). Apparently, in this case, thinking makes it so.

Interpretation

Throughout *De Anima*, Aristotle treats mental capacities as inseparable from their physical basis. The two are separable only in account, because the soul is the form of the body. Matter and form are inseparable, except in account. Because of this, it seems that Aristotle's views on active reason are incompatible with the rest of *De Anima*. In short, his otherwise biological view of the mind seems to conflict with his view that active reason is divine and immortal.

How can we reconcile the two? First, let us remind ourselves of *Metaphysics* XII, where Aristotle argues for the necessary existence of an unchanging, unmoved mover, whose essence is pure actuality. This unmoved mover cannot be material for various reasons, but principally because it is pure actuality and matter is potentiality. Pure actuality must belong to the unchanging nonmaterial realm. This much is already implicit in the earlier parts of the *Metaphysics*, in which Aristotle argues that substance is form, which is actuality, and that matter is potentiality. Anything that is untainted or pure actuality cannot contain potentiality; therefore, it must be free of matter and therefore, it is unchanging.

This reminder indicates that Aristotle's metaphysics has two radically different parts, the changeable world of nature and the unchanging divine. This suggests that we should view the cryptic passages of *De Anima* Book III, chapter 5, in a similar light: Aristotle is characterizing the divine aspect of the human soul as opposed to the soul as the natural essential functions of the living human body. In other words, when, in Book II, chapter 1, he asserts that the soul is the form of the body, and when he affirms that the soul is hence inseparable from the body except in account, Aristotle means these comments to be applicable only to the changing natural world. The unchanging and nonmaterial is altogether a different case.

In fact, there are passages in the earlier parts of *De Anima* that anticipate the possibility of the rational soul as form without matter. For example, in Book II, chapter 1, Aristotle asserts that some aspects of the soul might be separable from the body because they pertain to functions that do not involve an organ (413a6). In Book II, chapter 2, Aristotle says that thought or the power of reflection "seems to be a different kind of soul, differing as what is eternal from what is perishable; it alone is capable of being separated" (413b25–414a3).

Conclusion

Aristotle's *Metaphysics* tries to define and defend metaphysics or "the science of first philosophy" as the study of being qua being. Such understanding is necessary for wisdom. Aristotle defends metaphysics by characterizing it in three ways:

First, it consists of the study of fundamental principles, such as the principle of non-contradiction.

Second, metaphysics involves identifying what exists primarily or as a substance. To specify what is a substance, Aristotle appeals to his distinction between form and matter. He argues that a substance is embodied form on the grounds that a substance must be a unity and that such unity must be provided by the essence of a substance, which is its form. Although it is very difficult to interpret Aristotle, he may mean that primary substances are individuals or particulars insofar as they are members of a natural kind.

Third, in Book XII of the *Metaphysics*, Aristotle defines metaphysics as the study of the eternal source of all change, the unmoved mover. He argues that the unmoved mover must exist and that its nature is pure actuality. It is divine.

In his work *De Anima*, Aristotle characterizes the soul as the principle of animation, which is different in plants, animals and humans. Each person is an individual substance that can be conceived as both form and matter. The soul is form or organizing principle. Thus, it is not some thing distinct from the individual person. Yet, as such a principle, it cannot be reduced to the matter out of which it is composed, namely the body.

Within this general framework of the form/matter distinction, Aristotle describes the nature of perception and thought. Form and matter are inseparable aspects of individual substances and function as such perception and thought or reason. However, Aristotle contends that we participate in the divine-like active intellect, which is pure form and does not depend on matter. This last point has great importance for our lives and for ethics.

Study Questions

1. Aristotle provides four different characterizations of metaphysics. What are they?
2. According to Aristotle, what is wisdom?
3. What does he mean by "being *qua* being?"
4. How does the analogy of "healthy" help us to understand the nature of metaphysics?
5. What kind of support can one give for the principle of non-contradiction? What kind of support can one *not* give the principle?
6. How does Protagoras's claim that all appearances are true contravene the principle of non-contradiction? How does Aristotle respond to this?
7. How can perception be mistaken?
8. How does Aristotle define substance in Book V of the *Metaphysics*?
9. Why does Aristotle think that metaphysics involves identifying substance?
10. In chapter 17 of Book VII of the *Metaphysics*, Aristotle provides an argument that substance is form. What is the argument?

11. What is the difference between a pile and a substance?
12. What are Aristotle's main criticisms of Plato's *Theory of Forms*?
13. How does Aristotle argue for the claim that metaphysics must study the eternal substance?
14. Why is this substance pure actuality?
15. Why is what is pure actuality essentially good?
16. Aristotle characterizes form in four ways. What does he mean by claiming that the soul is the form of the body?
17. How does Aristotle explain perception?
18. What is the common-sense? How does this relate to the self-reflective capacity of the senses?
19. What is the distinction between passive and active intellect?
20. What is the problem with reconciling what Aristotle says about active intellect with what he says about the other aspects of the soul? How can we make such a reconciliation?

Discussion Questions

1. How does Aristotle portray the nature of reality? Is this portrayal justifiable?
2. Does Aristotle's view of the soul help solve the contemporary mind-body problem?
3. Can we reconcile Aristotle's view of the natural sublunary world with the more theological aspects of his metaphysics?

12

Aristotle
Ethics, Politics, and Poetics

The *Nicomachean Ethics* is one of the greatest works in moral philosophy. Its main aim is to define the good life for a human being. Every natural thing has a nature, which defines the final end of its development. The good of human life is the fulfillment of human nature. The distinctive characteristic of a human is the rational faculty of the soul. The highest good for human life, therefore, consists in the improvement and actualization of rationality.

An Outline of the *Nicomachean Ethics*

The work is divided into ten books. In Book I, Aristotle tries to establish that the best life for a human being consists of activity of the soul in accordance with virtue. Aristotle argues that the most general thing people want purely for itself is a happy life. The relevant Greek term *eudaimonia* indicates a life that is good to live. From I.7, Aristotle tries to discover the nature of the good life by specifying the distinctive functions of human beings. These functions define various traits of excellence or virtues that enable us to live well.

At the beginning of Book II, Aristotle distinguishes between moral virtues, the theme of Books II–V, and the intellectual virtues, the topic of Book VI. Book II is a general explanation of the moral virtues. Chapter 6 of Book II explains Aristotle's famous Doctrine of the Mean, according to which virtues, or excellences of character, are a mean between two extremes, which constitute vices. Aristotle also emphasizes the unity of the virtues.

Within this framework, Book III concerns the voluntary and the involuntary, and the nature of choice. Aristotle's main concern is to show how the virtues are voluntary states. Towards the end of Book III, Aristotle analyzes two specific virtues, courage and temperance, especially with regard to their voluntary nature. In Book IV, he extends this analysis to the other ethical virtues such as generosity, magnanimity, friendliness, and truthfulness. Book V is devoted to justice.

Book VI contains an important discussion of practical wisdom, or *phronesis*, which guides us to act in the right way. Practical wisdom not only includes the ability to find the best means to certain ends, but also a person with such wisdom understands how happiness or flourishing is formed by the virtues. In Book VI, Aristotle also discusses the intellectual virtues.

The first chapters of Book VII contain a discussion of incontinence or *akrasia*, which is sometimes misleadingly referred to as "weakness of the will" (see chapter 4, page 105). Aristotle argues that someone who thinks that X is good is necessarily disposed to choose it. Given this, he must explain how *akrasia* or incontinence is possible. Books VIII and IX contain an examination of the nature of friendship. In Book X, Aristotle returns to the nature of the human good, arguing that theoretical contemplation is the highest function of a person, corresponding to the activity of the divine-like active intellect.

This very brief summary is meant merely orientate the reader of the *Nicomachean Ethics*. It does *not* reveal the shape of the overall argumentation of the book, which is something we will return to later.

HAPPINESS AS THE ULTIMATE END

Aristotle argues that all activities are pursued for the sake of goals even when the goal is the activity itself. Humans have many goals and these are arranged in a hierarchy, and at the pinnacle of this pyramid is the ultimate end for a human: *eudaimonia* or happiness. Aristotle supports these contentions with a complex argument, which we shall now go through step by step. There are five steps as follows:

Ends and Good

An end is that for the sake of which an activity is performed. This might be some product or goal external to the activity itself, such as a bridle or a house, or it might be the activity itself. Ends guide us with regard to which actions need to be performed. For instance, the goal of constructing a house guides what needs to be done, and when (e.g., when and how the walls floors and roofs are made). Roof making and other construction activities are *part* of the act of constructing a house.

> Every craft and every inquiry, and likewise every action and decision, seems to aim at some good. For which reason people have rightly concluded that the good is that at which all things aim. (I.1 1094a1–3)

In the sentence above, Aristotle apparently defines something as good insofar as it is the end of an action. Can we also conclude that Aristotle thinks that there is a single ultimate good at which all actions ultimately aim?

Ends Are Structured

Ends or goals define activities in a pyramid-like structure, with the lower ones for the sake of the fewer higher ones. In other words, the end of a set of activities can contribute as a means towards or as part of another activity. For example, consider the commanding of an army for the sake of victory. There is a host of other activities (such as planning the strategy) that are performed directly for the sake of a higher end, in this case victory. Also, there are many other activities that aren't performed directly for that end, but which nevertheless contribute to that end and are shaped by it (e.g., bridle making, which has as its end bridles that are used for horse riding).

> Bridle-making and the other crafts of riding equipment fall under the craft of cavalry riding, and this and every other military action fall under the craft of strategy, and in the same way other crafts fall under still others. In all these cases, the ends of the commanding crafts are more worth choosing than all the ends under their power. For the latter are pursued for the sake of the former. (I.1 1094a10–16)

Aristotle's theory assumes that the end of one activity can be the means towards another activity, and also that an activity can be part of the end of another activity.

The Value of Ends

Aristotle claims that ends are more valuable than the actions that lead to them. If an action is performed for the sake of an end, then the end is more valuable because the actions were done for the sake of it. Furthermore, in a chain of ends, the ones that are higher up are more valuable than those that are lower in the chain because the lower ones are performed for the sake of the higher ones. Bridle making can't be more important than horse riding because the former is done for the sake of the latter.

Chains of Means Must Come to an End

Aristotle argues that every chain of means must come to an end. He says:

> We do not choose everything for the sake of something else, for if we did, it would go on to infinity, so that desire would be empty and frivolous. (I.2 1094a19–21)

All chains must terminate in some final end. Given the idea of a single ultimate end, the philosophical task is to define its nature, which is the next step.

However, first, we need to point out a potential problem. Of course, that all chains of ends must come to an end does not logically entail that all chains come to rest in one single common end. It would be a fallacy to argue from "each chain of ends must have an end" to "all chains of ends have the same end."

Does Aristotle think that he has shown by argument that all chains end in one final end? It seems not, because to make the point about the single final end he indicates that there is general agreement that happiness is the ultimate end of human action, even though there is disagreement about what happiness is. In other words, Aristotle appeals to popular opinion and not to a fallacious argument.

Happiness

Aristotle identifies the ultimate end as happiness, or *eudaimonia*. As we saw in earlier chapters, *eudaimonia* means living well. It shouldn't be translated as "happiness," if what we mean by the latter is simply hedonic feelings of happiness and pleasure. The Greek term is often translated as "flourishing" and sometimes as "self-actualization." It is sometimes rendered as "successful" in accordance with the idea that Aristotle's concern is how to live successfully as a human being.[1]

Aristotle argues for the conclusion that the ultimate end is happiness or *eudaimonia* on the grounds that the ultimate end must have two features: completeness and self-sufficiency.[2] The most complete end is worth pursuing for its own sake and not for the sake of something else. Happiness or *eudaimonia* is the only such good. Wealth is not an ultimate end, because it is good for the sake of something else and not for its own sake. The same point applies to honor, pleasure and virtue: they contribute to living well, but we choose living well or happiness for its own sake and not for the sake of something else. *Eudaimonia* also is self-sufficient because it is enough and is not lacking. Aristotle says, "We define "sufficient of itself" as that which, taken by itself, makes life worth living and is lacking in nothing." This apparently entails that there can be only one ultimate end because, if there were two, then the first on its own would not be sufficient for a good life (*NE* 1097a15–b21). Aristotle says:

> Fulfillment, counted as one good thing among others, would be still more worth having if even the least of the others were added to it. . . . (I, 7, 1097b14–20)

In short, happiness cannot be counted as one good thing among others.

Let us summarize the overall argument so far:

1. If X is for the sake of Y then Y is more valuable than X.
2. There is an ultimate end of all human activity.
3. The most ultimate end must comply with the following four conditions: (a) it is desired for itself; (b) it is not for the sake of anything else; (c) it is lacking in nothing; and (d) all other goods are desired for its sake.

4. The only thing that satisfies these four conditions in human life is happiness or *eudaimonia*.

5. Therefore, *eudaimonia* is the most valuable end for humans.

Happiness and Virtue

Having described flourishing as the final or ultimate end, Aristotle needs to characterize the happy or flourishing life more substantially. He has provided the teleological bones or structure, and now he will provide the flesh or content. He does this by introducing the idea of the function (or *ergon*) of a human being. Remember that, for Aristotle, the soul is the way in which an organism is organized naturally for certain purposes. For example, part of the natural function of some plants is to produce leaves, flowers, seeds and fruit. Aristotle's idea is that if we can characterize the natural functions of the human being then we can describe what constitutes functioning well as a human being. To function well as a human being is to exercise the relevant human capacities well or in an excellent way. This point will enable us to describe the flourishing life or *eudaimonia* as carrying out the relevant activities in an excellent manner.

Aristotle claims that we need to identify the natural functions of the human soul, and by this he means those capacities that are essentially and distinctively human or that aren't shared with animals. The functions in question are part of the human essence and, therefore, not just any uniquely human characteristic would count as part of our *ergon*.[3] For example, joke telling might be a uniquely human activity, but if it were not part of our essence then it wouldn't count as part of our *ergon*.

Aristotle claims that the function of humans is activity of the soul in accordance with, or not without, *logos*. In this context the term *logos* is usually translated as reason or rational principle. By "reason" Aristotle means a full range of capacities that involve rationality, such as the capability to make decisions, carry out logical deductions, understand first principles, and deliberate.

The ancient Greek term *logos* can also mean order or arrangement, and consequently, Aristotle might also mean that humans have the distinctive capacity to arrange or bring a certain kind of order to the soul.[4] Following this train of thought, Aristotle's view is that there are parts of the human soul that are indirectly rational. Our emotions and desires are not rational themselves; they don't think, but they can be guided by—or listen to voice of—reason. In other words, "activity of the soul in accord with *logos*" also contains the idea of the soul being organized harmoniously in accordance with reason.

Aristotle defines the human good as follows:

> The human good consists in the activity of soul in accordance with excellence (or virtue); and if there are several excellences, then in accordance with the one which is best and closest to the human goal (*telos*). (1098a15–16)

The argument for this conclusion (at 1098a 9–17) is as follows:

1. A good X is one that performs its function well.
2. The human function is to live in a way such that the activities of the soul conform with reason.
3. Each activity is performed well when it accords with or expresses a virtue.
4. Therefore, the human good life is activity of the soul that expresses virtue.

When Aristotle uses the Greek word *areté*, which is usually translated as "virtue," he means something close to the English word "excellence." He does not mean "virtue" with the religious and moral implications that the word often carries today. It is important to remember that Aristotle's ethics is pre-Christian and that the word *ethics* doesn't contain moralistic undertones. Indeed, we might distinguish morality and ethics along something like the following lines. Morality is often understood as the requirements of duty as set against the desires of self-interest; the idea is that we have certain moral obligations that can require us to limit what we do for the sake of self-interest. On the other hand, ethics, as understood in a broadly Aristotelian way, is concerned with how one lives a life that is valuable for the person living it. Thus, concerning Aristotle, the virtues are habitual dispositions that serve or constitute our happiness or flourishing rather than being moral requirements imposed on us by duty.

Is Happiness Inclusive or Exclusive?

How should we understand Aristotle's notion of *eudaimonia*? Many commentators, such as John Ackrill, believe that Aristotle has an inclusive view, according to which the ultimate end, *eudaimonia*, is a like a basket that includes a range of activities, all of which are themselves ends. In short, these activities are equally ultimate, and they form parts or constituents of the happy life. When we say that we value them for the sake of happiness, this means that they are valued as components of the happy life. In contrast, the exclusive view claims that there is one ultimate activity type which constitutes the happy life, for the sake of which we do everything else. Richard Kraut, among others, defends this kind of interpretation of Aristotle. This issue concerns the relationship between Books I and X of the *Ethics*; it is better to return to it later when we examine Book X.

Virtues and the Mean

According to Aristotle, there are two kinds of virtue (1103a1–10): those pertaining directly to reason (the intellectual virtues), and those concerning the parts of the soul merely capable of following reason (the ethical virtues). As we have seen, in humans, part of the animal aspect of the soul that is concerned with desire and emotion is not rational, but nevertheless it is not non-rational either; it is capable of responding or listening to reason (1102 b 13–14). The ethical virtues concern the functioning of these aspects of the human function. Aristotle's discussion of virtue is divided into three parts: first, he discusses ethical virtues in general; second, he examines particular ethical virtues such as courage; third, he looks at the intellectual virtues.

Aristotle offers the following definition of ethical virtue:

> A virtue is a habitual disposition connected with choice, lying in a mean relative to us, a mean which is determined by reason, by which the person of practical wisdom would determine it. (II, 6, 1106b36–1107a2)

Aristotle claims that virtues are habitual dispositions, which he calls *hexis*. This means that when we have a virtue, we are disposed or have a tendency towards certain habits. For example, the generous person is disposed as a matter of habit to give to others even when it is not strictly required that he or she do so. Likewise, defective character states, what we might call "vices," are also a matter of habitual training.[5]

Although Aristotle claims that virtuous character traits are acquired through training, he distinguishes skills from virtues. Both are habitual tendencies; but whereas skills pertain to the quality of a product, virtues pertain also to how the agent performs the action (II, 4). In particular, the ethical virtues involve how we feel—the appropriateness of the emotional response in a given context. Each ethical virtue is a disposition concerning an emotion, but it is not itself an emotion. Virtues and vices are habitual tendencies towards having emotions that are appropriate or inappropriate in the context. So, for example, a person is bad tempered when he or she has the tendency to react in an angry way that is inappropriate given the circumstances. This implies that if a person is angry in circumstances in which such anger is appropriate, then this does not count towards his or her being bad tempered.

Aristotle claims that the virtues are a mean between two extremes: one of excess and the other of deficiency (1106a26–b28). The courageous person, for example, lies somewhere on a continuum between the cowardly and foolhardy. Likewise, each virtue is an intermediate between two extremes. This view needs three qualifications.

First, the manifestation of each virtue as action is circumstance specific, as this famous quote from the *Ethics* shows:

The one who is angry at the right things and towards the right people, and also in the right way, at the right time, and for the right length of time, is praised. (NE IV 5 1125b31)

Aristotle's *Doctrine of the Mean* characterizes the general nature of each virtue, but not the specific acts that the virtuous person would perform or that the virtue in question demands.

Second, for this reason, although the virtues are a mean, they do not necessarily require moderation. For example, in special circumstances the virtue of courage might require a person to act in a way that we would normally consider foolhardy or rash, and in other contexts to act in a way that we would typically regard as cowardly. Aristotle's view of the virtues permits strong feelings when circumstances require it.

Third, Aristotle also claims that each virtue is relative to the person's capacities. For example, for a person who cannot swim well, crossing the river may constitute in certain circumstances an act of courage. For the experienced swimmer, it may not.[6] There is much discussion about what kind of relativity is at issue here. However, most commentators agree that Aristotle does not mean that the virtues are relative to a person's opinions; he doesn't make them subjective in that sense.

Specific Ethical Virtues

In Book II, chapter 7 of the *Nicomachean Ethics*, Aristotle lists the following 10 ethical virtues: courage, temperance, generosity, magnificence, magnanimity, a virtue concerned with honor on a small scale, mildness, truthfulness, wit, and friendliness. We should note that this list does not include justice, which is the topic of Book V. It does not contain the intellectual virtues, which receive a separate treatment in Book VI. Furthermore, Aristotle claims that there are means concerned with the passions, such as shame and righteous indignation, which are nevertheless not virtues (1108a31–1108b10).

Each of the ethical virtues has a domain or sphere of human life to which it is applicable. For example, courage is concerned with fear. Generosity and magnificence are both concerned with money, but the former with small sums and the latter with large ones. Traditionally, commentators, from St. Thomas Aquinas on, have classified the ethical virtues in accordance with their corresponding spheres. However, listing the spheres is not sufficient on its own as a method for generating the list of virtues.[7] Aristotle himself acknowledges this in Book VI, as we shall see.

For each of these virtues there are two associated states of vice, one to do with deficiency and the other with excess. Based on what Aristotle says, we can make a diagram or table of each virtue, its sphere of concern, and its two associated vices. (See the table at the end of the chapter.)

Aristotle refers to the second five of the 10 virtues as nameless (II, 7) even though he actually gives four of them names. The five nameless ones are: the virtue concerning honor on a small scale, mildness (*praotēs*), truthfulness (*alētheia*), wit (*eutrapelia* or *epidexiotēs*) and friendliness (*philia*). The reason for calling them "nameless" is that the relevant Greek terms are fundamentally misleading. The Greek for mildness (*praotēs*) errs towards the deficiency and doesn't accurately capture the virtue (IV 5 1125b26–9). The term "truthfulness" in Greek (*alētheia*) suggests that the virtuous person will simply say what is true; but Aristotle's idea of this virtue is that one won't boast or indulge in false modesty with regard to one's own judgments about oneself. Aristotle's virtue "wit" includes the idea that one knows when and how to joke appropriately, and his notion of *philia* is not captured well by the Greek word or its English translation, as we shall see when we discuss friendship later.

Responsibility

In Book III, Aristotle is concerned with to what extent, or under what conditions, a person is responsible for his or her actions and character state. To this effect, he discusses the voluntary and involuntary. The relevant Greek words *hekousion* and *akousion* applied to actions are sometimes translated as willingly and unwillingly, as well as voluntary and involuntary.[8]

Aristotle begins his discussion by examining a commonly accepted theory according to which one can show that an action was performed unwillingly only by demonstrating that it was performed (1) under compulsion or (2) because of ignorance (1109b35).

In the *Eudemian Ethics*, Aristotle claims that the term *voluntary* is applied only to those things of which the person himself is cause and origin (*EE*, 1223a15–18). For this reason, in the *Nicomachean Ethics*, he claims that a behavior is compelled if its causal origin is entirely outside the agent. For example, if sailors are blown off course by a storm, then this is not an action at all (1110a1–4). Actions must be caused by internal factors, such as the desires and choices of the agent. According to this definition, a person cannot refuse responsibility for an action by claiming that he or she was overcome by anger or desire, since the cause is internal (1110b9–17). Aristotle points out that, nevertheless, sometimes we might absolve someone of responsibility for his or her actions "when human nature is strained beyond anyone's capacity to endure" (1110a23–26). Perhaps phobias might count as such. In such cases we might call the behavior compulsive even though the cause is internal. Aristotle provides other examples in this category when we excuse a person's behavior as compulsive without impugning moral weakness, such as in cases of madness and brutishness.

Finally, he discusses instances of actions performed under threat, such as when a person complies with a tyrant's demands to save his family or when a sailor jettisons the cargo to save the ship from a storm. In such cases, the person acts voluntarily or willingly since the actions are chosen. Such actions do not qualify as compelled behavior. They have inner psychological causes. However, Aristotle also says that when they are described without qualification, one might be inclined to say that such actions were performed involuntarily because no one would choose them for their own sake (III, 1, 1110a9–19). In other words, Aristotle appeals to the idea that the action that a person performs depends on what the person saw him- or herself doing at the time. In this way, threat is fundamentally different from compulsion and madness.

With regard to ignorance, Aristotle provides several examples of actions performed in ignorance, such as giving a person medicine with fatal results (III, 1, 1111a10–13). He claims that such actions are not performed willingly, and they are performed unwillingly when the agent regrets what happens (III, 1, 1111a10–9). However, in such cases, the agent must not be responsible for his or her ignorance. For this reason, Aristotle distinguishes such actions performed *because of* ignorance from those done *in* ignorance—for example, when someone is drunk or in a rage.

Aristotle claims that there are actions done willingly but are not judged morally as proper objects of praise and blame. Such category includes the actions of animals and of young children.

Practical Wisdom

Aristotle begins Book VI by asserting that his earlier claim, that the virtues are an intermediary state determined by reason, is not sufficiently illuminating. Because of this, after having examined the ethical virtues, he proposes to investigate the excellences of reason, or the intellectual virtues, especially *phronesis* or practical wisdom (1138b17–1138b35).

The human soul's essential distinctive feature is activity in accordance with *logos* or reason. Aristotle divides reason into two parts: practical and theoretical. Accordingly, the intellectual virtues are in turn divided into two sorts: those that pertain to practical thinking or deliberation and those that pertain to theoretical reasoning or inquiry (1139a3–8). The main intellectual virtues are practical wisdom (*phronesis*), which we have already mentioned, and theoretical wisdom *(sophia)*.

As the definition of virtue given earlier points out, the virtuous person is guided by reason, as the practically wise person would determine it (1107a1–2). Given that each virtue is in part defined by the person having the appropriate feelings and desires in each circumstance, this means that the ethically right action cannot be defined completely in terms of a set of rules. Aristotle claims that some emotions, such as envy and spite, and some actions, such as murder and theft, are always wrong, irrespective of the context (1107a8–12). However, judgments about what is ethically right are circumstance specific and cannot be determined alone with a set of rules.

What is ethically right is determined by reason as the person who has practical wisdom would determine it. Aristotle says that the wise person:

> ... sees the truth in each case, being as it were a standard and measure of them. (1113a32–3)

In other words, what is ethically right in a particular context is best thought of in terms of how the practically wise person would judge it after deliberation. But Aristotle is not saying that what the wise person judges actually *defines* what is best. He says that what the wise person sees is *as it were* a standard and measure.

What is practical wisdom? The practically wise person can think well about what one ought to do for the sake of living a life of excellence or *eudaimonia*. This involves being able to deliberate well about one's goals or ends, as well as means, and to "see the truth in each case." Thinking about means involves discovering which means are necessary and best for achieving one's goals. Deliberation about ends is more complex. Aristotle thinks that the practically wise person will know what to do in any circumstances, but this may often require deliberation about what goals one should have. For example, it may not be clear what kindness or courage require of me in a particular situation. In making such a judgment, I might be misled by my own desires, emotions, or weaknesses.[9]

In this sense, practical wisdom is the most important of the virtues.[10] Nevertheless, it depends on the ethical virtues. For example, temperance helps to preserve our sense of what is best to be done. Aristotle says that practical wisdom is a state developed "in the eye of the soul" only in the presence of the ethical virtues. He continues:

> For instances of reasoning about practical matters have as their starting point viz "since the end is of such and such a kind" (whatever— anything will do as an example). But the end is not clear except to a good person. Wickedness distorts [our judgment] and leads to our being deceived about the starting points of action. Obviously, then, one cannot be a person of practical wisdom without being a good person. (VI, 12, 1144a26–b1)

Aristotle says when the wise person acts virtuously, he or she does so for the sake of the noble or fine (1120a23–4). The Greek term he uses is *kalon*, which can also mean the beautiful.

These points bring out two important aspects of Aristotle's ethical theory: the unity of the virtues and ethical realism.

Unity of the Virtues

Aristotle affirms some version of the unity of the virtues, a view that we discussed in relation to Socrates in chapter 4. In other words, the practically wise person must have all the virtues to be perfectly good. For example, to be kind may on occasion require one to be courageous. Likewise, to be able to see what action is courageous may require, in some circumstances, that one is kind.

This is a relatively mild version of the thesis of the unity of the virtues. Aristotle does not assert that there is only one virtue. He clearly thinks that there are many of them, distinguished by their spheres. Thus, Aristotle seems to embrace the reciprocity of the virtues rather than the identity of the virtues, as discussed in chapter 7.

Ethical Realism

Aristotle's use of the word *see* (when he says that the practically wise person "sees the truth in each case") suggests that he has what we call today a *cognitivist view* of the virtues. According to the contemporary cognitivist, ethical claims are assertions that can be either true or false and can be believed or judged to be so. In other words, a person can have cognitive states pertaining to ethical claims. Aristotle affirms that to have a virtue is to have a suitable range of cognitive capacities or sensibilities, such that one can see what one ought to do and perceive what the ethically relevant features of a situation are.[11]

In this regard it is worth contrasting Aristotle's position about ethical judgments with those of the Sophists and Plato. Plato regards the good as an absolute entity. This implies that certain things are good full stop or without qualification. In sharp contrast, the Sophists regarded the good as subjective; what is good depends on the judgments of the subject. Aristotle denies both Plato's absolutist and the Sophists' subjectivist views, and he develops an intermediary position. Rejecting Sophism does not require embracing Plato's absolutist views.

Against Plato, ethical claims are not absolutely true; what is ethical is often circumstance specific, as we have already seen. Furthermore, Aristotle treats the term *good* as what is sometimes called today an *attributive predicate*.[12] The word *good* essentially qualifies a noun in the sense that, for instance, a good carpenter is quite different from a good athlete. What counts towards being a good X depends on the X in question. Of course, Aristotle is primarily concerned with what counts as a good life for a human. But, in effect, he is rejecting the Platonic question of what counts as goodness *simpliciter*. Against the Sophist, as we have seen, Aristotle thinks that there can be true and false ethical judgments.

The Practical Syllogism

In Aristotle's practical syllogism, the major premise consists of a universal judgment, recommending that one perform a certain type of action; for example: "Everything sweet ought to be tasted." The minor premise is a particular judgment, grounded in perceptual experience, that this is an action of the recommended type; for example: "This is sweet." The conclusion of the syllogism is the action itself of tasting the sweet

(VII-3, 1147a4–32). If the person judges the two premises to be true, then he or she will draw the conclusion and perform the relevant action.

THE INTELLECTUAL VIRTUES

In Book VI, after an examination of *phronesis*, Aristotle discusses the intellectual virtues concerned with inquiry or theory, which are: expertise in the crafts (*techne*), scientific knowledge (*epistêmê*), intuitive understanding (*nous*), and theoretical wisdom (*sophia*). The underlying idea is that the function of each part of the understanding is truth, and consequently, the virtue of each part will be what enables that part to grasp the truth best (1139b).

Craft (*techne*) is true reason concerned with production. As we saw in chapter 9, scientific knowledge (*epistêmê*) is knowledge of what is not capable of being otherwise. It is knowledge of what we call today *necessary truths*. Thus, it is the capacity to demonstrate or deduce from first principles, which cannot be demonstrated themselves. In contrast, intuitive understanding (*nous*) is the state of the soul that allows us to capture first principles. *Sophia* is the combination of *epistêmê* and *nous*. In other words, a person has theoretical reason when he or she can grasp first principles and what follows from them (Book VI, 7). Aristotle characterizes it as "knowledge of the highest objects that has received as it were its proper completion." (1141a19). Immediately after this, he makes the following suggestive claim:

> For it would be strange to think that the art of politics, or practical wisdom, is the best knowledge, since man is not the best thing in the world. (1141a20)

This suggests that theoretical wisdom is a more valuable good than practical wisdom because it involves cognition of the divine or eternal. This claim will be important for understanding Aristotle's conclusions in Book X of the *Nicomachean Ethics* and their relation to Book I.

INCONTINENCE OR *AKRASIA*

Book VII begins with Aristotle making a fresh start by discussing incontinence and brutishness. A person is incontinent when he or she typically does things which he or she believes to be bad. Aristotle claims that incontinence is different from vice, even though they may lead to similar actions, because vice is in accordance with one's choices and incontinence is not (VII, 8, 150b29–151a10).

Incontinence, or *akrasia*, is when a person knows that he or she ought to perform A but does not do A. We will refine this definition later.

As we saw in chapter 4 of this book, Socrates thought that incontinence is impossible: no one can do wrong knowingly. Since a person always desires the good and virtue is knowledge, what appears to be incontinence is really ignorance.

Following this, one might ask: How is *akrasia* even possible? Aristotle claims that apparently people do sometimes knowingly perform wrong actions, noting that Socrates's view "contradicts the plain phenomena" (VII, 2,1145b22-28). To approach the issue of how this phenomenon is possible, Aristotle distinguishes three different ways in which a person might be said to both know and not know.

1. The word *know* is ambiguous: it can refer to a person who has knowledge and uses it or to a person who has knowledge and does not use it. In other words, one can bear in mind what one knows or not bear it in mind (1146b31-35).
2. One can know both premises of a practical syllogism but only use the major premise and not the minor one. For instance, I know that dry foods are good for my health, but I do not use the knowledge that the food in front of me is dry. (1146b35-1147a10).
3. One can both know and not know something in several very different ways, such as a person who is drunk, who is half asleep, or who is mad. There is the person who is overcome by strong emotions, and ones who have not assimilated what they have been told. Sometimes we know only as someone who recites his lines, such as an actor (1147a 10-24).

Having drawn these distinctions, Aristotle applies them to the practical syllogism (VII.3.1147a24-b19).[13] Remember that the conclusion of a practical syllogism is the relevant action according to Aristotle; hence, the need for a solution regarding *akrasia* couched in terms of such a syllogism.

A person has rationally chosen to eat a healthy diet. He or she knows that dry food is healthy and performs the following syllogistic reasoning:

1. All dry food is healthy for humans.
2. I am a human.
3. This food in front of me is dry food.

From these three premises, he or she ought to draw the appropriate conclusion which, according to Aristotle, consists in performing the action of eating the dry food. However, let us suppose the person rejects the healthy food and eats something tasty and oily instead. Aristotle's analysis of this situation is that the person both knows and does not know that he ought to eat the dry food. This is the way that he analyses incontinence. However, Aristotle *also* uses a different kind of language to describe incontinence, namely, that of having but not using one's knowledge.

Interpretations of the key passages in Aristotle (i.e., in Book VII, 3) are contested. One of the problems is that it is not clear exactly what the problem of incontinence is for Aristotle. The idea that a person might act contrary to his or her ethical beliefs shouldn't be much of a puzzle because Aristotle has a complex psychological theory, which allows for the idea that a person's emotions might exercise a stronger motivational force than his or her beliefs.

Another problem is that we can distinguish at least two kinds of *akrasia*: soft and hard. Soft *akrasia* is when the agent intentionally performs an action that he or she knows he should not perform. Hard *akrasia* is when an agent performs an action intentionally and yet judges that, all things considered, it would be better to perform an alternative action.[14] The difference is that the second involves a judgment with all things considered, and the first does not. Can Aristotle's theory explain the more difficult hard kind of incontinence in which an agent knows that the action he should perform is the best action in the circumstances, all things considered?

Aristotle is interested in incontinence as a type of ethical defect that is different from the vices. He classifies different kinds of incontinence, and he discusses incontinence with respect to different kinds of pleasures, appetites, and emotions, such as anger (Book VII, chapters 4–14).

FRIENDSHIP

In Books VIII and IX, Aristotle turns to the nature of friendship. The relevant Greek word is *philia*, which can also be translated more broadly as relationships to people we get on well with. Apart from family, friends, and lovers, Aristotle includes in this category members of the same club or religious group, business contacts, and people one sees on a daily basis—for example, in shops. Aristotle claims that such relationships must be mutual, mutually recognized, and must involve goodwill (VIII, 3, 1155b26–56a5). He says:

> So people in a relationship must have goodwill for each other, know of each other's goodwill, and wish good things for one another, on one of the three grounds already mentioned. These grounds differ from one another in kind. So then do the ways of relating, and the kinds of relationship. There are therefore three types of relationship, corresponding to the three grounds, which are their objects. (VIII, 2, 1156a3–8)

One of Aristotle's main points is to argue that there are three kinds of friendship, and that the third is the most perfect. The three types are:

1. Those based on mutual advantage
2. Those based on mutual pleasure
3. Those based on mutual admiration

These relationships can overlap. Thus, the third kind can also include the first two. Aristotle claims that the third kind is the most perfect for several reasons. First, such friendship arises because of the character or intrinsic qualities of the other and not just because the person is useful or fun. Second, because of this, the nature of such friendships is good without qualification. Finally, such relationships are more likely to endure (VIII, 3–6).

That Aristotle claims that the third kind of friendship is best does not mean that the other two are reducible to ways of using people. He notes with approval that "it is commonly said that one should wish for good things for a friend for the friend's sake" (1155b31). This can be understood as follows. Having mutual goodwill is a necessary condition for any kind of friendship at all, and this requires that one would want good things for one's friend for his or her sake. Therefore, even in friendships based on usefulness or mutual pleasure, one would have goodwill towards the other and want things for his or her good for their sake.

Pleasure and Contemplation

The first six chapters of Book X are concerned with pleasure and pain, which Aristotle also discusses in Book VII in relation to incontinence (chapters 11–14). The first three chapters of Book X are concerned with the views of previous thinkers about the nature of pleasure and pain, and their value.

In chapter 4, Aristotle argues that pleasure supervenes activities such as those of seeing, listening, and sensing in general, as well as thought and contemplation (1175a2–1856). For this reason, we speak of sights and sounds as pleasant. Pleasure supervenes on such activities when the sense is active in relation to its object, and the object is the most appropriate. In other words, the feeling of pleasure is not a thing or mental state separable from the pleasurable nature of the activities in question: the pleasure is involved or bound up with the activity.

Aristotle claims that pleasure completes an activity. However, he hastens to qualify this point. The most complete activity is "that of a well-conditioned organ in relation to the worthiest of its objects." This means, for example, that listening to beautiful sounds attentively and with a finely tuned ear will count as a complete activity. This point *defines* the completeness and value of the activity. However, he also says:

> Pleasure completes the activity not as the inherent state does, but as an end which supervenes as the bloom of youth does on those in the flower of their age. So long, then, as both the intelligible or sensible object and the discriminating or contemplative faculty are as they should be, the pleasure will be involved in the activity. (1175a5)

In short, the accompanying pleasure sweetens and enhances good or complete activities, but it doesn't define their completeness or value.

Because pleasure supervenes on activities of which there are many different types, there are also different kinds of pleasures. For example, the pleasure of listening to the flute is quite different from that of joining in a discussion (X, 5, 1175a28–1176a3). The point about the supervening nature of pleasure also helps explain in what ways pleasures can be bad. Aristotle says, "The pleasure proper to a worthy activity is good and that proper to an unworthy activity bad" (1176a3).

In summary, Aristotle's position is that pleasure doesn't define what is good, although it enhances what is already good. Aristotle claims that we should try to find pleasurable the valuable activities that constitute *eudaimonia*. We should train ourselves to find the exercise of the virtues pleasurable.

In chapter 6 of Book X Aristotle turns to the nature of happiness, summarizing the relevant discussions of the earlier parts of the *Ethics*. In chapter 7 he advances the thesis that the best activity is contemplation that accords with the highest virtue—*Sophia*, or intellectual wisdom. He says:

> If happiness is activity in accordance with virtue, it is reasonable that it should be in accordance with the highest virtue; and this will be that of the best thing in us . . . the activity of this in accordance with its proper virtue will be happiness. That this activity is contemplative we have already said. (1177a)

He also explicitly states that a life of only ethically virtuous activity is less valuable than one that is contemplative (1178a–1179a).

The Problem

How are we to reconcile the main claims of Book I with that of Book X?[15] The major part of the *Ethics* seems to follow the conclusion of Book I that ethically virtuous activity is an essential part of *eudaimonia*. However, the claims in Book X about the superiority of contemplation seem to contradict this view.

Some writers have claimed that Aristotle does indeed contradict himself, arguing that according to Book I the best kind of activity is ethically virtuous; and that according to Book X, it is contemplation.[16] Among those who think that there is no contradiction, there is nevertheless disagreement about how to read the relationship between Book I and Book X (or more precisely, between activity of the soul in accordance with the ethical virtues and activity of the soul in accordance with theoretical wisdom [i.e., contemplation]. This returns us to the discussion between the inclusive and the dominant view; the latter is also called the *intellectualist* view. In summary, the intellectualist or dominant view claims that Aristotle identifies *eudaimonia* with contemplation alone, and the inclusive view identifies *eudaimonia* with a package of activities that includes both the ethically virtuous and the contemplative.[17]

One of the weaknesses of the dominant view is that it contains an apparently implausible element, namely, the claim that all other activities are for the sake of contemplation. Remember that, according to Aristotle, the highest good, *eudaimonia*, must not only be for its own sake and for the sake of anything else, *but also* that everything else is for the sake of it. Thus, the scholars who identify *eudaimonia* with contemplation must claim that all human activities, including ethically virtuous activities, are for the sake of contemplation in accord with intellectual wisdom. The implausibility of this view can be seen on a few counts. First, it seems to imply that all the other excellent human activities are merely means to contemplation or that they are merely instrumentally valuable. For if they were also intrinsically valuable or for their own sake, then they would be part of *eudaimonia*.[18] Second, it apparently implies that Aristotle's conception of *eudaimonia* is reduced to one single type of activity. The inclusive view allows for the claim that human flourishing includes many kinds of activities for their own sake, including contemplation.[19] The dominant view seems to reduce *eudaimonia* to one kind of activity. Of course, we might conclude that Aristotle held an implausible view, but if there is textual evidence for a more charitable interpretation then we have good reason to adopt it. For this reason, let us briefly review the overall argument of the *Ethics*.

The Overall Argument

Aristotle's aim is to understand the ultimate end of humans. His answer in Book I was that happiness consists in virtuous or excellent activity, which he describes in Books II–V. However, these books describe the virtues of the part of the soul that is not rational *per se* but which can respond or listen to reason, such as the emotions and desires. In other words, these virtues are not the most important component of *eudaimonia* because they are only derivatively rational. To comprehend the ultimate end, we need to understand the virtuous activity of reason *per se* or the intellectual virtues. This is why Aristotle introduces *phronesis* (or practical wisdom) at the start of Book VI. Nevertheless, Aristotle thinks that *phronesis* is not the ultimate human end or "the best and most perfect virtue" because theoretical wisdom (*sophia*) is even more ultimate.

We can construct an argument implicit in the text to that effect. *Sophia* is a more ultimate end than *phronesis* for humans because *phronesis* is that part of reason that directs the emotions and desires. It is part of the ethically virtuous life. In other words, it is how reason helps the person to live in accordance with the ethical virtues. It doesn't constitute what reason would do on its own account. What the rational soul does for itself is constituted by the activities of reason that accord with *sophia* or theoretical wisdom.

On closer inspection, the conclusion of Book I was not simply that happiness consists of ethically virtuous activity because Aristotle also adds to the phrase, "and if there are several excellences, then in accordance with the one which is best and closest to the human end." In other words, this final clause anticipates or permits the conclusion of Book X. Furthermore, in Book X Aristotle echoes this very point by claiming that a life in accord with the ethical virtues is a happy life, but that the contemplative life is better still.

These textual points indicate the outlines of a broad solution to the conflict between the inclusive and dominant view. After all, both views agree that for Aristotle the ideal life comprises both the activities of the soul in accordance with the ethical excellences, and the activities of the soul in accordance with the theoretical virtues. They disagree on how these two are related: the dominant view claims that the ethical virtues enter as means to better contemplation, and the inclusive view denies this.

However, three points should help to clarify this difference. First, Aristotle's text is clear that contemplation is superior to or more desirable than the activities of the ethical virtues. Second, Aristotle is also clear that a person with theoretical wisdom will also have practical wisdom. In this sense, what Aristotle means by "the contemplative life" cannot conflict with ethically virtuous activity. Finally, the dominant view looks implausible because one needs to separate two ideas: the first is that contemplation is superior to, or more valuable than, merely ethically virtuous activity; and the second is that the latter is for the sake for the former. In other words, the first idea is clearly Aristotle's. If the second is also his, it is less plausible. If we can separate these two ideas then we can affirm that contemplation is better without denying that living according to the ethical virtues is also good in itself.

POLITICS

As the final sentences of the *Ethics* reveal, for Aristotle, ethics without politics is incomplete. The individual's aim of achieving the good is impossible outside of the state, or, more specifically, the best kind of state, a city-state or *polis*. As we shall see, this is fundamentally because humans are social and political animals. The main goal of Aristotle's *Politics* is to describe the best kind of city-state. However, more broadly, the aim is to describe statesmanship, the political application of practical wisdom, to all kinds of city-states. As we shall see, Aristotle distinguishes governing as a statesman from ruling as a master (1324b23–35). Only the first is appropriate for free people.

OVERVIEW

The *Politics* has eight books. The first concerns the household, the roots of the city-state. In Book II, Aristotle initiates the search for the ideal city-state by discussing some false ideals. He criticizes the politics of the dialogues of Plato, namely, the *Republic* and the *Laws* (in chapter 6). In the last four chapters of Book II, (i.e., 9–12), he investigates existing imperfect city-states, especially Sparta, Crete, and Carthage.

In Book III he characterizes the constitution and the nature of citizenship, and he identifies six main types of government: kingship, aristocracy, polity, tyranny, oligarchy, and democracy. In Book IV Aristotle identifies the ways in which states can be defective, focusing on democracy and oligarchy. Books V and VI examine other defective regimes, such as monarchy and tyranny. In these books Aristotle is concerned, among things, with how defective regimes might be improved.

Book VII starts the discussion of the best regime by looking at the virtuous life and pre-conditions for an ideal *polis*, such as its size, class structure, and territory. In chapter 13 Aristotle describes the goal that the best form of the *polis* should have. The remainder of Books VII and VIII is dedicated to the type of education the best state should have.

To avoid confusion, please note that some editors and commentators advance another order for the books of the *Politics*. According to this alternative idea, Books IV, V, and VI are placed at the end of the work, and Books VII and VIII are placed in the middle, after Book III. In this alternative proposal, the order would be I, II, III, VII, VIII, IV, V, VI.[20] The intent of the proposal is that Aristotle's discussion of the ideal regime should follow immediately after Book III. The standard complete works of Aristotle gives the order described above, and not the alternative one.

The Household and the *Polis*

In Book I, chapter 2, Aristotle presents some of the key ideas of his political theory. He begins by charting the natural development of the *polis*. People naturally form families or households (*oikia*), which is the simplest political unit. The household arises from two relations: male and female, and master and slave. These are natural relations because they arise from two instincts: the desire to procreate, and the instinct for self-preservation (1252a26–34).

The village is formed from a community of several households, and the natural extension of the village is the *polis*. Individually, people lack self-sufficiency, and so they combine to form increasingly complex associations, from household to village, until the only self-sufficient community is reached, namely, the *polis*. The *polis* is the association or community capable of self-sufficiency. Aristotle says that it exists for the sake of the good life of its citizens.

One of Aristotle's key ideas developed in Book I is that the *polis* is a natural entity. The basis of this idea is his claim that humans are by nature political. By this he means, in part, that by nature we live in groups. He also means that we work together for common goals. We aren't simply gregarious, as other animals are: our sense of community goes deeper due to our capacity for rational speech. Because of this capacity we can perceive the good, and hence, common goods such as justice (1252a15–20).

In claiming that the *polis* is a *natural* entity, Aristotle is denying that it is purely conventional. It is not artificial. In this sense, we might contrast Aristotle's views with those of Hobbes's *Leviathan* (1651). Hobbes claims that, in a state of nature, individuals live solitary lives and that, for the sake of survival, they agree to a social contract according to which they are governed by a king. According to Hobbes, this is the way in which the state is formed and justified. There are several points of difference between the two thinkers. The first is that, according to Hobbes, the state is an artificial creation; it is not a natural entity as it is for Aristotle. The second contrast is that, for Hobbes, in a state of nature prior to the social contract, people lived as individuals and not in social groups. In contrast, Aristotle stresses our lack of self-sufficiency both physically and psychologically. Individuals who live alone are either beasts or gods. Humans live naturally in groups. Third, although Aristotle might agree with Hobbes that the *polis* is formed for the sake of self-preservation, Aristotle's account of the formation of the state is fundamentally different from his. Aristotle stresses continuously that the historical process by which the state is formed is a natural one, based on our nature as political animals. Finally, Aristotle doesn't limit the function of the city-state to its sources or origins. It exists for the sake of the *eudaimonia* of its citizens.

For Aristotle, the *polis* is a natural entity. His argument for this conclusion (at 1252b27–1253a4) seems to be:

1. Something is natural if it develops naturally (that is, according to an inner principle of change) from something natural, and towards an end that is complete or self-sufficient.
2. The city-state develops naturally in stages, according to an inner principle of change, from the household.
3. The household has its basis in natural instinctive relations.
4. The development of the city-state has an end that includes self-sufficiency.

---

5. Therefore, the city-state is natural.

Aristotle also argues that the *polis* is prior in nature to the individual (1253a19). He says that the whole is prior to the parts, comparing the relationship of the individual to the state with that of functioning organs to the living body.

The analogy is unfortunate. Since a hand has no interests beyond contributing to the functioning of the organism as a whole, the analogy would imply that the individual has no interests beyond their contribution to the state. In fact, Aristotle doesn't adopt such a totalitarian approach.[21] On the contrary, he stresses that the state exists for the sake of the good life of its citizens, and he argues that the free person cannot be ruled over by a master. A state is a community of freemen (1279a22).

Slaves

Aristotle defines a slave as property that is an assistant for action. Being property, a slave does not belong to himself. At the start of chapter 5 Book I, Aristotle asks whether there are any natural slaves. He answers that the natural slave is capable of listening to reason but does not *have* reason, echoing the distinction between the two parts of reason drawn in the *Nicomachean Ethics*. Natural slaves lack the deliberative part of the soul, and thus are:

> Those people who are as different from others as body is from soul or beast from human, and people whose task, that is to say, the best thing to come from them, is to use their bodies. (1254b16–18)

The natural slave is to be contrasted with the natural master who has full possession of reason. In chapter 6 of Book I, Aristotle also distinguishes the natural slave from the slave by law. This distinction suggests that Aristotle might have been, or at least could have been, critical of the institution of slavery in the Athens of his time: the fact that people are legally slaves does not mean that this is their natural condition.[22] On the other hand, Aristotle thinks that the people of Greek descent are superior to foreigners from the North and East partly because of climatic conditions. In short, he thinks that only the Greeks tend to have both the spirit of independence of the peoples from the North and the intelligence of the peoples from the East. These passages suggest that Aristotle thinks that some peoples are more apt to be natural slaves.[23]

Male–Female

According to Aristotle, the household involves the subordination of women to men. He thinks that, in general, the deliberative part of the soul of a woman "lacks authority" (126013), and consequently women ought to be ruled by men.

Of course, Aristotle's views about women and slaves have attracted much critical comment. One of the issues that needs to be considered is whether these views are integral to his political philosophy or whether they can be set aside, leaving the rest of his philosophy more or less intact. There are different concerns to be addressed in thinking about this question. First, there is the ethical claim that the highest and happiest life is one of contemplation. Does this view of the human function already imply implicitly the claim that the happiest life is reserved for the few people who have the education and who can afford the time to exercise the virtue *sophia*? Second, can Aristotle's naturalism about the growth and nature of political institutions survive criticisms of his views about women and slaves? Can such naturalism provide adequate grounds for claims about the political equality of all persons? Third, can Aristotle's account of the ideal state be made exempt from criticisms of his views about slaves and women?

KINDS OF CITY-STATES

Book III attempts to answer the question, "Who should govern?" Aristotle begins by defining a *polis* as a community of citizens, and a constitution as the way they allocate powers. A citizen is a person who is eligible to participate in the policy making and judiciary of the city-state (III, 1, 1275b20). Aristotle notes, however, that what counts as good citizenship and the relevant virtues depends on the kind of *polis* in question. Different city-states have different conceptions of the civic virtues and of the required education for citizenship.

For these reasons, at Book III, 7, Aristotle classifies the different kinds of city-states. First, we can follow the traditional classification according to the numbers of the governing class: one, few, or many. But, second, we can also classify according to whether or not the *polis* is deviant.

We should think of a *polis* as a community of free people, and it is not comparable to the rule of a master. Thus, the constitution of a city should be directed towards the common good. For this reason, city-states that are directed towards the benefit of the rulers are deviant (1279a16–21).

On this basis, we arrive at six forms of government. The three directed towards the benefit of everyone are: kingship (rule by one), aristocracy (rule by few) and polity (rule by many). The corresponding deviant forms are: tyranny (monarchy for the benefit of the king), oligarchy (the rich ruling for the benefit of the rich), and democracy (the poor ruling for the benefit of the poor). Aristotle makes it clear that the key idea in the deviant forms is the aim and wealth of the governing class rather than merely the size of the governing class. It just so happens that everywhere the rich are few, the poor are many.

Most fundamentally, these constitutions have different aims, mainly because they have different conceptions of the good life and of justice (III, 9). To see this, let us consider the contrast between an oligarchy and a democracy. First, the oligarchy sees the principal aim of the state as the increasing of wealth. Consequently, the poor should have no power in the city, being ignorant in these matters. In contrast, in a democracy the main aim of the state is to promote the freedom of the people. Consequently, power should reside with the many. Second, based on this difference, justice is differently conceived in the two kinds of state. Aristotle says it is generally agreed that justice consists in awarding political power according to one's contribution towards the aims of the state.

However, the city-states differ in their understanding of these aims, and consequently they have varying conceptions of justice. The oligarchy thinks that the rich deserve more benefits because their merit is greater: they contribute more to the wealth of the city. The democrat thinks that the many deserve at least as much as the rich because, as citizens, they are equal.

Aristotle tries to show that both of these views are incorrect, fundamentally because they involve a mistaken view of living well and its relation to the city. The good life does not consist of increased wealth or freedom to do as one wants. Therefore, the city is not merely an instrument for wealth or self-protection. The good life is excellent or virtuous activity. The city is an organization that is dedicated to the living well of a community as a whole. There is a shared goal, which is the common good. Thus, the statesmen who run the city must have the required virtues and wisdom to understand and achieve this common good.

In Book III, Aristotle is working under the realistic assumption that the city will *not* be composed only of virtuous people (III, 4, 1276b37). Under this assumption, Aristotle thinks that, of the three correct constitutions, the best ones are those managed by the most virtuous person or group of people (III, 18). In other words, so long as the people in charge are truly virtuous, Aristotle concludes that kingship and aristocracy are a better form of government than polity or the rule of the many. He favors these two on the grounds that it is easier to find the highest virtues in the few rather than in the many. The relevant criterion is that the leaders should have a virtuous quality and a good understanding of human well-being. Aristotle also suggests that kingship would be the best constitution, but only if the monarch were like a god or a hero (III, 13, 1284a10–11). Since this condition is not readily fulfilled, it seems that aristocracy is the best constitution.

However, these conclusions about kingship and aristocracy assume that not everyone is virtuous and understands happiness; Aristotle has not yet constructed the profile of the ideal *polis*, free of this limiting assumption.

The Ideal City-State

In Books VII–VIII, Aristotle constructs a vision for the most ideal form of government. He starts from the premise that the happy life is one of virtue and that theoretical contemplation is the most valuable form of activity for humans. He says:

> What is most choice-worthy for each individual is always this: to attain what is highest. (1333b30)

Ideally, a political organization should make the highest activity available as much as possible.

> It is evident that the best constitution must be that organization in which anyone might do best and live a blessedly happy life. (1324a24)

In chapter 4 of Book VII, Aristotle begins to examine the necessary conditions for the existence of the ideal city-state. He argues that the city-state must not be excessive in size because the ideal state must be well organized: the limit in size is "the greatest size of multitude that promotes life's self-sufficiency, and that can be easily surveyed as a whole." For the best state, the population should be both spirited and intelligent. They should be equally capable of governing and being governed.

Under these ideal conditions, the power of the city should reside with the assembly of all citizens, and because they are equals, all of them would take turns in occupying the offices of the city (1329a2–4). This kind of arrangement fits well with what Aristotle says in Book I of the *Nicomachean Ethics* (*NE*, 10947b7–10): *eudaimonia* for the individual requires a life directed by *phronesis*, and the highest exercise of practical wisdom is in the state. Human wisdom requires that we participate in a self-governing community of equals. This arrangement also fits with the ideals implicit in the definitions of the *polis* and citizen, given at the start of Book III: the *polis* is a community of citizens, and citizens are eligible to participate in the deliberations and judiciary of the city.

However, the participatory arrangements of the ideal *polis* of Book VII seem to conflict with the conclusions of Book III, namely, that kingship or aristocracy is preferable to a polity. The difference may be due in part to the fact that the rule of the many is desirable only under the ideal conditions that every citizen is equally virtuous. When the city is *not* composed of equally virtuous people, as in Book III, then kingship or aristocracy is preferable.[24] But when everyone is equal, the many should rule (1332b26–9). Three important comments about this apparent conflict follow.

First, underlying the conflict between Books III and VII is the fact that Aristotle appeals to two very different political principles: first, the best forms of constitution involve the governance by the most virtuous rulers or statesmen; and second, the idea that the *polis* is a participatory community. These two principles are in conflict except under the ideal condition when the ruler and ruled are equal in virtue.[25]

Second, the issue is complicated by some remarks in Book IV, which suggest that Aristotle favors a mixed constitution with elements from different constitutions (IV, 8, 1294a9–29).[26] In other words, such a mixed constitution would recognize both the rich and the poor in assigning political roles.

Third, the rule of the many only applies to citizens. Aristotle excludes women, slaves, and manual workers from being citizens in his ideal city. The latter are excluded on the grounds that their work has not allowed them to develop their reason and the virtues. Furthermore, in Aristotle's ideal *polis*, the necessary economic production is the responsibility of the non-citizens, who are excluded from political participation.

Citizens enjoy leisure only because the women, the slaves, and the resident aliens do all the work in the *polis*.

Much of Books VII and VIII is dedicated to describing the education of citizens. However, Aristotle does not prescribe an education devoted to producing philosophers, as Plato does.

Commentary

Aristotle's politics largely circumvents one of the main issues of modern political theory, namely the justification for the authority of the state. What right does the state have to impose demands on us? What obligations do we have towards the state? These questions arise from a set of presuppositions and concepts quite different from Aristotle's. They assume that the individual has rights, primarily a right to freedom. The modern questions also assume that we have duties or obligations to the state, and that the state is external to its citizens. These assumptions don't get a grip on Aristotle's conception of the *polis*. For him, the city is ideally a community of self-governing individuals, who enable each other to live excellently.

THE *POETICS*

Aristotle's aim is to investigate the poetic craft, its power, and how plots should be composed. The *Poetics* is concerned with the fictional or dramatic work of the time, especially the epic and the tragedy. The work begins with a survey of different kinds of poetry and artistic imitation (chapters 1–3) and a history of the development of artistic imitation (chapters 4–6). Most of the work is concerned with tragedy (chapters 6–22). There follows a discussion of the epic (chapters 23–24), literary criticism (chapter 25), and a comparison of epic and tragedy. Part of the work is lost, including the second book, on comedy.[27]

Art as Imitation

In chapter 1, the different modes of art are mimetic or imitations. Aristotle classifies poetry in three ways, according to the means, the objects, and the manner of imitation. In terms of the means of representation Aristotle mentions: language, rhythm, and melody, or some combination of these. For instance, while instrumental music is mimesis through rhythm and melody, comedy, tragedy and lyrical poetry represent through rhythm, melody, and language. Aristotle claims that the objects of representation are actions, and their agents who are represented are good or bad. For example, comedy portrays a person as worse than average and tragedy as better (chapter 2). Within poetry, the manner of representation can be narrative, as in epic poems, or drama (as if the characters were really doing the things described).

It is important to note that, according to Aristotle, art as mimesis (or as an imitation of life) has two sources in human nature. First, as we see in babies, it is natural for us to imitate. Second, humans naturally love to learn, and therefore we take delight in imitation (chapter 4). Furthermore, as we saw in Book I, 1 *Metaphysics*, we love the senses for themselves, such as the perception of colors, tunes, and rhythm. From this point, Aristotle traces the development of different kinds of poetry, including epic poetry and drama, and comedy and tragedy, presumably to show how these art forms have their roots in our human nature.

Tragedy and Catharsis

At the beginning of chapter 6, Aristotle defines tragedy as the serious imitation of action in a plot of some magnitude and in a dramatic form, which accomplishes the catharsis of emotions such as pity and fear (chapter 6, 1449b22–1449b31).

He notes that it is primarily an imitation of actions rather than of characters. The plot of a tragedy must be complete and serious. To be complete, it must have a beginning, a middle, and an end; and to be a beautiful plot, it must be organic, like a living creature with an order in the arrangement of its parts (chapter 7, 1450b22–1451a15), with "its several incidents so closely connected that the transposition or withdrawal of any one of them will disjoin and dislocate the whole" (1451a30). To be a complex plot, it should include a reversal of fortune and a discovery (chapter 10, 1452a13–1452a21). To evoke the relevant emotions of pity and or fear, the plot should involve the downfall of a good person (chapter 11) through the actions of friends or family (chapter 14, 1453b12–1453b37).

Over the generations, readers have puzzled what Aristotle means by *catharsis*. In its most basic version Aristotle is portrayed as claiming that a tragedy must cause feelings of pity and/or fear in the audience, and through this, the play must purify them. In part, the problem is that the two terms (*catharsis* and *purification*) have both ritualistic and moral implications, and one might wonder which of the two kinds of implications requires the most emphasis. Furthermore, the idea of purification might be seen to imply that such emotions are impurities that one needs to shed. We might question whether this implication fits Aristotle's understanding of the emotions. If it doesn't, then how should we understand *catharsis*? Is it the release from an excess of such emotions? Is it a clarification of such emotions?[28]

∾
Conclusion

The central idea of Aristotle's *Ethics* is that happiness is the ultimate end, and it consists in the activities of the soul in accordance with virtue or excellence. Virtue must be defined in terms of the good for the kind of being in question. The human way of being necessarily includes various spheres of life, for each of which there corresponds a virtue that lies between two extremes.

These activities are defined by the human function which Aristotle identifies as reason or *logos*. In humans, the animal aspect of the soul, which is concerned with desires and emotions, is capable of responding to reason even it isn't directly rational. The ethical virtues concern the functioning of these aspects of the human function. The intellectual virtues concern the excellent functioning of reason. The main intellectual practical virtue is practical wisdom or *phronesis*. It guides practical reasoning and the ethical virtues. The main theoretical intellectual virtue is *sophia* or theoretical wisdom.

Aristotle claims that theoretical wisdom is a more valuable good than practical wisdom possibly because it involves cognition of the divine or eternal. In this way the activity of contemplation is the highest human activity. However, this doesn't necessarily mean that all the other human activities virtues and their corresponding virtues are merely means to contemplation.

The individual cannot attain happiness outside of the state because humans are social and political animals. The main goal of Aristotle's *Politics* is to describe the best kind of city-state and to characterize statesmanship, the political application of practical wisdom. After identifying six main types of government (kingship, aristocracy, polity, and tyranny, oligarchy and democracy) Aristotle argues that, in the ideal city state, the power of the city should reside with the assembly of all citizens, who would take turns in occupying the offices of the city. This type of government is a polity. According to Aristotle, it requires that the majority of the citizens are virtuous.

Study Questions

1. How does Aristotle argue for the claim that *eudaimonia* is the most valuable end?
2. How does Aristotle characterize *eudaimonia* in terms of the human function?
3. How does Aristotle support the claim that the good life consists of activities that accord with virtue?
4. How does Aristotle distinguish intellectual and ethical virtue?
5. What is the meaning of his claim that a virtue is a mean?
6. What are the 10 virtues that Aristotle lists? How does he arrive at that list? What is missing from the list?
7. What is Aristotle's main point with regard to the nature of responsibility?

Chapter Twelve—Aristotle: Ethics, Politics, and Poetics   321

8. What is *phronesis* or practical wisdom? Why is it important for Aristotle's ethical theory?
9. What is the practical syllogism?
10. What are the intellectual virtues? What is *sophia*? Why is it more valuable than *phronesis*?
11. How does Aristotle answer the question "How is incontinence possible?"
12. How does Aristotle classify friendship? What is the point of this classification?
13. According to Aristotle, what is the relationship between an activity and pleasure?
14. How does Aristotle characterize *eudaimonia* in Book X of the *Nicomachean Ethics*?
15. What is the difference between an exclusive and inclusive understanding of *eudaimonia*?
16. How can we best reconcile Book I and Book X of the *Nicomachean Ethics* with regard to *eudaimonia*?
17. How does Aristotle argue that the *polis* is a natural entity?
18. How does Aristotle classify the different kinds of state?
19. How does Aristotle characterize the ideal city-state?
20. When citizens are not equally virtuous, what is the best form of government?
21. What does Aristotle say about slavery?
22. How does Aristotle characterize art?
23. How does Aristotle describe tragedy?
24. How does Aristotle characterize catharsis?

Discussion Questions

1. In principle, could we provide a rule that defines what would count as a virtuous act? How would Aristotle answer this question? If such a rule is impossible, what implications would this have for ethics?
2. Is Aristotle right to define *eudaimonia* in terms of the *distinctive* function (or *ergon*) of humans?
3. Aristotle defines the ideal city-state in terms of the participation of citizens and in terms of the virtues of the rulers. Can these two characterizations be reconciled?

The Virtues

SPHERE	VIRTUE	EXCESS	DEFICIENCY
Fear	Courage	Rashness	Cowardice
Pleasure and pain	Temperance	Licentiousness	Insensibility
Spending (minor)	Generosity	Prodigality	Illiberality
Spending (major)	Magnificence	Vulgarity	Pettiness
Honor (major)	Magnanimity	Vanity	Pusillanimity
Honor (minor)	Proper ambition	Ambition	Unambitiousness
Anger	Mildness	Irascibility	Lack of spirit
Self-expression	Truthfulness	Boastfulness	Understatement
Conversation	Wittiness	Buffoonery	Boorishness
Social conduct	Friendliness	Obsequiousness	Cantankerousness

PART IV

Introduction to Hellenistic and Roman Philosophy

*I*n 323 BC, Alexander the Great died. A year later, Aristotle passed away. In nine years, Alexander, who had been Aristotle's most well-known pupil, had conquered much of the known world, as far east as the Indus River. These events mark the end of the classical Greek period and the demise of Greece as a collection of autonomous city-states. They denote the beginning of the so-called Hellenistic period, which lasted until the second century BC. During this time, Greece was no longer a collection of self-ruling cities but rather a small part of a large empire.

Although the schools established by Plato (the Academy) and Aristotle (the Lyceum) continued working during this period, the content of their work was often quite different from what it was when Plato and Aristotle were alive. Hellenistic philosophy consists of thought that is in many ways independent of Plato and Aristotle. This means that Hellenistic philosophy can be seen in part as a continuation of the Pre-Socratic or early ancient Greek traditions.

However, there is a very important addition. The main Hellenistic philosophers also draw deep inspiration from Socrates, but *not* through the lineage of Plato and Aristotle. For example, the Cynic movement derives from Antisthenes, who was a companion of Socrates according to the Socratic dialogues of Xenophon. The Cynics take from Socrates the key idea that virtue is living in accordance with nature. However, they interpret this in a way that is very different from Aristotle. According to Cynics, to live in accordance with nature should be understood as rejecting the arbitrary nature of convention or *nomos*. So, for example, according to Diogenes of Sinope, this rejection of convention involves redefining what is worthy of shame. Diogenes denies the idea that one should feel shame when one performs bodily functions in public, including, for instance, masturbation. Living in accordance with nature requires overthrowing and transcending convention.

Likewise, Diogenes is well known for his fearless truth-telling or *parrhēsia*. According to legend, Alexander the Great approached Diogenes when Diogenes was enjoying the sun. Alexander asked Diogenes what he might want, and Diogenes replied that Alexander should "stand out of my light."[1] There is a similar story regarding Diogenes and Plato: when Plato saw Diogenes washing lettuces, Plato said to him that if he had paid court to Dionysius (the ruler of Syracuse in Sicily) then he wouldn't be washing lettuces. Diogenes replies immediately to Plato: if you had washed lettuces then you wouldn't have had to pay court to Dionysius.[2]

These stories bring out two aspects of Cynic philosophy relevant to understanding Hellenistic thought generally, and its Socratic roots. First, the Cynics value *eleutharia* or freedom, and *autarkeia* or self-sufficiency. The idea of being able to tell the truth frankly and fearlessly (*parrhēsia*) is part of this personal freedom from authority. This emphasis on individual moral development is a very important theme in Hellenistic thinking, which has its source in Socrates.

Second, the Cynics affirm the view that practice matters more than theory. Many Hellenistic philosophers treat the kind of metaphysical questions discussed by the early ancient philosophers as secondary to the fundamental question, which is how one should live. Philosophy should serve life, which means the individual's quest to be free. The Cynics advocate *askēsis*, a constant training to be free from the false demands of custom. Just like Socrates before him, Diogenes walked barefoot in the snow and lived simply in order to be free from the commodities that are mistakenly thought to be needs. Philosophical ideas are only important insofar as they serve or facilitate this kind of practice.

These two aspects of Cynicism directly influenced Stoicism. They are also indicative of the broad spirit of the age. In summary, some of the important elements of Hellenistic thought draw inspiration from Socrates, but not through the lineage of Plato and Aristotle.

The Three Main Branches

Hellenistic philosophy has three main branches that are of special interest: Epicureanism, Stoicism, and Skepticism. Although Epicureanism and Stoicism were both founded in Athens, Hellenistic philosophy was not concentrated solely in Athens or even mainland Greece. There were centers of learning in other parts of the empire, including Alexandria in Egypt and Rhodes.

Epicurus (341–270 BC) was born in Samos, the birthplace of Pythagoras, but he established his school, the Garden, in Athens around 307 BC. To better understand the ethical teaching of Epicureanism, we need to examine the poem of Lucretius (99–55 BC), *On the Nature of Things*, in addition to the writings of Epicurus himself.

Zeno of Citium (334–262 BC) founded Stoicism around 300 BC under a porch or *stoa* in the marketplace of Athens. Because there are only fragments concerning the thought of Zeno, to understand Stoicism we need to examine the work of later writers: Seneca (4 BC–65 AD), Epictetus (55–135 AD), and the Emperor Marcus Aurelius (121–180 AD).

Pyrrho of Elis (367–275 BC) inspired the movement that has his name: Pyrrhonism or Pyrrhonean skepticism. This philosophy is first articulated in writing by Sextus Empiricus (175–225 AD). There are also some fragments concerning Pyrrho himself.

Although we will focus on these three movements, by no means do they exhaust Hellenistic thought. For instance, there is the Academic skepticism developed in Plato's Academy under Arcesilas (315–241 BC) and Carneades (213–129 BC), which we discuss in chapter 15. There is also Cynicism, which we mentioned earlier. There are other so-called "minor Socratic schools" such as the Cyrenaic and the Megaric, founded respectively by Aristippus of Cyrene (c. 435–356), and Eucleides of Megara (c. 450–380).

The Cyrenaic school embraced a strong form of hedonism according to which bodily pleasures are preferable to mental ones, and according to which we have reason only to pursue our own present pleasure as opposed to the pleasure of others and one's own future pleasure. This hedonism was influential on Epicurus in the sense that he tried to develop a form of hedonism that avoided the problems and extremism inherent in the egoistic present-moment hedonism of the Cyrenaics (see chapter 13).

The Cyrenaics were also what we call today "skeptical empiricist philosophers." This means that they think we have access only to our own private experiences, and consequently, that we don't know what causes those experiences. This view influenced the Pyrrhonean skeptics, as we shall see in chapter 15.

Their Common Features

Do Epicureanism, Stoicism, and Pyrrhonism have common elements? First, despite the differences between them, these three major schools share the central aim of showing why it is important for the individual to attain inner peace or happiness, and how to do so. This is an aim that is also inherited from Socrates. It is the idea that philosophy concerns the health of the soul. As Martha Nussbaum stresses, this implies that Hellenistic philosophy has at its roots a medical analogy of the soul and a view of philosophical practice as therapy, especially as applied to desire and emotion.[3]

Second, the political thought of Hellenistic philosophy is quite different from that of Plato and Aristotle, for whom ethics is more intimately connected with the politics and institution of the city-state. According to both Plato and Aristotle, the city-state provides a community governed by a wise elite so that people will attain a flourishing life insofar as they can. In contrast, the Hellenistic schools are at the same time more individualistic and more egalitarian. Each person works through his or her own journey towards tranquility, as equals within a framework of the institutions of the Empire. The Hellenistic thinkers tend to emphasize how the individual must practice personal detachment from the desire for wealth, and they tend to think less about how to reform the sociopolitical institutions for the sake of happiness. In these ways, while it would be mistaken to think of Hellenistic thought as apolitical, nevertheless it is more individualistic and less directly political than the communitarian thought of Plato and Aristotle.[4]

It is important to note that, in the case of Stoicism, this greater individualism, when coupled with the claim that only virtue is good and that social status is irrelevant, entails some form of egalitarianism. A slave and an emperor are equally possessors of reason, and their social status is irrelevant with respect to the good, virtue. They are naturally equals. Again, in the case of Stoicism, the egalitarian claim that all people should be treated as equals leads to a cosmopolitan view, namely, that all people should be regarded equally as citizens of the world. This Stoic claim has its roots in Cynicism and Socrates. When asked where he was from, Diogenes famously replied: "I am a citizen of the world." In contrast, Plato and Aristotle seem to be committed to the idea that a person's political affiliation, commitment, and identity should be tied primarily to the city-state.[5]

The individualism of Hellenistic philosophy is perhaps more fitting for a large empire in which individual happiness cannot depend deeply on a small self-governing community, such as a city-state.[6] Perhaps in part for these reasons, both Epicureanism and Stoicism continued to attract followers in the Roman period. Stoicism in particular had great influence on the thought and social life of Rome. In some ways, it became almost like a religion in Rome.

Third, another feature of Hellenistic philosophy is that metaphysics and science play a less central role than they do in the thought of Aristotle, Plato, and the earlier Greek thinkers. Nevertheless, both the Epicureans and the Stoics devote considerable effort to natural philosophy; indeed, in some ways they seem to continue the naturalist tradition of the Pre-Socratics. However, this claim needs to be qualified in two ways. First, both the Epicureans and the Stoics do draw on elements of the philosophies of Plato and Aristotle. They don't merely return to the earlier naturalistic traditions of the Pre-Socratics. Second, the Epicureans' and the Stoics' primary concern is individual happiness or tranquility. Natural philosophy should serve this interest because our happiness depends on the nature of the universe we live in, or at least on our understanding it properly. In other words, for both the Epicureans and Stoics, natural philosophy should serve the primary aim of helping the individual to attain tranquility.

In conclusion, the three major types of Hellenistic philosophy do have some common features. Although it has roots in the early ancient philosophy of the Pre-Socratics, it draws much inspiration from Socrates, quite independently of Plato and Aristotle.

Back to History

In 196 BC, Rome defeated Macedonia and began to conquer the eastern Mediterranean. By 188 BC, Rome was the power of the Mediterranean, and in 146 BC Greece became a protectorate of Rome. The last bastion of the Hellenistic empire was Ptolemic Egypt, which fell with the defeat of Cleopatra in 31 BC.

By the time Augustus established the Roman Empire in 30 BC, the initial period of Hellenistic philosophy was at an end. Soon afterwards, Christianity began to spread over the Empire. Plotinus (204–270 AD) developed a new interpretation of Plato, which became known as Neo-Platonism, and which became a rival to Christianity in the fourth century. By the third century AD, the cities, which were once the cultural centers of the Roman Empire, began to collapse economically due to the pressures of financing constant military campaigns. Many of the wealthier citizens fled to escape the steadily rising taxes; health standards began to deteriorate and, within a fairly short period, about a third of the population died either from wars or the plague. The militaristic elements of the Roman Empire gained supreme power, even over the emperors.

This disintegration of the Roman Empire was due largely to the continuous attacks by German tribes from the north and the Persians from the east. Finally, in 529 the Emperor Justinian closed the four philosophical schools in Athens (the Academy, the Lyceum, the Garden, and the Stoa), which were already only remnants of a bygone age.

The Texts

As with the early ancient philosophers, to know the thinking of the Hellenistic philosophers we have to rely largely on a few surviving fragments and on the testimonial of later writers. We do have summaries of Epicurus's letters and of his *Principal Doctrines*, and fragments from his work *On Nature*. However, we do not have writings from any of the early Stoic thinkers except for some fragments and reports from later writers, such as Diogenes Laërtius. Since later Stoic thinking differs from the early philosophy, there is uncertainty as to how and to what extent one can trust these later reports. Furthermore, the later summaries tend to provide us with doctrines but less often with the arguments for those conclusions. The situation is similar with respect to Pyrrho. Apart from some reports, we have to rely largely on the Roman Sextus Empiricus to understand Pyrrhonean skepticism, which makes it difficult to know the differences between Pyrrho's thought and that of Sextus.

Cicero, the great Roman statesman and orator (106–43 BC), wrote several philosophical works, in addition to his famous speeches and letters. These works are an important source for our knowledge of Hellenistic thinking. But Cicero was a philosopher in his own right, and one needs to remember that he had his own agenda to pursue, which influenced his reports of earlier writers.[7] He was critical of Epicureanism.

Plutarch (AD 46–120) was a Greek historian, biographer, and writer who became a Roman citizen. He is famous for his *Parallel Lives*, which sketches the lives of famous Greeks and Romans. He is critical of both Epicureanism and Stoicism, being Platonic in his philosophical approach.

As we mentioned in the introduction to Part I, sometime after 100 AD Aetius wrote a *Placita* summarizing the views of the early philosophers, which was lost. However, it formed the basis of two later doxographies: that of pseudo-Plutarch (third to fourth century AD) and Stobaeus (fifth century AD), which contain testimonies referring to the Hellenistic thinkers.

Diogenes Laërtius (third century AD) is the author of *The Lives of the Philosophers*. Very little is known about the life of Diogenes. However, his text is an important source of information about the lives of the philosophers, even though many of the stories he tells are probably false or exaggerated. Diogenes is a very important source of material from Epicurus, and also of Pyrrhonism.

The standard collection of Hellenistic philosophical sources is the one edited by A. A. Long and D. N. Sedley in two volumes, first published in 1987.[8] In this work, the selections from the original texts are organized thematically. Brad Inwood and L. P. Gerson's *Hellenistic Philosophy: Introductory Readings* is organized according to the sources.[9] So, for instance, in Long and Sedley, Epicurus's *Letter to Heredotus* is divided and the parts positioned according to their content; in Inwood and Gerson, the letter is given as a single piece.

13

Epicureanism
Epicurus and Lucretius

After the demise of Athenian democracy, Greek philosophy took a new turn. In a less democratic political climate, several thinkers searched for conceptions of the ethical life less explicitly and directly linked to political ideals. For example, Epicureanism is a philosophy dedicated to the pursuit of individual happiness through the cultivation of a state of tranquility achieved through freedom from desire. The concern for the good life and tranquility is central to the three philosophies we examine in this part, and in each case this concern tends to take precedence over more traditional metaphysical and epistemological questions. For example, drawing inspiration from the early atomists, such as Democritus, Epicurus argues for atomism. However, he does so mainly for the reason that this metaphysics is required to free persons from superstitious fears. Natural philosophy should help the individual attain happiness rather than be an end in itself. Epicureanism became popular in Greece, and to some extent in Rome, and its most famous exponent was the great Latin poet Lucretius (99–55 BC), whose poem *On the Nature of Things* preserved and popularized Epicurus's ideas for a Roman audience.

EPICURUS (341–270 BC)

Epicurus was born in Samos, the birthplace of Pythagoras. At the age of 18, he moved to Athens to serve for two years in the military, after which he taught near his hometown. In 307 BC, at the age of 35, he returned to Athens to establish a philosophical school, known as the Garden, which was open to women and persons from all social classes including slaves. It was not only an academic institution, but also a community of persons dedicated to living in accordance with Epicurean principles. He remained in the city until his death, living simply and quietly.

Epicurus was a prodigious writer but, unfortunately, not much of his work survives. We have three letters to his disciples, two collections of his doctrines, and various papyrus rolls, in addition to various fragments and reports.[1]

Diogenes Laërtius's *Lives of the Philosophers* devotes the whole of Book 10 to Epicurus. As well as describing his life, it includes the three letters and a collection of 40 of Epicurus's doctrines. Also, Diogenes summarizes in his own words some of Epicurus's main doctrines. Epicurus's letter to Herodotus contains an overall summary of Epicurus's philosophy. The letter to Pythocles contains a description of Epicurus's views on astronomy, and the letter to Menoeceus outlines Epicurus's ethical system.

The papyrus rolls are from the library of a first-century BC Roman Epicurean, Philodemus, who worked in Herculaneum. These rolls were preserved in liquid mud, now solidified, when Vesuvius erupted in 79 AD. From this source, we have some fragments of Epicurus's *On Nature*, which was his principal work, as well as works by other Epicureans such as Philodemus himself.

In the second century AD, Diogenes of Oenoanda, which is now in Southern Turkey, built a portico which has inscribed some of Epicurus's doctrines, including the famous Epicurean fourfold remedy: "God is not to be feared, death should cause no apprehension and the good is easily obtained, the terrible easily endured." As sources, we also have various fragments from non-Epicureans such as Cicero, Plutarch, Seneca, Sextus Empiricus, and various Greek commentators on Aristotle.[2] Of special importance is Lucretius's poem *De Rerum Natura*, or *On The Nature of Things*, which expounds Epicureanism, and which we discuss throughout this chapter.

Epicurus's philosophy covers three broad areas: a materialist metaphysics, an empiricist theory of knowledge, and a hedonistic ethic. Epicurus believes that philosophy should be primarily the search for individual happiness and that science, virtue, and knowledge are subservient to this search. He himself was supposed to have attained a state of real happiness and freedom from anxiety. He was considered by his followers to be "a god among men" and the founder of a new religion.

Physics

Let us start with the physics of Epicurus. As we have said, the main aim of his philosophy is to aid the individual in finding a happy life. His physics serves this purpose. He postulates that the universe consists only of material atoms and the void. This ontology is supposedly sufficient to explain natural events and psychological phenomena. According to Epicurus, understanding the exclusively physical nature of the universe is important for two reasons. First, it obviates the need for religious explanation and for extravagant metaphysics, and hence it helps us to avoid superstition that would disturb us. Second, he argues that this materialism requires denying the possibility of life after death; and thus it removes the fear and anxiety of divine punishment, which is one of the principal causes of unhappiness. This is the reason why the *Letter to Herodotus*, which outlines the basic doctrines of Epicurus, contains an exposition of his physics.

Like Leucippus and Democritus before him, Epicurus is an atomist (see chapter 3), He affirms that all bodies are either atoms or composites made up of atoms and void. In the *Letter to Herodotus*, Epicurus outlines an argument for this conclusion. He says that we need to be able to explain the objects of sense perception as simply as possible in accordance with various principles. These principles he lists as follows: nothing can come from what it is not; nothing can be destroyed; and there is nothing outside the universe to cause it to change (*Letter to Herodotus* [*LH*] 38–9). Since nothing can come from nothing, the basic constituents of the universe have always existed.

What could satisfy this requirement for a simple explanation of what we observe? The simplest explanation is that there are only two kinds of bodies: the basic constituents and the compounds that are formed out of them (*LH* 40)[3]. Of the basic constituents he says:

> And these are atomic and unchangeable, if indeed they are not all going to be destroyed into not being but will remain firmly during the dissolutions of compounds, being full by nature and not being subject to dissolution in any way or fashion. Consequently the principles of bodies must be atomic natures. (*LH* 41)

In brief, on the one hand, the existence of compounds is required to explain the facts that the things we perceive change and can be destroyed. On the other hand, the existence of indivisible, indestructible atoms is required to avoid the conclusion that everything can be infinitely divided into non-being.

Lucretius presents a different argument for the conclusion that the existence of indivisible atoms is necessary. Body and void must be mutually exclusive since they are two kinds of things. This means that body *as such* doesn't contain or include empty void. However, nothing can be divided unless it contains empty space. Therefore, anything that can be divided cannot be a simple body because it contains void. The divisible must be a complex. Because of this, there must be simples that don't contain void and cannot be divided. Hence, if anything exists then indivisible atoms do (Luc. I, 503–35).[4]

The void must exist because if all space were occupied, then solid objects would have no space to move into. There are an unlimited number of atoms and so the void is unlimited too (*LH* 42–44).

Epicurus was well aware of the criticisms of a purely materialistic ontology, and more specifically of atomism, directed against Democritus by Plato and Aristotle. Partly for this reason, his atomism has some important differences from that of Democritus. First, Democritus places no limits on the sizes and shapes that atoms might have. Epicurus does. In paragraph 56 of the *Letter to Herodotus*, he says that the atoms only need have the shapes and sizes required for explaining sensible qualities. In other words, Epicurus limits the shape and size of atoms according to the explanation of sense-experience. Democritus doesn't appeal to sense-experience. Lucretius adds to this point of difference. He says that if atoms could have an infinite number of shapes then there would be an indefinite number of sensible qualities, which there aren't (Luc. II, 500–521).

Second, Epicurus replies to a critique of atomism from Aristotle. As we saw in chapter 10, Aristotle rejects atomism arguing that space is continuous and infinitely divisible, and thus anything in space must be divisible, at least conceptually. It must be so, argues Aristotle, in order that any object is able to move across spatial boundaries. An object cannot cross a boundary all at once, and thus it must have parts.[5] Consequently, argues Aristotle, an atom without parts would not be able to move at all.

Probably in reply to this argument, Epicurus postulates ultimate minimal parts.[6] Lucretius also argues for minimal parts, which are the units of measurement, inseparable from the whole. As such, these minimal parts do not enter into physical interactions. Thus, according to the Epicureans, the atom cannot be physically divided or split, but it has notional parts. These minimal parts define a minimal unit of extension (*LH* 56–9). In other words, according to the Epicureans, space is not infinitely divisible.

Aristotle himself explores this idea as a possible reply to Zeno's paradoxes, but only to reject it. He argues that this solution would require that time too be granular, and that all motion would have to be in jumps of the same speed. In other words, the atom would have to pass from one minimal unit of space in one minimal unit of time all at once in a jump or jerk (*Physics* Book VI, 1). Thus, according to Aristotle, all atoms would have the same speed if space and time were granular.

Epicurus does ascribe to atoms the natural tendency to fall at a uniform velocity; this may indicate that he is accepting the point made by Aristotle.[7] Epicurus says:

> It is necessary that the atoms move at equal speed, when they move through the void and nothing resists them. For heavy things will not move faster than small and light ones when that is nothing stands in their way. (*LH* 61)

Although Epicurus doesn't explicitly cite avoiding Zeno's arguments as a reason for thinking that there must be minimal finite spatial units, nevertheless, parts of the *Letter to Herodotus* do strongly suggest this. As we saw in chapter 2, Zeno presents an argument to show that nothing can have parts: for if something did, then it would be infinitely divisible with infinite parts, each of which would have a size. The sum of an infinite number of magnitudes must be infinite, and so everything would have infinite size.

Apparently in order to reject a similar Zeno-like reasoning regarding mass, Epicurus says:

> As soon as one says that there is in some thing an unlimited number of masses, no matter how small, then one cannot think how this magnitude could any longer be limited. For obviously these unlimited masses must be of some size or other; and no matter how small they might be, the magnitude (of the whole object) would for all that be unlimited. (*LH* 57)

In other words, Epicurus is arguing that, in order to explain how things have finite mass, it is necessary that objects should not be infinitely divisible, which requires that there are minimal finite spatial units. In summary, the Epicureans hold that although atoms are physically indivisible, they have notional parts, but that there must be a minimal unit of space and time, smaller than which cannot be conceived.

Third, Epicurus apparently introduces the concept of the swerve of atoms, which is absent from the thought of Democritus. Lucretius makes the idea explicit. If atoms moved and fell only according to their weight, then they wouldn't interact with each other and couldn't form complexes or compounds. Free-falling atoms in the void wouldn't collide. To explain their collisions, we must suppose that they have a natural or spontaneous but tiny swerve (Luc. II, 184–293). Lucretius also says that this swerve is also necessary to explain the free actions and voluntary decisions of people. Furthermore, the concept of the swerve seems to be necessary for the Epicureans to oppose the view that all things happen by necessity, which was explicitly part of the philosophy of the Stoics, and perhaps of Democritus (DK68A1).[8]

Although Lucretius and other writers attribute the idea of the swerve to Epicurus, there is no evidence in his surviving works that he held such a view. Some recent commentators have speculated that Epicurus came to this idea late in life. Nevertheless, there is some evidence that Epicurus does hold that there is chance in the universe, which would fit with the idea of the atomic swerve.[9] The idea is that the universe isn't entirely mechanical, not in the sense that there are purposes or intelligent forces at work, but rather in the sense that spontaneous changes of direction can occur at the atomic level.

Even if Epicurus allows for chance or contingency in his physics, nevertheless, he claims that physical laws explain the order and regularities in the world. Again, this point is more explicit in Lucretius. At the level of aggregates, or as we would say today, at the macro-level, there are deterministic physical laws. Indeterminacy occurs only at the level of atoms and thus has no perceivable effect on dense solids, even if it has an effect on individual atoms and on the finer material of the soul.[10] Thus, even if there are atomic swerves, Epicurus nevertheless still has a mechanistic view of the universe, governed by natural laws, without the need for quasi-intelligent forces, such as Anaxagoras's *Nous* and Empedocles's Love and Strife (see chapter 3).

Epicurus's atomism challenges the metaphysics of Plato and Aristotle, both of whom see purposes and teleological explanation as essential for understanding the universe. Plato and Aristotle would regard a universe without purposes as impossible because it must be formless. Following the lead of Democritus, Epicurus answers this kind of objection based on the need for form by showing how atoms can aggregate and conjoin to form what we would regard as a solid object. All atoms move at the same speed, but when they collide and deflect each other's motions, they conjoin to form a solid object. Such compound bodies have properties, which the atoms from which they are made do not possess. Atoms have only shape, size, and weight.[11] Compounds have other properties.

To defend their theory, Epicureans need to show how it can explain in principle all natural phenomena, such as the formation of the planets, of living things and of conscious properties, such as perception and reasoning. However, Epicurus doesn't advocate that we should try to find the true cause and exact explanation of such phenomena. Such a search would cause anxiety and would defeat the main purpose of science. To avoid anxiety, it is enough to have a number of different plausible explanations that fit with the overall general atomistic theory and with sense-experience.

Like Democritus, Epicurus distinguishes the infinite universe as a whole from a cosmos, of which there are an unlimited number (*LH* 45). A cosmos is a "circumscribed" portion of the universe (*Letter to Pythocles* 88–9). It is a collection of stars and planets as a limited world. It is limited both in space and time. Both Epicurus and Lucretius reject the idea that a cosmos must have a particular shape, such as spherical. Furthermore, they reject the supposition that there must be a universal explanation of how the cosmoses have been formed, such as Democritus's swirling vortex (see chapter 3). However, they do argue that cosmoses are formed by conglomeration of atoms in a space that is largely void. Also they claim that this process requires "suitable seeds" to form the required structures. These "suitable seeds" are probably complex structures of atoms necessary for the causal laws to operate at a macro-level, such as the regular motion of planets.[12] Lucretius refers to seeds of fire and water. We should not take the term *seed* as indicating that there are biological purposes in the world. In a similar fashion, although both Epicurus and Lucretius use biological and poetic language to describe the birth, decay, and death of a cosmos, this does not mean that the cosmos has inherent purposes. It is formed only by blind mechanical processes.

The same point applies to the formation of living beings. Lucretius tries to explain why only members of the same species can interbreed in terms of fixed atomic structures. In other words, reproduction requires the suitable seeds that transmit the characteristics of the species to the offspring (Luc. I, 159–214). Also, this helps explain why members of species tend to grow according to fixed patterns, and why there are no hybrids of species. In each case, the reproductive seed can only interact appropriately with atoms of determinate and fixed shapes. Lucretius argues that such biological fixity is an argument for the unchanging nature of atoms. Epicurus also claims that species which were not well adapted for their environment would have perished and that only those that were well suited to the environment would have survived to reproduce.

According to Epicurus, the soul is composed of physical atoms; it is finely structured and diffused throughout the whole body. It is born, grows, and dies with the body. Epicurus thinks that the atoms of the soul most resemble those of "breath mixed with heat" (*LH* 63). However, the soul must consist of atoms that are even finer and more mobile than those of air (Luc. III, 238–40). Epicurus argues that the soul must be physical, because otherwise it would have to be void or nothing. Since it is changed by and affects changes in physical things, it cannot be immaterial. This is an important argument that can be represented as follows:

1. The soul is effected by and can affect the body.
2. Only physical things can cause interactions with other physical things.
3. Therefore, the soul is a physical thing.

It is worth noting that the materialism of the Epicureans had an important impact on the thinking of the early scientific philosophers of the Renaissance. Such ideas were nourishment for the early scientific philosophers who were struggling to break free of medieval scholasticism. For example, the philosopher rebel Bruno (1548–1600), who was burned at the stake for his heresy, was inspired by the materialism of Lucretius. Galileo noted that Lucretius challenged Aristotle's claim that a body falls in proportion to its weight. Epicurean thinking reached the zenith of its influence through the French philosopher Pierre Gassendi, who wrote three major works on Epicurus from 1647 to 1649, which were read by Hobbes, Locke, and Newton and which continued to have an important impact up to the French Enlightenment of the late eighteenth century.

The claim that the soul is material is important for the Epicureans. It is part of the basis of their argument that there is no reason for us to fear death. Given that death is the end of one's life, there is no reason to fear punishment or suffering in an afterlife. And given that death is the end of one's life, then it consists in not existing. Lucretius argues that not existing after having lived is no different from not existing prior to one's conception. In neither case is there reason for anxiety. In neither case can anything disturb or hurt us (Luc. III, 830–68). Death provides no reason for anxiety because if we are alive, then death is not present and when death is present, we do not exist. Either way it is irrelevant.[13]

Surprisingly, the Epicureans do not deny the existence of the gods. Epicurus thinks that the best explanation of why nearly everyone believes in the gods is that people have mental perceptions of the gods

(Cicero, *On the Nature of the Gods* 43–4). In other words, people are perceiving something. However, most popular religious beliefs are misconceived. In particular, according to Epicurus, the gods have no influence on human life. He argues for this conclusion on the basis that divine beings have the traditional properties of being immortal and supremely happy (*Letter to Menoeceus* [*LM*] 123). Such properties are incompatible with the involvement in human affairs because happiness requires uninterrupted tranquility. As we have seen, Epicurus also rejects the Aristotelian claim that divine beings are responsible for the movement of the stars and planets; such motions are mechanically caused. In summary, Epicurus argues for an atomistic materialism, which, together with a set of ethical principles, is designed to liberate humanity from the superstitious terrors of traditional Greek religion.

Given his atomistic ontology, Epicurus must assert that the gods are made of atoms. However, how then does he account for the immortality of the gods? Anything that is a compound must be destructible, as indeed is the human soul. So if the gods are made of atoms then they shouldn't be immortal. The best reply in the Epicurean texts is the report of Cicero that, according to the Epicureans, the gods lack solidity and numerical identity, and that the gods consist in innumerable atoms that flow towards them, which generate images that our intelligences pick up on (Cicero, op. cit., 49). In this way, the gods in Epicurean philosophy have been likened to waterfalls, constituted by a continuous flow.[14] These gods, constituted by constant flows of atoms, exist in the void between the cosmoses.

Theory of Knowledge

According to Epicurus, all knowledge is based on sense-perception. Towards the beginning of his *Letter to Herodotus*, Epicurus sets out his theory of perception. Perception consists of our having sensations or sense-impressions, such as color, sound, and smell, which are caused by objects that have those qualities. These sense-impressions are the conscious reception of the atoms emanated from the surfaces of solid objects around us. These atoms or emanations preserve the shape and other properties of the bodies and affect the sense organs accordingly. So, so long as this causal chain is not interrupted, the relevant sense organ will receive an impression that corresponds to the structure of the surface of the object perceived. Consequently, our sense-impressions generally will be reliable, so long as we do not add anything to this stimulus.

This last qualification is important. Epicurus distinguishes the receiving of impressions from the subsequent judgment that one makes about the object based on those impressions. He says:

> Falsehood or error always resides in the added opinion. . . . (*LH* 50)

Therefore, we should not confuse perception with fallible interpretation. To avoid false belief, we should believe truths based only on sense impressions that are clear. When impressions are blurred or confused, this is because the causal chain of atoms from the object to the sense organs has somehow been interrupted—for example, when the object is far away from us.

Diogenes Laërtius reports that in his *Canon*, a work that has since been lost, Epicurus provides three criteria for truth: sensation, preconception, and feelings. By *preconceptions* Epicurus means concepts, which are formed by the memory of repeated sensations of the same kind and which help us anticipate future impressions.

The Epicureans realize that their atomic theory requires a strong epistemology or theory of knowledge because atoms aren't directly perceived. When our judgments relate to objects that can be perceived, their truth is established by confirmation or their falsity by non-confirmation. In the case of things that cannot be perceived, beliefs can be infirmed or non-infirmed, which requires some connection between the hidden and the perceivable. For example, the existence of atoms is required to explain how compounds come into being even though they cannot be seen. Likewise, the existence of the void is required to explain how motion is possible even though it cannot be perceived.

Reason itself is founded on the senses. If one follows this theory of knowledge, then one will not quarrel with the senses and will have the confidence of a person who has well-formed conceptions.

Ethical Theory

Epicurus has a hedonistic ethics, according to which happiness is the sole intrinsic good (*LM* 128–9).[15] The happy life is one that is full of pleasure. According to Epicurus, pleasure is simply the absence of pain. In contrast, as we saw in chapter 7, according to Plato pleasure and pain are contraries: pleasure is a positive state distinct from the mere absence of pain. According to Epicurus, they are contradictories: pleasure is the absence of pain. There is no neutral state between the two.

Epicurus thinks that people have a natural and innate desire for pleasure. Nevertheless, we have to make rational choices about which pleasures to choose:

> Sometimes we pass up many pleasures when we get a larger amount of what is uncongenial from them. And we believe many pains to be better than pleasures when a greater pleasure follows for a long while if we endure the pains. So every pleasure is a good thing since it has a nature congenial to us but not every one is to be chosen. (*LM* 129)

Epicurus asserts that we must evaluate the sources of our pleasure and calculate which are the greatest.

In this regard, Epicurus distinguishes two kinds of pleasure, the most valuable of which is simply the absence of physical and mental pain. This he calls *static pleasure*. Pain is a disturbance from our natural state of pleasure, and freedom from such disturbances can be attained only through a state of nearly perfect tranquility. This static pleasure is like an enjoyment of one's well-being or of a state of complete freedom from pain in the body and disturbance in the mind (*LM* 131–2). This tranquility or lack of mental distress is called *ataraxia*. Freedom from physical pain is called *aponia*. In contrast, active pleasure comes from satisfying one's desires. Desires arise because of a perceived lack. For instance, one desires to eat fish, and the act of eating fish produces pleasurable sensations. Such kinetic or active pleasures are more short-lived than a sense of well-being that constitutes a static pleasure.

There are two other possible reasons why static pleasures are more valuable than active ones. The first has to do with the limits of pleasure. If one has calmness of mind and freedom from physical pain, then one has already reached the limit of happiness. One cannot add to it by pursuing other goods in the hope that they will bring more pleasure.

The second reason relates to desire. Epicurus distinguishes three types of desires. These are: (1) natural and necessary, (2) natural and unnecessary, and (3) groundless, which are neither natural nor indispensable (*PD* XXIX).[16] He divides natural and necessary desires into those that are necessary for life itself, for bodily health and for happiness (*LM* 127). Epicurus says that "the unwavering contemplation" of these distinctions helps us to refer every choice to "the health of the body and the freedom of the soul from disturbance" (*LM* 128). The basic point seems to be that desires or wants tend to disturb the natural calm of the body and mind (*PD* XVIII). Therefore, we should avoid cultivating groundless desires, and we should cultivate prudence in relation to unnecessary natural desires (*PD* XXVI). Once we have freedom from mental disturbance . . .

> all the mind's turmoil is removed since a creature has no need to wander as if in search of something it lacks, nor to look for some other thing by means of which it can replenish the good of the mind and the body. (*LM* 128)

In short, for the second and third kinds of desire, pleasure caused by the satisfaction of desire is less than that caused by the absence of desire.

Epicurus famously advocates a simple lifestyle. However, he does so purely on the grounds of prudence and not from ascetic or puritanical motives. He isn't against luxury or dynamic pleasures *per se*.[17] Rather he is against their cost, their potential damaging effects on *aponia* and *ataraxia* (*PD* X).

Epicurus's ethical theory is very different from that of Plato and Aristotle, who view virtue as a part or essential ingredient of *eudaimonia*. As we saw in chapter 12, for Aristotle, the exercise of virtue is constituted by the activities of the soul performed in an appropriately excellent way. So, *eudaimonia* is not simply a feeling of happiness or pleasure. It is more akin to excellent activity in accordance with our human nature. In contrast, for Epicurus, virtue is solely a means to happiness, and happiness is solely a feeling of pleasure, albeit of the static kind. Nevertheless, the virtues are very important for happiness. Epicurus stresses the primary need for prudence; the other virtues, such as nobility and justice, are necessary as contributors to prudence (*LM* 132). Prudence is primary as a virtue because we need judgment to evaluate the different sources of pleasure and pain, and because we need the capability to control our desires when these lead to "storms in the soul."

It is common to regard Epicurus's ethics as self-interested and individualistic. We need to be careful with regard to both of these claims. Is it self-interested? Clearly, Epicurus's ethics is self-interested in the sense that he regards the primary good of each individual to attain happiness. This aspect of his thought is evident in his treatment of justice. Epicurus regards the basis of justice as a social contract that serves the interests of all (*PD* XXVII). Justice is instrumentally valuable because it is a pact that we make to not harm each other (*PD* XXXIII). It promotes happiness, and in this sense it is generally the same for all political associations (*PD* XXXVI). In short, justice is not a good in itself. People do not have an intrinsic moral obligation to act justly. Instead, justice is a question of obeying rules that advance the happiness of all concerned. Rules or laws that satisfy this criterion of usefulness are just, and the wise person will obey them in order to secure tranquility for him or herself.

However, this self-interested aspect of Epicurus's theory needs to be balanced with his view of friendship. Epicurus claims that friendship is most important for living happily. He does so in a way that suggests that friendship is valuable for its own sake. Certainly, given the testimony of Cicero, it would be a travesty or oversimplification to say that Epicurus regards friends simply as a means to one's own pleasure.[18] This is because Epicurus thinks that friendship can require regarding the pleasure and interests of one's friend as equal to one's own (Cicero, *On Goals* I, 68). In this regard, Epicurus's view may require a subtle but important distinction. On the one hand, friendship is not to be regarded purely egoistically. It seems that, like Aristotle, Epicurus regards friendship as requiring one to recognize the interests of one's friend as reasons for action in themselves. Friendship requires altruism and self-sacrifice. Indeed Cicero reports that, according to Epicurus, a wise person "will have just the same feelings for his friend as for himself and will undertake the same labors for a friend's pleasure as he would for the sake of his own" (*On Goals* I, 68). On the other hand, Epicurus's views on friendship do not lead him to abandon his self-interested hedonism. Friendship is valuable because it is enjoyable. He claims that "it is more pleasant to confer a benefit than to receive it." How should we reconcile these two apparently contradictory claims? Cicero encapsulates this tension when he reports that because we cannot possibly secure stable and long-lasting pleasantness in our lives without friendship and cannot maintain friendship itself unless we cherish our friends as much as we do ourselves, it follows both that this kind of thing [i.e., empathy] does occur in friendship and that friendship is linked with pleasure. (*On Goals* I, 67)

While Epicurus's ethics is fundamentally based on hedonistic self-interest, his analysis of friendship shows that friendship can require one to recognize the interests of others and make them part of one's own interests.[19]

Is his ethics individualistic? In this regard, one might contrast Epicurus's views with those of Plato and Aristotle. While they regard living in a community as part and parcel of the virtuous and happy life, Epicurus's view seems more individualistic. For him, ethics is primarily a question of individual happiness. While this claim is true, nevertheless, it needs to be tempered with other points. First, we have already seen how Epicurus's analysis of friendship contradicts the idea that his ethics is individualistic. To be happy, one needs to have friends whom one cares about and for whom one would make sacrifices. Second, Epicurus doesn't advocate a withdrawal from society and its benefits. Although the *Letter to Menoeceus* suggests an individualistic approach, the *Principal Doctrines* indicate that Epicurus is well aware that the happy life requires the security and other benefits that a stable political state provides (*PD* XL). This is evident from his discussion of justice in the *Principal Doctrines*. Third, Epicurus famously advocates that one should "liberate oneself from . . . politics" (Vat. 58).[20] However, many contemporary scholars do not see this claim as expressing a disdain for all politics. Rather, Epicurus is advising that the wise person would steer clear of political life that is based on the desire for power and honor. Such ambitions would count as prime examples of groundless desires that lead to loss of tranquility. Indeed, if we combine what Epicurus says about friendship and justice, there is implicit a communitarian political ideal of a just community of wise friends.[21]

Summary of Key Texts

Epicurus describes the *Letter to Herodotus* as "an adequate summary of the entire system" (i.e., the Epicurean philosophy) for those who are unable to work through the details and to help his followers remember the system as a whole (*LH* 35). He says that the outline is based on certain general principles. Epicurus recommends continuous study of nature to his student because "with this sort of activity more than any other, I bring calm to my life." First, Epicurus points out the need for a clear definition for each word (37–8). Second, he points out the importance of making inferences based on sense perception. He proceeds to outline the basic principles of physics, such as "nothing can come from what is not." He claims that everything is composed of atoms and void (40). Atoms are unchangeable and the principles of bodies must be their atomic natures (41). Afterwards, he turns to the production of images and the nature of perception (46–55). After that, he discusses the magnitude of bodies, arguing against infinite indivisibility of things with mass, and also their motion (55–62). Returning to the theme of perception (63), he argues that the soul is material. In section 75, he discusses the origin of language.

The *Letter to Menoeceus* consists in a brief summary of Epicurus's moral philosophy that is probably intended for the general reader. In the letter, Epicurus stresses the two central principles of his ethical thought: the right understanding of the gods (*LM* 123) and freedom from the fear of death (125). He claims that we need to understand which desires are necessary and which are vain (127) in order to attain the aim of a blessed life, which is the body's health and the soul's freedom from disturbance (128). Epicurus claims that the pleasure that arises out of the freedom from desire is greater and more valuable than the pleasures that result from the satisfaction of desires. This is because the former consists of freedom from suffering and pain, which is more self-sufficient. In contrast, the second results in more pain and suffering. For this reason, Epicurus advocates the virtuous life, which has at its core prudence. He says that the pleasant life is inseparable from the virtues (133).

The *Principal Doctrines* makes it clear that Epicurus's philosophy is not egoistic despite its individualism. It recognizes the interests of others and extols the virtues and great importance of friendship (*PD* XXVII). The *Principal Doctrines* also contains a clear exposition of the three kinds of desire, which were mentioned earlier (XXIX), as well as a brief outline of his theory of knowledge and its importance for the life of tranquility (XXII–XXV).

LUCRETIUS (99–55 BC)

Titus Lucretius Carus, the great Latin poet, is the most influential Epicurean. Little is known of his life except that he came from a wealthy Roman family, and that he may have committed suicide as the result of insanity due to the consumption of a love potion. He was a contemporary of Cicero.

Like the works of Epicurus, the main aim of Lucretius's poem *De Rerum Natura* (*On the Nature of Things*) is to help people attain happiness and peace of mind through a proper understanding of nature, which liberates us from the superstitious fear of the gods and of death. Lucretius's poem is the most complete extant statement of Epicurean philosophy. It aims to, and probably does, well reflect the thought of Epicurus himself, despite the difference of over two hundred years. Lucretius says that he follows Epicurus alone, and it is very probable that he consulted Epicurus's large work *On Nature*. We have already signaled some important differences between the two. First, the theory of atomic swerves may be specific only to Lucretius; there is no sign of it in the extant works of Epicurus. Second, Lucretius has a more developed theory of causal laws than Epicurus.

Book I is devoted to explaining how the boundless universe consists only of indestructible atoms and void. Book II explains how the motion of these atoms constitutes the world and its observable qualities, such as color, heat, and smell. In Book III, Lucretius argues that the human soul is composed of matter and that the fear of death is irrational because death itself is not bad. Since one's nonexistence prior to birth is not bad, neither is nonexistence after death. Book IV advocates an Epicurean view of knowledge as sense perception. Visual images consist of thin films emanating from the surfaces of objects. Book V contains Lucretius's view of the origin of the earth and of the development of species and human institutions. These provide an alternative account of history to those advanced by Plato. Book VI, which shows signs of being unfinished, discusses a wide range of topics, such as the nature of thunder, magnets, and volcanoes.

Conclusion

The basis of Epicureanism is that one should aim to live a happy life. According to Epicurus, happiness is the sole intrinsic good. However, the Epicurean conception of happiness is different from what one might think. It is a static pleasure and a feeling of tranquility, which consists of not feeling pain or any mental disturbance. According to the Epicureans, this static pleasure is more valuable than the active pleasure that comes from satisfying desires. As well as being short-lived, such active pleasures are based on unnecessary and groundless desires, which tend to disturb the natural calm of the body and mind. For this reason, Epicurus advocates a simple lifestyle in which friendship is important.

Like Democritus before him, Epicurus argues for an atomistic ontology according to which everything is either a simple or a composite of atoms and void. He tries to show how atomism is sufficient to explain the observable features of the world without the need of Platonic Forms and Aristotelian purposes. Epicurus sees indivisible atoms as needed to answer Zeno's arguments with regard to infinite divisibility. Epicurus also defends atomism from the criticisms of Aristotle. In elaborating his theory, he postulates minimal parts of space and time, and introduces the notion of an atomic swerve to explain contingency.

Epicurus defends a materialist account of the soul. For Epicurus and Lucretius, this account is important because it implies that there is no reason to fear death. Because there is no afterlife, death is simply nonexistence. Since one had no reason to lament one's nonexistence before one's conception, likewise one has no reason to fear it after death.

Study Questions

1. How does Epicurus argue for the claim that everything that exists is either atoms or void or composites?
2. How does Epicurus respond to Aristotle's criticism of atomism that an atom without parts would not be able to move?
3. Why did Aristotle reject the possibility that space and time might be granular (rather than continuous)?
4. How does Epicurus respond to Zeno's arguments for the conclusion that nothing can have parts?
5. Why does Epicurus introduce the idea of the swerve of atoms?
6. How does Epicurus seek to explain all natural phenomena in terms of atoms?
7. How do Lucretius and Epicurus explain biological phenomena?
8. What is the relation between Epicurus's physics and his ethics?
9. How does Epicurus argue that the soul is physical?
10. How do Epicureans argue that there is no reason to fear death?
11. How do the Epicureans conceive of the gods?
12. What are the gods composed of?
13. How does Epicurus distinguish a perceptual impression from a judgment?
14. How does Epicurus distinguish active and static pleasure?
15. Why is static pleasure preferable to active pleasure?
16. How do some desires disturb tranquility?
17. What does Epicurus say about friendship?
18. Is Epicurus's philosophy individualistic?

Discussion Questions

1. Is Epicurus right to claim that we have no reason to fear death?
2. Is Epicurus's distinction between active and passive pleasure defensible? What are the implications of this distinction?
3. Is Epicurus's philosophy too self-centered?

14

Stoicism
Zeno of Citium, Seneca, Epictetus, and Marcus Aurelius

Around 300 BC, Zeno of Citium began teaching from a *stoa*, or porch, in the marketplace of Athens, and in so doing he founded the philosophical movement, Stoicism, which lasted six centuries. In part, Stoicism can be regarded as a reaction against the Epicurean view of happiness as a life of pleasure. Like Epicurus's philosophy, Stoicism is dedicated to the ethical question, "What is the good life?" But, unlike the Epicurean view, the Stoic answer draws on a metaphysical view of the universe as rationally governed by a divine element. The good life consists in living virtuously and, since humans are part of the universe, this requires following the dictates of nature as reflected in our divine-like reason. It does not consist in the pursuit of pleasure, but rather in our adapting our ends to the rational laws of nature. It requires us to follow reason, becoming free of the passions and indifferent to all misfortune.

The second head of the Stoa was Cleanthes (ca. 330 BC–230 BC), who lived in ascetic poverty. We have one surviving work by Cleanthes, the *Hymn to Zeus*. The third head was the prolific and influential Chrysippus (ca. 279 BC–206 BC), who synthesized Stoic thought into a system. After Chrysippus, Stoicism spread widely in the ancient world. Stoic views appealed to all classes, from slaves to rulers, and it exerted a great influence upon the Roman Empire; one of its greatest adherents was the Roman Emperor Marcus Aurelius.

The history of Stoicism is divided into three phases: Early, Middle, and Late. Apart from the *Hymn to Zeus*, no Stoic work survives from the Early and Middle periods (i.e., from Zeno, Cleanthes, and Chrysippus, nor from Panaetius in the Middle Period [ca. 185–110 BC]). Much of our knowledge of these two periods comes secondhand from later reporters, such as Cicero (45 BC), Diogenes Laërtius (third century AD), and Stobaeus (fifth century AD). The only remaining full-length Stoic works, such as the well-known writings of the Romans Seneca (ca. 1 BC–AD 65), Epictetus (AD ca. 55–135), and Marcus Aurelius (AD 121–180), all come from the last of the three periods of Stoicism. By this time, during the

Roman Empire, Stoicism had become a popular philosophy of life: a set of doctrines and of practices akin to a religion.

From these later Roman writers, we can appreciate how it was to live as a Stoic, but not the full range of philosophical concerns of early Stoicism. For this reason, it is important to also consider the fragments that preserve the ideas of Zeno and other early Stoics, such as the fragments from Cleanthes and especially Chrysippus, who wrote 165 works.

Zeno of Citium (334–262 BC)

Zeno was born in Citium, on the island of Cyprus. In 314 BC, the young man moved to Athens, possibly to work as a merchant. At the time, the city was still a flourishing philosophical center: Plato's academy was thriving, and Theophrastus was in charge of the Lyceum, Aristotle's school. There were Pythagorean thinkers and many Cynic philosophers, who claimed to be followers of Socrates. Zeno was attracted to philosophy when, after losing his fortune in a shipwreck, he sat by a bookstall reading the description of Socrates in Xenonphon's *Memorabilia*. It is said that he asked to meet someone like Socrates, and that, at this moment, Crates, a Cynic, was passing by; Zeno enrolled in Crates's school. He studied there for fourteen years but was also influenced by the ideas of Socrates and Heraclitus. In 300 BC, Zeno founded his own school, discussing philosophy with students under the porch in the marketplace of Athens. He taught in the Stoa for nearly forty years. He became famous as the living embodiment of his own teachings, and the Athenian Assembly honored him with a golden crown and a statue.

Stoic philosophy has three branches: logic, physics, and ethics. However, these categories should be understood broadly: logic relates to *logos*, or to language, thought, and rationality, and physics pertains to the study of nature. We shall divide our exposition according to these three parts of philosophy in the following order: physics, ethics, and logic.

Philosophy of Nature

Since the Stoics build their ethics on their view of nature, both metaphysics and physics are very important parts of their philosophy. Their ethics is supposed to follow from their claims about the nature and organization of the universe. The universe is fundamentally a cohesive unity directed by an active, rational and divine principle, which constitutes our human nature.

Following Diogenes, we can divide the natural philosophy of the Stoics into seven parts: bodies, principles, elements, limits, gods, place, and void (DL VII, 132). Our exposition will roughly follow this division.

According to the Stoics, everything that exists is corporeal. Something exists only if it can exercise a causal influence on, and be influenced by, other things that exist. The only things that can do that are three-dimensional bodies that resist external pressure. However, there are also non-corporeal things that subsist, such as place, time, and void; linguistic meaning, or what can be said, also fits into this category. These subsisting things do not exercise any causal influence on what exists.

Despite their physicalism, the Stoics view the universe as a living being that is rational and has soul. In this regard, they distinguish the active and the passive principles of the universe. The passive is unqualified matter, while the active is the rational principle embodied in it (Diogenes Laërtius [DL] VII, 134). Any physical body consists in passive matter, which makes it capable of being acted on, and an active principle, which makes it capable of acting on other things. Both the active and passive principles are physical.

In this manner, the Stoics are both physicalists *and* vitalists,[1] a combination that is slightly unusual. Usually, philosophers who are vitalists make some dualistic distinction, affirming that the soul is some nonphysical principle or entity that governs the material. However, the Stoics maintain that the active, intelligent, and creative principle of the universe is corporeal or physical. Their argument is that something non-corporeal cannot act upon or affect anything corporeal. Thus, if the active principle has causal effects on passive matter then it too must be physical.

Physically, what is the active principle? According to early Stoic sources, among the four elements, fire is the most divine. It is the intelligent, ever-present, guiding force in the universe, similar to how it is described by Heraclitus (see chapter 1). However, some of the Stoics think that there are two kinds of fire: the finer, subtler one, which is the divine creative principle, and the other, one of the four elements generated by the creative power. This distinction between the two kinds of fire is motivated by the idea that, as one of the four elements, fire would be destructible like the other three. Thus, creative fire must be something distinct.

However, after Chrysippus, the Stoics claim that *pneuma* directs natural processes. *Pneuma* is usually translated as "breath" or "hot breath," and it is characterized as being made of air and fire. Apparently, in the later Stoics, it has the same function as the earlier notion of creative fire; it acts as the soul in animals or the reason in humans, and as the cohesive force that makes the universe rational and organized. It has an inherent tension because it has simultaneously an inward and an outward tendency of movement.

There is a difficulty here, an apparent contradiction. On the one hand, the Stoics think that the traditional four elements are not fundamental. They can be transformed into one another, and they are destroyed in the cosmic cycle (see below). This implies that the divine active principle cannot be identified with any of the elements, a point that is supported by Diogenes Laërtius when he indicates that the divine active principle generated the four elements and thus is distinct from them (DL VII, 136). [2] For these reasons, some contemporary commentators suggest that the Stoic notion of the active principle is similar to the modern idea of force field.[3] Such a proposal doesn't fit well with the Stoic idea that the active principle is intelligent and divine, which are characteristics far removed from contemporary physics. However, it does express the idea that, for the Stoics, the active principle cannot be composed of one of the four elements.

On the other hand, the Stoics seem to claim that the active principle can be identified with some of the elements. They seem to have associated the active principle with air and fire, and the passive with earth and water. For instance, if the active principle is *pneuma*, then it is made of air and fire. Since the elements fire and air are associated with the qualities hot and cold, and elements earth and water with dry and wet, this implies that the active principles are hot and cold, and the passive principles are dry and wet. Hot and cold activate changes on dry and wet things. This point suggests that the active principle might be similar to the rarefaction and condensation referred to by some of the early ancient thinkers, especially Anaximenes (see chapter 1).[4]

There are four points to bear in mind regarding the active principle in Stoicism. First, the Stoics need the creative power to function as an organizing principle for diverse kinds of phenomena. It is supposed to explain the following: the cohesion of the universe as a whole, the organizational structure of things and the soul (*psuchê*) of animals, as well as the reason (*logos*) of persons. It is the force that provides physical cohesion and organizational regularity in the universe. However, to have these explanatory roles, it needs to have a physical presence. Thus, it functions both as a formal cause, in a more or less Aristotelian sense, and a physical cause.[5]

Second, because it has several explanatory roles, nature as the active principle manifests itself variously in different kinds of things. For instance, in plants it expresses itself as the nature of the plant. In animals it is manifest as the animating principle or soul. In humans, it expresses itself as reason or *logos*. Furthermore, for the Stoics, nature as the active principle is itself rational. This is why the principle itself is also called *logos*. Of course, even though the active principle is rational and intelligent, it manifests itself as reason only in humans, who have the capacity for articulate thought.

Third, the active principle thoroughly permeates every part of the passive. This is how it controls, shapes, and guides physical processes. It has its effects through physical contact by pervading coarser forms of matter. This physical presence allows it to form the cosmos as an organized whole. Chrysippus describes this permeation as analogous to the way the soul infuses the body, "although more in some places and less in others" (DL VII, 138). Furthermore, *pneuma* can have different tensions, which determine the kind of being in question. For instance, the differences between plants, animals, and humans hinges on the tension of the *pneuma* in each case.

Fourth, because the active principle is the intelligent organizing power of the whole cosmos, Stoics often claim it to the divine. Furthermore, they identify this aspect of the whole universe with God or Zeus. The existence of God is the divinity of Nature. He or it does not consist in an incorporeal creator, who stands outside the universe or is transcendent, but rather as an intelligent and immanent power.

These points in Stoicism about the divine had an important influence on the seventeenth-century thinker, Spinoza (1632–1677). The Stoics claim that the universe is entirely material but, at the same time, it has a divine aspect; and that, because we humans are part of this greater whole, we should aim to live in accordance with the laws of nature, which reflect its divine aspect. In his *Ethics,* Spinoza develops an understanding of human ethical development based on a non-dualist metaphysics that has some striking similarities to Stoicism. In particular, both are deterministic, non-dualistic, and quasi-pantheistic in their metaphysics; and both stress that liberating oneself from negative passions requires a proper understanding of the natural world. For early modern thinkers, such as Spinoza and Montaigne, Stoicism represented a noble, ethical vision of human life that was free from Church doctrine and Medieval scholasticism.

For the Stoics, theology is a sub-branch of physics because the active principle is physical as well as divine.[6] Nevertheless, theology plays a prominent and indispensable role in Stoic thought as a basis for their ethics. As we shall see later, this basis consists fundamentally in the claim that human nature consists in the divine active principle that permits us to reason and act autonomously.

The Stoic point that Zeus or God is the active and divine aspect of the universe needs to be more carefully articulated. Is Zeus simply the active organizing intelligence of the universe? Or is God rather the universe as a whole? The answer needs to take into account the Stoic view of the eternal cosmic cycles. According to the Stoics, the universe passes through cycles. During one period, it consists only of creative fire. According to Chrysippus's *On Providence,* during such a period.

> When the cosmos is fiery throughout, it is simply its own soul and controlling principle, whenever there is the conflagration. (Plutarch *St. Rep.* 1053b)[7]

During this phase, the deity is in its purest form. However, the cosmos passes through a different phase of the cycle during which it is constituted by the four elements. During this phase, the divine is immanent as a controlling principle of the cosmos. Given this account of the cosmic cycle, it would be misleading to claim that the divine is the creator of the cosmos, though that is true in a sense, and it would be misleading to claim that God is Nature as a whole, though that too is true in a sense. According to many Stoics, the universe's cycles were fixed and lasted what was called "the Great Year." In other words, after a fixed period, when the planets return to their original positions, the great conflagration (or the engulfing of the cosmos in fire) occurs again, and the cycle repeats itself.

The Stoics identify the action of the active principle with fate, and fate with the antecedent causes of an event. The early Stoics also claim that everything happens in accordance with antecedent causes (Aëtius, 1, 28.4).[8] Therefore, everything happens by fate. Fate is the unalterable chain of causes. Alexandra of Aphrodisias seems to have drawn deterministic conclusions from these points when he claims:

> Everything which has come to be is followed by something else which of necessity depends on it as a cause, and everything which comes to be has something preceding it to which it is connected as a cause. For nothing either is or comes to be in the universe without a cause, because there is nothing of the things in it that is separated and disconnected from all the things that have preceded. For the universe would be torn apart and divided and not remain single forever, organized according to a single order and organization, if any causeless motion were introduced. (Alexander of Aphrodisias, *Fat.* 192, 3–14)[9]

Because of this, events that seem to happen by chance must be caused by some unknown causal factor. These are sometimes called *non-evident causes*. When an event looks random or as if it happened by chance, there must be some hidden or unknown cause that brought it about. This point applies to human action, as much as to any other natural event. The early Stoics, such as Chrysippus, seem to think that this strong determinism is a logical consequence of the claim that the universe is a cohesive unity organized according to rational principles.

In this regard, Stoic philosophy has to tread a delicate path to avoid contradiction. On the one hand, as we have seen, the idea that the universe is a cohesive unity controlled by rational principles seems to imply determinism. Some occurrence that wasn't determined by prior causes would be an event that didn't happen in accordance with rational principles. On the other hand, Stoic ethics requires the idea that humans have the autonomy to make choices. For instance, it requires that a person have the autonomous choice of what attitude to take towards any misfortune that befalls him. This autonomy seems to require that determinism is not always true. To be able to accept both ideas, some Stoics may argue for what we call today *soft determinism*. According to soft determinism, the claim that every event has a cause is compatible with the claim that persons can make free choices. Soft determinism is often called *compatibilism*. However, these terms (soft determinism and compatibilism) are contemporary ones. In the context of Stoic philosophy, these issues played out through distinctions between different kinds of causes. So, for example, Chrysippus distinguishes total causes from proximate ones. While the former determine their outcome, the latter don't.

According to the Stoics, human beings have a body and a soul, but the soul itself is corporeal, consisting of *pneuma*, which permeates the whole body. Part of the function of the soul is the capacity to receive impressions and to issue impulses. These explain animal movements. Central to Stoic philosophy is the idea that all animals are "well-disposed towards themselves" (*SVF* II, 178–88)[10]; and central to this idea is the concept of *oikeiôsis*, which means roughly "belonging to and akin to." Because animals have *oikeiôsis*, they are naturally well-disposed to themselves, and this determines how they perceive and the nature of their impulses. For instance, an animal will perceive certain things as food— that is, as something that belongs to itself. Another Stoic idea key to the explanation of the actions of animals is that for a sense-impression to have relevance as source of an impulse, it needs to be assented to (*SVF* III, 171). Any act of perception requires assenting to impressions.

Central to the human soul is the "governing principle" (*SVF* II, 827), which has the capacity to command the body and which is the location of consciousness. As Epictetus says:

> God has introduced man to be an observer of himself and his works, and not merely an observer but an interpreter too. Therefore, it is shameful for man to begin and cease where animals do; he should rather begin where they do. (I, 6)

Reason governs the animal-like nature of humans. It is "the craftsman of impulse" (DL VII, 86). This means that we have desires that take precedence over our animal-like wants, such as those desires associated with the virtues. This Stoic assertion denies the Platonic division of the soul into three parts: the rational, the spirited, and the appetitive (see chapter 7). According to the Stoics, *all* facets of human life are influenced by the fact that we are rational animals who have language.

This is especially important for our relationship to our own desires or impulses. As we have just seen, perception requires assenting to the relevant impressions, which may include seeing something as a reason for action. In other words, for an impression to be a perception, it must be assented to. This applies to perceptions that have an appetitive element, such as seeing something as food to be eaten. Thus, in order for impulses to affect behavior, they need to be based on impressions that have been assented to. But humans have the capacity to dissent from impressions, just as we have the capability to disagree with a proposition that we think is false. Thus, we have the freedom to *not* assent to the impressions that form the basis of our animal-like impulses. In this way, we can control our impulses and passions.

The Stoics define the passions as the irrational and excessive movements of the soul. Passions usually cloud our judgment and bring us into conflict with nature and reason. However, this does not mean that the Stoics characterize all feeling as unhealthy. Indeed, they claim that all functions of the soul have both a cognitive and an affective, or emotive, element. However, the truly wise person uses knowledge to achieve independence from both the external world of social and political forces and the internal world of his or her own passions and emotions.

Ethics

We have three main sources for early Stoic ethics: Cicero's *De finibus*, Book VII of Diogenes Laërtius, and Stobaeus from the fifth century AD. Here is how Stobaeus reports Zeno's ethical position:

> Of things which exist some are good, some bad, some indifferent. Good are the following sorts of item: wisdom, moderation, justice, courage, and all that is virtue or participates in virtue. Bad are the following sorts of item: folly, intemperance, injustice, cowardice, and all that is vice or participates in vice. Indifferent are the following sorts of item: life, death, reputation, ill-repute, pleasure, exertion, wealth poverty, health, sickness, and things like these. (*Ecl.* II, 57.18–58.4)[11]

We need to build towards an understanding of this position in six steps. First, Zeno defines "good" in terms of being in accord with Nature, and "bad" in terms of being in discord (DL VII, 87). Zeno also formulates the goal of life as "living consistently." There is some debate as to whether these are distinct principles or different formulations of the same idea.[12] Later Stoic thinkers, such as Chrysippus, articulate the point in terms of "reason consistent and firm" (Plutarch, *Virt. Mor.* 441C).[13] These other formulations bring out different aspects of the basic idea that the good is being in accord with Nature.

Second, humans are rational beings. What counts as being in accord with Nature depends on the kind of being in question; it is different for plants, animals, and humans. According to Cicero, it is also different for humans at different ages and stages of development. For fully developed adult humans, being in accord with Nature consists of living in accordance with reason. It is a life governed by reason.

Third, because of their rational nature, it is a special function of humans to be virtuous (DL VII, 94). Thus, for humans to live in accordance with Nature is to live virtuously (DL VII, 87). This is because we are primarily rational beings and, as we have seen, according to Diogenes Laërtius's report, "reason supervenes as craftsman of impulse" (DL VII, 86). This means that we have the capacity for discovering wisdom or *phronesis*, and for being in proper or ethical relations to our own impulses.[14] Such relations constitute the virtues. In this way, the function of a human is the perfection of his or her nature.

Humans have certain natural propensities. According to Chrysippus, these are "the foundations of appropriate behavior" and the raw material for virtue (Plutarch, *Com Not* 1069e).[15] These propensities or affinities (*oikeiôsis*) include behaviors concerned with self-interest, such as health and wealth. The relevant virtues would comprise moderation and courage. The natural propensities also include the social principles that bind us together for "civic association" (*Fin* III, 66).[16] In other words, it is part of human nature to for us to form family and social relationships, and to live in communities. When humans acquire rationality, we can perform appropriate acts, which have their origin in reason and which can be justified rationally.[17] In other words, because we have a rational nature, we are capable of performing ethically appropriate acts, which define the virtues.

Fourth, virtue requires that we, as rational beings, live in accordance with the rational, active aspect of the universe (i.e., with Nature as a whole), rather just our limited human nature (DL VII, 88). Chrysippus says that this is because we are a part of Nature. In the words of Diogenes Laërtius, this means that if we abide by right reason, then we will follow the divine, active principle of the universe. This implies that we must adopt the wider perspective of universal reason. Given these claims, we can represent an important Stoic argument as follows:

1. The good is what accords with Nature.
2. Humans are rational by nature.
3. Reason is the universal active principle that brings order to Nature as a whole.

---

4. Therefore, it is good for humans to accord their actions with the universal active principle of Nature.

The first premise states Zeno's definition of the good, given in step 1 above. The second premise provides the Stoic view of human nature, which we discussed in step 2 above. The third premise claims that reason, which is part of human nature, is also the active guiding principle of the universe as a whole.

Fifth, returning to the initial quotation from Stobaeus, we are now in a better position to understand Zeno's claim that natural benefits and harms are not good or bad, but rather indifferent. The only thing that is good in all contexts is virtue. Only virtue has the kind of value that is not relative to circumstances. In contrast, the value of natural advantages, such as wealth, is relative; such benefits need not be advantageous in all circumstances. To mark this distinction, the Stoics reserve the term "good" for virtue and "bad" for vice, and "preferred" or "preferable" for natural advantages.[18] So, although wealth is preferable to poverty, morally speaking it isn't good *per se* and it does not form part of virtue. This is why such benefits are indifferent.

The ultimate or comprehensive goal in life for a human should be to be virtuous. However, the person may have other particular life goals, such as to have a family and to engage in public life, but these do not add to the ultimate goal of being virtuous. The virtuous person would pursue his or her particular goals by acting in accordance with right reasoning (DL VII, 88).

Sixth, and finally, the Stoics argue that virtue constitutes *eudaimonia* or well-being, which Zeno characterized as "a smooth current of life" (*Ecl.* II, 77.20–1). A person attains *eudaimonia* when his or her volition accords with or is harmonious with the divine will of the universe. Virtue is necessary and sufficient for *eudaimonia*. This is because reason dictates that what is good must benefit the person who has it, irrespective of circumstances. The sole thing that fits these criteria is virtue, which is under our own power. Persons are responsible only for their character and for the right intentions of their actions and not for the results of those acts.

Although *eudaimonia* is constituted by virtue, the Stoics argue that pleasure is of secondary value. On this important point, their thought is fundamentally different from that of the Epicureans. Pleasure is the product of a life that is suited to the animal's constitution. In the case of humans, as soon as a person "has seen the regularity and harmony of conduct, he (or she) values this far higher than everything . . ." (*Fin* III, 20–1). Therefore, although virtue produces "a smooth current of life," a person should aim to be virtuous; pleasure will be a by-product.

Virtue is a disposition of the soul that has four aspects: practical wisdom, justice, moderation, and courage. Each of these consists of knowledge. For example, courage is knowledge of what should be endured (*SVF* III, 285). The Stoics accept the Socratic theory of the unity of the virtues, as well as the claim that the virtues are based on knowledge of what is good and bad. Thus, to have the knowledge that constitutes courage, one must also have the knowledge that constitutes practical wisdom. In the final analysis, all of these virtues consist in knowing what accords with the divine principle of Nature.

Concerning things that are beyond our control, Stoicism advocates acceptance. As we mentioned earlier, a person is a part of the whole universe, which is guided by reason or *logos*. Thus, the virtuous person will accept those aspects of his or her circumstance that he or she cannot change, however unfortunate they may be from his or her limited point of view. Furthermore, this acceptance will be happy because he or she understands that those circumstances contribute to the well-being and harmony of the universe as a whole. Of course, the person may prefer that things turn out differently, and these preferences may be rational in the sense that they form part of human nature.

However, the sage does not regard the objects of those preferences as good because from the perspective of Nature, whatever happens is good. The Stoics claim that, from the perspective of Nature as a whole, everything that happens accords with Nature. Given this, how should they explain the unnatural? In part, the answer lies in a distinction between partial and complete views. For example, we prefer to avoid illness and death in reference to the ends that are natural for human beings. However, these preferences reflect a limited perspective from part of the universe. However, from the perspective of the whole, death is not bad.

> Many external things can prevent individual natures from perfecting themselves, but nothing can stand in the way of universal Nature because it holds together and maintains all natures. (Cic., *ND* II, 35)[19]

This is why Marcus Aurelius counsels us to welcome everything that happens because it contributes to the well-being of the universe (V, 8). However, the claim that everything is natural from the point of view of the universe as a whole generates a version of the problem of evil. The claim implies that everything is right from the perspective of the whole, and nothing is wrong. In reply, the Stoics reply that the wrong actions of people are not the responsibility of Nature. Although humans have the capacity to live in accordance with the rationality of Nature, they also have the capability to act disharmoniously.

Despite the fact that we are rational beings, not all persons are sages. Thus, one needs to distinguish right and wrong reason. Only the sage has right reason (*SVF* III, 560). To have right reason implies that one's governing principle will not waver from the good. The person who has less than perfect rationality will always be susceptible to the influence of the passions; this is because the *pneuma* of his or her soul is not at the right tension. When the soul is at the right tension, our inclinations and emotions will always be consistent with right reason.

In summary, for the Stoics, ethics is the study of the good life. According to Zeno, something is good if and only if it accords with Nature. Because we are rational beings, the good life consists of following the dictates of reason. Reason guides us to live virtuously by teaching us to adapt our ends to the nature of the world. Such a life accords with the universal perspective of the cosmos; we humans are part of the universe as a whole, which is governed by divine reason. This universal perspective requires us to cultivate a firm and noble indifference to the many vicissitudes of life, which is beneficial in a lasting way. This is why virtue is necessary and sufficient for *eudaimonia*.

Cosmopolitanism

Although the term *cosmopolitanism* has several definitions, roughly, it is the claim that all persons are equally citizens of the world. The cosmopolitan view of the Stoics has its roots in Socrates, but most explicitly in Diogenes the Cynic, who claimed to be a citizen of the cosmos. Cosmopolitanism is inherent in the ethical theory of the Stoics because, as we have seen, their view of the good is based on the reasoning nature of human beings; and reason is a universal force of the cosmos. Therefore, it accords with reason to adopt a universal view, according to which all persons are part of the cosmos equally. It would contradict this to benefit only oneself or a selected few. In other words, virtue requires that we are just and act as if all humanity is one, while still recognizing one's limitations (Cic., *Fin* III, 62).

According to Plutarch, this strand of Stoic thought starts with Zeno himself:

> The much admired *Republic* of Zeno is aimed at this one main point: that we should not organize our daily lives around the city . . . but we should regard all human beings as . . . our fellow citizens, and there should be one way of life and order. (LS 67A)[20]

Zeno may have postulated an ideal city-state in which all citizens were virtuous. However, it is difficult to be certain what this amounts to because Zeno's work, the *Republic*, has not survived. Likewise, neither has Chrysippus's work of the same name. According to Chrysippus, goodness requires that we should help others without prejudice in favor of one's own *polis* or city-state. Indeed it seems to imply that one should try to benefit more rather than fewer people (all other things being equal).[21] This may require a person to serve states and communities other than his own, if he or she can.

We might contrast this kind of view with that of Plato and Aristotle, for whom the *polis* is a local community that forms part of or the framework for the individual's moral development. According to this communitarian view, an Athenian should think of himself primarily as an Athenian, and this defines primarily who should count as a foreigner or barbarian, such as the Persians. In terms of classical Greece, the specifics of this point are not so cut and dry because members of the different city-states would have also identified themselves as Greeks, especially towards the end of the Archaic period (around 500 BC) and after. However, it remains true that, for Plato and Aristotle, one has obligations primarily to other members of one's local community, but not to strangers.

The later Roman Stoics make the cosmopolitanism and impartiality inherent in early Stoicism still more explicit. They stress the universal nature of reason in three ways. First, according to a universal ethical view, all persons are citizens of the world simply by virtue of their shared humanity or rational nature. Seneca expresses this claim when he writes:

> Let us take hold the fact that there are two communities—the one which is truly great and truly common . . . (which) measure the boundaries of our state by sun; the other which we have been assigned to by our birth. (*On Leisure* 4.1)

Second, the ethical status of persons has nothing to do with their social status. The Stoics admit the revolutionary idea that the prince and the slave are naturally equal. Seneca declares and expresses this equality in his Letter 47 to Lucilius, a slaveholder, which is named "On Master and Slave." In this work, Seneca says to Lucilius:

> It is just as possible for you to see in him a free-born man as for him to see in you a slave. (Letter 47)

Although Seneca criticizes the maltreatment of slaves, it is noteworthy that he never argues explicitly against the institution of slavery.[22]

Third, the Stoics liken the cosmos to a *polis* because the law of reason rule and bring order to the universe, and likewise it would have the same role in the ideal *polis*. Does this mean that the Stoics think that ideally there should a worldwide state in which all persons participate? Or does it mean that they think of the ideal state more abstractly, as comprised only of virtuous souls who are willing to follow the dictates of reason?

In understanding Stoic views of cosmopolitanism, there are at least two basic interpretative problems. First, the Stoics regard virtue as the sole good. Thus, they have no problem in advocating political engagement when the state is, or its rulers are, virtuous. Likewise, there is no problem with advocating universal beneficence as a moral virtue. The difficult question is: Should the Stoic engage in politics even when the state is corrupt? To do so might require the compromise of virtue. In contrast, in a corrupt state, should the Stoic who is a wise person withdraw from politics? There are texts that suggest different answers to these questions.[23]

The second interpretative question is: do the Stoics advocate a single worldwide state? It is one thing to refer to our common humanity and equality as a moral property that all persons ideally should respect, and it is another to argue that this implies there should be a single worldwide state. In other words, it is not clear to what extent the various Stoic writers are willing to affirm that their moral values should also be a political ideal.

Stoic cosmopolitan ideas were very influential partly because of geopolitical events of the period. The local identities of the classical Greek period were transformed by the Hellenistic Empire of Alexander the Great, and later by the Roman Empire. Stoic cosmopolitanism may have many features in common with the philosophy of the Roman republic, especially as characterized by Cicero (106–43 BC), who became consul of Rome in 63 BC. While Cicero stresses the need for a balance between different forms of government, he emphasized that the republic is a common wealth—a common property of the people, based on agreement on law and mutual interest.

Logic

The Stoics understood *logic* very broadly, to comprise all studies of language and reasoning. This includes the nature and use of language. So, for instance, they incorporate the practice of both public speaking and the discovery of truth within their broad conception of rhetoric, which is part of logic. The Stoics' interest in logic was motivated largely by the idea that the proper use of reason has great ethical importance.

The mind is blank at birth. Language begins with the development of concepts through the repeated occurrences of the same sense impressions in the mind. The mind performs various mental operations on those concepts derived from primary sense experiences to form other concepts. According to the Stoics, humans are rational beings because their governing principle is rational—which implies, among other things, that they have the capacity for linguistic thought. Thinking and speaking are two sides of a single mental capability. Humans differ from other animals in having internal speech.

The Stoics distinguish the receiving of impressions from the interpretation of impressions. The former is a passive awareness and the latter is an active linguistic or articulate thinking process. However, thinking always involves having impressions from the senses or from memory. It involves making connections between impressions through combination and inferences of the form "If this then that" (Sextus Empiricus, *Adv. Math.* VIII, 275).[24] So although articulate thought is born from impressions, language allows us to create new ideas and express our relations to the world.

Perception is a mental act in which we assent to an impression. Perception is a three-step process. First, when we receive a sense impression, an object causes changes to the environment around it that affect our sense organs, and these changes are transmitted to the governing principle located in the heart (*SVF* II, 56). The impression is a change in the governing principle. Second, the mind actively interprets or classifies the impression according to its concepts. Thus, it interprets a set of impressions as being of a dog, for instance. Third, it assents to the impressions so interpreted as corresponding to some external object. In other words, it assents to the impressions as being caused by and representing some external object (*SVF* II, 54).

The Stoics recognize that perceptual judgments can be mistaken. However, the early Stoics argue that there must be a set of impressions that are immune from error. These they called the *cognitive impression*. Such an impression is "stamped and molded out of the object from which it came," such that they couldn't have come from another object (Cic. *Acad* II, 18 and Sextus, *Adv. Math.* VII, 402).[25] The Stoics argue that these cognitive impressions that are immediately trustworthy are a necessary condition of knowledge. They are so clear and striking that assent to them is almost irresistible (Sextus, *Adv. Math.* VII, 253–7). Later Stoics are a little more cautious and add the condition that cognitive impressions will be reliable unless there is "some obstacle" in the external circumstances (Sextus, *Adv. Math.* VII, 258). Later Stoics argue that a person must do everything to ensure that they have a "clear and striking impression."

Zeno defines knowledge as the apprehension of something that cannot be removed by argument (*SVF* I, 68; *DL* VII, 4). In general the Stoics claim that knowledge must be secure. This point defines the contrast between knowledge and belief. The terms are mutually exclusive. A belief is an assenting that is not secure and which does not count as knowledge. Even if it is true, it nevertheless fails to be knowledge because it is a weak assent that can be swayed by argument.

This point is illuminated by the Stoic distinction between the true and truth (Sextus, *Adv. Math.* VII, 38). "The true" refers simply to any judgment or proposition that happens to state what is the case. In contrast, the truth is something that can only be had by the wise person, and it consists of a special combination of true propositions, the knowing of which would constitute wisdom. It refers to the divine principle, the *logos* and fate that determines what is true. In other words, the truth refers to "the first cause of all that is true" (Aurelius IX, 2).[26] To know it is to know why what is true must be true. This point shows us that, although the Stoics think that knowledge must be grounded in clear impressions, their conception of knowledge extends beyond sensory impressions because of our capacity for language.

As we saw earlier, the Stoics claim that everything that exists must be corporeal because such things can be acted on and can affect other things. Things that are incorporeal merely subsist and have no causal effects. This distinction applies to language. Voice is a vibration of air, and as such it is corporeal and it exists. In contrast, what is said, the meaning of the utterance, is incorporeal and merely subsists. The Greek word used for this is *lekton* or what is said. The Stoics distinguish two kinds of *lekta*: the incomplete ones such as "is walking" and the complete ones, which include a nominative—or in contemporary language, a subject term—and which alone can be true or false.

The difference between corporeal existence and incorporeal subsistence has important implications for the semantic notion of the *lekton*. A word such as a noun or adjective can refer to an existent. However, what is said by a whole assertion, such as "Cato is walking," isn't itself an existent. Cicero says:

> Then I say "Cato is walking." It is not a material object which I now state, but a certain affirmation about a material object. . . . Thus if we say "wisdom" we take this to refer to something material; but if we say "he is wise" we make an assertion about a material object. It makes a very great difference whether you refer to the person directly or speak about him. (*Ep.* 117, 13)[27]

An assertion about a material object or a *lekton* itself isn't a corporeal existent. Nevertheless, the thing referred to by a word, such as "Cato," is an existent. This point alludes to two important modern distinctions. First, there is the distinction, pioneered by Frege (1848–1925) between sense and reference. The meaning of a word isn't what the word refers to. The word *wisdom* has a certain meaning but it also refers to something in the world. These two are distinct. Second, there is the allied, but more general distinction between language and the world. The Stoics seem to be claiming that one thing is an assertion or statement. This is semantic and has no corporeal existence. Another thing is the state of the world, which has corporeal existence. The Stoics seem to be arguing that these are things are separate, and that the first cannot be reduced to the second.[28]

The recognition of this distinction is important because it allows the Stoics to investigate language as a phenomenon that has corporeal and non-corporeal aspects. Thus, for example, the Stoics investigate grammar as a feature of spoken language, as an existent, but they study logic as an aspect of the semantics of language or as non-corporeal *lekton*.

The complete *lekton* consists of a complete assertion that has a subject and a predicate. The Stoics argue that there are several types of complete *lekta* that satisfy this criterion; these include prayers, questions, commands, oaths, and statements or propositions (*axioma*). The terms *true* and *false* only and must apply to propositions.

The Stoics divide simple propositions into three kinds: definite ("this man is walking"); categorical ("Socrates is walking"); and indefinite ("someone is walking") (DL VII, 70). They take the first of the three as the most basic. This is because the statement involves a direct reference to a physical object, similar to the way that cognitive impressions pick out objects when assented to.[29] Sextus Empiricus says, "The simple definite statement is true when the predicate (e.g., walking) belongs to the thing falling under the demonstrative (*Adv. Math.* VIII, 100). The truth of the categorical and indefinite simple statements depends on that of some definite one.

Because all existing things are corporeal, the Stoics denied that there is a universal thing in the world corresponding to the general term "human"; they reject the existence of Platonic Forms. They claim that the reference of the assertion "Humans are rational animals" is the content of someone's thought, and they argue that such assertions really have a conditional form. In other words, the assertion's form would be: "If anything is a human then it is a rational animal" (Sextus, *Adv. Math.* XI, 8).

The Stoics claim that there are different kinds of compound statements. These include conditional statements, constructed by means of the conditional connection *if*, which "asserts that the second part follows from the first, for instance, 'if it is day, it is light'." (DL VII, 71) The disjunction is a statement disjoined by the connector *or*. Diogenes Laërtius reports: "This connection shows that one of the statements is false."

The Stoics study inferences governed by terms that connect two or more assertions, such as *and, if, or,* and *not*, which today are called the *propositional connectives*. The Stoics claim that all such inferences can be reduced to five fundamental forms. These are:

1. If p then q, p therefore q.
2. If p then q, not q, therefore not p.
2. Not (both p and q), p therefore not q.
4, Either p or q, p therefore not q.
5. Either p or q, not q, therefore p.

These five forms are indemonstrable; their validity is self-evident (Sextus VIII, 223). Although we have very little of his work remaining, Chrysippus proves many theorems on the basis of these axioms. In these, basic inferences are represented by letters for the propositions. In the writings of the Stoics, argument form 1 above is written: 'If the first then the second, the first, therefore the second (Sextus, *Adv. Math.* VII, 227). In carrying out such proofs, Chrysippus employs four inference rules, which are called *themata*. Of these four, we have only two:

> If from two propositions a third is deduced, then either of the two together with the denial of the conclusion yields the denial of the other.
>
> If from two propositions a third is deduced and there are propositions from which one of the premises may be deduced, then the other premise together with these propositions will yield the conclusion.[30]

The Stoics define an argument as a system composed of premises and conclusion. They recognize that valid arguments can have true or false premises, and thus they understand the distinction between valid and sound arguments. The propositional connectives can be defined in terms of each other. For instance, we can define "p and q" as "not (not p or not q)." As Benson Mates points out, Chrysippus saw this kind of inter-definability because he recommends that "if p then q" should be written as Not (p and not q).[31] Most importantly, the Stoics recognize that any valid argument form must be derivable from the five axioms given the four inference rules. This means that they conceived of propositional logic as a deductive system, albeit that they did so perhaps in an embryonic form.

In conclusion, we can see why Stoic logic is an important development by comparing it to the logic of Aristotle. As we saw in chapter 9, Aristotle's logic concerns inferences governed by the terms *all*, *some*, and *none*, which today are called the *quantifiers*. In contrast, the Stoics developed an entirely different branch of logic based on the connectives between whole assertions. They conceived of this branch of logic as a deductive system based on axioms and inference rules. Furthermore they saw that these connectives are inter-definable.

As we said earlier, the early Stoic thinkers such as Zeno, Cleanthes, and Chrysippus articulated the fundamental principles of Stoic thought. Chrysippus, especially, synthesized these into a coherent system of Stoic philosophy. However, we have only fragments and testimonials for the early Stoics. For the full-length Stoic works, we must turn to later writings of three Romans: Seneca (ca. 1 BC–AD 65), Epictetus (AD ca. 55–135), and Marcus Aurelius (AD 121–180). These later Roman writers are particularly important to help us appreciate how it was to live as a Stoic. In their writings, we see the philosophical implications and richness of Stoic philosophy in practice.

SENECA (1 BC–65 AD)

Seneca was born of a wealthy family in Cordoba, Spain, but he was educated in Rome, where he stayed with his aunt. He entered politics, but in 41 AD he was exiled to Corsica, allegedly for adultery with the Emperor Caligula's sister. When he returned to Rome in 49 AD, it was as the tutor of the 12-year-old Nero at the behest of Nero's mother, Agrippina the Younger, the fourth wife of the Emperor Claudius. When Nero became Emperor of Rome in 54 AD, Seneca became his advisor. Nero's life became politically complicated, and in 59 AD, Nero ordered the killing of his own mother. Modern commentators consider Seneca to have been a politically moderating force on the Emperor, and Seneca was seriously compromised in this role as advisor to the Emperor.[32] For example, Seneca had to write the speech in which Nero excuses himself for murdering his own mother. In 62 and 64 AD Seneca tried to distance himself from the court of Nero and retire from his advisory role, but he was unable to do so. In 65 AD there was a plot against the life of Nero in which Seneca's nephew Lucan was implicated. Nero ordered Seneca to commit suicide. Seneca modeled his death on that of Socrates. He was perfectly calm and discussed philosophy as he died. According to Tacitus, Seneca cut his own veins and took poison to hasten his end. When neither of these was effective, he took a hot bath to speed on his own death.[33]

Seneca's major writings include 8 or 10 tragic dramas.[34] We have around 127 of his letters that deal with ethical and philosophical issues. These include a collection of 124 letters to Lucilius Junior and three letters on consolation: one to Marcia on the death of her son, one to Polybius on his missing son, and one to his mother Helvia, consoling her for his own absence during exile. He also wrote 12 philosophical treatises, which include *On Anger*, *On the Shortness of Life*, *On the Happy Life*, *On Benefits*, and *On Clemency*.[35]

Most of Seneca's writings concern his own attempt to apply Stoic ideas to his own troubled life. His struggle is primarily how to free himself from the passions of anger and grief, and how to benefit others in order to become wiser. This struggle is poignant especially because of the political compromises that he had to make. Being close to Nero's megalomania, Seneca had to act in ways that might be seen as complicit and hypocritical. Although Seneca's primary concern is how to put Stoic ideas into practice rather than with theoretical philosophy, this doesn't mean that he is uninterested in philosophical theory. The point is that he is primarily concerned with practice. Indeed, Seneca is willing to depart from Stoic teachings when his experience seems to require him to do so. Because his primary concern is practice, Seneca's writings are mostly about ethics.

The early Stoics tend to think of ethics in terms of what an idealized sage would do and think. In contrast, Seneca tends to discuss ethics from within the moral problems and difficulties that he personally, and those close to him, face. For example, *On Benefits* discusses the problems of giving and receiving gifts well, such as how to avoid ingratitude (10.5). He classifies different kinds of gifts: necessary, useful, and pleasant (11.1), and discusses when and how to give them. This is a typically insightful claim that Seneca makes:

> The law that governs benefits between two people is this: one of them should immediately forget that the benefit was given; the other should never forget that it was received. (10.4)

Seneca's writings often have an addressee. This applies obviously to the letters but also to the philosophical treatises. This gives them a personable tone and directness, which is lacking from tracts that argue for abstract conclusions through sustained pieces of reasoning. For instance, *On Peace of Mind* is addressed to a person who is suffering from a sickness of the soul, which Seneca tries to address as what we would call today a therapist. *On Mercy* is addressed to the Emperor Nero, arguing that clemency is a virtue that rulers must exercise even towards enemies. [36]

Much of Seneca's writings concern the emotions or passions. For instance, he writes much on anger, fear, and grief. In *On Anger*, Seneca defines anger as the desire to take vengeance for a perceived wrong, describing it as "brief madness" (Book I, 1.2). He claims that "no pestilence has been more costly for the human race" (I, 2.1), and he persistently tries to disarm the idea that anger is sometimes good or useful or appropriate. He argues that anger is not part of human nature; a good person does not wish to cause harm and does not delight in payback (I, 6.1–6.5). Seneca argues that we are swept along by anger when the mind consents to the impression that one has been wronged (II, 1–3) Thus, "we should never give anger entry" (Book II, 14.1); the best course is to reject straightaway the initial prickings of anger (I, 8.1); and because of this, the great cure for anger is delay (II, 29.1). Seneca also discusses the causes of anger. For example, he recognizes that we tend to become angry with those dearest to us, and this because we feel that they have given us less than we imagined they would (III, 30). He also claims that no one who looks at another's possessions is pleased with his own. However much money one has, one tends to count it as an injury that we could have received more; hence "there's no end to shouting about money" (III, 31–33). Seneca praises peace of mind and consuls that injuries should be healed rather than revenged.

In his letters Seneca gives life to the Stoic idea that only virtue is good and that it alone is sufficient for happiness. In other words, through examples, he tries to show that preferred indifferents, such as wealth, health, and fame, are not good and do not contribute to happiness. He doesn't claim that such preferred indifferents have no value. He wants to show by considering examples that they are not good. In Letter 71, he says:

If the mind is content with its own self, if it understands that all those things for which men pray, all the benefits which are bestowed and sought for, are of no importance in relation to a life of happiness, under such conditions it is sound.

In Letter 66, he says that all virtues are equal because nothing can be added to make them better: "The ability to increase is proof that a thing is still imperfect." Nothing can be more fitting than that which is fitting. Therefore, virtue in pleasant circumstances is equal to virtue in adverse circumstances. Therefore, although I prefer pleasure to suffering, the virtue in each case is the same. It cannot be made better. To illustrate this point, Seneca asks us to compare the value of two equally virtuous persons: one wouldn't say that one is better than the other based on the differences in their hairstyles. Such considerations are quite irrelevant.

Epictetus (55–135 AD)

Epictetus was born as a Roman slave in Hieropolis, in Asia Minor. As a youth he was passed from one owner to another. Finally, an administrator of importance in Nero's court in Rome, Epaphroditus, purchased Epictetus and allowed him to study with the Stoic philosopher Musonius Rufus. Epictetus soon surpassed his teacher, and his philosophical abilities so impressed his master that he was freed. He began teaching philosophy. In 89 AD, when the Emperor Domitian banned the philosophers from Italy, Epictetus fled. Afterwards, he founded his own Stoic school in Nicopolis on the coast of northwest Greece. One of his students, Arrian, transcribed and published his lectures as the *Enchiridion* (or the Manual or Handbook) and the *Discourses*. Despite being physically weak and lame from his period as a slave, Epictetus developed a large following, even among the early Christians. In later life he adopted a baby that he rescued from exposure.

Epictetus never wrote. However, scholars are confident that Arrian's transcriptions of the *Discourses* and the *Enchiridion* are faithful to Epictetus's own ideas. In large part this is because the writing style of these texts is quite different from the elegant sophisticated Greek of Arrian's other works. The simple, direct language of the *Enchiridion* and the *Discourses* most likely reflects well Epictetus's own voice. Arrian says in the Preface to the *Discourses*:

> Whatever I heard him say I used to write down, word for word, as best I could, endeavouring to preserve it as a memorial, for my own future use, of his way of thinking and the frankness of his speech.

The *Discourses* is a work with four books; the *Enchiridion* is an abridgement.

It is worth noting that, although historically the Stoic master is Zeno, Epictetus draws heavily on Socrates as a paradigm example of a Stoic sage.

The core of Epictetus's thinking is the claim that humans are rational animals. This means that we have the capacity to assent (or not) to our sense impressions. In this capacity, we are guided by logic: if two propositions are contradictory, we reject one of them. By nature, we find the irrational intolerable, and we are attracted by the rational (*Discourses* I, 2). But because the rational may appear differently to different people, we need to learn discipline:

> We must discipline ourselves in the winter for the summer campaign, and not rashly run upon that which does not concern us. (I, 2)

This rational aspect of human nature mirrors the universe itself. Supreme and immanent Zeus guides the universe rationally so that it has a natural order, which human beings can grasp with suitable effort. In effect, our minds are parts of the mind of Zeus; and when we act from our own will, we are using the same power that guides the universe. This will constitutes the true self or the real person. This freedom to choose constitutes the non-contingent feature of our person. Everything else is external. This applies even to our own bodies.[37]

The distinction between the internal sphere of volition and the external circumstances of one's life comprises the basis of Epictetus's theory of what is good. Virtue is a disposition of the volition. Thus, it is directly under our control, and because of this it is the sole good. The virtuous disposition is the right exercise of our will, and this constitutes a proper expression of our rational nature. Virtue consists in acting correctly on the basis of what we know, given that we are witness to the rational order of the universe and have kinship with God or Zeus. The sole good is to will morally or in accord with the rational nature of oneself and the universe.

External things, such as one's status, health and wealth, do not have value. They are indifferent. Basically, this is because while it is natural to protect our self-interest, it is a mistake to identify this *self*-interest with external conditions because the essence of the self is only our volition. The point about the indifference of externals is subject to two clarifications. First, the external circumstances of our lives are what the will has to work with, and the use that our will makes of them is not indifferent. Second, although they don't have unconditional value, some external things are more natural than others. For example, it is more natural for a plant to continue growing than to be cut. Likewise, humans seek to avoid harm and to gain material advantage. Although none of the external things that we pursue have unconditional value, nevertheless, this does not automatically imply that it is inconsistent with reason for us to pursue them. Epictetus makes this point through the analogy of playing a ball game: the result of the game has no value in itself, but this doesn't mean that it is irrational for the players to play energetically (II, 5).

The main purpose of philosophy is to train us to achieve virtue, and as a consequence inner peace, through a proper understanding of the world. A major part of this training is to learn to not identify oneself with the external conditions of our lives. We are our will; anything outside that is not part of oneself. Thus, according to Epictetus, virtue requires detachment from these externals. Epictetus realizes that normally we are careless with respect what is good and bad and are often very active with regard to what is indifferent. To highlight this, he asks us to imagine being deprived of sight (I, 20). Clearly, we need to train ourselves deeply in order to attain indifference to what has no value. This implies that we must not identify with what is not ours. What is properly ours is only our own will. Therefore, we must detach all our desires from what is external or is not ours.

Such training does not require us to abandon feelings, but rather to adjust them. We can change the emotions that we feel because our feelings are partly constituted by our judgments of value. Emotions are expressions of a feeling of what is right. Consequently, by adjusting our judgments to reflect the fact that the external circumstances of life don't have value, we can change our emotions. This means, for example, that anger towards others is an inappropriate emotion. The behavior of others is an external that has no value. What has value is the reaction of one's will towards that external factor. According to Epictetus, this means that we can control how we evaluate the impressions of sensation and thought. In other words, for instance, when we see another person as angry, we have the capability to adjust the meaning of the impressions we receive so that we judge the situation as neutral or indifferent. In short, we are able to evaluate the significance of all impressions and thoughts that enter our minds, and correct any tendency to interpret them in a way that is in discord with reality, and which detracts from virtue and inner peace. This is why Epictetus says:

> The substance of goodness is the proper use of impressions. (*Dis* I, 20)

So far we have characterized Epictetus's views primarily in terms of a training through which we learn to align our volition so as to will what is good, to ignore what is indifferent, and to eschew what is bad. How does this relate to our duties to others? To explain Epictetus's view on this point, the contemporary scholar A. A. Long introduces the term *integrity*.[38] Integrity is the way in which a good will manifests itself in relation to other people. It links cultivation of the self to one's duties to others. Thus, it includes justice, shame, trustworthiness, conscience, and respect. According to Long, integrity is the concept in Epictetus that is equivalent to moral sense.

In contemporary thought, we often understand happiness and morality as opposites. This is because morality requires altruism, which involves giving up some self-interest. For much ancient thinking, this conception is a mistake. Proper concern for others is part of our *eudaimonia*, and in this way ethics is the road to flourishing. In part this is why it is misleading to translate *eudaimonia* as happiness: *eudaimonia* is the good or flourishing life, and it encompasses much more than feelings of pleasure. These points apply to the Stoics in general and to Epictetus in particular.

To understand why integrity is a manifestation of the will, we need to consider the following:

> Wherever "I" and "mine" are placed, to there the creature inevitably inclines. . . . Accordingly, if I am there, where my volition is, thus and only thus shall I be the friend and son and father that I should be. For this will then be my interest—to preserve my integrity, patience, abstemiousness, and cooperation, and to preserve my human relationships. (*Dis* II, 22)

In other words, when we identify ourselves with the will or volition, then we thereby identify ourselves with a universal point of view that allows us to perform social duties properly. For this reason, Epictetus can identify us as world citizens. In other words, Epictetus expands our conception of our self-identity so as to include the universal community of humans and the cosmos as a whole. Because we are the will, we are part of the greater whole in much the same way that a foot is part of a body: it cannot be detached from the rest of the body and remain a foot (II, 5).

The *Encheiridion* provides different methods for interpreting all external impressions and thoughts wisely and beneficially. For instance, if something is not under one's control, then one must accept it as it is and not complain. Paragraph 17 says that one is responsible for playing the role assigned to one admirably, but not for the selection of the role, which the divine Playwright determines. On the other hand, one must not relinquish what is under one's own control. For example, Epictetus says that if someone irritates you, be assured that it is really your judgment that is making you irritated (20).

Marcus Aurelius (121–180 AD)

Marcus Aurelius was born to a prominent Spanish family in Rome. When he was only three months old his father died, and he went to live with his grandfather, who was consul. The Emperor Hadrian knew the child well and thought that he was a born leader. Aurelius received an excellent education. By the age of 12, he was mastering geometry, music, mathematics, painting, literature and, most of all, philosophy. He showed so much promise and talent that when the emperor Hadrian chose Aurelius's uncle Antoninus as his successor, he also specified that Antoninus should designate Aurelius to be the next emperor. Despite being the heir apparent to the imperial throne of Rome, Marcus Aurelius lived the simple life of a Stoic. In 161, at the age of 39, he became the fourteenth Roman Emperor. During his nineteen-year-long reign he brought about many legal, social, educational, and economic reforms. He championed the poor, improved the condition of slaves, and initiated programs to aid young children. After years of peace, it was Marcus Aurelius's misfortune that, during his reign the Roman Empire came under attack from many quarters. He successfully resisted the threats of invasion in Syria, Spain, Egypt, Britain, and Italy, as well as from the Germanic tribes along the Rhine-Danube frontier. He appointed his son, Commodus, as his successor.

During the tumult of war, Marcus Aurelius wrote the *Meditations*, probably for personal reasons rather than for a readership, in order to nourish himself with noble thoughts during a seven-year military campaign. The book reveals the eloquence of a Stoic philosopher on a path of self-discovery and enlightenment through a regime of self-examination and self-discipline. The overarching theme of the *Meditations* is that there is only one thing to keep a person free: philosophy. The *Meditations* constitute a structured reflection that puts this claim into practice, as well as being an exercise in self-discipline.

Marcus Aurelius articulates three fundamental principles of Stoicism: first, external matters do not affect the soul; second, everything changes; third, all things are one (40). Several of the early sections elaborate and draw out the implications of these first two principles. For example, the first principle is amplified at section 7, where Aurelius says that if one discards the thought of injury, the injury will be gone. It is our judgment of events that harms us rather than the events themselves (39). The second principle is expounded in various ways. For instance, at section 17 Marcus Aurelius reminds himself that his life is short as a spur to practice virtue diligently. In several passages Aurelius emphasizes that he is a being with reason (e.g., 13 and 14). Reason can grasp the order in all changes, and in this way a person can be in tune with the universe rather than being a stranger (e.g., 22, 27, 29, and 36).

Conclusion

The Stoics regard the universe as entirely physical but animated by an active principle of reason. This active principle is itself physical but it is the intelligent organizing power of the whole cosmos. It is divine. This divine principle is also present in the human soul as reason, which pervades the whole of our life. It permits us to control our impressions and desires. This point has great ethical importance.

Following their founder, Zeno, the Stoics argue that the only good is virtue and the only bad thing is vice. Pleasure, wealth, reputation, and life itself are morally indifferent, although they are preferred. Such contingencies are not good, even though we prefer them. The Stoics define the good as living in accordance with Nature, which in the case of humans means living in accordance with reason, which in turn means living in accordance with the active principle of the universe as a whole. From this perspective, the fortunes and misfortunes of one's life are indifferent.

According to the Stoics, a life in accordance with reason is virtuous and happy. It has an unconditional value that doesn't depend on external circumstances. Virtue alone is good in all circumstances. Persons are responsible only for what is in their power to control, namely, their character and the right intentions of their actions. Concerning what is beyond our control, the Stoics advocates acceptance.

Study Questions

1. How do the Stoics distinguish what exists from what subsists? Why is this distinction important for their thought?
2. What is the distinction between the active and the passive principles in Stoicism?
3. What is the active principle physically composed of?
4. What is the problem with the claim that the active principle is composed of one or more of the elements?
5. What is the role of the active principle?
6. Why do the Stoics regard the active principle as divine?
7. What is the Stoic idea of fate?
8. What is the Stoic idea of *oikeiôsis*?
9. Explain the Stoic conception of the soul.
10. How do the Stoics define the good?
11. Humans are rational animals. What does this mean for the Stoics?
12. The active principle of the universe is the same as human reason. Why is this point important for Stoic ethics?
13. Why do the Stoics claim that only virtue is good and that natural benefits and harms are indifferent? How would they support such a claim?
14. How does Zeno support the claim that virtue is necessary and sufficient for *eudaimonia*?
15. What is the difference between receiving impressions and perception according to the Stoics?
16. What is the Stoic distinction between the true and the truth?
17. What is the Stoic conception of the *lekton*?
18. Explain the Stoic conception of propositional logic.
19. What is Epictetus's distinction between the internal and external? How is this distinction the basis of his theory of the good?

20. How does Epictetus arrive at the conclusion that we are all citizens of the world?

Discussion Questions

1. Can the claim that natural benefits and harms are indifferent be justified?
2. Are the Stoics right to claim that we can assent or dissent from our impressions?
3. Are humans rational animals in the way that the Stoics think?

15

Skepticism
Pyrrho and Sextus

*P*yrrho of Elis (367–275 BC) inspired the movement that has his name. Pyrrho was a sage who refused to pass judgment on anything in order to acquire tranquility and peace. Pyrrhonism went through a decline in popularity after his death. However, Aenesidemus revived it in the first century BC, and he distinguished Pyrrhonism from Academic skepticism. The latter was developed in Plato's Academy under Arcesilaus (315–241 BC) and Carneades (213–129 BC).

The difference between the two is philosophically important. Academic skepticism consists primarily in skeptical theses about what we cannot know and why. As such, it is constituted by claims or judgments, which need to be supported with argumentation. In contrast, Pyrrhonean skepticism is a practice of refusing to pass judgments of any kind in order to attain a tranquility of mind. Ideally, it doesn't consist of judgments or claims that need support. On the contrary, it is a practice comprised of refusing to make such judgments.

In the course of this chapter, we shall see that this standard way of distinguishing between the two types of skepticism is historically and philosophically problematic. It is philosophically problematic because it is not clear that Pyrrhonean skepticism can commit itself consistently to such a refusal. It is historically problematic because in practice the lines are blurred: the Academics were interested in tranquility and some of their claims look Pyrrhonic, and Pyrrho seems to advance skeptical theses.

The differences are least blurred in the writing of Sextus Empiricus (175–225 AD), whose writings are the only complete Pyrrhonist works to have survived. It is to Sextus that we should look for a clear statement of Pyrrhonism, which we can contrast with the later Academic skepticism of Carneades.

PYRRHO OF ELIS (367–275 BC)

We know little about Pyrrho himself. Elis is on the Northwestern side of the Peloponnesian peninsula in southern Greece, quite close to

Olympia. Pyrrho may have been a pupil of Bryson, who followed the Megarian school of thought. But Pyrrho was attracted by the Cynic philosophy, which advocates simplicity, living in accord with Nature, and freedom from social conventions. It is reported that Pyrrho traveled to India as part of the entourage of Alexander the Great. We have stories from Diogenes Laërtius that recount how Pyrrho was so indifferent that he would have died from falling or being run over by a cart, had friends not kept him from harm. These stories are perhaps not credible and may have been invented by dogmatist detractors. Since Pyrrho was famous as a sage, his followers played down such unflattering stories. Other stories tell of Pyrrho's calmness on a boat in the face of a huge storm, and his general imperturbable tranquility. In general, we can affirm that Pyrrho was greatly admired during his lifetime for his calm.

Pyrrho wrote nothing. This means that we are tempted to rely heavily on later writers, such as Aenesidemus and especially Sextus Empiricus (175–225 AD) for our understanding of Pyrrho. This is open to challenge.[1] However, one of Pyrrho's pupils, Timon of Phlius (320–230 BC), did write extensively, and some fragments from his work have survived. A preliminary approach to Pyrrho would be to focus on these more dependable fragments rather than simply assuming that the works of Sextus reflect the views of Pyrrho.

The most substantial fragment originating from Timon and that purports to reflect the views of Pyrrho is reported in a work by Aristocles of Messene in Sicily from the second century AD.[2] In this passage, Pyrrho is reported as claiming that the person who wants to be happy should consider three questions: what are things really like, what attitude should we have towards them, and what will the consequences of these attitudes be?

In answer to the three questions, Pyrrho first argues that things are indistinguishable, unmeasurable, and indeterminable. For this reason, our judgments and perceptions are neither true nor false.

> Things are equally indifferentiable and unmeasurable and undecidable; because of this neither our perceptions nor opinions tell the truth or lie. Because of this, then, we must not trust them, but we must be without opinions. . . . (Eusebius, 14.18.3–4)[3]

Concerning the second question, we should be without judgments by refusing to commit ourselves to any claim. Concerning the third question, the consequences of such an attitude will be a refusal to make judgments at all, and freedom from disturbance.

The first part of this passage can be read in two ways. First, objectively: Pyrrho is asserting something about reality, namely, that it is undifferentiated or indeterminate and that, because of this, our opinions are neither true nor false; they lack truth-value. According to this reading, Pyrrho is making a positive assertion about reality and is drawing skeptical conclusions from that. Second, we can read the passage subjectively: Pyrrho isn't asserting anything about reality; he is claiming that we cannot know or decide how reality is. He isn't asserting that our opinions lack truth-value. Instead, the crucial sentence in the above passage affirms that our opinions don't tell us about reality.[4]

Traditionally, Pyrrho is taken to be a Pyrrhonist! Accordingly, Pyrrho shouldn't be taken as making judgments about reality but rather as refusing to judge how things are. This traditional interpretation of Pyrrho best fits a subjective reading of the above passage. In contrast, the objective reading of the passage would contradict the kind of Pyrrhonean skepticism that Sextus Empiricus advances. It implies making the affirmation about reality that things are indeterminate.

In answer to his second question, in the fragment from Aristocles, Pyrrho says:

> We should be without opinions and lean to neither side and remain unwavering, saying concerning each individual thing that it no more is than is not, or both is and is not, or neither is nor is not. (Eusebius, 14.18.4)

Here Pyrrho characterizes the resultant attitude in three different ways. The sage should be "without opinions." With regard to any question, he or she should be inclined towards neither side of the debate and shouldn't waver in this decision to remain uncommitted. Finally, Pyrrho expresses this commitment to being uncommitted in terms of 'no more," meaning no more to this than to that. What Pyrrho seems to be saying is that we shouldn't be committed to any one of the following claims more than any of the others: X is F; X is not F; X is both F and not F; X is neither F nor not F. These explanations of the Pyrrhonist attitude are in many ways similar to those of Sextus.

Regarding the third point, the consequence of the attitude is twofold. The person will experience non-assertion or *aphasia*, which will result in tranquility or *ataraxia*. This state is said to be "freedom from confusion" and disturbance.

Other sources indicate that Pyrrho argues that we cannot apprehend objects except through sense perception, which provides no guarantee of veracity. Sense perception tells us how things appear, but this is not good evidence for how things are. Diogenes Laërtius reports that, in *On Perceptions*, Pyrrho's pupil Timon of Phlius writes: "I do not affirm that honey is sweet, but agree that it appears so."[5] There is some evidence to suggest that Pyrrho thinks that appearances provide no evidence for how reality is because appearances conflict. Because things can appear differently to different people, appearances don't provide evidence for how things are (DL IX, 78–9).[6]

This point is explicit in Sextus Empiricus in his description of the skeptical method. The different appearances or opinions have equal force of conviction (*isostheneia*). More precisely, they are experienced as such by the skeptic. Since they are contradictory, one cannot assent to all of them. Thus, one should assent to none or suspend assent (*epoché*). A similar form of reasoning applies in the moral case, as we shall now see.

According to Diogenes Laërtius, Pyrrho "denied that anything was morally good or bad" (IX, 61).[7] Diogenes attributes to Pyrrho the claim that

> ... equally in all cases that nothing is in truth, but that people do everything by law and custom, for each thing is no more this than that. (DL IX, 61)

The Pyrrhoneans argue as follows: since the different opinions about what is good have equal strength of conviction, one cannot assent to just one. This implies either that anything that is held to be good is good, or that one cannot say that anything is good. The first alternative, however, must be ruled out because people have contradictory views about what is good. Therefore, we are left with the second alternative, which is that one cannot claim that anything is good (DL IX, 101).

ACADEMIC SKEPTICISM

Arcesilaus became head of Plato's Academy in 268 BC. He was drawn more to the dialectics and uncertainties of Socratic questioning than to the metaphysical theories of Plato. Remember how Socrates disavows having knowledge, and how many of the Socratic dialogues end inconclusively in *aporia* (see chapter 4). These aspects of Plato's work and the Socratic method inspired Arcesilaus.

However, the Socratic method doesn't amount to a skeptical philosophy. It consists in the practice of challenging views and the arguments for them, and withholding judgment until a decisive argument has been found. It doesn't consist of the positive claim that no such argument can be found, nor of the attempt to prove that knowledge is impossible. It is more like a therapeutic practice than a set of conclusions.

It is debatable to what degree Arcesilaus argues for positive skeptical conclusions.[8] First, according to Cicero, Arcesilaus tries to refute aspects of particular philosophies, especially Stoicism. As we saw in the previous chapter, the Stoics claim that there are some impressions that are beyond doubt. Arcesilaus contends that such impressions would be indistinguishable from false ones. Second, Arcesilaus may advance considerations for the skeptical conclusion that we do not have secure knowledge, employing the arguments in Plato's *Parmenides* against the existence of transcendent Forms (see chapter 8). If we cannot be sure that the Forms exist, then we are left with uncertainty without the possibility of knowledge. He also may accept the thesis of Democritus and other Pre-Socratics that the appearances are not reliable sources of knowledge of reality.

Should we attribute such skeptical arguments and conclusions to Arcesilaus? If we do, then we place him in the kind of dilemma that we discussed in relation to Socrates himself: a person cannot claim to know that he doesn't know anything. It would seem to be more in accordance with the evidence to claim that, like Socrates, Arcesilaus practiced the arts of skeptical inquiry without arguing for positive skeptical conclusions.[9] If this is so, then this makes Arcesilaus's thinking more akin to the traditional interpretation of Pyrrho's thought. Indeed, Sextus Empiricus claims that Arcesilaus's skepticism was similar to Pyrrhonism (*PH* 1, 232).[10]

For a more stark contrast between Pyrrhonism and Academic skepticism, we must turn to Carneades. According to Sextus Empiricus, Carneades is clearer that truth cannot be known (*PH* 1, 226). In this way he is different from the Pyrrhonists and even from Arcesilaus. Whereas Arcesilaus's thinking seems to be motivated by the desire to avoid error, which implies that there are truths to be known, Carneades's position entails that there is no point investigating anything because knowledge is impossible. In contrast, according to the Pyrrhonean, such a claim is itself too dogmatic. This is because such finality is premature: we do not know that nothing can be known. Instead, according to the Pyrrhoneans, we should merely suspend judgment, without affirming or denying anything. Things appear a certain way, and the Pyrrhonean skeptic accepts this without judging whether reality really is how it seems.

Sextus Empiricus (175–225 AD)

Sextus Empiricus is the only Pyrrhonean skeptic whose writings have survived. He was trained as a medical doctor and teacher, and he became the last leader of the Pyrrhonean movement. His written works provide an overview of the arguments worked out by previous skeptics. We have three works by Sextus: *Outlines of Pyrrhonism, Against the Dogmatists*, and *Against the Professors*.

- The treatise *Against the Professors* is sometimes also called *Against the Learned*, and it contains six books, namely, *Against the Grammarians, Against the Rhetoricians, Against the Geometers, Against the Arithmeticians, Against the Astrologers*, and *Against the Musicians*.
- *Against the Dogmatists* contains five books, two called *Against the Logicians*, two called *Against the Physicists*, and one named *Against the Ethicists*.

Sometimes these two works are placed together as *Adversus Mathematicos*, containing 11 books. These contain detailed arguments against the claim to knowledge in the liberal arts (such as grammar, geometry, astronomy, and music), as well as in philosophy. Ironically, these works are two important sources of knowledge about the early history of astronomy, geometry, grammar, and Stoic theology.

Although we have a lot of his writing, it is difficult to disentangle when Sextus asserts for himself and when he is merely repeating what earlier skeptics have said.

Sextus begins his *Outlines of Pyrrhonism* (Pyrrhoniae Hypotyposes, or *PH*) by dividing those who inquire into three groups. First are those who claim to have found the answer, such as the Stoics. Second are thinkers who claim that questions cannot be answered, such as the Academic skeptics. Finally are those who think that questions have not yet been answered, the Pyrrhoneans. Only this third group carries on with the relevant inquiries. This is philosophically the healthiest position: not to draw premature and final conclusions. Sextus defines skepticism as the ability to place our sense impressions and our intellect in opposition to each other. It is an ability that

> because of the equal force which characterizes opposing objects and reasonings, we arrive first at suspension of assent and after that, at tranquility. (*PH* I, 8)

Sextus usually opposes skepticism with dogmatism. In this context, the term *dogmatism* doesn't have the contemporary implication that someone holds views stubbornly or without reason. A dogmatist is simply someone who makes judgments based on opinions.

The *Outlines of Pyrrhonism* is a general summary of the various Pyrrhonean arguments organized as a philosophical method to aid the skeptic in maintaining his healthy and quiet skeptical attitude of neither affirming nor denying anything beyond the immediate sense impressions that "induce our assent involuntarily" (10).

The skeptic is the person who exercises the abilities that are outlined in the Pyrrhonean method in order to attain tranquility. Such a person must have sought tranquility through holding opinions or searching for truth in the past, and of course failed through dogmatism. The skeptic will experience the diverse opinions about something as being equal in force of conviction (*isostheneia*). This means that the skeptic must find the diverse opinions equally plausible. The method helps the skeptic to attain *isostheneia* and thereby suspension of assent (or *epoché*). Just as medical doctors use varying remedies of different strengths to cure the sick depending on the severity of their illness, so the skeptical philosopher must use arguments of appropriate strength and measure to cure the philosophical ills of dogmatic belief and to find diverse opinions equally plausible. The strongest skeptical arguments should be applied to the more entrenched beliefs with the aim of showing that one does not really know what one thinks one knows. The *Outlines of Pyrrhonism* helps the skeptic to apply the appropriate skeptical reasoning at the right time.

The ultimate aim of this skeptical attitude is to achieve tranquility or quietude. This state requires the suspension of judgment because the person who judges that anything is by nature good or bad is always being disquieted (12). According to Sextus, freedom from disturbance is "a consequence of suspending judgment (about the inconsistency which belongs to appearances and judgments)" (29).

These points enable us to make three important clarifications with regard to Pyrrhonean skepticism. First, unlike the dogmatist, the skeptic limits himself to describing appearances or his experiences as they appear to him. He says:

> what appears to himself and reports his own experience without holding opinions, making no firm pronouncements about external objects. (*PH* I, 15)

A person who feels warm in the shade and cold in the sun is not mistaken in those feelings, even though those feelings conflict with those of other people (DL IX, 80; Sextus *PH* I, 82). In short, the Pyrrhonists draw a sharp distinction between statements of the form "X appears to be F to person A" and those of the form "X is F" (DL IX, 103). The former don't provide a good reason for asserting judgments of the latter kind. We can't infer the nature of reality from how it appears to us. Because of this, we should avoid making judgments about how external objects are.

The Pyrrhonean would regard judgments about things appear simply as reports of one's perceptual experience (DL IX, 78). Such claims do not purport to tell us how the world itself actually is. Therefore, such claims are not subject to the suspension of judgment. In other words, the skeptic does not suspend judgment about immediate experience. This is an important point, as we shall see.

Second, we navigate the world practically, on the basis of the "objects as perceived" (or appearances) without making the further step of making judgments about how things really are (DL IX, 106). This means that, for practical purposes, Pyrrhonists can present their view as siding with common sense and as suspending judgment solely towards philosophical positions that make assertions about the world. In this way, the Pyrrhonists try to have the best of both worlds: escape the confusion surrounding philosophical positions regarding the nature of reality and the gods, but without giving up the practical reliance on perceptions and appearances for functional purposes.

Third, we can see Sextus's own philosophy as a recipe book or as descriptions of his own experiences rather than as a set of philosophical assertions. For example, when he says that every opinion on a subject-matter has equal force, these phrases are not to be understood as philosophical assertions, but rather merely as an expression of the decision to not make any judgments, or as a description of Sextus's own experience (*PH* I, 203). Thus, if a Pyrrhonean skeptic says, "snow is no more white than non-white," this itself is not to count as a judgment that provides a description or determination. It is merely an expression of his or her decision not to make judgments about how things are. Likewise, as the first book of the *Outlines of Pyrrhonism* suggests, Sextus's method doesn't consist in a set of philosophical assertions, but rather in guidance or a recipe for the person who wants to find tranquility.

In fact, Sextus explicitly adopts nonassertive speech, which he defines as "an affect that precludes us from saying that we posit or deny anything" (*PH* I, 192). He adds:

> Hence it is clear that we adopt non-assertion, too, not with the idea that things are by nature such as to drive us absolutely to non-assertion. (I, 193)

This quote should be compared with the objective reading of the fragment from Timon, which we discussed in the section on Pyrrho.

Influences

The Greek term *skepsis* means inquiry, and the Pyrrhonean skeptics were thinkers who argued for persistence in inquiry. They claimed that one should not accept anything as true until it has been subjected to exhaustive and rigorous scrutiny. In contrast, today, the English word *skeptic* means, roughly, "doubter."

Pyrrhonean skepticism had a liberating effect on early modern thought. In his popular *Essays* (1580), the French Renaissance thinker Montaigne takes his reader on a tour of ancient philosophy. Initially, he finds wisdom in the ethics of Stoicism but, as the *Essays* proceed, he is drawn increasingly towards skepticism. Like Pyrrho, Montaigne decides to suspend all judgment and simply to observe. His *Essays* present skepticism with a very human and reasonable face; they oppose any religious dogmatism and articulate the humanism and the freedom of thought of the Renaissance.

Descartes, who knew of Pyrrhoneanism through Montaigne's *Essays*, revolutionized philosophy with his method of doubt in his *Meditations on First Philosophy* (1641). Descartes argued that it was reasonable to suspend judgment as to the veracity of our perceptions, fundamentally because there is no independent way to check them. Descartes' skeptical arguments set a fundamental problem that many later philosophers tried to solve: how can we have justified knowledge of the external world?

Conclusion

The skepticism of Pyrrho is a method for achieving tranquility or *ataraxia*. This method consists of refusing to pass judgment on any claim that transcends how things appear to oneself. Therefore, according to a Pyrrhonean skeptic, one wouldn't affirm or deny that honey is sweet, but one might agree that it appears sweet to oneself. This method consists of suspending judgment and experiencing diverse opinions as equally convincing. The method enables the sage to remain undisturbed and tranquil, especially when it is applied to judgments about what is good and bad.

Study Questions

1. How is academic skepticism different from Pyrrhonean skepticism?
2. What does Pyrrho mean when he says that things are indifferentiable and unmeasurable and undecidable? What implications does this claim have for judgments?
3. What does Pyrrho mean by "no more this than that?"
4. Why does Pyrrho think that sense perception doesn't give us evidence for how things are?
5. In what ways does the Socratic method *not* amount to a skeptical philosophy?
6. Why would a Pyrrhonean not claim that knowledge is impossible?
7. How does Sextus Empiricus contrast skepticism with dogmatism?
8. What is *isostheneia*?
9. According to Sextus Empiricus, how can a Pyrrhonean skeptic live practically without making judgments about how things are?
10. According to Sextus Empiricus, how can a Pyrrhonean skeptic affirm his or her own philosophical view about non-assertion without contradiction?

Discussion Questions

1. Is the Pyrrhonean skeptic committed to the assertion that tranquility is good? Why is this point important?
2. Is it possible to suspend judgment in the way that the Pyrrhonean claims?
3. Is Pyrrhonism a more defensible philosophical position than dogmatic skepticism?

Timeline

BCE

ca. 800	End of Dark Age and beginning of Archaic Period
776	First Olympian Games
ca. 750	Homer's *Iliad* and *Odyssey*
ca. 700	Hesiod composes *Theogony* and *Works and Days*
ca. 624	Thales
585	Eclipse that was predicted by Thales
ca. 580	Anaximander
ca. 550	Anaximenes
ca. 540	Xenophanes
	Pythagoras
525	Persians conquer Egypt
ca. 500	Heraclitus
499	Ionian revolt against Persia
494	Persians sack Miletus
490	Persian Wars: Battle of Marathon
480	Persian Wars: Battle of Salamis
ca. 480	Parmenides
479	Persian Wars: Battle of Plataea
477	Formation of Delian League under Athens
469	Socrates born
460	Start of First Peloponnesian War
ca. 460	Anaxagoras
	Empedocles
458	Aeschylus's *Oresteia*
ca. 450	Zeno
	Melissus
	Democritus born
450	Great Panathenaia, probable dramatic date of Plato's *Parmenides*
447	Pericles initiates the construction of the Parthenon
445	End of First Peloponnesian War: Thirty Years' Peace

Timeline

441–39	Samos revolts from Athens
ca. 440	Leucippus
431	Start of the second Peloponnesian War
430–29	Plague in Athens
ca. 430	Diogenes of Apollonia
	Philolaus
429	Death of Pericles
ca. 428	Plato born
428	Sophocles's *Oedipus*
423	Aristophanes's *Clouds* first performed
415–413	Sicilian Expedition under leadership of Alcibiades
411	Aristophanes's *Lysistrata*
410	Democracy restored in Athens
404	End of Second Peloponnesian War: surrender of Athens
404–403	Thirty Tyrants in Athens
399	Death of Socrates
384	Aristotle born
360	Philip II became king of Macedon
352	Philip II becomes commander of Thessalian League
ca. 360	Death of Democritus
ca. 347	Death of Plato
338	Philip II wins battle against Athens and Thebes at Chaeronea
336	Philip II assassinated; Alexander the Great begins his reign
334	Alexander begins conquest of Asia
331	Alexander conquers Egypt
ca. 335	Aristotle begins teaching in the Lyceum
ca. 320–230	Timon of Phlius
326	Alexander wins Battle of the Hydraspes
323	Alexander the Great dies
322	Death of Aristotle
321	Death of Perdiccas; Antipater controls regency
300	Zeno of Citium teaches in the Stoa
367–275	Pyrrho of Elis
341–270	Epicurus
268	Arcesilaus becomes head of Academy
262	Death of Zeno of Citium; Cleanthes heads the Stoa
285	Death of Theophrastus
ca. 280	Three Macedonian kingdoms
232	Chrysippus becomes the third head of the Stoa
196	Rome defeats King of Macedonia

146	Greece is a protectorate of Rome
106–43	Cicero
99–55	Lucretius
31	Defeat of Cleopatra
30	Augustus establishes the Roman Empire

AD

55–135	Epictetus
65	Death of Seneca
ca. 50–ca.120	Plutarch
79	Eruption of Vesuvius
1st–2nd century	Aëtius
130	Death of Epictetus
161	Marcus Aurelius becomes Emperor
180	Death of Marcus Aurelius
	Clement of Alexandria
	Dionysius of Corinth
129–ca. 199	Galen
175–225	Sextus Empiricus
204–270	Plotinus
2nd–3rd century	Eusebius of Caesarea
	Hippolytus of Rome
3rd century	Diogenes Laërtius
4th century	Themistius
5th century	Stobaeus
529	Emperor Justinian closes the four philosophical schools in Athens
6th century	Simplicius

Endnotes

Preface
[1] Bernard Williams, *The Sense of the Past* (Princeton University Press, 2006, 3).

Historical and Cultural Introduction
[1] Bernard Williams (2006, 6) claims that the only two substantial general themes of contemporary philosophy removed from ancient philosophy are idealism and historical consciousness.

Part I: Early Ancient Greek Philosophy
[1] Charles Kahn divides the Pre-Socratics into three phases. See Kahn, "The Achievement of Early Greek Philosophy," *Early Greek Philosophy*, ed. Joe McCoy (Catholic University of America Press, 2013).
[2] See Trevor Curnow, *The Philosophers of the Ancient World, An A–Z Guide* (Bristol Classical Press, 2011).
[3] James Warren, *Presocratics* (Acumen, 2007), 3.
[4] Warren, 3.
[5] *Physics* I, 2–9. See also *Metaphysics* A, 3–10 and *De Anima* I, 2–5.

Chapter 1
[1] That claim is anachronistic because no such distinction existed 2,500 years ago; the early ancients did not separate philosophy (conceptual questions that are answered through reasoning) and science (empirical questions that are best addressed through observation).
[2] Diogenes Laërtius, *Lives of the Philosophers* I, 22–28.
[3] Herodotus, *Histories* I, 170.3.
[4] Herodotus, *Histories* I, 75.4.
[5] Diogenes Laërtius, *Lives of the Philosophers* I.
[6] DK stands for Hermann Diels and Walther Kranz, *Die Fragmente der Vorsokratiker* (Zurich: Weidmann, 1985).
[7] Joe McCoy, ed., introduction to *Early Greek Philosophy: The Presocratics and the Emergence of Reason* (Catholic University of America Press, 2013), xv.
[8] Keimpe Algra, "The Beginnings of Cosmology," *Cambridge Companion to Early Greek Philosophy*, ed. A. A. Long (Cambridge University Press, 1999), 50–52.
[9] Aristotle, *De Anima* 411a7 and 405a19.
[10] Jonathan Barnes, *The Presocratic Philosophers* (Routledge and Kegan Paul, 19830), 5.
[11] Hippolytus, *Refutation of all Heresies* I, vi, 1–7.
[12] Aristotle makes a report similar to Simplicius's at *Metaphysics* 1069b19 but does not directly attribute the argument to Anaximander.
[13] Aristotle, *On the Heavens* (De Caelo) II, 295b10–16.
[14] Simplicius, *Phys.* 24, 26.

15. Hippolytus, *Refutation of all Heresies* I, vi, 1–9.
16. Plutarch, *On the Scientific Beliefs of the Philosophers*, 876 AB.
17. Herodotus II, 81 and Isocrates, *Busiris*, 28.
18. Iamblichus, *Life of Pythagoras*, 81 (written around 300 AD).
19. Carl Huffman, "The Pythagorean Tradition," in Long, *Cambridge Companion*, 67–70.
20. Isocrates, *Busiris*, 28–9, quoted in J. Barnes, *Early Greek Philosophy* (Penguin Books, 1987), 84.
21. Porphyry, *Life of Pythagoras*, 19.
22. Charles Kahn, *Pythagoras and the Early Pythagoreans* (Hackett, 2001), 9.
23. Kahn, *Pythagoras*, 19–22.
24. Diogenes Laërtius, *The Lives of the Philosophers* VIII, 4–5.
25. Diodorus, *Universal History* X, vi, 1–3.
26. Walter Burkert, *Love and Science in Ancient Pythagoreanism*, trans. Edwin L. Minar, Jr. (Harvard University Press, 1972).
27. Plato, *Republic* Book VII, 530d.
28. Plato, *Republic* Book X, 600a.
29. Sextus Empiricus, *Against the Mathematicians* VII, 94–5.
30. Kahn, *Pythagoras*, 31.
31. Aristotle, *On the Heavens* 293a18–24 and 293b18–25.
32. Huffman, *Archytas of Tarentum: Pythagorean, Philosopher and Mathematician King* (Cambridge University Press, 2005).
33. Aristotle, *Metaphysics*, 1080b16–21 and 1090a20–25.
34. Aristotle, *Metaphysics*, 987a13–19.
35. The first view is argued for by Carl Huffman, "The Pythagorean Tradition," in Long, *Cambridge Companion*, and the second by Kahn, *Pythagoras*.
36. B25 and B26 in Simplicius, *Commentary on the Physics* 22.26–23.20.
37. Of these, about 89 qualify as citations from Heraclitus's text; the rest are partial quotations and reports of doctrine.
38. James Warren, *Presocratics* (Acumen, 2007), 61–63.
39. Such as B50.
40. Plato, *Cratylus*, 402A.
41. Aristotle, *Metaphysics*, 987a32–b1.
42. Aristotle *Metaphysics*, 1010a12–15.
43. Barnes, *The Presocratic Philosophers*, 68–69.
44. This doesn't mean that the soul is composed of fire. Heraclitus may conceive the soul as composed of air; see Charles Kahn, *The Art and Thought of Heraclitus* (Cambridge University Press, 1981), 128.
45. Kahn, *The Art and Thought*, 14–16, 21.
46. Kahn, *The Art and Thought*, 183.
47. Kahn, *The Art and Thought*, especially 240.
48. Kenneth Dorter, "The Problem of Evil in Heraclitus," in McCoy, ed., *Early Greek Philosophy*.

Chapter 2

1. A. H. Coxon, *The Fragments of Parmenides: A Critical Text with Introduction and Translation, the Ancient Testimonia and a Commentary* (Parmenides, 2009).
2. R. D. McKirahan, *Philosophy Before Socrates: An Introduction with Texts and Commentary* (Hackett, 1994), 177.
3. Theophrastus, *On Sensation* I, 3, DK28A46. See also McKirahan, *Philosophy Before Socrates*, 177.
4. Plato, *Parmenides*, 127a.
5. *Physics*, VI, 9.
6. Simplicius, 139.9–11 (DK29B2) and 141.2. Simplicius wrote his commentary around 530 AD.
7. Simplicius, 140.29.
8. McKirahan, *Philosophy Before Socrates*, 185.
9. See N. Huggett, *Stanford Encyclopedia of Philosophy* (http://plato.stanford.edu/entries/paradox-zeno/).

10. Aristotle, *Physics* IV, 3, 210b22–3 and Simplicius, 562, 3–6 (DK29B5).
11. Aristotle, *On Generation and Corruption*, 316a9 and Simplicius, 139.24.
12. Plato, *Parmenides*, 127e.
13. Plato, *Parmenides*, 129a–d.
14. Jonathan Barnes, *The Presocratic Philosophers* (Routledge and Kegan Paul, 1983), 234–36.
15. For example, Barnes (*The Presocratic Philosophers*, 285) argues that Zeno's argumentation does not depend on such assumptions.
16. For an exploration of some of these issues see Mary Tiles, *The Philosophy of Set Theory* (Dover, 1989).
17. See B. Dowden, "Zeno's Paradoxes," *Internet Encyclopedia of Philosophy* (http://www.iep.utm.edu/zeno-par/).
18. See F. Arntzenius, "Are There Really Instantaneous Velocities?" *The Monist* 83 (2000): 187–208.
19. D. Bohm, *Wholeness and the Implicate Order* (Routledge, 1983).
20. See, e.g., A. Papa-Grimaldi, "Why Mathematical Solutions of Zeno's Paradoxes miss the Point," *Revue of Metaphysics* 50 (December 1996).

Chapter 3

1. C. Osborn, ed., *Rethinking Early Greek Philosophy* (Cornell University Press, 1987) and B. Inwood, ed., *The Poem of Empedocles* (University of Toronto Press, 1992).
2. See James Warren, *The Presocratics* (Routledge), 136.
3. See R. D. McKirahan, *Philosophy Before Socrates* (Hackett, 1994), 256.
4. McKirahan, 260.
5. McKirahan, 261.
6. Advocates of some version of the standard view include W. K. C. Guthrie, J. Barnes, and R. McKirahan.
7. Aristotle, *On the Heavens* III, 2, 301a14–20.
8. Aristotle, *Physics* 1, 4, 187a23–b6.
9. Warren, *The Presocratics*, 122.
10. McKirahan, 204.
11. This is Zeno's fourth argument, which is given in chapter 2 on page 54.
12. McKirahan, 218.
13. See chapter 4 and chapter 11.
14. There are about 300 extant fragments from Democritus; of these, 220 concern ethics. See *Early Greek Philosophy*, ed./ trans. J. Barnes (Harmondsworth, 1987), 530.
15. McKirahan, 315.
16. This is the first of five arguments that we listed in chapter 2 on pages 52–53.
17. This is the fourth of the five arguments.
18. *Histories* III, 38.
19. The main difference concerns the semantics of justice: Callicles thinks that pursuing one's own interest is naturally just, and Thrasymachus thinks that such rational self-interest is unjust but that justice is to be avoided for the sake of self-interest.
20. J. Barnes, *The Presocratic Philosophers* (Routledge, 1983), 448.
21. Diogenes Laërtius IX, 53–4.
22. Plato, *Phaedrus*, 267c and Aristotle, *Rhetoric*, 1407b6–7.
23. His views are also discussed without his presence in the *Cratylus* and *Euthydemus*.
24. *Theaetetus*, 152b–d and 167b–d.
25. See, e.g., DK80A1 (Diogenes Laërtius, *Lives of the Philosophers*, 9.53). However, Aristotle thinks that Protagoras does deny the principle of non-contradiction (*Metaphysics* IV, 4–5).
26. Barnes, *Presocratic Philosophers*, 547–50.
27. Sextus Empiricus, *Against the Mathematicians* VII, 389–90.
28. Aristotle, *Metaphysics*, 1007b, 20–22.
29. Aristotle, *Rhetoric* II, 24, 1402a24–26.

30 J. Lavery, "Protagoras," in *The Sophists: An Introduction*, ed. P. O'Grady (Bloomsbury Academic Press, 2008), chapter 3.
31 C. C. W. Taylor and M. Lee, "The Sophists," *The Stanford Encyclopedia of Philosophy* (Spring 14th ed.), ed. Edward N. Zalta (http://plato.stanford.edu/archives/spr2014/entries/sophists/).
32 Aristotle, *On Melissus, Xenophanes and Gorgias*, and DK82B3.
33 See Barnes, *Presocratic Philosophers*, 173.
34 Please compare this point with that of Zeno's third argument given on pages 53–54 of chapter 2.
35 McKirahan, *Philosophy Before Socrates*, 382.
36 P. Woodruth, "Rhetoric and Relativism," *The Cambridge Companion to Early Greek Philosophy*, ed. A. A. Long (Cambridge University Press, 1999), 306. See also G. B. Kerford, *The Sophistic Movement* (Cambridge University Press, 1981), who has a different interpretation.
37 G. B. Kerford, "The Sophists," *From the Beginning to Plato, Routledge History of Philosophy, Volume I*, ed. C. C. W. Taylor (Routledge, 1997), 255.

Part II: Introduction to Socrates and Plato

1 Plato, *Symposium*, 219e–221b. Plato's dialogue the *Laches* also mentions his bravery in the battle of Delium (181b).
2 Many of these details of Plato's life come from his Seventh Letter, the authenticity of which is disputed.
3 Dion's sister Arisomache was married to Dionysius I.
4 Deborah Nails, "The Life of Plato of Athens," in *A Companion to Plato*, ed. Hugh Benson (Blackwell, 2006).

Chapter 4

1 See William Prior, "The Socratic Problem," *A Companion to Plato*, ed. H. Benson (Blackwell, 2006).
2 G. Vlastos, "The Paradox of Socrates," *The Philosophy of Socrates*, ed. G. Vlastos (Doubleday, 1971).
3 See Aristotle, *Metaphysics*, 987a32.
4 See T. Penner, "Socrates and the Early Dialogues," in *Cambridge Companion to Plato*, ed. R. Kraut (Cambridge University Press, 2006), 123 and ff.
5 G. Vlastos, *Socrates, Ironist and Moral Philosopher* (Doubleday, 1991).
6 This view is represented by C. H. Kahn, *Plato and the Socratic Dialogue* (Cambridge University Press, 1996).
7 Prior, *The Socratic Problem*, 46–47.
8 Prior, 34.
9 In *Euthydemus*, 293b-c, Socrates affirms that he knows many trivial things. In the *Apology*, 22-ce, he professes ignorance of "the most important things."
10 Hugh Benson, *Socratic Wisdom* (Oxford University Press, 2000).
11 Vlastos (*Socrates, Ironist*, ch. 1) argues for this strong claim; Benson (1995) and Brickhouse and Smith (1994) criticize Vlastos's view. See Gregory Vlastos, "The Socratic Elenchus" and "Socrates' Disavowal of Knowledge," *Plato 1: Metaphysics and Epistemology, Oxford Readings in Philosophy*, ed. Gail Fine (Oxford University Press, 2000); T. Brickhouse and N. Smith, *Plato's Socrates* (Clarendon Press, 1994); Benson, "The Dissolution of the Problem of the Elenchus," *Oxford Studies in Ancient Philosophy*, Vol. XIII, ed. C. C. W. Taylor (Clarendon Press, 1995), 45–112.
12 Not (P and Q) is equivalent to Not P or Not Q.
13 *Euthydemus*, 278e; *Meno*, 77b–78b; *Gorgias*, 468b.
14 An argument against the thesis that Socrates was a hedonist may be found in Donald J. Zeyl, "Socrates and Hedonism," *Phronesis* 25 (1980): 250–269. See Gail Fine's introduc-

tion in *Plato 2: Ethics, Politics, Religion and the Soul*, Oxford Readings, ed. Gail Fine (Oxford University Press, 1999).
15. This is the standard view defended in Irwin (1977, 1995). Brickhouse and Smith (1994) and Devereux (1995) argue against it as an interpretation. See T. H. Irwin, *Plato's Moral Theory: The Early and Middle Dialogues* (Oxford and New York: Clarendon Press, 1977); T. C. Brickhouse and N. D. Smith, *Plato's Socrates* (Oxford University Press, 1994); and Daniel Devereux, "Socrates' Kantian Conception of Virtue," *Journal of the History of Philosophy* 33, no. 3 (1995): 381–408; see also T. Brickhouse and N. Smith, "The Socratic Paradoxes," *A Companion to Plato*, ed. H. Benson (Blackwell, 2006).
16. Thank you to Professor Elizabeth Schiltz for this comment.
17. For a different view see T. H. Irwin, "Who Discovered the Will?" *Philosophical Perspectives*, Vol. 6, Ethics, Ridgeview (1992): 453–73.
18. T. Penner, "The Unity of Virtue," *Philosophical Review* 80 (1971), reprinted in Fine (ed.), *Plato 2.*; D. Devereux, "The Unity of the Virtues in Plato's Protagoras and Laches," *Philosophical Review* 101 (1992): 765–89.
19. Fine (Ed.), *Plato 2*.
20. *Apology*, 25d–e.
21. See Brickhouse and Smith, "The Socratic Paradoxes," 274–5.
22. See "The Socratic Paradoxes," 275.
23. Diogenes Laërtius, *Lives of Eminent Philosophers*, Loeb Classical Library, 1925, Vol. II.4.
24. A. A. Long, "How Does Socrates' Divine Sign Communicate with Him?" *A Companion to Socrates*, ed. S. Ahbel-Rappe and R. Kamtekar (Blackwell, 2009), 68–72.
25. This comes from Diogenes Laërtius, who heard it from another person (Favorinus, who saw the public record of the indictment).
26. D. Nails, "The Trial and Death of Socrates," in *A Companion to Socrates* (Blackwell, 2009).

Chapter 5

1. Leonard Brandwood, "Stylometry and Chronology," *The Cambridge Companion to Plato*, ed. R. Kraut (University of Cambridge Press, 1992).
2. Terry Penner, "Plato and the Early Dialogues," in Kraut, *Cambridge Companion to Plato*, 123.
3. Apart from some of the later dialogues, which do have a clear chronology.
4. For a more complete list see Penner, "Plato and the Early Dialogues," 125–30.
5. See Penner, 125.
6. This view is defended by Irwin, *Plato's Moral Theory: The Early and Middle Dialogues* (Oxford University Press, 1979).
7. Gail Fine, *Plato on Knowledge and Forms: Selected Essays* (Clarendon Press, 2003), 3.
8. The Greek phrase is *aitios logismos*.
9. The phrase *aitios logismos* is best translated as an explanatory account and not as "justification." So Plato's view is not quite the same as the more contemporary (and disputed) claim that knowledge is justified true belief. Plato's theory is more is akin to the claim that knowledge is true belief that p for which one can give an explanatory account as to why p is true. See G. Fine, p. 9 (especially footnote 29) in *Plato 1*, ed. G. Fine (Oxford University Press, 2000).

Chapter 6

1. Please see chapter 3 for an overview of Sophism and chapter 5 for some of Plato's arguments against Sophism.
2. In the Analogy of the Divided Line in the *Republic*, Plato draws a distinction between the Forms and mathematical objects (see below).
3. Not all commentators agree with this. Plato himself does not use the term *approximately* in this context. See N. White, "Plato's Metaphysical Epistemology," in *Cambridge Companion to Plato*, ed. Richard Kraut (Cambridge University Press, 1992), 283–84.

4 For the view that the forms are meanings, see D. Bostock, *Plato's* Phaedo (Oxford University Press, 2002).
5 Gail Fine, "Plato: Metaphysics and Epistemology," *Oxford Readings in Philosophy* (Oxford University Press, 2000), 19–20.
6 Fine, "Plato: Metaphysics," p. 18; Gail Fine, *On Ideas* (Oxford University Press, 2004); and S. Peterson, "A Reasonable Self-Predication Premise for the Third Man Argument," *Philosophical Review* 82 (1973).
7 White, "Plato's Metaphysical Epistemology," 292–97.
8 G. E. L. Owen, "A Proof in the Peri Ideon," *Journal of Hellenic Studies* 77 (1957). Owen's interpretation is discussed critically in White, "Plato's Metaphysical Epistemology," 285.
9 These contexts include *Symposium*, 199d–200a and *Parmenides*, 133e–134a. See White, 285.
10 Aristotle, *Metaphysics*, 987a32–b1.
11 For the view that if words are to be meaningful then the Forms exist, see N. P. White, *Plato on Knowledge and Reality* (Hackett, 1976).
12 Gail Fine, "Knowledge and Belief," in *Plato on Knowledge and Forms: Selected Essays*, ed. Gail Fine (Clarendon Press, 2003), 66–84.

Chapter 7

1 C. D. C. Reeve, *Philosopher Kings: The Argument of Plato's* Republic (Hackett, 2006), 19–24.
2 Bernard Williams, *Sense of the Past* (Princeton University Press, 2006), chapter 6.
3 Nicholas White, "Plato's Conception of Goodness," *A Companion to Plato*, ed. Hugh Benson (Blackwell, 2006).
4 David Sachs, "A Fallacy in Plato's *Republic*," *The Philosophical Review* 72.2. (April, 1963): 141–58. For a reply see Norman Dahl, "Plato's Defence of Justice," *Plato 2: Ethics, Politics, Religion and the Soul*, ed. Gail Fine (Oxford University Press, 1999), chapter 8.
5 Fine, *Plato 2*, 21.
6 Rachel Singapurwalla, "Plato's Defense of Justice in the *Republic*," *The Blackwell Guide to Plato's Republic*, ed. G. Santos (Blackwell, 2006), 263–82.
7 This representation of Plato's argument owes much to R. Kraut, "The Defense of Justice in The *Republic*," *The Cambridge Companion to Plato*, ed. R. Kraut (Cambridge University Press, 1999), chapter 10.
8 Kraut, "The Defense of Justice," 320.
9 Fine, ed., *Plato 2*, 20–21.
10 Singapurwalla, "Plato's Defense of Justice," 273.
11 Another possibility is that the view defended in the *Protagoras* is different from those rejected in other dialogues. See J. C. B. Gosling and C. C. W. Taylor, *The Greeks on Pleasure* (Clarendon Press, 1982) chapter 4.
12 Christopher Taylor, "Plato's Totalitarianism," Fine, ed., *Plato 2*, 280–96.
13 See Julia Annas in Fine, ed., *Plato 2*, 265–79.
14 G. Ferrari, "Platonic Love," *The Cambridge Companion to Plato*, 252–53.
15 Martha Nussbaum, "The Speech of Alcibiades: A Reading of the Symposium," *Philosophy and Literature* 3, no. 2 (1979).

Chapter 8

1 This view is also supported by David Bostock, *Plato's Theaetetus* (Clarendon Press, 1988).
2 R. Kraut, "Introduction to the Study of Plato," *The Cambridge Companion to Plato*, ed. R. Kraut (Cambridge University Press, 1992), 15–19.
3 See Samuel Rickless, "Plato's *Parmenides*," *The Stanford Encyclopedia of Philosophy* (Winter 2012), ed. N. Zalta (http://plato.stanford.edu/archives/win2012/entries/plato-parmenides/).
4 C. Meinwald, "Good Bye to the Third Man," *The Cambridge Companion to Plato*, 365.
5 See *Plato's Theaetetus*, trans. John McDowell (Oxford University Press, 2014).
6 See David Bostock, *Plato's Theaetetus* (Clarendon Press, 1988).

7 The father would be either Antoine Lavoisier (1743–1794) or John Dalton (1766–1844), who developed atomic theory.
8 G. E. L. Owen, "Plato on Not–Being," *Plato 1: Metaphysics and Epistemology*, ed. G. Fine (Oxford University Press, 1999), 416–54. See *Plato's Parmenides*, trans. Samuel Scolnicov (University of California Press, 2003).
9 Using a contemporary example, not from Plato, it does not make sense to ask, "How many nonexistent elephants are there in the room?" Any answer would face grave epistemological problems: how does one know that there are N non–existent elephants in the room (where N = any number)? The original question falsely presupposes that non–existent things can *be*.
10 Although Plato uses the term *contrary*, he probably means *contradictory*. Two claims are contradictory if and only if they cannot both be true and they cannot both be false. Two claims are contraries if and only if they cannot both be true, but they could both be false. "X is large" and "X is small" are contraries. For further explanation of the difference, see chapter 9.

Chapter 9

1 The birth of Plato was 428 BC and the death of Aristotle 322 BC.
2 Diogenes Laërtius, *Lives of the Philosophers* V, 22–27.
3 Some of the titles are: *Politicus, Sophistes, Menexenus, Symposium, Gryllus* (on Rhetoric), *Eudemus*.
4 *On Justice, On the Poets, On Wealth, On Prayer, On Good Birth, On Education, On Pleasure*, the *Nerinthus*, and the *Eroticus*.
5 Cicero, Ac. Pr. 38.119.
6 From *The Lives of the Philosophers*, V, 22–27. The list is cited in "Fragments," *Complete Works of Aristotle: The Revised Oxford Translation*, Vol. 2 (Bollingen Series LXXI-2),Sept. 1, 1984, by Aristotle and Jonathan Barnes.
7 This grouping includes *On the Universe, On Colors, On Things Heard, Physiognomonics, On Plants, On Marvelous Things Heard, Mechanics, Problems, On Indivisible Lines, The Situation and Names of Winds, On Melissus, Xenophanes and Gorgias, Magna Moralia, On Virtues and Vices, Economics*, and *Rhetoric to Alexander*.
8 This characterizes Plato's work in the middle period. His methodology in the later *Sophist* and *Statesman* is more empirical.
9 C. Shields, *Aristotle* (Routledge, 2007), 57.
10 The divine might constitute an exception to this claim.
11 Julie Ward, *Aristotle on Homonymy* (Cambridge University Press, 2008), 1.
12 This is probably why he says at *Metaphysics* 1003a34 that this is not an instance of homonymy.
13 Shields, *Aristotle*, 137–42. A contemporary term for a similar phenomenon might be *polysemy*.
14 Shields, *Aristotle*, 147–49.
15 *Posterior Analytics* 83b15 and *Physics* 225b5–9.
16 Robin Smith, "Logic," *The Cambridge Companion to Aristotle*, ed. J. Barnes (Cambridge University Press, 1995), 56–57.
17 The law of excluded middle is different from the principle of bivalence. The law says, "P or not–P." The principle of bivalence says that any proposition will be either true or false.
18 See Robin Smith, "Logic," 46.
19 Note that this definition of the first figure is order indifferent.
20 Alternatively, "A is predicated of B" or "A belongs to every B." For this reason, "all Bs are A" is often written as AaB. Please see the appendix.
21 AaB and BeC.
22 Robin *Smith, Aristotle, Prior Analytics* (Hackett, 1989), xxiii.
23 Smith (*Prior Analytics* xiv) says that Book II is more difficult to characterize because it appears that Aristotle has achieved most of his aims in Book I.
24 Aristotle takes this theme up again in Book I, chapters 19–20.

25 Myles Burnyeat, "Aristotle on Understanding Knowledge," *Aristotle on Science: The Posterior Analytics*, ed. E. Berti, Proceedings of the 8th Symposium Aristotelicum (Editrice Antenore, 1981), 97–139.
26 We must distinguish the two distinctions: particular versus universal from specific versus general.
27 But see chapter 24 where Aristotle discusses the relative merits of universal versus particular demonstrations.
28 Michael Ferejohn, "Empiricism and the First Principles of Aristotelian Science," *A Companion to Aristotle*, ed. G. Anagnostopoulos (Blackwell, 2009), 66–80.

Chapter 10

1 For an explanation of the term *sublunary*, please see page 253.
2 See J. Lear, *Aristotle: the Desire to Understand* (Cambridge University Press, 1988), 59–60.
3 C. Shields, *Aristotle* (Routledge, 2007), 47.
4 Sir David Ross, *Aristotle* (Routledge, 1995), 74–75.
5 See Aristotle, *Physics*, ed. W. Charlton (Clarendon Press, 1992), xvii.
6 Shields, *Aristotle* (Routledge, 2007), 76–85.
7 Lear, *Aristotle*, 39–40.
8 Sometimes Aristotle uses the term *motion* to mean change generally; at other times he uses it to refer more specifically to change of place or position. Sometimes he uses the term *locomotion* to refer specifically to change of spatial position.
9 Ross, *Aristotle*, 86–87.
10 Ursula Cope, *Time for Aristotle* (Oxford University Press, 2005), 89–91.
11 Helen Lang, *The Order of Nature in Aristotle's Physics* (Cambridge University Press, 1998), 212.
12 See G. E. R. Lloyd, *Aristotle: the Growth & Structure of his Thought* (Cambridge University Press, 1968), 148–52.
13 For more regarding Aristotle's rejection of atomism, please see chapter 13.
14 See Lloyd, *Aristotle*, 72–174.
15 And also *On Generation and Corruption*, especially II.
16 This is discussed by Lloyd, *Aristotle*, 74–76.
17 Lang, *The Order of Nature*, 265.

Chapter 11

1 They may have been compiled in the first century BC by Andronicus of Rhodes, who is credited with compiling the first reliable edition of the works of Aristotle.
2 Except Books V and XI; See Sir David Ross, *Aristotle* (Routledge, 1995), 155.
3 See chapter 9, page 211.
4 The three types of plurality: otherness, dissimilarity, and inequality, and the three types of unity are: sameness, similarity, and equality (1004a10–31).
5 Probably, Aristotle also rejects the very idea of an indeterminate substratum.
6 In the *Categories* and *On Interpretation*. However, these are not the words he uses.
7 D. Wiggins, *Sameness and Substance* (Blackwell, 1980); W. Charlton, Aristotle, *Physics: Books I and II* (Clarendon Press, 1992).
8 But all the way down, which is impossible because even particles are wholes that have unity.
9 C. Shields, *Aristotle* (Routledge, 2007), 278–85; G. Thomson and M. Misner, *On Aristotle* (Wadsworth Press, 2001), chapter 7.
10 M. C. Nussbaum and H. Putnam, "Changing Aristotle's Mind," *Essays on Aristotle's De Anima*, eds. M. C. Nussbaum and A. O. Rorty (Clarendon Press, 1992).
11 Pavel Gregoric, *Aristotle on the Common Sense* (Oxford University Press, 2007).
12 Ronald Polansky, *De Anima: A Critical Commentary* (Cambridge University Press, 2007), 439–41.

Chapter 12

[1] See D. S. Hutchinson, "Ethics," in *The Cambridge Companion to Aristotle*, ed. J. Barnes (Cambridge University Press, 1995), 199; and Gabriel Lear, "Happiness and the Structure of Ends," in *Blackwell Companion to Aristotle*, ed. G. Anagnostopoulos (Blackwell, 2009), chapter 24.
[2] G. Lear, "Happiness," 388.
[3] C. D. C. Reeve, *Practices of Reason* (Clarendon Press, 2002), 126.
[4] Jonathan Lear, *Aristotle: The Desire to Understand* (Cambridge University Press, 2007), 163.
[5] The word *vice* has misleading Christian connotations.
[6] P. Gottlieb, *The Virtue of Aristotle's Ethics* (Cambridge University Press, 2009), 29–39.
[7] Gottlieb, 74–77.
[8] Gerard Hughes, *Routledge Guidebook to Aristotle on Ethics* (Routledge, 2001), 118.
[9] Hughes, *Routledge Guidebook*, 108.
[10] But note that it isn't one of the ethical virtues. It is an intellectual virtue.
[11] J. McDowell, "Virtue and Reason," *Aristotle's Ethics: Critical Essays*, ed. Nancy Sherman (Rowan and Littlefield, 1999) and *Aristotle and Moral Realism*, ed. R. Heinaman (Westview Press, 1995).
[12] P. Geach, "Good and Evil," *Analysis* 17 (1956–57): 30–42.
[13] A. W. Price, "Acrasia and Self Control," *The Blackwell Guide to Aristotle's Nicomachean Ethics*, ed. R. Kraut (Blackwell, 2006), 234.
[14] J. Lear, 176.
[15] Hope May, *Aristotle's Ethics: Moral Development and Human Nature* (Continuum, 2010), chapter 1.
[16] W. Hardie, *Aristotle's Ethical Theory* (Oxford, 1980), 279; John Cooper, *Reason and the Human Good* (Harvard University Press, 1975), 65–80.
[17] This classification is a bit simplistic because there are several variants in each camp. Please see May, *Aristotle's Ethics*, 12–17.
[18] Kraut claims that ethical virtue is an intrinsically desirable good, but that it is not a component of *eudaimonia*. See R. Kraut, *Aristotle on the Human Good* (Princeton University Press, 1989), 215. Irwin points out that this claim is problematic. He asks rhetorically: why should one choose ethical virtue for its own sake, if it is not a component of *eudaimonia*? See T. Irwin, "The Structure of Aristotelian Happiness," *Ethics* 101 (1991): 382–91.
[19] Although inclusivists agree that *eudaimonia* contains a plurality of virtues, they may disagree about which goods comprise *eudaimonia*. For instance, J. L. Ackrill claims that all intrinsically desirable goods comprise *eudaimonia*. See J. Ackrill, "Aristotle on Eudaimonia," *Essays on Aristotle's Ethics*, ed. A. O. Rorty (University of California Press, 1980), 15–33. In contrast Keyt and Purinton disagree, claiming instead that all and only virtuous activities comprise *eudaimonia*. See D. Keyt, "Intellectualism in Aristotle," *Essays in Ancient Greek Philosophy*, Vol. II, eds. A. Prius and J. Anton (State University of New York Press, 1983), 364–87; and J. Purinton, "Aristotle's Definition of Happiness," *Oxford Studies in Ancient Philosophy*, Vol. 16 (Oxford University Press, 1998), 259–378.
[20] See, for example, Peter Philip Simpson, *A Philosophical Commentary on the Politics of Aristotle* (University of North Carolina Press, 1998).
[21] C. W. W. Taylor, "Politics," *The Cambridge Companion to Aristotle*, ed. Barnes, 240.
[22] The suggestion that Aristotle is critical of the institution of slavery as practiced in his day is present in J. Lear, 192; and Kraut contends that Aristotle argues for reforms to the institution of slavery. See R. Kraut, *Aristotle: Political Philosophy* (Founders of Modern Political and Social Thought), (Oxford University Press, 2002), 278.
[23] Kraut, *Aristotle: Political Philosophy*, 290–94.
[24] Kraut, *Aristotle: Political Philosophy*, 359–61.
[25] Taylor, "Politics," 246–47.
[26] Fred Miller, "Aristotle on the Ideal Constitution," in *Blackwell Companion to Aristotle*, ed. G. Anagnostopoulos, 548.

27. Janko tries to reconstruct the missing book from the remaining fragments. See Richard Janko, *Aristotle on Comedy: Towards a Reconstruction of Poetics II* (Gerald Duckworth & Co., Ltd., 2002).
28. See Christopher Shields, *Aristotle* (Routledge, 2007), 387–91.

Part IV - Introduction to Hellenistic and Roman Philosophy

1. Diogenes Laërtius, *Lives of the Eminent Philosophers*, VI, 60.
2. Diogenes Laërtius, *Lives of the Eminent Philosophers*, VI, 58.
3. Martha Nussbaum, *The Therapy of Desire: Theory and Practice in Hellenistic Ethics* (Princeton University Press, 1994).
4. Eric Brown, "Hellenistic Cosmopolitanism," in *A Companion to Ancient Philosophy*, ed. M. Gill and P. Pellegrin (Blackwell, 2006), chapter 28.
5. Though we should remember that Aristotle wasn't an Athenian and that Plato was willing to help Dionysius I and II of Syracuse become a philosopher king. In other words, the reality was more ambiguous and complicated.
6. Some people were able to participate politically and actively in the running of local communities within the Empire.
7. Robert Sharples, "The Problem of Sources," *A Companion to Ancient Philosophy*, 433–34.
8. A. A. Long and D. N. Sedley, *The Hellenistic Philosophers*, Vols. I and II (Cambridge University Press, 1987).
9. Brad Inwood and L. P. Gerson, *Hellenistic Philosophy: Introductory Readings* (Hackett, 1997).

Chapter 13

1. The first collection is the *Principle Doctrines* from Diogenes Laërtius, and the second is called the *Vatican Sayings*, preserved in a fourteenth-century manuscript in the Vatican Library. Some of the Vatican sayings are the same as the *Principle Doctrines* and some are from Epicurean followers.
2. R. W. Sharples, *Stoics, Epicureans and Skeptics: An Introduction to Hellenistic Philosophy* (Routledge, 1996), 5–7; and R. W. Sharples, chapter 22 in *A Companion to Ancient Philosophy*, ed. M. Gill and P. Pellegrin (Blackwell, 2006).
3. LH stands for *Letter to Herodotus*.
4. See A. A. Long, *Hellenistic Philosophy: Stoics, Epicureans and Sceptics* (University of California Press, 1986), 33.
5. Aristotle, *Physics* VI, 10, 240b8.
6. Pierre-Marie Morel, "Epicureanism," in *A Companion to Ancient Philosophy*, ed. Gill and Pellegrin), 488–90.
7. David Konstan, "Epicureanism," *Blackwell Guide to Ancient Philosophy*, ed. C. Shields (Blackwell, 2003), 239–41.
8. Democritus says, "Necessity is the principle of all things."
9. This point is debated. See A. A. Long, "Chance and Laws of Nature," *From Epicurus to Epictetus: Studies in Hellenistic and Roman Philosophy* (Clarendon Press, 2006), 161–62, and 164. Apart from Lucretius, the best evidence is from Plutarch who says, "In order that stars and animals and chance might slip in and human autonomy not be destroyed."
10. Long, *Hellenistic Philosophy*, 166–68 and 171–73.
11. It is possible that the early atomist Democritus did not include this latter property, weight, among the features of atoms.
12. Long, *Hellenistic Philosophy*, 169–70; and Pierre-Marie Morel, "Epicurean Atomism," *The Cambridge Companion to Epicureanism*, ed. James Warren (Cambridge University Press, 2009).
13. It is worth noting that these arguments apply to death but not necessarily to the process of dying.
14. Long, *Hellenistic Philosophy*, 47.
15. LM stands for *Letter to Menoeceus*.
16. PD stands for Epicurus's *Principal Doctrines*.

[17] Raphael Woolf, "Pleasure and Desire," *The Cambridge Companion to Epicureanism*, 158–78.
[18] Cicero, *On Goals* I, 65–70.
[19] Long, *From Epicurus to Epictetus*, 201. See also Tim O'Keefe, *Epicureanism* (University of California Press, 2010), 151–54.
[20] *Vat* refers to Epicurus's *Vatican Sayings*; these are saying of Epicurus from a fourteenth-century manuscript found in the Vatican library.
[21] Eric Brown, "Politics and Society," *The Cambridge Companion to Epicureanism*, 191–96.

Chapter 14

[1] It is less misleading to call the Stoics *physicalist* than *materialist* for two reasons. First, the term *matter* has a special meaning for the Stoics, as the passive principle. Second, in contemporary usage, the term *materialist* may suggest a reductive thesis.
[2] *DL* refers to Diogenes Laërtius's *Lives of the Philosophers*.
[3] Samuel Sambursky, *The Physics of the Stoics* (Routledge and Kegan Paul, 1959), 31–32.
[4] Michael J. White, "Stoic Natural Philosophy," *The Cambridge Companion to the Stoics*, ed. Brad Inwood (Cambridge University Press), 134–36.
[5] D. E. Hahm, *The Origins of Stoic Cosmology* (Ohio State University Press, 1977), 34–36; and White, "Stoic Natural Philosophy," 132.
[6] Kiempe Algra, "Stoic Theology," *The Cambridge Companion to the Stoics*.
[7] *St. Rep.* refers to Plutarch's *On Stoic Self-Contradictions* (Stoicorum Repugnatiis).
[8] Aëtius's *Placita*.
[9] Alexander of Aphrodisias's *On Fate*.
[10] *SVF* refers to the collection by H. von Arnim (1903–5), *Stoicorum Veterum Fragmenta*, Vols. 1–3.
[11] *Ecl* refers to Stobaeus, *Anthologium*. This work is referred to as "Eclogae" (abbreviated as *Ecl*).
[12] Malcolm Schofield, "Stoic Ethics," *The Cambridge Companion to the Stoics*, 242.
[13] *Virt Mor* refers to Plutarch's *De virtute morali* (On Moral Virtue).
[14] Schofield, "Stoic Ethics," 244.
[15] *Com Not* refers to Plutarch's *On Common Conceptions* (De communibus notitiis adversus Stoicos).
[16] *Fin* refers to Cicero's *On Ends* (De finibus bonorum et malorum).
[17] A. A. Long, *Hellenistic Philosophy* (University of California Press, 1986), 190.
[18] Long, *Hellenistic Philosophy*, 193.
[19] ND is the standard abbreviation for Cicero's *On the Nature of the Gods* (De natura deorum).
[20] LS refers to *The Hellenistic Philosophers*, ed. A. A. Long and D. N. Sedley (Cambridge University Press, 1987).
[21] Cicero, *Fin.* III, 65.
[22] M. T. Griffin, *Seneca: A Philosopher in Politics* (Clarendon, 1992), 256–85.
[23] For example, compare Seneca, *De Otio*, 8.1 and *Ep.* 68.2 with Chrysippus at Diogenes Laërtius VII, 121.
[24] *Adv. Math.* refers to *Against the Professors or Against the Mathematicians* (Adversus mathematicos).
[25] See note 24 above.
[26] This refers to Aurelius's *Meditations*.
[27] This refers to the letters of Cicero.
[28] Long, *Hellenistic Philosophy*, 136–37.
[29] Long, *Hellenistic Philosophy*, 140.
[30] Benson Mates, *Stoic Logic* (University of California Press, 1961), 77.
[31] Mates, *Stoic Logic*, 55.
[32] *On Benefits: The Complete Works of Lucius Anneus Seneca* (University of Chicago Press, 2010), viii.
[33] *Brill's Companion to Seneca*, eds. Gregor Damschen and Andreas Heil (Brill, 2014).
[34] *Agamemnon, Thyestes, Oedipus, Medea, Phaedra, Phoenissae* (The Phoenician Women), *Troades* (The Trojan Women), and *The Madness of Hercules*.

35 *De Ira* (*On Anger*), *De Brevitate Vitæ* (*On the Shortness of Life*); *De Otio* (*On Leisure*); *De Tranquillitate Animi* (*On Tranquillity of Mind*); *De Providentia* (*On Providence*), *De Constantia Sapientis* (*On the Firmness of the Wise Person*); *De Vita Beata* (*On the Happy Life*); *De Clementia* (*On Clemency*); *De Beneficiis* (*On Benefits*).
36 Katja Vogt, "Seneca," *The Stanford Encyclopedia of Philosophy* (Summer 2013 ed.), ed. Edward N. Zalta (http://plato.stanford.edu/archives/sum2013/entries/seneca/).
37 A. A. Long, *Epictetus: A Stoic and Socratic Guide to Life* (Oxford University Press, 2002), 29.
38 Long, *Epictetus*, 30–31.

Chapter 15

1 See Svavar Svavarsson, "Pyrrho and Early Pyrrhonism," T*he Cambridge Companion to Ancient Scepticism*, ed. Richard Brett (Cambridge University Press, 2010), 36.
2 This text is quoted by Eusebius, Bishop of Caesaria, in *Praeparatio Evangelica* (Preparation for the Gospel), XIV, 18, 758c–d. See A. A. Long, *Hellenistic Philosophy* (University of California Press, 1986), 80–81.
3 A. A. Long and D. N. Sedley, *The Hellenistic Philosophers*, Vol. 1, (Cambridge University Press, 1987), 15.
4 Svavarsson, "Pyrrho," 41–46.
5 Timon, *On Perception*, in Diogenes Laërtius IX, 105.
6 *DL* refers to Diogenes Laërtius's *The Lives of the Philosophers*.
7 Long, *Hellenistic Philosophy*, 85.
8 Harald Thorsrud, "Arcesilaus and Carneades," *The Cambridge Companion to Ancient Scepticism*, 58–60.
9 Thorsrud, "Arcesliaus," 60–62.
10 *PH* refers to Vol. I of the collected works of Sextus Empiricus. Vol 1 is the *Outlines of Pyrrhonism* or *Purrhôneiôn Hupotupôseis*. The whole four-volume work is *Sexti Empirici Opera*.

Glossary of Some Key Greek Terms

Aisthêsis	Perception
Aition	Cause or explanation
Aporia	Puzzlement
Apodeixis	A deduction in which the premises are necessary
Akousion	Involuntary
Akrasia	
Alētheia	Truthfulness
Archê	First principle
Areté	Virtue, excellence
Askēsis	Training of the self
Atomos	Something that cannot be cut
Ataraxia	Tranquility; freedom from mental disturbance
Aponia	Freedom from physical pain
Autarkeia	Self-sufficiency
Daimōn	Divine spirit
Dialektikê	Dialectic
Doxa	Belief
Eidos	Form or species
Einai	To exist
Entelecheia	Actuality
Epagôgê	Induction
Epistêmê	Knowledge or science
Eudaimonia	Happiness, flourishing, well-being
Elenchus	Questioning, cross examination (the Socratic Method)
Eleutharia	Freedom or liberty
Epoché	Suspension of beliefs or judgments
Endoxa	What we think about the world, reputable opinions
Ergon	Function or what something is for

Hêdonê	Pleasure
Hekousion	Voluntary
Hulê	Matter
Isostheneia	Equipollence; the equal weight of opposing views
Kinêsis	Change or motion
Oikeiôsis	Appropriation: the perception of something as one's own
Ousia	Substance
Lekton	What is said, meaning
Logos	Word, narrative, reckoning, reasoning, evaluation, principle
Mimesis	Imitation
Nomos	Social convention, custom,
Nous	Mind, reason, the capacity to know what is real
Onta	What exists
Parrhēsia	Frank truth-telling
Pathê	Emotions and passions
Polis	City-state
Phainomena	Things that appear
Phusis	Nature
Philia	Friendship
Prohairesis	Choice, volition
Psuchê	Soul, that which animates
Sophia	Wisdom, intellectual wisdom
Sophon	Cleverness
Stoicheia	Elements
Techne	Craft
Telos	End

Bibliography

INTRODUCTION

Blackson, T., *Ancient Greek Philosophy*, Wiley-Blackwell, 2011.
Gill, Marie L., and Pellegrin, P., *A Companion to Ancient Philosophy*, Blackwell, 2006.
Kenny, Anthony, *Ancient Philosophy: A New History of Western Philosophy Volume 1*, Oxford University Press, 2006.
Roochnik, David, *Retrieving the Ancients*, Blackwell, 2004.
Shields, Christopher, ed., *The Blackwell Guide to Ancient Philosophy*, Blackwell, 2003.
Shields, Christopher, *Classical Philosophy*, Routledge, 2003.
Williams, Bernard, *The Sense of the Past*, Princeton University Press, 2006.

PART I

Primary Texts

Early Greek Philosophy, ed./trans. J. Barnes, Harmondsworth, 1987.
Freeman, Kathleen, *Ancilla to the Presocratic Philosophers*, Basil Blackwell, 1956.
McKirahan, Richard, *Philosophy Before Socrates*, Hackett, 1994.
Waterfield, Robin, *The First Philosophers: The Presocratics and Sophists*, Oxford University Press, 2000.

Secondary Texts

Barnes, J., *The Presocratic Philosophers (Arguments of the Philosophers)*, Routledge, 1983.
Guthrie, W. K. C., *A History of Greek Philosophy*, Volumes I and II, Cambridge, 1965.
Hussey, E., *The Presocratics*, London, 1972.
Kirk, G. S., Raven, J. E., and Schofield, M., *The Presocratic Philosophers*, 2nd ed., Cambridge, 1983.
Long, A. A., ed., *The Cambridge Companion to Early Greek Philosophy*, Cambridge University Press, 1999.
McCoy, J., *Early Greek Philosophy: The Presocratics and the Emergence of Reason*, the Catholic University of America Press, 2013.
McKirahan, R., *Philosophy Before Socrates: An Introduction with Texts and Commentary*, Hackett, 1994.
Taylor, C. W. W., ed., *From the Beginning to Plato*, The Routledge History of Philosophy, Vol. 1, Routledge, 1997.
Warren, James, *Presocratics*, Acumen, 2007.

Milesians
Kahn, C. H., *Anaximander and the Origins of Greek Cosmology*, Columbia University Press, 1962.

Pythagoras
Burkert, W., *Love and Science in Ancient Pythagoreanism*, Harvard University Press, 1972.
Huffman, C., *Philolaus of Croton: Pythagorean and Presocratic*, Cambridge University Press, 1993.
Kahn, Charles, *Pythagoras and the Pythagoreans*, Hackett, 2001.

Heraclitus
Kahn, C. H., *The Art and Thought of Heraclitus*, Cambridge University Press, 1981.
Robinson, T. M., *Heraclitus Fragments*, University of Toronto Press, 1987.

Parmenides
Cornford, F. M., *Plato and Parmenides*, Routledge, 1939.
Gallop, D., *Parmenides of Elea: Fragments: A Text with an Introduction*, University of Toronto Press, 1984.
Mourelatos, A. P., *The Route of Parmenides*, Yale University Press, 1971.

Zeno
Arntzenius, Frank, "Are there Really Instantaneous Velocities?" *The Monist* 83, 2000: 187–208.
Bohm, David, *Wholeness and the Implicate Order*, Routledge, 1983.
Dowden, Bradley, "Zeno's Paradoxes," *Internet Encyclopedia of Philosophy* (http://www.iep.utm.edu/zeno-par/).
Grunbaum, Arthur, *Modern Science and Zeno's Paradoxes*, Allen and Unwin, 1968.
Papa-Grimaldi, Alba, "Why Mathematical Solutions of Zeno's Paradoxes Miss the Point," *Revue of Metaphysics* 50, December 1996.
Salmon, W., ed., *Zeno's Paradoxes*, Bobbs Merrill, 1970.
Tiles, Mary, *The Philosophy of Set Theory: An Introduction to Cantor's Paradise*, Basil Blackwell, 1989.

The Pluralists and Atomists
Furley, D. J., *Two Studies in the Greek Atomists*, Princeton University Press, 1967.
Inwood, Brian, *The Poem of Empedocles: A Text and Translation with an Introduction*, University of Toronto Press, 1992.
Schofield, Malcolm, *An Essay on Anaxagoras*, Cambridge University Press, 1980.
Wright, M. R., *Empedocles: The Extant Fragments*, Yale University Press, 1981.

The Sophists
de Romilly, J., *The Great Sophists in Periclean Athens*, Clarendon Press, 1992.
Guthrie, W. K. C., *The Sophists*, Cambridge University Press, 1971.
Kerferd, G. B., *The Sophistic Movement*, Cambridge University Press, 1981.
O'Grady, Patricia, ed., *The Sophists: An Introduction*, Bloomsbury Academic Press, Duckworth, 2008.

PART II

Primary Texts
Euthyphro, Apology, and *Crito*, trans. Hugh Trednnick, Penguin, 1969.
Gorgias, trans. T. H. Irwin, Clarendon Press, 1979.
Meno, trans. J. M. Day, London, 1994.
Parmenides, trans. Kenneth Sayre, University of Notre Dame, 1996.
Phaedo, trans. David Gallup, Clarendon Press, 1975.
Phaedrus, trans. J. C. Rowe, Aris and Philips, 1986.
Plato: Collected Dialogues, ed. E. Hamilton and H. Cairns, Princeton, 1961.
Plato: Complete Works, ed. John Cooper, Hackett, 1997.
Protagoras, trans. C. C. W. Taylor, Clarendon Press, 1991.
Republic, trans. R. Waterfield, Oxford University Press, 1993.
Symposium, trans. R. Waterfield, Oxford University Press, 1994.
Theaetetus, trans. John McDowell, Oxford University Press, 2014.
Timaeus, trans. F. M. Cornford, Routledge, 1937.

Secondary Texts: Socrates
Ahbel-Rappe, Sara, and Kamtekar, Rachana, eds., *A Companion to Socrates*, Blackwell, 2006.
Benson, H., *Essays on the Philosophy of Socrates*, Oxford University Press, 1992.
Benson, H., *Socratic Wisdom*, Oxford University Press, 2000.
Brickhouse, T., and Smith, N., *The Philosophy of Socrates*, Westview, 2000.
Brickhouse, T., and Smith, N., *Plato and the Trial of Socrates*, Routledge, 2004.
Brickhouse, T., and Smith, N., *Plato's Socrates*, Clarendon, 1994.
Rappe, Sara, and Kamteker, Rachana, *A Companion to Socrates*, Blackwell, 2006.
Santas, Gerasimos, *Socrates, The Arguments of the Philosophers*, Routledge, 1979.
Taylor, Christopher, *Oxford Studies in Ancient Philosophy*, Vol. XIII, Clarendon Press, 1995.
Taylor, Christopher, *Socrates, Past Master Series*, Oxford University Press, 1998.
Vlastos, Gregory, ed., *The Philosophy of Socrates*, Doubleday, 1971.
Vlastos, Gregory, *Socrates: Ironist and Moral Philosopher*, Doubleday, 1991.

Secondary Texts: Plato, General
Benson, Hugh, ed., *A Companion to Plato*, Blackwell, 2006.
Fine, Gail, *On Ideas*, Oxford University Press, 2004.
Fine, Gail, ed., *Plato 1: Metaphysics and Epistemology*, Oxford Readings in Philosophy, Oxford University Press, 2000.
Fine, Gail, ed., *Plato 2: Ethics, Politics, Religion and the Soul*, ed., Oxford University Press, 1999.
Fine, Gail, ed., *Plato on Knowledge and Forms: Selected Essays*, Clarendon Press, 2003.
Gosling, J. C. B., *Plato, The Arguments of the Philosophers*, Routledge, 1973.
Gosling, J. C. B., and Taylor, C. C. W., *The Greeks on Pleasure*, Clarendon Press, 1982.
Grube, G. M. A., *Plato's Thought*, Hackett, 1980.
Hare, R. M., *Plato*, Oxford University Press, *Past Master Series*, 1982.
Irwin, T. H., *Plato's Ethics*, Clarendon Press, 1995.

Irwin, T. H., *Plato's Moral Theory: The Early and Middle Dialogues*, Clarendon Press, 1977 and 1985.
Kahn, C. H., *Plato and the Socratic Dialogue*, Cambridge University Press, 1996.
Kraut, Richard, ed., *The Cambridge Companion to Plato*, Cambridge University Press, 1992.
Owen, G. E. L., *Logic, Science, and Dialectic: Collected Papers in Greek Philosophy*, ed. Martha Nussbaum, Cornell University Press, 1986.
Vlastos, Gregory, *Plato's Universe*, University of Washington Press, 1975.

Secondary Texts: Plato's *Republic*

Annas, Julia, *An Introduction to Plato's* Republic, Clarendon Press, 1981.
Kraut, Richard, ed., *Plato's* Republic: *Critical Essays*, Rowan and Littlefield, 1997.
McPherran, Mark, *Plato's* Republic: *A Critical Guide*, Cambridge University Press, 2010.
Pappas, N., *Plato and the* Republic, Routledge, 1995.
Reeve, C. D. C., *Philosopher Kings: The Argument of Plato's* Republic, 2006.
Santos, G., ed., *The Blackwell Guide to Plato's* Republic, Blackwell, 2006.
Sheppard, D. J., *Plato's* Republic, Edinburgh University Press, 2009.

Secondary Texts: Other Specific Plato Dialogues

Bostock, David, *Plato's* Phaedo, Oxford University Press, 2002.
Bostock, David, *Plato's* Theaetetus, Clarendon Press, 1988.
Burnyeat, M., *The* Theaetetus *of Plato*, Hackett, 1990.
Griswold, Charles L., *Knowledge in Plato's* Phaedrus, Yale University Press, 1986.
Meinwald, C., *Plato's* Parmenides, Oxford University Press, 1991.
Sayre, K., *Metaphysics and Method in Plato's* Statesman, Cambridge University Press, 2006.
Scott, Dominic, *Plato's* Meno, Cambridge University Press, 2005.

Part III

Primary Texts

Aristotle, *The Complete Works*, ed. J. Barnes, Princeton, 1984 (two volumes).

Secondary Texts: General

Ackrill, J. L., *Aristotle the Philosopher*, Oxford University Press, 1981.
Allan, D. J., *The Philosophy of Aristotle*, Oxford, 1970.
Anagnostopoulos. G., ed., *Blackwell Companion to Aristotle*, Blackwell, 2009.
Barnes, J., *Aristotle*, Oxford University Press, 1982.
Barnes, J., ed., *The Cambridge Companion to Aristotle*, Cambridge University Press, 1995.
Barnes, J., Schofield, M., and Sorabji, R., *Articles on Aristotle* (4 volumes), Duckworth, 1975.
Furley, David, *From Aristotle to Augustine, The Routledge History of Philosophy*, Vol. II, Routledge, 1999.
Gill, M., *Aristotle on Substance: The Paradox of Unity*, Princeton, 1989.

Graham, D., *Aristotle's Two Systems*, Oxford, 1987.
Irwin, Terence, *Aristotle's First Principles*, Clarendon Press, 1988.
Jaeger, Werner, *Aristotle: Fundamental of the History of His Development*, Clarendon Press, 1948.
Lear, Jonathan, *Aristotle: The Desire to Understand*, Cambridge, 2007.
Lloyd, G. E. R., *Aristotle: The Growth & Structure of His Thought*, Cambridge, 1968.
Nussbaum, Martha, *The Fragility of Goodness*, Cambridge, 1986.
Ross, Sir David, *Aristotle*, Methuen, 1923.
Shields, C., *Aristotle*, Routledge, 2007.
Thomson, G., and Missner, M., *On Aristotle*, Wadsworth, 2000.
Veatch, Henry, *Aristotle: A Contemporary Appreciation*, Indiana University Press, 1974.

Secondary Texts: Aristotle on Logic

Berti, E., ed., *Aristotle on Science: The Posterior Analytics*, Proceedings of the 8th Symposium Aristotelicum, Editrice Antenore, 1981.
Crivelli, Paolo, *Aristotle on Truth*, Cambridge University Press, 2004.
Lear, Jonathan, *Aristotle and Logical Theory*, Cambridge University Press, 1980.
Long, Christopher, *Aristotle on the Nature of Truth*, Cambridge University Press, 2010.
Modrak, Deborah, *Aristotle's Theory of Language and Meaning*, Cambridge University Press, 2009.
Shields, Christopher, *Order in Multiplicity: Homonymy in the Philosophy of Aristotle*, Clarendon Press, 1999.
Smith, Robin, ed., *Aristotle: Prior Analytics*, Hackett, 1989.
Ward, Julie, *Aristotle on Homonymy*, Cambridge University Press, 2008.

Secondary Texts: Aristotle's *Physics*

Cope, Ursula, *Time for Aristotle*, Oxford University Press, 2005.
Judson, Lindsay, ed., *Aristotle's* Physics*: A Collection of Essays*, Clarendon Press, 2003.
Lang, Helen, *The Order of Nature in Aristotle's* Physics, Cambridge University Press, 1998.
Roark, Tony, *Aristotle on Time: A Study of the* Physics, Cambridge University Press, 2011.
Waterlow, Sarah, *Nature Change and Agency in Aristotle's* Physics*: A Philosophical Study*, Clarendon Press, 1982.

Secondary Texts: Aristotle's Philosophy of Nature

Falcon, Andrea, *Aristotle and the Science of Nature*, Cambridge University Press, 2005.
Johnson, Monte Ransome, *Aristotle on Teleology*, Clarendon Press, 2005.
Leunissen, Mariska, *Explanation and Teleology in Aristotle's Science of Nature*, Cambridge University Press, 2010.
Nussbaum, Martha, *Aristotle's* de Motu Animalium, Princeton University Press, 1987.
Wilson, Malcolm, *Aristotle's Theory of the Unity of Science*, University of Toronto Press, 2000.

Secondary Texts: Aristotle's Philosophy of Mind

Charles, David, *Aristotle's Philosophy of Action*, Duckworth, 1984.
Gregoric, Pavel, *Aristotle on the Common Sense*, Oxford University Press, 2007.
Johansen, T. K., *Aristotle on the Sense Organs*, Cambridge University Press, 1997.

Nussbaum, Martha, and Rorty, A., *Amelie, Essays on Aristotle's* De Anima, Clarendon Press, 1995.
Polansky, Ronald, De Anima: *A Critical Commentary*, Cambridge University Press 2007.

Secondary Texts: Aristotle's *Metaphysics*

Cohen, Marc, "Aristotle's *Metaphysics*," *Stanford Encyclopedia of Philosophy*, 2005 (http://plato.stanford.edu/entries/aristotle-metaphysics/).
Politis, Vasilis, *Routledge Philosophy Guide Book to Aristotle and the* Metaphysics, Routledge, 2004.
Reeve, C. D. C., *Substantial Knowledge: Aristotle's* Metaphysics, Hackett, 2000.
Wedin, M., *Aristotle's Theory of Substance*, Oxford University Press, 2000.

Secondary Texts: Aristotle's Ethics

Broadie, Sarah, *Ethics with Aristotle*, Oxford University Press, 1991.
Cooper, John, *Reason and the Human Good*, Harvard University Press, 1975.
Gottlieb, Paula, *The Virtue of Aristotle's Ethics*, Cambridge University Press, 2009.
Hardie, W., *Aristotle's Ethical Theory*, Oxford, 1980.
Heinaman, R., ed., *Aristotle and Moral Realism*, Westview Press, 1995.
Hughes, G., *Routledge Guidebook to Aristotle on Ethics*, Routledge, 2001.
Kraut, R., *Aristotle on the Human Good*, Princeton University Press, 1989.
Kraut, R., *The Blackwell Guide to Aristotle's* Nicomachean Ethics, Blackwell, 2006.
May, Hope, *Aristotle's Ethics: Moral Development and Human Nature*, Continuum, 2010.
Miller, Jon, ed., *Aristotle's* Nicomachean Ethics: *A Critical Guide*, Cambridge University Press, 2011.
Reeve, R., *Practices of Reason: Aristotle's* Nicomachean Ethics, Clarendon Press, 1992.
Rorty, A., *Essays on Aristotle's Ethics*, London, 1980.
Sherman, Nancy, ed., *Aristotle's Ethics: Critical Essays*, Rowan and Littlefield, 1998.

Secondary Texts: Aristotle's *Politics*

Keyt, David, *Aristotle's* Politics: *A Critical Reader*, Blackwell.
Keyt, David, and Miller, Fred, *A Companion to Aristotle's* Politics, Blackwell, 1991.
Kraut, Richard, *Aristotle: Political Philosophy* (Founders of Modern Political and Social Thought), Oxford University Press, 2002.
Miller, Fred, *Nature, Justice, and Rights in Aristotle's* Politics, Clarendon Press, 1997.
Simpson, Peter Philip, *A Philosophical Commentary on the* Politics *of Aristotle*, University of North Carolina Press, 1998.
Swanson, Judith A., and Corbin, C. David, *Aristotle's "Politics": A Reader's Guide*, Continuum, 2009.

Part IV

Primary Texts

Inwood, Brad, and Gerson, L. P., *Hellenistic Philosophy*, Hackett, 1988.
Irwin, Terence, *Hellenistic Philosophy*, Garland Publishing, 1995.
Long, A. A., and Sedley, D. N., *The Hellenistic Philosophers*, Volumes I and II, Cambridge University Press, 1987.

Oates, Whitney, ed., *The Stoic and Epicurean Philosophers: The Complete Extant Writings of Epicurus, Epictetus, Lucretius and Marcus Aurelius*, Random House, 1940.

Secondary Texts
Annas, Julia, *The Morality of Happiness*, Oxford, 1993.
Furley, David, *From Aristotle to Augustine*, Routledge History of Philosophy, Vol. II, Routledge, 1999.
Long, A. A., *From Epicurus to Epictetus: Studies in Hellenistic and Roman Philosophy*, Clarendon Press, 2006.
Long, A. A., *Hellenistic Philosophy: Stoics, Epicureans and Sceptics*, University of California Press, 1986.
Nussbaum, M. C., *The Therapy of Desire: Theory and Practice in Hellenistic Ethics*, Princeton University Press, 1994.
Sharples, R. W., *Stoics, Epicureans, and Sceptics: An Introduction to Hellenistic Philosophy*, Routledge, 1996.

Epicureanism
Primary Texts
Lucretius, *On the Nature of Things*, trans. W. Rouse and M. Smith (Loeb ed.), Cambridge University Press, 1975.

Secondary Texts
Diskin, Clay, *Lucretius and Epicurus*, Cornell University Press, 1983.
Fish, Jeffrey, and Sanders, Kirk, eds., *Epicurus and the Epicurean Tradition*, Cambridge University Press, 2011.
Kenny, E. J., *Lucretius*, Oxford University Press, 1977.
O'Keefe, Tim, *Epicureanism*, Acumen, 2010.
Rist, J. M., *Epicurus: An Introduction*, Cambridge University Press, 1972.
Strozier, Robert, *Epicurus and Hellenistic Philosophy*, University Press of America, 1985.
Warren, James, *The Cambridge Companion to Epicureanism*, Cambridge University Press, 2009.
Warren, James, *Facing Death: Epicurus and His Critics*, Clarendon Press, 2006.

The Stoics
Primary Texts
Epictetus, *Discourses*, Volume I, Books 1–2, ed. W. A. Oldfather, Loeb Classical Library, 1925.
Epictetus, *Discourses*, Volume II, Books 3–4, ed. W. A. Oldfather, Loeb Classical Library, 1928.
Epictetus, *The Discourses*, ed. C. J. Gill, Dent, NuVision, 2006.
Epictetus, *Encheiridion*, trans. W. A. Oldfather, Loeb Version, Harvard University Press, 1928.
Farquharson, A. S. L., ed., *The Meditations of the Emperor Marcus Aurelius*, Clarendon Press, 1944.
Inwood, B., and Gerson, L., *The Stoics Reader*, Hackett, 2008.
Marcus Aurelius, *Meditations*, trans. Maxwell Standford, Penguin, 1964.
Seneca, *Seneca: Moral and Political Essays*, trans. and ed. J. M. Cooper and J. F. Procopé, Cambridge University Press, 1995.

Seneca, *Seneca: On Benefits, The Complete Works of Lucius Anneaus Seneca*, ed. E. Asmis, S. Bartsch and M. Nussbaum, University of Chicago Press, 2011.
Seneca, *Seneca: Selected Philosophical Letters*, trans. B. Inwood, Oxford University Press, 2007.

Secondary Texts
Graver, Margaret R., *Stoicism and Emotion*, University of Chicago Press, 2007.
Hahm, D. E., *The Origins of Stoic Cosmology*, Ohio State University Press, 1977
Inwood, Brad, *The Cambridge Companion to the Stoics*, Cambridge University Press, 2003.
Inwood, Brad, *Ethics and Human Action in Early Stoicism*, Oxford University Press, 1985.
Long, A. A., *Problems in Stoicism*, Althone Press, 1971.
Long, A. A., *Stoic Studies*, Cambridge University Press, 2001.
Mates, Benson, *Stoic Logic*, University of California Press, 1961.
Sanbach, F. H., *The Stoics*, Hackett Publishing, 1994.
Sellars, John, *Stoicism: Ancient Philosophies*, 2006.

Epictetus
Brouwer, René, *The Stoic Sage: The Early Stoics on Wisdom: Sagehood and Socrates*, Cambridge University Press, 2014.
Long, A. A., *Epictetus: A Stoic and Socratic Guide to Life*, Oxford University Press, 2002.

Seneca
Griffin, M., *Seneca: A Philosopher in Politics*, Oxford University Press, 1992.
Inwood, Brad, *Reading Seneca: Stoic Philosophy at Rome*, Oxford University Press, 2005.
Williams, G., *The Cosmic Viewpoint: A Study of Seneca's Natural Questions*, Oxford University Press, 2012.

Marcus Aurelius
Rutherford, R. B., *The Meditations of Marcus Aurelius: A Study*, Oxford University Press, 1989.
van Ackeren, Marcel, *A Companion to Marcus Aurelius*, Wiley-Blackwell, 2012.

The Skeptics
Primary Texts
Sextus Empiricus, *Outlines of Pyrrhonism*, trans. J. Annas, and J. Barnes, Cambridge University Press, 1994.

Secondary Texts
Annas, J., and Barnes, J., *The Modes of Scepticism*, Cambridge University Press, 1985.
Bett, R., ed., *The Cambridge Companion to Ancient Scepticism*, Cambridge University Press, 2010.
Harkinson, R., *The Sceptics*, Routledge, 1995.
Mates, Benson, *The Skeptic Way: Sextus Empiricus's Outlines of Pyrrhonism*, Oxford University Press, 1995.

Index

Abstract objects, 14, 34, 96, 133, 147, 149, 185, 278–279
Academic skepticism
 of Arcesilaus, 325, 374–375
 of Carneades, 371, 375
 Pyrrhonism vs., 371, 375
Acceptance, Stoic advocacy of, 354–355
Accidental predication, 273
Achilles paradox, 51–52
Ackrill, John, 298
Active principle (Stoic), 346–350, 353. *See also* Divine intelligence
Aenesidemus, 371
Aether, 69, 72, 252, 256, 280, 284. *See also* Elements
Aetius, 20
Akousmatikoi, 30–32
Akrasia (incontinence), 105, 294, 305–307
Alcibiades, 8–9, 91–92, 98, 110, 169–171
Alētheia (truthfulness), 301
Alexander the Great, 10–11, 13
Alexandra of Aphrodisias, 350
Amphiboly, as a kind of fallacy, 230
Anaxagoras, 18, 78
 on motion, 72
 naturalism of, 67–72
 on *Nous*, 71–72
 on substance, 67–70
Anaximander
 biographical information, 17
 cosmology of, 26–28
 natural philosophy of, 26–28
 ontology of, 69
 on the problem of the stability of the earth, 28
 on Simplicius, 27
 on substance-stuff, 26–27, 41
 on unity of opposites, 27
 on the universe, 26–27
Anaximenes, 17, 28–29, 41
Anaxoragas, 72
Ancilla to the Presocratic Philosophers (Freeman), 21
Anger, Seneca on, 363
Animals
 Anaximander on, 28
 Aristotle on, 257–261
  anatomical descriptions/physiological processes of, 259–260
  classification of species, 257–259
  movement and perception of, 261
  reproduction, inheritance, and growth, 260
 Empedocles on, 65–66
 Pythagoras on, 31
 Stoics on, 351
Animate (*empsuchos*), 25
Aphasia (non-assertion), 373
Aponia (freedom from physical pain), 338
Aporia (irresolvable contradiction), 97, 151, 154, 374
Appearances
 Arcesilaus on, 374
 Aristotle on, 270–271, 275
 Parmenides on, 44, 47–49
 Protagoras on, 83
 Pyrrho on, 373
 vs. reality. *See* Perception(s); Reality
 Skeptic view of, 373, 377
Appetitive desires, 117, 119, 156–157, 163–164, 355

408 ∾ Index

Arcesilaus, 325, 371, 374–375
Archytas, 33
Argument
  Aristotle on common fallacies in, 230
  deductive, Parmenides on, 49
  fallacies in, 230
  and refutation (*elenchus*), 97
  Stoic definition of, 361
Aristocles of Messene, 372–373
Aristophanes, 7, 95
Aristotle
  on *akrasia* (incontinence), 305–307
  on Anaxagoras, 72
  on animals, 257–261
  on argument, common fallacies in, 230
  on art as imitation, 318–319, 323
  on causes/explanation, 238–239
  on change, 234, 237, 246, 248
  classification, use of, 208, 257–259
  on compounds, 254–256, 262
  on contemplation, 308–311
  on continuity of motion, 246–247
  cosmology of, 252–253
  critique of Protagoras's view about appearances, 270–271
  on dialectic, 229–230
  on early ancient Greek philosophers, 24–29
  on elements, 27, 251–255, 258, 262, 284
  on empirical investigation of nature, 207
  on empirical knowledge, 226–227, 229
  on *endoxa* (credible beliefs), 207–208
  on essence
    forms as, 208–209, 237–238, 256, 273–275, 289–290
    of natural kinds of objects, 227
    relation to the individual, 273–274, 277
    soul as, 283–284, 286
    substance as, 271, 273–274
    of unmoved mover, 290
  ethical realism of, 304
  on eudaimonia/happiness, 293–294, 296–298, 303, 309–311

  "first principles" of, 207, 223, 230, 265–291
  on form and matter, 208–209, 236–237, 254, 256, 274–275, 279, 283
  on friendship (*philia*), 301, 307–308
  on function (*ergon*) of human beings, 103, 297–298, 301
  on God, 267, 280–281
  on happiness, 296–298, 309
  on the household and the *polis*, 312–315
  hylomorphism of, 208–209
  on indivisibility of now, 247
  on infinity(ies)/infinitesimals, 26, 55–56, 242–243
  on intellect, passive vs. active, 289
  on intellectual virtues, 302–305
  life of, 202–203
  logic of, 215–221
  on meaning, 269–270
  metaphysics of, 265–290
    on accidental predication,
    on being qua being, 267, 269–271
    brief overview, 265–266
    vs. Plato and the Pre-Socratics, 278–279
    principle of non-contradiction, 269–271
    on substance, 271, 277–278
    as theology, 279–281
  on motion, 241–242, 247, 249–251, 253
  on natural phenomena, 255–256
  Nicomachean Ethics
    ethical virtues, 300–301
    happiness and virtue, 297–298
    happiness as the ultimate end, 294–297
    outline of, 293–294
    on practical wisdom, 302–305
    on responsibility, 301–302
    virtues and the mean, 299–301
  on numbers, 34
  on Parmenides's view of change, 235–236
  on perception, 228, 231, 270–271, 275, 287–288

philosophy of science, 210–212
physics of, 238, 249–257
on place, 243–244
Plato and, 96, 147, 207–210
on pleasure and contemplation, 308–311
on the *polis*/city-state, 311–318. *See also* Polis/city-state
practical syllogism of, 304–305
on practical wisdom, 302–303
on Pre-Socratics, 20, 25, 238
primary substances as forms, 277
on Pythagorean concept of numbers, 34
qua, use of, 209
on reason, 289–290, 301–306
on responsibility, 301–302
on scientific demonstration, 221–222, 224–226
scientific method of, 210–215
scientific understanding, 222–223
on slavery, 314
on Socrates, 96
on *sophia*, 79, 302, 305, 309–310, 314, 320
on the soul, 25, 282–285, 290, 297
   in terms of actuality, 283
   in terms of essence, 283
   in terms of the final cause, 284
   in terms of motion/animation, 284–285
on subordination of women to men, 314–315
on substance(s), 25, 212, 236, 256, 268, 271–275, 279–280
   as essence, 273–274
   as form, 274–276
   as a form/matter complex (hylomorphism), 208–209
   matter as potential and form as actuality, 275
   primary substances as forms, 276. *See also* Forms
   as subject or substratum, 272–273
   as universals, 274
on teleological explanation of nature, 239–240
theory of demonstration, 221–223

theory of the syllogism, 210, 215–221, 229, 232
on time, 244–246, 250
on tragedy and catharsis, 319
on the universe, 27, 250–257
   sublunary world, 253–257
   superlunary world, 251–252
on the void, 244
on wisdom, 266–267
on Zeno's paradoxes, 50, 55–56, 247–248, 332
Aristotle, works
   Categories, 210–212
   De Anima, 229, 281–290
   Eudemian Ethics, 206, 301
   Generation of Animals, 228, 259–261
   History of Animals, 257–258, 260,
   Metaphysics, 211, 228–229, 250, 265–281
   Meteorology, 255–257,
   Movement of Animals, 261
   Nicomachean Ethics, 293–311, 322
   On Generation and Corruption, 253–255
   On Interpretation, 212–215
   On the Heavens, 29, 251–253
   Parts of Animals, 258, 259–260
   Physics, 20, 26–27, 233–250
   Poetics, 318–319
   Politics, 311–318
   Posterior Analytics, 221–229
   Prior Analytics, 215–221, 227, 232
   Sophistical Refutations, 230
   Topics, 229–230
Armstrong, David, 147
Arrow argument (that no motion is possible), 52, 56
Art
   as imitation, Aristotle on, 318–319, 323
   Plato on, 142–143
Arts and Sciences, Plato's analogy of, 118–120
Askēsis (self-discipline), 324
Ataraxia (tranquility), 338, 373, 378
Atomism
   Aristotle's argument against, 253–254, 332
   of Democritus, 72–77, 331–332

Epicurean, 331–337, 341
    of Leucippus, 61, 73–74
    of Lucretius 331, 333, 335
    Plato on, 192–193
Augustine, attempt to reconcile Platonism and Christianity, 148
Axioms, 223, 360–361

Barnes, Jonathan, 55, 387
Begging the question, 230
Being/existence
    Aristotle on, 267–272
    homonymousness of, 211
    Parmenides on, 44–47
    Plato on, 193–194
    See also Nonexistence/non-being
Belief (*doxa*), Plato on, 144
Biology of Aristotle, 210, 257–260
Boyle, Robert, 191
Brickhouse, T., 106
Burkert, Walter, 32, 34

Callicles, 86, 123, 164
Canon (Epicurus), 337
Cantor, Georg, 55–57
Carneades, 325, 371, 375
Categories (Aristotle), 210–212, 272–273
Catharsis, Aristotle on, 319
Causation/causes
    Alexandra of Aphrodisias on, 350
    Aristotle on, 238–239, 249–250, 267
    Chrysippus on, 350–351
    Epicureans on, 334
    Stoics on, 350
Cave, Analogy of, 144–146, 170
Change
    Anaxagoras on, 70
    Anaximander on, 26–27
    Anaximenes on, 29
    Aristotle on, 234–237, 246, 248
    Empedocles on, 64–65
    Heraclitus on, 35–36
    Parmenides's argument against, 43, 46, 48, 235–236
Choice
    Aristotle on, 105, 293
    Epicurus on, 337
    Stoics on, 350, 365

Chronology of events, 381–383
Chrysippus, 345, 349, 351–352, 356, 361
Cicero, 339, 352, 357, 339–340, 359
City-state. *See* Polis/city-state
Classification, Aristotle's use of, 208, 257–259
Cleanthes, 345
Clouds (Aristophanes), 95
Cognition, Plato's four types of, 144
Cognitive impression, Stoics on, 358
Commentary on Aristotle's Physics (Simplicius), 52
Compatibilism/soft determinism, 350
Compounds
    Aristotle on, 254–256, 262
    Democritus on, 75
    Empedocles on, 63–65, 70
    Epicurus/Epicureans on, 331, 333–334, 336
    Plato on, 190–191
Concerning Nature (Anaximander), 26
Contemplation, Aristotle on, 308–311
Continuums, 57
Convergent series, 55
Conviction (*osostheneia*), 376
Core-dependent homonymy, 211
Cosmogony
    of Anaxagoras, 72
    of Empedocles, 65–66
    See also Universe
Cosmology
    of Anaxagoras, 72
    of Anaximander, 27–28
    of Anaximenes, 29
    of Aristotle, 252–253
    atomists' view of, 73, 75–76
    of Democritus, 76
    of early ancient Greek philosophers, 14, 23
    of Empedocles, 61–67, 71–72
    Epicurean, 334, 336
    of Heraclitus, 35–40
    mathematical (mathematikoi), 32
    of the Milesians, 28–29
    of Parmenides, 47–48
    of Philolaus, 33
    of Pythagoras/Pythagoreans, 33–34
    of the Stoics, 347, 349–350, 355

of Thales, 25
See also Cosmogony; Universe
Cosmopolitanism, Stoic, 355–357
Craft (*techne*), 305
Cratylus (Heraclitus), 36, 92, 96, 116, 139
Creation, Plato on, 188–189
Credible beliefs (*endoxa*), 207–208
Critias (Plato), 187
Cultural relativism, 78, 81, 86
Cyrenaics, skeptical empiricist philosophy of, 325

Darius III, 10–11
De Anima (Aristotle), 25, 281–285
De Rerum Natura (Lucretius), 341, 350
Death
   early ancient Greek philosophers on, 17
   Epicureans on, 334–335, 339
   Lucretius on, 346
   Plato on, 129
   Socrates on, 128–129
   Stoics on, 359
   See also Transmigration of the soul
Deductive argument, Parmenides on, 49
Deductive explanation, scientific demonstrations as, 226
Definitions
   Aristotle on, 223, 227
   Plato on the need for, 118
   universal, 96
Democritus, 18
   atomism of, 73, 75–77, 79
   cosmology of ("swirling vortex" theory), 72, 76, 338
   on motion, 73–74
   physics of, 76–77
   theory of perception, 76
Demonstration
   Aristotle's theory of, 221–223
   necessary premise required for, 224–225
   See also Scientific demonstration
Descartes, René, 378
Desire(s)
   Epicurus/Epicureans on, 338
   Socrates on, 173

Stoics on, 351, 366
   See also Appetitive desires
Determinism. *See* Causation/Causes
Dialectic, Aristotle on, 229–230
Diels, Alexander, 20, 62
Diogenes Laërtius, 31–32, 62, 72–73, 76, 79, 177, 205–206, 3328, 30, 337, 347, 352–353, 360, 372–374
Diogenes of Oenoanda, 330
Diogenes the Cynic, 355
Divided Line, Analogy of, 143–145
Divine active principle
   Heraclitus on, 37
   Stoic, 347–348
Divine intelligence
   Epictetus/Stoics on, 365
   Heraclitus on, 35–37
   Socrates on, 112, 190
   Stoics on, 345, 347, 349
   Unmoved mover, 250, 252, 280
   See also God/god(s)
Divisibility, infinite, 70, 73–75, 77, 333
Doctrine of the Mean, 300
Dogmatism vs. skepticism, 376–377, 380
Duality
   of appearance and reality, Parmenides on, 47
   of human experience, Heraclitus on, 39
   See also False Duality; Unity of opposites

Early ancient Greek philosophy, 17, 23–42
   Eleatics, 17, 43–60
   Ionians, 30–41
   Milesians, 24–29
   pluralists and atomists, 61–77
   Sophists, 77–87
   surviving texts of, 19–21
Earth, problem of the stability
   Anaximander on, 28
   Thales on, 25
Education
   Plato on, 147, 157–159, 163, 165–166, 168, 197, 199
   Protagoras on, 82
   Sophist, 77–78

Eleatics, 17, 43–60
  Melissus of Samos, 58–59
  Parmenides, 43–50
  Zeno, 50–57
Elements
  Anaxagoras on, 68
  Anaximander on, 26–27
  Anaximenes on, 29
  Aristotle on, 27, 251–255, 258, 262, 284
  Empedocles on, 18, 62–64
  Parmenides on, 47–48
  Plato on, 189–191, 193
  Socrates on, 190
  Stoics on, 347–348
  Thales on, 24–25
Elenchus/elenctic knowledge, 97, 99, 101, 118
Eleutharia (freedom), 324, 328
Emotion(s)
  Aristotle on, 297, 299, 302, 307, 310
  Plato on, 105
  Stoics on, 352, 355, 363, 366, 370
  See also Catharsis; Passions
Empedocles
  claim to divinity, 66
  cosmogony/cosmology of, 63–67
  on elements, 18, 62–64
  on love and strife/attraction and repulsion, 63–67, 71–72
  on natural phenomena, 240
  on the university, 63
  zoogony of, 65–66
Empirical knowledge, 226–227, 229
Empiricist Theory of Perception, 184
Empsuchos (animate), 25
Encheiridion (Epictetus), 364, 367
Endoxa (credible beliefs), 207–208
Ends
  for chains of means, 295–296
  good and, 294
  Plato on, 110
  pyramid-like structure of, 295
  value of, 295
Epictetus, 351, 364–367
Epicurus/Epicureans
  atomism of, 331, 333
  biographical information/works of, 329–330
  on cosmoses, 334
  ethical theory of, 337–340
  on hedonism, 325
  Letter to Herodotus, 340–341
  Letter to Menoeceus, 341
  physics of, 330–332
  on pleasure and pain, 337–338
  Principal Doctrines, 40, 341, 345
  on religion, 336
  on the soul, 335
  summary of key texts, 340–341
  swerve, concept of, 333, 342
  theory of knowledge, 336–337
  theory of perception, 336
  on the universe, 334
Epistêmê (scientific knowledge), 144, 221, 223–225, 227, 229, 231, 305, 309
Epistemology. *See* Knowledge
Epochê (suspension of assent/judgment), 374–376. *See also* Judgment
Equivocation, fallacy of, 230
Ergon (function) of human beings, Aristotle/Socrates on, 103, 297–298, 301
Essays (Montaigne), 378
Essence
  Aristotle on. *See* Aristotle, on essence
  early ancient Greek philosophers on, 23
  Plato on, 115, 133, 191, 274
Ethical realism, Aristotle on, 304
Ethical virtues, Aristotle on, 299–301, 322
Ethics
  Aristotelian, 298–300, 310–311. *See also Nichomachean Ethics*
  Epicurean, 342–344, 337–340
  Stoic, 352–356, 362
  Zeno on, 352–353
Eudaimonia
  Aristotle on, 293–294, 296–298, 303, 309–311
  Epictetus on, 367
  Epicurus on, 338
  Plato on, 161–162, 165
  Socrates on, 102–104

Stoics on, 354, 366
See also Happiness
Euthyphro (Plato), 100–101, 111–112
Eutrapelia/epidexiotēs (wit), 301, 305
Exemplary Self-predication Thesis, Plato's, 134
Existence/being. *See* Being/existence
Explanation, Aristotle on, 238–239. *See also* Causation/Causes

Fallacy of Irrelevance, 159–161
False belief, Plato on, 187
False dichotomy, 230
Falsity/error
  and non-being, Plato on, 193–195
  of perception, Aristotle on, 271
  of Sophist theory, Plato on, 119–120
  Stoic view of, 360
Fate, Stoics on, 350
Feminism, Plato as champion of, 168
Fifth element, Aristotle's, 251–252, 284
Fine, Gail, 105
First principle(s)
  Anaximander on, 26
  Aristotle on, 207, 223, 230, 265–291
Flux, Heraclitean doctrine of, 35–37
Forces
  Anaxagoras on, 72
  Empedocles on, 63–64
Form and matter
  Aristotle on, 208–209, 236–237, 254, 256, 274–275, 279, 283
  Plato on, 278
Form of Goodness, 132, 134, 136, 138, 143, 145, 151, 155, 157–158, 160–164, 166–169, 174, 191, 193, 202, 204
Forms
  Aristotle on, 15
  Exemplary Self-predication Thesis and reality of, 134, 136
  as neither particular nor universal, 276
  as the particular, 276
  Phaedo's argument for, 126–129
  Plato/Socrates on, 55, 117, 129–130, 144, 191

Plato's Theory of, 131–140. *See also* Theory of Forms
  Stoic rejection of, 360
  as universal, 276
Fragmente der Vorsokratiker (Diels-Kranz), 21
Freeman, Kathleen, 21
Frege, Gottlob, 147, 359
Friendship
  Aristotle on, 307–308
  Cicero on, 339–340
  Epicurus on, 339–340
  philia, 301, 307–308
Function (*ergon*) of human beings, 103, 297–298, 301

Gassendi, Pierre, 335
Gerson, L. P., 328
God/god(s)
  Aristotle on, 267, 280–281
  Epicureans on, 335–336, 345
  Heraclitus on, 39–40
  Hesiod's *Theogony* on, 23
  Milesian/Ionian view of, 24
  Plato on, 190
  Plotinus's Neo-Platonism and, 150
  Protagoras on, 83
  Socrates on, 109, 112, 190
  Stoics on, 349–350
  Xenophanes on, 34
  See also Divine Intelligence; Religion
Good life
  Aristotle on, 296
  Stoics on, 355
Good/goodness
  Aristotle on, 294, 304
  Epictetus on, 365–366
  Form of. *See* Form of Goodness
  Socrates on, 102–103, 105
  Stoic view of, 356
  See also Unity of the virtues; Virtue(s)
Gorgias, rhetoric of, 84–86, 123
Gorgias (Plato), 106, 108, 122–123
Government, Aristotle on six forms of, 315
Great World System (Leucippus), 61, 73

Greece
    age of the tyrants (650–500 BC), 4
    ancient, intellectual culture of,
        13–15
    Archaic period, 3–6
    Classical period, 6–9
    Dark Ages of, 1–2
    Hellenistic period, 11–13
    late Bronze Age, 1
    Macedonian Empire, 9–11
    post-Dark Ages renaissance, 2

Habit in training, Protagoras on, 82
Happiness
    Aristotle on, 296–298, 309
    commonality among Epicureanism,
        Stoicism, and Pyrrhonism
        (Hellenistic), 325
    Epicurus on, 340
    Plato on, 162, 165
    Pyrrho of Elis on, 372
    Socrates on, 102–105
    Stoics on, 363, 366
    as the ultimate end, Aristotle on,
        294–297
    See also Eudaimonia
Hard *akrasia*, 307
Harmony/ies
    early ancient Greek philosophers
        on, 33
    Empedocles on, 64
    mathematikoi on, 32–33
    Plato on, 157, 160–161, 194
    Pythagoreans on, 32–33
    Socrates on, 128, 130–131
    Stoics on, 358
Hedonism
    Cyrenaic school of, 325
    Epicurean, 337–340
    Plato on, 103, 121, 164–165
    Socrates on, 123, 125
    See also Pleasure
Hellenistic and Roman philosophy,
    323–379
    Epicureanism, 329–343
    importance of nature in, 326
    individualism of, 326
    political thought, contrasted with
        Plato and Aristotle, 326

Skepticism, 371–379
Stoicism, 345–370
surviving texts of, 327–328
Heraclitus, 34–41, 78
    cosmology of, 39
    on the cosmos, 36–37
    on divine intelligence, 37
    epistemology of, 40
    on learning, 40–41
    on *logos*, 35–36, 40
    naturalism of, 35
    on perspectival nature of human
        perception, 39
    on the soul, 37
    on unity of opposites, 35–39
    on wisdom, 38–39, 41
Herodotus, 7, 31, 78
Hesiod, 3–4, 23
Hexis (virtues as habitual disposi-
    tions), 299
Hippolytus of Rome, 20, 29
Histories (Herodotus), 31
History of Animals (Aristotle), 257,
    260
Hobbes, Thomas, 313, 335
Homer, 2–3
Homonymy, Aristotle on, 210–211
Household and polis, Aristotle on,
    312–315
Huffman, C. A., 34
Human beings
    as core of Sophist thought, 90
    Epictetus on, 365
    ergon (function) of, Aristotle/
        Socrates on, 103, 273,
        297–298, 301
    Heraclitus on dualities of human
        experience, 39–40
    as measure of all things, Protagoras
        on, 83
    Stoic view of, 351–352, 355, 358
Human nature
    Aristotle on, 281, 323
    Stoics on, 350, 352–353, 357–358,
        367, 369
Hylomorphism, 208–209
Hylozoism, 25
Hymn to Zeus (Cleanthes), 345
Hypothetical necessity, 240, 260, 262

Ignorance
  Aristotle on, 302
  Heraclitus on, 40
  Socrates on, 97–99, 105, 306
Iliad, The, 2–3
Impartial justice approach, 161
Impressions
  Epictetus on, 366
  Epicurus on, 336–337, 340
  Stoics on, 351, 358
Incontinence (*akrasia*), 105, 294, 305–307, 310
Indestructibility, 26, 62–63, 78, 208, 210, 251, 256, 284, 335
Individual subjectivism, 81–83, 86
Indivisibility, 18, 43, 47, 49–50, 54, 56, 58, 61, 70, 73–75, 77, 130, 246–247, 250–252, 258, 333, 335, 337, 345
Induction (*epagôgê*), 228
Infallibilism, 137
Infinity(ies)/infinitesimals
  actual, 57
  Anaxagoras on Zeno's argument for, 70
  Anaximander on, 26
  Aristotle on, 26, 53, 55–57, 242–243, 270
  Epicureans on, 331
  infinite divisibility, 70, 73–75, 77, 333
  Melissus on, 58
  Plato on infinite series of Forms, 179
  Zeno's paradoxes and, 54–57
Injustice, Socrates on, 106–107, 122–123
Inquiry (*skepsis*), 378
Integrity, 366, 370–371
Intellect, passive vs. active, Aristotle on, 289
Intellectualist theory of virtue, Socrates's, 105–106
Intellectual virtues, Aristotle on, 302–305
Intuitive understanding, 305
Involuntary vs. voluntary actions, Aristotle on, 301–302
Inwood, B., 328

Ionians
  akousmatikoi, 30–32
  Heraclitus, 34–41
  mathematikoi, 32–34
  Pythagoras, 30–34
Irwin, Terence, 104
Isostheneia (force of conviction), 374, 376

Judgment(s)
  Aristotle on, 275, 304, 306–308
  Heraclitus on, 38
  Plato and the Sophists on, 139, 155
  Plato on, 139–140, 187, 308
  Plato on Protagoras's view of, 80–81
  skeptics on, 372–373, 375–378, 381–382
  Socrates on, 172, 185, 188
  Sophists on, 86, 185, 304, 308
  Stoics on, 362, 370–372
Justice
  Epicurus on, 339
  Form of Goodness and, 160–162
  as harmonious working of the parts of the soul, 159–160, 162
  and the individual, 157–159
  the just city and the just soul, 162–163
  Plato on, 163–165
  Socrates on, 106–107, 122–123
  and the state, 155–156, 159
  See also Virtue(s)

Kahn, Charles, 38
Kant, Immanuel, 48
Kerferd, G. B., 86
Knowledge
  Academic skeptics on, 374–375
  Arcesilaus on, 374
  Aristotle on, 221, 305–307. *See also* Scientific demonstration
  elenctic, 97, 99, 101, 118
  empirical, Aristotle on, 227, 229
  Epicurus on, 336–337
  Form of Goodness as necessary for, 191–192
  Gorgias on, 86
  Heraclitus on, 40

and incontinence (*akrasia*), Aristotle on, 305–307
as perception, 183–185
Plato on, 108, 125–126, 141, 144, 147, 192
scientific (*epistêmê*), 144, 221, 223–225, 227, 229, 231, 305, 309
Sextus Empiricus on, 375–376
Skeptic view of, 374–375
Socrates on, 97–99, 121
Stoic view of, 354, 358–359
as true belief, 145, 185–187
See also Truth
Kranz, Walther, 20, 62
Kraut, Richard, 298

Language
Aristotle on fallacies based on, 232
Heraclitus on, 36, 40
mathematical, 57
Plato on, 183
Protagoras on, 79
Stoics on, 355, 357–364
Law of excluded middle, 213–215, 225
Laws, the, 195–197
Learning
Heraclitus on, 40–41
Plato on, 115, 124–125, 164–165, 192
Lekta, Stoics on, 359–360
Letter to Herodotus (Epicurus), 330–331
Letter to Menoeceus (Epicurus), 340
Leucippus, 61, 73–74
Leviathan (Hobbes), 313
Lives of the Philosophers, The (Diogenes Laërtius), 20, 62, 328, 330
Logic
of Aristotle, 215–221
Epictetus on, 365
propositional logic of Stoicism, 361
Stoic view of, 357–361
Logos
Ancient Greek philosophers on, 23
Aristotle on, 297, 301–302, 306
different meanings in different contexts, 21
early ancient Greek philosophers on, 23, 35

Gorgias on, 85
Heraclitus on, 35–36, 39–40
Plato on, 186, 188
as principle, Heraclitus on, 35
Stoic view of, 346, 348, 350, 352, 354, 359
See also Reason
Long, A. A., 328, 366, 370
Love
Plato on, 168–174
Socrates on, 171–173
and strife, in Empedocles's cosmology, 63–67, 71–72
Lucretius Carus, 325, 331, 333, 335, 341–342
Lyceum, 203, 206–207

Macedonian empire, 9–11
Marcus Aurelius, 355, 367–368
Mass, Epicurus on, 332
Materialism, Epicurean, 335
Mates, Benson, 361
Mathematical objects, 56–57, 278
Mathematics
Plato vs. Aristotle on, 210
Platonic philosophy of, 56–57
Mathematikoi, 30, 32, 34, 41
Matter. *See* Substance; Substance-stuff
McKirahan, R., 85
Meaning(s)
Aristotle on, 269–270
properties of Forms and, 135
referential theory of, 139
Means and ends, Plato on, 110
Mechanical necessity vs. teleology, 240
Medici, Cosimo, influence of Plato on, 148
Meditations on First Philosophy (Descartes), 378
Meinong, Alexius, 47
Memorabilia (Xenophon), 95
Meno, 123–126
knowledge and true beliefs, 125–126
learning as recollection, 124–125
overview of, 123–124
paradox of inquiry, 124
Metaphysics (Aristotle), 25, 211, 228–229, 250, 265–291

Metempsychosis. *See also* Transmigration of the soul
Meteorology (Aristotle), 255–257
Midway Problem (the dichotomy), 50–51
Milesians
  Anaximander, 26–28
  Anaximenes, 28–29
  Thales, 24–25
Mind. *See* Nous
Mixtures
  Aristotle on, 254–255
  Boyle on, 190
  Empedocles on, 67–69
Modal deductions, 220
Modal fallacy, 214
Monism
  of Anaximander, 26
  in Eleatic thought, 58–59
  of Heraclitus, 36–37, 40
  of Melissus of Samos, 58
  of Parmenides, 46–47, 49, 178
  Stoic, 346, 349
  of Thales, 25
  of Zeno, 50, 55
  See also Unity of opposites
Montaigne, Michel de, 378
Moral relativism, 86, 353
Morality
  vs. ethics, Aristotelian view of, 298
  vs. happiness, Stoics on, 366
  Sophist view of, 78
Motion
  Anaxagoras on, 72
  Aristotle on, 241–242, 246–247, 249–251, 253
  atomists on, 73–74
  Democritus and Leucippus on, 73–74
  Heraclitean doctrine of flux, 35–37
  Newton's theory of, 77
  Parmenides on, 46
  Zeno on, 50–56
    Achilles paradox, 51–52
    Arrow argument, 52, 248
    Midway Problem, 50–51, 247–248
    moving rows/stadium argument, 52

Motivation, Socrates's theory of, 105
Movement of Animals (Aristotle), 261
Moving rows argument, 52
Murdoch, Iris, 174
Muthos (myth), 23, 109

Naturalism/natural philosophy, 23–41
  of Anaxagoras, 67–72
  of Anaximander, 26–28
  of early ancient Greek philosophers, 23–29
  of Empedocles, 61–67
  of Heraclitus, 34–40
  in Hellenistic thought, 326
  Plato's rejection of, 131, 201
  Pre-Socratic, 278
  Stoic, 354–355
  See also Causation/cause(s); Change; Cosmology; Elements
Nature, empirical investigation/scientific demonstration, 226
Necessary truths (*epistêmê*), 221–225, 229
Necessity, occurrence through, 240
Neo-Platonism, 327
Newton, Isaac, 77
Nicomachean Ethics, 293–311
Nomos vs. *phusis*, Sophists on, 78
Non-assertion (*Aphasia*), 373
Non-contradiction, principle of, 269–270
Non-evident causes, Stoics on, 350
Nonexistence/non-being
  Gorgias on, 84–85
  Parmenides on, 45–47
  Plato on, 193–195
  See also Being/existence
Noumena vs. phenomena, 48
Nous, 67, 71–72, 229, 231, 305
Now, Aristotle on indivisibility of, 247
Numbers, Pythagoreans on, 33–34
Nussbaum, Martha, 325

Objectivism, 82, 86
Odyssey, The, 2–3
Oikeiosis, 351, 353
On Benefits (Seneca), 363
On Generation and Corruption (Aristotle), 54, 75, 253–254

On Interpretation (Aristotle), 212–215, 220, 269, 273
On Mercy (Seneca), 363
On Mind (Leucippus), 73
On Nature (Anaxagoras), 66–67
On Nature (Empedocles), 62
On Nature (Epicurus), 330
On Peace of Mind (Seneca), 363
On the Dignity of Man (Pico della Mirandola), 148
On the Heavens (Aristotle), 29, 251–253
On the Mind (Leucippus), 61
On the Nature of Things (Lucretius), 325, 330, 341
On the Political Constitution (Protagoras), 79
On the Senses (Theophrastus), 20
On the Soul (Aristotle). *See* De Anima
On the Virtues (Protagoras), 79
Opinions of the Philosophers, The (pseudo-Plutarch), 20
Organon (Aristotle), 210
Orpheus/Orphism, 31
Osostheneia (conviction), skeptic view of, 376
Outlines of Pyrrhonism (Sextus Empiricus), 376, 378
Owen, G. E. L., 117, 177, 179, 193

Paradoxes
    of inquiry, 123–124, 126, 129
    of motion (Zeno), 50–52
    solutions to, 56–57
Parity Assumption, 193–194
Parmenides, 17–18
    Aristotle's argument against, 235–236
    biographical information, 43
    on change, 46
    denial of the existence of change, 234
    on duality of appearance and reality. See also Way of Truth, Way of Opinion, 44
    on false duality of appearance and reality. See also Way of Truth, Way of Opinion, 47
    the journey, 44
    on motion, 46
    philosophically important implications of his poem, 49–50
    on reality, 48–49
    references by Plato and Aristotle to, 43
    on sensation, 48
    the Way of Seeming/Way of Opinion, 47–49
    the Way of Truth, 44–47
Parmenides (Plato), 50, 55, 178–182
Paronymy, Aristotle on, 210–211
Parrhēsia, 324
Parts of Animals (Aristotle), 258–259
Passions
    Seneca/Stoics on, 361, 363
    Stoic view of, 351–352, 355–356
Penrose, Roger, 147
Perception(s)
    Aristotle on, 228, 231, 270–271, 275, 287–288
    Democritus on, 76
    Epicurus on, 336
    Heraclitus on, 38–39
    knowledge as, 183–185
    Protagoras on relativity of, 80–81
    Pyrrho of Elis on, 372–373
    Pyrrhonian skeptics on, 377
    skepticism and, 377
    Sophists on, 183
    Stoics on, 351, 355–356, 358
    subjectivity of, 80
    See also Appearances
Perceptual experience, judgments as reports of, 377
Peripatetic philosophers, 206
Perspective, Heraclitus on, 38–39
Phaedo (Plato), 32, 111, 115, 126–128
Phaedrus (Plato), 109, 171–174
Phenomena vs. noumena, 48
Philia (friendship), 301, 307–308
Philip II of Macedonia, 9–10
Philip III, 12
Philolaus, 31–33
Philosophers, Plato's definition of, 168
Phronesis (wisdom) 302–303, 310, 317, 352
Phusis (nature), 23, 78

Physics
  of Aristotle, 238, 249–257
  of Democritus, 76–77
  of Epicurus, 330–332
  Stoic, 346–352
  Stoicism and, 349
Physics (Aristotle), 20, 26–27, 234
Piety, Euthyphro on, 100–101
Place
  Aristotle on, 243–244
  Zeno on, 53–54
Placita (Aetius), 20
Plato
  analogies
    of the Arts and Sciences, 118–120
    of the Cave, 142, 144–146, 170
    of the Divided Line, 143–145
    of the Sun, 143–144, 158
  arguments against Sophism, 118–123
    need for definitions, 118
    reductio ad absurdum arguments, 119–120
  Aristotle and, 96, 147, 207–210
  biographical information, 115
  on cognition, 144
  on creation, 188–189
  developmentalist/stylometric approach to dialogues of, 116–117
  direct influence on the history of philosophy, 147, 149
  on education, 147, 157–159, 163, 165–166, 168, 197, 199
  on essence, 115, 133, 191, 274
  Exemplary Self-Predication Thesis, 134
  on falsity and non-being, 193–195
  on government, 162–163, 196
  grouping of the middle and late dialogues, 117
  on hedonism, 121
  on the ideal city-state, 166–168
  on justice, 151–174
  on knowledge and true beliefs, 125–126, 185
  on learning and recollection, 124
  life of, 92–94
  on love, 151–174
  metaphysics and epistemology of, 131–149
  on pleasure, 163–165
  political philosophy of, 142
  on propositions as abstract entities, 147
  on recollection and learning, 124–127
  refutation of Sophism, 96, 107–108, 110, 119
  Socrates in the early dialogues of, 95–113
  Socrates vs., 117–118
  Socratic dialogues, 96–100
  on the soul, 117, 127–128, 130, 141, 156–157, 164–165
  Theory of Forms, 131–140. *See also* Theory of Forms
  theory of the government of the ideal state, 162–163, 165
  Third Man Argument, 179–180
  on tripartite division of the soul, 141
  Two-Worlds Theory of, 145
  on weakness of the will, 121
Platonic dialogues
  the *Apology*, 98, 103, 109, 106–113
  the *Cratylus*, 36, 135, 387
  the *Critias*, 187, 192
  the *Crito*, 113
  the *Euthedemus*, 105, 387
  the *Euthyphro*, 100–101, 111–112
  the *Gorgias*, 86, 103, 105, 106, 108, 122–123, 164
  the *Laches*, 99, 102, 388
  the *Laws*, 195–197
  the *Meno*, 105, 123–126
  the *Parmenides*, 50, 55, 178–182, 198
  the *Phaedo*, 32, 103, 108, 111, 115, 126–128, 136, 138–139, 164
  the *Phaedrus*, 109, 171–174
  the *Philebus*, 103, 164
  the *Protagoras*, 80, 82–83, 106, 108, 120–121, 164
  the *Republic*, 103, 107, 119, 135, 137, 139, 140–146, 151–165, 174, 196–197

Socratic, 96–100
the *Sophist*, 192–195, 258
the *Statesman*, 192, 195
the *Symposium*, 109, 168–171
the *Theaetetus*, 80–82, 111, 120, 182–187
the *Timaeus*, 187–191
Pleasure
    Aristotle on, 308–311
    Callicles on, 123
    Epicurus on, 337–340
    Plato on, 163–165
    Socrates on, 123, 125
    Stoics on, 354
    See also Hedonism
Plotinus, 148
Plurality/pluralists, 61–67
    Anaxagoras, 67–72
    Democritus, 72–77
    Empedocles, 61–67
    Leucippus and Democritus, 74
    Zeno, 52–55, 70
    See also Unity of opposites
Plutarch, 20, 29, 356
Pneuma (soul), 347–349, 351, 355
Poetics (Aristotle), 318–319
Polis/city-state
    in ancient Archaic Greece, 3–5
    Aristotle on, 311–314
        household and polis, 312–314
        ideal city-state, 316–317
        kinds of city-states, 315–316
    Aristotle vs. Hobbes on, 313
    as natural entity, Aristotle on, 313
    Plato and Aristotle vs. Chrysippus on, 356
    Plato's, 162–163, 168
    Socrates and Plato on, 155–156, 159
    Stoic view of, 356–357
    Zeno on, 356
Political realism, 154
Politics
    Epicurus on, 340, 344
    Stoic view of, 357
    See also Polis/city state
Politics (Aristotle), 311–318
Popper, Karl, 167
Positivism, 152

Possible world semantics theory, Platonic aspects of, 147
Posterior Analytics (Aristotle), 221, 225, 227
Power, 124, 199
Practical syllogism, 304–305
Practical wisdom, Aristotle on, 302–303
Pragmatism, 82–83, 86
Praotēs (mildness), 301
Preconceptions, Epicurus on, 337
Predication
    accidental, Aristotle on, 274
    arguments from, 138–139
    categories of, 212
Pre-Socratic philosophers, 19, 108–109, 278
Principal Doctrines (Epicurus), 40, 341, 345
Principle of Non-contradiction, 81, 269–270
Principle of Sufficient Reason, 28, 45–46
Prior Analytics (Aristotle), 215–221
Priority of Definitional Knowledge, 100
Properties/natural meanings of Forms, 135
Propositional connectives, Stoics on, 360–361
Propositional logic, 221
Propositions
    Anaxagoras on, 71
    Aristotle on, 215–217, 219, 223, 225, 232
    Gorgias on, 84–85
    Heraclitus on, 35–41
    Plato on, 147, 193
    Socrates on, 100–101
    Stoics on (*axioma*), 360
Protagoras, 79–83, 270
    agnosticism of, 83
    on education, 82
    humanism/pragmatism of, 80, 83
    moral subjectivism of, 79–83
    objectivism of, 82, 86
    subjectivism of, 81, 83
Protagoras (Plato), 106, 108, 120–121
Prudence, Epicurus on, 338–339
Psuchê (soul), 21, 25, 128, 282, 286, 289, 348. *See also* Soul

Psychological egoism, 103
Purifications (Empedocles), 62, 66
Pyrrhonian skepticism/Pyrrhonism
  academic skepticism vs., 371, 375
  Aenesidemus's revival of, 371
  Pyrrho of Elis, 338, 373,376, 371–374, 378
  Sextus Empiricus, 375–378
Pythagoras/Pythagoreans, 17, 30–34
  akousmatikoi, 30–32
  mathematikoi, 32–34
  numerical metaphysics, 33–34
  on the soul, 30–32, 41
  on the universe, 41

Qua, 209

Rationalism/rational egoism, 78, 86
Rationality, Epictetus on, 365
Reality
  Arcesilaus on, 374–375
  Aristotle on, 227, 289–290
  Eleatics on, 43
  Gorgias on, 85–86
  Parmenides on, 14, 43–44, 48–49
  Plato vs. the Pre-Socratics on, 278–279
  Pyrrho of Elis on, 372–373
Reason
  Anaximander on, 28
  Aristotle on, 289–290, 301–306
  early ancient Greek philosophers on, 23, 28
  Epictetus on, 351
  Heraclitus on, 37
  Parmenides on, 44–45, 49
  Socrates on, 110, 112
  Stoics on, 355
  See also Logos
Recollection, Plato's theory of, 124–127
Reductio ad absurdum arguments of Plato, 119–120
Referential theory of meaning, 139
Refutation of all Heresies, The (Hippolytus of Rome), 20
Reincarnation. *See* Transmigration of the soul
Relativism, moral/cultural, 78, 81, 86, 353

Relativity of perception. *See* Perception
Religion
  Aristotle on, 280–281
  early scientific Greek philosophers on, 78–79
  Epicurus on, 336
  Socrates on, 109–110
  See also Divine intelligence; God/god(s)
Republic, 140–146, 174
  Analogy of the Cave, 145–146
  Analogy of the Sun, 143
  Divided Line Analogy and priority of the Forms, 143–145
  on nature of justice, 151–165
  overview of, 141–143
Responsibility, Aristotle on, 301–302
Rhetoric
  of Gorgias, 84
  Socrates on, 112, 122–123, 173
Russell, Bertrand, 47

Science
  as investigation of nature (Aristotle), 238
  Pythagorean view of, 32
Scientific demonstration
  Aristotle on, 221–222, 224–226
  induction vs. deduction in, 228–229
Scientific knowledge (*epistêmê*), 144, 221, 223–225, 227, 229, 231, 305, 309
Scientific method, Aristotle's, 210–215
Sedley, D. N., 328
Self-discipline (*Askēsis*), 324
Self-interest, 161, 339
Self-predication, 134, 136, 179
Self-rule, Socrates on, 123
Self-sufficiency (*autarkeia*), 328
Seneca, 356–357, 362–364
Sensation/sense impression
  Aristotle on, 270–271, 275, 282
  Epicurus on, 336–337
  Parmenides on, 48–49
  Pyrrho on, 373
  Stoics on, 351

Sextus Empiricus, 375–378
  documentation of Pyrrhonism by, 325
  on knowledge, 375–376
  on Pyrrhonism vs. Academic skepticism, 375
  skepticism vs. dogmatism, 376–377, 380
  on tranquility, 376, 378
  works of, 375–376
Shields, Christopher, 211
Simplicius, 20, 26–28, 52
Skepticism, 371–379
  academic, 371, 374–375
  on conviction (*osostheneia*), 376
  Montaigne and Descartes on, 378
  persistence in inquiry, 378
  Pyrrho of Elis, 371
  Pyrrhonian, 371–374
  Sextus Empiricus on, 375–378
  Stoicism vs., 375
  Timon of Phlius, 372
Slavery
  Aristotle on, 312, 314, 317, 393
  Aurelius on, 368
  Epicurus on, 329
  instances of, 11, 93, 364
  Seneca on, 357
  Stoic view of, 356–357
Smith, M., 106
Society
  Chrysippus on, 353
  Plato on, 136, 141–143, 157, 165, 170, 199
  Protagoras on, 82
  Stoic view of, 356–357
  See also Polis/city-state
Socrates
  on *akrasia* (incontinence), 306
  Alcibiades on irony of, 98
  Analogy of the Chariot, 173
  Analogy of the Soul, 172, 174
  Aristophanes on, 95
  Aristotle and Plato on, 96
  disagreement with the Pre-Socratic philosophers, 108
  Divided line Analogy, 144
  in the early dialogues of Plato, 95–113
  on *elenchus*/elenctic knowledge, 97–99, 100–102, 121
  on function (*ergon*) of human beings, 103, 297–298, 301
  on the gods, 109–110
  on happiness, 102–105
  ignorance of, 98–99, 105
  on injustice, 106–107, 122–123
  irony of, 88
  life of, 91–92, 95
  on love, 171–173
  motivation and *akrasia*, theory of, 105
  philosophical method of, 100–102
  philosophical theses of, 102–107
    functions of the soul, 103
    happiness as the greatest good, 102–103
    harming others harms oneself, 106–107
    intellectualist theory of virtue, 105
    unity of the virtues, 105–106
    virtue and happiness, 103–105
  Plato vs., 117–118
  rejection of naturalism in Pre-Socratic thought, 108–109
  rejection of sophism, 107–108
  on the relative virtues of the spoken and written word, 173–174
  on religion, 109–110
  on rhetoric, 122, 173
  seeker of universal definitions, 96
  on the soul, 106, 126, 154, 172
  trial and death of, 110–113
    in *Apology*, 112–113
    in *Crito*, 113
    in *Euthyphro*, 111–112
    in *Phaedo*, 126–128
  on unity of the virtues, 121
  Xenophon on, 95, 110
Socratic dialogues, 96–100
  analogy from the arts, 118
  argument against Sophism, 118–128
Socratic knowledge paradox, 97–99
Soft *akrasia*, 307
Soft determinism/compatibilism, 350
Sophia (theoretical wisdom), 79, 302, 305, 309–310, 314, 320

Sophism
  origin of the term *sophist*, 79
  Platonic dialogues about, 79
  Plato's arguments against, 110, 118–120, 140
  Socrates's rejection of, 107–108, 118–128
Sophist (Plato), 192–193
Sophists
  Gorgias, 84–86
  on *phusis* vs. *nomos*, 78
  Plato's portrayal as moral relativists, 18
  Protagoras, 79–83, 120–121, 270
  rhetoric of, 77
  Thrasymachus, 152
Soul
  Anaximenes on, 29
  Aristotle on, 25, 282–285, 290, 297
  Epicureans on, 335
  Heraclitus on, 37
  justice as harmonious working of the parts of, 159–160, 162
  Plato on, 117, 127–128, 130, 141, 156–157, 164–165
  Protagoras on, 82
  Pythagoras/Pythagoreans on, 30–32, 41
  Simias on, 130
  Socrates on, 106, 126, 154, 172
  Stoic view of, 347–349, 351, 355
  Thales on, 25
  transmigration of, 17, 31–32, 66–67
Space
  Anaximander on, 28
  Epicurus on, 332
  Zeno on, 51
Speechwriting, Socrates on, 173
Spinoza, Baruch
  rationalism of, 148
  similarities to Stoics, 349
Stadium argument, 52
State (the), Stoics on, 357
Statesman (Plato), 135, 192
Static pleasures, 337–338
Stobaeus, 20, 352
Stoicism/Stoics, 37, 345–369
  active principle in, 346–350, 353
  advocacy of acceptance, 354–355
  cosmopolitan view of, 326, 355–357
  egalitarianism in, 326
  Epictetus, 364–367
  ethics of, 352–354
  lekton, semantic notion of, 359–360
  logic of, 357–361
  Marcus Aurelius, 367–368
  on perception, 358
  philosophy of nature, 346–348
  physics of, 346–352
  on pleasure, 354
  on propositions, 360
  Seneca, 362–364
  skepticism vs., 375
  on the soul (*pneuma*), 347–349, 351, 355
  stoic vs. Aristotelian logic, 361
  on virtue, 353–354
  Zeno of Citium, 346, 353–356
Strife, Empedocles on, 63–67, 71–72
Subjectivism, moral, 79–82, 86
Stylometry, 116
Sublunary world, Aristotle on, 253–255
Substance(s)
  Anaxagoras on, 67–69
  Aristotle on, 25, 208–209, 212, 236, 256, 268, 271–272, 274–275, 279–280
  Milesians on nature of, 41
  Plato on, 189–190. *See also* Forms
  as stuff, Anaxagoras on, 69
Substance-stuff/substance-kind
  Anaxagoras on, 68–70
  Anaximander on, 26–27
  Anaximenes on, 17, 28–29, 41
  pluralistic view of, 61
  Pre-Socratics on, 278
  Thales on, 25–27
Substance(s) as entity
  Aristotle on, 25, 208–209, 212, 236, 256, 268, 271–272, 274–275, 279–280
  Plato on, 189–190
  See also Forms
Substratum/subject as substance, Aristotle on, 272–273
Sun, Analogy of, 143–144, 158
Superlunary world, Aristotle on, 251–253

Syllogism, Aristotle's theory of, 210, 215–221, 229, 232
Synonymy, Aristotle on, 210

Teleological explanation vs. material necessity, 240
Teleology
  Aristotle's defense of, 240–241
  and nature, 239–240
  of Plato, 193–194
Thales, 17, 24–27
Themata, 361
Theogony (Hesiod), 3–4, 23
Theology, Stoicism and, 349
Theophrastus, as source of information about Pre-Socratics, 20
Theoretical wisdom (*sophia*), 305
Theory of Descriptions, 47
Theory of Forms, 55
  arguments against Sophism, 140
  arguments for
    epistemological arguments, 139
    from predication, 138–139
    from relativity, 136–138
    semantic arguments, 139–140
  Aristotle's rejection of, 208–209
  dualism inherent in, 146
  elements and the necessity of things, 190–191
  Exemplary Self-Predication Thesis, 134
  existence of the soul and, 127–128
  Forms as thoughts/patterns set in nature, 180–181
  ontological thesis, 132–133
  Parmenides and, 48, 178–182
  Plato's eventual abandonment of, 180
  problems of interpretation, 136
    Forms as meanings vs. properties, 135
    Forms for only natural properties, 135
    self-predication of the Forms, 136
  reality of the Forms, 134
  Unity Thesis, 133–134
  Zeno's, 55
Third Man Argument, 179–180

Thrasymachus, 78, 86, 98, 119, 141, 151–154
Timaeus, 145, 187–192
Time
  Aristotle on, 244–247, 250–252
  Empedocles on, 65
  indivisibility of, 56
  Plato on, 188–189
Timon of Phlius, 372–373
Tooley, Michael, 147
Topics, the, 212, 229–230
Totalitarianism, 167, 169
Tragedy, Aristotle on, 319
Tranquility
  Epicureans on, 329, 336, 338–339, 373, 376, 378
  skeptics on, 380–381
Transmigration of the soul, 17, 31–32, 66–67
True belief, 99, 101–102, 111, 125–128, 147, 149, 187–189, 192
Truth
  Carneades on, 375
  Parmenides on, 44–47
  Skeptics on, 375
  Stoics on, 359
  See also Knowledge
Truthfulness (*Alētheia*), 301
Two-Worlds epistemology of Plato, 145

Unity of opposites, 27, 35–39, 268
Unity of the virtues, 105–106, 121, 303–304, 354
Unity vs. plurality, Zeno on, 54–55
Universal definitions, 96
Universal History (Diodorus), 32
Universals, 274, 278
Universe
  Anaximander on, 26–27
  Aristotle on, 27, 250–257
  Empedocles on, 63
  Epicurus on, 333–334
  Heraclitus on, 36–37
  Parmenides on, 47
  Plato on, 189
  Pythagoreans on, 34, 41
  Stoics on, 345, 347–349
  Thales on, 24

Xenophanes on, 34
See also Cosmogony; Cosmology
Unlimited, the
   Anaxagoras on, 72
   Anaximander on, 26–27
   Democritus on, 76
   See also Infinity(ies)/infinitesimals
Unmoved mover, 250, 252, 280

Virtue(s)
   Aristotle on, 293, 297–305
   Epictetus on, 365–366, 369–370
   Epicurus on, 339, 343
   intellectualist theory of, 105, 305
   as knowledge, 121
   Plato on, 126, 144
   Protagoras on, 82
   reciprocity of, 106
   Seneca on, 363–364
   Socrates on, 103–106, 122–123
   Stoics on, 352–354. 357
   unity of, 105–106, 121, 303–304, 354
   See also Good; Justice
Vlastos, Gregory, 96, 99, 104
Void
   Aristotle on, 244
   atomists on, 73–76
   Epicureans on, 341
   Lucretius on, 331
   Melissus of Samos on, 58
Voluntary vs. involuntary actions, Aristotle on, 301–302

Way of Opinion, 44, 49
Way of Truth, Parmenides on, 44–47
Weakness of the will, Plato on, 121
Williams, Bernard, iii
Wisdom
   Aristotle on, 266–267, 302–311
   Heraclitus on, 38–39, 41
   Phronesis, 302–303, 310, 317, 352
   Plato on, 115, 144
   Socrates on, 123
   theoretical vs. practical, 305–311
Wit (*eutrapelia/epidexiotēs*), 301, 305
Women
   Aristotle on, 314
   Plato on, 142
Woodruth, Paul, 85
Works and Days (Hesiod), 3
World, The (Descartes), 29
Writing/written word, Socrates on, 173

Xenophanes, 34, 78
Xenophon on Socrates, 95

Zeller, E., 34
Zeno, 18, 353, 356, 358
   arguments against motion, 50–52
   arguments against plurality, 52–55
   biographical information, 50
   ethics of, 352–353
   on knowledge, 358–359
   on the nature of infinitesimals, 55–56
Zeno of Citium, 37, 346, 353–356
   cosmopolitanism, 355–357
   ethics, 352–355
   logic, 357–361
   philosophy of nature, 346–352
Zeno's paradoxes
   Achilles paradox, 51–52
   Aristotle's rejection of, 247–248, 332
   arrow paradox, 52, 248
   contemporary standard solution to, 56
   Midway Problem, 50–51, 247–248
   Moving Rows argument (the Stadium), 52
Zoogony. *See* Animals